lonely planet

Scotland

Tom Smallman
Graeme Cornwallis

D1007126

LONELY PLANET PUBLICATIONS
Melbourne • Oakland • London •Paris

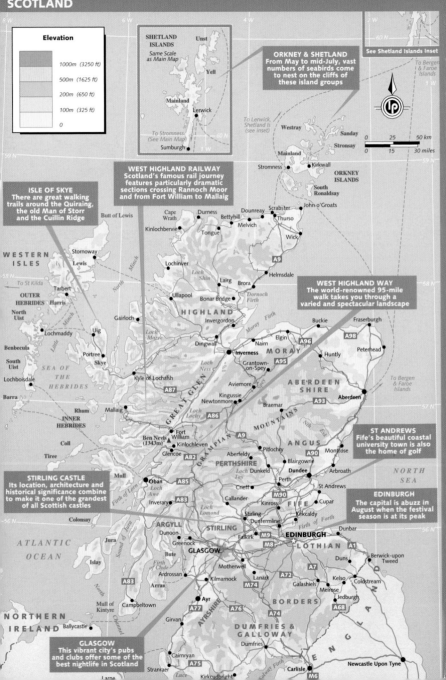

SCOTLAND

Elevation

1000m (3250 ft)
500m (1625 ft)
200m (650 ft)
100m (325 ft)
0

SHETLAND ISLANDS
Same Scale as Main Map

Unst
Yell
Mainland
Lerwick
To Stromness (See Main Map)
Sumburgh

ORKNEY & SHETLAND
From May to mid-July, vast numbers of seabirds come to nest on the cliffs of these island groups

See Shetland Islands Inset

To Bergen & Faroe Islands

Westray
Sanday
Stronsay
Mainland
Stromness
Kirkwall
ORKNEY ISLANDS
South Ronaldsay
John o'Groats

0   25   50 km
0   15   30 miles

WEST HIGHLAND RAILWAY
Scotland's famous rail journey features particularly dramatic sections crossing Rannoch Moor and from Fort William to Mallaig

ISLE OF SKYE
There are great walking trails around the Quiraing, the old Man of Storr and the Cuillin Ridge

Butt of Lewis

Cape Wrath
Durness
Bettyhill
Dounreay
Scrabster
Thurso
Kinlochbervie
Melvich
Wick
Tongue

WEST HIGHLAND WAY
The world-renowned 95-mile walk takes you through a varied and spectacular landscape

WESTERN ISLES

Stornoway
Lewis

To St Kilda

OUTER HEBRIDES Harris
Tarbert
North Uist
Benbecula
Lochmaddy
Uig
South Uist
Portree
Lochboisdale
Skye
Barra

SEA OF THE HEBRIDES

Lochinver
Loch Shin
Lairg
Ullapool
Bonar Bridge
Brora
Helmsdale
Dornoch Firth
Invergordon
Gairloch
HIGHLAND
Dingwall
Inverness
Loch Maree
Moray Firth
Buckie
Fraserburgh
Nairn
Elgin
A96
A98
MORAY
Grantown-on-Spey
Huntly
Peterhead
A95
Loch Ness
Aviemore
ABERDEEN SHIRE
Kyle of Lochalsh
A87
Kingussie
Newtonmore
Braemar
Aberdeen
A93
GREAT GLEN
Loch Lochy
A86
Nith
GRAMPIAN
MOUNTAINS

To Bergen & Faroe Islands

Rhum
INNER HEBRIDES
Mallaig
Ben Nevis (1343m)
Fort William
Kinlochleven
Coll
Tiree
Glencoe
A82
Aberfeldy
Pitlochry
ANGUS
Montrose
A90

ST ANDREWS
Fife's beautiful coastal university town is also the home of golf

STIRLING CASTLE
Its location, architecture and historical significance combine to make it one of the grandest of all Scottish castles

Mull
Oban
A85
Loch Awe
Inveraray
A83
Loch Tay
PERTHSHIRE
Dunkeld
Crieff
Callander
Dundee
Blairgowrie
Perth
Arbroath
St Andrews
Cupar
NORTH SEA

EDINBURGH
The capital is abuzz in August when the festival season is at its peak

Colonsay
Jura
Loch Lomond
STIRLING
Stirling
Dunfermline
Kinross
FIFE
Kirkcaldy
Firth of Forth
Dunbar

ARGYLL
Dunoon
Greenock
GLASGOW
Falkirk
M9
M8
EDINBURGH
LOTHIAN
A1
Duns
Berwick-upon-Tweed

ATLANTIC OCEAN

Bute
Islay
Firth of Clyde
Ardrossan
Arran
Motherwell
Lanark
A72
A7
Kelso
Coldstream
Kilmarnock
Galashiels
Melrose
A83
Mull of Kintyre
Campbeltown
Ayr
A77
AYRSHIRE
A76
BORDERS
Jedburgh
A68
A74
ENGLAND

GLASGOW
This vibrant city's pubs and clubs offer some of the best nightlife in Scotland

NORTHERN IRELAND
Ballycastle
Girvan
DUMFRIES & GALLOWAY
Cairnryan
A75
Dumfries
Stranraer
Luce
Kirkcudbright
Carlisle
M6
Newcastle Upon Tyne
Larne

THE HIGHLANDS

THE HEBRIDES

ORKNEY & SHETLAND ISLANDS   429

LANGUAGE   463

GLOSSARY   467

SOME ALTERNATIVE PLACE NAMES   469

ACKNOWLEDGMENTS   471

INDEX   480

MAP LEGEND   488

METRIC CONVERSION   inside back cover

Inset
Same Scale as Main Map

Hermaness
Keen of Herma
Fethaland
Eshaness
Muckle Roe
Foula
Noss
South West Mainland

SHETLAND ISLANDS

To Shetland Islands (see inset)

National Nature Reserve
National Scenic Area
Regional Park
Forest Park

Hoy & West Mainland

ORKNEY ISLANDS

NORTH SEA

0   25   50 km
0   15   30 miles

Invernaver
Dunnet Links
North West Sutherland
Gualin
Kyle of Tongue
Strathy Bogs
Achanarras Quarry
Loch a Mhuilinn
Blar Nam Faoileag
Assynt-Coigach
Inchnadamph
Inverpolly
Mound Alderwoods
To St Kilda National Scenic Area
Dornoch Firth
South Lewis, Harris & North Uist
Loch Maree Islands
Corrieshalloch Gorge
Nigg & Udale Bays
Trotternish
Beinn Eighe
Ben Wyvis
Monach Isles
Wester Ross
Rassal Ashwood
Forvie
Loch Druidibeg
Allt Nan Caman
Strathfarrar
South Uist Machair
The Cuillin Hills
Glen Strathfarrar
Kintail
Glen Affric
Cairngorms
Craigellachie
Abernethy Forest
Knoydart
Cairngorms
Muir of Dinnet
Rum
Glen Roy
Dinnet Oakwood
Glen Tanar
The Small Isles
Creag Meagaidh
The Cairngorm Mountains
Morrone Birkwood
Loch Shiel
Caenlochan
Morar, Moidart & Ardnamurchan
Clash Moss
Ariundle Oakwood
Ben Nevis & Glencoe
Rannoch
Deeside & Lochnagar
St Cyrus
Glencripesdale
Loch Tummel
Lynn of Lorn
Rannoch Moor
Loch Rannoch & Glen Lyon
Milton Wood
Den of Airlie
Gladrum Wood
Faskally
River Tay
Loch na Keal Isle of Mull
Glen Nant
Ben Lui
Ben Lawers
Morton Lochs
Tentsmuir Point
River Earn
Loch Lomond
The Trossachs
Queen Elizabeth
Loch Leven
Fife
Isle of May
Scarba, Lunga & the Garvellachs
Moine Mhor
Argyll
Flanders Moss
Taynish
Kyles of Bute
Loch Lomond
Jura
Knapdale
Blawhorn Moss
Pentland Hills
St Abbs Head
Mealdarroch
Clyde Muirshiel
Eilean Na Muice Duibhe
Glen Diomhan
Braehead Moss
North Arran
Clyde Valley Woodlands
Eildon & Leaderfoot
Upper Tweeddale
Whitlaw Mosses
Cragbank Wood
Galloway
Tynron Juniper Wood
Silver Flowe
Nith Estuary
Caimsmore of Fleet
East Stewartry Coast
Kirkconnell Flow
Caerlaverock
Fleet Valley

ATLANTIC OCEAN

NORTHERN IRELAND

ENGLAND

Scotland
1st edition – March 1999

Published by
Lonely Planet Publications Pty Ltd A.C.N. 005 607 983
192 Burwood Rd, Hawthorn, Victoria 3122, Australia

Lonely Planet Offices
Australia PO Box 617, Hawthorn, Victoria 3122
USA 150 Linden St, Oakland, CA 94607
UK 10a Spring Place, London NW5 3BH
France 1 rue du Dahomey, 75011 Paris

Photographs by
Glenn Beanland	Gareth McCormack	Bryn Thomas
Bethune Carmichael	Tom Smallman	Neil Wilson
Graeme Cornwallis	Jonathan Smith	Pat Yale

All of the images in this guide are available for licensing from
Lonely Planet Images.
email: lpi@lonelyplanet.com.au

Front cover photograph
A solitary kirk in the Highlands (Alan Becker, The Image Bank)

ISBN 0 86442 592 9

text & maps © Lonely Planet 1999
photos © photographers as indicated 1999

Printed by Colorcraft Ltd, Hong Kong

Contents – Text

2 Contents – Text

This Book

Material from the Scotland chapters of LP's Britain guide, first written by Bryn Thomas, was used for this book. Tom Smallman was the coordinating author and wrote the introductory chapters, Edinburgh, the Borders Region and Dumfries & Galloway sections of Southern Scotland, and the Shetland section of Orkney & Shetland Islands. Graeme Cornwallis wrote Glasgow, the Lanarkshire & Ayrshire sections of Southern Scotland, Central & North-Eastern Scotland, The Highlands, The Hebrides, and the Orkney section of Orkney & Shetland Islands.

From the Publisher

Craig MacKenzie was the coordinating editor of this first edition of Scotland. Coordinating designers were Louise Klep and Adrian Persoglia. Craig was assisted by Chris Wyness, Arabella Bamber, Jocelyn Harewood, Clay Lucas and Joyce Connolly. Piotr Czajkowski took the book through layout. Csanád Csutoros, Paul Dawson and Ann Jeffree assisted with map production. Mark Griffiths organised the colour wraps and Jenny Jones produced the colour country map. Thanks to Simon Bracken for the cover design, Patrick Watson for his illustrative talents, Matt King for his aesthetic appreciation, and Tim Uden for his QuarkXPress expertise. Quentin Frayne and our phrasebook department produced the Language chapter.

THANKS
Many thanks to the travellers who used the last edition of Britain and wrote to us with helpful hints, advice and interesting anecdotes.

7

Foreword

ABOUT LONELY PLANET GUIDEBOOKS

The story begins with a classic travel adventure: Tony and Maureen Wheeler's 1972 journey across Europe and Asia to Australia. Useful information about the overland trail did not exist at that time, so Tony and Maureen published the first Lonely Planet guidebook to meet a growing need.

From a kitchen table, then from a tiny office in Melbourne (Australia), Lonely Planet has become the largest independent travel publisher in the world, an international company with offices in Melbourne, Oakland (USA), London (UK) and Paris (France).

Today Lonely Planet guidebooks cover the globe. There is an ever-growing list of books and there's information in a variety of forms and media. Some things haven't changed. The main aim is still to help make it possible for adventurous travellers to get out there – to explore and better understand the world.

At Lonely Planet we believe travellers can make a positive contribution to the countries they visit – if they respect their host communities and spend their money wisely. Since 1986 a percentage of the income from each book has been donated to aid projects and human rights campaigns.

Updates Lonely Planet thoroughly updates each guidebook as often as possible. This usually means there are around two years between editions, although for more unusual or more stable destinations the gap can be longer. Check the imprint page (following the colour map at the beginning of the book) for publication dates.

Between editions up-to-date information is available in two free newsletters – the paper *Planet Talk* and email *Comet* (to subscribe, contact any Lonely Planet office) – and on our Web site at www.lonelyplanet.com. The *Upgrades* section of the Web site covers a number of important and volatile destinations and is regularly updated by Lonely Planet authors. *Scoop* covers news and current affairs relevant to travellers. And, lastly, the *Thorn Tree* bulletin board and *Postcards* section of the site carry unverified, but fascinating, reports from travellers.

Correspondence The process of creating new editions begins with the letters, postcards and emails received from travellers. This correspondence often includes suggestions, criticisms and comments about the current editions. Interesting excerpts are immediately passed on via newsletters and the Web site, and everything goes to our authors to be verified when they're researching on the road. We're keen to get more feedback from organisations or individuals who represent communities visited by travellers.

Lonely Planet gathers information for everyone who's curious about the planet – and especially for those who explore it first-hand. Through guidebooks, phrasebooks, activity guides, maps, literature, newsletters, image library, TV series and Web site we act as an information exchange for a worldwide community of travellers.

Research Authors aim to gather sufficient practical information to enable travellers to make informed choices and to make the mechanics of a journey run smoothly. They also research historical and cultural background to help enrich the travel experience and allow travellers to understand and respond appropriately to cultural and environmental issues.

Authors don't stay in every hotel because that would mean spending a couple of months in each medium-sized city and, no, they don't eat at every restaurant because that would mean stretching belts beyond capacity. They do visit hotels and restaurants to check standards and prices, but feedback based on readers' direct experiences can be very helpful.

Many of our authors work undercover, others aren't so secretive. None of them accept freebies in exchange for positive write-ups. And none of our guidebooks contain any advertising.

Production Authors submit their raw manuscripts and maps to offices in Australia, USA, UK or France. Editors and cartographers – all experienced travellers themselves – then begin the process of assembling the pieces. When the book finally hits the shops, some things are already out of date, we start getting feedback from readers and the process begins again ...

WARNING & REQUEST

Things change – prices go up, schedules change, good places go bad and bad places go bankrupt – nothing stays the same. So, if you find things better or worse, recently opened or long since closed, please tell us and help make the next edition even more accurate and useful. We genuinely value all the feedback we receive. Julie Young coordinates a well travelled team that reads and acknowledges every letter, postcard and email and ensures that every morsel of information finds its way to the appropriate authors, editors and cartographers for verification.

Everyone who writes to us will find their name in the next edition of the appropriate guidebook. They will also receive the latest issue of *Planet Talk*, our quarterly printed newsletter, or *Comet*, our monthly email newsletter. Subscriptions to both newsletters are free. The very best contributions will be rewarded with a free guidebook.

Excerpts from your correspondence may appear in new editions of Lonely Planet guidebooks, the Lonely Planet Web site, *Planet Talk* or *Comet*, so please let us know if you *don't* want your letter published or your name acknowledged.

Send all correspondence to the Lonely Planet office closest to you:

Australia: PO Box 617, Hawthorn, Victoria 3122
USA: 150 Linden St, Oakland, CA 94607
UK: 10A Spring Place, London NW5 3BH
France: 1 rue du Dahomey, 75011 Paris

Or email us at: talk2us@lonelyplanet.com.au

For news, views and updates see our Web site: www.lonelyplanet.com

HOW TO USE A LONELY PLANET GUIDEBOOK

The best way to use a Lonely Planet guidebook is any way you choose. At Lonely Planet we believe the most memorable travel experiences are often those that are unexpected, and the finest discoveries are those you make yourself. Guidebooks are not intended to be used as if they provide a detailed set of infallible instructions!

Contents All Lonely Planet guidebooks follow the same format. The Facts about the Country chapters or sections give background information ranging from history to weather. Facts for the Visitor gives practical information on issues like visas and health. Getting There & Away gives a brief starting point for researching travel to and from the destination. Getting Around gives an overview of the transport options when you arrive.

The peculiar demands of each destination determine how subsequent chapters are broken up, but some things remain constant. We always start with background, then proceed to sights, places to stay, places to eat, entertainment, getting there and away, and getting around information – in that order.

Heading Hierarchy Lonely Planet headings are used in a strict hierarchical structure that can be visualised as a set of Russian dolls. Each heading (and its following text) is encompassed by any preceding heading that is higher on the hierarchical ladder.

Entry Points We do not assume guidebooks will be read from beginning to end, but that people will dip into them. The traditional entry points are the list of contents and the index. In addition, however, there is a complete list of maps and an index map illustrating map coverage.

There's also a colour map that shows highlights. These highlights are dealt with in greater detail in the Facts for the Visitor chapter, along with planning questions and suggested itineraries. Each chapter covering a geographical region begins with a locator map and another list of highlights. Once you find something of interest in a list of highlights, turn to the index.

Maps Maps play a crucial role in Lonely Planet guidebooks and include a huge amount of information. A legend is printed on the back page. We seek to have complete consistency between maps and text, and to have every important place in the text captured on a map. Map key numbers usually start in the top left corner.

Although inclusion in a guidebook usually implies a recommendation we cannot list every good place. Exclusion does not necessarily imply criticism. In fact there are a number of reasons why we might exclude a place – sometimes it is simply inappropriate to encourage an influx of travellers.

Introduction

No visitor to Britain should miss the chance to visit Scotland. Despite its official union with England and Wales in 1707, it has managed to maintain an independent national identity that extends much further than the occasional display of kilts and bagpipes.

Almost without exception, it is also very beautiful. The wild, untamed Highlands, in particular, are extraordinary. There's a combination of exhilarating open space and a rain-washed quality to the light that illuminates a wonderful range of colours – subtle purples, browns and blues, interspersed with vivid greens and gold.

The weather is sometimes harsh, but 'bad' weather, with scudding clouds and water spilling from storm-wrapped hills and mountains, can be spectacular. It's not an easy country, and even Scottish engineers and modern technology have failed to tame it completely. When the winds howl, a human being can still feel extremely vulnerable.

Then the clouds break, and shafts of sunlight play across the landscape, highlighting spectacular snow-capped mountains and heather-covered hills, vast lochs and fast-running streams. And then come the balmy, sunny days, when the countryside is as seductive as anywhere on earth.

Scotland is hardly a secret, but for a country with an interesting history and some of the world's most dramatic scenery, it's curiously underrated and unknown.

Scottish culture is alive and well, particularly in the countryside and on the islands, but the urban centres are also unique: Edinburgh is one of the world's most beautiful cities; Glasgow is a vibrant cultural centre, vigorously reinventing itself after the collapse of its traditional industries; St Andrews is a beautiful coastal university town in the ancient Pictish kingdom of Fife; and prosperous Aberdeen surveys the North Sea (and its oilfields) with proprietorial interest.

Facts about Scotland

HISTORY
First Immigrants

Scotland's earliest inhabitants were hunter-gatherers who began arriving about 6000 years ago from England, Ireland and northern Europe. Over the next few thousand years these colonisers came in waves to different parts of the country. There are indications of Baltic cultures in east Scotland and Irish cultures on the islands of the west. Mesolithic flints from northern France have been found at many sites.

Prehistoric Civilisations

The Neolithic era, beginning in the 4th millennium BC, brought a new way of life, with agriculture, stock breeding and trading. Unprecedentedly large populations were the result and more complex patterns of social organisation evolved to control them. With organised groups of workers, more ambitious construction projects were now possible.

Neolithic people usually built wooden houses. It's only in treeless regions where they were forced to use stone that their architecture has survived. These northern islands contain rare examples of Neolithic domestic architecture; there's an entire village at Skara Brae in Orkney dating from around 3100 BC.

Between the late Neolithic and the early Bronze Age the Beaker People reached the British Isles from mainland Europe. They were so named from the shape of their earthenware drinking vessels which were customarily buried with their dead. They also introduced bronze for knives, daggers, arrowheads and articles of gold and copper. Many of Scotland's standing stones and stone circles can be accredited to the Beaker People. Some sources claim that they were the original Celts.

The Iron Age reached Scotland around 500 BC, heralding the arrival of Celtic settlers from Europe. In the Highlands, which escaped Roman influence, it lasted well into the Christian era.

Roman Attempts at Colonisation

The Romans didn't have much success in the north of Britain. In 80 AD, the Roman governor Agricola (whose son-in-law, Tacitus, named this region Caledonia) marched north and spent four years trying to subdue the wild tribes the Romans called the Picts (from the Latin pictus, meaning painted). The Picts were the most numerous of many Celtic peoples occupying this area at the time and probably reached Scotland via Orkney.

In the far north, Orkney was a centre of maritime power and posed a threat not only to the Romans, but also to the other northern tribes. For defence against raiding parties, brochs (fortified stone towers) were constructed. Broch architecture was perfected in Orkney in the 1st century BC, and there are over 500 examples, concentrated in Shetland, Orkney, the Western Isles and the north of Scotland. The best preserved, at Mousa in Shetland, dates from around 50 BC.

By the 2nd century, Emperor Hadrian decided, for reasons of defence, to build the wall (122-28 AD) that took his name. Two decades later Hadrian's successor, Antoninus Pius, invaded Scotland again and built the turf rampart, the Antonine Wall, between the Forth and the Clyde. Roman legions were stationed there for about 40 years, before they again withdrew. Apart from one more brief incursion by Septimus Severus early in the 3rd century AD to quell an uprising of Scottish tribes, the Romans abandoned attempts to subdue Scotland.

Feuding Celtic Tribes & Christianity

When the Romans finally left Britain in the 4th century, there were two indigenous Celtic tribes in the northern region of the British isles, then known as Alba: the Picts, and the Britons from the south.

The historian, Bede, attributes Christianity's arrival in Scotland to St Ninian who established a centre in Whithorn (in Dumfries & Galloway) in 397. It's more than likely, however, that some of the Romanised Britons in southern Scotland adopted Christianity after the religion was given state recognition in 313. St Columba founded a second important early Christian centre on the tiny island of Iona, off Mull, in 563.

In the 6th century a third Celtic tribe, the Scotti (the name given to them by the Romans), reached Scotland from northern Ireland (Scotia) and established a kingdom in Argyll called Dalriada. These Irish Celts spoke Q-Celtic or Gaelic which they introduced into Scotland. In the 7th century Anglo-Saxons from north-east England colonised south-east Scotland.

Despite their differences, all these tribes had converted to Christianity by the late 8th century at which time a new invader appeared.

In the 790s, raiding Norsemen in longboats sacked the religious settlement at Iona, causing the monks to flee inland with St Columba's bones to found a cathedral in the Pictish Kingdom at Dunkeld. The Norsemen continued to control the entire western seaboard until Alexander III broke their power at the Battle of Largs in 1263.

Kenneth MacAlpin & the Makings of a Kingdom

The Picts and Scotti were drawn closer together by the threat from the Norsemen and by their common Christianity. In 843 Kenneth MacAlpin, king of the Scotti of Dalriada and son of a Pictish princess, took advantage of the Pictish custom of matrilineal succession to make himself king of Alba. Thereafter the Scotti gained cultural and political ascendancy, the Pictish culture disappeared and Alba eventually became known as Scotia.

The only material evidence of the Picts comprises their truly unique symbol stones which were set up to record Pictish lineages

and alliances. These boulders, engraved with the mysterious symbols of an otherwise unknown people, can be found in many parts of eastern Scotland.

Canmore Dynasty

Shakespeare's Malcolm was Malcolm III, who was a Canmore. He killed Macbeth at Lumphanan in 1057. With his English queen, Margaret, he founded a dynasty of able Scottish rulers.

They introduced new Anglo-Norman systems of government and religious foundations, and David I (1124-53) increased his influence by adopting the Norman feudal system, granting land to great Norman families in return for their acting as what amounted to a government police force. By 1212 Walter of Coventry remarked that the Scottish court was 'French in race and manner of life, in speech and in culture'.

Clans & Feudalism

The old society was based on ties of kinship between everyone in the tribe, or clan, and its head. Unlike a feudal lord, a chief might still command the loyalty of his clan whether he was a landowner or not. The feudal system, despite the initial bloody reception,

Tanistry: Finding a King

Unlike the matrilineal Picts, the Scots preferred tanistry – the selection of a suitable male heir from anyone in the family who could claim a king as great grandfather. The chosen successor was known as the *tanist*. This had dire consequences for Scottish history, with many successions decided by the murder of one's predecessor. Shakespeare demonstrated this to great effect in *Macbeth*, but seen in a historical context Macbeth was no more a villain than anyone else. While the play isn't historically or geographically accurate, it certainly manages to evoke the dark deeds, bloodshed and warring factions of the period.

was eventually grafted onto the old system, creating families and clans who were enormously powerful in terms of land ownership and loyal fighting men.

Highlands & Lowlands

However, inaccessible in their glens, the Highland clans remained a law unto themselves for another 600 years. A cultural and linguistic divide grew up between Gaelic-speaking Highlanders, and the Lowland Scots who spoke Lallans, a language made up of English, Norse and Gaelic constituents.

In the Lowlands, small commercial centres like Berwick, Roxburgh, Stirling, Edinburgh and Forfar grew up through the trading activities of Angles, Scandinavians and Flemings. These centres later became independent, self-governing burghs, trading wool from the monasteries of the Borders for Flemish cloth or wine from Burgundy. Most of the population, however, eked out a subsistence from the land. Until the 20th century, the rural Scots' diet consisted largely of oatmeal, barley, milk, cheese, herrings, rabbits, grouse and kail (cabbage).

Wars of Independence

Two centuries of the Canmore dynasty effectively ended in 1286 when Alexander III fell to his death into the Firth of Forth at Kinghorn, Fife. He was succeeded by his four year old granddaughter, Margaret (the Maid of Norway), who was engaged to the son of England's Edward I, but she died in 1290.

There followed a dispute over the succession to the throne for which there were 13 tanists or contestants, but in the end it came down to two: Robert Bruce of Annandale and John Balliol. Edward I, as the greatest feudal lord in Britain, was asked to arbitrate and chose Balliol.

Instead of withdrawing, Edward I sought to formalise his feudal overlordship and travelled the country forcing clan leaders to sign a declaration of allegiance to him. Balliol allied himself with the French in 1295, thus beginning the enduring Auld Alliance with France.

In a final blow to Scottish pride Edward I removed the Stone of Destiny, the coronation stone on which the kings of Scotland had been invested for centuries, and sent it from Scone to London. Resistance broke out throughout the country, some of it serious, and Edward's response earned him the title Hammer of the Scots. In 1296 he laid siege to and captured Berwick.

In 1297, William Wallace's forces succeeded in defeating the English at the Battle of Stirling Bridge. After further skirmishes Wallace was betrayed, captured and executed – hanged, drawn, emasculated, burnt and quartered – at Smithfield in London in 1305. He's still remembered as the epitome of patriotism and a great hero of the resistance movement.

Robert the Bruce (grandson of Robert Bruce of Annandale) emerged as a contender for the throne. Early in 1306 he murdered his rival John Comyn (also called Red Comyn) and had himself crowned king of Scotland.

That same year Bruce's forces were defeated in battle at Methven and Dalry. According to myth, while Bruce was on the run he was inspired to renew his own efforts by a spider's persistence in spinning its web. He later went on to defeat the English at the Battle of Bannockburn in 1314, a turning point in Scotland's fight for independence from England.

After his death, the country was ravaged by civil disputes and plague epidemics. The Wars of Independence cemented links with France and Europe; the Auld Alliance with France was constantly renewed up to 1492.

The Stewarts & the Barons

Bruce's son became David II of Scotland, but was soon caught up in battles with Scots disaffected by his father and aided by England's Edward III. He suffered exile and imprisonment, but was released after agreeing to pay a huge ransom. He appointed Edward's son as his heir, but when David II died in 1371 the Scots quickly crowned Robert Stewart (Robert the Bruce's grandson), the first of the Stewart dynasty.

The early Stewart kings were ruthless in their attempts to break the power of the magnates. These were not peaceful years. Time and again the king met with an untimely death and clans like the Douglases and the Donalds (Lords of the Isles after the Norsemen were driven from the Hebrides in 1266) grew to wield almost regal power.

James IV & the Renaissance

James IV married the daughter of Henry VII of England, the first of the Tudor monarchs, thereby linking the two families. This didn't, however, prevent the French from persuading James to go to war with his in-laws. He was killed at the battle of Flodden Hill in 1513, along with 10,000 of his subjects.

Renaissance ideas flourished in Scotland during James IV's reign. Scottish poetry thrived. The intellectual climate was fertile ground for the ideas of the Reformation, a critique of the medieval Catholic church, and the rise of Protestantism.

Much graceful Scottish architecture dates from this time, and examples of the Renaissance style can be seen in alterations made to the palaces at Holyrood, Stirling, Linlithgow and Falkland. The building of collegiate churches and universities brought opportunities for education at home, along French lines. St Andrews University was founded in 1410, Glasgow in 1451 and Aberdeen in 1495.

Mary Queen of Scots & the Reformation

In 1542, James V died – broken-hearted, it is said, after his defeat by the English at Solway Moss. His baby daughter, Mary, became Queen of Scots.

At first the country was ruled by regents, who rejected Henry VIII's plan that Mary should marry his son, and sent her to France.

Henry was furious, and his armies ravaged the Borders and sacked Edinburgh in a failed attempt to force agreement – the Rough Wooing, as it was called. Mary eventually married the dauphin and became queen of France as well as Scotland.

While Mary, a devout Catholic, was in France, the Reformation of the Scottish church was under way. The wealthy Catholic church was riddled with corruption and the preachings of John Knox, pupil of the Swiss reformer, Calvin, found sympathetic ears. In 1560 the Scottish Parliament created a Protestant church that was independent of Rome and the monarchy. The Latin mass was abolished and the pope's authority denied.

Following her husband's death, Mary returned to Scotland. Still only 18 and a stunning beauty, she was a headstrong Catholic and her conduct did nothing to endear her to the Protestants. She married Henry Darnley and gave birth to a son. However, domestic bliss was shortlived and, in a bizarre train of events, Darnley was involved in the murder of Mary's Italian secretary Rizzio (rumoured to be her lover). Then Darnley himself was murdered, presumably by Mary and her lover and future husband, the Earl of Bothwell.

Forced to abdicate in favour of her son, James VI, Mary was imprisoned in the castle in the middle of Loch Leven, but escaped to England and her cousin, the Protestant Elizabeth I. Since Mary had claims to the English throne, and Elizabeth had no heir, she was seen as a security risk and Elizabeth kept her locked in the Tower of London. It took her 19 years to agree to sign the warrant for Mary's execution. When Elizabeth died in 1603, James VI of Scotland united the crowns by also becoming James I of England.

Religious Wars of the 17th Century

Religious differences led to civil war in Scotland and England. The fortunes of the Stuarts (spelt the French way following Mary's Gallic association) were thereafter bound up with the church's struggle to establish its independence from Rome. To complicate matters further, the movement for religious reform in Scotland was divided between Presbyterians, who shunned all ritual and hierarchy, and less-extreme

Protestants who were more like the Anglicans south of the border. The question of episcopacy (rule of the bishops) was particularly divisive.

Earning himself the nickname of the Wisest Fool in Christendom, James VI/I pursued a moderate policy despite the reformers' fervour. But he also insisted that his authority came directly from God (the Divine Right of Kings) and was therefore incontestable, and encouraged the paranoia which led to witch hunts, with many innocent people, set up as scapegoats, suffering appalling deaths by torture and burning.

In 1625 James was succeeded by his son, Charles I, a devout Anglican who attempted to impose a High Anglican form of worship on the church in Scotland.

In 1637 the Dean of St Giles Cathedral in Edinburgh was reading the English prayer book (a symbol of episcopacy) when he was floored by a stool thrown by Jennie Geddes, an Edinburgh greengrocer. The common people wanted a common religion and riots ensued which ended with the creation of a document known as the National Covenant. The Covenanters sought freedom from Rome and from royal interference in church government, the abolition of bishops and a simpler ritual.

The dispute developed into civil war between moderate royalists and radical Covenanters. The Marquis of Montrose is still remembered as a dashing hero who, though originally a Covenanter, eventually held out for the king. He was betrayed to the English Republicans while hiding at Ardvreck Castle in Loch Assynt and executed as a traitor.

In the meantime, civil war raged in England. Charles I was defeated by Oliver Cromwell and beheaded in 1649. His exiled son, Charles, was offered the crown in Scotland as long as he signed the Covenant. He was crowned in 1650 but soon forced into exile by Cromwell.

After Charles II's restoration in 1660, episcopacy was reinstated. Many of the clergy rejected the bishops' authority and started holding outdoor services, or Conven-

ticles. His successor, James II, a Catholic, appeared to set out determinedly to lose his kingdom. Among other poor decisions, he made worshipping as a Covenanter a capital offence.

The prospect of another Catholic king was too much for the English Protestants, so they invited William of Orange, a Dutchman who was James' nephew and married to his oldest Protestant daughter, to take power. In 1689 he landed with a small army; James broke down and fled to France. In the same year, episcopacy was abolished.

Union with England in 1707

The wars had left the country and economy ruined. During the 1690s, famine killed up to a third of the population in some areas.

Anti-English feeling ran high. Graham of Claverhouse (Bonnie Dundee) raised a band of Highlanders and routed the English troops at Killiecrankie (1689), near Pitlochry. The situation was exacerbated by the failure of an investment venture in Panama set up by the Bank of England to boost the economy, which resulted in widespread bankruptcy in Scotland.

In 1692, people were horrified by the treacherous massacre, on English government orders, of MacDonalds by Campbells in Glencoe, for failing to swear allegiance to William. The massacre became Jacobite (Stewart) propaganda that still resonates today.

In this atmosphere, the lure of trade concessions to boost the economy and the preservation of the Scottish church and the legal and education systems (along with financial inducements to ensure the compliance of the powerful nobility) persuaded the Scottish Parliament to agree to the Act of Union of 1707. This act united the two countries under a single parliament, but the union was very unpopular with most ordinary Scots.

The Jacobites

The Jacobite rebellions, most notably of 1715 and 1745, were attempts to replace the Hanoverian monarchy (chosen by Parliament to succeed the house of Orange) with Catholic Stuarts. Despite Scottish disenchantment with the Act of Union, however, there was never much support for the Jacobite cause outside the Highlands, owing to the fear of inviting Catholicism back into Scotland.

James Edward Stuart, known as the Old Pretender, was the son of the exiled James VII. With support from the Highland clans he made several attempts to regain the throne but fled to France after the unsuccessful 1715 rebellion. In an effort to impose control on the Highlanders, General Wade and the English military (the Redcoats) were sent to construct roads into the previously inaccessible glens.

In 1745, James' son, Charles Edward Stuart (Bonnie Prince Charlie) landed in Scotland to claim the crown for his father. He was at first successful, getting as far south into England as Derby, but back in Scotland after retreating north, the Young Pretender and his Highland supporters suffered catastrophic defeat at Culloden in 1746. Dressed as a woman, the prince escaped via the Western Isles assisted by Flora MacDonald.

After 'the '45' (as it became known), the government banned private armies, wearing the kilt and playing the pipes. Many Jacobites were transported or executed, or died in prison; others forfeited their lands. Those who still raise their glasses in a toast to The King over the Water are expressing a nostalgia for a way of life, the inevitable disappearance of which was accelerated by these events.

Beginnings of the Industrial Revolution

From about 1750 onwards, Lowland factories began to draw workers out of the glens. The tobacco trade with America boomed before the American War of Independence (1776-83) and then gave way to the textile industry. People came to work in the cotton and linen mills in Glasgow and Lanarkshire. Established in 1759, the Carron ironworks became the largest ironworks in Britain. The jute trade developed in Dundee and shipyards opened on the Clyde in the early 19th century.

Scottish Enlightenment

In the flowering of intellectual life known as the Scottish Enlightenment of the 18th century, the philosophers David Hume and Adam Smith emerged as influential thinkers nourished on generations of theological debate.

After the bloodshed and fervent religious debate of the Reformation, people applied themselves with the same energy and piety to the making of money and the enjoyment of leisure. There was a revival of interest in vernacular literature, reflected in Robert Fergusson's satires and Alexander MacDonald's Gaelic poetry. The poetry of Robert Burns, a man of the people, achieved lasting popularity. Sir Walter Scott, the prolific poet and novelist, was an ardent patriot.

Highland Clearances & the 19th Century

With the banning of private armies, the relationship of chief to clansman in the late 18th and early 19th centuries became one of economic, not military, consideration. The kelp industry (the production of soda ash from seaweed) was developed and Highland populations continued to grow.

By the mid-19th century, overpopulation, the collapse of the kelp industry and the potato famine of the 1840s led to the Highland Clearances. People were forced off the land and shipped or tricked into emigrating to North America, Australia and New Zealand. Those who remained were moved to smallholdings, known as *crofts*. Rents were extortionate and life for the crofters was extremely precarious. Common grazing ground was confiscated for sheep or deer runs. In 1886, however, the Crofters Commission was set up to ensure security of tenure and to fix fair rent for smallholders.

In the 19th century, it became fashionable for wealthy southerners to holiday in the Highlands to shoot deer and grouse. Queen Victoria had Balmoral built in 1848 and spent a great deal of time there, disguising herself as a simple Scotswoman and promenading in the company of her Scots servant, John Brown. Their relationship was depicted in the 1997 film, *Mrs Brown*.

Elsewhere, the new urban society saw a growing bourgeoisie take precedence in politics over the still powerful landed aristocracy. Political life was more closely integrated with England. Two Scotsmen had a significant impact on British politics. The popular Liberal, William Gladstone, was prime minister four times and Keir Hardie was the first leader of the British Labour Party.

There was much constitutional and parliamentary reform throughout the Victorian era. Legislation to improve the education system was connected with reform and dissension in the church. Desire for betterment might send a farmer's child, barefoot and with a sack of oatmeal on their back, to the university. The education system remains distinct from that of England.

In the great industrial cities, conditions among the working classes were hard. In the notorious Glasgow Gorbals, where typhoid epidemics were rife, people lived in overcrowded tenements on barely subsistence wages. Despite prosperity from the thriving shipyards, coal mines, steel works and textile mills, Glasgow and Clydeside still harboured many unemployed, unskilled immigrants from Ireland and the Highlands.

The Economy in the 20th Century

Industry continued to thrive through WWI, with Clydeside a munitions centre. The postwar slump didn't make itself felt in Scotland until the 1920s, but the Great Depression of the 1930s hit so hard that heavy industry never recovered. In fact, the seeds of Scotland's 20th century economic failure could be said to lie in the success of the preceding industrial era.

The discovery of oil and gas in the North Sea in the 1970s brought prosperity to Aberdeen and the surrounding area, and to the Shetland Islands. However, most of the oil revenue was siphoned off to England. This, along with takeovers of Scots companies by English ones (which then closed the Scots operation, asset-stripped and transferred jobs to England), fuelled increasing nationalist sentiment in Scotland.

Light engineering and high-tech electronics companies have replaced the defunct coal mines and steel works of the Central Lowlands, but many are foreign owned. The fishing industry, profitable until Britain joined the European Union (EU), is in decline, crippled by fishing quotas imposed from Brussels and by over-fishing.

Depopulation of the rural areas continues although grant schemes subsidise new business initiatives away from agriculture and fishing.

Self-Rule

From 1979 to 1997, the Scots were ruled by a Conservative government for which the majority of Scots hadn't voted. Nationalist feelings, always present, grew stronger. In 1967 the Scottish National Party (SNP) won its first seat, and support for it grew in this period.

Both the Labour Party and the Conservatives had toyed with offering Scotland devolution, or a degree of self-government. In 1979 Scots voted in a referendum on whether to set up a directly elected Scottish Assembly, but failed to get the necessary majority. Following the landslide victory of the British Labour Party in May 1997, another referendum was held over the creation of a Scottish Parliament. This time voters chose overwhelmingly in favour. The new parliament will be in Edinburgh and, following elections in 1999, will convene in the year 2000. Although devolution is occurring *within* the UK, the prospect of a totally independent Scotland doesn't seem as unlikely as it once did.

GEOGRAPHY & GEOLOGY

Scotland covers 30,414 sq miles, about half England's size. It can be divided into three areas: Southern Uplands, Central Lowlands, and northern Highlands and Islands.

South of Edinburgh and Glasgow are the Southern Uplands, with fertile coastal plains and ranges of hills bordering England. The Central Lowlands comprise a triangular slice from Edinburgh and Dundee in the east to Glasgow in the west, and contain the industrial belt and most of the population.

The Highland Boundary Fault, a geographical division, runs north-east from Helensburgh (west of Glasgow) to Stonehaven (south of Aberdeen) on the east coast. North of it are the Highlands and Islands, roughly two-thirds of the country and an area that includes mountain ranges of sandstone, granite and metamorphic rock. Mountains over 3000 feet (914m) – there are almost 300 of them in Scotland – are known as Munros, after the man who first listed them. Some rise directly from the steep sea fjords, or lochs, of the west coast. Ben Nevis, in the western Grampians, is Britain's highest mountain at 4406 feet (1343m).

The main Highlands watershed is near the west coast, giving long river valleys running east, many containing freshwater lochs and some arable areas. The Great Glen is a fault line running north-east from Fort William to Inverness, containing a chain of freshwater lochs (including Loch Ness) connected by the Caledonian Canal.

Of Scotland's 790 islands, 130 are inhabited. The Western Isles comprise the Inner Hebrides and the Outer Hebrides. To the north are two other island groups, Orkney and Shetland, the northernmost reaches of the British Isles.

Edinburgh is the capital and financial centre, Glasgow the industrial heart and Aberdeen and Dundee the two largest regional centres.

CLIMATE

'Varied' is a vague but accurate way to describe the many moods of Scotland's cool temperate climate. The weather changes quickly – a rainy day is often followed by a sunny one. There are also wide variations over small distances; while one glen broods under a cloud, the next may be basking in sunshine. As some locals are wont to say, 'If you don't like the weather just wait five minutes'. May and June are generally the driest months, but expect rain at any time. Storms are rare April to August.

Considering how far north the country lies (Edinburgh is on the same line of latitude

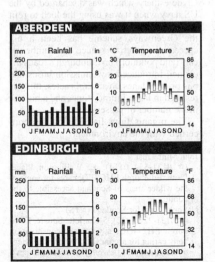

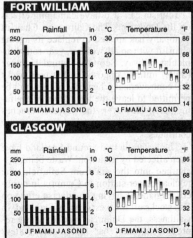

as Moscow), you might expect a colder climate, but the winds from the Atlantic are warmed by the Gulf Stream. The east and west coasts have relatively mild climates.· The east coast tends to be cool and dry – rainfall averages around 650mm, and winter temperatures rarely drop below 0°C, although winds off the North Sea can rattle your teeth. The west coast is milder and wetter, with over 1500mm of rain and average summer highs of 19°C.

In the Highlands rainfall can be as much as 3000mm; the average summer high is 18°C.

ECOLOGY & ENVIRONMENT

Though Scotland's wild, open countryside looks natural, it isn't. It's almost entirely 'spoilt' in so far as much of the original forest (ie 99%) has gone. However, the grassy hillsides 'laid bare' are very beautiful.

In much of Scotland you'll notice thick evergreen plantations. In recent decades governments encouraged landowners to plant these fast-growing trees, despite serious ecological drawbacks. As well as destroying wildlife habitat, conifers increase acidity in soil and may have a detrimental effect on weather patterns. In the far north, bogland has been destroyed. This also causes increased water run-off and, hence, flooding downstream.

Tourism can also have damaging effects on the landscape. The Cairngorm Chairlift Company has applied to replace its ageing chairlift with an all-weather, year-round funicular railway. Scottish Natural Heritage (SNH) initially opposed it, but now backs this controversial scheme (visitors won't be permitted to leave the top station of the funicular!). However, the project breaches certain EU regulations and the controversy continues.

The waters in and around Scotland have been affected by pollution. Waste being discharged into the sea from Sellafield, the nuclear power station in Cumbria in northern England, is having an adverse effect on fish stocks off the west coast of Scotland. In Caithness, the Dounreay nuclear waste reprocessing plant has had a poor safety

record over several decades. Following a recent series of accidents and disclosures about errors and cover ups the British government decided to close it down. However, reprocessing will continue until about 2006 when the waste runs out; after that it'll take another 100 years to clean up the plant, dismantle it and encase the remains in concrete.

Toxic chemicals have been put into lochs, to control sea lice which eat the flesh of salmon. Environmentalists fear that dosages will increase as lice become more resistant.

The seas around St Kilda are Britain's only World Heritage Site and ocean wilderness with 21 species of whale and dolphin. Greenpeace says the site is threatened by oil exploration and has applied to put it on a UNESCO list of sites in danger. Shetland appears to have pretty much recovered from the sinking of the oil tanker *Braer* in 1993; the coastline was spared serious damage because storms spread the spilled oil over a wide area. Marine biologists are monitoring what long-term effects the pollution has had on marine life. Oil tankers still plough the waters around Shetland so the threat of a similar accident remains real.

On a more positive note, there are plans to clean up toxic waste at Holy Loch on the Clyde estuary which was discharged by the US navy when it was using the loch to refit nuclear submarines (1961-92). In Edinburgh, the Greenways scheme has been a big success. In order to reduce the number of cars (and pollution) on Edinburgh's roads the council introduced low emission buses and bus priority lanes on several routes; this has resulted in faster journey times and a big rise in the number of passengers.

The organisations listed below are concerned with the environment.

John Muir Trust
(☎ 0131-554 0114), 12 Wellington Place, Leith, Edinburgh EH6 7EQ; cares for some of the wilder areas of Scotland accessible to the public.
National Trust for Scotland (NTS)
(☎ 0131-226 5922), 5 Charlotte Square, Edinburgh EH2 4DU; a voluntary conservation body caring for around 185,000 acres of countryside (as well as owning historic buildings);

reciprocal membership agreements with the National Trust (for England, Wales and Northern Ireland).

Royal Society for the Protection of Birds (RSPB) (☎ 0131-557 6275), 12 Regent Terrace, Edinburgh EH7 5BN; has a number of reserves around Scotland which are open to the public.

Scottish Natural Heritage (SNH) (☎ 0131-447 4784), 12 Hope Terrace, Edinburgh EH9 2AS; a government agency responsible for the conservation of Scotland's wildlife, habitats and landscapes; designates and manages National Nature Reserves (NNRs) and Sites of Special Scientific Interest (SSSIs).

Scottish Wildlife Trust (☎ 0131-312 7765), 16 Cramond Glebe Rd, Edinburgh EH4 6NS; a voluntary agency that owns and runs 116 nature reserves.

The Woodland Trust (☎ 01764-662554), Glenruthven Mill, Abbey Rd, Auchterarder, Perthshire PH3 1DP; buys and cares for native woodlands and potential forest land for conservation and public access.

FLORA & FAUNA
Flora

Although much of the country was once covered by the Caledonian forest – a mix of Scots pine, oak, silver birch, willow, alder and rowan, with heather underfoot – deforestation has reduced this mighty forest to a few small pockets of indigenous trees. Only 1% remains.

Almost three-quarters of the country is uncultivated bog, rock and heather. In mountainous areas like the Cairngorms, alpine plants thrive, while in the far north there are lichens and mosses found nowhere else in Britain.

Acidic peat covers almost two million acres, most notably in the Flow Country of Caithness and Sutherland, a conservation area.

Although the thistle is commonly associated with Scotland, the national flower is the harebell or bluebell. Yellow flag, wild thyme and yarrow abound in the summer. Purple coloured heather, which flowers in August is probably the most noticeable of Scots flowering plants. Other flowering plants include bluebells in May and the heather's arch enemy, strong-yellow gorse, also in May.

Fauna

Red deer are found in Scotland in large numbers, but the reindeer, beaver and auroch (wild ox) are all now extinct. The last wolf was shot in Morayshire in 1743 but there's talk of reintroducing the species. Once nearly extinct, wild boars have been reintroduced in the south-west. There are still some wildcats but, like wild goats, they're rarely seen.

Sheep graze the grass-covered hills, and much of the Lowlands is given over to agriculture. Hairy Highland cattle are well adapted to survive the cold. Take care in approaching these diminutive bovines – they look cuddly but have foul tempers.

Foxes and red squirrels are found throughout the country, with pine martens in the forests. Otters are rare, though less so than in England; and minks, escaped from fur farms, are multiplying fast. Scotland contains almost the entire British population of blue mountain hares.

Native reptiles include the adder (poisonous) and the common lizard.

Scotland has an immense variety of avifauna. Large numbers of grouse graze the heather on the moors, and gamekeepers burn vast areas to encourage the new shoots that attract this small game bird. In heavily forested areas you may be lucky enough to see a capercaillie, a black, turkey-like bird, the largest member of the grouse family. Birds of prey such as the eagle, osprey, peregrine falcon and hen harrier are protected. Millions of greylag geese winter on the Lowland stubble fields.

Since 80% of Britain's coastline is in Scotland, it's not surprising to find millions of sea birds including gannets, kittiwakes, puffins, shags, fulmars and guillemots. Whale-watching trips follow more substantial photographic prey and seals are quite frequently seen. The fabled wild Scottish salmon and varieties of trout are found in many rivers and lochs.

Endangered Species

Scotland is home to many animals and birds that are rare elsewhere in the UK, but they too are constantly threatened by the changing environment. The habitat of the once common corncrake, for example, was almost completely destroyed by modern farming methods. Farmers now receive a subsidy for mowing in a corncrake-friendly fashion and there are good prospects for its survival. Other threats don't even have an economic justification; the osprey nest at Boat of Garten has to be watched continuously to prevent egg collectors whipping the eggs.

Wildlife species that were slaughtered to the point of extermination in the 19th century – golden eagles, buzzards, pine martens, polecats and wildcats among them – are protected by law and only now recovering. However, many of these species are a natural enemy of game birds and in order to preserve the latter as targets for sporting shooters, some unscrupulous estate owners and gamekeepers poison birds like the golden eagle.

Furthermore, the Agriculture, Environment & Fisheries Department of the Scottish Office has licensed the culling of fish-eating birds like the cormorant and goosander to preserve fish for anglers. Some fear that the level of culling could threaten the survival of these species.

To combat these threats, Scottish Natural Heritage has established a Species Action Programme to restore populations of endangered species.

Conservation Areas

Scotland doesn't have national parks, but it does have a range of designated protected areas.

National Scenic Areas (NSAs) are regions of exceptional natural beauty, especially in the Highlands, and are considered of national significance. National Nature Reserves (NNRs), also of national importance, protect habitats and species. The largest of these is in the Caingorm Mountains. Sites of Special

The Monarch of the Glen

The red deer, the Monarch of the Glen, is causing a serious ecological problem in Scotland. Unlike many species, it isn't hurtling towards extinction but multiplying way out of control. There are over 300,000 and huge areas of vegetation are being damaged.

Fencing off woodland isn't the answer as it reduces the territory of the deer and leads to even heavier grazing of these areas. In some parts of Scotland, no new trees have been able to grow since deer populations started to increase about 300 years ago.

The balance of nature was upset when the natural predator of the red deer, the wolf, was eradicated in the 17th century and there's now talk of reintroducing the species. In recent years, too few deer have been culled by farmers and estate managers, and, with milder winters, fewer deer have died from lack of food. If nothing is done to reduce deer numbers, the last few areas of indigenous forest in the country may be destroyed.

Scientific Interest (SSSIs) are significant for their geology, flora, fauna or habitats or combinations thereof. All NNRs are also SSSIs and are managed by the SNH. (Keeping up with the acronyms?)

Local Nature Reserves (LNRs) cover sites of local conservation interest for public use, while Regional Parks are large areas of countryside set aside for public recreation. Country Parks are smaller and usually close to towns.

GOVERNMENT & POLITICS

Until the new Scottish Parliament is up and running Scotland will still largely be ruled from London. The Secretary of State for Scotland, a member of the British Cabinet, is responsible for Scotland's administration in the form of five departments – education and health; development; planning; agriculture and fisheries; and the judicial system. The secretary operates from the Scottish Office in Edinburgh. Some laws in the British Houses of Parliament are passed exclusively for Scotland.

There are 72 Scottish members in the House of Commons and all Scottish peers have a seat in the House of Lords.

There are 32 administrative regions, roughly corresponding to the old counties (eg Argyll, Perthshire etc) which existed prior to the 1974 reforms.

The main political parties are the same as for the rest of Britain – Conservative, Labour, Liberal Democrat – with the addition of the Scottish National Party. As a result of the 1997 British general election there were no remaining Conservative MPs in Scotland. The Conservative Party was largely opposed to devolution (the transfer of government powers from Westminster to Scotland), and the long-term goal of the Scottish Nationalists is complete independence.

In a landmark referendum in 1997 Scots voted overwhelmingly for a separate Scottish Parliament. Elections for this new parliament (under a system of partial proportional representation) will be held in 1999 and the parliament will convene in 2000. It'll have 129 members, will sit for four-year terms and be responsible for levying income tax, education, health and other domestic affairs. Westminster will still control areas like defence, foreign affairs and social security.

The Scottish Parliament will sit in Edinburgh. Its temporary home will be the Assembly Rooms of the Church of Scotland on the Royal Mile until a new purpose-built building is completed near the Palace of Holyroodhouse.

ECONOMY

Scotland's economy is in a process of transition. Many coal mines and steel works have closed. Oil and gas are still extracted from North Sea platforms, but the oil-boom days in Shetland, Invergordon and Aberdeen are over. The old heavy industries are being replaced by less labour-intensive high-tech engineering projects (Scotland has its Silicon Glen), electronics, finance and service industries. There are some traditional industries that survive and thrive. Woollens, tweeds and tartans from Harris and the Borders are world renowned, as are the whisky distilleries. Edinburgh is an important international finance centre.

Tourism is now Scotland's largest industry, with over £2.5 billion injected into the Scottish economy in 1997, and continues to grow. A lot of future growth will be via the Internet.

In the Highlands some sheep and cattle farming continues, although tourism means that grouse moors, deer forests and salmon rivers are a better bet economically. The fertile lowland plains produce barley, oats, wheat, potatoes, turnips, cattle and sheep. EU policy, however, requires farmers to put around 15% of arable land out of production. Scotland catches over two-thirds of UK fish and shellfish even with EU fishing quotas.

Unemployment is generally higher than the UK average and some regions, eg the Highlands and Islands, are much higher. The Scottish Enterprise Network, a quasi-government body, has been set up to promote businesses and jobs at a local level.

Radical Politics

The radical Scottish tradition that produced John Knox and other church reformers also generated some later influential political thinkers.

The trade unions produced James Keir Hardie, who helped form the Scottish Labour Party (1888), the Independent Labour Party for Great Britain (1893) and the Labour Representative Committee (1900), forerunner of the British Labour Party. Ramsay MacDonald, like Hardie, came from a poor background. He joined the Labour Representative Committee and in 1923-24 led the first Labour government. He was later to move to the centre politically, and many of his Labour supporters felt betrayed when he formed a coalition with the Tories in 1931-35.

The economic distress of the 1930s pushed Scottish political opinion further to the left and several major players in the Communist Party of Great Britain were Scots.

James Keir Hardie's efforts led to the formation of the Labour Party in Britain.

The formation in 1934 of the Scottish National Party (SNP) was initiated by several distinguished men of letters – Hugh MacDiarmid, Eric Linklater, Sir Compton Mackenzie, Neil Gunn and Lewis Grassic Gibbon. This party achieved political success only relatively recently, most Scots being traditional Labour supporters. After the elections to the new Scottish Parliament it may well be the majority party. It sees the new parliament as only a stepping stone to complete independence, for which it has a target date of 2007 – the 300th anniversary of the Act of Union.

POPULATION & PEOPLE

Scotland has around five million people, which equates to just 9% of the UK's total population. Scotland's population has been declining steadily since the 1920s largely through migration (mainly because of lower job opportunities) and, in more recent times, through birth control.

Glasgow is the largest city with 689,000 people, followed by Edinburgh which has 409,000, Aberdeen with 217,260, and Dundee with 177,540. The Highland region is Britain's most sparsely populated administrative area, with an average of 20 people

per square mile – 30 times fewer than the UK average.

Early history describes a belligerent people of mixed origin. Invading Romans, raiding Vikings, avaricious English kings and clan warfare never gave them a chance to settle down.

Centuries-old disagreements between clans are remembered, and even today a Colquhoun won't sit with a MacGregor because of the massacre of Colquhouns by Rob Roy and a band of MacGregors over 300 years ago. Religious differences also play a part (see Religion later in this chapter).

Influences from different parts of Europe have created a country of people who are far from homogeneous. The 'hurdy-gurdy' accent of Shetlanders and Orcadians betrays their Scandinavian roots. Gaelic is still spoken in parts of the Highlands and Islands, and Highland society is very different to the anglicised Lowlands. In the 20th century, immigrants, including Irish, Italians, Jews, Poles and Asians, have settled mostly in the larger towns.

EDUCATION

Scotland's education system was one of the best in the world, the Scottish love of learning and their pride in education being a by-product of the church reformation. Education was controlled by the church for a long time and the great universities were set up to provide a source of educated churchmen. By the 17th century there was a school in every parish and standards continued to rise until the Industrial Revolution, when the use of child labour increased. Basic education became compulsory in 1872.

The 1962 Education Act introduced a uniform system preserving the broader-based Scottish system from erosion by anglicisation. Schools today are run by the Scottish Education Department under the auspices of the Scottish Office and follow a curriculum and examination system different from England's.

There are many independent, fee-paying schools along English lines. At tertiary level there are over a dozen universities, the most prestigious being Aberdeen, St Andrews, Dundee, Edinburgh, Glasgow and Stirling.

Many young people leave school without qualifications, but educational standards aren't really falling as some have claimed. It's just that the educational results of other countries are improving.

SCIENCE & PHILOSOPHY

It's not overstating it to say that the intellectual output of Scottish scientists has transformed modern civilisation. Scottish

---

Scots Abroad

'The Scotsman is never at home but when he's abroad', goes the saying. This reflects the fact that the Scots' sense of Scottishness and national identity is often more keenly felt when they're away from the land of their birth. That's perhaps one reason why someone like Sean Connery, for example, can claim to be a Scottish nationalist while living abroad. The yearning from afar for their homeland resulted in many songs, a good number of them over-sentimentalised.

Scots have emigrated to all corners of the globe for hundreds of years. There are now about 25 million people of Scottish extraction living outside the country, compared to only five million within it.

Evicted Highlanders were sent to Canada, Free Church supporters went to Dunedin in New Zealand, while others joined the Hudson's Bay Company and the East India Company. Large numbers of Scots were among those who colonised the countries of the British Empire, well prepared by the hardship of existence in Scotland for the pioneering life. The missionary zeal of the Presbyterians was great in Africa; Dr Livingstone, explorer of the source of the Nile, is one example of many. Some Scots, like Andrew Carnegie in the USA, had a disproportionate influence on their adopted country.

One of Scotland's greatest exports has been its intellect. Alexander Graham Bell, for example, was living and working in the USA when he invented the telephone. And most of the country's Nobel Prize winners received the award for work they had done outside Scotland.

scientists include John Napier, the inventor of logarithms; Lord Kelvin, who revealed the second law of thermodynamics; and James Clerk Maxwell, who described the laws of electromagnetism. James Hutton is considered the founder of modern geology.

The technologists include James Watt, who revolutionised steam power and John Dunlop, who invented the pneumatic wheel. John McAdam invented the road surface that bears his name (but spelt differently) and Charles Macintosh invented waterproof material.

Alexander Graham Bell invented the telephone, John Logie Baird TV and Sir Robert Watson Watt radar. The list goes on.

The doctors include John and William Hunter, who pioneered anatomy; Sir Joseph Lister, who pioneered the use of antiseptics; and Sir Alexander Fleming, who discovered penicillin.

The philosophers and thinkers include David Hume and Adam Smith.

Many reasons have been given for this extraordinary roll-call, but one of the most obvious is the long tradition of high-quality education that can be traced back as far as the earliest monastic institutions.

ARTS

Between them, Edinburgh and Glasgow dominate the arts in Scotland. Both have an energetic cultural scene, partly reflected by

Scottish Inventions & Discoveries

The inventiveness of the Scots is remarkable, given the size of Scotland's population. Some academics say that the Scots have produced more geniuses than any other people. Perhaps it was the weather that caused thinking Scots to remain indoors pondering life, the universe and all that is within it.

It would be difficult to imagine life without many of the long list of things they either discovered or invented.

James Watt (1736-1819) didn't invent the steam engine (that was done by an Englishman, Thomas Newcomen), but it was Watt's modifications and improvements that led to its widespread use in industry. Perhaps it's not surprising, given the amount of rainfall in Scotland, that a Scot would invent a fabric-waterproofing process. This was done by chemist and dyeist Charles Macintosh (1766-1843) whose name was given to the first rainproof coat.

James Watt's modifications to the steam engine led to its widespread use in industry.

Not only did John Logie Baird (1888-1946) from Helensburgh invent television, but his own company produced with the BBC the world's first broadcast, the first broadcast with sound and the first outside broadcast. Alexander Graham Bell (1847-1922) made a series of inventions but his most famous was the telephone in 1876. James Dewar (1842-1923) used his expertise in the storing of liquid gases to invent the vacuum flask.

their respective festivals, which showcase an extraordinary range of performers and artists. Historically, however, although the Scots have had a disproportionate impact on science, technology, medicine and philosophy, they are, with the notable exception of literature, under-represented in the worlds of art and music.

The arts never seem to have caught the Scottish popular imagination – or at least not in a form recognised by modern culture vultures. Perhaps the need for creative expression took different, less elitist paths – in the *ceilidh* (see Society & Conduct later in this chapter), in folk music and dance, oral poetry and folk stories.

Literature

Scotland's literary heritage is so rich that most parts of the country have a piece of writing that captures its spirit.

Sir Walter Scott's prodigious output did much to romanticise Scotland and its historical figures. *Rob Roy* portrays the cattle rustler/blackmailer rather rosily; the descriptions of the Trossachs, in which the MacGregor family operated, are more accurate. The Lammermuir Hills between the Borders and East Lothian were the setting for *The Bride of Lammermoor*. In the *Heart of Midlothian* he used an existing house in St Leonard's, Edinburgh, as the home of the fictional character, Jennie Deans.

John Dunlop (1840-1921) invented the pneumatic tyre while experimenting on his son's tricycle. Metereologist Robert Watson Watt (1892-1973) first helped to develop a storm-warning device for pilots which later evolved into radar. A network of radar tracking stations was set up in the late 1930s which were to prove crucial in the RAF's fight against the German Luftwaffe during WWII.

In 1996, a team of Scottish embryologists working at the Roslin Institute near Edinburgh scored a first when they successfully cloned a sheep, Dolly, from the breast cell of an adult sheep. They added to this success when Dolly was mated naturally with a Welsh ram; in April 1998 she gave birth to a healthy lamb, Bonnie.

Other inventions and discoveries include:

- anaesthetics
- carbon dioxide
- electric light
- grand pianos
- lawnmowers
- morphine
- refrigeration
- steel ships
- ultrasound
- breech-loading rifles
- colour photography
- fire alarms
- golf
- logarithms
- penicillin
- shrapnel
- tarmacadam roads (McAdam)
- water softeners
- bicycles
- decimal fraction point
- gas-masks
- insulin
- marmalade
- postage stamp (adhesive)
- speedometers
- telescopes

Scotland has also had a significant number of Nobel Prize winners. Sir William Ramsay (1852-1916), whose work helped in the development of the nuclear industry, received the prize in 1904 for chemistry. Physiologist, John Macleod (1876-1935) received it for medicine in 1923; his work led to the discovery of insulin. Sir Alexander Fleming (1881-1955), co-discoverer of penicillin, also received it for medicine (in 1945). Other prize winners include: Charles Wilson, John Orr, Alexander Robertus Todd and Sir James Black.

Several Robert Louis Stevenson novels have Scottish settings; *Kidnapped*, set on the island of Mull, Edinburgh and Rannoch Moor, captures the country most vividly. Although *The Strange Case of Dr Jekyll and Mr Hyde* is set in London, Stevenson drew inspiration from the streets of Edinburgh. The island in *Treasure Island* is said to be based on Unst in the Shetlands.

Arthur Conan Doyle, creator of Sherlock Holmes, was inspired by his daily walk to Edinburgh University as a student past Salisbury Crags for the setting of his novel *The Lost World*.

Many of John Buchan's adventure stories, of which *The Thirty Nine Steps* is the most famous, are set at least partly in Scotland.

Sir Compton Mackenzie's *Whisky Galore* is required reading for long Hebridean ferry rides; it's the witty tale of what happens when a cargo of whisky runs aground on one of the islands during WWII, something that really happened. Derek Cooper's more serious *Hebridean Connection* is also recommended.

If you're visiting Orkney, you should try to read at least one of George Mackay Brown's novels. *Greenvoe* is a wonderfully poetic description of an Orkney community. His short story collection, *A Calendar of Love*, is delightful.

Muriel Spark's shrewd portrait of 1930s Edinburgh, *The Prime of Miss Jean Brodie*, was made into an excellent film. In sharp contrast, Irvine Welsh's novels, like *Trainspotting* which was also made into a successful film, take the reader on a guided tour of the modern city's underworld of drugs, drink, despair and violence. His latest novel is called *Ecstasy*. Sometimes compared to Welsh is Alan Warner whose two novels *Marver Callar* and *These Demented Lands* cover similar themes but are set in the Highlands.

St Leonard's Hall, just outside Holyrood Park, was once occupied by a girl's school, called St Trinnean's (reputedly the inspiration for the St Trinian stories of Robert Earle whose daughter was a pupil there).

The grim realities of contemporary Glasgow are vividly conjured up in James Kelman's short story collection, *Not Not While the Giro*. Kelman won the 1994 Booker Prize with *How Late It Was, How Late*, but the language it was written in provoked much controversy. Alasdair Gray's acclaimed *Lanark* is also set in a run-down city based on modern Glasgow. Duncan McLean's *Bucket of Tongues* is an equally disturbing short story collection set in assorted depressed urban locations.

Journalist Isla Dewar's novels are spirited accounts of small town life in modern Scotland. Titles include *Women Talking Dirty* and *Giving up on Ordinary*.

In *A Scot's Quair*, Lewis Grassic Gibbon evocatively recaptures early 20th century village life in Aberdeenshire. His *Sunset Song* is a literary classic.

Nigel Tranter is a prolific historical novelist whose books are set in Scotland. His most recent novel *High Kings and Vikings* is set in the 10th century and tells the story of one Cormac Mac Farqhar, Thane of Glamis.

Emma Blair is a popular romantic historic novelist whose books are set in Scotland. Her most recent, *The Flower of Scotland*, tells the story of a family that owns a whisky distillery around the time of WWI. The most successful author of light fiction is Rosamunde Pilcher whose novels, *The Shell Seekers*, *September* and *Coming Home* have sold in their millions.

Neil Munro's *Para Handy* about a steamship captain who sails the west coast gives an insight into Gaelic life in the early 20th century. His *Erchie & Jimmy Swan* is also well worth considering.

Other writers to look out for are Alisdair Gray, AL Kennedy, Elizabeth McNeill and Laura Hird.

Collections of ballads and poems by the popular national bard Robert Burns are widely available. Another 18th century poet, Alexander MacDonald, wrote in Gaelic. Sorley MacLean and Norman McCaig were also exceptional poets. Scotland's finest modern poet is Hugh MacDiarmid, cofounder of the Scottish National Party.

Perhaps the worst is William MacGonagall, who is celebrated for the sheer awfulness of his rhymes. His *Poetic Gems* offers a taster.

Architecture

Scottish architecture can be divided into six periods: Celtic (up to the 11th century), Anglo-Norman (up to the 16th century), post-Reformation or Renaissance (up to the 17th century), Georgian (18th century), Victorian Baronial (19th century), and 20th century (which so far evades simple characterisation).

Interesting buildings can be viewed throughout Scotland, but Edinburgh has a particularly remarkable heritage of superb architecture from the 12th century to the present day.

Celtic Few Celtic buildings survive, although the islands have some of the best surviving examples in Europe. The best known are the stone villages of Skara Brae (from 3100 BC) in Orkney, Jarlshof (from 1500 BC) in Shetland, and the characteristic stone towers *(brochs)*, probably built by chieftains, that can be seen in a number of places, including Carloway in Lewis and Mousa in Shetland.

The crofters' blackhouses of the Highlands and Islands were probably little changed from Celtic times through to the 19th century, but only a few remain. Originally they were circular, but at some point they came to be long, low rectangular buildings. They had thick dry-stone walls, and thatched roofs, sometimes augmented with skins and canvas, tied down with ropes and nets. There were no chimneys; smoke from a central peat fire simply leaked through the thatch. The kitchen and communal area was in the centre; the family slept to one side, the animals to the other.

Anglo-Norman The Normans were great builders, and their Romanesque style – with its characteristic round arches – can still be seen in David I's church at Dunfermline (1128) and the church at Leuchars (12th century).

Military architecture was also influenced by the Normans in castles like Caerlaverock (1290) and, later, at Stirling (1496). Most feudal lords, however, built more modest tower, or peel, houses, like Threave and Smailholm (14th century). These had a single small entrance, massively thick stone walls and a single room at each of about five levels.

As the Gothic style developed in England and Europe, it was brought to Scotland and adapted by the religious orders. The characteristic pointed arches and stone vaulting can be seen in Glasgow Cathedral (13th century) and the ruins of great Borders abbeys like Jedburgh (12th century).

Post-Reformation After the Reformation most churches were modified to suit the new religion, which frowned on ceremony and ornament.

In some areas, tower houses and castles became less relevant because of the increasing effectiveness of artillery. The gentry therefore had the luxury of expanding their houses and at the same time making them more decorative. Features like turrets, conical roofs, garrets and gables became popular in buildings like Castle Fraser (1636) and Thirlestane Castle.

Georgian The greatest exponent of the austere, symmetrical Georgian style in Scotland was the Adam family, in particular Robert Adam. Among other buildings, he designed Hopetoun, Mellerstain and Culzean Castle in the mid-18th century.

Victorian Baronial As the Scottish identity was reaffirmed by writers like Burns and Scott, architects turned to the towers and turrets of the past for inspiration. Fanciful buildings like Balmoral, Scone Palace and Abbotsford were created, and the fashion was also exhibited in many civic buildings.

20th Century Scotland's most famous 20th century architect and designer is Charles Rennie Mackintosh of Glasgow, one of the most influential exponents of the

Art Nouveau style. The most acclaimed example of his work is Glasgow School of Art, which still looks modern 90 years after it was built.

In general, the quality of modern building has not been high, although there are notable exceptions like the impressive gallery housing the Burrell Collection in Glasgow. On the whole, however, the larger towns and cities have suffered badly under the onslaught of the motor car and the unsympathetic impact of large-scale, shoddy council housing. Traditional houses suffered badly from dampness. They've been demolished in large numbers but many remain.

Painting

There are few internationally known figures in the visual arts, although the National Gallery in Edinburgh and the galleries in Glasgow, Aberdeen, Perth and Dundee have important Scottish collections.

Scottish painting only really emerged in the mid-17th century with portraits by George Jameson and John Wright. Scottish portraiture reached its peak during the Scottish Enlightenment in the second half of the 18th century in the figures of Alan Ramsay and Henry Raeburn.

At the same time, Alexander Nasmyth emerged as an important landscape painter whose work had immense influence on the 19th century. One of the greatest artists of the 19th century was David Wilkie whose paintings depicted simple, rural Scottish life.

The Trustees' Academy in Edinburgh, particularly under the direction of William Scott Lauder, was very influential and taught many of the great painters of the 19th century, most notably William McTaggart. Exhibitions at the Royal Scottish Academy in Edinburgh also helped to promote Scottish painters.

Since the end of the 19th century, Glasgow has dominated the Scottish scene, partly thanks to the Glasgow School of Art, which has produced several outstanding artists. These included Charles Rennie Mackintosh, whose Art Nouveau style upset

more traditionalist painters, and Mary Armour who was a student there in the 1920s.

In the 1890s, the Glasgow Boys, which included James Guthrie and EA Walton in their ranks, were stylistically influenced by the French impressionists. They were succeeded by the Scottish Colourists whose striking paintings drew upon French post-impressionism and Fauvism. In the same period the Glasgow Girls, exponents of decorative arts and design, drew upon Art Nouveau and Celtic influences. Among their members were Jessie Newbery, Anne Macbeth and the MacDonald sisters, Margaret and Frances.

The Edinburgh School of the 1930s were modernist painters who depicted the Scottish landscape. Chief among them were William Gillies, William MacTaggart (not to be confused with his earlier namesake) and Ann Redpath. Following WWII, artists such as Alan Davie and Eduardo Paolozzi gained international reputations in abstract expressionism and pop art, but their work isn't particularly 'Scottish'. Today's new wave of painters include the New Glasgow Boys whose work is characterised by a concern for social issues.

Music

In the 1950s and 60s many people's idea of Scottish music was represented by the likes of Kenneth McKellar and Andy Stewart, who sang mostly sentimental ballads often accompanied by the accordion and occasionally the bagpipes. They often wore the kilt when they performed. In the 70s the most recognised Scottish pop band was the Bay City Rollers (the Spice Girls of their day) who sang simple ditties and wore short baggy tartan trousers. They can still be seen performing in small venues.

Scotland has always had a strong folk tradition and in the 60s and 70s Robin Hall and Jimmy MacGregor, the Corries and the hugely talented Ewan McColl worked the pubs and clubs up and down the country. The Boys of the Lough were one of the first to successfully blend Scottish (and Irish) folk music with pop/rock music and they have been followed by the Battlefield Band, Runrig (who write songs in Gaelic), Alba, Capercaillie and others. Rock musicians like Simple Minds and the Pogues borrowed from Scottish themes.

Other Scottish artists who have been successful in rock music include Gerry Rafferty, who wrote *Baker St*, and Midge Ure, who helped organise the Band Aid famine relief in the 1980s. Iain Anderson, front man for Jethro Tull, was born in Edinburgh. Barbara Dickson, Nazareth and Vipond all hail from Dunfermline. Sheena Easton came from Bellshill and now lives in Beverley Hills and Aberdeen's greatest musical export is Annie Lennox. The Jesus & Mary Chain came from East Kilbride. Glasgow has shown an amazing depth of musical talent, producing such performers as the BMX Bandits, Aztec Camera, Hue & Cry, Simple Minds, Tears for Fears, Wet Wet Wet, Texas – and Lulu.

Cinema

Scotland has been the setting for many films. Earlier ones include *The Prime of Miss Jean Brodie* (1969) and *Kidnapped* (1972). *Local Hero* (1983) is Bill Forsyth's gentle story of an oil magnate turned conservationist for love of the scenery. His other great success was *Gregory's Girl* (1980), about an awkward teenage schoolboy's romantic exploits.

Highlander (1986), starring Sean Connery and Christopher Lambert, was set in 16th century Scotland and filmed around Fort William and in Glen Coe and Glen Uig.

When *Braveheart*, the Mel Gibson spin on the William Wallace saga, won an Oscar in 1996 the Scottish Tourist Board (STB) cheered, anticipating a boom in tourists lured by the glorious scenery in the background. What the STB wasn't shouting about, however, was that though it was partly filmed around Fort William, most of *Braveheart* was shot in Ireland which had been wooing Hollywood film makers with tax breaks.

The same year saw the release of *Loch Ness*, a romantic comedy focussing on the monster myth, following fast on the success of *Trainspotting*. All this, when memories of *Rob Roy*, the 1995 rendition of the outlaw's tale, starring Liam Neeson and Jessica Lange with wonky Scottish accents, were only just fading.

Billy Connolly's accent was real enough when he played John Brown, Queen Victoria's Scottish servant in *Mrs Brown* (1997).

Scottish actors who have achieved international success include Sean Connery, who played the quintessential Englishman, James Bond; Robert Carlyle whose film *The Full Monty* (1997) was the UK's most commercially successful film ever; Ewan McGregor who appeared in *Trainspotting*; and John Hannah whose films include *Four Weddings & a Funeral* and *Sliding Doors*. Others are Ian Bannen, Gordon Jackson, Alistair Sim, James Robertson Justice, Dame Flora Robson, Finlay Currie and Andrew Cruickshank.

SOCIETY & CONDUCT

Outside Scotland, Scots are often stereotyped as being a tight-fisted bunch, but nothing could be further from the truth – most are in fact extremely generous. Scots may appear reserved, but they are passionate in their beliefs whether it's politics, religion or football. They generally treat visitors courteously, and the class distinctions that so bedevil England are less prevalent. The influence of religion is declining. But in the Highlands and Islands it still affects daily life, and sectarian tension between Protestant and Catholic occasionally erupts in violence. Scotland is mainly an urban society with most people living in the south from the Firth of Clyde to the Firth of Forth.

The Scots take their drinking seriously, spending an average 9% of their weekly income on booze and cigarettes, the highest consumption in Britain.

Traditional Culture

Bagpipes One of the oldest musical instruments still used today is the bagpipe. Although no piece of film footage on Scotland is complete without the drone of the pipes, their origin probably lies outside the country. The Romans used bagpipes in their armies, and modern versions can be heard as far away from the Highland glens as India and Russia.

The Highland bagpipe is the type most commonly played in Scotland. It comprises a leather bag inflated by the blowpipe and held under the arm; the piper controls the flow of air through the pipes by squeezing the bag. Three of the pipes, appropriately known as the drones, play all the time without being touched by the piper. The fourth pipe, the chanter, is the one on which tunes can be played.

Queen Victoria did much to repopularise the bagpipe, with her patronage of all things Scottish. When staying at Balmoral she liked to be wakened by a piper playing outside her window.

Ceilidh The Gaelic word *ceilidh* (pronounced kaylee) means 'visit' since a ceilidh was originally a social gathering in the house after the day's work was over. A local bard (poet) presided over the telling of folk stories and legends, and there was also music and song. These days, a ceilidh means an evening of entertainment including music, song and dance.

Clans A clan is a group of people who claim descent from a common ancestor. In the Highlands and Islands, where the Scottish clan system evolved between the 11th and 16th centuries, many unrelated families joined clans to be under the clan chief's protection. So, although they may share the same name, not all clan members are related by blood. Clan members united in raiding parties into the more prosperous Lowlands or into neighbouring glens to steal other clans' cattle.

After the 18th century Jacobite rebellions the suppression of Highland culture brought the forced breakdown of the clan system, but the spirit of clan loyalty remains strong, especially among the 25 million Scots living abroad. Each clan still has its own chief, like the Queen merely a figurehead, and its own tartan (see Tartans later in this chapter).

Crofting In the Highlands and Islands, a few acres of land supporting some sheep or cows, or a small market garden, are known as a croft. Crofting has always been a precarious way of life. In the 19th century crofters were regularly forced off the land by landlords demanding extortionately high rents. In the 20th century, unrealistic demands upon the land by agricultural economists almost killed off the crofting tradition.

Today, however, there is increased interest in crofting, and some communities now support more people than they have done since the mid-19th century.

Highland Games Highland Games take place throughout the summer, and not just in the Highlands. Assorted sporting events with piping and dancing competitions attract locals and tourists alike.

The original games were organised by clan chiefs and kings who recruited the strongest competitors for their armies and as bodyguards. Even now the Queen never fails to attend the Braemar Gathering, the best known, and most crowded, of all Highland Games in September.

Some events are peculiarly Scottish, particularly those that involve the Heavies in bouts of strength testing. The apparatus used can be pretty primitive – tossing the caber involves heaving a tree trunk into the air. Other popular events in which the Heavies take part are throwing the hammer and putting the stone.

Tartans The oldest surviving piece of tartan, a patterned woollen material now made into everything from kilts to key-fobs, dates back to the Roman period. Today, tartan is popular the world over, and beyond – astronaut Al Bean took his MacBean tartan to the moon and back.

The *plaid* is the traditional Scottish dress, with a long length of tartan wrapped around the body and over the shoulder. Particular

A selection of distinctive pub signs

A Bay City Rollers fan?

Hairy, horny and typically Highland

Haggis, central to Burns Night celebrations

Piper in full Highland regalia

More about Tartans

There's some contention over the origin of the word 'tartan', but according to the Scottish Tartans Society, the word originally described the *way* a woollen thread was woven to make the fabric – a single thread passed over two threads then under two threads etc. The tartan textile that it created, however, was too light to keep the wearer warm.

Today, tartan is the name given to the colourful pattern of cloth that derives from Highland dress. A tartan pattern is created from a list of coloured threads called a thread count. Broad strips of colour called the 'under check' are often decorated with narrower lines of colour called the 'over check'. Reading a tartan involves locating two unique points within the pattern called 'pivots'. Over 2500 tartan patterns have been recorded in the Register of All Publicly Known Tartans. Two of the largest groups of tartans are the Black Watch (named after the Highland regiment) and Royal Stewart.

If you'd like to learn more about tartans or whether your family has one contact the Scottish Tartans Society (☎ 044-01796 474079, fax 01796 474090, www.tartans.electricscotland .com), Port-na-Craig Rd, Pitlochry PH16 5ND. New tartans can't be declared genuine without its approval. It's a charity which offers both academic and individual research on tartans and is keeper of the Register of All Publicly Known Tartans. It also runs the Scottish Tartans Museum (☎ 0131-556 1252), 3rd Floor, The Scotch House, Princes St, Edinburgh.

setts (patterns) didn't come to be associated with certain clans until the 17th century, although today every clan, indeed every football team, has a distinctive tartan.

The wearing of Highland dress was banned after the Jacobite rebellions but revived under royal patronage in the following century.

For their visit in 1822, George IV and his English courtiers donned kilts. Sir Walter Scott, novelist, poet and dedicated patriot, did much to rekindle interest in Scottish ways. By then, however, many of the old setts had been forgotten – some tartans are actually Victorian creations. The modern kilt only appeared in the 18th century and was reputedly invented by Thomas Rawlinson, an Englishman!

Dos & Don'ts

Labelling locals as British is fine for some Scots, but anathema to others. The Scots don't like being called English, especially in the Highlands and Islands where Scottish nationalism is strongest.

The mixture of religion and football (soccer) creates intense rivalry especially between Protestant Glasgow Rangers and Catholic Glasgow Celtic. If someone approaches you, in a bar for example, and asks which team you support it may be wisest to tell them you don't follow football. Whenever subjects like religion or Scottish nationalism come up, as a visitor it's probably a good time for you to practise your listening skills, at least until you're sure of the situation.

Treatment of Animals

Some rare, protected birds of prey are killed illegally (see Ecology & Environment earlier in this chapter). Contact the Royal Society for the Protection of Birds (☎ 0131-557 3136), 17 Regent Terrace, Edinburgh EH7. For information on injured birds and animals contact the Scottish Society for the Prevention of Cruelty to Animals (☎ 0131-339 0222), Braehead Mains, 603 Queensferry Rd, Edinburgh EH4.

RELIGION

It's probably true that religion has played a more influential part in Scotland's history than in other parts of Britain. This remains true today. While barely 2% of people in England and Wales regularly attend church services, the figure for Scotland is 10%.

Christianity reached Scotland in the 4th century although in some places vestiges of older worship survived. As recently as the 18th century, Hebridean fishing communities conducted superstitious rites to ensure a good catch. With the Reformation the Scottish Church rejected the pope's authority. Later a schism developed among Scottish Protestants, the Presbyterians favouring a simplified church hierarchy without bishops, unlike the Episcopalians.

Two-thirds of Scots belong to the Presbyterian Church (or Kirk) of Scotland. There are also two Presbyterian minorities: the Free Church of Scotland (known as the Wee Frees) and the United Free Presbyterians, found mainly in the Highlands and Islands. The Episcopal (Anglican) Church of Scotland, once widespread North of the Tay, now has only about 35,000 members, many of them from the landed gentry.

There are about 800,000 Catholics, mainly in the Glasgow area and many of them descended from 19th century Irish immigrants. Some islands, like Barra, and areas of Aberdeenshire and Lochaber, were converted to Roman Catholicism as a result of secret missionary activity after the Reformation. Although not remotely on the scale of Northern Ireland, sectarian tensions can be felt in Glasgow, especially when the Protestant Rangers and Catholic Celtic football teams play.

LANGUAGE

The ancient Picts spoke a language that may have been of non Indo-European origin; Pictish is described as P-Celtic (the same family as Welsh, Cornish and Breton). It survives mainly in place names prefixed by 'Pit' (eg Pitlochry).

With the coming of Gaelic-speaking Celts (Gaels or Scotti, later called Scots) from northern Ireland from the 4th to 6th centuries, Gaelic became the language spoken in almost all Scotland. This predominance lasted until the 9th or 11th century when Anglo-Saxon arrived in the Lowlands. Gaelic then went into a long period of decline, and it was only in the 1970s that it began to make a comeback.

Lallans or Lowland Scots evolved from Anglo-Saxon and contains Dutch, French, Gaelic, German and Scandinavian influences. It too is undergoing a revival.

And then there's English, whose influence grew following union in 1707. Aye, but the Scots accent can make English almost impenetrable to the *Sassenach* (an English person or a Lowland Scot) and other foreigners, and there are numerous Gaelic and Lallan words that linger in everyday English speech. Ye ken?

See the Language section at the back of the book for more information on Scottish Gaelic and for useful words and phrases.

Facts for the Visitor

PLANNING
When to Go
Whenever you visit Scotland, you're likely to see both sun and rain. The best time to visit is May to September. April and October are also acceptable weather risks, though many things close in October. In summer, daylight hours are long; the midsummer sun sets around 11 pm in the Shetland Islands and even in Edinburgh there are seemingly endless evenings.

Edinburgh becomes impossibly crowded during the festival in August. Book well ahead if you plan to visit then; alternatively, stay in Glasgow (or elsewhere) and travel into Edinburgh.

In winter the weather's cold and daylight hours are short. Though travel in the Highlands can be difficult, roads are rarely closed and Scotland's ski resorts are popular then. Although many facilities close for the season, there's always one tourist information centre (TIC) open for an area (though several within that area may close) and more B&Bs and hotels are staying open year-round. Travel in the islands can be a problem then because high winds easily disrupt ferries. Edinburgh and Glasgow are still worth visiting in winter.

What Kind of Trip?
Your particular interests will have a large bearing on the kind of trip it'll be, as will the amount of time and money at your disposal. Many visitors to Scotland restrict themselves to Edinburgh, but the rest of the country is too beautiful to overlook. You'll get more out of your visit if you take time to explore some of the less touristy towns, and the wonderful, more remote parts of Scotland are best appreciated on a longer stay.

It's easy enough to get to the main centres by bus or train, but some attractions have no public transport so walking or cycling may be your only way to see them. If you're driving, the country's A roads offer plenty to see and can be travelled at the national speed limit of 60/70mph. However, getting around remote parts of the country is time-consuming because of twisty, single-track roads; give yourself time to do them justice, especially if you want to take in some of the islands too.

With limited time your best bet might be to take a coach tour, or one of the hop on, hop off bus transport only tours operated by Go Blue Banana or Haggis Backpackers (see the Getting Around chapter).

Maps
If you're driving north from England you'll probably already have a road atlas to Britain showing Scotland in adequate detail for touring. There's a range of excellent road atlases and not much to distinguish between them in terms of accuracy or price, though the graphics differ – pick the one you find easiest to read. If you plan to go off the beaten track, you'll need one that shows at least 3 miles to the inch.

Alternatively, TICs have free maps at a scale of at least one inch to 10 miles which are adequate for most purposes. For general touring the clear *Leisure Map – Touring Scotland* (£3.50) shows most of the tourist attractions.

What to Bring
Since anything you think of can be bought in Scottish cities, pack light and pick up what you need as you go along. Clothing in particular is good value.

A travelpack – a combination of a backpack and shoulder bag – is the most popular item for carrying gear, especially if you plan to do any walking. A travelpack's straps zip away inside the pack when not needed, making it easy to handle in airports and on crowded public transport. Most travelpacks have sophisticated shoulder-strap adjustment systems and can be used comfortably, even for long hikes.

Highlights

Planning a trip can be difficult for the first-time visitor. Scotland may be small but its long, turbulent history has left it with a rich heritage of medieval castles and cathedrals, historic cities and towns, stately homes and elegant gardens. Added to this are the Lowland hills, the beautiful coastal regions, and the spectacular Highlands and Islands.

Historic Cities & Towns

Edinburgh	One of the world's great cities with a dramatic site and extraordinary architectural heritage.
Melrose	Charming market town in the heart of the Borders, with a ruined abbey and good walks (the Borders).
St Andrews	Old university and golfing town, with ruined castle and harbour, on a headland overlooking a sweeping stretch of sand (Fife).
Dunfermline	Visit the abbey and the palace in the city that was once Scotland's capital (Fife).
Kirkwall	The original part of the city is a fine example of an ancient Norse town (Orkney).
Scone	Traditionally the place where Scotland's kings were crowned (Perthshire & Kinross).
Stirling	An ancient fortress city that played a pivotal role in Scotland's history, with a castle more interesting than Edinburgh's.

Cathedrals & Churches (Kirks)

St Giles' Cathedral	A Norman-style cathedral from where John Knox launched the Scottish Reformation (Edinburgh).
Greyfriars Kirk	In one of Edinburgh's most evocative locations and where Greyfriars Bobby sat in vigil over his master's grave (Edinburgh).
Glasgow Cathedral	This Gothic cathedral was the only mainland cathedral to survive the Scottish Reformation intact.
Dunkeld Cathedral	One of the most beautifully sited cathedrals in Scotland (Perthshire & Kinross).
St Magnus Cathedral	This red sandstone cathedral was built by the same masons who built Durham Cathedral in England (Kirkwall, Orkney).

Museums & Galleries

Burrell Collection	A fascinating moderate-sized collection developed by a wealthy shipowner, housed in a superb museum sited in parkland (Glasgow).
National Gallery of Scotland	Houses a large collection of European art from 15th century Renaissance to 19th century postimpressionism; special section on Scottish art (Edinburgh).
Scottish National Portrait Gallery	Tells the story of Scottish history through its portraits (Edinburgh).
National Gallery of Modern Art	Concentrates on 20th century art with works by Picasso, Magritte, Matisse etc (Edinburgh).
Kelvingrove Art Gallery and Museum	Has an excellent collection of European and Scottish art (Glasgow).

Highlights

Historic Houses

Tenement House	Small apartment giving a vivid insight into late 19th/early 20th century middle-class life (Glasgow).
Traquair	Extraordinary building dating from the 10th century, seemingly untouched by time (the Borders).
John Knox's House	One of the most interesting buildings on the Royal Mile (Edinburgh).
Hopetoun House	One of Scotland's finest stately homes, overlooking the Firth of Forth (Edinburgh).
Mellerstain House	Considered Robert Adam's finest mansion (the Borders).
Provost Skene's House	A pre-Reformation gem (Aberdeen).

Medieval Castles

Blair	One of the most popular tourist attractions in Scotland (Perthshire & Kinross).
Caerlaverock	Unusual triangular castle, surrounded by a moat (Dumfries & Galloway).
Glamis	Where Shakespeare set Macbeth (Dundee & Angus).
Edinburgh	Former royal residence atop an extinct volcano, overlooking the city centre.
Hermitage	Brutal but romantic castle surrounded by bleakly beautiful country-side (Dumfries & Galloway).
Stirling	Favoured royal residence of the Stewarts (Central Scotland).
Thirlestane	A fairy-tale castle that's still inhabited (the Borders).

Coast

The Scottish coast ranges from beautiful (Berwick-upon-Tweed to John o'Groats on the east coast, and Gretna to Glasgow on the west) to extraordinary (in the north-west). From Oban to John o'Groats it is one of the world's greatest natural spectacles. Some of the most spectacular cliffs in Britain are to be found in Orkney and Shetland.

Islands

Colonsay	Fine sandy beaches, good walks and a mild climate with only half as much rain as on the mainland (Argyll).
Harris	Mountainous and spectacular, with beautiful beaches and isolated crofts (Outer Hebrides).
Iona	Very touristy during the day, but spend the night here to experi-ence the magic of this holy island (Argyll).
Jura	Wild and remote, with dramatic scenery, superb walks, few people and just one road (Argyll).
Orkney	Beautiful beaches, wildflowers and the unique Stone Age ruins at Skara Brae (off north coast).
Staffa	Boat trips from Mull to see Fingal's Cave and the incredible rock formations that inspired Mendelssohn's Hebridean Overture (Argyll).

Highlights

Barra	Tiny but beautiful, it encapsulates the Outer Hebridean experience (Outer Hebrides).
St Kilda	A World Heritage Site with prolific bird life (Outer Hebrides).
Fair Isle	Famous for its sweaters, it's an important birdwatching site (Shetland).
Shetland	Famous for its varied, teeming birdlife (Shetland).

Prehistoric Remains

Callanish Standing Stones	A cross-shaped avenue and circle on a dramatic site (Lewis).
Mousa Broch	The best preserved *broch* (defensive tower) in Britain (Shetland).
Ring of Brodgar	Well-preserved stone circle, part of an extensive ceremonial site that includes standing stones and a chambered tomb (Orkney).
Skara Brae	The extraordinarily well-preserved remains of a village inhabited 3000 years ago – including dressers, fireplaces, beds and boxes all made from stone (Orkney).

Train Journeys

West Highland Railway	Scotland's most famous railway line, with particularly dramatic sections crossing Rannoch Moor and from Fort William to Mallaig.
Strathspey Steam Railway	Operates between Aviemore, Boat of Garten and Nethy Bridge; to be extended to Grantown.

SUGGESTED ITINERARIES

Depending on the time at your disposal, you might want to see and/or do some of the following:

One week	Visit Edinburgh, Glasgow, Oban, Glencoe, Fort William.
Two weeks	Visit Edinburgh, Glasgow, Isle of Arran, Oban, Glencoe, Fort William, Kyle of Lochalsh, Isle of Skye.
One month	Visit Edinburgh, Glasgow, Isle of Arran, Oban, Glencoe, Fort William, Kyle of Lochalsh, Isle of Skye, Ullapool, Outer Hebrides, Inverness, the Orkneys, the Shetlands.
Six weeks	As for one month but stay put in one place for a week or so. Explore Ben Nevis or perhaps walk a long-distance path like the West Highland Way.

A tent is unlikely to be very useful; the weather hardly encourages camping and long-distance walks are well served by hostels, camping barns and B&Bs.

A sleeping bag is useful in hostels and when visiting friends; get one that doubles as a quilt. A sleeping sheet with a pillow cover is necessary for staying in Scottish Youth Hostel Association (SYHA) hostels – if you don't bring one you'll have to hire or purchase one.

A padlock is handy for locking your bag to a train or a bus luggage rack, and may also be needed to secure your hostel locker.

A Swiss Army knife (or any pocketknife that includes a bottle opener and strong corkscrew) is useful for all sorts of things. For city sightseeing, a small daypack is harder for snatch thieves to grab than a shoulder bag. Other possibilities include a compass, a torch (flashlight), an alarm clock, an adaptor plug for electrical appliances, a universal bath/sink plug, sunglasses and an elastic clothes-line.

Use plastic carrier bags to keep things organised, and dry, inside your backpack. Airlines lose bags from time to time, but there's a much better chance of getting them back if they're tagged with your name and address *inside* as well as on the outside.

Don't forget some form of waterproof clothing (a mackintosh perhaps) or an umbrella. If you're going to be walking, it's worth treating your boots with a waterproofing agent as some trails cross boggy ground.

RESPONSIBLE TOURISM

Except in Scotland's remote and mountainous reaches, congestion on the roads and in the cities and towns can be a major problem – even before the peak tourist season brings more traffic. Visitors will do residents, themselves and the environment a favour if, wherever possible, they forego driving in favour of using public transport, cycling or even walking.

If the natural environment is to support the growing number of visitors, especially the remote and fragile areas, then human activity will need to be sensitive to that environment. The country code involves some important principles – minimising your impact, leaving no trace of your passing (not damaging wildlife, plants or trees), leaving no litter (take out what you take in), and sticking to the walking trails.

TOURIST OFFICES
Local Tourist Offices

The Scottish Tourist Board (STB, ☎ 0131-332 2433, fax 0131-315 4545, www .holiday.scotland.net) has its headquarters at 23 Ravelston Terrace (PO Box 705), Ed-

inburgh EH4 3EU. In London, contact the STB (☎ 0171-930 8661; from 22 April 2000 ☎ 020-7930 8661), 19 Cockspur St, London SW1 5BL, off Trafalgar Square.

Most towns have TICs that open weekdays from 9 am to 5 pm, often opening at weekends in summer. In small places, particularly in the Highlands, TICs only open from Easter to September.

Tourist Offices Abroad

Overseas, the British Tourist Authority (BTA, www.bta.org.uk) represents the STB and stocks masses of information, much of it free.

Contact the BTA before leaving home because some discounts are available only to people who have booked before arriving in Britain. Travellers with special needs (disability, diet etc) should also contact the nearest BTA office. Addresses are listed on its Web site. Some overseas offices are:

Australia
  (☎ 02-9377 4400, fax 02-9377 4499)
  Level 16, The Gateway, 1 Macquarie Place, Circular Quay, Sydney, NSW 2000
Canada
  (☎ 416-925 6326, fax 416-961 2175)
  Suite 450, 111 Avenue Rd, Toronto, Ontario M5R 3JD
France
  (☎ 01 44 51 56 20)
  Tourisme de Grand-Bretagne, Maison de la Grande Bretagne, 19 Rue des Mathurins, 75009 Paris (entrance in Rues Tronchet and Auber)
Germany
  (☎ 069-238 0711)
  Taunusstrasse 52-60, 60329 Frankfurt
Ireland
  (☎ 01-670 8000)
  18-19 College Green, Dublin 2
Netherlands
  (☎ 020-685 50 51)
  Stadhouderskade 2 (5e), 1054 ES Amsterdam
New Zealand
  (☎ 09-303 1446, fax 09-377 6965)
  3rd Floor, Dilworth Building, corner Queen and Customs Sts, Auckland 1
USA
  (☎ 1 800 GO 2 BRITAIN)
  625 N Michigan Ave, Suite 1510, Chicago IL 60611 (personal callers only) 551 Fifth Ave, Suite 701, New York, NY 10176-0799

VISAS & DOCUMENTS
Passport

Your most important travel document is a passport, which should remain valid until well after your trip. If it's about to expire, renew it before you go. This may not be easy to do abroad, and some countries insist your passport remain valid for a specified minimum period (usually three to six months) after your visit.

Applying for or renewing a passport can be an involved process taking from a few days to several months, so don't leave it till the last minute. Bureaucracy usually grinds faster if you do everything in person rather than relying on the mail or agents. First check what is required: passport photos, birth certificate, population register extract, signed statements, exact payment in cash, whatever.

Australian citizens can apply at post offices, or the passport office in their state capital; Canadians can apply at regional passport offices; New Zealanders can apply at any district office of the Department of Internal Affairs; and US citizens must apply in person (but may usually renew by mail) at a US Passport Agency office or some courthouses and post offices.

Citizens of European countries may not need a valid passport to travel to Britain. A national identity card can be sufficient, and usually involves less paperwork and processing time. Check with your travel agent or the British embassy.

Visas

A visa is a stamp in your passport permitting you to enter a country for a specified period of time. Depending on your nationality, the procedure may be a mere formality. Sometimes you can get a visa at borders or airports, but not always – check first with the embassies or consulates of the countries you plan to visit.

There is a variety of visa types, including tourist, transit, business and work visas. Transit visas are usually cheaper than tourist or business visas, but they only allow a very short stay and can be difficult to extend.

Visa requirements can change, and you should always check with embassies or a reputable travel agent before travelling. If you're travelling widely, carry plenty of spare passport photos (you'll need up to four every time you apply for a visa).

Access the Lonely Planet Web site (www .lonelyplanet.com.au) for more information.

British Visas Visa regulations are always subject to change, so it is essential to check the situation with your local British embassy, high commission or consulate before leaving home.

Currently, if you are a citizen of Australia, Canada, New Zealand, South Africa or the USA, you are given 'leave to enter' Britain at your place of arrival. Tourists from these countries are generally permitted to stay for up to six months, but are prohibited from working. To stay longer you need an entry clearance certificate; apply to the high commission.

Citizens of the European Union (EU) can live and work in Britain free of immigration control – you don't need a visa to enter the country.

The immigration authorities have always been tough and are getting even tougher; dress neatly and carry proof that you have sufficient funds with which to support yourself. A credit card and/or an onward ticket will help. People have been refused entry because they happened to be carrying papers (like references) that suggested they intended to work.

No visas are required for Scotland if you arrive from England or Northern Ireland. If you arrive from the Republic of Ireland or any other country, normal British customs and immigration regulations apply.

Visa Extensions To extend your stay in the UK contact the Home Office, Immigration and Nationality Department (☎ 0181-686 0688; from 22 April 2000 ☎ 020-8686 0688), Lunar House, Wellesley Rd, Croydon, London CR9 *before* your existing permit expires. You'll need to send your passport or ID card with your application.

Onward Tickets

Although you don't need an onward ticket to be granted 'leave to enter' on arrival (see Visas above), this could help if there's any doubt over whether you have sufficient funds to support yourself and purchase an onward ticket in Britain.

Travel Insurance

This not only covers you for medical expenses, theft or loss, but also for cancellation of or delays in any of your travel arrangements. There's a variety of policies and your travel agent can provide recommendations. The international student travel policies handled by STA Travel and other reputable student travel organisations are usually good value.

Make sure the policy includes health care and medication in the countries you may visit to/from Scotland. Go for as much as you can afford, especially if you're also visiting the Channel Islands, the USA, Switzerland, Germany or Scandinavia, where medical costs are high.

Always read the small print carefully:

- Some policies specifically exclude 'dangerous activities' like scuba diving, motorcycling, skiing, mountaineering, even trekking.
- You may prefer a policy that pays doctors or hospitals directly rather than forcing you to pay on the spot and claim the money back later. If you have to claim later, make sure you keep all documentation. Some policies ask you to call back (reverse charges) to a centre in your home country where an immediate assessment of your problem is made.
- Not all policies cover ambulances, helicopter rescue or emergency flights home.
- Most policies exclude cover for pre-existing illnesses.

Driving Licence & Permit

Your normal driving licence is legal for 12 months from the date you last entered Britain; you can then apply for a British licence at post offices.

Ask your automobile association for a Card of Introduction. This entitles you to services offered by British sister organisations (touring maps and information, help with breakdowns, technical and legal advice etc), usually free of charge.

Camping Card International

Your local automobile association also issues a Camping Card International, basically a camping ground ID. It's also issued by local camping federations, and sometimes at camp sites. It incorporates third party insurance for damage you may cause, and many camping grounds offer a small discount if you have one. Some hostels and hotels also accept carnets for signing-in purposes, but won't give discounts.

Hostel Card

If you're travelling on a budget, membership of the Scottish Youth Hostel Association/ Hostelling International (SYHA/HI) is a must (£10 over-18, £5 under-18). There are almost 80 hostels in Scotland and members are eligible for a wide list of discounts.

Student & Youth Cards

The most useful is the plastic ID-style International Student Identity Card (ISIC), which displays your photograph. This can perform wonders, including producing discounts on many forms of transport. Even if you have your own transport, the card soon pays for itself through cheap or free admission to attractions, and cheap meals in some student restaurants.

There's a worldwide industry in fake student cards, and many places now stipulate a maximum age for student discounts or, more simply, substitute a 'youth discount' for a 'student discount'. If you're aged under 26 but not a student, you can apply for a Federation of International Youth Travel Organisations (FIYTO) card or a Euro26 Card which give much the same discounts. Your hostelling organisation should be able to help with this.

Both types of card are issued by student unions, hostelling organisations or student travel agencies. They don't automatically entitle you to discounts, but you won't find out until you flash the card.

Seniors' Cards

Discount cards for over 60s are available for rail and bus travel. See the Getting Around chapter.

International Health Card

You may need this yellow booklet if you're travelling onwards through parts of Asia, Africa and South America, where yellow fever is prevalent.

· If you're a national of another EU country, Form E111 (available from post offices) entitles you to free or reduced-cost medical treatment in Britain.

Other Documents

If you're visiting Britain on a Working Holiday Entry Certificate bring any course certificates or letters of reference that might help you find a job.

Photocopies

It's wise to keep photocopies of all your important documents (passport, air tickets, insurance policy, travellers cheques serial numbers) in a separate place in case of theft; stash £50 away with the photocopies just in case.

EMBASSIES & CONSULATES

Don't expect much from your embassy in Britain, or in any other country for that matter.

They're probably not going to start worrying about you unless you get into trouble with the police or inconvenience them by expiring while on holiday. They will, however, help you replace a lost passport or offer advice on other emergencies. They won't hold mail for travellers, but will help someone in your home country get in touch with you in an emergency.

UK Embassies Abroad

Some UK embassies abroad include:

Australia
  High Commission:
  (☎ 02-6270 6666)
  Commonwealth Ave, Yarralumla, Canberra, ACT 2600

Canada
  High Commission:
  (☎ 613-237 1530)
  80 Elgin St, Ottawa K1P 5K7
France
  Consulate:
  (☎ 01 42 66 38 10)
  9 Ave Hoche, 8e, Paris
Germany
  Embassy:
  (☎ 0228-23 40 61)
  Friedrich-Ebert-Allee 77, 53113 Bonn
Ireland
  Embassy:
  (☎ 01-205 3700)
  29 Merrion Rd, Ballsbridge, Dublin 4
Japan
  Embassy:
  (☎ 03-3265 5511)
  1 Ichiban-cho, Chiyoda-ku, Tokyo
Netherlands
  Embassy:
  (☎ 070-427 0427)
  Lange Voorhout 10, 2514 ED, The Hague
New Zealand
  High Commission:
  (☎ 04-472 6049)
  44 Hill St, Wellington 1
South Africa
  High Commission:
  (☎ 27-21-461 7220)
  91 Parliament St, Cape Town
USA
  Embassy:
  (☎ 202-462 1340)
  3100 Massachusetts Ave NW, Washington DC 20008

Consulates & High Commissions in Scotland

Most foreign diplomatic missions are in London, but some also have consulates or high commissions in Edinburgh:

Belgium
  (☎ 01968-679969)
  21b The Square, EH26 8LH
Denmark
  (☎ 0131-556 4263)
  4 Royal Terrace, EH7 5AB
Canada
  (☎ 0131-245 6013)
  30 Lothian Rd, EH1 2DH
France
  (☎ 0131-225 7954)
  11 Randolph Crescent, EH3 7TT

Germany
(☎ 0131-337 2323)
16 Eglinton Crescent, EH12 5DG
Italy
(☎ 0131-226 3631)
32 Melville St, EH3 7HA
Japan
(☎ 0131-225 4777)
2 Melville Crescent, EH3, 7HW
Netherlands
(☎ 0131-220 3226)
53 George St, EH2 2HT
Spain
(☎ 0131-220 1843)
63 North Castle St, EH2 3LJ
Sweden
(☎ 0131-554 6631)
6 Johns Place, Leith, EH6 7EP
Switzerland
(☎ 0131-226 5660)
66 Hanover St, EH2 1HH
USA
(☎ 0131-556 8315)
3 Regent Terrace, EH7 5BW

CUSTOMS

Entering Britain, if you have nothing to declare go through the green channel; if you have something to declare go through the red channel. For imported goods there's a two-tier system: the first for goods bought duty-free, the second for goods bought in an EU country where tax and duty have been paid.

The second tier is relevant because a number of products (eg alcohol and cigarettes) are much cheaper on the continent. Under single market rules, however, as long as tax and duty have been paid somewhere in the EU there is no prohibition on importing them within the EU provided they are for personal consumption. The result has been a thriving market for day trips to France where Brits can load up their cars with cheap beer, wine and cigarettes – the savings can more than pay for the trip.

Duty-Free

If you buy from a duty-free shop, you can import 200 cigarettes or 250g of tobacco, 2L of still wine plus 1L of spirits or another 2L of wine (sparkling or otherwise), 60cc of perfume, 250cc of toilet water, and other duty-free goods (eg cider and beer) to the value of £145.

Tax & Duty Paid

If you buy from a normal retail outlet, customs will nod through 800 cigarettes or 1kg of tobacco, 10L of spirits, 20L of fortified wine, 90L of wine (not more than 60 sparkling) and 110L of beer as legitimate personal imports.

MONEY
Currency

The British currency is the pound sterling (£), with 100 pence (p) to a pound. One and 2p coins are copper; 5p, 10p, 20p and 50p coins are silver; the £1 coin is gold-coloured; and the new £2 coin is gold and silver-coloured. Like its written counterpart the word pence is usually abbreviated and pronounced 'pee'.

Notes (bills) come in £5, £10, £20 and £50 denominations and vary in colour and size. Notes issued by several Scottish banks – the Clydesdale Bank, Royal Bank of Scotland and Bank of Scotland – including a £1 note are legal tender in other parts of the UK. You shouldn't have trouble changing them in shops etc immediately south of the Scotland-England border, but elsewhere it may be difficult. However, any bank will exchange them.

Exchange Rates

country	unit		sterling
Australia	A$1	=	£0.38
Canada	C$1	=	£0.39
euro	€1	=	£0.71
France	FF1	=	£0.11
Germany	DM1	=	£0.36
Ireland	IR£1	=	£0.91
Japan	¥100	=	£0.52
New Zealand	NZ$1	=	£0.32
USA	US$1	=	£0.60

Changing Money

Be careful using *bureaux de change*; they may offer good exchange rates but frequently levy outrageous commissions and fees. Make sure that you establish the rate, the percentage commission and any fees in advance.

The *bureaux de change* at the international airports are exceptions to the rule. They charge less than most High St banks and cash sterling travellers cheques for free. They also guarantee that you can buy up to £500 worth of most major currencies.

Personal cheques are still widely used in Britain, but they're validated and guaranteed by a plastic cheque card. Increasingly, retail outlets are linked to the Switch/Delta debit card networks; money is deducted direct from your current account. Look for a current account that pays interest (or at least doesn't charge for ordinary transactions while you're in credit), gives you a cheque book and guarantee card, and offers access to ATMs and the Switch/Delta network.

Cash Nothing beats cash for convenience ... or risk. It's still a good idea, though, to travel with some local currency in cash, if only to tide you over until you get to an exchange facility. There's no problem if you arrive at Edinburgh, Glasgow or Aberdeen airports; all have good-value exchange counters open for incoming flights.

If you're travelling in several countries, some extra cash in US dollars is a good idea; it can be easier to change a small amount of cash (when leaving a country, for example) than a cheque.

Banks rarely accept foreign coins, although some airport foreign exchanges will. Before you leave one country for the next, try to use up your change.

Travellers Cheques Travellers cheques offer some protection from theft. American Express or Thomas Cook cheques are widely accepted and have efficient replacement policies. Keep a record of the cheque numbers and the cheques you've cashed somewhere separate from the cheques themselves.

Although cheques are available in various currencies, there's little point using US$ cheques in Britain (unless you're travelling from the USA), since you'll lose on the exchange rate when you buy the cheques and again each time you cash one. Bring pounds sterling to avoid changing currencies twice. In Britain, travellers cheques are rarely accepted outside banks or used for everyday transactions; you need to cash them in advance.

Take most cheques in large denominations. It's only towards the end of a stay that you may want to change a small cheque to make sure you don't get left with too much local currency.

Plastic Cards & ATMs If you're not familiar with the options, ask your bank to explain the workings and relative merits of credit, credit/debit, debit and charge cards.

Plastic cards are ideal for major purchases and can allow you to withdraw cash from selected banks and automatic telling machines (ATMs – called cashpoints in Britain). ATMs are usually linked to international money systems such as Cirrus, Maestro or Plus, so you can insert your card, punch in a personal identification number (PIN) and get instant cash. But ATMs aren't fail-safe, especially if the card was issued outside Europe, and it's safer to go to a human teller – it can be a headache if an ATM swallows your card.

Credit cards usually aren't hooked up to ATM networks unless you specifically request a PIN number from your bank. You should also ask which ATMs abroad will accept your particular card. Cash cards, which you use at home to withdraw money from your bank account or savings account, are becoming more widely linked internationally – ask your bank at home for advice.

Charge cards like American Express and Diners Club don't have credit limits but may not be accepted in small establishments or off the beaten track. If you have an American Express card, you can cash up to £500 worth of personal cheques at American Express offices in any seven-day period.

Credit and credit/debit cards like Visa and MasterCard (known as Access in

Britain) are more widely accepted. If you have too low a credit limit to cover major expenses like car hire or airline tickets, you can pay money into your account so it's in credit when you leave home.

Visa, MasterCard, Access, American Express and Diners Club cards are widely recognised although some places make a charge for accepting them. B&Bs usually require cash. MasterCard is operated by the same organisation that issues Access and Eurocards and can be used wherever you see one or other of these signs.

You can use MasterCard in ATMs belonging to the Royal Bank of Scotland and Clydesdale Bank; with a Visa card you can use the Bank of Scotland, Royal Bank of Scotland, Clydesdale Bank and TSB; American Express card holders can use the Bank of Scotland.

If you have a UK bank account in England or Wales, then you can use a National Westminster or Midland cash card at the Clydesdale Bank, and a Lloyds or Barclays cash card at the Royal Bank of Scotland or Bank of Scotland.

Combine plastic and travellers cheques so you have something to fall back on if an ATM swallows your card or the local banks don't accept your card.

International Transfers You can instruct your home bank to send you a draft. Specify the city, the bank and the branch to which you want your money directed, or ask your home bank to tell you where there's a suitable one.

The whole procedure will be easier if you've authorised someone back home to access your account.

Money sent by telegraphic transfer (usually at a cost of £15) should reach you within a week; by mail, allow at least two weeks. When it arrives, it will most likely be converted into local currency – you can take it as it is or buy travellers cheques.

You can also transfer money by either American Express or Thomas Cook. American travellers can also use Western Union (☎ 0800-833833).

Security

Keep your money in a money-belt or something similar, out of easy reach of snatch thieves. You might want to stitch an inside pocket into your skirt or trousers to keep an emergency stash; keep about £50 apart from the rest of your cash in case of an emergency. Take care in crowded places, and never leave wallets sticking out of trouser pockets or daypacks.

Costs

Scotland is expensive, but backpacker accommodation is widely available, so backpackers will be able to keep their costs down. Edinburgh is more expensive than most other mainland towns, but prices also rise quite steeply in remote parts of the Highlands and Islands where supplies depend on ferries. Petrol can cost 10p to 15p a litre more on the Islands than in the central Lowlands.

While in Edinburgh you'll need to budget £16 to £25 a day for bare survival. Dormitory accommodation costs from £8.50 to £14 a night, a one-day bus travel card is £2.20, and drinks and the most basic sustenance cost at least £6, with any sightseeing or nightlife costs on top. To enjoy some of the city's life, if possible add another £10 to £15.

Costs obviously rise if you stay in a central B&B or hotel and eat restaurant meals. B&B rates cost around £18 to £25 per person and a restaurant meal will be at least £8. Add a couple of pints of beer (£2 each) and entry fees to a tourist attraction or nightclub and you could easily spend £50 per day – without being extravagant.

Once you start moving around the country, particularly if you have a transport pass or are walking or hitching, the costs drop. Fresh food costs roughly the same as in Australia and the USA. However, without including long-distance transport, and assuming you stay in hostels and an occasional cheap B&B, you'll still need around £25 per day.

If you hire a car or use a transport pass, stay in B&Bs, eat one sit-down meal a day and don't stint on entry fees, you'll need

£40 to £50 per day. Most basic B&Bs cost from £15 to £20 per person and dinner £8 to £15; add £3 for snacks and drinks, £4 for miscellaneous items and at least £5 for entry fees. If you're travelling by car you'll probably average a further £7 to £12 per day on petrol and parking (not including hire charges).

Unless otherwise indicated, this book gives the adults/children admission price to attractions.

Tipping & Bargaining

In general, if you eat in a Scottish restaurant you should leave a tip of at least 10% unless the service was unsatisfactory. Waiting staff are often paid derisory wages on the assumption that the money will be supplemented by tips. If the bill already includes a service charge of 10 to 15%, you needn't add a further tip.

Taxi drivers expect to be tipped (about 10%). It's less usual to tip minicab drivers.

Bargaining is virtually unheard of, even at markets, although it's fine to ask if there are discounts for students, young people, or youth hostel members. Some 'negotiation' is also OK if you're buying an expensive item such as a car or motorcycle.

Taxes & Refunds

Value-Added Tax (VAT) is a 17.5% sales tax that is levied on all goods and services except food and books. Restaurant prices must by law include VAT.

It's sometimes possible to claim a refund of VAT paid on goods – a considerable saving. You're eligible if you've spent *less* than 365 days out of the two years prior to making the purchase living in Britain, and if you're leaving the EU within three months of making the purchase.

Not all shops participate in the VAT refund scheme, and different shops have different minimum-purchase conditions (normally around £40).

On request, participating shops give you a special form/invoice; they'll need to see your passport. This form must be presented with the goods and receipts to customs when you depart (VAT-free goods can't be posted or shipped home). After customs has certified the form, it should be returned to the shop for a refund less an administration fee.

Several companies offer a centralised re-funding service to shops. Participating shops carry a sign in their window. You can avoid bank charges for cashing a sterling cheque by using a credit card for purchases and asking to have your VAT refund credited to your card account. Cash refunds are sometimes available at major airports.

POST & COMMUNICATIONS
Post

Most post offices open weekdays from 9 am to 5.30 pm, Saturday 9 am to 12.30 pm.

First-class mail is quicker and more expensive (26p per letter) than 2nd-class mail (20p). Air-mail letters to EU countries are 30p, to the Americas and Australasia 43/63p (up to 10/20g). An air-mail letter generally take less than a week to get to the USA or Canada; around a week to Australia or New Zealand.

If you don't have a permanent address, mail can be sent to poste restante in the town or city where you're staying. American Express offices also hold card-holders' mail free.

Telephone

Although British Telecom (BT) is still the largest telephone operator, with the most public phone booths, there are also several competing companies.

Red phone booths survive in conservation areas. More usually you'll see glass cubicles of two types: one takes money (and doesn't give change), while the other uses prepaid, plastic debit cards and credit cards.

All phones come with reasonably clear instructions and if you're likely to make several calls (especially international) and don't want to be caught out, buy a BT phonecard. Ranging in value from £2 to £20, they're widely available from all sorts of retailers, including post offices and newsagents.

Some codes worth knowing are:

0345	local call rates apply
0500	call is free to caller
0800	call is free to caller
0891	premium rates apply; 39p cheap rate, 49p at other times
0990	national call rate applies

Local & National Calls Local calls are charged by time; national calls are charged by time and distance. Daytime rates are from 8 am to 6 pm, Monday to Friday; the cheap rate is from 6 pm to 8 am, Monday to Friday and the cheap weekend rate from midnight Friday to midnight Sunday. The latter two rates offer substantial savings.

For directory inquiries call ☎ 192. These are free from public telephones but are charged at 25p from a private phone. To get the operator call ☎ 100.

International Calls Dial ☎ 155 to get the international operator. To get an international line (for international direct dialling) dial 00, then the country code, area code (drop the first zero if there is one) and number. Direct dialling is cheaper, but some budget travellers prefer operator-connected reverse-charge (collect) calls.

You can also use the Home Country Direct service to make a reverse-charge or credit card call via an operator in your home country which should avoid language problems. If you need to get a message overseas urgently, call ☎ 0800-190190.

For most countries (including Europe, USA and Canada) it's cheaper to phone overseas between 8 pm and 8 am Monday to Friday and at weekends; for Australia and New Zealand, however, it's cheapest from 2.30 to 7.30 pm and from midnight to 7 am every day. The savings are considerable.

Emergency Dial ☎ 999 or ☎ 112 (free calls) for fire, police or ambulance.

Fax, Email & Internet Access
Most hotels have faxes and the larger ones also have email access. Some hostels, too, offer Internet access to their customers or you can try one of the cybercafés in Edinburgh or Glasgow. Some shops also offer fax services, advertised by a sign in the window.

INTERNET RESOURCES
There are plenty of sites of interest to cyber travellers. In this guide, Web sites are given with addresses where appropriate.

The best place to start is the Lonely Planet Web site (www.lonelyplanet.com.au) which offers a speedy link to numerous sites of interest to travellers to Britain. The Scottish Tourist Board has its own site (see Tourist Offices earlier), or if you'd like to find out about Scotland's museums go to www.museum.scotland.net.

BOOKS
Lonely Planet
The information in Lonely Planet's *Edinburgh* city guide is similar to the information in this guidebook, but if you're reading this in a bookshop and plan to visit only Edinburgh, check it out. Lonely Planet's *Walking in Britain* has two chapters on Scottish walking trails. For travel elsewhere in Britain, Lonely Planet publishes guides to *Britain* and *London*.

Guidebooks
For detailed information on history, art and architecture, *Scotland* in the Blue Guide series is excellent, with a wealth of scholarly information on all the important sites, including good maps.

People of a literary bent might like to look at the *Oxford Literary Guide to Great Britain and Ireland* which details the writers who have immortalised the towns and villages.

There are numerous local guidebooks, the most useful being mentioned in the text. See the Activities chapter for details of cycling and walking guidebooks and books on tracing your ancestors.

For specialist guides on accommodation and food see those sections later in this chapter.

Travel

One of the greatest Scottish travelogues is *The Journal of a Tour to the Hebrides with Samuel Johnson*, by James Boswell. This famous lexicographer and his Scottish biographer visited Skye, Coll and Mull in 1773, and met Flora MacDonald (who had helped Bonnie Prince Charlie escape after the battle of Culloden).

More recently, *Native Stranger*, by Alistair Scott (1995), recounts the efforts of a Scot who knew 'more about the Sandinistas' but got to grips with the realities of modern Scotland by travelling the length and breadth of the land.

In Bill Bryson's highly entertaining and perceptive modern travelogue covering Britain, *Notes from a Small Island*, the author visits Scotland. *The Kingdom by the Sea* by Paul Theroux and Jonathan Raban's *Coasting*, both written in 1982 are now a little dated, but nonetheless readable. Older but also still readable is John Hillaby's *Journey Through Britain* which describes a walk from Land's End to John o'Groats in 1969, great for measuring the changes which have taken place since then.

For a look behind the tourism gloss, Nick Danziger's *Danziger's Britain* should be required reading. The picture it paints of modern Britain is thoroughly depressing, and includes descriptions of life for the marginalised in the Highlands and Glasgow. This guy has seen the world and if this is how he says it is, then it's hard to argue with him.

History & Politics

A Short History of Scotland, by Richard Killeen, is a concise up-to-date introduction. Michael Lynch's large tome, *Scotland – A New History*, provides a good in-depth historical background up to the early 1990s. Andrew Marr's *The Battle for Scotland*, is an interesting political history of Scotland from the 19th century to 1992. Tom Steel's *Scotland's Story* is readable and well illustrated but stops in the early 1980s.

If you were wondering what happened to the Stewart dynasty, *The Forgotten Monarchy of Scotland* (1998) gives a history of the royal line up to the present day. It's written by Prince Michael of Albany, current head of the House of Stewart.

To flesh out some of the great figures of Scottish history, there are many well-written biographies, including Antonia Fraser's *Mary Queen of Scots* and Fitzroy Maclean's *Bonnie Prince Charlie*. John Prebble has written passionate accounts of the Highland Clearances, the massacre in Glen Coe and the battle of Culloden.

In Bed with the Elephant, by Sir Ludovic Kennedy, himself a Scot, is an entertaining, sometimes personal account of Scottish culture, Scotland's turbulent history and the country's relationship with its powerful southern neighbour, England (the elephant referred to in the title).

General

Gavin Maxwell wrote several books about his life among otters and other wildlife in the Highlands; *Ring of Bright Water* is probably best known. The naturalist, Mike Tomkies, wrote an evocative series of books, including *A Last Wild Place*, about his experiences while living in a remote West Highland cottage in the 1980s.

The Silver Darlings, Neil Gunn's story of the north-east's great fishing communities in the days before EU quotas, is worth seeking out.

With some beautiful photographs, *Wild Scotland* by James McCarthy, is an informative guide to Scotland's natural heritage and conservation.

For information on all things Scottish consult the *Collins Encyclopaedia of Scotland* edited by Julia & John Keay.

NEWSPAPERS & MAGAZINES

The Scots have published newspapers since the mid-17th century. Scotland's home-grown dailies include the *Scotsman*, a Liberal Democrat paper, and the popular tabloid *Daily Record*. The *Herald*, formerly the *Glasgow Herald*, is the oldest daily newspaper in the English-speaking world having been founded in 1783. The *Sunday*

Post is the country's best-selling Sunday paper with a circulation of over 2½ million.

If you visit the Highlands or Islands take a look at the weekly broadsheet the *Oban & West Highlands Times*, which gives a wonderfully parochial view of local goings on.

Most papers sold in England and Wales are available in Scotland, some of them designed specifically for Scottish readership (the *Scottish Daily Mail*, the *Scottish Express* etc).

The monthly *Scots Magazine*, with articles on all aspects of Scottish life, has been in circulation since the 18th century. *Scottish Memories* is a monthly magazine that highlights people and moments from Scottish history.

You can also buy many foreign papers, including the *International Herald Tribune*, especially in central Edinburgh. *Time* and *Newsweek* are also readily available.

RADIO & TV

Radio and TV stations are linked to the national networks, although there are considerable regional variations.

Radio

The BBC caters for most tastes though much of the material comes from England. Its main pop music station, Radio 1, aims at a young audience; Radio 2 is mostly middle of the road but also plays music by 'dinosaur' bands like Status Quo; Radio 3 spins the classics; Radio 4 offers a mix of drama, news and current affairs for a mostly mature audience; Radio 5 Live intersperses sport with current affairs.

BBC Radio Scotland provides a mix of music, drama, news and sport from a Scottish point of view. It also oversees regional stations in Aberdeen, the Highlands, the Orkneys and the Shetlands and a Gaelic language channel, Radio nan Gaidheal.

There are numerous independent radio stations throughout Scotland; wherever you go there'll be a local commercial station offering local news alongside the music. However, picking up radio stations in the Highlands can be a nightmare.

UK-wide commercial stations can be picked up in the main urban centres. These include Classic FM (classical music), Virgin Radio (pop) and Talk Radio ('shock jock' chat and phone-ins).

Radio frequencies and programs are published in the daily press.

TV

Britain still turns out some of the world's best TV, although increasing competition as channels proliferate seems to be resulting in standards slipping. BBC1 and BBC2 are publicly funded by a TV licence and don't carry advertising; ITV and Channels 4 and 5 are commercial stations and do.

There are two Scotland-based commercial TV broadcasters. Scottish Television (STV) covers southern Scotland and some parts of the western Highlands while Grampian TV transmits from Fife northward to Shetland. Both broadcasters include Gaelic-language programs. Border TV covers Dumfries & Galloway and the Borders as well as north-west England.

These channels are up against competition from Rupert Murdoch's satellite TV, BSkyB, and assorted cable channels. Cable churns out mostly missable rubbish but BSkyB is slowly monopolising sports coverage with pay-per-view screenings of the most popular events.

VIDEO SYSTEMS

With many tourist attractions selling videos as souvenirs it's worth bearing in mind that Britain, like much of Europe, uses the Phase Alternative Line (PAL) system which isn't compatible with other standards (NTSC or SECAM) unless converted.

PHOTOGRAPHY & VIDEO
Film & Equipment

Although print film is widely available, slide film can be more elusive; if there's no specialist photographic shop around, Boots, the High St chemist chain, is the likeliest stockist. Thirty-six exposure print films cost from £4.30 for ISO 100 to £5 for ISO 400. With slide film it's usually cheapest to go for process-inclusive versions although these will usually need to be developed in Britain: 36-exposure films cost from £7 for ISO 100 to £10.50 for ISO 400.

Technical Tips

With dull, overcast conditions common, high-speed film (ISO 200, or ISO 400) is useful. In summer, the best times of day for photography are usually early in the morning and late in the afternoon when the glare of the sun has passed.

Restrictions

Many tourist attractions either charge for taking photos or prohibit it altogether. Use of flash is frequently forbidden to protect delicate pictures and fabrics. Video cameras are often disallowed because of the inconvenience they can cause to other visitors.

Airport Security

You'll have to put your camera and film through the X-ray machine at all British airports. The machines are supposed to be film-safe, but you may feel happier if you put exposed films in a lead-lined bag to protect them.

TIME

Wherever you are in the world, the time on your watch is measured in relation to Greenwich Mean Time (GMT) – although, strictly speaking, GMT is used only in air and sea navigation, and is otherwise referred to as Universal Time Coordinated (UTC).

Daylight-saving time (DST) muddies the water so that even Britain itself is ahead of GMT from late March to late October. But to give you an idea, San Francisco is eight hours and New York five hours behind GMT, while Sydney is nine hours ahead of GMT. Phone the international operator on ☎ 155 for the exact difference.

Most public transport timetables use the 24 hour clock.

ELECTRICITY

The standard voltage in Scotland, as in the rest of Britain, is 240V AC, 50Hz. Plugs have three square pins and adapters are widely available.

WEIGHTS & MEASURES

In theory Britain has now moved to metric weights and measures although non-metric equivalents are still used by much of the population. Distances continue to be given in miles except on some Scottish islands where hostel locations are indicated in kilometres. In most cases this book uses miles to indicate distance although the heights of mountains are given in metres.

Most liquids other than milk and beer are sold in litres. For conversion tables, see inside the back cover.

LAUNDRY

Most High Sts have a laundrette, usually a disheartening place to spend much time. The average cost for a single wash and drying will be about £3. Bring soap powder with you; it can be expensive if bought in a laundrette. A service wash where someone does it for you costs about £1 more.

TOILETS

Although many city-centre facilities can be grim (graffitied or rendered vandal-proof in solid stainless steel), those at main stations, bus terminals and motorway service stations are generally good, usually with facilities for the disabled and children.

Many disabled toilets can only be opened with a special key which can be obtained from some tourist offices or by sending a cheque or postal order for £2.50 to RADAR (see Disabled Travellers), together with a brief description of your disability.

HEALTH

Travel health largely depends on predeparture preparations, day-to-day health care while travelling and how you handle any medical problem or emergency that does develop.

Dial ☎ 999 or ☎ 112 for an ambulance or ☎ 0800-665544 for the address of the nearest doctor or hospital.

Predeparture Planning

Make sure that you have adequate health insurance; see Travel Insurance earlier for details. No immunisations are necessary to visit Scotland.

Make sure you're healthy before you start travelling. If you're going on a long trip make sure your teeth are OK. If you wear glasses be sure to take a spare pair and your prescription.

If you require a particular medication take an adequate supply, as it may not be available locally. Take part of the packaging showing the generic name, rather than the brand, which will make getting replacements easier. It's a good idea to have a legible prescription or letter from your doctor to show that you legally use the medication to avoid any problems.

Basic Rules

Care in what you eat and drink is the most important health rule; stomach upsets are the most likely travel health problem (between 30% and 50% of travellers in a two-week stay experience this) but the majority of these upsets are relatively minor. Unfortunately, food poisoning can sometimes be a problem so it's important not to become complacent.

Water Tap water is always safe unless there's a sign to the contrary (eg on trains). Don't drink straight from a stream – you can never be certain there are no people or cattle upstream.

Medical Problems & Treatment

Sunburn Even in Scotland, and even when there's cloud cover, it's possible to get sunburnt surprisingly quickly – especially if you're on water, snow or ice. Use 15+ sunscreen, wear a hat and cover up with a long-sleeved shirt and pants.

Heat Exhaustion Dehydration or salt deficiency can cause heat exhaustion. In hot conditions and if you're exerting yourself make sure you get sufficient nonalcoholic liquids. Salt deficiency is characterised by

fatigue, lethargy, headaches, giddiness and muscle cramps. Vomiting or diarrhoea can rapidly deplete your liquid and salt levels.

Fungal Infections To prevent fungal infections, wear loose, comfortable clothes, wash frequently and dry carefully. Be sure to always wear thongs (flip-flops) in shared bathrooms.

If you get an infection, consult a chemist. Try to expose the infected area to air or sunlight as much as possible and wash all towels and underwear in hot water as well as changing them often.

Cold Hypothermia can occur when the body loses heat faster than it can produce it, resulting in the body's core temperature falling. It's surprisingly easy to progress from very cold to dangerously cold through a combination of wind, wet clothing, fatigue and hunger, even if the air temperature is above freezing.

Walkers in Scotland should always be prepared for difficult conditions. It's best to dress in layers, and a hat is important as a lot of heat is lost through the head. A strong, waterproof outer layer is essential. Carry basic supplies, including food that contains simple sugars to generate heat quickly.

Symptoms of hypothermia are exhaustion, numb skin (particularly toes and fingers), shivering, slurred speech, irrational or violent behaviour, lethargy, stumbling, dizzy spells, muscle cramps and violent bursts of energy.

To treat it, get the person out of the wind and rain, remove wet clothing and replace it with dry, warm clothing. Give them hot liquids – not alcohol – and some high-calorie, easily digestible food. Do not rub victims; instead, allow them to warm themselves. This should be enough to treat the early stages of hypothermia.

Diarrhoea A change of water, food or climate can cause the runs; diarrhoea caused by contaminated food or water is more serious. Dehydration is the main danger with any diarrhoea, particularly in children with any diarrhoea, particularly in children or the elderly, and it can occur quite quickly. *Fluid replacement* (at least equal to the volume being lost) is the most important thing to remember. Weak black tea with a little sugar, soda water, or soft drinks allowed to go flat and diluted 50% with clean water are all good. With severe diarrhoea a rehydrating solution is preferable to replace minerals and salts lost. Keep drinking small amounts often and stick to a bland diet as you recover.

Motion Sickness Eating lightly before and during a trip will reduce the chances of motion sickness. If you are prone to motion sickness try to find a place that minimises disturbance – near the wing on aircraft, close to midships on boats, near the centre on buses. Fresh air usually helps; reading and cigarette smoke don't. Commercial motion-sickness preparations, which can cause drowsiness, have to be taken before the trip commences; when you're feeling sick it's too late. Ginger (available in capsule form) and peppermint (including mint-flavoured sweets) are effective natural preventatives.

HIV & AIDS The Human Immunodeficiency Virus (HIV) develops into Acquired Immune Deficiency Syndrome (AIDS), which is fatal. Any exposure to blood, blood products or body fluids may put the individual at risk. The disease is often transmitted through sexual contact or dirty needles – vaccinations, acupuncture, tattooing and body piercing can be potentially as dangerous as intravenous drug use. HIV/AIDS can also be spread through infected blood transfusions; but in Scotland these are screened and safe.

Sexually Transmitted Diseases (STDs) Gonorrhoea, herpes and syphilis are among these diseases; sores, blisters or rashes around the genitals, discharges or pain when urinating are common symptoms. In some STDs, such as chlamydia, symptoms may be less marked or not observed at all

especially in women. Syphilis symptoms eventually disappear completely, but the disease continues and can cause severe problems in later years. While abstinence from sexual contact is the only 100% effective prevention, using condoms is also effective. The treatment of gonorrhoea and syphilis is with antibiotics. Each individual STD requires specific antibiotics. There is no cure for herpes or AIDS.

Insect Bites & Stings Bee and wasp stings are usually painful rather than dangerous. However, in people who are allergic to them severe breathing difficulties may occur and require urgent medical care. Calamine lotion or Stingose spray will give relief and ice packs will reduce the pain and swelling.

Midges – small blood-sucking flies – are a major problem in the Highlands and Islands during summer. Bring mosquito repellent and some antihistamine.

Women's Health

Gynaecological Problems Use of antibiotics, synthetic underwear, sweating and contraceptive pills can lead to fungal vaginal infections. Fungal infections, characterised by a rash, itch and discharge, can be treated with a vinegar or lemon-juice douche, or with yoghurt. Nystatin, miconazole or clotrimazole pessaries or vaginal cream are the usual treatment.

STDs are a major cause of vaginal problems. Their symptoms include a smelly discharge, painful intercourse and sometimes a burning sensation when urinating. Male sexual partners must also be treated. Medical attention should be sought. Remember that in addition to these diseases HIV or hepatitis B may also be acquired during exposure. Besides abstinence, the best thing is to practise safe sex using condoms.

Medical Emergency

Dial ☎ 999 or ☎ 112 (both free) for an ambulance. Not all hospitals have an accident and emergency department; look for red signs with an 'H', followed by 'A&E' (Accident & Emergency).

Pharmacies should have a notice in the window, advising where you'll find the nearest late-night branch.

WOMEN TRAVELLERS
Attitudes Towards Women

The occasional wolf-whistle and groper aside, women will find Scotland reasonably enlightened. There's nothing to stop women going into pubs alone, although not everyone likes doing this; pairs or groups of women blend more naturally into the wallpaper. Some restaurants persist in assigning the table by the toilet to lone female diners, but fortunately such places are becoming fewer.

Safety Precautions

Solo travellers should have few problems, although common-sense caution should be observed in big cities, especially at night, and hitching is unwise.

While it's certainly not essential, it can help to go on a women's self-defence course before setting out on your travels, if only for the increased feeling of confidence it's likely to give you.

Condoms are increasingly sold in women's toilets. Otherwise, chemists and many service stations stock them. The contraceptive pill is available only on prescription, as is the 'morning-after' pill (effective for up to 72 hours after unprotected sexual intercourse). Family planning associations are listed in the phone book.

Organisations

Most big towns have a Well Woman Clinic which can advise on general health issues. Find their addresses in the local phone book or ask in the library. Rape Crisis Centres can offer support after an attack.

GAY & LESBIAN TRAVELLERS

In general, Scotland is fairly tolerant of homosexuality. That said, there do remain pockets of hostility and overt displays of affection aren't necessarily wise if conducted away from acknowledged 'gay' venues or districts. MPs at Westminster have voted to reduce the age of homosexual consent from 18 to 16.

Edinburgh and Glasgow have a small but flourishing gay scene. *Gay Scotland* magazine (☎ 0131-557 2625), 58A Broughton St, Edinburgh EH1, is a good source of information. *Scotsgay* is a newspaper for gays, lesbians and bisexuals.

The *List*, the Edinburgh and Glasgow listings magazine, is also useful. For more information contact the Gay Switchboard (☎ 0131-556 4049) or the Lesbian Line (☎ 0131-557 0751).

DISABLED TRAVELLERS

For many disabled travellers, Scotland is a mix of user-friendliness and unfriendliness. Few new buildings aren't accessible to wheelchair users, so large, new hotels and modern tourist attractions are usually fine. However, most B&Bs and guesthouses are in hard-to-adapt older buildings. This means that travellers with mobility problems may pay more for accommodation than their more able-bodied fellows.

It's a similar story with public transport. Newer buses sometimes have steps that lower for easier access, as do trains, but it's always wise to check before setting out. Tourist attractions sometimes reserve parking spaces near the entrance for disabled drivers.

Many ticket offices, banks etc are fitted with hearing loops to assist the hearing impaired; look for the symbol of a large ear. A few tourist attractions, cathedrals etc have braille guides or scented gardens for the visually impaired.

Information & Organisations

If you have a physical disability, get in touch with your national support organisation (preferably the travel officer if there is one).

These often have complete libraries devoted to travel, and can put you in touch with travel agents who specialise in tours for the disabled.

The STB produces a guide, *Accessible Scotland*, for disabled travellers and many TICs have leaflets with accessibility details for their area. For more information, including specialist tour operators, contact Disability Scotland (☎ 0131-229 8632), Princes House, 5 Shandwicke Place, Edinburgh EH2 4RG.

The Royal Association for Disability and Rehabilitation (RADAR) publishes a guide on travelling in the UK which gives a good overview of facilities. Contact RADAR (☎ 0171-250 3222; from 22 April 2000 ☎ 020-7250 3222), Unit 12, City Forum, 250 City Rd, London EC1V 8AF. The Holiday Care Service (☎ 01293-774535), 2 Old Bank Chambers, Station Rd, Horley, Surrey RH6 9HW, also publishes a guide to accessible accommodation and travel in Britain and can offer general advice.

Rail companies offer a Disabled Persons' Railcard.

SENIOR TRAVELLERS

Senior citizens are entitled to discounts on things like public transport, museum admission fees etc, provided they show proof of their age. Sometimes they need a special pass. The minimum qualifying age is generally 60 to 65 for men, 55 to 65 for women.

In your home country, a lower age may entitle you to special travel packages and discounts (on car hire, for instance) through organisations and travel agents that cater to senior travellers. Start hunting at your local senior citizens advice bureau.

In Scotland, rail companies offer a Senior Citizens Railcard for people of 60 and over, giving 33% discounts.

TRAVEL WITH CHILDREN

Successful travel with young children requires effort but can certainly be done. Try not to overdo things and consider using self-catering accommodation as a base. Children under a certain age can often stay free with their parents in hotels, but be prepared for hotels and B&Bs that won't accept children. Modern, purpose-built hotels can usually provide a cot.

Include children in the planning process; if they've helped to work out where you'll be going, they'll be more interested when they get there. Include a range of activities – balance a visit to Edinburgh Castle with one to the Museum of Childhood.

The *List* magazine has a section on children's activities and events in and around Glasgow and Edinburgh; also check the local newspapers.

See Lonely Planet's *Travel with Children* by Maureen Wheeler for more information.

USEFUL ORGANISATIONS

Membership of Historic Scotland (HS) and the National Trust for Scotland (NTS) is worth considering, especially if you're going to be in Scotland for a while. Both are non-profit organisations dedicated to the preservation of the environment, and both care for hundreds of spectacular sites.

Historic Scotland

Historic Scotland (HS) (☎ 0131-668 8800), Longmore House, Salisbury Place, Edinburgh EH9 1SH, manages more than 330 historic sites, including top attractions like Edinburgh and Stirling castles. A year's membership costs £22/16 for an adult/child, giving free entry to HS sites and half-price entry to English Heritage properties in England, and Cadw properties in Wales. It also offers short-term 'Explorer' membership – seven/14 days for £12.50/17.

There are standard HS opening times. April to September properties open daily from 9.30 am to 6.30 pm. October to March they close two hours earlier. Last entry is 30 minutes before closing time.

In this book, initials HS indicate an Historic Scotland property. Unless indicated otherwise, standard opening times apply.

National Trust for Scotland

The National Trust for Scotland (NTS, ☎ 0131-226 5922), 5 Charlotte Square, Edinburgh EH2 4DU, is separate from the National Trust (England, Wales and Northern Ireland), although there are reciprocal membership agreements. The NTS cares for over 100 properties and 185,000 acres of countryside.

A year's membership of the NTS costing £25 (£10 if you're aged under 26) offers free access to all NTS and NT properties. Short-term membership (touring ticket) costs £16/24 for one/two weeks. YHA members and student-card holders get half-price entry to NTS properties.

In this book, the letters NTS indicate a National Trust for Scotland property.

DANGERS & ANNOYANCES
Crime
Scotland has the usual big-city crimes (often drug related), so normal caution is advised. Pickpockets and bag snatchers operate in crowded public places, although this isn't a big problem. To make it harder for them, place your wallet in a front pocket when in cities and large towns.

Carry valuables next to your skin or in a sturdy pouch on your belt. Carry your own padlock for hostel lockers. Be careful even in hotels; don't leave valuables lying around in your room. Never leave valuables in a car, and remove all luggage overnight. Report thefts to the police and ask for a statement, or your travel insurance won't pay out; thefts from cars are often excluded anyway.

Midges
The most painful problem facing visitors to the Highlands and Islands is the tiny, blood-sucking midges which are related to mosquitoes. They're at their worst in the evening or in cloudy or shady conditions and proliferate late May to mid-September, but especially mid-June to mid-August. It's at least partly thanks to them that much of Scotland remains sparsely populated.

Cover yourself up, particularly in the evening; wear light-coloured clothing (midges are attracted to dark colours); and, most importantly, buy a reliable insect repellent containing DEET or DMP.

Beggars
The cities have their share of beggars. If you must give, don't wave a full wallet around – carry some change in a separate pocket. If you don't want to give them money, but would like to help the homeless and long-term unemployed, you could buy a copy of the magazine the *Big Issue* (80p) from homeless street vendors who benefit directly from sales. Also, consider giving to Shelter Scotland (☎ 0131-313 1550), 8 Hampton Terrace, Edinburgh EH12, a charity that helps the homeless and gratefully accepts donations.

Church Regulations
In the Highlands and Islands the Free Church of Scotland (the Wee Frees) and the United Free Presbyterians, adhere so strictly to the scriptures that in some areas on Sundays the public toilets are padlocked and ferries aren't always allowed to operate.

RAF Jets
One of the most annoying and frightening aspects of touring the Highlands is the sudden appearance and sound of RAF jets. It's something you never get used to.

Racial Discrimination
In general, tolerance prevails and visitors are unlikely to have problems associated with their skin colour. However, though few visitors will be aware of anti-English feelings they do exist, fanned by organisations like Scottish Watch and Settler Watch which try to dissuade the English (and other nationalities) from buying property in the Highlands.

LEGAL MATTERS
The 1707 Act of Union preserved a Scottish legal system separate from England and Wales, although there has been considerable mergence since then.

A barrister in Scotland is called an advocate and the Scottish Bar is known as the Faculty of Advocates. Scottish law places more importance on principle rather than precedence and doesn't separate equity (jurisprudence based on principles of natural justice and fair conduct) and law. The court system is also different. The criminal courts in Scotland are the High Court of Justiciary (the supreme criminal court), the Sheriff Court and District Court. The two main civil courts are the Court of Session and the Sheriff Court.

Most crimes and offences may be prosecuted only by the Lord Advocate, the crown's chief law officer in Scotland.

Some young people still head north to Gretna Green because in Scotland you only need to be 16 to marry without parental consent; in the rest of the UK it's 18.

If you need legal assistance contact the Scottish Legal Aid Board (☎ 0131-226 7061), 44 Drumsheugh Gardens, Edinburgh.

Drugs

The importation of illegal drugs is prohibited and could result in prison. Possession of small quantities of cannabis usually attracts a fine (still a criminal conviction) or a warning; harder drugs are treated much more seriously.

Driving Offences

The legal drinking age is 18. You're allowed to have a maximum blood-alcohol level of 35mg/100ml when driving, but the safest approach is not to drink at all.

Traffic offences (illegal parking, speeding etc) usually incur a fine for which you're usually allowed 30 days to pay.

See also Road Rules under Car & Motorcycle in the Getting Around chapter.

BUSINESS HOURS

Offices generally open weekdays from 9 am to 5 pm. Shops may open longer hours, and most open Saturday from 9 am to 5 pm. An increasing number of shops also open Sunday, perhaps from 10 am to 4 pm. In country towns, shops may have an early-closing day – usually Tuesday, Wednesday or Thursday afternoon. Late-night shopping is usually on Thursday or Friday.

Bank hours vary, but you'll be safe if you visit weekdays from 9.30 am to 3.30 pm. Friday afternoons get very busy. Some banks open Saturday, generally from 9.30 am till noon.

PUBLIC HOLIDAYS & SPECIAL EVENTS
Public Holidays

Although bank holidays are general public holidays in the rest of the UK, in Scotland they only apply to banks and some other commercial offices.

Bank holidays occur at the start of January, the first weekend in March, the first and last weekend in May, the first weekend in August and Christmas Day and Boxing Day.

Christmas Day, New Year's Day and 2 January are also general public holidays. Scottish towns normally have their own spring and autumn holiday; dates vary from year to year and from town to town.

Special Events

Countless diverse events are held around the country all year. Even small villages have weekly markets, and many still enact traditional customs and ceremonies, some dating back hundreds of years.

The STB publishes a comprehensive list, *Events in Scotland*, twice a year. Historic Scotland (see Useful Organisations earlier in this chapter) also publishes an annual list of events at its sites.

January
Hogmanay
Celebrations to greet New Year, including huge street party in Edinburgh
The Ba'
Two teams chase each other and a ball until one team reaches its goal, New Year's day, Kirkwall, Orkney
Up Helly Aa
Re-enactment of Viking fire festival, last Tuesday in January, Shetlands
Burns Night
Suppers all over the country celebrating Robbie Burns, 25 January

April
Rugby Sevens
Seven a side rugby tournament, the Borders

May
Maydaze
High-quality arts festival; runs for three weeks, Glasgow

Scottish FA Cup Final
Deciding match in Scotland's premier football knock-out tournament, Hampden Park, Glasgow

Orkney Folk Festival
Concerts, ceilidhs, workshops, Orkney

June to August
Riding of the Marches
Horse riding, with parades, brass bands etc, commemorating conflict with England, various towns in the Borders

June
West End Festival
Two huge weeks of music and the arts, Glasgow

Royal Highland Show
Scotland's national agricultural show, Edinburgh

July
International Jazz Festival
Jazz from around the world, Glasgow

August
Edinburgh Military Tattoo
Pageantry and military displays, runs for three weeks

Edinburgh International and Fringe Festivals
Premier international arts festivals, run for three weeks

World Pipe Band Championships
Gathering of over 100 pipe bands, Glasgow

September
Braemar Royal Highland Gathering
Kilts, cabers and bagpipes, attended by the Queen, Braemar; other games held all over Scotland, June to September

October
National Mod
A largely competitive Gaelic music festival, various locations

LANGUAGE COURSES
With the remarkable revival of Scottish Gaelic since the 1980s there is a growing number of courses in the language and culture. A number of places offer courses including:

An Ceathramh
(☎ 0148-641474), Muie East, Rogart Sutherland IV28 3U8 – centre for adult tuition in Gaelic, intensive courses throughout summer

Cothrom na Fèinne
(☎ 01599-566240), Balmacarra Mains, Kyle IV40 8DN – residential courses first week of month, May to October, individually tailored week/ends November to April

Sabhal Mór Ostaig
(☎ 01471-844 373, www.sino.uhi.ac.uk), Sleat, Isle of Skye, IV44 8RQ – courses in Gaelic language learning, song, piping and fiddle

WORK
Despite the fact that large numbers of locals are jobless, if you're prepared to do anything and work long hours for poor pay, you'll almost certainly find work. Lowly paid seasonal work is available in the tourist industry, usually in restaurants and pubs. Hostel noticeboards sometimes advertise casual work and hostels themselves sometimes employ travellers to staff the reception, clean etc. Without skills, though, it's difficult to find a job that pays well enough to save money.

Jobcentres (government employment offices) are scattered around and are listed in the telephone book. Whatever your skills, it's worth registering with a number of temporary agencies.

EU citizens can work in Scotland without a work permit. Citizens of Commonwealth countries aged 17 to 27 can apply for a Working Holiday Entry Certificate that allows them to spend up to two years in the UK and to take work that is 'incidental' to a holiday. Commonwealth citizens with a UK-born parent may be eligible for a Certificate of Entitlement to the Right of Abode, which entitles them to live and work in the UK free of immigration control.

Commonwealth citizens with a UK-born grandparent, or a grandparent born before 31 March 1922 in what's now the Republic of Ireland, could qualify for a UK Ancestry-Employment Certificate, allowing them to work full time for up to four years in the UK.

Visiting US full-time students aged 18 and over can get a six-month work permit through the Council on International Educational Exchange (☎ 212-822 2600, www.ciee.org), 205 East 42nd St, New York, NY 10017. British Universities North America Club (BUNAC, ☎ 203-264 0901,

Special Events

Following its inception in 1947 as a counterpoint to the austerity and problems of reconstruction after WWII, the **Edinburgh International Festival** has grown into the world's largest, most important arts festival. It attracts top performers in 'serious' music, dance and drama who play to capacity audiences.

The **Fringe Festival** began unofficially at the same time and grew in tandem to become the largest such event in the world. It showcases wannabe stars, and over 500 amateur and professional groups present every possible kind of avant-garde performance in venues all around the city.

A separate event but a major attraction in its own right, the **Edinburgh Military Tattoo** is held in the same period and takes place on the Esplanade of Edinburgh Castle. The show is an extravaganza of daredevil displays, regimental posturing and swirling bagpipes and ends with a single piper playing a lament on the battlements.

To make sure that every B&B and hotel room for over 40 miles is full, several other festivals take place at roughly the same time. The nine-day **Edinburgh International Jazz & Blues Festival** attracts top musicians from around the world who perform at various venues in early August. The two-week **Edinburgh International Film Festival**, dating from 1947, is Britain's chief film festival. Authors and many literary enthusiasts gather in Charlotte Square during the **Edinburgh Book Festival**. These latter two festivals are during the second half of the month.

The festival period is a great time to be in Edinburgh. The city is at its best, and the Fringe isn't at all elitist. In most cases the performers and front-of-house people are friendly and relaxed – they're grateful to have an audience – so there's no need to feel intimidated. Just be prepared to take the bad with the good ...

The International Festival runs from mid-August to early September. If you're more interested in this festival the last week is a good time to go, because the Fringe and Tattoo finish at the end of August, reducing the number of visitors. If you want to attend the International Festival, it's best to book ahead; the program is published in April and is available from the

www.BUNAC.org), PO Box 49, South Britain 06487 can also help organise a permit and find work.

ACCOMMODATION

This will almost certainly be your single greatest expense. Even camping can be expensive at some official sites. For budget travel, the two main options are hostels and cheaper bed and breakfasts (B&Bs). Mid-range B&Bs are often in beautiful old buildings and some rooms have private bathrooms. Guesthouses and small hotels are more likely to have private bathrooms, but they also tend to be less personal. If money's no object, there are some superb

hotels, the most interesting in converted castles and mansions.

TICs have local booking services (usually £1) and a Book-A-Bed-Ahead scheme (£3). A refundable deposit is also required for most bookings. The service is worth using in July and August, but isn't necessary otherwise, unless you plan to arrive in a town after business hours when the local TIC is closed. If you arrive late, it may still be worth going to the TIC, since some leave a list in the window showing which B&Bs had rooms free when they closed.

Regional tourist boards publish reliable (if not comprehensive) accommodation lists which include camp sites, hostels, self-catering accommodation and STB approved

Special Events

Edinburgh Festival Office (☎ 0131-226 4001, 473 2000), 21 Market St, EH1 1BW. Prices are generally reasonable, and any unsold tickets are sold half-price on the day of performance (1 to 5 pm) from the venue one hour before each performance or from the Festival Box Office in Market St. (The box office is scheduled to move to the Highland Tolbooth Kirk on the Royal Mile; check with the TIC.)

The Fringe is less formal, and many performances have empty seats left at the last moment. It's still worth booking for well-known names, or if the production has received good reviews. Programs are available, from June, from the Festival Fringe Society (☎ 0131-226 5257, www.edfringe.com), 180 High St, EH1 1QS.

To book for the Military Tattoo contact the Tattoo Office (☎ 0131-225 1188; fax 225 8627), 33-34 Market St, EH1 1QS.

Hogmanay, the Scottish celebration of the New Year, is another major fixture in Edinburgh's festival calendar with concerts, street parties and a massive bonfire on Calton Hill. Plans are under way to celebrate the year 2000 with the mother of all street parties. For details contact Unique Events (☎ 0131-557 3390, fax 557 8566), 17-23 Calton Rd, Edinburgh EH8 8DL.

For all these festivals, booking accommodation months ahead is strongly advised.

Glasgow too has a series of major festivals, the largest of which is the **West End Festival** with open-air concerts and other events during two weeks from the middle of June. Contact The White House (☎ 0141-341 0844, fax 341 0855), Downhill Park, Havelock St, Glasgow G11 5JE.

Highland games occur all over Scotland, but the biggest and most famous is the **Braemar Gathering** in Aberdeenshire in the north-east. Thousands, including the royal family, descend on Braemar on the first Saturday in September to watch Scotland's finest take part in these traditional sports in Memorial Park. There's also music and dancing and less traditional activities like parachute jumping. For information contact WA Meston (☎/fax 01339-755377), Coilacriech, Ballater, Aberdeenshire AB35 5UH.

and graded guesthouses, B&Bs and hotels. Places participating in the STB system have a plaque at the front. Some of the best B&Bs don't participate at all because they have to pay to do so. In practice, seeing the place, even from the outside, will give a clue as to what to expect. Always ask to look at your room before checking in.

Single rooms are in short supply and many accommodation suppliers are reluctant to let a double room (even when it's quiet) to one person without charging a hefty supplement.

Camping

You can camp free on public land (unless it's specifically protected). Commercial camping grounds are geared to caravans and vary widely in quality. A tent site costs from around £6.50. If you plan to use a tent regularly, invest in *Scotland: Camping & Caravan Parks* (£3.99), available from most TICs. Camping and caravan parks are graded by the STB, reflecting the level and quality of facilities.

Bothies, Camping Barns & Bunkhouses

Bothies are simple shelters, often in remote places. They're not locked, there's no charge, and you can't book. Take your own cooking equipment, sleeping bag and mat. Users should stay one night only, and leave it as they find it.

A camping barn – usually a converted farm building – is where walkers can stay for around £3 per night. Bunkhouses are a grade or two up from camping barns, have stoves for heating and cooking and may supply utensils. They may have mattresses, but you'll still need a sleeping bag. Most charge from £6.50.

Hostels

If you are travelling on a budget, the numerous hostels offer cheap accommodation and are great centres for meeting fellow travellers. Hostels have facilities for self-catering and some provide cheap meals. May to September and on public holidays, hostels can be heavily booked but so are most other things. Booking in advance is advisable.

Scottish Youth Hostel Association (SYHA) The SYHA (☎ 01786-891400, fax 01786-891333, www.shya.org.uk), 7 Glebe Crescent, Stirling FK8 2JA, is separate from the YHA in England and Wales. Its hostels are generally cheaper and often better than in those countries. The SYHA produces a handbook (£1.50) giving details on around 80 hostels, including transport links. In big cities, costs are £11.50/9.95 for seniors/juniors while the rest range from £4.65/3.85 to £8.60/7.10. Throughout this book, higher hostel prices for seniors are given first, followed by the reduced price for juniors.

SYHA hostels aren't always in town centres; fine if you're walking the countryside or have your own transport, a pain if you're not. Some are still run dictatorially, you're usually locked out between 10 am and 5 pm, the front door is locked at 11 pm.

The SYHA markets an Explore Scotland and a Scottish Wayfarer ticket, that represent a worthwhile saving on transport and accommodation, especially if you're not a student; see the Getting Around chapter for details.

Independent & Student Hostels There's a fast growing number of independent hostels/bunkhouses, most with prices around £9.50. The *Independent Hostel Guide – Backpackers Accommodation*, available from some TICs, lists over 90 hostels in Scotland. Alternatively, send a stamped, addressed envelope to Pete Thomas, Croft Bunkhouse & Bothies, 7 Portnalong, Isle of Skye IV47 8SL.

University Accommodation

Many Scottish universities offer their student accommodation to visitors during the holidays (vacations). Most rooms are comfortable, functional single bedrooms with shared bathroom. Increasingly, however, there are rooms with private bathroom, twin and family units, self-contained flats and shared houses. Full-board, half-board, B&B and self-catering options are available. Rooms are usually available late June to late September. B&B costs around £18 to £25 per person.

Local TICs have details.

B&Bs, Guesthouses & Hotels

B&Bs provide the cheapest private accommodation. At the bottom end (£12 to £18 per person) you get a bedroom in a private house, a shared bathroom and an enormous cooked breakfast (juice, cereal, bacon, eggs, sausage, baked beans and toast). Small B&Bs may only have one room to let. More upmarket B&Bs have private bathrooms and TVs in each room.

Guesthouses, often large converted houses with half a dozen rooms, are an extension of the B&B concept. They range from £12 to £50 a night, depending on the quality of the food and accommodation. In general, they're less personal than B&Bs, and more like small budget hotels. Pubs may also offer cheap B&B and can be good fun since they often place you at the hub of the community. However, they can be noisy and aren't always ideal for lone women travellers.

At the other end of the scale, however, there are some wonderfully luxurious places, including country-house hotels in superb settings, and castles complete with crenellated battlements, grand staircases and the obligatory rows of stags' heads. For these you can pay from around £60 to well over £100 per person. The *Which? Hotel Guide* (£14.99) covering Britain lists many of the finest hotels. Recommendations are generally trustworthy because hotel owners don't have to pay to appear in the guide.

Short-Term Rental

There's plenty of self-catering accommodation and staying in a house in the city or cottage in the country gives you an opportunity to get a feel for a region and a community. The minimum stay is usually one week in the summer peak season, three days or less at other times.

Outside weekends and July/August, it's not essential to book a long way ahead. Details are in the accommodation guides available from TICs. Alternatively, buy a copy of the STB's *Scotland: Self-Catering Accommodation* (£5.99). Expect a week's rent for a two bedroom cottage to cost from £150 in winter, £175 April to June, and £250 July to September. Places in the city range from £175 to over £700 per week.

FOOD

Scotland's chefs have an enviable range of fresh meat, seafood and vegetables at their disposal. And the country has gone a long way to shake off its once dismal culinary reputation. Most restaurants are reasonably good while there are some which are internationally renowned.

The Scots' high rate of heart disease partly results from their high consumption of alcohol and cigarettes, but also from many poorer Scots eating a less healthy diet – high on fried foods, refined sugar and white bread – than previous generations. However, restaurants don't usually serve greasy, fatty foods.

The quality of cooking at hotel restaurants and B&Bs that provide evening meals is variable. In small villages the alternatives are usually bleak, although village bakeries have a good range of pies, cakes and snacks. In towns there are Indian and Chinese alternatives, as well as fast-food chains.

Most pubs do food, with either a cheap bar menu or a more formal restaurant or both. Many supermarkets and department stores have reasonable (and reasonably priced) cafés.

Lunch is served from 12.30 to 2 pm, dinner 7 to around 9 pm. An alternative to dinner is high tea (from about 4.30 to 6.30 pm), when a main dish is served with tea and cakes.

Some of the best places to eat are members of the Taste of Scotland scheme. The STB's annual *Taste of Scotland Guide* (£7.99) is worth buying to track down these restaurants and hotels.

For vegetarians, if you like pizza, pasta and curry you should be able to get a reasonable meal pretty well anywhere. Most restaurants have at least a token vegetarian dish, although vegans will find the going tough. *The Vegetarian Travel Guide*, published annually by the UK Vegetarian Society covers hundreds of places to eat and stay in Britain.

The cheapest way to eat is to cook for yourself. Even if you lack great culinary skills, you can buy good quality pre-cooked meals from supermarkets.

Scottish Breakfast

Surprisingly few Scots eat porridge and even fewer eat it in the traditional way as a savoury dish not a sweet one; that is with salt to taste, then eaten with milk, but no sugar. You'll rarely be offered porridge in a B&B. Generally, a glass of fruit juice accompanies a bowl of cereal or muesli, followed by a cooked breakfast which may include: bacon, sausage, black pudding (a type of sausage made from dried blood), grilled tomato, grilled mushrooms, fried bread or tattie (potato) scones (if you're lucky), and an egg or two.

More upmarket hotels may offer porridge followed by kippers (smoked herrings). As well as toast, there may be oatcakes (oatmeal biscuits) to spread your marmalade upon. In the Aberdeen area there may also be butteries – delicious butter-rich bread rolls.

Snacks

As well as ordinary scones (similar to American biscuits), Scottish bakeries usually offer milk scones, tattie scones and girdle scones.

Bannocks are a cross between scones and pancakes. Savoury pies include the *bridie* (a pie filled with meat, potatoes and sometimes other vegetables) and the Scotch pie (minced meat in a plain round pastry casing – best eaten hot). And a *toastie* is a toasted sandwich.

Dundee cake, a rich fruit cake topped with almonds, is highly recommended. Black bun is another type of fruit cake, eaten over Hogmanay (New Year's Eve).

Soups

Scotch broth, made with barley, lentils and mutton stock, is highly nutritious and very good. Cock-a-leekie is a substantial soup made from a cock, or chicken, and leeks.

You may not be drawn to *powsowdie* (sheep's-head broth) but it's very tasty. More popular is *cullen skink*, a fish soup containing smoked haddock.

Meat & Game

Steak eaters will enjoy a thick fillet of world-famous Aberdeen Angus beef, while beef from Highland cattle is much sought after. Venison, from the red deer, is leaner and appears on many menus. Both may be served with a wine-based or creamy whisky sauce.

Gamebirds like pheasant and the more expensive grouse, traditionally roasted and served with game chips and fried breadcrumbs, are also available. They're definitely worth trying, but watch your teeth on the shot, which is not always removed before cooking.

Then there's haggis, Scotland's much-maligned national dish ...

Fish & Seafood

Scotland offers a wide variety of fish and seafood. Scottish salmon is well known but there's a big difference between farmed

---

Haggis – Scotland's National Dish

Scotland's national dish is frequently ridiculed by foreigners because of its ingredients which don't sound too mouth watering. However, once you get over any delicate sensibilities towards tucking in to chopped lungs, heart and liver mixed with oatmeal and boiled in a sheep's stomach, with the accompanying glass of whisky it can taste surprisingly good.

Haggis should be served with tatties and neeps (mashed potatoes and turnips, with a generous dollop of butter and a good sprinkling of black pepper).

Although it's eaten year round, haggis is central to the celebrations of 25 January in honour of Scotland's national poet, Robert Burns. Scots worldwide unite on Burns Night to revel in their Scottishness. A piper announces the arrival of the haggis and Burns' poem *Address to a Haggis* (otherwise known as the Selkirk Grace) is recited to this 'Great chieftan o' the puddin-race'. The bulging stomach is then lanced with a *dirk* (dagger) to reveal the steaming offal within.

Vegetarians (and quite a few carnivores, no doubt) will be relieved to know that veggie haggis is available in some restaurants in Scotland.

salmon and the leaner, more expensive, wild version.

Both are available either smoked (served with brown bread and butter) or poached. Wild brown trout is cheaper than salmon and almost as good; there's also a farmed variety and it's often served fried in oatmeal.

As an alternative to kippers (smoked herrings) you may be offered Arbroath smokies (lightly smoked fresh haddock), traditionally eaten cold. Herrings in oatmeal are good if you don't mind the bones. *Krappin heit* is cod's head stuffed with fish livers and oatmeal. Mackerel paté and smoked or peppered mackerel (both served cold) are also popular.

Prawns, crab, lobster, oysters, mussels and scallops are available in coastal towns and around lochs, although much is exported.

Cheeses

The Scottish cheese industry is growing. Cheddar is its main output but there are speciality cheese-makers whose products are definitely worth sampling. Many are based on the islands, particularly Arran, Bute, Gigha, Islay, Mull and Orkney. Brodick Blue is a ewes' milk blue cheese made on Arran. Lanark Blue is rather like Roquefort. There are several varieties of cream cheese (Caboc, St Finan, Howgate) which are usually rolled in oatmeal.

Scottish oatcakes make the perfect accompaniment for cheese.

Puddings

Traditional Scottish puddings are irresistibly creamy, calorie-enriched concoctions. *Cranachan* is made with toasted oatmeal, raspberries, or some other fresh fruit, and whisky, all mixed into thick cream. *Atholl brose* is similar but without the fruit – rather like English syllabub. *Clootie dumpling* is delicious, a rich steamed pudding filled with currants and raisins.

DRINKS
Nonalcoholic Drinks

On quantity drunk, tea probably qualifies as Scotland's national drink, but coffee is widely available and it's easy to get a cappuccino or espresso in large towns. Definitely an acquired taste is the virulent orange-coloured fizzy drink, Irn-Bru; it's 100% sugar plus some pretty weird flavouring.

Alcoholic Drinks

Takeaway alcoholic drinks are sold from neighbourhood off-licences (liquor stores) rather than pubs. Opening hours vary, but although some stay open daily to 9 or 10 pm, many keep ordinary shop hours. Alcohol can also be bought at supermarkets and corner shops.

Most restaurants are licensed to sell alcoholic drinks which are always expensive. There are a few BYO (Bring Your Own booze) restaurants. Most charge an extortionate sum for 'corkage' – opening your bottle for you.

See Pubs under Entertainment.

Whisky Whisky (always spelt without an 'e' if it's Scottish) is Scotland's best-known product and biggest export. The spirit was first distilled in Scotland in the 15th century and over 2000 brands are now produced.

There are two kinds of whisky: single malt, made from malted barley, and blended whisky, which is distilled from unmalted grain (maize) and blended with selected malts. Single malts are rarer (there are only about 100 brands) and more expensive than blended whiskies.

Although there are distilleries all over the country, there are concentrations around Speyside and on the Isle of Islay.

As well as blends and single malts, there are also several whisky-based liqueurs like Drambuie.

If you must mix your whisky with anything other than water try a whisky-mac (whisky with ginger wine). After a long walk in the rain there's nothing better to warm you up.

When out drinking, Scots may order a 'half' or 'nip' of whisky as a chaser to a pint of beer. Only tourists say 'Scotch' – what else would you be served in Scotland? The standard measure is 50ml.

Beer There's a wonderfully wide range of beers, from light (almost like lager) to extremely strong and treacly. What New Worlders call beer is actually lager; to the distress of local connoisseurs, lagers constitute a huge chunk of the market. Fortunately, thanks to the Campaign for Real Ale (CAMRA) organisation, the once threatened traditional beers are thriving.

The best ales are hand-pumped from the cask, not carbonated and drawn under pressure. They're usually served at cellar temperature, which may come as a shock to lager drinkers, and have subtle flavours that a cold, chemical lager can't match. Most popular is what the Scots call 'heavy', a dark beer similar to English bitter. Most Scottish brews are graded in shillings so

The Malt Whisky Trail

Roughly 45 Scottish whisky distilleries open to the public and you should certainly try to visit one while you're in Scotland.

In some, showing tourists around has become a slick marketing operation, complete with promotional videos, free drams (whisky measures), gift shops that rival the distillery in size and an entry charge of around £3. Eight Speyside distillers – Glenfiddich, Cardhu, Glenfarclas, Glen Grant, The Glenlivet, Strathisla, Tamdhu and Tamnavulin – promote themselves in the Malt Whisky Trail, a pleasant drive around Speyside, although visiting all eight might be overkill. You can also create your own malt whisky trail by visiting six distilleries on the Isle of Islay.

The process of making malt whisky begins with malting. Barley is soaked in water and allowed to germinate so that enzymes are produced to convert the starch in the barley to fermentable sugar. The barley is then dried in a malt kiln over the peat fire that gives malt whisky its distinctive taste. Since most distilleries now buy in their malted barley, tourists rarely see this part of the process.

This huge copper-pot still plays a pivotal role in the age-old art of making malt whisky.

The malt is milled, mixed with hot water and left in a large tank, the *mash tun*. The starch is converted into sugar and this liquid, or 'wort', is drawn off into another large tank, the washback, for fermentation.

This weak alcoholic solution, or wash, is distilled twice in large copper-pot stills. The process is controlled by the stillman, who collects only the middle portion of the second distillation to mature in oak barrels. The spirit remains in the barrels for at least three years, often much longer. During bottling, water is added to reduce its strength.

Some recommended distillery tours include: Glenfiddich, The Glenlivet and Strathisla on Speyside; any of the Islay distilleries; and Highland Park on Orkney, one of the few distilleries where you still see the barley malting process.

Edinburgh Castle at sunset in winter

St Giles Cathedral, Parliament Square, Edinburgh

Castle Hill, Old Town, Edinburgh

Players and supporters of Hearts celebrate the club's 1998 Scottish Cup triumph

Patisserie Florentin, St Giles St, Edinburgh

Edinburgh Festival box office

you can tell their strength, the usual range being 60 to 80 shillings (written 80/-). The greater the number of shillings, the stronger the beer.

The market is dominated by the big brewers – Youngers, McEwans, Scottish & Newcastle and Tennent's. Look out for beer from local breweries, some of it very strong – the aptly-named Skullsplitter from Orkney is a good example. Caledonian 80/, Maclays 80/- and Belhaven 80/- are others worth trying.

Long before hops arrived in Scotland, beer was brewed from heather. Reintroduced, heather ale is surprisingly good and available in some pubs.

Stout is a dark, rich, foamy drink; Guinness is the most famous brand.

Beers are usually served in pints (from £1.50 to £2), but you can also ask for a 'half' (a half pint). The stronger brews are usually 'specials' or 'extras'. Potency can vary from around 2 to 8%.

Wines For centuries people made wine from wild flowers, fruits and tree saps. This cottage industry is continued at Moniack Castle, near Beauly in the Highlands, and at Cairn o' Mohr winery in the Carse of Gowrie.

Good international wines are widely available and reasonably priced (except in pubs and restaurants). In supermarkets an ordinary but drinkable bottle can be found for around £4.

ENTERTAINMENT

Scotland has its own national ballet, opera and orchestra as well as many fine theatres and repertory companies. Cinemas are found throughout the country showing commercial films, and the big cities have independent cinemas showing arthouse, foreign and cult movies. Glasgow and Edinburgh have lively club scenes, but nightclubs are by no means confined to the major cities. Many pubs offer entertainment ranging from live traditional Scottish folk music, to pop, rock and jazz music to disco and quiz nights.

In Glasgow and Edinburgh, look out for the *List*, a twice-monthly listings magazine.

Pubs

The local pub is the place to go for a drink and often live music; you'll get a warm reception at most. Given how much Scotland is epitomised by its pubs, it's odd how unenthusiastic the big breweries seem to be in hanging on to them.

Not only are High Sts vanishing beneath a plethora of brewery-owned bars and brasseries, but traditional pubs are being reinvented as Irish or Australian theme bars. Just ask at your hostel, B&B or hotel for recommendations.

Some pubs in the more depressed areas of big towns have a reputation for late-night brawls and should be avoided by the non-pugnacious visitor.

Pubs generally open Monday to Saturday, from 11 am to 11 pm, Sunday from 12.30 pm. Some have a late licence at weekends. The bell for last orders rings about 15 minutes before closing time. Infuriatingly, many pubs in the Highlands and Islands close for two hours mid-afternoon (usually 2 to 4 pm). There's nothing worse, especially if you've been travelling for some time.

Ceilidhs

Many tourist centres stage a ceilidh or Highland show featuring Scottish song and dance, most nights during the summer. Some local restaurants also combine a floor show with dinner.

If you fancy trying an eightsome reel, ceilidhs with dancing you can join in usually take place on Friday or Saturday. Ask at the local TIC for details. It's not as difficult as it looks and there's often a 'caller' to lead everyone through their paces.

SPECTATOR SPORTS

The Scots love their games, watch them with fierce, competitive dedication and identify closely with teams and individuals that compete both locally and internationally. The most popular games are football (soccer), rugby union, shinty, lawn bowls, curling and golf, the last of which the Scots claim to have invented.

Football

Also known as soccer to distinguish it from rugby football, this is Scotland's largest spectator sport. The Scottish Football League is the main national competition and has a number of divisions. The best clubs form the Scottish Premier League. In the 1990s it has been dominated by Glasgow Rangers who, in 1997, equalled the record of nine successive championships set by its main rival Glasgow Celtic in the 1960s and 70s. Celtic was the first British team to win the European Cup (1967) and, so far, the only Scottish club to have done so.

The Scottish Football Association (SFA) Cup is a knock-out competition. The final is held mid-May, traditionally at Hampden Park in Glasgow which, after major renovations, again hosts this important annual sporting event. The national team has resumed playing home internationals at Hampden.

The domestic football season lasts from August to May and most matches are played at 3 pm on Saturday or 7.30 pm on Tuesday or Wednesday.

When the Scots play abroad, the game unites the country; at home it highlights differences and trouble can occur, especially when Catholic Celtic plays Protestant Rangers in Glasgow.

Rugby Union

Rugby union football is administered by the Scottish Rugby Union based at Murrayfield in Edinburgh, where international games are played. Each year, starting in January, Scotland takes part in the Six Nations Rugby Union Championship. The most important fixture is the clash against England for the Calcutta Cup.

At club level, the season runs from September to May, and among the better union teams are those from the Borders like Hawick, Kelso and Melrose. At the end of the season teams play a Rugby Sevens

(seven a side) variation of the 15-player competition.

Golf

Although games that involve hitting a ball with a stick have been played in Europe since Roman times, it was the Scottish version that caught on. Apparently dating from the 15th century, golf was popularised by the Scottish monarchy. St Andrews in Scotland is the home of golf, since the Royal and Ancient club (the recognised authority on the rules) and the famous Old Course are both there.

Shinty

Shinty (*camanachd* in Gaelic) is an amateur ball-and-stick sport similar to Ireland's hurling. It's fast, very physical and played most of the year. It's administered by the Camanachd Association and the Camanachd Cup is the most prized trophy. The final, a great Gaelic get-together, draws a large crowd and is televised on STV.

Curling

Scotland is the home of curling which involves propelling circular polished granite stones over ice as close to the centre of a target as possible. A team is made up of four players. Almost all games are played indoors and the Royal Caledonian Curling Club, in Edinburgh, is the governing body.

SHOPPING

Making things to sell to tourists is big business in Scotland, and almost every visitor attraction seems to have been redesigned to funnel you through the gift shop. Among the tourist kitsch are some good-value, high-quality goods, but check labelling thoroughly as many 'Scottish' products are made in other countries.

If you're interested in visiting mills, factories and craftshops, pick up a copy of the STB publication *See Scotland at Work*.

Tartan, Tweed & Other Fabrics

Scottish textiles, particularly tartans, are popular and tartan travelling rugs or scarves are often worth buying. There are said to be over 2000 designs, some officially recognised as clan tartans. Many shops have a list and can tell you if your family belongs to a clan, but these days if you can pay for the cloth you can wear the tartan. There are some universal tartans, like the Flower of Scotland, that aren't connected with a clan.

For about £350 to £400, you can have a kilt made in your clan tartan, but this shouldn't be worn without a *sporran* (purse), which can cost from £40 for a plain version up to £1000 for an ornate silver-dress sporran. Full kilts are traditionally worn only by men, while women wear kilted or tartan skirts.

There are mill shops in many parts of Scotland, but the best-known textile manufacturing areas are the Borders and Central regions, particularly around Stirling and Perth. Scotland is also renowned for a rough woollen cloth known as tweed – Harris tweed is world famous. There are various places on this Hebridean island where you can watch your cloth being woven.

Sheepskin rugs and jackets are also popular.

Knitwear

Scottish knitwear can be great value and is sold throughout Scotland. Shetland is most closely associated with high-quality wool, and at knitwear factory shops you can buy genuine Shetland sweaters for as little as £11. The most sought-after sweaters bear the intricate Fair Isle pattern – the genuine article from this remote island costs at least £25.

Jewellery & Glassware

Silver brooches set with cairngorms (yellow or wine-coloured gems from the mountains of the same name) are popular. Jewellery decorated with Celtic designs featuring mythical creatures and intricate patterns is particularly attractive, although some pieces are actually made in Cornwall. Glassware, particularly Edinburgh crystal and Caithness glass, is another good souvenir.

Food & Drink

Sweet, butter-rich Scottish shortbread makes a good gift. The biggest manufacturer, Walkers, is famous for baking such prodigious quantities of the stuff that the Speyside town of Aberlour smells of nothing else. Dark, fruity Dundee cake lasts well and is available in a tin, but heavy to take home by air. Heather honey can give you a reminder of Scotland when your visit is over.

If you haven't far to go, smoked salmon or any other smoked product (venison, mussels etc) is worth buying, but some countries don't allow you to import meat and fish.

You're better off buying duty-free souvenir bottles of whisky at the airport rather than in High St shops, unless it's a rare brand. If you go on a distillery tour, you may be given £1 or so discount to buy a bottle there. Miniature bottles make good presents.

Activities

Pursuing a favourite activity or interest is one of the best ways of escaping the beaten track. Becoming part of a country's life, and preferably an active participant, is more rewarding than remaining a spectator viewing the world through a camera lens or car window.

Scotland is a great place for outdoor recreation and although it isn't cheap to travel in, many activities open up some of the most beautiful corners of the country and are often within the reach of the tightest budget. In fact, budget travellers may find themselves hiking or cycling out of necessity. Fortunately, a walk or ride through the countryside will almost certainly be a highlight (as well as a cheap part) of a Scottish holiday. For those who have the money, other activities like golf or fishing are available as part of holiday packages that include bed, board and transport.

Most activities are well organised and have clubs and associations that can give visitors invaluable information and, sometimes, substantial discounts. Many of these organisations have national or international affiliations, so check with local clubs before leaving home. The Scottish Tourist Board and British Tourist Authority have brochures on most activities, which can provide a starting point for further research.

WALKING

Every weekend many people invade the countryside for short and long walks often ending up somewhere that sells tea or beer. Villages and towns are often surrounded by footpaths. Keen walkers should consider a week based in one interesting spot (perhaps in a self-catering cottage, or a hostel or camp site) with a view to exploring the surrounding countryside.

The best time is usually May to September for mountains, although walking the West Highland Way or Southern Upland Way is normally OK between April and October. (Winter walking in the higher areas of Scotland is 'technical' – requiring, at the very least, an ice-axe, crampons and mountaineering experience.)

July and August is holiday time in Britain, so everywhere is likely to be busier than normal – although only a few parts of Scotland ever get *really* crowded. Midges can also be a problem at this time. The most pleasant time is May to mid-June – before the midges emerge. September (and sometimes October) is also good, although days are colder and shorter.

Highland hikers should be properly equipped and cautious as the weather can become vicious at any time of year. After rain peaty soil can become boggy; always wear stout shoes and carry a change of clothing.

Some of the walks described here are quite serious mountain/wilderness undertakings, and shouldn't be embarked upon lightly.

Access

Scotland doesn't have a formal system of registered rights of way, but there is a tradition of relatively free access to open country, especially on mountains and moorlands. There is much cooperation between organisations such as the Scottish Landowners' Federation, the Mountaineering Council of Scotland and the Ramblers' Association to promote responsible access to the countryside.

Providing you don't cause damage and that you leave the land if (in the unlikely event) you're asked to do so by the owner, you shouldn't have any trouble. You should, however, avoid areas where you might disrupt or disturb wildlife, deer stalking and grouse shooting (mainly 12 August to the third week in October), and lambing (generally mid-April to the end of May).

Rights of way exist, but local authorities aren't required to list and map them so they're not shown on Ordnance Survey

(OS) maps. However, in its guide, *Scottish Hill Tracks*, the Scottish Rights of Way Society publicises those routes which have, or deserve to have, legal status and defends those under threat.

Nor does Scotland have national parks, although development is controlled in a number of areas that have been designated as National Scenic Areas (NSAs) and National Nature Reserves (NNRs). Access is free at all times to areas owned by the National Trust for Scotland (NTS) and to most owned by the Forestry Commission.

Information

Every TIC has details (free or for a nominal charge) of suggested walks that take in local points of interest. Other useful sources of information are:

Mountaineering Council of Scotland
(☎ 01738-638227), 4A St Catherine's Rd, Perth PH1 5SE
Scottish Rights of Way Society
(☎ 0131-652 2937), John Cotton Business Centre, 10 Sunnyside, Edinburgh EH7 5RA
Ramblers' Association Scotland
(☎ 01592-611177), 23 Crusader House, Haig Business Park, Markinch, Fife KY7 6AQ

Guides Scores of books are available that describe walks ranging from half-hour strolls to week-long expeditions.

Lonely Planet's *Walking in Britain* has a chapter covering short walks and one on long-distance paths including the Southern Upland Way and West Highland Way.

For general advice, the STB produces a *Walk Scotland* booklet, describing numerous routes in various parts of the country, plus safety tips and other information.

Great Walks Scotland by Hamish Brown et al describes a good range of routes of varying difficulty all over the country. Or try *100 Best Routes on Scottish Mountains* by Ralph Storer.

The Scottish Mountaineering Club publishes a series of guides including *The Munros Hillwalkers Guide*. It also publishes several *District Guides* listing mainly high-level walks for those with experience.

The High Mountains Companion is a condensed text of Irvine Butterfield's *The High Mountains of Britain & Ireland*. Both books cover the British Isles, but concentrate on the mountains of Scotland.

Highly recommended if you like mountains, but can't stomach the intensity of Munro-bagging is *The First Fifty* by Muriel Gray.

She likes to debunk the mystique and fastidiousness that can sometimes envelope other writers and books concerning walking in Scotland.

And just in case you thought all walks in Scotland were up the biggest mountains, there's *Exploring Scottish Hill Tracks* by Ralph Storer, with a marvellous range of circular routes and longer expeditions for walkers and mountain bikers.

Recommended if you don't want to attack high peaks are the Pathfinder Guides to *Loch Lomond & The Trossachs*, *Fort William & Glen Coe* and *Skye*.

These books each cover about 30 routes, with OS map excerpts, colour photos and background information.

For short day walks, the spiral-bound *Bartholomew Map & Guide* series is recommended. They come with good maps and descriptions; most walks described take around two to three hours.

The OS caters to walkers with a wide variety of maps at different scales. Its Landranger series at 1:50,000 – or about 1¼ inches to 1 mile – is good, but if you want more detail it also publishes Pathfinder/ Tourist maps at 2½ inches to 1 mile. TICs usually stock a selection.

Alternatively, look out for the excellent walkers' maps published by Harveys; they're at scales of 1:40,000 and 1:25,000. And unlike the OS equivalents these maps include tourist information.

Munro-baggers should look out for the Bartholomew map of the Munros (£3.99).

Organised Walks

There are plenty of operators offering guided walks and the STB has a comprehensive list. Scot Trek (☎ 0141-334 9232),

9 Lawrence St, Glasgow G11 5HH, organises walking holidays from February to March in places such as the Cairngorms, and on the West Highland Way. Contact Fred Chatterton.

Southern Upland Way

Coast to coast the Southern Upland Way is 212 miles from Portpatrick in the west to Cockburnspath in the east. It's for walkers of different abilities and passes through varied countryside which contains a wealth of local history, literature and wildlife.

The route includes some long, extremely demanding stretches, so walkers tackling the entire length must be both experienced and fit. Parts of the route are sparsely populated, with shelter and transport virtually nonexistent. Proper equipment is essential; in summer you can expect to experience everything from snow to a heat wave. Although the entire route is waymarked, walkers must be able to navigate with map and compass when the visibility is bad.

Walkers are advised to walk south-west to north-east and the walk could take anything between 12 and 20 days. The way incorporates clifftop paths, old Roman roads, hill ridges and droving trails. It passes over high hilltops and wide moors, through valleys, forests, farms and villages.

Shorter, less demanding sections of the walk can be undertaken. Two are Portpatrick to New Luce (23 miles) and Yair Bridge to Melrose (7½ miles).

The excellent official guide to the walk, *Southern Upland Way*, is published by the government Stationery Office and comes complete with two 1:50,000 OS route maps. Aurum Press also publishes the *Southern Upland Way* by Anthony Burton.

Accommodation is quite difficult to find in parts, and many walkers use tents. Book accommodation in advance, especially in the busy summer months. Local TICs can help, and supply a free accommodation leaflet.

West Highland Way

This 95-mile hike through the Scottish Highlands runs from Milngavie (pronounced mullguy), 7 miles north of the centre of Glasgow, north along Loch Lomond to Fort William.

The route passes through a tremendous range of landscape that includes some of Scotland's most spectacular scenery. It begins in the Lowlands, but the greater part of this trail is among the mountains, lochs and fast-flowing rivers of the Highlands. In the far north the route crosses wild Rannoch Moor and reaches Fort William via Glen Nevis, in the shadow of Britain's highest peak, Ben Nevis.

The path is easy to follow and it uses the old drove roads along which cattle were herded in the past, the old military road (built by troops to help control the Jacobites in the 18th century) and disused railway lines. Best walked from south to north, the walk can be done in about six or seven days.

You need to be properly equipped with good boots, maps, a compass, and food and drink for the northern part of the walk. Midge repellent is also worth bringing.

The Harveys map, *West Highland Way*, is the most accurate and contains tourist information. *The West Highland Way* (Stationery Office) by Robert Aitken comes with a 1:50,000 OS route map and is the most comprehensive guide. *West Highland Way* (Aurum Press) by Anthony Burton also contains OS maps.

Accommodation shouldn't be too difficult to find, though between Bridge of Orchy and Kinlochleven it's quite limited. In summer, book B&Bs in advance. There are some youth hostels on and near the path, as well as bunkhouses. It's also possible to camp in some parts. A free accommodation list is available from TICs.

The Speyside Way

This is a lowland route, running alongside the 'silvery' River Spey, one of Scotland's famous salmon-fishing rivers. It starts on the coast at Spey Bay, east of Elgin, and runs inland to Tomintoul, on the northern edge of the Cairngorm Mountains. At only 45 miles, it can be done in three or four days. With more time it could possibly be

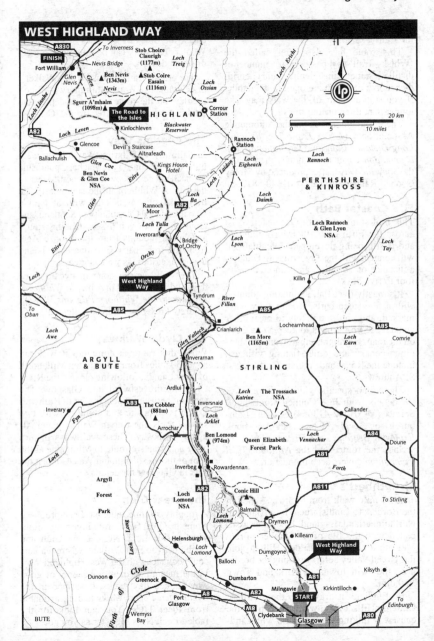

combined with some high-level walking in the Cairngorms.

This route has also been called the 'Whisky Trail' as it passes near a number of distilleries, including Glenlivet and Glenfiddich, some of which are open to the public. If you stop at them all, the walk may take longer than three or four days!

There's no guidebook but the Automobile Association's (AA's) *Exploring Britain's Long Distance Paths* and the *National Trail Companion* cover most things; there's also the *Speyside Way* leaflet produced by Moray Council Ranger Service (☎ 01340-881266).

Fife Coastal Path

This trail starts at North Queensferry just across the Firth of Forth from Edinburgh and is still being developed. Eventually, it will connect with the Tay Bridge to Dundee, a distance of 78 miles, and can be done in four to five days.

It's mostly over flat, undulating country, with a few steep parts. It isn't fully way-marked, and you're unlikely to meet other walkers, so you'll need to keep a close eye on the map. Highlights, apart from the stunning scenery and quiet fishing villages, include the Royal and Ancient Golf Club at St Andrews.

There's no specific guidebook yet. Ask for details from Fife Council Community Services (☎ 01592-413664) or at the Edinburgh or local TICs. The AA book *Exploring Britain's Long Distance Paths* describes the route, and the *National Trail Companion* covers accommodation.

St Cuthbert's Way

This 62-mile walk from Melrose Abbey in the Borders to Lindisfarne (Holy Island) in Northumberland, England, links sites associated with the life of St Cuthbert. From Melrose it crosses the Eildon Hills to join the Tweed Valley before crossing the border near the twin towns of Kirk and Town Yetholm.

In England it traverses the northern Cheviot Hills to Fenwick and on to the causeway linking the mainland with Lind-

isfarne. Before crossing the causeway check the times of the tides at the TIC in Wooler. The walk can be done in about six or seven days.

The official trail guide is Harvey Walker's *St Cuthbert's Way* (Stationery Office). Leaflets on the route, accommodation and facilities are available free from TICs.

The Pilgrims Way

In Galloway, the Pilgrims Way follows a 25-mile trail through The Machars peninsula from Glenluce Abbey in the north-west to the Isle of Whithorn in the south-east. The trail links sites associated with St Ninian who introduced Christianity to Scotland, and along the route you'll see standing stones and burial mounds from the Bronze Age, Iron Age forts, early Christian chapels and medieval castles, as well as great scenery.

The walk can be done in two to three days and is described in *A Way to Whithorn: A Guide to the Whithorn Pilgrims Way* (St Andrew Press) by Andrew Patterson.

The Clyde Walkway

When this route is complete it will run about 30 miles from Bonnington Mill, north of New Lanark, following closely the River Clyde north-westward into Glasgow. The section between Glasgow and Bothwell Castle is complete and connects with two shorter trails, the Kelvin Walkway and Allander Walkway. These walkways in turn offer an attractive route to Milngavie at the start of the West Highland Way. Contact the TIC in Glasgow for details.

The Great Glen

A roughly 50-mile route has been proposed along the Great Glen, from Inverness southward beside Loch Ness, Loch Oich and Loch Lochy to Fort William, where walkers could connect with the West Highland Way. In the meantime, there are plenty of good way-marked day walks, described in the *Great Glen Forest Walks* leaflet, available from local TICs. You can look for the fabled Loch Ness Monster as you go!

Short Walks

As well as those mentioned here, descriptions of other walks are given throughout this guide.

Isle of Arran Arran is called 'Scotland in miniature' and there's enough there to keep any walker happy for quite a few days. When the sun shines, Arran masquerades as an island in the Mediterranean, but it can get cold, wet and windy, so come well prepared. From the TIC in Brodick get a copy of the leaflet *Walks on Arran*.

The island's highest mountain, Goat Fell (874m, 2866 feet), near Brodick, is one of the most visited points on the island and there are several routes up to the summit. The most popular are from Brodick Castle and from Corrie on the east side of the mountain. A quieter, more pleasing approach goes from The Saddle, at the heads of Glen Rosa and Glen Sannox, on the west side. Allow seven to eight hours. There are numerous possibilities for linking up with paths to other peaks including Cir Mhor, Ciogh na h'Oighe, Castheal Abhail and Beinn Tarsuinn.

In the north-west of Arran are the Pirnmill Hills. Although not quite as high as Goat Fell, and less rugged in appearance, they are far less frequently visited. Finally, there are some lovely coastal walks, worthwhile at any time, but particularly when the hills are shrouded in cloud. Possibly the best of these is the walk from Lochranza to Sannox, called the Cock of Arran Coast Walk. Even in miserable weather, this 8-mile route is interesting. It takes about four to five hours.

Glen Coe & Ben Nevis These famous places lie in the West Highlands, near Fort William. The complex geology of this part of Scotland has bequeathed great scenery and many great walking opportunities. Contact Fort William TIC for information.

The lofty peaks and ridges which flank Glen Coe should be left to the mountaineer, but there's a good rough walk circumnavigating Buachaille Etive Beag. The appeal of this route is the remote, rugged landscape. The 9-mile walk itself is quite a challenge and you might be glad of a stick for balance when negotiating stream crossings. Allow at least five hours.

There's something irresistible about an attempt on Ben Nevis (1343m, 4406 feet), the highest peak in the country. Despite its popularity, the walk, which begins virtually at sea level, shouldn't be undertaken lightly. You should be well equipped, have adequate food and drink, and be aware that it can be dangerous. The route is about 4½ miles each way, but the ascent (and descent) and inevitable stops along the way mean that up to eight hours should be allowed for the round trip. Ionad Nibheis Visitor Centre or the SYHA hostel are good starting points. If you don't want to go to the summit there's the Ben Nevis Low-Level Circuit from Halfway Lochan.

Cairngorms The Cairngorms may be better known as a winter ski area, but this extensive mountain range is popular with climbers and hill-walkers year-round. These are the wildest uplands anywhere in Britain, with arctic tundra, superb high corries and awesome rock formations. The wildlife is pretty good too.

Cairn Gorm (1245m, 4083 feet) is the most accessible summit, but the high plateau is not the place for a casual stroll. You're only about 650 miles from the Arctic Circle here, and at altitudes of 1000m or more you're certainly in an arctic environment. Weather conditions are notoriously bad. Unless you're an experienced mountaineer the routes should only be attempted in summer. Even then, walkers should be prepared for the worst.

The Cairn Gorm High Circuit is one of the most popular routes in the Cairngorms, not only because of its easy access, but also because of the chairlift which allows walkers to ascend Cairn Gorm without even raising a sweat. From the upper chairlift station it takes about 30 minutes to walk up to the start of the circuit, which runs around the top rim of Coire an t-Sneachda and Cairn

Lochan, then down the ridge that runs alongside Lurcher's Gully and back to the lower chairlift station. The total distance is around 5 miles.

Don't be put off if you're not a peak-bagger. On the north side of the range near Aviemore, Rothiemurchus Estate and Glenmore Forest Park provide many walking opportunities suitable for all walkers.

Check with the TIC in Aviemore.

CYCLING

Travelling by bicycle is an excellent way to explore Scotland. Bikes aren't allowed on motorways, but you can cycle on all other roads (on the left!) unless the road is marked 'private'. A-roads tend to be busy and are best avoided. B-roads are usually quieter and many are pleasant for cycling. The best roads are the unclassified roads, or country lanes linking small villages together; they're not numbered – you simply follow the signposts. Lanes are clearly shown on OS maps. There are also forest trails and dedicated routes along canal towpaths and disused railway tracks. Cycle routes have been suggested throughout this book.

You can bring your own bike or hire one when you arrive.

Information

The STB publishes a useful free booklet, *Cycling in Scotland*, with some suggested routes, lists of cycle holiday companies and other helpful information. Many regional TICs have information on local cycling routes and places to hire bikes. They also stock cycling guides and books – look for those produced by the OS.

The Cyclists' Touring Club (CTC, ☎ 01483-417217, fax 01483-426994, cycling @ctc.org.uk, www.ctc.org.uk), 69 Meadrow, Godalming, Surrey GU7 3HS, is a membership organisation offering comprehensive information about cycling in Britain. It provides suggested routes, lists of local cycling contacts and clubs, recommended accommodation, organised cycling holidays, a cycle hire directory, and a mail-order service for maps and books.

For up-to-date detailed information on Scotland's cycling trail network contact Sustrans (☎ 0117-929 0888), 53 Cochrane St, Glasgow G1 1HL.

There are plenty of operators hiring out bikes from around £6 to £15 a day, or £50 a week, plus a refundable deposit when the bike is returned.

Beware the midge, prevalent during summer and early autumn, and especially annoying if you're camping.

Transporting Your Bicycle

Ferries transport bicycles for a small fee and airlines usually accept them as part of your 20kg/44lb luggage allowance. When buying your ticket, check with the ferry company or airline about any regulations or restrictions that apply on the transportation of bicycles.

Bicycles can be transported by bus provided there's enough room in the luggage compartment and that they're folded or dismantled and boxed.

Generally, bikes can be taken free on local rail services on a first-come, first-served basis. On most long-distance routes it's necessary to make a reservation (usually around £3.50) for your bike. Some trains carry only one or two bikes so make your reservation (and get your ticket) at least 24 hours before travelling.

Check bike-carriage details with the rail company for the whole of your planned journey as far in advance as possible.

Where to Cycle

Cyclists in search of the wild and remote will enjoy north-west Scotland. Its majestic Highlands and mystical islands offer quiet pedalling through breathtaking mountainscapes. There are fewer roads in this part of Scotland and generally less traffic. Roads are well graded, but sometimes very remote, so carry plenty of food. Of the isles, Skye has a bridge to the mainland and suffers the worst of seasonal traffic; good ferries between the islands offer easy escape routes.

For the less intrepid cyclist, the beautiful forests, lochs, glens and hills in the central and southern areas of Scotland are more easily accessible and have a more intimate charm. Cyclists can seek out the smaller roads and tracks to avoid the traffic.

Hebridean Islands The scenic Hebridean Islands off the west coast, linked by a comprehensive ferry system, provide superb cycling opportunities. Allow two to three weeks to give yourself time to enjoy the scenery. Interesting circular routes are possible on most islands. The route outlined here comprises some 280 miles of cycling, and any tour will need to be planned around the timings of the ferry crossings; some are summer only.

Ardrossan, near Ayr, is a good starting point since the ferry to the Isle of Arran leaves from here. On Arran, cycle north to Lochranza for another ferry to the Kintyre peninsula. You can cycle north to Lochgilphead and Oban to catch the ferry to Tobermory on the Isle of Mull.

Mull is worth exploring before taking the ferry across to Kilchoan. Cycle eastwards along the Ardnamurchan peninsula to Salen, then north to Mallaig. Ferries leave from here to Armadale on the Isle of Skye.

You can then cycle north to Uig, or follow numerous other routes around the island.

From Uig, take a ferry to Tarbert (Isle of Harris) in the Outer Hebrides. These outer isles are wild and remote places with quiet lanes to explore. Cycle south to Benbecula and onto South Uist where you can catch the ferry back to Oban.

Land's End to John o'Groats The best known long-distance route in Britain runs from the extreme south-west tip, Land's End in Cornwall, to the north-east corner, John o'Groats, in Scotland. Along quiet roads, this is a distance of some 1000 miles. The ride is a classic British favourite.

The route is challenging and goes via the scenic western side of England and Scotland, crossing to the east eventually. Many cyclists do the ride in two to three weeks, following one of the CTC's three recommended routes. The main road route runs via Exeter, Cheddar, Shrewsbury, Carlisle, Dumfries, Fort William and Bonar Bridge. The 14-day youth hostel route follows quiet roads via Exeter, Wells, Leominster, Chester, Slaidburn, Windermere, Dumfries, Glasgow, Loch Lomond, Fort William and

Sustrans & the National Cycle Network

Sustrans is a civil-engineering charity whose goal is the creation of a 6500-mile National Cycle Network of paths in Britain that will pass through the middle of most major towns and cities.

When Sustrans announced this objective in 1978 the charity was barely taken seriously, but increasingly congested roads have made the public reconsider the exalted place given to the car in modern Britain. Sustrans has received £43.5 million from the Millenium Commission to ensure that at least 2500 miles of routes will be opened by the year 2000. The whole network will be completed in 2005.

Half the network is to be on traffic-free paths (including disused railways and canal-side towpaths) the rest of the system along quiet minor roads. Cyclists will share the traffic-free paths with wheelchair users and walkers. Many useful sections are already open. The Scottish National Cycle Route runs 425 miles from Carlisle in northern England to Inverness and there are other local cycle networks being developed in places like Edinburgh, Glasgow and Fife which will connect with the National Cycle Network.

For up-to-date information on Scotland's cycling network contact Sustrans (☎ 0117-929 0888, www.sustrans.org.uk), 53 Cochrane St, Glasgow G1 1HL.

Loch Ness. The B&B route also follows quiet roads through North Devon, Cheddar, Ludlow, Slaidburn, Brampton, Peebles, Edinburgh, Crieff, Dunkeld and Inverness.

Glasgow to Gourock There's a 14-mile cycling route that starts in Glasgow and runs west via Paisley, Kilmacolm and Greenock to Gourock on the peninsula jutting into the Firth of Clyde. It's partly on minor roads, partly on a disused railway line.

Loch Leven There's a lovely 20-mile circuit around Loch Leven in the West Highlands (near Glencoe), taking in Kinlochleven, Glencoe, North Ballachulish and Ballachulish and the views are stunning.

The Machars Peninsula You can cycle around The Machars peninsula in Galloway between Newton Stewart and Glenluce via Whithorn.

The quiet 50-mile route is off the beaten track and goes through rich green pastures and attractive villages with the coast visible most of the way. It's easy cycling, but it can be windy and you should be prepared for rain.

Tweed Cycle Way This is 62 miles along minor roads through the beautiful Tweed Valley from Biggar in the Borders, to Berwick-upon-Tweed in Northumberland.

GOLF

Scotland is the home of golf. The game has been played here for centuries and there are more courses per capita in Scotland than in any other country.

Courses are tested for their level of difficulty, and most are playable year-round. Some private clubs only admit members, friends of members, or golfers who have a handicap certificate or a letter of introduction from their club, but the majority welcome visitors.

Most clubs give members priority in booking tee-off times; it's always advisable to book in advance. It should be easier to book a tee-off time on a public course but

weekends, on all courses, are usually busy. Also, check whether there's a dress code, and whether the course has golf clubs for hire (not all do) if you don't have your own.

For most people St Andrews is the home of golf. It's the headquarters of the game's governing body, the Royal and Ancient Golf Club, and the location of the world's most famous golf course, the Old Course. Muirfield is home to the world's oldest golf club, the Honourable Company of Edinburgh Golfers. Carnoustie, east of Dundee, has one of the longest courses and toughest finishes in golf, which has been played here since at least 1650. The course at Loch Lomond is home to the World Invitational Championship. Other major courses are Troon and Turnberry in Ayrshire, Gleneagles in Perthshire and Musselburgh in East Lothian.

Information

The British Tourist Authority (BTA) has a useful *Golfing Holidays* booklet that focuses on golfing holidays and major golf tournaments in Britain. *Golf in Scotland* is a free brochure listing 400 courses and clubs with details of where to stay. Contact the Scottish Tourist Board (☎ 0131-332 2433), 23 Ravelston Terrace, Edinburgh EH4 3EU, for a copy.

The Golf Club of Great Britain (☎ 0181-390 3113; from 22 April 2000 ☎ 020-8390 3113) is at 3 Sage Yard, Douglas Rd, Surbiton, Surrey KT6 7TS.

Costs

A round of golf on a public course costs about £7. Private courses are more expensive with green fees ranging from £12 to £20 – and up to £40 on championship courses. However, many clubs offer a daily or weekly ticket. For example, a Golf Pass in Scotland costs between £46 and £70 for five days (Monday to Friday) depending on the area.

A set of golf clubs is about £5 (per round) to hire.

TRACING YOUR ANCESTORS

For visitors with Scottish ancestors a trip here is a good chance to find out more about them and their lives; you may even discover relatives you never knew about.

You should first go to the General Register Office (GRO, ☎ 0131-334 0380), New Register House, 3 West Register St, Edinburgh EH1 3YT. This office holds birth, marriage and death records since 1855, the census records and old parochial registers. Contact the GRO for leaflets giving details of its records and fees. The office opens weekdays, 9 am to 4.30 pm. Before you go, contact the office to reserve a search-room seat, particularly if you have limited time.

Next door is part of the Scottish Record Office (☎ 0131-535 1314), HM General Register House, 2 Princes St, Edinburgh EH1 3YY. There are two search rooms: the historical search room, where you should go to research ancestors (no charge), and the legal search room, where you can see records for legal purposes (a fee is payable). Staff will answer simple inquiries by correspondence, if you give precise details. If you want more research done for you (perhaps before you come), the office will send a list of professional searchers. All correspondence should be addressed to: The Keeper of the Records of Scotland, Scottish Record Office, and sent to the above address.

The other place to try is the Scottish Genealogy Society (☎ 0131-220 3677), 15 Victoria Terrace (above Victoria St), Edinburgh EH1, which has a library, microfiche, books for sale and helpful staff.

Visiting graveyards may seem morbid but it's something many tourists do as part of tracing their ancestors (and paying their respects). This address is useful: Anne King, Scottish Ancestral Research (aking53104@aol.com), Tigh Righ, 4 Esplanade Terrace, Joppa, Edinburgh EH15 2ES.

If you're serious about ancestry research, it may be worth buying one or more of the following: *Tracing Your Scottish Ancestors* (Stationery Office) by Cecil Sinclair; *Tracing Your Scottish Ancestry* (Polygon, Edinburgh), by Kathleen B Cory; and *My Ain Folk – an Easy Guide to Scottish Family History*, by Graham S Holton & Jack Wind;

and *Surnames of Scotland* by George F Black, published by the New York Library.

SURFING & SWIMMING

Most overseas visitors don't think of Scotland as a place for a beach holiday – for good reasons, notably climate and water temperature. You definitely have to be hardy, or equipped with a wetsuit, to do anything more than take a quick dip. On the other side of the equation, there is some truly magnificent coastline and some wonderful sandy beaches.

Summer water temperatures are roughly around 55°F (13°C); winter temperatures are about 10°F colder. So getting in the water, at least in summer, is feasible if you have a wetsuit. A 3mm fullsuit (steamer) plus boots is sufficient in summer, while winter requires a 5mm suit, plus boots, hood and gloves.

Sadly, many beaches suffer from pollution, often thanks to local towns draining their storm water and sewage offshore. It's worth checking with a local before taking the plunge.

For most visiting surfers, the most unusual aspect of surfing here is the impact of the tides. The tidal range is huge, which means there are often a completely different set of breaks at low and high tides. As is usually the case, the waves tend to be biggest and best on an incoming tide. Sadly, the waves in spring, autumn and winter tend to be bigger and more consistent than in summer. The conditions in summer are pretty unreliable.

Northern Scotland has Britain's biggest and best surf, and although the outside temperatures are considerably lower than in the south, the water temperatures are only marginally lower. The entire Scottish coast has surf but it's the north, particularly around Thurso, that has outstanding world-class possibilities. The west coast is mainly sheltered by islands, and although there are no doubt untapped possibilities on the islands, they're difficult and expensive to get to. Islay is occasionally surfed. The east coast is easily accessible, but the swells are unreliable and short-lived.

There's quite a large surfing community in Thurso, thanks to several famous breaks. There are two breaks, one in front of the harbour wall with lefts and rights, known as Reef, and one at Beach. Thurso East (Castle Reef) is the big one – a huge right that works up to 15 feet (close to 5m).

For more information contact the British Surfing Association (BSA, ☎ 01736-60250, fax 01736-331077), Champion's Yard, Penzance, Cornwall TR18 2TA.

FISHING

Coarse, game and sea fishing are enormously popular in Scotland, whose waters are filled with salmon, trout (sea, brown and rainbow), pike, arctic char and many other species. Its streams, rivers, lochs and firths have probably the greatest variety of marine habitats and cleanest waters in Europe.

There's no close season for coarse fishing or sea angling, but for wild brown trout the close season is early October to mid-March. The close season for salmon and sea trout varies between districts and between net and rod fishing. It's generally from late August to early February for net fishing, early November to early February for rod fishing.

You don't need a licence to fish in Scotland, but most land and its waters are privately owned so you must obtain a permit from the owners or their agents. These are often readily available at the local fishing tackle shop. Permits usually cost from around £15 but some rivers can be much more expensive.

The STB's booklet *Fish Scotland* is a good introduction and is stocked by TICs. For more in-depth information you should try *Scotland for Game, Sea and Coarse Fishing* which is available from Pastime Publications (☎ 0131-556 1105), 6 York Place, Edinburgh EH1 3EP.

Organisations which can also help are:

Scottish Federation of Sea Anglers
(☎ 01292-264735) Brian Burn, Flat 2, 16 Bellevue Rd, Ayr KA7 2SA

Scottish National Anglers Association
(☎ 0131-339 8808) David Wilkie, Administration Office, Caledonia House, South Gyle, Edinburgh EH12 9DQ

HORSE RIDING & PONY TREKKING

Seeing the country from the saddle is highly recommended, even if you're not an experienced rider. There are riding schools catering to all levels of proficiency.

Pony trekking is a popular holiday activity; a half-day should cost around £10, and hard hats are included. Many pony trekkers are novice riders so most rides are at walking speed with the occasional trot. If you're an experienced rider there are numerous riding schools with horses for hire – TICs have details.

The STB publishes a *Trekking & Riding* brochure which lists riding centres around Scotland. For more information contact:

Trekking & Riding Society of Scotland
(☎ 01796-481543) Horse Trials Office, Blair Atholl, Perthshire
British Horse Society
(☎ 01203-414288) British Equestrian Centre, Stoneleigh Park, Kenilworth, Warwickshire CV8 2LR; publishes *Where to Ride* (£5.99) which lists places throughout the UK; also can send lists specific to a particular area

CANAL & WATERWAY TRAVEL

Scotland's network of canals and waterways rose during the Industrial Revolution as a method of transporting freight (passengers were always secondary). But they were short-lived, trimmed back by railways and killed off by modern roads. By WWII, much of the waterway system was in terminal decline. Today, however, the canals are reviving as part of the tourist industry. Canals lead you to a Scotland of villages, beautiful countryside and convenient and colourful waterside pubs.

Exploring Scotland by canal can be immensely rewarding. Narrowboats (barges carried coal, longboats carried Vikings) can be rented and for a family or a group they can provide surprisingly economical transport and accommodation. Canals are also used by yachts, motorboats and fishing boats. Canal towpaths have become popular routes for walkers and cyclists who can enjoy the same hidden perspective as people out on the waterways.

At 60 miles, the Caledonian Canal which slices through the Great Glen is Scotland's longest, and connects Corpach north of Fort William with Clachnaharry near Inverness. The 9-mile Crinan Canal in Argyll links Ardrishaig with Crinan.

In the Lowlands the Forth and Clyde Canal runs 35 miles between Grangemouth in the east and Bowling near Dumbarton in the west. The 31-mile Union Canal connects Port Downie close to Falkirk with Lochrin in Edinburgh. At one time these two canals were connected at Falkirk and, as part of the Millennium Project to restore the canals, that link will again be available.

Information

The British Tourist Authority publishes a brochure on boating holidays in Britain and Ireland. More information on the canal system is available from the Inland Waterways Association (☎ 0171-586 2510; from 22 April 2000 ☎ 020-7586 2510), 114 Regent's Park Rd, London NW1 8UQ. It publishes *The Inland Waterways Guide*, a general guide to holiday hire.

The Caledonian and Crinan canals are operated by the British Waterways Board (www.british-waterways.org) which publishes *The Waterways Code for Boaters*, a free booklet packed with useful information and advice. It also publishes a complete list of hire-boat and hotel-boat companies. Its offices in Scotland are:

Caledonian Canal
   (☎ 01463-233140, fax 01463-710942) Seaport Marina, Muirtown Wharf, Inverness IV3 5LS
Crinan Canal
   (☎ 01546-603210, fax 01546-603941) Pier Square, Ardrishaig, Argyll PA30 8DZ

Locks

A lock enables boats to go up or down a hill. It's a bathtub-shaped chamber with a single door at the top end and a double door at the bottom. Sluices in the doors let water flow into or out of the lock when the paddles over the sluices are opened. A winding handle or key is used to open or close the paddles and this is one of the essential pieces of equipment for narrowboat travel. The process of going through a lock is known as 'working' the lock.

On narrow canals the locks are usually wide enough and long enough for just one boat at a time. On rivers or wider canals they may be large enough for two or more boats. In a wider lock it's essential to keep your boat roped to the side to prevent it yawing around as the water flows in or out of the lock. But don't tie it up tightly – the

The Millenium Link

This £78 million project will provide a continuous waterway along the routes of the Forth and Clyde Canal (built in 1790) and the Union Canal (built in 1822). Once again boats will travel between Lochrin in Edinburgh in the east and the Forth and Clyde estuaries in the west.

The world's first revolving boat waterwheel will be built at the Port Downie interchange near Falkirk replacing the 11 abandoned locks. The wheel will take boats from the higher Union Canal and lower them 33m (110 feet) into a new tunnel which will connect with the Forth & Clyde Canal. The other major construction will be the realignment of the Union Canal under the M8 motorway; part of the existing canal will be filled in and a new canal loop built. These two projects probably represent the first construction of canals in Scotland since the 1800s.

It's estimated that the link will create several thousand jobs and increase tourism spending by £10 million. For more detailed information you should contact Millenium Link (☎ 0345-952000), PO Box 15067, Glasgow G4 9BR.

ropes will need to be shortened or lengthened as the water level changes.

Narrowboats

Typically, a narrowboat is 40 to 70 feet (12m to 21m) in length and no more than 7 feet (2m) wide. Narrowboats are usually comfortable and well equipped with bunks and double beds, kitchen and dining areas, a fridge, cooker, flush toilet, shower and other mod-cons. Usually they're rented out by the week, although shorter periods are sometimes available.

As narrowboats usually come so well equipped for everyday living, food supplies are all you need to worry about and there are plenty of shopping opportunities along the waterways. Alternatively, careful planning can see you moored at a riverside pub or restaurant for meals.

Boats can accommodate from two or three people up to 10 or 12. Costs vary with the size of boat, the standard of equipment and the time of year.

At the height of the summer season, a boat for four varies from around £500 to £1000 per week. Larger boats work out cheaper per person; a boat for eight might cost £1000 per week. This means canal travel can cost not much over £100 per person for a week's transport and accommodation, a terrific travel bargain.

Travelling the Waterways

No particular expertise or training is needed, nor is a licence required to operate a narrowboat. You're normally given a quick once over of the boat and an explanation of how things work, a brief foray out onto the river or canal and then you're on your way. Proceed with caution at first, although you'll soon find yourself working the locks like a veteran.

SKIING

There are five ski centres in Scotland, but the slopes are far less extensive and the weather considerably less reliable than anything you'll find in the Alps or Pyrenees. On a sunny day, however, and with good snow, it can be very pleasant.

Scotland offers both alpine (downhill) and nordic (cross-country) skiing as well as other snow-related sports. The high season is from January to April, but it's sometimes possible to ski from as early as November to as late as May. Package holidays are available but it's easy to make your own arrangements, with all kinds of accommodation on offer in and around the ski centres.

Information

Contact the Scottish Tourist Board (☎ 0131-332 2433) for its detailed *Ski Scotland* brochure and accommodation list. General information can be obtained from the Scottish National Ski Council (☎ 0131-317 7280), Caledonia House, South Gyle, Edinburgh EH12.

Alternatively, you can phone the skiing information centre for each area: Nevis Range (☎ 01397-705825), Glencoe (☎ 01855-851226), Glenshee (☎ 013397-41320), The Lecht (☎ 01975-651440), and Cairngorm (☎ 01479-861261). There's an answerphone service for calls outside business hours.

The Ski Hotline weather-report service can be useful. Phone ☎ 0891-654 followed by 654 for all centres, 660 for Nevis Range, 658 for Glencoe, 656 for Glenshee, 657 for The Lecht, and 655 for Cairngorm. For nordic the number is ☎ 0891-654659. Alternatively you can check the Web site at www.ski.scotland.net which is updated daily during the ski season.

Costs

It's easy to hire ski equipment and clothes when you arrive but you should book lessons, if you want them, in advance. The prices vary in each centre but on average expect to pay £11 to £13 per day for skis, sticks and boot hire; and £8 to £12 per day for ski clothes.

Lift passes cost £12 to £17 per day, or £65 to £68 for a five-day pass (photo required). In a group, ski lessons cost £13 to £20 for a day, and £50 to £65 for five days; private lessons cost £18 per hour.

Packages including ski-hire, tuition and pass cost from £90 for three days (midweek). Two, four or five day, and weekend packages are also available.

Charges are less for juniors – under 18 (Nevis Range and Cairngorm), under 16 (Glencoe, Glenshee, The Lecht).

Resorts

The biggest ski centres are **Glenshee** (920m, 3019 feet) and **Cairngorm** (1097m, 3600 feet). Glenshee offers the largest network of lifts and selection of runs in Scotland. It also has snow machines for periods when the real thing doesn't appear. Cairngorm has almost 30 runs spread over an extensive area.

Aviemore is the main town and there's a ski bus service from here and from the surrounding villages to the slopes.

Glencoe (1108m, 3636 feet) is the oldest of the resorts and opens seven days a week. The **Nevis Range** (1221m, 4006 feet) offers the highest ski runs, the only gondola in Scotland to take you to the foot of the main skiing area, and a dry (plastic) ski slope. **The Lecht** (793m, 2600 feet) is the most remote centre. However, the runs are good for beginners and families, as well as for nordic skiers.

Access to the centres is probably easiest by car – there are plenty of car parks. Slopes are graded in the usual way, from green (easy) through blue and red to black (very difficult); and each centre has a ski patrol. You should ensure that your travel insurance covers you for winter sports.

All ski resorts have facilities for snowboarding. The Lecht is best for beginners and the other four resorts are best for intermediates. They're all OK for advanced snowboarders.

DIVING

Scotland has thousands of dive sites around its shores which have distinct ecosystems and yield a rich variety of marine life, wrecks and wonderful scenery. They can be divided into three broad areas: the east coast, the Highlands and Islands and the west coast sea lochs.

The *Diving & Snorkelling Guide to Scotland* (Pisces Books) by Lawson Wood, describes some of the best sites and lists operators offering dive services and boat charters. For more information contact:

Scottish Sub Aqua Club
(☎ 0141-425 1021) 40 Bogmoor Place, Glasgow G51 47Q
British Sub Aqua Club (Scottish Federation)
(☎ 0131-664 4381) 67 Moredun Park, Gilmerton, Edinburgh EH17

BIRDWATCHING

Scotland is a birdwatcher's paradise. There are over 80 ornithologically important nature reserves managed by Scottish Natural Heritage, the Royal Society for the Protection of Birds and the Scottish Wildlife Trust. (See Ecology & Environment in the Facts about Scotland chapter for addresses.) Further information can be obtained from the Scottish Ornithologists Club (☎ 0131-556 6042), 21 Regent Terrace, Edinburgh EH7.

In the Highlands there are finches, jackdaws and birds of prey such as the peregrine falcon and golden eagle. Good locations to view them are the Craigellachie Nature Reserve and Boat of Garten both near Aviemore. Seabirds can be seen at Duncansby Head near John o'Groats and at the Clo Mor Cliffs on Cape Wrath.

The islands are home to thousands of seabirds as well as a stopover to migrating birds. In the Hebrides, Islay is a wintering ground for barnacle geese and North Uist has huge populations of migrant waders including curlews, lapwings and oystercatchers.

Orkney has colonies of nesting seabirds at Mull Head and Gultak, and Deer Sound attracts wildfowl. Other Orkney islands – Stronsay, Westray and North Ronaldsay – also attract breeding seabirds and migratory birds.

The Shetland Islands are also famous for their varied birdlife. On Sumburgh Head, Shetland, there are puffins, kittiwakes, fulmars, guillemots, razorbills and shags. Fair Isle, Whalsay and Out Skerries are in the path of thousands of migrating birds and

Munros & Munro Bagging

The Scottish Highlands cover the most extensive tract of hill country in the British Isles. In addition to their appeal to scenery seekers, they present many challenges for hillwalkers, rock, snow and ice climbers and mountaineers.

Unpredictable weather conditions at any time of year and often remote summits, together with few opportunities for shelter, mean that those who venture into the hills should be properly equipped and aware of their own capabilities.

The Scottish mountains are relatively modest in height with the highest, Ben Nevis, reaching only 1343m (4406 feet) above sea level.

At the end of the 19th century, Sir Hugh Munro compiled a list of summits over 3000 feet with nearly 300 gaining the status of 'Munros'. After various revisions to the list since then there are now 284 Munros in the eponymous tables. 'Munro bagging' is a popular leisure activity, not to say obsession.

Sir Hugh himself narrowly failed to complete the full round and the first person to succeed in this monumental task was the Reverend AE Robertson in 1930, a Scottish Gaelic-speaking minister of the church. Since then, his feat has been matched by about 2000 others and the number continues to increase.

Munro bagging has created a boom in books devoted to walking and climbing in the Scottish mountains so there's no shortage of advice on the subject.

To the uninitiated, it may seem curious that Munro baggers see a day (or longer) plodding around in the mist and cloud in driving rain to the point of exhaustion as time well spent. However, for those who can add one or more ticks to their list, the vagaries of the weather are part of the enjoyment – at least in retrospect.

Munro bagging is, of course, more than merely ticking names on a list. It takes you to some of the wildest, most beautiful parts of Scotland and, for many, provides years of healthy enjoyment and spiritual reward.

Visitors to Scotland may wish to experience something of the magic of the Scottish mountains, but, with limited time, choices must be made. All parts of the Highlands and Islands have their own devotees and there are many Munros within easy reach of Scotland's major cities.

Some areas are outstanding for their own particular reasons. These include the Torridon Hills in Wester Ross, ancient mountains rising steeply from sea level; Ben Nevis and Glencoe, offering an infinite variety of walks and climbs as well as the highest peak and biggest cliffs in Britain; and the Cairngorms, a sub-arctic wilderness of stoney plateau far from public roads. The traverse of the Cuillin Hills on the Isle of Skye provides the finest mountaineering challenge of all, taking in seven Munros with serious rock climbing punctuating the route. Completion of the traverse in a day is a considerable achievement, but is really only possible in good settled weather.

The weather is the key. When the sun shines, it's easy to understand the lure of the Scottish mountains, but wind, rain and even snow are likely at any time of year. Skill and judgement are then at a premium in deciding whether to carry on, to turn back or even not to set out at all. On such occasions, it's worth reminding yourself that the hills will be there for another day.

Hugh Gore

Foula has around 500,000 seabirds including great skuas.

Mousa Broch is home to many waders and seabirds and Fetlar has large numbers of auks and is home to the rare red-necked phalarope.

CLIMBING

The Cairngorms and Cuillins provide challenging climbing as do the classic routes of Ben Nevis, Glencoe, Arran and Lochnagar. Arrochar is a popular destination with Glasgow climbers, and Edinburgh citizens practise their skills on the Salisbury Crags in Holyrood Park.

The Climbing Guide to Scotland, by Tom Prentice, describes over 600 crags for summer and winter climbing throughout the country. *The Munros* by Cameron McNeish, lists all the Munros; royalties from sales of the book go to the Scottish Mountain Rescue Service. *Mountaineering in Scotland* (1947) and *Undiscovered Scotland* (1951) both by WH Murray, are classic personal accounts

of climbing adventures and mountain walks. (See also Guides under Walking earlier.)

For more detailed information you should contact the Mountaineering Council of Scotland (☎ 01738-638227), 4A St Catherine's Rd, Perth PH1 5SE.

CANOEING

Scotland, with its islands. mountains, rivers, lochs and indented coastline is great for canoeing or kayaking. Rivers vary from the slow, winding River Forth near Stirling to the white-water River Nith in the southwest. The numerous freshwater and sea lochs vary from small, sheltered, secluded, remote lochans to the open stretches of water like Loch Lomond.

For information contact the Scottish Canoe Association (☎ 0131-317 7314, www .scot-canoe.org), Caledonia House, South Gyle, Edinburgh EH12 9DQ. It publishes coastal navigation sheets as well as organising tours including introductory ones for beginners.

Getting There & Away

Whichever way you're travelling, make sure you take out travel insurance. (See Visas & Documents in the Facts for the Visitor chapter.)

For travel to/from Europe or other parts of the UK, buses are the cheapest and most exhausting method of transport, although discount rail tickets are competitive, and budget flights can be good value. Bear in mind a small saving on the fare may not adequately compensate you for time spent travelling that leaves you exhausted.

Travelling from Europe you'll often be best off flying to London, then taking the train or bus north. Flying time from London to Edinburgh or Glasgow is about one hour, but once you add the time taken to get between the airports and the city centres, and boarding time, the four hour centre-to-centre rail trip takes only about an hour more than flying in actual travelling time.

And when making an assessment, don't forget the hidden expenses: getting to/from airports, departure taxes, and food and drink consumed en route.

AIR
Airports & Airlines
The three main international airports are Glasgow (☎ 0141-887 1111), Edinburgh (☎ 0131-333 1000) and Aberdeen (☎ 01224-722331). Other airports include Prestwick (☎ 01292-479822), Dundee (☎ 01382-643242), Inverness (☎ 01463-232471) and Sumburgh (☎ 01950-60654). There are frequent direct flights to other parts of the UK and Ireland, Europe and North America and a limited number of services to Africa, the Middle East and Asia. There are no direct air services from North America to Edinburgh.

The main operators are British Airways (☎ 0345-222111, www.british-airways.com), British Midland (☎ 0345-554554, www.iflybritishmidland.com), and KLM UK (☎ 0990-074074, www.klmuk.com). There are several other smaller companies, including easyJet (☎ 01582-445566 or ☎ 0870-600 0000, www.easyjet.com) and EuroScot Express (☎ 0870-607 0809).

Buying Tickets
The plane ticket may be the single most expensive item in your budget, and buying it can be an intimidating business.

There's a multitude of travel agents hoping to separate you from your money, and it's always worth researching the current state of the market. Start early; some of the cheapest tickets have to be bought months in advance, and some popular flights sell out early.

Cheap tickets are available in two distinct categories: official and unofficial. Official ones are advance-purchase tickets, budget

---

Warning

The information in this chapter is particularly vulnerable to change: prices for international travel are volatile, routes are introduced and cancelled, schedules change, special deals come and go, and rules and visa requirements are amended. Airlines and governments seem to take a perverse pleasure in making price structures and regulations as complicated as possible. Check directly with the airline or a travel agent to make sure you understand how a fare (and ticket you may buy) works. In addition, the travel industry is highly competitive and there are many lurks and perks.

The upshot of this is that you should get opinions, quotes and advice from as many airlines and travel agents as possible before you part with your hard-earned cash. The details given in this chapter should be regarded as pointers and are not a substitute for your own careful, up-to-date research.

fares, Apex, super-Apex, or whatever other brand name airlines care to use.

Unofficial tickets are discounted ones that airlines release through selected travel agents. Airlines can supply information on routes and timetables, and their low-season, student and senior citizens' fares can be competitive, but they don't sell discounted tickets. Remember that normal, full-fare airline tickets sometimes include one or more side trips to Europe free of charge, and/or fly-drive packages, which can make them good value.

Return tickets usually work out cheaper than two one-ways – often *much* cheaper. In some cases, a return ticket can even be cheaper than a one-way. Round-the-World (RTW) tickets can also be great bargains, sometimes cheaper than an ordinary return ticket. RTW prices start at about UK£900, A$2000 or US$1900 depending on the season. An RTW might take you directly to Edinburgh or Glasgow or as a side trip from London.

Official RTW tickets are usually put together by two airlines, and permit you to fly anywhere on their route systems so long as you don't backtrack. There may be restrictions on how many stops you are permitted, and on the length of time the ticket remains valid. Travel agents put together unofficial RTW tickets by combining a number of discounted tickets.

Discounted tickets are usually available at prices as low as or lower than the official Apex or budget tickets. When you phone around, find out the fare, the route, the duration of the journey, the stopovers allowed and any restrictions on the ticket (see the boxed text 'Air Travel Glossary'), and ask about cancellation penalties.

You're likely to discover that the cheapest flights are 'fully booked, but we have another one that costs a bit more'. Or the flight is on an airline notorious for its poor safety standards and liable to leave you confined in the world's least favourite airport for 14 hours in mid-journey. Or the agent claims to have the last two seats available, which they'll hold for you for a maximum

of two hours. Don't panic – keep ringing around.

If you're travelling from the USA or South-East Asia, or leaving Britain, you'll probably find that the cheapest flights are advertised by small, obscure agencies. Most are honest and solvent, but a few rogue ones will take your money and disappear. If you feel suspicious about a firm, leave a deposit (no more than 20%) and pay the balance when you get the ticket. You could phone the airline direct to check you actually have a booking before picking up the ticket. If the travel agent insists on cash in advance, go somewhere else or be prepared to take a very big risk.

You may decide to pay more than the rock-bottom fare by opting for the safety of a better known travel agent. Firms such as STA Travel, which has offices worldwide, Council Travel in the USA, Travel CUTS in Canada and Trailfinders in London offer good prices to most destinations, and are competitive and reliable.

Use the fares quoted in this book as a guide only. They're likely to have changed by the time you read this.

Travellers with Special Needs

If you have special needs – you've broken a leg, you require a special diet, you're taking the baby, or whatever – let the airline people know as soon as possible. Remind them when you reconfirm your booking and again when you check in at the airport.

Children aged under two travel for 10% of the standard fare (or free on some airlines) if they don't occupy a seat, but they don't get a baggage allowance either. 'Skycots', baby food and nappies (diapers) should be provided if requested in advance. Children aged between two and 12 usually get a seat for half to two-thirds of the full fare, and do get a baggage allowance.

England & Wales

Trailfinders (☎ 0171-938 3939; from 22 April 2000 ☎ 020-7938 3939), 194 Kensington High St, London W8 6FT, produces a brochure which includes air fares.

Air Travel Glossary

Baggage Allowance This will be written on your ticket and usually includes one 20kg item to go in the hold, plus one item of hand luggage.

Bucket Shops These are unbonded travel agencies specialising in discounted airline tickets.

Bumped Just because you have a confirmed seat doesn't mean you're going to get on the plane (see Overbooking).

Cancellation Penalties If you have to cancel or change a discounted ticket, there are often heavy penalties involved; insurance can sometimes be taken out against these penalties. Some airlines impose penalties on regular tickets as well, particularly against 'no-show' passengers.

Check-In Airlines ask you to check in a certain time ahead of the flight departure (usually one to two hours on international flights). If you fail to check in on time and the flight is overbooked, the airline can cancel your booking and give your seat to somebody else.

Confirmation Having a ticket written out with the flight and date you want doesn't mean you have a seat until the agent has checked with the airline that your status is 'OK' or confirmed. Meanwhile you could just be 'on request'.

Courier Fares Businesses often need to send urgent documents or freight securely and quickly. Courier companies hire people to accompany the package through customs and, in return, offer a discount ticket which is sometimes a phenomenal bargain. In effect, what the companies do is ship their freight as your luggage on regular commercial flights. This is a legitimate operation, but there are two shortcomings - the short turnaround time of the ticket (usually not longer than a month) and the limitation on your luggage allowance. You may have to surrender all your allowance and take only carry-on luggage.

Full Fares Airlines traditionally offer 1st class (coded F), business class (coded J) and economy class (coded Y) tickets. These days there are so many promotional and discounted fares available that few passengers pay full economy fare.

ITX An ITX, or 'independent inclusive tour excursion', is often available on tickets to popular holiday destinations. Officially it's a package deal combined with hotel accommodation, but many agents will sell you one of these for the flight only and give you phoney hotel vouchers in the unlikely event that you're challenged at the airport.

Lost Tickets If you lose your airline ticket an airline will usually treat it like a travellers cheque and, after inquiries, issue you with another one. Legally, however, an airline is entitled to treat it like cash and if you lose it then it's gone forever. Take good care of your tickets.

MCO An MCO, or 'miscellaneous charge order', is a voucher that looks like an airline ticket but carries no destination or date. It can be exchanged through any International Association of Travel Agents (IATA) airline for a ticket on a specific flight. It's a useful alternative to an onward ticket in those countries that demand one, and is more flexible than an ordinary ticket if you're unsure of your route.

No-Shows No-shows are passengers who fail to show up for their flight. Full-fare passengers who fail to turn up are sometimes entitled to travel on a later flight. The rest are penalised (see Cancellation Penalties).

On Request This is an unconfirmed booking for a flight.

Air Travel Glossary

Onward Tickets An entry requirement for many countries is that you have a ticket out of the country. If you're unsure of your next move, the easiest solution is to buy the cheapest onward ticket to a neighbouring country or a ticket from a reliable airline which can later be refunded if you do not use it.

Open Jaw Tickets These are return tickets where you fly out to one place but return from another. If available, this can save you backtracking to your arrival point.

Overbooking Airlines hate to fly empty seats and since every flight has some passengers who fail to show up, airlines often book more passengers than they have seats. Usually excess passengers make up for the no-shows, but occasionally somebody gets bumped. Guess who it is most likely to be? The passengers who check in late.

Point-to-Point Tickets These are discount tickets that can be bought on some routes in return for passengers waiving their rights to a stopover.

Promotional Fares These are officially discounted fares, available from travel agencies or direct from the airline.

Reconfirmation At least 72 hours prior to departure time of an onward or return flight, you must contact the airline and 'reconfirm' that you intend to be on the flight. If you don't do this the airline can delete your name from the passenger list and you could lose your seat.

Restrictions Discounted tickets often have various restrictions on them - such as needing to be paid for in advance and incurring a penalty to be altered. Others are restrictions on the minimum and maximum period you must be away, such as a minimum of 14 days or a maximum of one year.

Round-the-World Tickets RTW tickets give you a limited period (usually a year) in which to circumnavigate the globe. You can go anywhere the carrying airlines go, as long as you don't backtrack. The number of stopovers or total number of separate flights is decided before you set off and they usually cost a bit more than a basic return flight.

Stand-by This is a discounted ticket where you only fly if there is a seat free at the last moment. Stand-by fares are usually available only on domestic routes.

Travel Agencies Travel agencies vary widely and you should choose one that suits your needs. Some simply handle tours, while full-services agencies handle everything from tours and tickets to car rental and hotel bookings. If all you want is a ticket at the lowest possible price, then go to an agency specialising in discounted tickets.

Transferred Tickets Airline tickets cannot be transferred from one person to another. Travellers sometimes try to sell the return half of their ticket, but officials can ask you to prove that you are the person named on the ticket. This is less likely to happen on domestic flights, but on an international flight tickets are compared with passports.

Travel Periods Ticket prices vary with the time of year. There is a low (off-peak) season and a high (peak) season, and often a low-shoulder season and a high-shoulder season as well. Usually the fare depends on your outward flight - if you depart in the high season and return in the low season, you pay the high-season fare.

STA Travel (☎ 0171-361 6262; from 22 April 2000 ☎ 020-7361 6262), 86 Old Brompton Rd, London SW7, has a number of branches in the UK.

The London listings magazine *Time Out*, the Sunday papers and the *Evening Standard* carry ads for cheap fares. Also look out for free magazines like *TNT Magazine* which you can often pick up outside main train and tube stations.

All travel agents should be covered by an Air Travel Organiser's Licence (ATOL). This scheme is operated by the Civil Aviation Authority (CAA) and means that in the event of either the agent or the airline going bust, you are guaranteed a full refund or, if you are already abroad, to be flown back. It's worth noting that under existing consumer protection legislation, the only way that you can lose out is if you book directly from a scheduled airline – even a bucket shop gives you more protection. To be covered by the scheme, however, when you hand over money, you must be given either the ticket or an official ATOL receipt.

The Globetrotters Club (BCM Roving, London WC1N 3XX) publishes the *Globe* newsletter which can help in finding travelling companions.

British Airways has flights from London's Heathrow, Gatwick and Stansted, and also from Birmingham, Manchester and Cardiff; British Midland flies from Heathrow, Manchester, the East Midlands and Leeds, KLM UK flies from Stansted; easyJet flies from London's Luton airport. Most airlines offer a range of tickets.

Prices vary enormously. The standard economy return ticket from London to Edinburgh on British Airways costs £266; British Airways' and British Midlands' lowest return fare is £59 but there are restrictions. EasyJet and KLM UK offer no-frills flights for £29 one way between London (Luton/Stansted) and Edinburgh, Glasgow and Aberdeen.

Ireland

The Union of Students in Ireland (USIT) (☎ 01-679 8833 or ☎ 677 8117), 19 Aston Quay, O'Connell Bridge, Dublin 2, the Irish youth and student travel association, has offices in most major cities in Ireland.

Aer Lingus (☎ 0645-737747) is the main operator between Ireland and Scotland. It flies from Dublin, Cork, Donegal and Shannon to Edinburgh and Glasgow; British Airways flies from Dublin, Belfast and Derry to Edinburgh and Aberdeen. The one-way fare between Edinburgh and Dublin is from around £80.

Continental Europe

Discount charter flights are often available to full-time students aged under 30 and all young travellers aged under 26 (you need an ISIC or official youth card) and are available through the large student travel agencies.

Edinburgh, Glasgow and Aberdeen are connected with major cities and some regional centres in Europe. Discount return fares from Glasgow and Edinburgh to Amsterdam cost £137, from Edinburgh to Rome £234. Official tickets with carriers like British Airways can cost a great deal more.

The USA & Canada

Flights from North America put down in Glasgow and Aberdeen, but because competition on flights to London is much fiercer, it's generally cheaper to fly to London first.

As well as British Airways, major airlines operating across the North Atlantic to Scotland are Air Canada (☎ 0990-247226), American Airlines (☎ 0345-789789) and Continental Airlines (☎ 0800-776464). They connect Glasgow directly with many cities including Boston, Calgary, Chicago, Denver, Las Vegas, Los Angeles, Miami, Montreal, New Orleans, New York City, Philadelphia, San Francisco, Seattle, Toronto, Vancouver and Washington. The return fare from New York City to Glasgow is around US$600 (£390).

British Airways connects Aberdeen with New York and Toronto.

Check the Sunday travel sections of papers like the *New York Times*, the *LA*

Times, the *Chicago Tribune*, the *San Francisco Chronicle* and the *San Francisco Examiner* for the latest fares. The *Globe & Mail*, *Toronto Star* and *Vancouver Sun* have similar details from Canada. Offices of Council Travel and STA Travel in the USA or Travel CUTS in Canada are good sources of reliable discounted tickets.

The *Travel Unlimited* newsletter, PO Box 1058, Allston, MA 02134, USA, publishes monthly details of the cheapest airfares and courier possibilities for destinations all over the world from the USA and other countries.

Australia & New Zealand

Flights from Australia and New Zealand arrive via London.

STA Travel and Flight Centres International are major dealers in discounted airfares from Australia and New Zealand. Check the travel agents' ads and ring around.

The Saturday travel sections of the *Sydney Morning Herald* and Melbourne's *Age* newspapers have ads offering cheap fares to London, but don't be surprised if they happen to be sold out when you contact the agents: they're usually low-season fares on obscure airlines with conditions attached.

Discounted return fares on mainstream airlines through a reputable agent like STA Travel cost between A$1800 (low season) and A$3000 (high season). Flights to/from Perth are at least a couple of hundred dollars cheaper.

A Britannia charter service also is in operation between Britain and Australia/New Zealand. November to March, prices can drop as low as £499 return from London to Sydney and £698 return from Sydney to London. Contact UK Flight Shop (☎ 02-9247 4833), 7 Macquarie Place, Sydney, or, in the UK, Austravel (☎ 0171-838 1011; from 22 April 2000 ☎ 020-7838 1011), 152 Brompton Rd, Knightsbridge, London SW3 1HX.

The cheapest fares from New Zealand will probably take the eastbound route via the USA, but an RTW ticket may be cheaper than a return.

Africa

There are direct flights from Edinburgh and Glasgow to Cairo, Johannesburg and Nairobi. Nairobi, Kenya, is probably the best place in Africa to buy tickets to Britain, thanks to the many bucket shops and the strong competition between them. A typical one-way/return fare to Scotland would be about US$750/950. If you're thinking of flying from Cairo, it's often cheaper to fly to Athens and to proceed with a budget bus or train from there.

Two travel agents in South Africa with keen prices are: Student Travel, Rosebank, Johannesburg (☎ 011-447 5551; Cape Town 021-418 6570) and The Africa Travel Centre (☎ 021-235555) on the corner of Military Rd and New Church St, Tamboerskloof, Cape Town.

Asia

There are direct flights from Aberdeen, Edinburgh and Glasgow to Singapore, and from Glasgow to Beijing.

Ask the advice of other travellers before buying a ticket. Many of the cheapest fares from South-East Asia to Europe and Britain are offered by eastern European carriers. STA Travel has branches in Tokyo, Singapore, Bangkok and Kuala Lumpur.

To/from India, the cheapest flights tend to be with eastern European carriers like LOT and Aeroflot, or with Middle Eastern airlines such as Syrian Arab Airlines and Iran Air. Bombay is the air transport hub, with many transit options to/from South-East Asia, but tickets are slightly cheaper in Delhi.

LAND
Bus

Long-distance buses (coaches) are usually the cheapest method of getting to Scotland. The main operator is Scottish Citylink (☎ 0990-505050), which is part of the Britain-wide National Express (☎ 0990-808080; www.nationalexpress.co.uk) group with numerous regular services from London and other departure points in

England and Wales (see the Edinburgh and Glasgow chapters).

Fares on the main routes are competitive, with many smaller operators undercutting Scottish Citylink/National Express. The cheapest London to Glasgow route is Silver Choice (☎ 0141-333 1400) at £13/25 a single/return. The fare with Scottish Citylink is £18/28, but its services are more frequent. For information on bus passes and discount cards see the Getting Around chapter.

The budget bus company Slowcoach (☎ 0171-373 7737; from 22 April 2000 ☎ 020-7373 7737; www.straytravel.com) operates between youth hostels in England and ventures into Scotland as far as Edinburgh, Glasgow and Stirling. You can get on and off the bus where you like (and there's no compulsion to stay at a hostel). Buses leave London three times a week throughout the year; the price (£119) includes some activities and visits en route.

Train

Trains are a deservedly popular mode of transport: they're good meeting places, comfortable, frequent, generally reliable, and rail passes and discount cards make them affordable (see the Getting Around chapter).

InterCity services can whisk you from London's King's Cross or Euston stations to Edinburgh in as little as four hours, to Glasgow in five hours.

The cheapest adult return ticket between London and Edinburgh or Glasgow is the SuperApex, which costs only £35. Numerous restrictions apply to these tickets, which must be purchased 14 days in advance and are difficult to get hold of in summer. Apex tickets (£49 return) must be bought seven days in advance and are much more readily available. Phone the general inquiry line (☎ 0345-484950, open 24 hours) for timetables, fares and the numbers to ring for credit card bookings.

Car & Motorcycle

See the Getting Around chapter for details of road rules, driving conditions and information on renting and buying vehicles.

The main roads into Scotland are busy and quick. Edinburgh is 373 miles north of London, Glasgow 392 miles. Allow eight hours for the trip.

It makes more sense to break the journey en route, perhaps in York or Chester, or in the Lake District.

From Carlisle in north-west England the main road into Scotland is the A74(M) which passes through Dumfries & Galloway and South Lanarkshire before finally arriving in Glasgow. The main road to Edinburgh is the A7.

From Newcastle upon Tyne in England's north-east there are several routes north to Edinburgh. The A1 follows the east coast while the A696 and A697 join the A68 through the central Borders region.

Hitching

It's easy enough, if not necessarily wise, to hitch into Scotland along the A7, or A696 and A697 which become the A68 (to Edinburgh), or on the A74 (to Glasgow). The coastal route (A1) to Edinburgh is slow. See also Hitching in the Getting Around chapter.

SEA

Ferry companies can have a host of different prices for the same route, depending upon the time of day or year, the validity of the ticket, or the size of a vehicle. Return tickets may be much cheaper than two single fares, and vehicle tickets may also cover a driver and passenger. It's worth planning (and booking) ahead where possible as there may be special reductions on off-peak crossings.

Northern Ireland

Scotland has ferry links to Larne, north of Belfast, from Stranraer and Cairnryan both south-west of Glasgow. High-speed catamarans operate between Stranraer and Belfast. There's also a ferry from Campbeltown in Argyll to Ballycastle in County Antrim.

On some routes the cost for a car includes up to four or five passengers at no additional cost. If you can hitch a ride in a less than full car, it costs the driver nothing extra. Figures quoted are one-way fares for one adult, for two adults with a car and for four adults with a car.

Stranraer to Belfast The Stena Line and SeaCat high-speed catamarans race across in just 1½ hours at a cost of £27/170/180 at peak times; for bookings, call SeaCat (☎ 0990-523523), SeaCat Terminal, West Pier, Stranraer, or Stena Line (☎ 0990-707070).

Stranraer and Cairnryan to Larne There are as many as 15 sailings daily on this route which takes about 2½ hours and costs £27/190/190 at peak times; Stena Line (☎ 0990-707070) operates Stranraer-Larne, P&O (☎ 0990-980666) operates Cairnryan-Larne.

Campbeltown to Ballycastle The three hour crossing from Campbeltown in Argyll to Ballycastle in County Antrim costs £25/163/179; operated by Argyll & Antrim Steam Packet Company (☎ 0990-523523).

Scandinavia

Until you see the ferry possibilities, it's easy to forget how close Scandinavia and Scotland are, and why the Vikings found British villages so convenient to pillage.

From late May to early September the Smyril Line (the agent is P&O; ☎ 01244-572615) operates its 'North Atlantic Link' between Shetland (Lerwick), the Faroe Islands (Torshavn), Iceland (Seydisfjordur), Norway (Bergen) and Denmark (Hantsholm). It leaves from Lerwick on Mondays and Tuesdays.

First things first, however. You have to get to Shetland from Orkney, or from Aberdeen. P&O has sailings Monday to Friday from Aberdeen to Lerwick. A reclining seat costs £49/55 (one way) in the low/high season.

On the Smyril Line link, one-way couchette fares (a couchette is a sleeping berth) from Shetland to Norway are £45/63, to the Faroes £45/63, to Denmark £95/135, and to Iceland £98/139.

DEPARTURE TAXES

People taking flights from Britain have to pay an Air Passenger Duty, which is built into the price of an air ticket. Those flying to countries in the European Union (EU) pay £10; those flying beyond pay £20. There's no departure tax if you leave by sea or tunnel. See Money in the Facts for the Visitor chapter for details on how to reclaim Value-Added Tax when you depart.

ORGANISED TOURS

There are many companies offering general interest or special-interest tours of Scotland. See your travel agent, check the small ads in newspaper travel pages or contact the British Tourist Authority or Scottish Tourist Board for the names of tour operators.

One operator, Outback UK (☎ 01327-704115, fax 01327-703883), The Cottage, Church Green, Badby, Northants, NN11 3AS, offers two to 14-day tours round Britain with departures every Saturday (March to November) from London, though it's possible to join at any point. Other companies with trips pitched at a young crowd include Drifters (☎ 0171-262 1292; from 22 April 2000 ☎ 020-7262 1292), Contiki, (☎ 0171-637 0802; from 1 June 1999 ☎ 020-7637 0802), Insight (☎ 0990-143433) and Acacia (☎ 01797-344164).

If you don't fit into this category, try Shearings Holidays (☎ 01942-824824), Miry Lane, Wigan, Lancashire, WN3 4AG. It has a wide range of coach tours and also offers Club 55 holidays for the more mature holiday-maker.

For the over 60s, Saga Holidays (☎ 0800-300500), Saga Building, Middleburg Square, Folkestone, Kent CT20 1AZ, offers a wide range of holidays.

Saga also operates in the USA (☎ 617-262 2262), 222 Berkeley St, Boston, MA 02116, and in Australia (☎ 02-9957 4266), Level 1, 10-14 Paul St, Milsons Point, Sydney 2061.

Getting Around

Public transport is generally of a high standard, but can be expensive and doesn't reach many of the interesting places.

Buses are usually the cheapest way to get around. Unfortunately, they're also the slowest, and on main routes you're often confined to major roads which screen you from the small towns and landscapes that make travelling in Scotland worthwhile. With discount passes and tickets bought in advance, trains can be competitive in price; they're also quicker and often take you through beautiful countryside.

The British Tourist Authority (BTA) distributes an excellent brochure, *Getting about Britain for the Independent Traveller*, which covers bus, train, plane and ferry transport around Britain and into Europe.

It's worth considering car rental for at least part of your trip. However, even if you're not driving, with a mix of buses, trains, ferries, the occasional taxi, plenty of time, walking and occasionally hiring a bike, you can get almost anywhere.

PASSES

If you're not a student, it's worth considering the Freedom of Scotland Travelpass – see the passes table on the facing page for details. For more information contact ScotRail (☎ 0345-484950), which administers the scheme. Tickets are available from the Scottish Travel Centre, at London's Victoria and King's Cross train stations, and from the main stations in Glasgow and Edinburgh.

The Scottish Youth Hostels Association (SYHA, ☎ 01786-891400) markets an Explore Scotland ticket. It includes a Citylink bus pass as well as seven nights SYHA accommodation, a bus timetable, a Scotpass discount card, free SYHA membership and a handbook and a Historic Scotland pass for £155/250 for five/eight days travel. Its Scottish Wayfarer ticket gives a similar package but includes travel by rail and on Caledonian MacBrayne's west-coast and Strathclyde

PT ferries. It costs £160/270/299 for four/eight/12 days travel.

AIR

It might be worth flying to Barra to experience landing on a beach. Otherwise, flying is a pricey way to get round relatively short distances. Unless you're going to the outer reaches of Scotland, in particular the northern Highlands and Islands, planes are only marginally quicker than trains if you include the time it takes to get to/from airports. It's worth checking whether any passes are available.

The British Airports Authority (BAA) publishes a free *Scheduled Flight Guide* to Scotland with information on flight schedules and carriers and on Aberdeen, Edinburgh and Glasgow airports.

Several carriers, including British Airways/Logan Air (☎ 0345-222111, www. british-airways.com), Gillair (☎ 0191-214 6666) and British Midland (☎ 0345-554554, www.iflybritishmidland.com), connect the main towns, the Western Isles, Orkney and Shetland.

Most airlines offer a range of tickets including full fare (very expensive but flexible), Apex (for which you must book at least 14 days in advance) and special offers on some services (British Airways calls these Seat Sale fares). There are also youth fares (for under 25s) but Apex and special-offer fares are usually cheaper.

An Apex fare to Kirkwall in the Orkneys on British Airways costs £126 from Glasgow, £113 from Inverness. The full return economy fare to Sumburgh in the Shetlands is £261 from either Edinburgh or Glasgow. Flights between the Orkneys and the Shetlands cost £88 return.

Air Passes

If you're flying into the UK on BA you may be eligible for a UK Airpass. This costs an additional £57 per internal flight between

SCOTTISH TRANSPORT PASSES

Pass name	Cost (prices for adults/ discount card holders)	Bus/train/ferry services offered
Freedom of Scotland Travelpass	£64 for 4 days out of 8 consecutive days £93 for 8 days out of 15 consecutive days £122 for 12 days out of 15 consecutive days	Unlimited travel on trains, CalMac ferries and Strathclyde ferries. 33% discount on postbuses and most important regional bus lines. 33% discount on P&O Orkney to Scrabster ferry, 20% discount on P&O Aberdeen to Shetland, Aberdeen to Orkney. £1.50 off Guide Friday city tours of Edinburgh, Glasgow and Dundee
National Express Tourist Trail Pass	£49/39 for 2 days in a 3-day period £120/94 for 7 days in a 21-day period 187/143 for 14 days in a 30-day period	All National Express and Scottish Citylink buses
National Express Discount Coach Card (full time students; under 26; over 50)	£8	30% off adult fares on all Scottish Citylink buses
Explore Scotland (SYHA)	£155 for 5 days £250 for 8 days	Includes Citylink bus pass, with 7 nights SYHA accommodation and a Historic Scotland pass, plus other benefits
Scottish Wayfarer (SYHA)	£160 for 4 days £270 for 8 days £299 for 12 days	Similar to Explore Scotland, but includes rail travel, CalMac west coast and Strathclyde PT ferries
Young Person's or Senior's Railcard	£18 per annum	33% off rail throughout Britain
Go Blue Banana Haggis Backpackers	Both £85	Jump on, jump off circuit route
Flexipass Britain (must be bought outside Britain)	US$219/175 for 4 days in a month US$315/253 for 8 days in a month US$480 (adult) for 15 days in a month US$385 (youth) for 15 days in 2 months	Unlimited rail travel throughout Britain

each zone in the country, and must be arranged at least seven days prior to arrival in the UK.

Domestic Departure Tax

There's a £10 airport departure tax added to the price of tickets – check that this is included in the price you're quoted.

BUS

Scotland's internal bus network has one major player, Scottish Citylink (☎ 0990-505050), part of the Britain-wide National Express group, and numerous smaller regional companies. Long-distance express buses are usually referred to as coaches, and over short distances are quicker though more expensive than buses.

Some regions operate telephone inquiry travel lines which try to explain the fast-changing situation with timetables; where possible, these numbers have been given. Before starting a journey off the main routes it's advisable to phone for the latest information.

Passes & Discounts

The National Express Explorer Pass allows unlimited coach travel within a specified period. It's available to all overseas visitors but must be bought outside Britain. You'll be given a travel voucher which can be exchanged at any of the larger National Express agencies. For adults/concessions they cost £59/45 for three days travel within five consecutive days, £110/80 for seven days in a 21-day period and £170/130 for 14 days in a 30-day period.

National Express Tourist Trail Passes are available to UK and overseas citizens. They provide unlimited travel on all services for two days travel within three consecutive days (£49/39 for an adult/discount cardholder), any five days travel within 10 consecutive days (£85/69), any seven days travel within 21 consecutive days (£120/94) and any 14 days travel within 30 consecutive days (£187/143). The passes can be bought overseas, or at any National Express agent in the UK.

Citylink also honours European under-26 cards, including the Young Scot card (£7), which provides discounts all over Scotland and Europe.

If they don't have one of these cards, full-time students and people aged under 26 can buy the so-called Smart Card. On presentation of proof of age, or student status (an NUS or ISIC card), a passport photo and an £8 fee, you get the Smart Card to add to your collection. It entitles you to a 30% discount, so chances are you'll be ahead after buying your first ticket.

Hop On, Hop Off Buses

June to September, Haggis Backpackers (☎ 0131-557 9393), 11 Blackfriars St, Edinburgh, runs a daily service on a circuit between hostels in Edinburgh, Perth, Pitlochry, Aviemore, Inverness, Loch Ness, Isle of Skye, Fort William, Glencoe, Oban, Inverary, Loch Lomond and Glasgow (although there's no obligation to stay in the hostels). You can hop on and off the minibus wherever and whenever you like, booking up to 24 hours in advance. There's no fixed time for completing the circuit, but you can only cover each section of the route once. At other times of year there are still five or six departures a week.

Go Blue Banana (☎ 0131-556 2000), 16 High St, Edinburgh, also runs a jump on, jump off service on the same circuit. See the Scottish Transport Passes table for more information.

Both companies also offer excellent-value three-day Highlands tours for £75, leaving from Edinburgh.

Postbus

Many small places can only be reached by Royal Mail postbuses – minibuses that follow postal delivery routes. These are circuitous routes through many of the most beautiful areas of Scotland, and are particularly useful for walkers. For the free *Postbus Guide to Scotland* contact Postbus Services (☎ 01463-256273) Royal Mail, 7 Strothers Lane, Inverness IV1 1AA.

TRAIN

Scotland has some stunning train routes but they're limited and expensive, so you'll probably have to use other modes of transport too. The West Highland line through Fort William to Mallaig, and the routes from Stirling to Inverness, Inverness to Thurso, and Inverness to Kyle of Lochalsh are some of the best in the world.

ScotRail operates most train services, but a separate company, Railtrack, owns and maintains the tracks and stations. You can make ScotRail bookings by credit card on ☎ 0345-550033. Phone the general inquiry line (☎ 0345-484950, open 24 hours) for timetables and fares; or try the Web site www.rail.co.uk for rail services.

For short journeys, just buy tickets at the station before you go.

Train Passes

Unfortunately, Eurail passes are not recognised in Britain. There are local equivalents, but they in turn aren't recognised in the rest of Europe. The BritRail pass, which includes travel in Scotland, must be bought outside Britain. ScotRail's Freedom of Scotland Travelpass (see Scottish Transport Passes) and Regional Rover tickets can be bought in Britain, including from most train stations in Scotland.

The Highland Rover ticket covers the West Highlands and Inverness-Kyle line (£42 for four out of eight consecutive days). The Festival Cities Rover covers the central

---

Rail Itinerary

The following itinerary is for four days.

Journey Times

Edinburgh	to Glasgow	1 hour
Glasgow	to Fort William	3¾ hours
Fort William	to Mallaig	1½ hours
Mallaig	to Kyle of Lochalsh	2 hours by boat, summer only
Kyle of Lochalsh	to Inverness	2½ hours
Inverness	to Perth	2½ hours
Perth	to Edinburgh	1½ hours

Route

This route includes the West Highland Line, arguably the most scenic rail journey in the country, and the Kyle Line across the Highlands from Kyle of Lochalsh to Inverness. The Scot-Rail Flexi Rover ticket (£64) allows travel on this route for four days out of eight.

It takes less than one hour from Edinburgh to Glasgow's central station. Nearby, from Queen St station, trains depart on the West Highland Line. The route passes Loch Lomond on the way to Crianlarich, then climbs over wild Rannoch Moor, with views of Ben Nevis, Britain's highest peak. From Fort William, the train crosses the River Lochy. There are superb views of Loch Shiel and, after Glenfinnan station, Loch Eilt. The rails run through tunnels along the edge of the sea lochs to Arisaig, Britain's most westerly train station, then north to Morar with views across to the islands of Skye, Rhum and Eigg. The line follows the coast from Morar to Mallaig.

In the summer there are ferry services for the two-hour voyage to Kyle of Lochalsh, the terminus of the Kyle Line from Inverness. From Inverness there are frequent departures south to Perth, where it's worth stopping to see nearby Scone Palace before continuing to Edinburgh.

area (£26 for three out of seven consecutive days).

The ScotRail Rover covers all the Scot-Rail network and costs £60 for four out of eight consecutive days, £88 for eight consecutive days, or £115 for 12 out of 15 consecutive days. Holders of either the Young Person's or Senior Citizen's Railcard get a 30% discount.

Reservations for bicycles (£3.50) are compulsory on many services.

Railcards

You can get discounts of up to 33% on most off-peak fares if you're aged 16 to 25, or over 60, or studying full-time, or disabled – but you must first buy the appropriate railcard. There is also a railcard for families.

The cards are valid for one year and most are available from major stations. You'll need two passport photos, and proof of age (birth certificate or passport) or student status.

Young Person's Railcard – costs £18 and gives you 33% off most tickets and some ferry services; you must be aged 16 to 25, or a student of any age studying full-time in the UK.
Senior Railcard – available to anyone over 60, this card costs £18 and gives a 33% discount.
Disabled Person's Railcard – costs £16 and gives a 33% discount to a disabled person and one person accompanying them; pick up an application form from a station and then send it to Disabled Person's Railcard Office, PO Box 1YT, Newcastle-upon-Tyne, NE99 1YT; it can take up to three weeks to process this card so you should apply early.
Family Railcard – costs £20 and allows discounts of 33% (20% for some tickets) for up to four adults travelling together, providing a cardholder is a member of the party; up to four accompanying children pay a flat fare of £2 each. A couple of journeys can pay for the card.

Tickets

If the various train passes and railcards aren't complicated enough, try making sense of the different tickets.

Children under five years old travel free; aged between five and 15 they pay half-price for most tickets. However, when

travelling with children it is almost always worth buying a Family Railcard.

Single ticket – valid for a single (ie one-way) journey at any time on the particular day specified; expensive
Day Return ticket – valid for a return journey at any time on the particular day specified; relatively expensive
Cheap Day Return ticket – valid for a return journey on the day specified on the ticket, but there are time restrictions and it is usually only available for short journeys; often about the same price as a single; you're not usually allowed to travel on a train that leaves before 9.30 am
Open Return – for outward travel on a stated day and return on any day within a month
Apex – one of the cheapest return fares; usually for distances of more than 100 miles; you must book at least 48 hours in advance, but seats are limited so book as soon as possible (ASAP)
SuperSaver – the cheapest ticket where advance purchase isn't necessary; can't be used on Fridays after 2.30pm, Saturdays in July and August or on bank holidays, or on days after these before 2.30pm. The return journey must be within one calendar month
SuperAdvance – similarly priced to the Super-Saver but with fewer time/day restrictions; however, tickets must be bought before 2 pm on the day before travel and both the outward and return journey times must be specified; limited availability so book ASAP
Saver – higher priced than the SuperSaver, but can be used any day and there are fewer time restrictions

Classes

There are two classes of train travel: 1st, and what is now officially referred to as standard (although in class-conscious Britain this will always be called 2nd class). First class costs 30 to 50% more than 2nd and, except on very crowded trains, isn't really worth the extra money.

On overnight trains there are sleeping compartments, with one berth in 1st and two in 2nd. These cost extra and must be reserved in advance.

CAR & MOTORCYCLE

Travelling by private car or motorcycle enables you to get to remote places, and to

Road Distances (in miles)

	Aberdeen	Dundee	Edinburgh	Fort William	Glasgow	Inverness	Kyle of Lochalsh	Mallaig	Oban	Scrabster	Stranraer	Ullapool
Aberdeen	–											
Dundee	70	–										
Edinburgh	129	62	–									
Fort William	165	121	146	–								
Glasgow	145	84	42	104	–							
Inverness	105	131	155	66	166	–						
Kyle of Lochalsh	188	177	206	76	181	82	–					
Mallaig	189	161	180	44	150	106	34	–				
Oban	180	118	123	50	94	115	125	90	–			
Scrabster	228	250	279	185	286	119	214	238	235	–		
Stranraer	228	171	120	184	80	250	265	232	178	374	–	
Ullapool	150	189	215	90	194	60	88	166	166	125	158	–

travel quickly, independently and flexibly. Unfortunately, the independence you enjoy tends to isolate you and cars are nearly always inconvenient in city centres.

Scotland's roads are generally good and far less busy than in England, so driving is more enjoyable.

Motorways and main A-roads are triple or dual carriageways and deliver you quickly but you miss the most interesting countryside. The fast A9, which runs up the centre, is the busiest. Be particularly careful if you use them in foggy or wet conditions. Minor A-roads are single carriageways and are likely to be clogged with slow-moving trucks.

Life on the road is more relaxed and interesting on the B-roads and minor roads. These wind through the countryside from village to village. You can't travel fast, but you won't want to. In some areas, roads are only single track, with passing places indicated by a pole. It's illegal to park in these places. In the same areas petrol stations are few and far between and sometimes closed on Sunday.

In the Highlands and Islands the main hazards are suicidal sheep (be particularly wary of lambs) ... and the distracting beauty of the landscape!

At around 67p per litre (equivalent to £2.54 for a US gallon), petrol is expensive by American or Australian standards; and diesel is only a few pence cheaper. Distances, however, aren't great. Petrol prices also tend to rise as you get farther from main population centres.

Road Rules

Anyone using the roads should get hold of the *Highway Code* (99p), which is often available in TICs.

A foreign driving licence is valid in Britain for up to 12 months from the time of your last entry into the country. If you're bringing a car from Europe make sure you're adequately insured.

Briefly, vehicles drive on the left-hand side of the road; front-seat belts are compulsory and if belts are fitted in the back seat then they must be worn; the speed limit is 30mph (48kph) in built-up areas, 60mph

(96kph) on single carriageways, and 70mph (112kph) on dual or triple carriageways; you give way to your right at roundabouts (traffic already on the roundabout has the right of way); and motorcyclists must wear helmets.

See Legal Matters in the Facts for the Visitor chapter for information on drink-driving rules.

Rental

Rates are expensive and often you'll be better off making arrangements in your home country for a fly/drive deal. The big international rental companies charge from around £150 a week for a small car (Ford Fiesta, Peugeot 106).

The principle companies include Avis (☎ 0990-900500), Europcar (☎ 0345-222525), Budget (☎ 0800-181181), Hertz (☎ 0990-996699) and Thrifty Car Rental (☎ 01494-442110). TICs have lists of local car-hire companies.

Purchase

It is possible to buy a reasonable vehicle for around £1000; a reliable van could be up to twice as much.

Vehicles require a Ministry of Transport (MOT) safety certificate (the certificate itself is usually referred to simply as an MOT) valid for one year and issued by licensed garages; full third party insurance – shop around but expect to pay at least £300; registration – a standard form signed by the buyer and seller, with a section to be sent to the Ministry of Transport; and tax (£150 for one year, £82 for six months) – from main post offices on presentation of a valid MOT certificate, insurance and registration documents. Note that cars that are 25 or more years old are tax exempt.

You're strongly recommended to buy a vehicle with valid MOT and tax. MOT and tax remain with the car through a change of ownership; third-party insurance goes with the driver rather than the car, so you'll still have to arrange this (and beware of letting others drive the car). For further information about registering, licensing, insuring and testing your vehicle, contact a post office or Vehicle Registration Office for leaflet V100.

Car Parking

Many places in Scotland, big and small, could easily be overrun by cars. As a result, there are often blanket bans on, or at least active discrimination against, bringing cars into the centre. It's a good idea to go along with it even if, sometimes, you will have to walk farther.

The parking will be easier and you'll enjoy the places more if it's not cluttered up with cars, yours and others. This particularly applies in small villages – park in the car parks, not on the street.

In bigger cities there are often short-stay and long-stay car parks. Prices are often the same for stays of up to two or three hours, but for lengthier stays the short-stay car parks rapidly become much more expensive. The long-stay car parks may be slightly less convenient but they're much cheaper.

A yellow line painted along the edge of the road indicates there are parking restrictions. The only way to establish the exact restrictions is to find the nearby sign that spells them out.

A double line means no parking at any time; a single line means no parking for at least an eight hour period somewhere between 7 am and 7 pm; and a broken line means there are some restrictions. In some cities there are also red lines, which mean no stopping or parking.

Motorcycle Touring

Scotland is simply ideal for motorcycle touring, with lots of winding roads of good quality and stunning scenery to stimulate the senses. Just make sure your wet-weather gear is up to scratch. Crash helmets are compulsory.

The Auto-Cycle Union (☎ 01788-566400, fax 01788-573585, admin@acu. org.uk, www.acu.org.uk), ACU House, Wood St, Rugby, Warwickshire, CV21 2YX, publish-

Driving Itinerary

If you're only visiting Scotland for a short holiday, you can pack in a lot more if you have your own set of wheels and plan your itinerary carefully. The following itinerary is for seven days.

Road Distances

Edinburgh	to St Andrews	58 miles
St Andrews	to Aberdeen	83 miles
Aberdeen	to Inverness	106 miles
Inverness	to Fort William	65 miles
Fort William	to Glasgow	102 miles
Glasgow	to Stirling	26 miles
Stirling	to Edinburgh	35 miles

Route

Take the A90 out of Edinburgh over the Forth Road Bridge. The A90 becomes the M90 soon after the bridge, and you should turn onto the A91 north of Kinross, following signs to St Andrews. It's worth spending the night in this interesting seaside town, best known as the home of golf.

From St Andrews, turn off the A91 along the A919 and A92 following signs for Tay Bridge and Dundee. Stop to see Scott's Antarctic research ship *Discovery*, conveniently moored beside the bridge in Dundee. Continue on the A929 and the smaller A928 to Glamis Castle, one of the most famous of Scotland's many castles. From Glamis take the A94 to the affluent granite city of Aberdeen.

You could take one of several routes from Aberdeen to Inverness. The direct route is along the A96 via Elgin, a distance of 106 miles. Alternatively, and if you have an extra day to spare, consider taking the route through the Grampian Mountains, via the A93, A939, A95 and A9 – about 150 miles. Balmoral Castle, the Queen's Scottish residence, which can be visited when the royal family is not at home, is a short distance off this route.

From Inverness, follow Loch Ness on the A92, stopping at Urquhart Castle and the nearby Loch Ness Monster Exhibition at Drumnadrochit. Continue on the A82 to Fort William, leaving yourself time for an evening walk in Glen Nevis. To climb Ben Nevis, Britain's highest peak, you'd need to allow a whole day.

Take the A82 south from Fort William, stopping in Glen Coe and then continuing past Loch Lomond to Glasgow. Spend the following day in this lively city before taking the M80 to Stirling, a drive of under one hour. Look around Stirling's magnificent castle the next day before returning to Edinburgh.

es a useful booklet about motorcycle touring in Britain.

Motoring Organisations

It's well worth becoming a member of a British motoring organisation for 24 hour breakdown assistance. The two largest in the UK are the AA (☎ 0800-919595) and the RAC (☎ 0800-550550). One year's membership starts at £46 for the AA and £39 for the RAC. Both these companies can also extend their cover to include Europe.

If you're a member of a motoring organisation back home, you should check to see if it has a reciprocal arrangement with an organisation in Britain.

WALKING & BICYCLE

Walking and cycling are popular, rewarding ways to explore Scotland. For information see the Activities chapter.

HITCHING

Hitching is never entirely safe in any country, and we don't recommend it. Travellers who decide to hitch are taking a small but potentially serious risk. However, many people choose to hitch, and the advice that follows should help to make their journeys as fast and safe as possible.

Hitching is reasonably easy in Scotland, except around the big cities and built-up areas, where you'll need to use public transport. Although the north-west is more difficult because there's less traffic, waits of over two hours are unusual (except on Sunday in 'Sabbath' areas). Public transport doesn't stop on the A9 (except in villages); otherwise, buses usually stop and rescue you if they're not full. On some Scottish islands, where public transport is infrequent, hitching is so much a part of getting around that local drivers may stop and offer you lifts without you even asking.

It's against the law to hitch on motorways or the immediate slip roads; make a sign and use approach roads, nearby roundabouts, or the service stations.

Although hitching is probably safer than in many other western countries, it's obviously not without its dangers, and it's certainly not advisable for a woman to hitch alone. Two women will be reasonably safe but a man and a woman travelling together is probably the best combination.

If you don't like the look of someone who stops for you, don't get in the car. Likewise, if you're a driver, take care over who you pick up.

BOAT

Caledonian MacBrayne (CalMac, ☎ 0990-650000) is the most important ferry operator on the west coast, with services from Ullapool to the Outer Hebrides, and from Mallaig to Skye and on to the Outer Hebrides. Its main west-coast port, how-

ever, is Oban, with ferries to the islands of Barra, South Uist, Coll, Tiree, Lismore, Mull and Colonsay.

As an example, a single passenger fare from Oban to Lochboisdale, South Uist (Hebrides), is £17.30. However, it pays to plan your complete trip in advance since CalMac's Island Hopscotch tickets are usually the best deal, with ferry combinations over 15 set routes. CalMac also has Rover tickets, offering unlimited travel for eight and 15 days (£39/56).

P&O (☎ 01224-572615) has ferries from Aberdeen and Scrabster to Orkney, and from Aberdeen to Shetland. June to August, the cheapest one-way tickets to Stromness (Orkney) cost £14 from Scrabster, £37 from Aberdeen. Between Aberdeen and Shetland, the standard fare is £55. There's a 10% student discount.

Taking a car on the ferries is expensive. You can save some money by hiring one once you get onto the islands.

LOCAL TRANSPORT

There are comprehensive local bus networks in Edinburgh, Glasgow, Aberdeen and some other larger towns. Glasgow also has an extensive suburban rail network as well as an underground line. Taxis are reasonably priced and over a short distance may be competitive with a local bus, especially if there are three or four people to share the cost.

ORGANISED TOURS

Since travel is so easy to organise in Scotland, there's little need to consider a tour. Still, if your time is limited and you prefer to travel in a group, there are some interesting possibilities. See also Hop On Hop Off Buses earlier in this chapter.

There are plenty of coach tours available from the big cities, particularly Edinburgh and Glasgow. From Edinburgh, Lothian Regional Transport (LRT) has a variety of half and full day trips. A day tour of Loch Ness and the Grampians costs £26 (children £18) and includes lunch. LRT also does trips to Glencoe, Loch Lomond, St Andrews, Stirling, the Trossachs and the Isle of Arran. Call ☎ 0131-555 6363 or ☎ 554 4494.

Rabbie's Trail Burners (☎ 0131-226 3133), 207 High St, Edinburgh EH1 1PE, has one, two and three-day tours of Scotland in minibuses. Its three-day tour explores Glencoe, Lochaber, Kintail and Skye; it costs £79 and accommodation is extra.

ScotRail does short breaks including a week-long tour of the Highlands and Islands for £455 which covers rail, coach and ferry travel and accommodation. Call ☎ 0870-161 0161.

Scotsell (☎ 0141-772 5928), located at 2D Churchill Way, Bishopbriggs, Glasgow G64 2RH, organises car touring holidays to the islands including ferries and accommodation, plus wildlife, walking and cruising holidays.

Excellent Adventures (☎/fax 0131-669 4418, d001533@infotrade.co.uk), PO Box 13859, Edinburgh E7H15 1UF, runs four-day trips to the Highlands and Islands, which include sea kayaking, climbing or canyoning, for £99 per person.

Caledonian Discovery Ltd (☎ 10397-772167, fax 01397-772765, fingal@sol.co.uk, www.lochaber.co.uk/fingal) has a 37m (120 feet) barge, *Fingal of Caledonia*, which sails from mid-April to mid-October between Inverness and Fort William on the Caledonian Canal. It costs £428 per person per week in the high season (June to August) which includes activities such as canoeing, windsurfing, swimming and cycling, and full board. There's also a 10% discount for children under 14.

Edinburgh

• pop 409,000 ☎ 0131

Studded with volcanic hills, Edinburgh has an incomparable location on the southern edge of the enormous Firth of Forth. The city's superb architecture ranges from the Greek-style monuments on Calton Hill (for which it was called the 'Athens of the North'), to extraordinary 16th century tenements to monumental Georgian and Victorian masterpieces. All are dominated by the castle on a precipitous crag in the city's heart. Sixteen thousand buildings are listed as architecturally or historically important, in a city which is a World Heritage Site.

The geology and architecture combine to create an extraordinary symphony in stone. The Old Town, with its crowded tenements and bloody past, stands in contrast to the orderly grid of the New Town with its disciplined Georgian buildings. There are vistas from nearly every street – sudden views of the Firth of Forth, the castle, the Pentland Hills, Calton Hill with its memorials, and rugged Arthur's Seat.

After becoming a royal capital in the 11th century, all the great dramas of Scottish history played at least one act in Edinburgh. Following the union of 1707 with England it remained the centre for government administration (now the Scottish Office), the separate Scottish legal system and the Presbyterian Church of Scotland.

In some ways, however, it's the least Scottish of Scotland's cities – partly because of the impact of tourism, its closeness to England, and because of its multicultural, sophisticated population.

Edinburgh has a reputation for being civilised and reserved, especially in comparison with intense, gregarious Glasgow. Nevertheless, there's a vibrant pub scene, and the dynamism unleashed every August creates the world's greatest arts festival.

The flipside to the gloss, however, is the grim reality of life in the bleak council

HIGHLIGHTS

- Savour the views from Arthur's Seat, Salisbury Crags and Calton Hill
- Stroll along the world-famous Royal Mile
- Treat yourself to performances at the Fringe Festival
- Cruise the Firth of Forth to Inchcolm Island
- Visit Hopetoun House, one of Scotland's finest stately homes
- Walk or cycle in Holyrood Park
- Gain a fascinating insight into the Old Town's past at Gladstone's Land
- Enjoy the vibrant pub scene

ATLANTIC
OCEAN

Central Edinburgh p114-5
● Bruntsfield p118
Greater Edinburgh p113

housing estates surrounding the city, the thriving drug scene and a distressing AIDS problem.

HISTORY

Castle Rock, a volcanic crag with three vertical sides, dominates the city centre. This natural defensive position was probably what first attracted settlers; the earliest signs of habitation date back to 850 BC.

The Northumbrian Angles captured Lothian in the 6th century, rebuilding a fortress, known as Dun Eadain, on Castle Rock.

This served as the Scots' southern outpost until 1018 when Malcolm II established a frontier at the River Tweed. Nonetheless, the English sacked the city no less than seven times.

Edinburgh really began to grow in the 11th century when markets developed at the foot of the fortress, and from 1124 when David I held court at the castle and founded the abbey at Holyrood.

The first effective town wall was constructed around 1450 and circled the Old Town and the area around Grassmarket. This restricted, defensible zone became a medieval Manhattan, forcing its densely packed inhabitants to build tenements that soared to 12 storeys.

A golden era that saw the foundation of the College of Surgeons and the introduction of printing ended with the death of James IV at the Battle of Flodden in 1513. England's Henry VIII attempted to force a marriage between Mary (James V's daughter) and his son, but the Scots sent the infant Mary to France to marry the dauphin. The city was sacked by the English, and the Scots turned to the French for support.

The Scots were increasingly sympathetic to the ideas of the Reformation, and when John Knox returned from exile in 1555 he found fertile ground for his Calvinist message.

When James VI/I succeeded to the Scottish and English crowns he moved the court to London and, for the most part, the Stuarts ignored Edinburgh. When Charles I tried to

introduce episcopacy (the rule of the bishops) in 1633 he provoked the National Covenant (see St Giles' Cathedral later in this chapter) and more religious turmoil which eventually ended in triumph for the Presbyterians.

The Act of Union in 1707 further reduced Edinburgh's importance, but cultural and intellectual life flourished.

In the second half of the 18th century a new city was created across the ravine to the north. The population was expanding, defence was no longer vital and the thinkers of the Scottish Enlightenment planned to distance themselves from Edinburgh's Jacobite past.

The population exploded in the 19th century – Edinburgh quadrupled in size to 400,000, not much less than it is today – and the old city's tenements were taken over by refugees from the Irish famines. A new ring of crescents and circuses was built to the south of the New Town, and grey Victorian terraces sprung up.

In the 20th century the slum dwellers were moved into new housing estates which now foster massive social problems. However, a new era is beginning with the decision to locate the new Scottish Parliament in Edinburgh.

ORIENTATION

The most important landmark is Arthur's Seat, the 251m (823 feet) rocky peak southwest of the city centre. The Old and New Towns are separated by Princes St Gardens, with the castle dominating both of them.

The main shopping street, Princes St, runs along the north side of the gardens. Buildings are restricted to the north side of Princes St, which has the usual High St shops. At the east end, Calton Hill is crowned by several monuments. The Royal Mile (Lawnmarket, High St and Canongate) is the parallel equivalent in the Old Town.

The TIC is between Waverley train station and Princes St, above the Waverley Market shopping centre. The bus station in the New Town is trickier to find; it's off the north-east corner of St Andrew Square, north of Princes St.

Bear in mind that the same street may be subdivided into a few different names. For example Leith Walk is variously called Union Place and Antigua St on one side, Elm Row and Greenside Place on the other.

Maps

The foldout maps produced by the Scottish Tourist Board, A-Z, Bartholomew (a local cartographic company) and Collins, are good for most purposes. For more detail A-Z, Bartholomew and Collins also produce handy street atlases; there's also the *Super Red Book of Edinburgh* which is two colour and easy to read.

If you really want to explore the wynds, loans and closes of the city the Ordinance Survey *Edinburgh Street Atlas* is the most comprehensive. The print in the pocket-size version, though, may be too small for some users. It's testimony to the intricacies of the Old Town that not even the OS includes some of its tiniest nooks and crannies.

INFORMATION
Tourist Offices

The busy main TIC (☎ 557 1700), Waverley Market, 3 Princes St, opens November to March, Monday to Saturday from 9 am to 6 pm, plus Sunday 1 to 6 pm in April and October. May, June and September it opens Monday to Saturday from 9 am to 7 pm, Sunday 11 am to 7 pm; July and August, Monday to Saturday from 9 am to 8 pm, Sunday 11 am to 8 pm. There's also a branch at Edinburgh airport (☎ 333 2167). These TICs have information about all of Scotland, and sell an *Essential Guide to Edinburgh* (50p).

At the Backpackers Centre (☎ 557 9393), 6 Blackfriars St beside Haggis Backpackers, you can get information about hostels and tours, and book tickets for National Express, Stena Line, P&O and many other services.

Consulates & High Commissions

Scotland's capital houses several consulates and high commissions; see the Facts for the Visitor chapter.

Money

The TIC *bureau de change* opens the same hours as the TIC; it charges 2.5% commission with a minimum of £2.50. There's also a *bureau de change* in the post office. American Express (☎ 225 7881), 139 Princes St, opens Monday to Friday from 9 am to 5.30 pm, Saturday to 4 pm. Thomas Cook (☎ 465 7700), 26-28 Frederick St, opens Monday to Saturday from 9 am to 5.30 pm.

Most banks also change money. The Royal Bank of Scotland (☎ 556 8555) and the Bank of Scotland (☎ 442 7777) both have branches in St Andrew Square.

Post & Communications

The main post office (☎ 0345-223344) is inconveniently tucked away inside the sprawling St James' Shopping Centre, off Leith St. It's open Monday from 9 am to 5.30 pm, Tuesday to Friday 8.30 am to 5.30 pm, and Saturday 8.30 am to 6 pm. Items addressed to poste restante are automatically sent here and can be picked up from any counter.

There are plenty of public telephones around Edinburgh, all of which have STD or international access.

Web 13 Internet Café (☎ 229 8883), 13 Bread St near the corner of Lothian Rd, offers online access for £5 per hour. It opens weekdays from 9 am to 10 pm, Saturday to 6 pm, and Sunday noon to 6 pm. Cyberia Cyber Café (☎ 220 4403), 88 Hanover St, is similar.

Internet Resources

Edinburgh & Lothians Tourist Board's Web site is at www.edinburgh.org. For information on the city's changing program of exhibitions at museums and galleries check www.cac.org.uk.

For information on music, theatre, art and things to see in and around Edinburgh, check www.eae.co.uk.

Travel Agencies

Two travel agencies specialise in budget and student travel. Campus Travel (☎ 225 6111),

53 Forrest Rd, opens Monday to Friday from 9 am to 5.30 pm, Saturday 10 am to 5 pm; it's often busy. Close to the university campus, Edinburgh Travel Centre (☎ 668 2221), 3 Bristo Square, opens Monday to Friday from 9 am to 5.30 pm; it issues ISIC cards. American Express and Thomas Cook also have offices in the city. See Money earlier in this chapter.

Going Places (☎ 225 5373), 30 George St on the corner of Hanover St, is a general travel agent which opens on Sunday.

Bookshops
The Stationery Office Bookshop (☎ 228 4181), 71 Lothian Rd, has an excellent selection of books and maps on Scotland.

A good general bookshop with several locations is James Thin. The main shop (☎ 556 6743) is at 53-59 South Bridge St on the corner of Infirmary St. There's a branch (☎ 539 7757) at 35 South Gyle and another (☎ 225 4495) at 57 George St which also has a small café.

Waterstone's (not to be confused with George Waterston office supply shops) has two branches at either end of Princes St – at No 13 (☎ 556 3034) near the Royal British Hotel, and at No 128 (☎ 226 2666). They're both well stocked and well organised. There's another branch (☎ 225 3436) at 83 George St.

McNaughtan's Bookshop (☎ 556 5897) downstairs at 3A Haddington Place on Leith Walk, just near the corner of Annandale St, deals in second-hand books. It's closed on weekends.

Bauermeister Bookseller (☎ 226 5561) at 19 George IV Bridge is Edinburgh's largest independent bookseller.

Libraries
The Central Library (☎ 225 5584), George IV Bridge, has one room devoted to all things Scottish, another to Edinburgh. The library opens Monday to Thursday from 10 am to 8 pm, Friday to 5 pm, Saturday 9 am to 1 pm.

The National Library of Scotland (☎ 226 4531) opposite the Central Library houses the reference-only, general reading room. It opens weekdays from 9.30 am to 8.30 pm (from 10 am Wednesday), Saturday 9.30 am to 1 pm. There's a branch south of the city in Newington at 33 Salisbury Place on the corner of Causewayside, which contains the Scottish science library and a map room.

Universities
Edinburgh has three universities. The oldest and most prestigious is the University of Edinburgh. Its information centre (☎ 650 1000) on Nicolson St (the southern extension of South Bridge), next to the Festival Theatre, opens weekdays from 9.15 am to 5 pm.

Herriot-Watt University's (☎ 449 5111) main location is south-west of town at the Riccarton Campus in Currie, but it has a site in the centre at the Mountbatten Building south of Grassmarket. Napier University (☎ 444 2266), 219 Colinton Rd, is southwest of Bruntsfield in Craiglockhart.

Laundry
For those staying in Pilrig St, there's Bendix Launderette & Dry Cleaners just round the corner (toward Leith) on Leith Walk at No 342-46. Canonmills Dry Cleaners & Launderette, 7 Huntly St, is convenient for people staying in Eyre Place; a service wash costs £3.60.

The pick of the laundrettes is Sundial Launderette in New Town at the junction of Broughton and East London Sts. It's bright, clean and has an adjacent café. The laundrette opens daily and charges £2.80 for a wash.

South of the centre in Bruntsfield is Tarvit Launderette on Tarvit St opposite Gilmore Place.

Left Luggage
Left-luggage facilities are available at Waverley train station (from £2.50 all day) opposite Edinburgh Rail Travel Centre. At St Andrew Square bus station, the left-luggage department is in the ticket office building and charges £1 to £2 depending on size. Both also have left-luggage lockers for £4 per day.

Medical Services

Chemists can advise you on minor ailments. Medications are readily available either over the counter or on prescription. At least one local chemist opens round the clock and other chemists post details of this in their window. Alternatively, look in the local newspaper or in the yellow pages. Boots (☎ 225 6757), 48 Shandwick Place (the extension of Princes St in the West End), opens Monday to Saturday from 8 am to 9 pm, Sunday 10 am to 5 pm.

The Royal Infirmary of Edinburgh, 1 Lauriston Place south of Grassmarket, has a 24 hour accident and emergency department (☎ 536 4000). It also has its own dental hospital (☎ 536 4900). On Crewe Rd South in the city's north, the Western General Hospital's minor injuries unit (☎ 537 1330/31) opens daily from 9 am to 9 pm.

Emergency

For help from the police, ambulance, fire brigade or coastguard call ☎ 999 or ☎ 112 (both free). Edinburgh's police headquarters (☎ 311 3131) is on Fettes Ave north of the centre near the Western General Hospital.

Western General Hospital operates an emergency dental service (☎ 537 1338) weekday evenings from 7 to 9 pm, weekends 10 am to noon and 7 to 9 pm. There's a casualty dental clinic (☎ 543 4903) at the Edinburgh Dental Hospital, 31 Chambers St off South Bridge. Some other useful emergency numbers are:

Gay and Lesbian Switchboard
 ☎ 556 4049
National AIDS Helpline
 ☎ 0800 567123 (24 hours)
Rape Crisis Centre
 ☎ 556 9437
Samaritans
 ☎ 0345-909090 (24 hours)

Dangers & Annoyances

Edinburgh is safer than most cities of a similar size. Nevertheless, the usual big city precautions apply.

Rose St and the west end of Princes St at the junction with Shandwick Place and Queensberry and Hope Sts, can get a bit rowdy on Friday and Saturday night after people have been drinking. Calton Hill offers good views during the day, but is probably best avoided at night.

If you lose anything check with the lost property department (☎ 311 3141) at the police headquarters on Fettes Ave.

ROYAL MILE

Following a ridge that runs from Edinburgh Castle to Holyrood Palace, the Royal Mile is one of the world's most fascinating streets. From the west end you can see beyond craggy Arthur's Seat and over the waters of the Firth of Forth, with tantalising glimpses of the Old and New Towns through the *closes* (entrances) and *wynds* (alleyways) on either side. Although there are tourists and shops stuffed with tacky Scottish souvenirs aplenty, the street still feels a real part of a thriving city. It's lined with extraordinary buildings, including multistoreyed *lands* (tenements) dating from the 15th century.

To see the numerous sites would take several days, but even with limited time it's worth ducking through a *pend* (arched gateway) or close to explore the narrow wynds and courts beyond.

Edinburgh Castle

Edinburgh Castle dominates the city centre. It sits astride the core of an extinct volcano, its three sides scoured almost vertical by glacial action.

There was a settlement here as early as 850 BC, although the first historical references date from the 6th century when the Northumbrian king, Edwin, rebuilt a fortress here as a defence against the Picts.

A favoured royal residence from the 11th to the 16th centuries, Edinburgh only became Scotland's capital at the end of the Middle Ages. The oldest surviving part of the castle is St Margaret's Chapel.

Although it looks impregnable, the castle often changed hands between the Scots and English. It last saw action in 1745, when Bonnie Prince Charlie's army tried, but failed, to breach its walls.

During the Wars of Independence (1174 to 1356), the English captured it several times. In 1313 it was demolished by the Scots as part of Robert the Bruce's scorched earth policies and wasn't rebuilt (by David II) until 1371. Little of this work survives, however, because the castle was strengthened and renovated in the 16th, 17th and 18th centuries.

From the 16th century the royal family built more comfortable domestic accommodation at places like Holyrood, and the castle developed as a seat of government and military power. However, in 1566 Mary Queen of Scots underlined its continuing symbolic importance when she chose to give birth to her son in the castle. In 1573 much of it was destroyed when loyalists attempted to hold it for Mary; the oldest substantial work – including the Half Moon Battery and Portcullis Gate – survives from the subsequent rebuilding. The castle was then taken in turn by the Covenanters (in 1640), Cromwell (in 1650) and King William and Queen Mary (the last true siege, in 1689). In 1715 and 1745 the Stuarts tried unsuccessfully to recapture it. In the gaps between sieges more defences were added, and by the mid-18th century the castle looked much as it does today.

Partly thanks to Sir Walter Scott, in the 19th century the castle began to recover its importance as a Scottish symbol. Efforts were made to improve its appearance and to restore important buildings.

The castle crawls with tourists, and although the views are great, you may decide it's more impressive from the outside looking in.

Visitors enter from the **Esplanade**, a parade ground where the Military Tattoo takes place each August. The changing of the guard occurs on the hour, and on summer evenings a piper plays here.

After entering the castle proper through the Gatehouse (added in the late 19th century), the pathway curves round to the right. It passes through Portcullis Gate before coming to **Argyle Battery** then **Mills Mount Battery** from where the weekday 1 pm gun

salute takes place. There are good views to the north from both batteries.

Continuing round you enter the central defensive area through Foog's Gate.

Here you'll find the small Norman **St Margaret's Chapel**, the oldest building in Edinburgh. It's a simple stone edifice, probably built by David I or Alexander I in memory of their mother sometime around 1130. Following Cromwell's capture of the castle in 1650 it was used to store ammunition until Queen Victoria had it restored; it was rededicated in 1934.

On the eastern end of Crown Square is the **Palace** built between the 15th and 16th centuries. Among the royal apartments is the bedchamber where Mary Queen of Scots gave birth to her son James, who was to unite the crowns of Scotland and England. Another room is used to house the Scottish crown jewels, made up of sceptre, sword and crown; with them now lies the Stone of Destiny (see the boxed text 'Stone of Destiny').

Adjacent to the Palace is the **Great Hall**, built for James IV as a ceremonial hall and used as a meeting place for the Scottish Parliament until 1639. In former barracks opposite, the massive, sombre **Scottish National War Memorial** was added to the castle complex in the 1920s and is a memorial to the Scots dead of WWI.

From the western end of Crown Square you can descend into the dark, dank **Vaults**, a former prison. One of its rooms contains **Mons Meg**, a huge 15th century siege cannon.

The castle (☎ 225 9846) opens April to September, daily, from 9.30 am to 6 pm (5 pm in winter). The admission price of £6/1.50 includes provision of an audio tape commentary.

Scotch Whisky Heritage Centre

If you'd like to know how whisky is manufactured the Scotch Whisky Heritage Centre (☎ 220 0441), Castle Hill, offers a tour with several audiovisual presentations followed by a ride in a car past a tableau explaining the history of the 'water of life'. You can

The Stone of Destiny

Alleged to have accompanied the Scots in all their mythical journeyings, the original Stone of Destiny (the Fatal Stone) was a carved block of sandstone on which the Scottish monarchs placed their feet during the coronation.

Stolen by Edward I in 1296, this venerable talisman was incorporated into the Coronation Chair, used by English (and later British) monarchs, in London's Westminster Abbey. Apart from being taken to Gloucester during air raids in WWII, the Stone lay undisturbed for centuries.

On Christmas Eve 1950, however, a plucky band of Scottish students drove down from Glasgow, jemmied the door of Westminster Abbey and made off with the Stone. English officialdom was outraged. The border roads had roadblocks on them for the first time in 400 years, but while Scots living in London jeered the English police as they searched the Serpentine Lake and the River Thames, the Stone was being smuggled back to Scotland.

King George VI was 'sorely troubled about the loss', but the students issued a petition affirming their loyalty to him, stating that they would give back the Stone as long as it could remain on Scottish soil. The authorities refused to negotiate and, three months after it was stolen, the Stone turned up on the altar of the ruined Abbey of Arbroath. It was here, in 1320, that the Arbroath Declaration had been signed, reaffirming the right of Scots to self-rule and independence from England. Before the public were aware that the Stone had even been found, it was back in London. No charges were brought and Ian Hamilton, the student who led this jolly caper, published his story in *The Taking of the Stone of Destiny*.

Many Scots, however, hold that the original Stone is safely hidden somewhere in Scotland, and that Edward I was fobbed off with a shoddy imitation. This is possibly true, for descriptions of the original state that it was decorated with carvings, not that it was a plain block of sandstone. Given that Scottish nationalism is running high, this powerful symbol of Scotland would surely have been brought out by now if it hadn't been quite so safely hidden.

Imitation or not, the then Scottish Secretary and Conservative MP, Michael Forsyth, arranged for the return of the sandstone block to Edinburgh Castle, with much pomp and circumstance, in 1996. If it was an attempt to boost his flagging political standing, it failed dismally: Forsyth lost his seat in the House of Commons in the May 1997 general election.

take the ride only (15 minutes) for £3.80/2, but it's not really worth it. It's better value to do the full tour or put the money toward the purchase of one (or more) of the hundreds of different brands of whisky sold in the shop. The centre opens daily from 10 am to 5.30 pm; the full experience including a tasting costs £4.95/2.50.

Camera Obscura

Just beyond Ramsay Lane, the Camera Obscura (☎ 226 3709) offers great views over the city. The 'camera' itself is a curious device (originally dating from the 1850s, al-

though improved in 1945) a bit like a periscope, which uses lenses and mirrors to throw a 'live' image onto a large interior bowl. The accompanying 'guided tour' is entertaining, and the whole exercise has a quirky charm. It's open Monday to Friday from 9.30 am to 6 pm, weekends from 10 am; £3.85/1.95, family £11.50.

Highland Tolbooth Kirk

With the tallest spire (72.8m, 239 feet) on one of Edinburgh's highest points, the Highland Tolbooth Kirk is an important feature of the skyline. It was built in the

1840s by James Graham and Augustus Pugin (architect of the London Houses of Parliament). It gets its name from the Gaelic services that were held here for Edinburgh's Highland congregations (which now occur at Greyfriars Kirk). It's being refurbished and will eventually be the home of the Edinburgh Festival office.

Opposite the kirk are the **Assembly Rooms** of the Church of Scotland, the temporary home of the new Scottish Parliament.

Ramsay Garden

Constructed around the mid-18th century home of the poet Alan Ramsay, the attractive apartments here overlook the Esplanade and the small garden from which they get their name. They were designed in the 1890s by an early town planner, Patrick Geddes, in an attempt to revitalise the Old Town. They're now very expensive, very wonderful private apartments.

Gladstone's Land

Gladstone's Land (☎ 226 5856, NTS), 477 Lawnmarket, gives a fascinating glimpse of the Old Town's past. The house was built in the mid-16th century and extended around 1617 by wealthy merchant Thomas Gledstanes. Its comfortable interior contains fine painted ceilings, walls and beams and some splendid furniture from the 17th and 18th centuries. It's open April to October, Monday to Saturday from 10 am to 5 pm, Sunday 2 to 5 pm; £2.80/1.90.

The Writers' Museum

The Writers' Museum (☎ 529 4901) is in Lady Stair's House, built in 1622, and contains manuscripts and memorabilia belonging to Robert Burns, Sir Walter Scott and Robert Louis Stevenson. The static displays will only entertain enthusiasts of these writers but it's open Monday to Saturday from 10 am to 5 pm and, during the Edinburgh Festival, Sunday 2 to 5 pm; free.

Brodie's Close

Brodie's Close (and nearby Deacon Brodies pub) is named after the father of the notorious William Brodie, a deacon and respected citizen by day, a burglar by night. William Brodie was the inspiration for Robert Louis Stevenson's *The Strange Case of Dr Jekyll and Mr Hyde* and, some would say, a dramatic reflection of Edinburgh's schizophrenic undercurrents. He met his end on the gallows in 1788.

Parliament Square

Lawnmarket ends at the crossroads of Bank St and George IV Bridge; at the south-east corner, brass strips set in the road mark the site of the scaffold where public hangings took place until 1864. From there the Royal Mile continues as High St.

Parliament Square, largely filled by St Giles Cathedral, the High Kirk of Edinburgh, is on the south side of High St. This was the heart of Edinburgh until the 18th century, and a cobblestone **Heart of Midlothian** is marked on the ground. Passers-by traditionally spit on it for luck. This was the site of the entrance to the Tolbooth, originally built to collect tolls, but subsequently a meeting place for parliament, the town council and the General Assembly of the Reformed Kirk, then law courts and, finally, a prison and place of execution.

The 19th century **Mercat Cross** replaced the original 1365 cross and marks the spot where merchants and traders met to transact business and Royal Proclamations were read.

The square's southern side is flanked by **Parliament House**, the meeting place of the Scottish Parliament from 1639; its neoclassical façade was added in the early 19th century. After the Act of Union in 1707 the building became the centre for the Scottish legal system – the Court of Session and High Court – which retained its independence. The most interesting feature is **Parliament Hall**, where the parliament actually met, which is now used by lawyers and their clients as a meeting place.

St Giles' Cathedral

There has been a church on this site since the 9th century. A Norman-style church was built in 1126, but this was burnt by the

English in 1385; the only substantial remains are the central piers that support the tower. The present church was then built in stages, with the crown spire completed in 1495.

Inside, near the entrance, is a life-size statue of John Knox, minister from 1559-72; from here he preached his uncompromising Calvinist message and launched the Scottish Reformation. The new austerity this ushered in led to changes in the building's interior – decorations, stained glass, altars and the relics of St Giles were thrown into the Nor Loch.

The High Kirk of Edinburgh was at the heart of Edinburgh's struggle against episcopacy (the rule of the church by bishops). In 1637 when Charles I attempted to re-establish episcopacy and made the kirk a cathedral, he provoked a possibly apocryphal outburst by Jenny Geddes which, according to popular belief, led to the signing of the National Covenant at Greyfriars the following year. Jenny hurled a stool at the dean who was using the English prayer book (a symbol of episcopacy); a tablet marks the spot and a copy of the National Covenant is displayed on the wall.

One of the most interesting corners of the kirk is the Thistle Chapel built 1909-11 for the Knights of the Most Ancient and Most Noble Order of the Thistle. The carved Gothic-style stalls have canopies topped with the helms and arms of the 16 knights.

Entry to the kirk is free, but a £1 donation is requested.

Edinburgh City Chambers

The City Chambers were originally built by John Adam (brother of Robert) in 1761 to replace the Mercat Cross and serve as a Royal Exchange. However, the merchants continued to prefer the street, and the building was taken over by the town council which has been using it since 1811.

Tron Kirk

At the south-western corner of the intersection with South Bridge, Tron Kirk owes its name to a salt *tron* or public weighbridge that stood on the site. It was built in 1637 on top of Marlin's Wynd which has been excavated to reveal a cobbled street with cellars and shops on either side. Run by the Edinburgh Old Town Renewal Trust (☎ 225 8818), the church acts as a visitor centre for the Old Town. It's open early April to mid June, Thursday to Monday from 10 am to 5 pm, and mid June to early September daily 10 am to 7 pm.

John Knox's House

Perhaps the most extraordinary building on the Royal Mile, John Knox's House (☎ 556 9579), 43-45 High St, dates from around 1490. The outside staircase, overhanging upper floors and crow-stepped gables are all typical of a 15th century town house. John Knox is thought to have occupied the 2nd floor from 1561-72.

The labyrinthine interior has an interesting display on his life including a recording of his interview with Mary Queen of Scots, whose mother was a target of his diatribe *First Blast of the Trumpet Against the Monstrous Regiment of Women*. It's open Monday to Saturday from 10 am to 4.30 pm; £1.95/75p.

Museum of Childhood

This museum (☎ 529 4142), 42 High St, attempts to cover the serious issues related to childhood – health, education, upbringing and so on – but more enjoyable is the enormous collection of toys, dolls, games and books which fascinate children and, for adults, brings childhood memories back. It includes a video history of the various Gerry Anderson puppet TV series, like *Thunderbirds*, made in the 1960s. The museum opens Monday to Saturday from 10 am to 5 pm, and, during the Edinburgh Festival only, Sunday 2 to 5 pm; free.

Netherbow Port & Canongate

High St ends at the intersection with St Mary's and Jeffrey Sts, where the city's eastern gate, Netherbow Port, part of the Flodden Wall, once stood. Though it no longer exists, it's commemorated by brass strips set in the road.

The next stretch of the Mile, Canongate, takes its name from the canons (priests) of Holyrood Abbey. From the 16th century, it was home to aristocrats attracted to the Palace of Holyroodhouse. Originally governed by the canons, it remained an independent burgh until 1856.

The People's Story

Canongate Tolbooth, with its picturesque turrets and projecting clock, is an interesting example of 16th century architecture. Built in 1591, it served successively as a collection point for tolls (taxes), a council house, a courtroom and a jail. It now houses a fascinating museum (☎ 331 5545) telling the story of the life, work and pastimes of ordinary Edinburgh folk from the 18th century to the present day. It opens Monday to Saturday from 10 am to 5 pm, and, during the Edinburgh Festival only, Sunday 2 to 5 pm; free.

Huntly House

Huntly House, built in 1570, is a good example of the luxurious accommodation that aristocrats built for themselves along Canongate; the projecting upper floors of plastered timber are typical of the time. It now contains a local history museum (☎ 529 4143) with some interesting displays, including a copy of the National Covenant of 1638 signed in protest against Charles I's attempt to re-establish episcopacy and the English prayer book. It opens Monday to Saturday from 10 am to 5 pm, and, during the Edinburgh Festival only, Sunday 2 to 5 pm; free.

Canongate Kirk

Attractive Canongate Kirk was built in 1688. In 1745 Prince Charles Stuart (Bonnie Prince Charlie, the Young Pretender) used it to hold prisoners taken at the Battle of Prestonpans. The churchyard has good views and several famous people are buried there. These include the economist Adam Smith, author of *The Wealth of Nations*, who lived nearby in Panmure Close, and the 18th century poet Robert Fergusson.

Abbey Lairds

On the left-hand side of Abbey Strand, flanking the entrance to the Palace of Holyroodhouse, the Abbey Lairds provided sanctuary for aristocratic debtors from 1128 to 1880. It was one of a number of hovels, most of which were pulled down when Queen Victoria occupied the palace. The debtors or 'lairds' could avoid prison as long as they remained within the palace and Holyrood Park, although they were allowed out on Sunday.

Queen Mary's Bath House

According to legend, Mary Queen of Scots used to bathe in white wine and goat's milk in this small, 16th century turreted lodge – but only twice a year! More likely, it was a dovecote or summer house.

Palace of Holyroodhouse & Holyrood Abbey

The Palace of Holyroodhouse developed from a guesthouse attached to medieval Holyrood Abbey. It was a royal residence at various times from the 16th century, and is still the Queen's official residence in Scotland, so access is very restricted. You're only allowed to view a few apartments, walk around part of the grounds and visit the abbey ruins.

The abbey was founded by David I in 1128, and was probably named after a fragment of the Cross (*rood* is an old word for cross) said to have belonged to his mother St Margaret. As it lay outside the city walls it was particularly vulnerable to English attacks, but the church was always rebuilt and survived as Canongate parish church until it collapsed in 1768. Most of the surviving ruins date from the 12th and 13th centuries, although a doorway in the far south-eastern corner survives from the original Norman church.

King James IV extended the abbey guesthouse in 1501 to create more comfortable living quarters than were possible in bleak and windy Edinburgh Castle; the oldest surviving section of the building, the north-west tower, was built in 1529 as a royal apartment.

Mary Queen of Scots spent 16 eventful years living in the tower. During this time she married Darnley (in the abbey) and Bothwell (in what is now the Picture Gallery), and this is where she debated with John Knox and witnessed the murder of her secretary Rizzio.

Although Holyrood was never again a permanent royal residence after Mary's son James VI/I departed for London, it was further extended during Charles II's reign.

Although you're carefully shepherded through a limited part of the palace, there's a certain fascination to following in Mary's footsteps and seeing the room where Rizzio was cut down.

Opening hours are normally April to October, daily, from 9.30 am to 5.15 pm; November to March, daily, from 9.30 am to 3.45 pm. Entry is £5.30/2.60. However, the complex is sometimes closed for state functions or when the Queen is in residence, usually in mid-May, and mid-June to around early July; phone ☎ 556 7371 to check.

Close to Holyroodhouse, construction is under way for the new purpose-built **Scottish Parliament** and the **Dynamic Earth** exhibition presenting the geology story of the planet.

Holyrood Park & Arthur's Seat

Edinburgh is blessed in having a real wilderness on its doorstep. Holyrood Park covers 650 acres of varied landscape, including mountains, moorland, lochs and fields. The highest point is the 251m (823 feet) extinct volcano, Arthur's Seat.

The park can be circumnavigated along Queen's Drive by car or bike, but it's closed to motorised traffic on Sunday. There are several excellent walks. Opposite the palace's southern gate, a footpath named Radical Rd runs up immediately along the base of the Salisbury Crags, but is partly blocked off because of danger from falling rocks. A fairly easy half-hour walk leads from Dunsapie Loch to the summit of Arthur's Seat. There are magnificent views of the city to the Pentland Hills and across the Firth of Forth.

Arthur's Seat

Arthur's Seat, the eroded stump of a lava flow that erupted around 325 million years ago, sits in Holyrood Park, the ancient hunting ground of Scottish kings. It forms part of a volcano that includes Calton Hill and Castle Rock and seen from the southwest isn't unlike a lion lying on its haunches.

It's not certain where the name derives from. There's no evidence to connect it with the King Arthur of Camelot and round table fame; it may have been named after the 6th-century Arthur of Strathclyde. Alternatively, it may come from the Gaelic *Ard-na-Saighead* which means 'Height of Arrows'.

To the south, Duddingston Loch, the one natural lake, is a bird sanctuary.

SOUTH OF THE ROYAL MILE

The area south of the Royal Mile includes some of the oldest and most crowded parts of the Old Town at the foot of Castle Rock and the Mile.

Around the university and the beautiful Meadows it opens up to run into sturdy Victorian suburbs like Bruntsfield, Marchmont and Grange.

One of the city's main traffic arteries (carrying traffic to/from the A68 and A7), with many shops, restaurants and guesthouses, runs down the eastern side – beginning as North Bridge and becoming successively South Bridge, Nicolson St, Clerk St, Newington Rd, Minto St, Mayfield Gardens and Craigmillar Park.

Grassmarket

Grassmarket is one of Edinburgh's nightlife centres, with numerous restaurants and pubs, including the White Hart Inn which was patronised by Robert Burns.

Continued on page 121

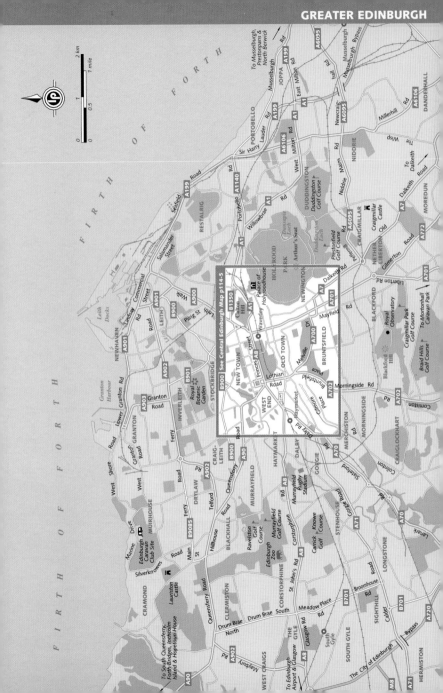

CENTRAL EDINBURGH

COMELY BANK

To Stockbridge & Royal Botanic Garden

NEW TOWN

Queensferry Road

A90

DEAN

Dean Gardens

To Scottish National Gallery of Modern Art

WEST END

West Princes Street Gardens

Edinburgh Castle

OLD TOWN

COATES

Haymarket

A8

A702

A70

A70

VIEWFORTH

See Bruntsfield Map p118

BRUNTSFIELD

Toll Cross

A700

Bruntsfield Links

Waverley Station

Castlehill

Lawnmarket

Grassmarket

Cowgate

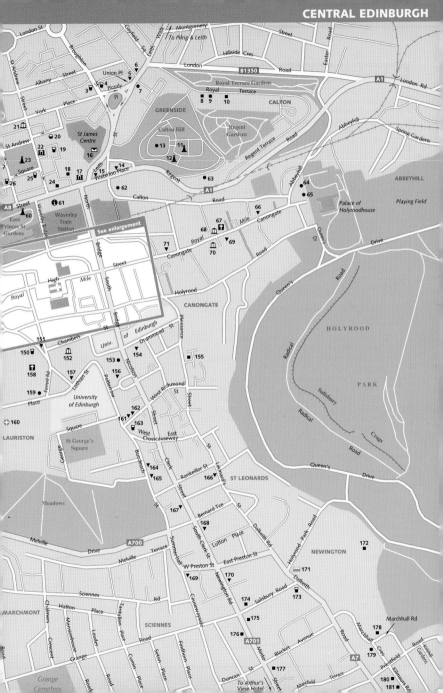

CENTRAL EDINBURGH

PLACES TO STAY

1 Sibbet House
8 Royal Terrace Hotel
9 Claymore, Halcyon, Greenside
   & Adria Hotels
10 Ailsa Craig Hotel
18 Princes St Backpackers
24 Old Waverley Hotel
40 Roxburghe Hotel
44 Belford Youth Hostel
45 Eglinton Youth Hostel
46 Palmerston Lodge
47 Kinnaird Christian Hostel
48 Princes St West
   Backpackers
53 Caledonian Hotel
78 Royal Mile Backpackers
80 Edinburgh Backpackers
   Hostel
109 Ibis Hotel
112 Bank Hotel & Logie Baird's
   Bar
113 Holiday Inn Crowne Plaza
115 High St Hostel
121 Central Youth Hostel
129 Thistle Inn Hotel
138 Sheraton Grand Hotel
148 Point Hotel & Monboddo
155 Pleasance Youth Hostel
172 Pollock Halls of Residence
174 Salisbury Guest House
175 Grange Guest House
176 Sherwood Hotel
177 Thrums Hotel
178 Millfield Guesthouse
179 Marchhall Hotel
180 Casa Buzzo
181 Kenvie Guest House

PLACES TO EAT

5 Giuliano's
6 Ferri's Italiano Pizzeria
14 Café 1812
15 Delifrance
29 Hard Rock Café
30 Bar Napoli
32 Henderson's
33 Gringo Bill's
34 Chez Jules
35 Singapura Restaurant
36 Vito's Ristorante
37 Café Rouge
43 Rafaelli's
49 The Granary
50 Ryan's Café-Bar
56 Bewley's
66 Clarinda's Tea Room

69 Brambles Tearoom
71 The Grange
75 Netherbow Theatre Café
77 Gustos Café
79 Dubh Prais
81 Viva Mexico
82 Doric Wine Bar & Bistro
90 Patisserie Florentin
95 Polo Fusion
102 Deacon's House Café
107 Elephant's Sufficiency
108 Bann's Vegetarian Café
118 Black Bo's
125 Beppe Vittorio
126 Pierre Victoire
130 Ristorante Gennaro
131 Pierre Victoire
133 Mamma's Pizzas
139 Verandah Restaurant
140 Howie's Restaurant
143 Lazio
144 Dario's Pizzeria Ristorante
145 Starbucks Café
147 Uluru
149 Jasmine
151 Elephant House
154 Khushi's
156 Kebab Mahal
157 Negociant's
161 Susie's Diner
162 Pigs Bistro
164 King's Balti
165 La Bonne Vie
166 Howie's Restaurant
167 Isabel's Café
168 Kalpna
169 Chinese Home Cooking
170 Metropole

PUBS

2 Wally Dug
3 Basement Bar
4 Mathers
19 Café Royal Bar
25 Tiles Bar-Bistro
26 Abbotsford
28 Rose St Brewery
51 Whigham's Wine Cellars
72 The Tass
73 World's End
85 Hebrides Bar
88 Malt Shovel Inn
92 Deacon Brodie's
94 Jolly Judge
110 Ceilidh House
119 Bannerman's Bar
122 Green Tree

127 Bow Bar
128 Last Drop
132 White Hart Inn
134 Beehive Inn
135 Fiddler's Arms
150 Greyfriars Bobby's Bar
163 Peartree House
173 Physician & Firkin

OTHER

7 Playhouse Theatre
11 National Monument
12 Nelson Monument
13 City Observatory
16 St James Shopping Centre &
   Main Post Office
17 Register House
20 St Andrew Square Bus
   Station
21 Scottish National Portrait
   Gallery & Museum of
   Antiquities
22 Dundas House
23 Melville Monument
27 St Andrew's & St George's
   Church
31 Cyberia
38 Thomas Cook
39 Tiso's
41 Georgian House
42 West Register House
52 American Express
54 St Cuthbert's Church &
   Watchtower
55 St John's Church
57 Waterstone's Bookshop &
   Starbucks Café
58 Royal Scottish Academy
59 National Gallery
60 Sir Walter Scott Monument
61 TIC
62 Venue Night Club
63 Royal High School
64 Queen Mary's Bath House
65 Abbey Lairds
67 Canongate Kirk
68 The People's Story
70 Huntly House Museum
74 Go Blue Banana
76 John Knox's House
83 Tattoo Office
84 LRT Travel Shop
86 Traveline
87 Edinburgh Festival Box Office
89 Edinburgh City Chambers
91 Lady Stair's House
93 Gladstone's Land

CENTRAL EDINBURGH

A Calton Hill-view of early morning Edinburgh. The Dugald Stewart monument is in the foreground.

GLENN BEANLAND

BRUNTSFIELD

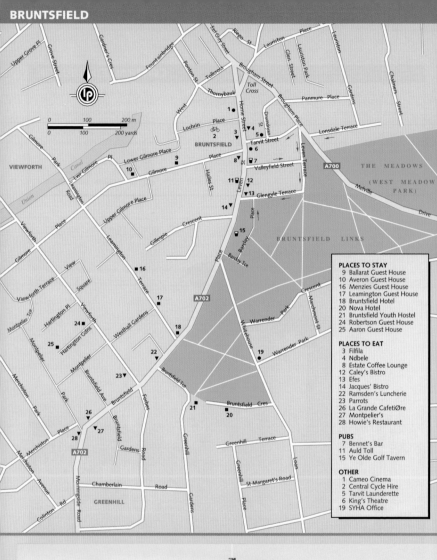

PLACES TO STAY
9 Ballarat Guest House
10 Averon Guest House
16 Menzies Guest House
17 Leamington Guest House
18 Bruntsfield Hotel
20 Nova Hotel
21 Bruntsfield Youth Hostel
24 Robertson Guest House
25 Aaron Guest House

PLACES TO EAT
3 Filfila
4 Ndbele
8 Estate Coffee Lounge
12 Caley's Bistro
13 Efes
14 Jacques' Bistro
22 Ramsden's Luncherie
23 Parrots
26 La Grande CafetiØre
27 Montpelier's
28 Howie's Restaurant

PUBS
7 Bennet's Bar
11 Auld Toll
15 Ye Olde Golf Tavern

OTHER
1 Cameo Cinema
2 Central Cycle Hire
5 Tarvit Launderette
6 King's Theatre
19 SYHA Office

Edinburgh Castle from Bruntsfield Links

TOM SMALLMAN

Bagpipes, balmorals, glengarries, sporrans and a shepherd's crook – and lots and lots of tartan. Gatherings like these provide colourful displays of traditional clan culture.

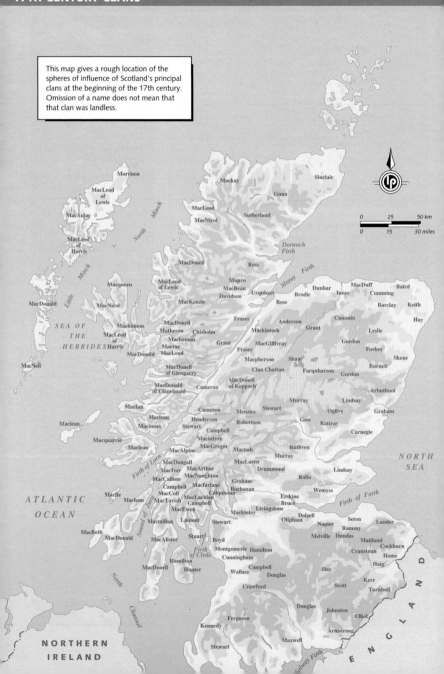

This map gives a rough location of the spheres of influence of Scotland's principal clans at the beginning of the 17th century. Omission of a name does not mean that that clan was landless.

0   25   50 km
0   15   30 miles

Morrison

MacLeod of Lewis

MacAulay

MacLeod of Harris

North Minch

Mackay

Gunn

Sinclair

MacLeod

MacNicol

Sutherland

Dornoch Firth

Little Minch

Macqueen

MacNicol

MacLeod of Lewis

MacDonald

MacDonell

Munro
MacBean
Davidson

Ross

Moray Firth

Urquhart

Rose

Brodie

Dunbar

Innes

MacDuff

Cumming

Baird

Barclay

Keith

Hay

SEA OF THE HEBRIDES

Mackinnon

MacLeod of Harris

MacKenzie

Fraser

Anderson

Grant

Cummin

Leslie

MacNeil

Matheson

Maclennan
Macrae
MacLeod

Chisholm

Grant

Mackintosh

MacGillivray

Forbes

Gordon

Skene

MacDonald

MacDonell of Glengarry

Fraser

Macpherson

Clan Chattan

Shaw

Farquharson

Burnett

Gordon

MacDonell of Clanranald

Cameron

MacDonell of Keppoch

Arbuthnot

Maclan

Maclean

Macinnes
Stewart

Cameron

Henderson
Stewart

Menzies

Robertson

Campbell

Stewart

Murray

Gow

Ogilvy

Rattray

Lindsay

Graham

Maclean

Macquarrie

Maclean

Macintyre

MacGregor

Macnab

Ruthven

Murray

Carnegie

MacAlpine

MacDougall

MacIver
MacCallum

MacArthur
MacNaughton

Campbell
MacColl
MacTavish

Macfarlane

MacLaren

Drummond

Graham

Buchanan

Rollo

Lindsay

NORTH SEA

Macfie

Maclean

MacLachlan
Campbell

Colquhoun

Erskine
Bruce

Wemyss

MacEwen

Lamont

Mackinlay

Livingstone

Firth of Forth

Macbeth

Macmillan

Stewart

Dalzell
Oliphant

Seton

Lauder

MacDonald

MacAlister

Stuart

Boyd

Napier

Melville

Ramsay
Dundas

Maitland

Cockburn

MacDonell

Hamilton

Montgomerie

Cunningham

Hamilton

Hunter

Campbell

Wallace

Douglas

Hay

Cranstoun

Home

Haig

Kerr

Scott

Turnbull

Crawford

Douglas

Johnston

Elliot

Kennedy

Ferguson

Maxwell

Armstrong

Stewart

Solway Firth

ATLANTIC OCEAN

Firth of Lorn

Sound of Jura

Firth of Clyde

North Channel

NORTHERN IRELAND

ENGLAND

Continued from page 112

An open area hedged by tall tenements and dominated by the looming castle, it can be approached from George IV Bridge, via Victoria St, an unusual two-tiered street clinging to the ridge below the Royal Mile, with some excellent shops.

The site of a market from at least 1477 to the start of the 20th century, Grassmarket was always a focal point for the Old Town. This was the main place for executions and over 100 hanged Covenanters are commemorated with a cross at the east end. The notorious murderers Burke and Hare operated from a now vanished close off the west end. In around 1827 they enticed at least 18 victims here, suffocated them and sold the bodies to Edinburgh's medical schools.

Leading off the south-east corner, Candlemaker Row climbs back up to George IV Bridge and Chambers St with the Royal Museum of Scotland and the University of Edinburgh's Old College.

Cowgate

Cowgate, which runs off the eastern end of Grassmarket parallel to the Royal Mile, is less a canyon than a bleak tunnel, thanks to the bridges that were built above it. Once a fashionable place to live, it now has a couple of Fringe Festival venues and one or two good pubs.

Royal Museum of Scotland

The Royal Museum of Scotland (☎ 225 7534), Chambers St, is a Victorian building whose grey, solid exterior contrasts with its large, bright, galleried entrance hall of slim wrought-iron columns and glass roof. The museum houses an eclectic, comprehensive series of exhibitions.

These range from the natural world (evolution, mammals, geo-logy, fossils etc) through scientific and industrial technological development, with one section featuring the world's oldest steam locomotive, *Wylam Dilly* (1813) to the decorative arts of ancient Egypt, Islam, China, Japan, Korea and the west.

The adjacent **Museum of Scotland**, opened in 1998, houses archaeological artefacts from the old Museum of Antiquities. It shows the history of Scotland in chronological order starting with the country's earliest history in the basement.

The museums open Monday to Saturday from 10 am to 5 pm (to 8 pm Tuesday), Sunday noon to 5 pm. Entry is £3 (free on Tuesday from 5 to 8 pm), children free.

University of Edinburgh

The University of Edinburgh is one of Britain's oldest, biggest and best universities. Founded in 1583, it now has around 17,000 undergraduates. The students make a major contribution to the lively atmosphere of Grassmarket, Cowgate, and the nearby restaurants and pubs. The university sprawls for some distance, but the centre is the **Old College** (also called Old Quad), at the junction of South Bridge and Chambers St, a Robert Adam masterpiece designed in 1789, but not completed till 1834.

Inside the Old College is the **Talbot Rice Art Gallery** (☎ 650 2210) which houses a permanent, small collection of old masters, plus regular exhibitions of new work.

Greyfriars Kirk & Kirkyard

At the bottom of a stone canyon made up of tenements, churches, volcanic cliffs and the castle, Greyfriars Kirkyard is one of Edinburgh's most evocative spots – a peaceful oasis dotted with memorials and surrounded by Edinburgh's dramatic skyline.

The kirk was built on the site of a Franciscan friary and opened for worship on Christmas Day 1620. In 1638, the National Covenant was signed inside near the pulpit. The Covenant rejected Charles I's attempts to reintroduce episcopacy and a new English prayer book, and affirmed the independence of the Scottish church. Many who signed were later executed in Grassmarket and, in 1679, 1200 Covenanters were held prisoner in terrible conditions in an enclosure in the yard. There's a small exhibition inside.

Tour groups, however, come to pay homage to a tiny statue of Greyfriars Bobby (in front of the nearby pub). Bobby was a Skye terrier who maintained a vigil over the grave of his master, an Edinburgh police officer, from 1858 to 1872. The story was immortalised (and distorted) in a novel by Eleanor Atkinson in 1912 and later turned into a film. In the kirk you can buy *Greyfriars Bobby – The Real Story at Last* (£3.50), Forbes Macgregor's debunking of some of the myths. Bobby's grave is just inside the entrance to the kirkyard.

CALTON HILL

Calton Hill, at the east end of Princes St, is another distinctive component of Edinburgh's skyline, 101.5m (333 feet) high and scattered with grandiose memorials mostly dating from the first half of the 19th century. Here you get one of the best views of Edinburgh, taking in the entire panorama – the castle, Holyrood, Arthur's Seat, the Firth of Forth, the New Town and Princes St.

Approaching from Waterloo Place, you pass the imposing **Royal High School**, Regent Rd, dating from 1829 and modelled on the Temple of Theseus in Athens. Former pupils include Robert Adam, Alexander Graham Bell and Sir Walter Scott. Now called St Andrew's House, it was at one time cited as a potential home for the new Scottish parliament, and houses the Scottish Office. Farther east, across Regent Rd, is the **Burns Monument** designed by Thomas Hamilton, another former pupil of the school.

The largest structure is the **National Monument**, an over-ambitious attempt to replicate the Parthenon, in honour of Scotland's dead in the Napoleonic Wars. Construction began in 1822, but funds ran dry when only 12 columns were complete.

The design of the **City Observatory** (1818) was based on the Greek Temple of the Winds. Here you'll find the **Edinburgh Experience** (☎ 556 4365), a 20 minute, 3-D audio-visual portrayal of Edinburgh's history. It's open April to October, daily, from 10 am to 5 pm; £2/1.20.

Looking a bit like an upturned telescope, the **Nelson Monument** was built to com-

memorate Nelson's victory at Trafalgar. It's open (for great views) April to September, Monday from 1 to 6 pm, Tuesday to Saturday 10 am to 6 pm; October to March, Monday to Saturday from 10 am to 3 pm; £2.

There are also two historic observatories, and the small, circular **Monument to Dugald Stewart** (1753-1828), an obscure professor of philosophy.

NEW TOWN

The New Town, dating from the 18th century, lies north of the Old Town, separated from it by Princes St Gardens and occupying a ridge that runs below, but parallel to, the Royal Mile.

It's in complete contrast to the chaotic tangle of streets and buildings that evolved in the Old Town, and typifies the values of the Scottish Enlightenment.

Despite being confined behind city walls, the Old Town was periodically sacked by the English or torn by civil wars and disputes. The overcrowding and the smoke from its chimneys gave it its nickname, Auld Reekie.

So when the Act of Union in 1707 brought the prospect of long-term stability, aristocrats were keen to find healthier, more spacious surroundings.

Cowgate was bridged to open up the south, Nor Loch at the northern foot of Castle Rock was drained and the North Bridge constructed.

In 1767, 23-year-old James Craig won a competition to design a New Town. His plan was brilliant in its simplicity. George St followed the line of the ridge between Charlotte and St Andrew Squares. Building was restricted to one side of Princes St and Queen St only, so the town opened onto the Firth of Forth to the north, and to the castle and Old Town to the south.

The New Town continued to sprout squares, circuses, parks and terraces, and some of its finest neoclassical architecture was designed by Robert Adam. Today, the New Town is the world's most complete and unspoilt example of Georgian town planning and architecture.

Princes St

Princes St was originally envisaged as the back of the New Town, as it was literally and figuratively turning away from its Jacobite past. However, the transport links and stunning outlook soon led to its development as Edinburgh's principal thoroughfare.

The main train station at the east end is now overshadowed by the uninspiring **Waverley Market** shopping centre. The entrance to the TIC is via the street level piazza which is frequently used by buskers and other street performers.

The street's north side is lined with standard High St shops, and few 18th century buildings survive. One exception is the beautiful **Register House** (1788), designed by Robert Adam, at the eastern end of Princes St, with the statue of the Duke of Wellington on horseback in front. It's home to the Scottish Record Office.

Back on the south side, about halfway along, the massive Gothic spire of the **Sir Walter Scott Monument**, built by public subscription after his death in 1832, testifies to a popularity largely inspired by his role in rebuilding pride in Scottish identity. At the time of research it was closed for refurbishment (costing about £2 million), but when it reopens you'll be able to climb the 287 steps to the top.

Behind the monument are the **Princes St Gardens**, a public park which stretches east to west from Waverley Bridge to Lothian Rd, and up the hillside to the castle. The Princes St Gardens are cut by **The Mound**, a pile of earth dumped during the construction of the New Town to provide a road link with the Old Town. It was completed in 1830. The Royal Scottish Academy and the National Gallery of Scotland are also here (see later).

St John's Church, at the west end of Princes St on the corner of Lothian Rd, stands above some interesting shops and is worth visiting for its fine Gothic Revival interior. It overlooks **St Cuthbert's Church** below, off Lothian Rd, which has a watchtower in the graveyard – a reminder of the Burke and Hare days when graves had to be guarded against robbers. Inside are ornate furnishings and many murals.

Royal Scottish Academy (RSA)

The RSA (☎ 225 6671), fronting Princes St, was designed by William Playfair and built in Grecian style in 1826, with its fluted Doric columns added later. It contains artwork by academy members and hosts temporary exhibitions throughout the year. It's open Monday to Saturday from 10 am to 5 pm, Sunday 2 to 5 pm; free (although there are charges for some exhibitions).

National Gallery of Scotland

Also designed by William Playfair, the National Gallery (☎ 556 8921) behind the RSA at the foot of The Mound, is an imposing classical building dating from the 1850s. It houses an important collection of European art from 15th century Renaissance to 19th century postimpressionism. There are paintings by Verrocchio (Leonardo da Vinci's teacher), Tintoretto, Titian, Holbein, Rubens, van Dyck, Vermeer, El Greco, Poussin, Rembrandt, Gainsborough, Turner, Constable, Monet, Pissaro, Gauguin and Cezanne.

The USA is also represented by the works of Frederick Church, John Singer Sargent and Benjamin West. The section specifically on Scottish art, in the basement, includes portraits by Allan Ramsay and Sir Henry Raeburn, rural scenes by Sir David Wilkie and impressionistic landscapes by William MacTaggart.

Antonio Canova's statue of the Three Graces (room X) is owned jointly with London's Victoria and Albert Museum. In Greek mythology the Three Graces – Aglaia, Euphrosyne and Thalia – daughters of Zeus and Euryonome, embodied beauty, gracefulness and youth.

The gallery opens Monday to Saturday from 10 am to 5 pm, Sunday 2 to 5 pm; free.

St Andrew Square & George St

Dominated by the fluted Doric column of the **Melville Monument**, St Andrew Square isn't architecturally distinguished (partly thanks to the bus station at the north-east corner). On the eastern side, however, is the impressive Palladian-style **Dundas House** which has a spectacular dome, visible from inside, and frieze. It's the head office of the Royal Bank of Scotland, which has been there since 1825.

George St, parallel to Princes St and connecting St Andrew Square with Charlotte Square, was originally envisaged as the main thoroughfare of the residential New Town. It's now Scotland's Wall St, home to highly successful Scottish financial institutions which control billions of pounds. **St Andrew's and St George's Church**, built in 1784, boasts a wonderful oval plaster ceiling, and was where the Church of Scotland split in two in 1843.

Charlotte Square

At the western end of George St, Charlotte Square, designed in 1791 by Robert Adam shortly before his death, is regarded as the architectural jewel of the New Town. St George's Church (1811) is now **West Register House**, an annexe to Register House in Princes St. It houses part of Scotland's official records which appear in occasional exhibitions in the entrance hall.

The north side of Charlotte Square is Robert Adam's masterpiece, and one of the finest examples of Georgian architecture anywhere. **Bute House**, at No 6, is the office of the Secretary of State for Scotland. Next door at No 7, the **Georgian House** (☎ 225 2160, NTS), has been beautifully restored and refurnished to show (albeit in idealised form) how Edinburgh's wealthy elite lived at the end of the 18th century. The walls are decorated with paintings by Allan Ramsay, Henry Raeburn and Sir Joshua Reynolds. A 35 minute video brings it all to life rather well. It's open April to October, Monday to Saturday from 10 am to 5 pm, Sunday 2 to 5 pm; £4.20/2.80, family £11.20.

Scottish National Portrait Gallery

The gallery (☎ 556 8921) at the junction of St Andrew and Queen Sts is in a large, red-sandstone, Italian-Gothic building dating from 1882. It records Scottish history through portraits and sculptures. Although the subjects are probably the main source of interest, some portraits are also well worth viewing.

The entrance hall is decorated with a frieze showing the chief protagonists in Scottish history and the balcony with frescoes of important moments in Scottish history painted by William Hole in 1897. The collection's subjects range from the kings, queens and nobles of earlier times to modern-day Scots from various walks of life.

There's a good café (see Places to Eat later in this chapter). The gallery opens Monday to Saturday from 10 am to 5 pm, Sunday 2 to 5 pm; free.

WEST END

The last part to be built, the West End is an extension of the New Town. Huge **St Mary's Episcopal Cathedral**, Palmerston Place, built in the 1870s, was Sir George Gilbert Scott's last major work.

If you follow Palmerston Place north over the Water of Leith, you come to **Dean Village** ('dean' means deep valley), an odd corner of Edinburgh. Once a milling community, it has been restored and taken over by yuppies. A pleasant walk begins by the Water of Leith at Belford Bridge. The footpath takes you up onto Dean Path, then onto Dean Bridge, from where you can look down on the village. You can continue on the south bank of the Leith, north-east through Stockbridge, then detour to the Royal Botanic Garden.

Scottish National Gallery of Modern Art

West of Dean Village, the Scottish National Gallery of Modern Art (☎ 556 8921), off Belford Rd, repays the effort of getting there (walk from Belford Bridge or take bus No 13 from George St). It's in an impressive classical Greek-style building surrounded by a sculpture park, which features work by Henry Moore and Barbara Hepworth among others.

Inside, the collection concentrates on 20th century art, with various European art movements represented by the likes of Matisse, Picasso, Kirchner, Magritte, Miro, Mondrian and Giacometti. American and English artists are also represented, but most space is given to Scottish painters – from the Scottish Colourists early in the 20th century to contemporary artists. The gallery is small enough not to overwhelm and opens Monday to Saturday from 10 am to 5 pm, Sunday 2 to 5 pm; free.

NORTH OF THE NEW TOWN

The New Town's Georgian architecture extends north to Stockbridge and the Water of Leith, a rewarding area to explore since it's well off the tourist trail.

Stockbridge is a trendy area with its own distinct identity, some interesting shops, and a good choice of pubs and restaurants.

The painter, Sir Henry Raeburn, was born in Stockbridge and is well known for developing part of the area, most notably **Ann St**, one of the most exclusive addresses in Edinburgh.

Just north of Stockbridge is the lovely **Royal Botanic Garden** (☎ 552 7171) on Inverleith Row. It's worth visiting for the different perspective you get on the Edinburgh skyline from the Terrace Café. The garden opens daily November to January from 10 am to 4 pm; February and October to 5 pm; March and September to 6 pm; April to August to 7 pm; free. Bus Nos 8, 19, 23, 27 and 37 will get you there.

ACTIVITIES

Edinburgh offers numerous opportunities for recreational activities and the TIC can provide particular details. Favourite outdoor venues are Holyrood Park, Meadow Park and Bruntsfield Links.

There are plenty of good walks. Following the Water of Leith offers a relaxed stroll through the city, while more strenuous climbs to Arthur's Seat or along the Radical Rd in Holyrood Park are rewarded with great views. For longer hill-walking head for the Pentland Hills in the south.

Edinburgh has a network of signposted cycle paths that can get you around the city and out into the surrounding countryside. Queen's Drive, that circles Holyrood Park, is popular especially on Sunday when it's closed to motorised traffic. The Innocent Railway Path from Holyrood Park takes you through Duddingston village to Craigmillar and Musselburgh.

Not surprisingly, golf is a favourite pastime and there are lots of courses around Edinburgh. Many people practise their golf stroke on Bruntsfield Links; others head for Braid Hills public course or the nearby floodlit driving range at Braid Hills Golf Centre (☎ 658 1755), 91 Liberton Drive. Some private courses also welcome visitors including Craigmillar Park Golf Club (☎ 667 0047), Observatory Rd, near the Royal Observatory.

Alien Rock (☎ 552 7211), Old St Andrew's Church, 8 Pier Place, Newhaven, is an indoor climbing centre open daily. Training courses are available. It costs £5 per session plus £3 for boots and harness hire.

On the southern boundary of the city off the A702 the Midlothian Ski Centre (☎ 445 4433), Hill End, is a large artificial ski area, open daily year-round. Take bus No 4 from the city centre.

Canoeing and sailing in the Firth of Forth are available from Port Edgar Marina & Sailing School (☎ 331 3330), in South Queensferry west of Edinburgh.

Indoor sports centres providing activities such as swimming, squash, badminton etc include Meadowbank Sports Centre (☎ 661 5351), 139 London Rd, off Leith Walk and the Royal Commonwealth Pool (☎ 667 7211), 21 Dalkieth Rd, Newington.

ORGANISED TOURS
Walking Tours

There are lots of organised walks of Edinburgh, many of them related to ghosts, witches and torture – and with appropriately dressed guides. Mercat Tours (☎ 661 4541) has a Ghost Hunter Tour of the Old Town's underground vaulted chambers which starts at 9.30 pm, lasts 1½ hours and costs £5. Other companies offering similar walks are Robin's Tours (☎ 661 0125), Auld Reekie Tours (☎ 557 4700) and Witchery Tours (☎ 225 6745). Mercat Tours and Robin's Tours also do straightforward historical guided walks of the Royal Mile.

One of the most popular tours is the Macallan Edinburgh Literary Pub Tour (☎ 226 6665) in which actors take you to the pubs frequented by Burns, Scott, Stevenson et al and give you a light-hearted lesson in Scottish literature.

Tours leave from the Beehive Inn in Grassmarket and cost £6.

Bus Tours

Open-topped buses leave from Waverley Bridge outside the main train station and offer hop-on, hop-off tours of the principal sights. Guide Friday (☎ 556 2244) charges £7.50 and LRT's (☎ 555 6363) Edinburgh Classic Tour costs £5.50. They're a good way of getting your bearings – although with a bus map and a Day Saver bus ticket (£2.20) you could do the same thing, without a commentary.

Scotline Tours (☎ 557 0162) does four-hour tours of the city for £4, leaving Waverley Bridge daily at 9 am. It also offers tours farther afield to St Andrews, the Borders and Loch Ness.

SPECIAL EVENTS

Edinburgh has an amazing series of festivals throughout the year, particularly the Edinburgh International Festival, the Fringe Festival and the Military Tattoo, which are all held about the same time. See the boxed text 'Special Events' in the Facts for the Visitor chapter.

PLACES TO STAY

Edinburgh has masses of accommodation, but the city can still fill up quickly over the New Year, at Easter and between mid-May and mid-September, especially while the festivals are in full swing. Book in advance if possible, or use an accommodation booking service.

The TIC's accommodation service (☎ 473 3855) charges a steep £4 fee and only books one night ahead ... hopeless during busy periods when forward planning is essential. Instead, get its free accommodation brochure and ring round yourself.

For £5, three branches of Thomas Cook also make hotel reservations: the Edinburgh airport office (☎ 333 5119); the office (☎ 557 0905) in Waverley Steps near the TIC; and the office (☎ 557 0034) on Platform One of Waverley train station.

Camping

Edinburgh has two well-equipped camp sites reasonably close to the centre. *Edinburgh Caravan Club Site (☎ 312 6874, Marine Drive)* overlooks the Firth of Forth 3 miles north-west of the centre, and has full facilities and tent sites for £3. From North Bridge take bus No 8A, 9A or 14A. *Mortonhall Caravan Park (☎ 664 1533, 38 Mortonhall Gate)* off Frogston Rd East, Mortonhall, is 5 miles south-east of the centre. Sites are £8 to £12 and it's open March to October. Take bus No 11 from North Bridge.

Hostels & Colleges

SYHA Hostels There are four good SYHA hostels. *Eglinton Youth Hostel (☎ 337 1120, 18 Eglinton Crescent)* is about 1 mile west of the city near Haymarket train station; beds cost £12.50/9.95. Walk down Princes St and continue on Shandwick Place which becomes West Maitland St; veer right at the Haymarket along Haymarket Terrace, then turn right into Coates Gardens which runs into Eglinton Crescent.

Bruntsfield Youth Hostel (☎ 447 2994, 7 Bruntsfield Crescent) has an attractive location overlooking Bruntsfield Links about 2½ miles from Waverley train station. Catch bus No 11 or 16 from the garden side of Princes St and alight at Forbes Rd. It's closed in January and rates are £8.60/7.10 (£9.60/8.10 in July and August).

The other two are summer only (late June to early September): *Central Youth Hostel (☎ 337 1120, Robertson's Close/College

Wynd), Cowgate, and ***Pleasance Youth Hostel*** *(☎ 337 1120, New Arthur Place)*.

Independent Hostels There's a growing number of independent backpackers' hostels, some of them right in the centre. The long-established, well-equipped ***High St Hostel*** *(☎ 557 3984, 8 Blackfriars St)* is popular although some have found it noisy. Beds cost £9.50 per night in a 10-bed dorm. It's opposite the Haggis Backpackers tour-booking office.

Not far away is ***Royal Mile Backpackers*** *(☎ 557 6120, 105 High St)*, which charges £9.90 for beds in dorms of up to 10 beds. ***Edinburgh Backpackers Hostel*** *(☎ 220 1717, 65 Cockburn St)* is close to the action; dorm beds cost from £10 and doubles are £35; a continental breakfast is available for £1.75.

Princes St Backpackers *(☎ 556 6894, 5 West Register St)* is well positioned behind Princes St and close to the bus station. It's a fun place, but you do have to negotiate 77 exhausting steps to reach reception. Dorm beds cost £9.50, doubles £24. A full breakfast costs just £2, and Sunday night dinner is free!

Princes St West Backpackers *(☎ 226 2939, 3-4 Queensferry St)* is close to the nightlife. Rates are £10 for a dorm bed or £13 per person in a double; the seventh night is free, and there's a free meal on Sunday.

Belford Youth Hostel *(☎ 225 6209, 6 Douglas Gardens)* is in a converted church and although some people have complained of noise, it's well run and cheerful with good facilities. Dorm beds cost £8.50.

Quiet ***Palmerston Lodge*** *(☎ 220 5141, 25 Palmerston Place)*, on the corner of Chester St, is in a listed building. There are no bunks, only single beds, and showers and toilets on every floor. The rates, which include a continental breakfast, start at £10 for a dorm bed; singles/doubles with bathroom are £30/40.

Women and married couples are welcome at the ***Kinnaird Christian Hostel*** *(☎ 225 3608, 13-14 Coates Crescent)* where beds in a Georgian house cost from £14. Singles/doubles cost £20/34.

Colleges Edinburgh has a large student population and during vacations colleges and universities offer accommodation on their campuses, though most are a fair way from the centre and cost as much as lower-end, more-central B&Bs.

Closest is ***Pollock Halls of Residence*** *(☎ 667 0662, 18 Holyrood Park Rd)*, which has Arthur's Seat as a backdrop. Modern (often noisy) single rooms cost from £23.90 per person including breakfast. ***Napier University*** *(☎ 455 4291)*, Colinton Rd (which runs south-west off Bruntsfield Place) in Craiglockhart offers B&B in summer from £18 per person. ***Queen Margaret College*** *(☎ 317 3310, 36 Clerwood Terrace)* is 3 miles west in Corstorphine near Edinburgh Zoo. From June to September, B&B with shared bathroom costs from £17.50.

B&Bs & Guesthouses
On a tight budget the best bet is a private house; get the TIC's free accommodation guide and phone around. Outside festival time you should get something for around £18, although it'll probably be a bus ride away in the suburbs.

Places in the centre aren't always good value if you have a car, since parking is restricted; when booking check whether the establishment has off-street parking.

Guesthouses are for the most part two or three pounds more expensive, and to get a private bathroom you can expect to pay around £25.

The main concentrations are around Pilrig St, Pilrig; Minto St (a southern continuation of North Bridge), Newington; and Gilmore Place and Leamington Terrace, Bruntsfield.

North of the New Town Pilrig St, left off Leith Walk has lots of guesthouses, all within about a mile of the centre. Take bus No 11 from Princes St or walk north from the east end of the street.

Balmoral Guest House (☎ 554 1857), No 32, is a comfortable terraced house with beds from £17 to £20 per person. Similar is the *Barrosa* (☎ 554 3700), No 21, where B&B costs from £19.50/23.50 without/with bath. At No 94, the attractive, detached, two-crown *Balquhidder Guest House* (☎ 554 3377) has rooms with bath from £18 to £30 a head. Next door, the larger *Balfour House* (☎ 554 2106) at No 92 has 19 mostly *en suite* rooms for £20/23 per person without/with bathroom.

There are several elegant places in Eyre Place, near Stockbridge and the Water of Leith, 1 mile from the centre. *Ardenlee Guest House* (☎ 556 2838), No 9, is a terraced Victorian townhouse with beds from £22 to £26 per person (£2 more for a private bath). The friendly, Georgian *Dene Guest House* (☎ 556 2700), No 7, has 10 rooms with B&B from £19.50/37 a single/double. If these are full try *Blairhaven Guest House* (☎ 556 3025), No 5, which does B&B from £18.

Newington There are lots of guesthouses on and around Minto St/Mayfield Gardens in Newington. It's south of the city centre and university on either side of the continuation of North/South Bridge, with plenty of buses to the centre. This is the main traffic artery from the south and carries traffic from the A7 and A68 (both routes are signposted). The best places are in the streets on either side of the main road.

Salisbury Guest House (☎ 667 1264, 45 Salisbury Rd), just east of Newington and 10 minutes from the centre by bus, is quiet, comfortable and nonsmoking. Rooms with private bath cost from £23 to £30 per person.

The welcoming, red sandstone *Avondale Guest House* (☎ 667 6779, 10 South Gray St), just west of Minto St, is a comfortable, traditional B&B with singles/doubles from £19/32.

In a quiet street, *Fairholme Guest House* (☎ 667 8645, 13 Moston Terrace), just east of Mayfield Gardens, is a pleasant Victorian villa with free parking. The range of rooms includes a single from £15.

Grange Guest House (☎ 667 2125, 2 Minto St), near the corner of Salisbury Rd, is a two storey, terrace house convenient for the centre, but only provides a continental breakfast. Rooms with shared bathroom cost £16/28 a single/double. One of the better guesthouses here is *Sherwood Guest House* (☎ 667 1200, 42 Minto St), a refurbished Georgian villa with off-road parking. B&B costs £25/40, or £40/64 with bathroom.

Millfield Guest House (☎ 667 4428, 12 Marchhall Rd), just east of Dalkeith Rd past Pollock Halls of Residence, is a pleasant, two-storey, Victorian house with singles/ doubles from £18/33.

Farther south, Kilmaurs Rd, also east of Dalkeith Rd, has several B&Bs. The spacious *Casa Buzzo* (☎ 667 8998), No 8, has two doubles for £16 per person with shared bathroom. If you prefer private facilities the nearby *Kenvie Guest House* (☎ 668 1964), No 16, has a couple of *en suite* rooms for £26/46 a single/double.

Bruntsfield Bruntsfield is less than a mile south-west of the centre; most places are on Gilmore Place and Leamington Terrace. Bus Nos 10 and 10A run to Gilmore Place from Princes St.

Busy *Averon Guest House* (☎ 229 9932, 44 Gilmore Place) has comfortable if small rooms from £20 per person. Named after a former gold-mining town in Australia, *Ballarat Guest House* (☎ 229 7024, 14 Gilmore Place) provides clean, nonsmoking rooms for £23 per person.

Menzies Guest House (☎ 229 4629, 33 Leamington Terrace) is well run and has rooms from £20 to £28 per person, though you only have one choice of breakfast cereal. The refurbished *Leaminton Guest House* (☎ 228 3879, 57 Leamington Terrace) has eight rooms, each with a different theme, and good breakfasts for £20/26 without/with bathroom.

There are several quiet guesthouses in Hartington Gardens, off Viewforth, itself off Bruntsfield Place. *Aaron Guest House*

(☎ 229 6459), at the end of the street, is handy for drivers since it has a private car park. Beds go for £20 to £35 per person in comfortable *en suite* rooms. The comfortable, friendly **Robertson Guest House** (☎ 229 2652), No 5, offers a good range of food at breakfast including yoghurt and fruit; and has rooms from £20 per person.

Hotels

Not surprisingly, the international hotels in the centre are extremely expensive, although there can be good deals outside summer, especially at weekends. Unless otherwise stated, rates include breakfast.

Old Town The **Thistle Inn Hotel** (☎ 220 2299, 94 Grassmarket) is in the heart of the Old Town in one of the city's nightlife centres. Singles/doubles with private bath and TV cost from £33/56. The entrance is next to Biddy Mulligan's pub, and every floor is accessible by lift. (Don't confuse it with the bigger, more expensive King James Thistle Hotel beside the shopping centre, off Leith St.)

The new **Ibis Hotel** (☎ 240 7000, 6 Hunter Square) is just off the Royal Mile, and offers a flat rate of £55 per room per night, but breakfast is an extra £5.25. The **Bank Hotel** (☎ 556 9043, 1 South Bridge) on the corner of the Royal Mile, has a good bar downstairs and singles/doubles for £70/100 including breakfast.

The **Holiday Inn Crowne Plaza** (☎ 557 9797, 80 High St) is a purpose-built hotel whose exterior mimics the Royal Mile's 16th century architecture. The interior is, nonetheless, as modern as you could hope for. Rates are from £125/145 a single/double.

New Town The **Old Waverley Hotel** (☎ 556 4648, 43 Princes St) has a prime site opposite Waverley station, and many rooms have castle views. Rooms with private bath cost from £90/144. The **Caledonian Hotel** (☎ 459 9988) at the west end of Princes St on the corner of Lothian Rd, is in a huge, sandstone building below the castle.

Singles/doubles cost £147/220 and hotel facilities include three restaurants.

Royal Terrace has a great position on the north side of Calton Hill, with views over Royal Terrace Gardens to Leith. **Ailsa Craig Hotel** (☎ 556 1022, 24 Royal Terrace) is a refurbished Georgian building where rooms, most with bath, cost from £30/55 a single/double. The **Claymore Hotel** (☎ 556 2693, 7 Royal Terrace), the **Halcyon** (☎ 556 1032, 8 Royal Terrace) and the **Adria Hotel** (☎ 556 7875, 11 Royal Terrace) are similar.

At the **Greenside Hotel** (☎ 557 0022, 9 Royal Terrace) the 15 huge rooms are each furnished differently, are all *en suite* and cost from £25 to £55 per person; snacks are available throughout the day. The swishest hotel and one of the best in Edinburgh is the **Royal Terrace Hotel** (☎ 557 3222, 18 Royal Terrace). It's full of fine furnishings and most rooms include a spa bath; it costs from £120/160 a single/double.

More personal than most hotels is the tastefully decorated **Sibbet House** (☎ 556 1078, 26 Northumberland St) where prices of £80 to £90 per person might include an impromptu bagpipe recital by your host.

The grand, traditional **Roxburghe Hotel** (☎ 225 3921, 38 Charlotte Square) is in one of Edinburgh's most prestigious locations. Rooms with bathroom cost from £100/135 a single/double.

North of the New Town The **Lovat Hotel** (☎ 556 2745, 5 Inverleith Terrace) near the Royal Botanic Garden is a small terrace hotel with off-street parking. Rooms cost £30/50. **Christopher North House Hotel** (☎ 225 2720, 6 Gloucester Place), Stockbridge, is a small, genteel Georgian hotel in a quiet area. Rooms cost from £40/60 a single/double, £60/100 with bathroom.

West End & Haymarket Good value given the location, the **West End Hotel** (☎ 225 3656, 35 Palmerston Place) has *en suite* rooms from £25 per person, and a bar with a wide selection of whiskies. **Rothesay Hotel** (☎ 225 4125, 8 Rothesay Place) is in a quiet, central street and has pleasantly spacious rooms, mostly with bathroom, from £30 to £80 per person.

There's a handy batch of mid-range places on Coates Gardens, off Haymarket Terrace near Haymarket train station. Comfortable *Boisdale Hotel* (☎ 337 1134), No 9, has rooms with private bath from £25 to £45 per person.

At the top of Coates Gardens in Eglinton Crescent, *Greens Hotel* (☎ 337 1565) at No 24 occupies four terrace houses and caters mostly to business people, but is reasonably priced from £35 per person.

Lothian Rd & Around The *Sheraton Grand Hotel* (☎ 229 9131, 1 Festival Square) is opposite the Royal Lyceum Theatre, off Lothian Rd, west of the castle. You pay for, and get, luxury. Rooms cost from £155/195. Farther south off Lothian Road the *Point Hotel* (☎ 221 5555, 34 Bread St) has a strikingly modern, stark, Art Deco interior, and a trendy café-bar. Rates are from £70/90.

Newington South of Holyrood Park, *Marchhall Hotel* (☎ 667 2743, 14-16 Marchhall Crescent), a three-storey Victorian terrace, offers B&B from £23 per person. *Thrums Hotel* (☎ 667 5545, 14 Minto St) is a small but popular place with off-street parking. B&B costs from £30 per person and it's advisable to book in advance. *Arthur's View Hotel* (☎ 667 3468) is on the corner of Mayfield Gardens and Bright's Crescent. Although its name is stretching credibility a bit, it's a friendly place with a private car park and evening meals. B&B costs from £40/70 a single/double.

Bruntsfield Hotels here have the advantage of being close to Bruntsfield Links and Meadow Park and to some good eateries.

Next to the SYHA hostel, the *Nova Hotel* (☎ 447 6437, 5 Bruntsfield Crescent) is in a quiet, three-storey Victorian terrace, with views across the links. Its 12 *en suite* rooms cost from £35.

Bruntsfield Hotel (☎ 229 1393) on the corner of Bruntsfield Place and Leamington Terrace charges £89/125 a single/double, but has a standby rate of £50 per person for the first night and other specials.

PLACES TO EAT

There are good-value restaurants and cafés scattered all round the city. For cheap eats, the best areas are Union Place, near the Playhouse Theatre; around Grassmarket, just south of the castle; near the university around Nicolson St, the extension of North/South Bridge, and in Bruntsfield. Most restaurants offer cheap set menus at lunchtime. Many close on Sunday evening, so ring ahead to make sure.

Royal Mile & Around

Despite being a tourist Mecca, the Royal Mile has lots of good-value, enjoyable eating oases.

Restaurants The excellent, small *Polo Fusion* (☎ 622 7722, 503 Lawnmarket) is reasonably priced by Edinburgh standards, and specialises in Asian dishes. Noodle dishes are good value at £5.50 to £6.50.

Viva Mexico (☎ 226 5145, Cockburn St) is a cheerful restaurant with a good atmosphere. Some tables have views across to the New Town, and the food is good quality. Nachos cost from £2.50, burritos from £8.95.

Doric Wine Bar & Bistro (☎ 225 1084, 15 Market St) has a good-value bar menu (meals from £2.50 to £3.50) from noon to 6.30 pm. The small upstairs bistro offers classic Scottish dishes like haggis, neeps and tatties for £8.95.

Pleasant *Black Bo's* (☎ 557 6136, 57 Blackfriars St) offers an imaginative vegetarian menu. Mains like mushrooms and olives in filo pastry cost around £8.95.

You can sample traditional Scottish cooking at the *Grange* (☎ 558 9992, 267 Canongate) where three-course lunches are £9.95; in the evening, venison in a prune and wine glaze costs £15.35. *Dubh Prais* (☎ 557 5732, 123 High St), considered one of the best places to try Scottish cuisine, is popular with locals and tourists. The menu features dishes like asparagus and parmesan risotto for £4.90 and aubergine with goat's cheese for £9.90.

Cafés *Deacon's House Café*, down Brodie's Close, serves traditional Scottish food like Dundee cake or Scottish salmon sandwiches for £3.95.

Patisserie Florentin (St Giles St) attracts a rather self-consciously Bohemian crowd, but has excellent light meals and pastries; filled baguettes are £3 and good coffee £1. It stays open till the early hours during the festival period.

The enormously popular *Elephant House* (☎ 220 5355, 21 George IV Bridge) is a café with delicious pastries, newspapers, some of the best variety of coffee and tea (£1.70) in Edinburgh ... and lots of elephants. *Lower Aisle Restaurant*, beneath St Giles' Cathedral in Parliament Square, is peaceful outside peak lunchtimes. Soup and a roll cost £1.50. *Elephant's Sufficiency* (☎ 220 0666, 170 High St) is a bustling lunch spot. Try the Orkney burger for £3.75. Open daily *Bann's Vegetarian Café* (Hunter Square), behind the Tron Kirk, is a relaxed Art Deco place. Most mains are under £7; vegetarian haggis with creamed turnip tartlets is £6.50.

Gustos Café (☎ 558 3083, 105 High St) does delicious gourmet sandwiches from £1.95. *Netherbow Theatre Café*, beside John Knox's House, serves cheap breakfasts in an outdoor courtyard until noon, then lunches (big portions), salads and quiche for £3.15.

Clarinda's Tea Room (69 Canongate) lurks at the quieter Holyrood end of the Mile. There are a variety of teas from 50p and delicious cakes from 93p. *Brambles Tearoom*, close to Huntly House, does soup and a roll for £1.50 and has a good selection of cakes.

Grassmarket

The lively pubs and restaurants on the north side of Grassmarket cater to a young crowd – it's a good starting point for a night out.

Ristorante Gennaro (☎ 226 3706, 64 Grassmarket) has standard Italian fare, with minestrone at £2.20, cannelloni at £6.20 and pizzas from £4.70 to £7. Popular *Mamma's Pizzas* (☎ 225 6464, 28 Grassmarket) does fine pizzas with imaginative toppings (from £3.95).

Pierre Victoire (☎ 226 2442, 38 Grassmarket) is part of the chain that serves good-value French food. There's also a branch at 10 Victoria St, which curves up to George IV Bridge from the north-east corner of Grassmarket. Also part of Pierre's empire, *Beppe Vittorio* (☎ 226 7267, 7 Victoria St) follows the same formula – authentic, good-value food – although in this case it's Italian. You can mix and match sauces and pastas from £5.

New Town

The New Town is neither particularly well endowed with eating places nor a particularly interesting part of town at night, but there are a few reasonable options, especially in Hanover and Frederick Sts.

Restaurants *Henderson's* (☎ 225 2131) downstairs at 94 Hanover St is an Edinburgh institution which has been churning out vegetarian food for more than 30 years. Hot dishes start at £3.50 but it's worth checking if there's a lunch or dinner special.

At No 110, *Gringo Bill's* (☎ 220 1205) is a good Mexican restaurant which serves food with an off-beat sense of humour. It does a huge meal and a drink at lunchtime for £5. *Bar Napoli* (☎ 225 2600), No 75, is a cheerful Italian restaurant, open until 3 am, with pasta and pizza for £4 to £6. Another reliable Italian option, the traditional *Alfredo's* (☎ 226 6090), No 109, is good value for money; it offers a three-course lunch for £4.95, and lets you BYO beer.

Chez Jules (☎ 225 7893, 61 Frederick St) is a Pierre Victoire spin-off offering similar simple, cheap, but good-quality French food. A three-course lunch is £5.90. In the same French vein there's a branch of the popular *Café Rouge* (☎ 225 4515, 43 Frederick St); lamb casserole here is £7.95.

Below street level, *Vito's Ristorante* (*☎ 225 5052, 55 Frederick St*), is a busy Italian restaurant specialising in seafood served in large portions. King prawns in garlic cost £5.95.

The long-standing *Singapura Restaurant* (*☎ 538 7878, 69 North Castle St*) serves an array of excellent Malaysian and Singaporian food while also offering a five-course banquet for £17.90. It's closed on Sunday.

Cafés Midway along Princes St are two pleasant cafés. On the 2nd floor of Waterstone's bookshop, near the corner of South Charlotte St overlooking Princes St, is a branch of the *Starbucks* chain, with good coffee. Nearby, *Bewley's Café* (*☎ 220 1969, 4 South Charlotte St*) is a branch of the traditional Irish chain. Sandwiches are £1.95 to £2.50, pastries £1.20; it also serves lunch and breakfast.

At the western end of Princes St on the corner of Lothian Rd, below St John's Church, *Cornerstone Coffee House* (*☎ 229 0212*), has good views of the castle and St Cuthbert's Church.

At the east end of Princes St the French-style *Delifrance* (*☎ 557 4171, 1 Waterloo Place*), does reasonably priced, good food; baguettes are £3.25 to £4.20. More upmarket French food is provided by *Café 1812* (*☎ 556 5766, 29 Waterloo Place*) with great views of Calton Hill and good-value two-course lunches for £5.40.

While you're in the Scottish National Portrait Gallery, Queen St, check out the delicious home-baked cooking at its *Queen Street Café*, open from 10 am to 4.30 pm.

The popular *Hard Rock Café* (*☎ 260 3000, 20 George St*) has huge burger meals for around £9.

Fast Food Princes St is the main area in Edinburgh for fast food. There are the usual international chains like *Burger King* plus food courts in Waverley train station, at the bottom level of Waverley Market shopping centre and in St James shopping centre.

Leith Walk & Broughton St

Restaurants A number of places on Leith Walk pitch for Playhouse Theatre-goers, including several Italian options. Pick of the bunch is friendly, informal *Giuliano's*

Edinburgh Oyster Bars

Dotted around Edinburgh are a number of oyster bars, part of a chain operated by Oyster Bar Enterprises whose head office (☎ 554 6200) is at 1 Quayside St in Leith. The bars are all casual places where you can eat or drink daily from noon till late, and the menu includes beef and chicken dishes as well. Half a dozen Loch Fyne oysters cost £4.60, snacks like nachos £4.20.

The largest of the chain is St James Oyster Bar (☎ 557 2925), 2 Calton Rd, down some steps below the Black Bull pub opposite the St James shopping centre. The Queen St Oyster Bar (☎ 226 2530), 16A Queen St, on the corner of Hanover St is more intimate. In the West End the West End Oyster Bar (☎ 225 2530) can be found at 28 West Maitland St near Haymarket station. The Bare Story (☎ 556 3953), 55 Cowgate, an anagram of the name, is a popular student hangout. Finally, Leith Oyster Bar (☎ 554 6294), 12 Burgess St, is near the Malt & Hops pub in Leith.

All of them serve real ale, while the St James has a juke box and the Queen St and West End bars have live music on weekends.

Of course, these aren't the only oyster bars in town and one of the best of the rest is at the Café Royal Bar (☎ 556 4124), 17 West Register St, in beautiful Victorian surroundings.

(☎ 556 6590, 18 Union Place) opposite the theatre. It's open to 2 am, and serves pasta and pizza for under £6. *Ferri's Italiano Pizzeria* (☎ 556 5592, 1 Antigua St) does pasta and pizza at similar prices, and has a good vegetarian selection.

Pierre Victoire (☎ 557 8451, 8 Union St) offers a relaxed style and main courses for around £8.

Cafés & Bars The informal *Café Libra* (☎ 556 9602), downstairs at 5A Union St, has all-day breakfasts for £4 and walls covered in posters advertising the latest events.

Nearby, Broughton St has a couple of organic food shops and a few interesting low-cost café-bars, that are good for a drink as well as a meal, and are especially busy on weekends.

The busy *Basement Bar* (☎ 557 0097, 10A Union St) has reasonable prices and opens from noon to 1 am. Most dishes are under £4.50 and its weekend Mexican menu is especially popular. *Blue Moon Café (36A Union St)* is a gay café but straights are welcome. It has a wide selection of dishes including vegetarian. Boldly painted in orange and purple, *Baroque* (☎ 557 0627, 39-41 Union St) is hard to miss. In fine weather it has tables outside and serves fare like toasted baguettes (£3.95) and salads (£2.95).

West End

Restaurants A few places on Dalry Rd are convenient for those staying in or near the West End. *Howie's Restaurant* (☎ 313 3334, 63 Dalry Rd) is so popular that advance booking is wise. A two-course lunch is a bargain at £6.95. House specialities include banoffi pie. At the north end of Dalry Rd, the *Verandah Restaurant* (☎ 337 5828), No 17, is an excellent tandoori restaurant with tasty food and three-course lunches for £5.95.

Raffaelli's (☎ 225 6060, 10 Randolph Place) is one of Edinburgh's top Italian restaurants, but its pastas are reasonably priced at £4.50 to £7.50.

Cafés & Bars *Ryan's Café-Bar* (☎ 226 7005), on the corner of Hope and Queensferry Sts, has an Irish name but is very much in the style of a Parisian street café. The food is a mix of traditional and French. Mussels in garlic cost £4.95. The *Granary*, next door on Queensferry St, is rather like a down-market Hard Rock Café, but is noted for its burger meals (£5.95) and the portions are generous.

Stockbridge & Around

Village-like, sleepy Stockbridge is popular with the young and affluent and has some interesting eateries.

Restaurants Upmarket *Lancers* (☎ 332 3444, 5 Hamilton Place) is reputed to be one of Edinburgh's best Indian restaurants; the food is mostly North Indian and mains like tandoori murgh (roasted chicken) cost £6.95 to £12.95.

Pizza Express (☎ 332 7229, 1 Deanhaugh St) overlooking the Water of Leith, offers above average pizzas from £3.85. Small *Passepartout* (☎ 332 4476, 24 Deanhaugh St) takes its name from Jules Verne's *Around the World in 80 Days* and reflects its international menu. A three-course dinner costs £6.

The *Watershed* (☎ 557 0627, 44 St Stephen St) is popular and serves good inexpensive food, some of it traditional like sausage and mash (£5.50), some of it more Mediterranean like seafood pasta (£4.85).

Near Stockbridge, *Ducks at Le Marché Noir* (☎ 558 1608, 2-4 Eyre Place) is a gourmet French-Scottish restaurant with mains like confit of duck for £12.25 to £17. Next door, the Spanish *Tapas Olé* (☎ 556 2754, 10 Eyre Place) mostly serves the dishes for which it is named; seafood tapas are £3 to £5, vegetarian ones £2 to £4.

Cafés & Bars *Caffe Italia* (☎ 332 3864, 1 Raeburn Place) on the corner of Dean St is a popular trattoria where pastas cost a modest £4 to £6. It's closed Sunday. *Patisserie Florentin* (☎ 220 0225, 5 North West Circus Place) has excellent quiche, pastries and coffee like its sister shop off the Royal Mile.

River Café (☎ 332 3322, 36 Deanhaugh St) offers ample all-day breakfasts for £2.75, but also includes a small range of Persian specialities.

The *Bailie Bar* (☎ 225 4673, 2 St Stephen St) has an excellent moderately priced, varied menu; stuffed baked aubergine is £4.85.

Lothian Rd & Around

Restaurants A few places around the southern end of Lothian Rd cater for the Royal Lyceum Theatre's clientele. Big, jolly *Dario's Pizzeria Ristorante* (☎ 229 9625, 85 Lothian Rd) opens until 5 am daily. Set lunches cost £4 and pasta and pizzas start from around £5.

Opposite the theatre, *Jasmine* (☎ 229 5757, 32 Grindlay St) has excellent Chinese cooking, especially seafood. You can eat well for under £15. A weekday three-course lunch costs only £6.

Lazio (☎ 229 7788, 95 Lothian Rd) has won awards for its pizzas and pastas (£4.80 to £6.20); it opens from noon onwards.

Cafés & Bars The *Starbucks* café on the corner of Lothian Rd and Bread St has a simple decor, a relaxed atmosphere and a variety of coffees and teas.

Open till late, *Uluru* (☎ 228 5407, 133 Lothian Rd) is a café-bar whose name and decor are Australian inspired. Pizzas cost from £3.20 and sandwiches £2.95; there's also a good selection of teas and coffees.

The *Monboddo* café-bar in the Point Hotel (☎ 221 5555, 34 Bread St), off Lothian Rd, is stylish but reasonably priced. Main dishes from the extensive menu cost £5.50.

Bruntsfield

There's a batch of moderately-priced eateries on Home and Leven Sts (which lead to Bruntsfield Place), but some of the more interesting places are farther south around the junction of Bruntsfield Place, Montpelier Park and Murchison Place.

Restaurants *Efes* (☎ 229 7833, 42 Leven St) sells various Turkish kebabs and pizzas. They're cheaper to take away but if you eat in, a doner kebab costs £6.50. *Caley's Bistro* (☎ 622 7170, 32 Leven St) provides contemporary Scottish cuisine, with its three-course lunch great value at £6.75. You can bring your own alcohol.

Jacques' Bistro (☎ 229 6080, 8 Gillespie Place) is a cosy French restaurant catering to the King's Theatre crowd. It offers a pre/post-theatre, two-course meal and coffee for £8.90.

Parrots (☎ 229 3252, 3 Viewforth), off Bruntsfield Place, is a deservedly popular nonsmoking restaurant selling excellent-value evening meals in very pleasant parrot-themed surroundings. The extensive menu offers everything from baltis for £5.95, to mushroom and nut fettucine for £3.75. It's even possible to eat alone here without feeling like a leper. It's closed Sunday and Monday.

Montpelier's (☎ 229 3115, 159 Bruntsfield Place) serves cappuccinos and cakes all day, and excellent Scottish breakfasts. The interesting dinner menu includes swordfish in mango sauce for £8.95. *La Grande Cafetière* (☎ 228 1188) opposite, is similar; it serves delicious meals for around £5.25 and agreeably wicked desserts.

There's a branch of *Howie's Restaurant* (☎ 221 1777, 208 Bruntsfield Place) in an old bank (see West End earlier in this chapter).

Cafés *Ramsden's Luncherie* (Bruntsfield Place) is a basic, friendly café with breakfasts for £2.30. The large *Estate Coffee Lounge* on Leven St opposite the King's Theatre has posters advertising the latest happenings. Sandwiches are £2 and the coffee is good.

On Home St, colourful *Filfila* serves mostly Middle Eastern food. Meals are filling but perhaps not as flavoursome as you'd expect. Beef with couscous is £3.60 and it has a good vegetarian selection. Young people are continually dropping into *Ndebele* (☎ 221 1141, 57 Home St), opposite, which serves healthy, good-value, tasty South African style food; sugar bean stroganoff is £3.50.

University

There are lots of places near the university. Many student favourites are between Nicolson St and Bristo Place at the end of George IV Bridge.

Restaurants *Kebab Mahal* (☎ 667 5214), in Nicolson Square, is a legendary source of cheap sustenance with excellent kebabs from £2.25, and curries from £3.25. You sit at a counter bathed in fluorescent light.

Vegetarian *Susie's Diner* (☎ 667 8729), in West Nicolson St (west off Nicolson St) has good, inexpensive food – mains costs £3.45 to £4.75 – and a belly dancer for entertainment in the evenings. Pigs feature in the decor at *Pigs Bistro* (☎ 667 6676, 41 West Nicolson St) but not on the diverse menu. Lunchtime mains are good value – chicken enchilada costs £3.95.

Spartan *Khushi's* (☎ 556 8996, 16 Drummond St) is the original Edinburgh curry house and little has changed since it opened in 1947. You can bring your pint in from the pub next door. Lamb bhuna at £4.60 is said to be the local favourite.

Kalpna (☎ 667 9890, 2 St Patrick's Square) is a highly acclaimed, reasonably priced Gujarati (Indian) vegetarian restaurant. Each week on Wednesday night it lays on a gourmet buffet (£8.95) of 20 dishes from a different region of India.

Cafés & Bars *Nile Valley Café* (☎ 667 8200), on Potterow, serves an interesting mix of Mediterranean and Sudanese food; you can bring your own beer. Mains cost £6 to £8. *Negociant's* (☎ 225 6313, 45 Lothian St) is a very hip café and music venue with good-value food – main courses cost around £6.50. The basement bar opens until 3 am.

Newington & Around

If you're staying in Minto St or Mayfield Gardens, you need to head back toward the centre to find several good choices on either side of the main road.

Restaurants *Chinese Home Cooking* (☎ 668 4946, 34 West Preston St) is an inexpensive BYO restaurant with spartan décor but filling, tasty food. Its three-course lunch is a real bargain at £4.

There's another branch of *Howie's Restaurant* (☎ 668 2917, 75 St Leonard's St) near the corner of Montague St.

La Bonne Vie (☎ 622 9111, 113 Buccleuch St) is a highly regarded French restaurant specialising in vegetarian and seafood. Vegetarian strudel is £5.75 and smoked haddock £6. Nearby at No 79 is *King's Balti* (☎ 622 9212, 79 Buccleuch St), a large BYO balti restaurant with a wide selection of dishes including vegetarian ones. Three-course lunch specials cost £6.95.

Cafés The *Metropole* (☎ 668 4999, 33 Newington Rd), a good place to relax with a newspaper, magazine or book, serves a wide choice of coffees and teas from 85p, plus delicious pies and pastries. *Isabel's Café* (☎ 662 4014, 83 South Clerk St) sells tasty, inexpensive vegetarian/vegan snacks and meals. Pasta and green vegetable bake is £3.50.

ENTERTAINMENT

For full coverage of films, theatre, cabaret, music and clubs, buy the *List* (£1.90) Edinburgh's and Glasgow's fortnightly events guide.

Theatre & Music

Probably because of the frantic festival activity, Edinburgh has more than its fair share of theatres in relation to its population size.

The *Edinburgh Festival Theatre* (☎ 529 6000, 13-29 Nicolson St) stages everything from ballet to the Chippendales. The *Royal Lyceum Theatre* (☎ 229 9697), opposite Festival Square, hosts concerts, children's shows and ballet. Nearby, the architecturally impressive *Usher Hall* (☎ 228 1155) puts on classical and popular concerts. Beside Usher Hall, *Traverse Theatre* (☎ *228 1404, Cambridge St*) is noted for its production of experimental drama.

The small *Netherbow Theatre* (☎ *556 9579, 43-45 High St*), on the Royal Mile, features modern drama, cabaret and children's story-telling. The program at slightly run-down *King's Theatre* (☎ *220 4349, 2 Leven St*), Bruntsfield, often features revivals. The restored *Playhouse Theatre* (☎ *557 2590, 18-22 Greenside Place*) in Leith Walk stages musicals, dance shows and Christmas pantomimes.

Tickets can be purchased from Ticketline (☎ 220 4349).

Cinema

Filmhouse (☎ *228 2688, 88 Lothian Rd*) is an excellent arthouse cinema which shows foreign, offbeat and current but less commercial films. Near Tollcross, the *Cameo Cinema* (☎ *228 4141, 38 Home St*) has late-night cult screenings as well as showing independent and arthouse films. Entry is £4. For mainstream films there's the *ABC Cinema* (☎ *228 1638, 120 Lothian Rd*).

Pubs

Edinburgh has over 700 pubs and bars which are as varied as the population ...

everything from Victorian palaces to rough and ready drinking holes.

Royal Mile & Around The pubs on the Royal Mile aren't very inspiring, although there are some classics along the side streets. The *Jolly Judge* (☎ *225 2669, 7A James Court*) retains its distinctive 17th century character, has live music and a cheering fire in cold weather. *Malt Shovel Inn* (☎ *225 6843, 11-15 Cockburn St*) has a good range of beers and whiskies and jazz on Tuesday nights.

One of Edinburgh's most entertaining pubs is the *Ceilidh House* (☎ *220 1500*), below the Tron Tavern, Hunter Square. It's home to the Edinburgh Folk Club. Most nights, there are informal, but high-quality, jam sessions. Entry to the more formal sessions is £7. The *Hebrides Bar* (☎ *220 4213, 17 Market St*) provides a mix of Scottish and Irish folk music, Friday and Saturday night; on Sunday afternoon anyone is invited to play.

Instead of watching TV you can sit and see the comings and goings along the Mile from the trendy *Logie Baird's Bar*, on the corner of High St and South Bridge.

The *Tass* (☎ *556 6338*), on the corner of High and St Mary's Sts, has guest ales each week and traditional Scottish music on

---

Give me a Firkin Pint!

To supplement the many traditional Scottish pubs and the growing number of trendy café-bars, Edinburgh has been invaded by theme pubs.

There are Irish pubs, like O'Neill's, on Hanover St, where they pull a good, slow pint of Guinness and put on folk music. There are Australian theme pubs like Bar Oz, on Forrest Rd, a big barn of a place, with clocks showing current times in Australia and New Zealand, and mileposts with distances to towns and suburbs in those countries. And of course, they sell antipodean as well as local beers.

You'll also see a number of pubs with 'Firkin' in the name; these are all part of a chain. The Physician & Firkin (☎ 662 4746), 58 Dalkieth Rd on the corner of Salisbury Rd in Newington, is the main one. It houses the brewery which supplies the Firkin beer for the other Firkin pubs – the Fiscal & Firkin, 7 Hunter Square off the Royal Mile; Fling & Firkin, 49 Rose St in the New Town; and Footlights & Firkin, 7 Spittal St, just south of the castle.

For those who don't know, a firkin is a small wooden barrel.

Thursday and Saturday night and Sunday afternoon. Opposite is the *World's End* (☎ 556 3628) where part of the Flodden Wall can still be seen in the basement.

Grassmarket & Around Traditional *Bow Bar* (☎ 226 7667, 80 West Bow) is a popular pub serving real ales and a huge collection of malt whiskies. Despite its picturesque name, the *Last Drop* (☎ 225 4851, 74 Grassmarket) actually commemorates the executions that used to take place nearby.

The *White Hart* (☎ 226 2688, 34 Grassmarket) is another traditional pub once visited by Robbie Burns. The *Fiddlers Arms* (☎ 229 2665, 9-11 Grassmarket) is an unpretentious pub with old fiddles lining the walls and live music during the week.

There's a couple of cheerful, friendly places on Cowgate. The *Green Tree* (☎ 225 1294, 182 Cowgate) is a student hang-out and one of Edinburgh's few pubs with a beer garden. *Bannerman's* (☎ 556 3254, 212 Cowgate) attracts students, locals and backpackers, and there's often live music or disco.

Greyfriars Bobby's Bar (☎ 225 8328, 34 Candlemaker Row) is popular with students and tourists, and serves inexpensive meals. *Peartree House* (☎ 667 7533, 38 West Nicolson St) is another student favourite partly because of the reasonably priced food, but also for the large outdoor courtyard which fills up in fine weather.

New Town & Around Rose St may have lots of pubs, but they're not all worth frequenting. One exception is the *Abbotsford* (☎ 225 5276, 3 Rose St), which has Victorian décor and a restaurant. Another is the *Rose St Brewery* (☎ 220 1227, 55 Rose St), which has a good range of beers, most brewed on the premises.

At the western end in Hope St between Princes St and Charlotte Square, *Whigham's Wine Cellars* (☎ 225 9717) is an old (and pricey) wine bar.

It's worth sticking your nose through the door of the *Café Royal Bar* (☎ 556 1884, 17 West Register St) to see its amazing stained-glass windows, Victorian interior and ceramic portraits of famous people. In Andrew St, *Tiles Bar-Bistro* (☎ 558 1507) is similarly lavish.

In stylish Broughton St, the friendly *Basement Bar* (☎ 557 0097, 10A Broughton St) is one of Edinburgh's busiest bars and the music (jazz funk, hip hop etc) is loud. By contrast, *Mathers* (☎ 556 6754, 25 Broughton St) is good for a quiet drink, and has inexpensive real ales and a huge selection of malts.

The *Wally Dug* (☎ 556 3271, 32 Northumberland St), is a small pub with cask conditioned ales where workers gather at the end of the day to wind down. Its name translates as 'woolly dog'.

At *Harry's Bar* (☎ 539 8100), downstairs at 7B Randolph Place, in the West End, you can drink (and eat) in the evenings until late.

Stockbridge Trendy *Maison Hector* (☎ 332 5328, 47 Deanhaugh St) is a café-bar with live music on Thursday nights from 10 pm to 1 am, and jazz on Sunday from 4.30 pm. The long-established *Antiquary* (☎ 225 2858, 72-78 St Stephen St), popular with students and locals, offers folk music on Thursday nights, when all comers are welcome to perform. The relaxed *Bailie Bar* (☎ 225 4673, 2 Stephen St) attracts a mixed clientele and serves good pub grub.

Bruntsfield *Bennet's Bar* (☎ 229 5143, 8 Leven St) beside the King's Theatre is a Victorian pub whose chief feature is the large curved mirrors with the tiled surrounds. Decorated with golfing memorabilia, *Ye Olde Golf Tavern* (☎ 229 5040, 30 Wright's Houses) dates from 1486 and overlooks Bruntsfield Links. The *Auld Toll* (☎ 229 1010, 39 Leven St) is an old unpretentious pub serving real ales.

Clubs

Old Town The Old Town has the largest concentration of nightclubs. There are some interesting music/club venues in old vaults under the George IV and South Bridges.

The **Vaults** (☎ *558 9052, 15 Niddry St*), under South Bridge, has a variety of reliable club nights offering reggae, rap and rhythm and blues. On the same street, **Whistle Binkie's** (☎ *557 5114*) has been around a long time and provides live music nightly till 3 am.

Venue Night Club (☎ *557 3073, 15 Calton Rd*) has live music and is well worth checking out. Its fortnightly **Disco Inferno** is one of the favourite sessions with disco music on three floors. It's open from 10 pm to 3 am and entry is £6.

It's a bit hard to know where to slot the **City Café** (☎ *220 0125, 19 Blair St*). It's a seriously cool bar, but there are also meals, and downstairs there's a dance floor, *City 2*, with different music depending on the night.

There are several clubs around the junction of Blair St and Cowgate. The **Honeycomb** (☎ *220 4381, 36-38A Blair St*) has a good range of music nights which includes house, garage, groove, disco and soul. The **Subway** (☎ *225 6766*), on Cowgate, has different music themes each night. Next door, **Legends** (☎ *225 8382*) has live bands on most nights; entry is £3 to £5. The **Kitchen** (☎ *226 6550, 233 Cowgate*) has a variety of performances including live bands and comedy acts.

New Town & West End Below Chez Jules' restaurant in Frederick St, **Fingers Piano Bar** (☎ *225 3026*) dishes up a mix of rock, pop and blues nightly till 3 am. Also in Frederick St, **Club 30** (☎ *220 1226*), for the over 25s, has disco music from the 1970s, 80s and 90s.

At the **Catwalk** (☎ *225 5583*), Broughton St, it's a blend of funk, garage and house from 9 pm to 1 am.

In the West End, **CC Blooms** (☎ *556 9331, 23-24 Greenside Place*) is a gay pub with a free club downstairs open from 11 pm to 3 am offering dance and house music. **Walkers** (☎ *476 7613, 12 Shandwick Place*) has a happy hour from 4 to 8 pm, free entry till 10.30 pm and DJs till 3 am.

Scottish Evenings

Several places offer an evening of eating, singing and dancing. The **Carlton Highland Hotel** (☎ *0131-472 3000*), North Bridge, has a *Hail Caledonia* night for £35.50 which includes five courses, entertainment and a nip of whisky. The action kicks off at 7.30 pm and ends around 10.20 pm, depending on how much the audience gets into the swing of things.

SPECTATOR SPORTS

Edinburgh has two rival football (soccer) teams that both play in the Scottish Premier Division: Heart of Midlothian (Hearts) and Hibernian (Hibs). Hearts' home ground is Tynecastle Park (☎ 337 6132), south-west of the centre on Gorgie Rd. The home ground of Hibs is Easter Rd Park (☎ 652 0630), about 1¼ miles east of the centre, north of London Rd.

International rugby union matches are played at Murrayfield Stadium (☎ 346 5000), about 1½ miles west of the centre and south of Corstorphine Rd.

Most other spectator sports, including athletics and cycling, are played at Meadowbank Sports Centre (☎ 661 5351), 139 London Rd.

Horse racing enthusiasts need to head 6 miles east to Musselburgh Racecourse (☎ 665 2859), where meetings occur throughout the year.

SHOPPING

Princes St, George St and the streets around them form Edinburgh's main shopping precinct. Princes St has many of the standard British High St stores. It also has two large shopping centres: the sprawling St James, just off its eastern end in Leith St, and the more upmarket Waverley Market, next to the train station. On the corner of David St, holding its own against this retail onslaught is Jenners (☎ 225 2442), the world's oldest independent department store. Opened in 1838 it sells a range of quality goods.

Behind Princes St, narrow and partly pedestrianised Rose St has lots of small, speciality craft shops. Les Cadeaux (☎ 225 9120), 121 Rose St, is one of Edinburgh's leading stores selling china and crystal. Tiso's (☎ 225 9486), 115 Rose St, is an excellent, well-stocked outdoor equipment shop.

George St has a number of upmarket stores. Aitken & Niven (☎ 225 1461), at No 79, is a clothing outfitter which specialises in tweeds, while the long-established Hamilton & Inches (☎ 225 4898), at No 87, sells antique and modern silver and gold jewellery.

North-west of the New Town, Stockbridge has some charming boutique and antique shops including Mon Trésor (☎ 220 6877), 35 St Stephen St, which has a wide range of antiques.

In the Old Town, the Royal Mile is the most tourist oriented shopping area, but it does offer a good selection of tartans, tweeds, whiskies and crafts. Hector Russell (☎ 558 1254), 137 High St, is a specialist kiltmaker; if you want one made, it will cost from £345. John Morrison (☎ 225 8149), 461 Lawnmarket, supplies tweeds and tartans, and can give you an off the peg kilt for £190. Royal Mile Whiskies (☎ 225 3383), 379 High St, offers a wide range of malt whiskies and miniatures.

Steep, curving Victoria St/West Bow, between the Royal Mile and Grassmarket, has some interesting shops. Byzantium (☎ 225 1768), 9A Victoria St, a flea market, is a great place to buy all sorts of things but we can't recommend the buffet in the upstairs café.

Along Bank St off Lawnmarket, Coda Music (☎ 622 7246) has a wide selection of CDs and tapes including a good selection of Scottish folk and traditional music. South-east of the Old Town in St Leonard's, Scayles Music (☎ 667 8341), 40-42 West Crosscauseway, sells, hires out and repairs musical instruments.

GETTING THERE & AWAY
Air
Edinburgh airport (☎ 333 1000), 6½ miles west of the city, has numerous services to other parts of the UK, Ireland and Europe and a limited number of services to Africa, the Middle East and Asia. Flights from North America arrive via Glasgow. Air UK (☎ 344 3325), British Airways (☎ 0345-222111) and British Midland (☎ 344 3302) have frequent services.

Bus
Buses from London are very competitive and you may be able to get cheap promotional tickets. See the Glasgow chapter; prices are the same and the journey to Edinburgh takes about 7½ hours.

There are numerous links with cities in England, including Newcastle (2¾ hours, £8 one way) and York (5½ hours, £20.25 one way).

Buses and coaches leave from St Andrew Square bus station where Scottish Citylink has an inquiry and ticket counter. Scottish Citylink (☎ 0990-505050) has buses to virtually every major town in Scotland. Most west-coast towns are reached via Glasgow. There are numerous buses to Glasgow, with peak/off-peak returns for £7/5, and to St Andrews, Aberdeen and Inverness.

Train
The main train station is Waverley in the heart of the city, although most trains also stop at Haymarket station, convenient for the West End.

Edinburgh Rail Travel Centre at Waverley station opens Monday to Saturday from 8 am to 11 pm, Sunday 9 am to 8 pm. For rail inquires, phone ☎ 0345-484950.

There are up to 20 trains a day from London's King's Cross; apart from Apex fares they're expensive, but they're quicker and more comfortable than buses.

ScotRail has two northern lines from Edinburgh: one that cuts across the Grampians to Inverness (3½ hours) and on to Thurso, and another that follows the coast to Aberdeen (three hours) and on to Inverness. All services are nonsmoking.

There are numerous trains to Glasgow (50 minutes, £7.10).

Car & Motorcycle

Glasgow is 46 miles west of Edinburgh on the M8. North from Edinburgh the A90 crosses the Firth of Forth on the Forth Rd Bridge into Fife from where it continues to Perth as the M90. The A1 runs east to the coast near Dunbar then follows it south to Newcastle upon Tyne. The A7 passes through the central Borders and skirts eastern Dumfries & Galloway before arriving in Carlisle. The A71 heads south-west to Kilmarnock.

GETTING AROUND
To/From the Airport

Frequent LRT buses run from Waverley Bridge near the train station to Haymarket and the airport, taking 35 minutes and costing £3.20/5 one way/return. Guide Friday's (☎ 556 2244) Air Bus Express provides a similar service. A taxi costs around £14 one way.

Bus

Bus services are frequent and cheap, but two main companies, Lothian Regional Transport (LRT) and Scottish Motor Traction (SMT), compete on some services and their tickets aren't interchangeable. SMT operates much of the service between Edinburgh and the Lothians. LRT is the main operator within Edinburgh, but also runs buses to East Lothian. You can buy tickets when you board buses, but on LRT buses you must have exact change.

For short trips on LRT, fares are 50p to 65p. A Day Saver (£2.20), available from bus drivers when you board, covers a whole day's travel. After midnight there are special night buses. The free *Edinburgh Travelmap* shows the most important services and is available from the TIC, or during weekdays from Traveline (☎ 225 3858 or ☎ 0800-232323), 2 Cockburn St, which has information on all of Edinburgh's public transport.

Train

Edinburgh doesn't have its own separate rail network. Those running through the city are part of the national rail system. Trains heading west and north link Waverley station with Haymarket, but it's cheaper to catch a bus down Princes St. Trains east to North Berwick stop at Musselburgh and Prestonpans.

Taxi

There are numerous central taxi ranks and costs are reasonable; £6 will get you almost anywhere. Local companies include Capital Taxis (☎ 228 2555), Central Radio Taxis (☎ 229 2468), City (☎ 228 1211) and Radiocabs (☎ 225 9000).

Car & Motorcycle

Though useful for day trips beyond the city, a car in central Edinburgh is as much a millstone as a convenience. There is restricted access on Princes St, George St and Shandwicke Place and a number of streets are one-way. On-street parking Monday to Saturday from 8 am to 6 pm is limited and meters expensive. Cars parked illegally may be towed away. The TIC has a map of off-street car parks, but these are expensive.

Motorcycles can be parked for free at designated areas in the city centre.

Car Rental In addition to the big national operators, the TIC has details of reputable local car rental companies.

Practical Car & Van Rental (☎ 346 4545), 23 Roseburn St, has weekly rates of £70 (plus insurance) for its smallest cars with unlimited mileage.

Bicycle

Although there are plenty of steep hills to negotiate, Edinburgh is an ideal place for cycling – nothing is more than half an hour away and outside the centre the traffic is fairly tolerable.

Edinburgh Cycle Hire (☎ 556 5560), 29 Blackfriars St, hires out city bikes for £5 a day, mountain and hybrid bikes for £10 to £15 a day, or £50 a week. It hires out tents and touring equipment, and arranges cycling tours of the city. It also sells used bikes and buys them back, the price depending on the state they come back in.

Central Cycle Hire (☎ 228 6333), Lochrin Place off Home St, near Tollcross, operates from the Bike Trax shop and has touring/mountain bikes for £10/15 per day.

Around Edinburgh

Outside the centre there are some worthwhile attractions in the suburbs and beyond. Edinburgh is small enough, that when you need a break from the city, the beautiful surrounding countryside isn't far away and is easily accessible by public transport.

GREATER EDINBURGH
Craigmillar Castle

Urban encroachment aside, massive Craigmillar Castle (☎ 244 3101, HS), about 2½ miles south of the city centre off the A68 to Dalkeith, is still impressive.

Dating from the 15th century, the tower house rises above two sets of walls that enclose an area of 1½ acres. Mary Queen of Scots took refuge here after the murder of Rizzio; it was here too that plans to murder her husband Darnley were laid. Look for the prison cell complete with built-in sanitation, something some 'modern' British prisons only finally managed in 1996.

It's open daily April to September from 9.30 am to 6.30 pm; October to March, Monday to Saturday from 9.30 am to 4.30 pm, Sunday 2 to 4.30 pm; £1.80/75p. Bus Nos 14, 21, C3 and C33 pass by.

Leith

Leith is and was Edinburgh's main port, although it remained an independent burgh until the 1920s. It's still among Britain's busiest ports, but in the 1960s and 70s it fell into decay. Since the 1980s a revival has been taking place and the area is now noted for its interesting restaurants and pubs. The royal yacht *Britannia* is docked here (see the boxed text 'Britannia No Longer Rules the Waves').

Parts are still rough, but it's a distinctive corner of Edinburgh. and the prettiest area

---

Britannia No Longer Rules the Waves

You'll find the former royal yacht *Britannia* (☎ 555 5566 for ticket reservation) moored in Leith harbour, just off Ocean Drive (the ship will be relocated at the new Ocean Terminal, also in Leith, in 2001). She's well worth visiting and you'll learn some surprising things in the visitors centre and on board. Allow at least 1½ hours to look around, and note that the use of cameras on board is prohibited.

After a four minute introductory video, you enter the visitors centre. Take care to have a good look around – you can't get back in once you've boarded the ship. Among other things, you'll discover that the Queen travelled with five tonnes of luggage when making state visits, shouting by officers and crew was forbidden, and a three month deployment required 2200 toilet rolls.

The ship was launched by the Queen at John Brown's shipyard, Clydebank, on 16 April 1953, then sailed 1.1 million miles over the next 44 years, calling at nearly every Commonwealth country and making 25 state visits. After decommissioning at Portsmouth on 11 December 1997 the final voyage took *Britannia* to Leith.

Britannia is open daily, except Christmas Day, from 10.30 am to 6 pm (last admission at 4.30 pm). Entry to the visitors centre and the ship costs £7.50/5.75/3.75 for adults/seniors/children and there's an £18 family ticket for two adults and two children. Tickets should be reserved in advance by telephone or purchased from the Tattoo Office, 32 Market St.

is around The Shore, where the Water of Leith path to Balerno starts.

Malmaison Hotel (☎ *555 6868, 1 Tower Place*) in a 19th century sailor's home, is a wonderfully stylish hotel, with rooms from £95. It has a café-bar and a brasserie where mains, including plenty of vegetarian options, cost £8.50 to £16.50.

There are other places to eat along The Shore, including the *Shore* (☎ *553 5080*), an informal place with three-course lunches for £7.95 and live traditional music Wednesday and Saturday at 9 pm. At up-market *Fishers Bistro* (☎ *554 5666*) in a 17th century signal tower, seafood mains (£12 to £16) include marinated swordfish. You can eat on the cruise ship *Edinburgh*, moored in the dock, on weekends; a full breakfast including haggis is £5.75.

Bar meals and real ales are available in two historic pubs, the *Malt & Hops* (☎ *555 0083*), the oldest in Leith, and *King's Wark* (☎ *554 9260*).

Take bus No 87, 88 or 88A from St Andrew Square.

Portobello

About 2¼ miles south-east of Leith along the coast, the suburb of Portobello is Edinburgh's seaside resort. Although its heyday has long passed, its beach still attracts crowds on warm summer days. Take bus No 15, 20, 26, 42 or 46 from the centre.

Newhaven

Immediately west of Leith is Newhaven, once a small, distinctive fishing community, now absorbed into the Edinburgh conurbation. The old fish-market building has a **Heritage Centre** which is worth a visit. A 15 minute video reveals the astonishingly tribal lifestyle that survived here until the 1950s when overfishing put paid to the traditional source of income. In a matriarchal society, women in distinctive dress dominated the fish market and life in the

---

Sir Harry Lauder

These days not everyone will have heard of the Scottish music hall entertainer Sir Harry Lauder (1870-1950), but they almost certainly have heard one or more of his songs.

Born in Portobello, he worked as a flax spinner in Arbroath while still at school then in his teens as a pitboy in a Lanarkshire coal mine. He travelled around entering and winning talent competitions before achieving professional success in Glasgow. When he moved to London he was an immediate hit, and he then went on to wow them in the US and around the world.

Two of his most famous songs are *'Roamin' in the Gloamin'* and *'I Love a Lassie'*, both written for his wife. Another, *'Keep right on to the End of the Road'* was written after their only son was killed in battle in WWI. Although he continued to perform he never fully recovered from this tragedy.

Sometimes derided for his stage persona of a stereotypical bekilted and thrifty Scot, he was enormously talented and his musical legacy endures.

home. The centre opens daily from noon to 5 pm; admission free.

Most people come here, however, to taste the delights of the enormously popular *Harry Ramsden's (☎ 551 5566)*, purveyor of fish and chips, next to the centre.

Take bus No 7 or 11 from Princes St.

Edinburgh Zoo

Parents of young children will be relieved to know there's a zoo (☎ 334 9171), 3 miles west of the centre on the A8, offering an alternative to the museums. It's open April to September, Monday to Saturday from 9 am to 6 pm, October and March to 5 pm, November to February to 4.30 pm (it opens Sunday at 9.30 am). Admission costs £6/3.20. Bus Nos 2, 26, 31, 69, 85 and 86 pass by.

Lauriston Castle

Three miles north-west of the centre, Lauriston Castle (☎ 336 2060), Cramond Rd South, started life in the 16th century but was 'modernised' in 19th century baronial style. There are 40-minute guided tours April to October, Saturday to Thursday from 11 am to 5 pm; November to March, weekends only, from 2 to 4 pm; £4/3. Bus Nos 40 and 41 from Hanover St pass by.

South Queensferry & the Forth Bridges

South Queensferry lies on the south bank of the Firth of Forth, at its narrowest point. From early times it was a ferry port, but ferries no longer operate and it's now overshadowed by two bridges.

The magnificent Forth Rail Bridge is one of the finest Victorian engineering achievements. Completed in 1890 after seven years work and the deaths of 58 men, it's over a mile long and the 50,000 tons of girders take three years to paint. The Forth Road Bridge wasn't completed until 1964 and is a graceful suspension bridge.

In the pretty High St there are several places to eat and the small **South Queensferry Museum** (☎ 331 5545) contains some interesting background information on the bridges. The prize exhibit is a model of the Furry Man; on the first Friday of August, some hapless male still has to spend nine hours roaming the streets covered from head to toe in burrs and clutching two floral staves in memory of a medieval tradition. It's open Thursday to Saturday from 10 am to 1 pm and 2.15 to 5 pm, Sunday noon to 5 pm; free.

The *Maid of the Forth* (☎ 331 4857) leaves from Hawes Pier and cruises under the bridges to Inchcolm Island and Deep Sea World (☎ 01383-411411), the huge aquarium in North Queensferry. There are daily sailings mid-July to early September (weekends only April to June and October). In summer, evening cruises with jazz or folk music cost £9.50 a head.

Inchcolm Island & Abbey Inchcolm Island has one of Scotland's best preserved medieval abbeys which was founded for Augustinian priors in 1123. In well-tended grounds stand remains of a 13th century church and a remarkably well-preserved octagonal chapter house with stone roof.

It's half an hour to Inchcolm, and you're allowed 1½ hours ashore. Admission to the abbey is £2.30/1, included in the £7.50/3.60 ferry cost (HS members should show their cards for reduction); nonlanding tickets cost £5.20/2.60 and allow you to see the island's grey seals, puffins and other seabirds.

Getting There & Away From St Andrew Square numerous buses (Nos 43, X43, 47, 47A) run to South Queensferry. From Edinburgh there are frequent trains to Dalmeny station (15 minutes).

Hopetoun House

Two miles west of South Queensferry, Hopetoun House (☎ 331 2451), one of Scotland's finest stately homes, has a superb location in lovely grounds beside the Firth of Forth. There are two parts, the older built to Sir William Bruce's plans between 1699 and 1702 and dominated by a splendid stairwell, the newer designed between 1720 and 1750 by three members of the

Adam family, William and sons Robert and John.

The rooms have splendid furnishings and staff are on hand to make sure you don't miss details like the revolving oyster stand for two people to share. The Hope family supplied a Viceroy of India and a Governor-General of Australia so the upstairs museum displays interesting reminders of the colonial life of the ruling class. Even farther up there's a viewing point on the roof, ideal for photos.

It's open April to September daily from 10 am to 5.30 pm; £4.70/2.60 (for the grounds only it's £2.60/1.60).

Hopetoun House can be approached from South Queensferry, or from Edinburgh – turn off the A90 onto the A904 just before the Forth Bridge Toll and follow the signs.

Edinburgh Canal Centre

The Edinburgh Canal Centre (☎ 333 1320) is beside the Union Canal in **Ratho** 8 miles south-west of Edinburgh. The centre offers 1½ hour sightseeing barge trips on the canal for £4.50/2.50 April to October. Take bus No 37 from St Andrew Square. By car, follow the Calder Rd (A71), then turn right (north) onto Dalmeny Rd.

EAST LOTHIAN & MIDLOTHIAN

East of Edinburgh, East Lothian stretches from Musselburgh along the coast to North Berwick and Dunbar. In the centre, attractive Haddington is worth visiting both in its own right and as a site from which to explore the hinterland; nearby Gifford is the gateway to the northern slopes of the Lammermuir Hills.

Midlothian, directly south of Edinburgh, is bordered in the south by the Moorfoot Hills and in the west by the Pentland Hills, both of which afford excellent walks and great views.

Trains stop in Musselburgh, Prestonpans, North Berwick and Dunbar and there are regular buses to these and other towns and villages. For information on public transport call the East and Midlothian Traveline (☎ 0800-232323).

Musselburgh to North Berwick

The small town of **Musselburgh** sits on the River Esk about 6 miles east of Edinburgh. There's not much here except for the small but pretty, terraced **Inveresk Lodge Garden** (☎ 01721-722502, NTS) open April to September, Monday to Friday from 10 am to 4.30 pm, weekends 2 to 5 pm; £1. There's also a riverside path and good views from the harbour.

In **Prestonpans**, 3 miles north-east of Musselburgh, coal was mined for centuries and at the former colliery you can visit the somewhat bleak **Prestongrange Industrial Heritage Museum** (☎ 0131-653 2904), open daily April to October from 11 am to 4 pm; free.

Past Port Seton the countryside opens up. At the mouth of the River Peffer 17 miles from Edinburgh, Georgian cottages stretch along the main street of the village of **Aberlady**. The mud flats and salt marshes here are the site of the **Aberlady Bay Nature Reserve**, where numerous seabirds nest and feed.

Next along the road, the fashionable resort town of **Gullane** is home to a number of golf courses including the prestigious Muirfield.

Two miles east lies **Dirleton Castle** (☎ 01620-850330, HS) surrounded by well-tended walled gardens. Originally built in the 13th century it was altered and added to over the next 300 years until destroyed by General Monk in 1650. Nevertheless, the ruins are still massive enough to dwarf Dirleton village. The castle opens April to September, daily, from 9.30 to 6.30 pm; October to March, Monday to Saturday, from 9.30 am to 4.30 pm, Sunday 2 to 4.30 pm. Entry is £2.30/1.

North Berwick & Around
• pop 4860   ☎ 01620

An easy day trip from Edinburgh, North Berwick is an attractive Victorian seaside resort with long sandy beaches, three golf courses and a small harbour. The TIC (☎ 892197) on Quality St opens Monday to Saturday from 9 am to 6 pm. The public toilets are very clean and even have flowers in vases beside the washbasins!

Things to See Off High St a short steep path climbs up **North Berwick Law** (187m, 613 feet), an extinct volcano, that dominates the town.

By the harbour are the remains of the **Auld Kirk**, the 12th century Church of St Andrews, the first parish church of North Berwick.

Several small islands lie offshore. **Bass Rock**, 3 miles east, was once used as a prison for Covenanters but is now home to thousands of gannets and other seabirds. To visit, you need to be a dedicated birdwatcher and not mind the smell of guano. Puffins nest in burrows on nearby **Craig Rock** and **Fidra Island**.

Fred Marr (☎ 892838) runs trips out daily in summer, on weekends the rest of the year. Trips around Bass Rock and Fidra Island cost £4.60/2.60 and take about 70 minutes. Fred will also drop you off on Bass Rock for two to three hours then return and pick you up (£10).

The Witches of North Berwick

In 1590, the Church of St Andrews was the scene of a gathering of witches of both sexes, under the leadership of 'the Devel', who was in reality Francis Stuart, Earl of Bothwell. He tried by means of witchcraft to cause a storm in the Forth which was to drown James VI as he returned by sea from Denmark, accompanied by Princess Anne of Denmark, his wife. The attempt failed and several witches were subsequently tortured, tried and executed. Bothwell was imprisoned but later escaped. The North Berwick events became widely known. James took a great interest in the trial and even wrote a book about witchcraft.

Nearly 200 years later, it's believed that Robbie Burns drew on stories about the witches when writing *Tam O'Shanter* and the *Old Kirk of Alloway*.

Places to Stay North Berwick has lots of places to stay, though they can fill quickly on weekends when golfers are in town.

Close to town and the beach, *Gilsland Caravan & Camping Park* (☎ 892205, Grange Rd) has sites from £6.50. *Palmerston* (☎ 892884, 115 High St) is a central B&B with spacious *en suite* rooms from £18 and private parking. Popular *Craigview* (☎ 892529, 5 Beach Rd) overlooks the harbour and Bass Rock and offers B&B from £16 per person.

Getting There & Away The bus stop outside the TIC is for Haddington (bus No 121) and Dunbar (bus No 120), the one at the other end of High St, is for Edinburgh (bus Nos 124, 125 and X5). There are frequent ScotRail trains to Edinburgh (33 minutes).

Tantallon Castle

Built around 1350, Tantallon Castle (☎ 01620-892727, HS), 3 miles east of North Berwick, was a fortress residence of the Douglas Earls of Angus (the 'Red Douglases'). On one side it's an almost sheer drop to the sea below, and fulmars nest in the cliffs. It opens daily April to September from 9.30 am to 6.30 pm; October to March, Monday to Saturday, from 9.30 am to 4.30 pm, Sunday 2 to 4.30 pm; £2.30/1.

Dunbar

- **pop 5800**　　☎ 01368

Attractive Dunbar is a holiday resort and small fishing port on the east coast, 30 miles from Edinburgh. It was the site of two important battles, both resulting in Scottish losses, one when Edward I invaded (1296), the other when General Monck defeated a larger Scots army (1650), facilitating Cromwell's entry into Edinburgh. John Muir (1838-1914), pioneer conservationist and 'father' of the US national park system, was born here.

The TIC (☎ 863353), 143 High St, opens October to March, weekdays, from 9 am to 5 pm; daily April to September (extended hours in July and August).

Things to See & Do In the Middle Ages, Dunbar was an important Scottish fortress town, but little remains of **Dunbar Castle** except for some small ruins, inhabited by seabirds, by the harbour.

From the castle a 2-mile clifftop trail follows the coastline west to the sands of Belhaven Bay and **John Muir Country Park** (☎ 863886), where there's sea fishing and horse riding.

John Muir House (☎ 862595), 128 High St, the man's childhood home, has a small exhibition and audio-visual display on his life. It opens June to September, Monday to Saturday, from 11 am to 1 pm, 2 to 5 pm, Sunday 2 to 5 pm; free. **Dunbar Town House Museum** (☎ 863734), also on High St, gives an introduction to local history and archaeology. It opens April to October, daily, from 2 to 4.30 pm, free.

Diving offshore to sites such as Johnson's Hole or Old Harbour Reef is popular. Cromwell Mariner (☎ 863354), Cromwell Harbour, Shore St, organises trips and provides equipment, showers and changing rooms.

Places to Stay There are several camping grounds in the Dunbar region including *Belhaven Bay Caravan & Camping Park* (☎ 01620-893348), in John Muir Country Park. Sites cost from £8.

South of the centre *Cruachan Guest House* (☎ 863006, East Links Rd) is a two-storey Victorian house close to East Beach. B&B with shared bathroom costs from £15 per person.

West of the harbour and close to the clifftop trail, *Overcliffe Guest House* (☎ 864004, 11 Bayswell Park) is a terraced, bay-windowed house with B&B from £17.50 per person (£19.50 with bathroom).

Getting There & Away Dunbar is well served by buses from Edinburgh including bus Nos 251, 253 and 256. The Great North Eastern Railway (GNER) has frequent trains to Edinburgh (40 minutes) and Berwick-upon-Tweed.

Haddington & Around
• pop 8000   ☎ 01620

Haddington, straddling the River Tyne 18 miles east of Edinburgh, dates back to the 12th century when it was made a royal burgh by David I. Most of the modern town, however, was built during the 17th to 19th centuries in a period of great prosperity resulting from the Agricultural Revolution. It's still a prosperous market town and the administrative centre for East Lothian.

The prettiest part of Haddington is the tree lined Court St, with its wide pavement and grand 18th and 19th century buildings. Haddington gets congested with traffic especially on Market and High Sts where, during the day at least, cars joust for limited parking spaces.

Protestant reformer, John Knox, was either born here or in nearby Gifford.

Things to See From the eastern end of High St, Church St leads to **St Mary's Collegiate Church** (1462), the largest parish church in Scotland; it opens daily from 11 am to 4 pm. Buried in the churchyard is Jane Welsh (1801-66), wife of Thomas Carlyle. **Jane Welsh Carlyle Museum** (☎ 823738), in the house in which she lived until her marriage, is off Lodge St and opens April to September, Wednesday to Saturday, from 2 to 5 pm; £1/75p.

Lennoxlove House (☎ 823720), a mile south of Haddington, is the seat of the Duke of Hamilton (since 1947). The oldest part of the house dates from around 1345 with extensions added over the following centuries. It contains some fine furniture and paintings, and memorabilia relating to Mary Queen of Scots. Chief among these are her death mask and a silver casket given to her by Francis II of France, her first husband. The house only opens Easter to October, Wednesday, Saturday and Sunday, from 2 to 5 pm; £4.50/2.50.

Places to Stay & Eat Close to town, the *Monk's Muir* (☎ 860340) is a secluded camping ground with sites from £6. *Mrs Hamilton* (☎ 822465, 28 Market St) offers

B&B in a central Victorian terrace with rooms with shared bathroom from £16 per person.

The *Waterside Bistro & Restaurant* (☎ 825764), has a great location beside the river near Nungate Bridge. When the weather is fine you can sit outside and watch the swans and ducks go by. It provides French cuisine with mains from £11 to £14.

Getting There & Away Bus Nos 123 and 128 run regularly between Edinburgh and Haddington. By road take the A1 east from Edinburgh.

Dalkieth & Around
• **pop 11,000**   ☎ **0131**

Lying between two rivers, the South and North Esk, Dalkieth is 8 miles south-east of Edinburgh. Once an important grain-market and coal transportation centre, today it's a busy commercial centre.

Dalkieth Country Park, at the northern end of High St, is made up of the 18th century landscaped estate surrounding the Palladian-style Dalkieth House (once the home of the Buccleuch family and now the Scottish campus of the University of Wisconsin). In the park spanning River North Esk, is the Robert Adam-designed Montague Bridge (1792). Near the entrance is St Mary's Church (circa 1835), a private chapel of the Buccleuch family. The park opens daily from 9 am to dusk; £2.

About 2 miles south of Dalkieth, the **Scottish Mining Museum** (☎ 663 7519) is in the Lady Victoria Colliery, Newtongrange. A series of tableaux depicts a day in the harsh life of a 19th century mining family, and former miners act as guides down to the coalface. It's open early March to October, daily, from 10 am to 4 pm; £3/2.

Bus Nos 80 and 80A run from Edinburgh to Dalkieth and Newtongrange.

Roslynn Chapel
This unique 15th century chapel (☎ 0131-440 2159), also called the Collegiate Church of St Matthew, in the quiet village of Roslin, 7 miles south-west of Edinburgh, is undergoing massive restoration. It's renowned for its wealth of intricate carvings and sculptures depicting biblical stories, most notable of which is the 'Apprentice Pillar'. Intriguingly, there are also carvings of plants from the Americas which predate Columbus' arrival there. It's open April to October, Monday to Saturday, from 10 am to 5 pm, Sunday noon to 4.45 pm; £2.50. The entrance is off Chapel Loan opposite Roslin Glen Hotel.

Bus No 315 runs hourly from Edinburgh.

Penicuik
This small town on the eastern slopes of the Pentland Hills, 10 miles south of Edinburgh, is where Edinburgh crystal is manufactured. At the **Edinburgh Crystal Visitor Centre** (☎ 01968-675128), off the A701, there's an exhibition and factory tour. It's open Monday to Saturday, from 9 am to 8 pm, Sunday 11 am to 5 pm; free.

Pentland Hills
Beginning about 3 miles south-west of Edinburgh's centre, these hills stretch 16 miles to near Carnworth in Lanarkshire. The hills are below 610m (2000 feet) at the highest point and offer excellent, not too strenuous walking with great views. There are several access points off the A702 including the village of Flotterstone from which there are short walks to nearby reservoirs. Take bus No 100 from Edinburgh.

WEST LOTHIAN
West Lothian is immediately west of Edinburgh and Linlithgow is its administrative centre. For detailed information on public transport call the council's travel helpline (☎ 01506-775288).

Linlithgow
• **pop 9500**   ☎ **01506**

This ancient royal burgh, 15 miles west of Edinburgh, is one of Scotland's oldest towns though much of it 'only' dates from the 15th to 17th centuries. Its centre retains a certain charm, except for the appallingly ugly modern buildings so inappropriately close to the palace and Cross (marketplace).

The TIC (☎ 844600) in the Burgh Halls at the Cross, opens Monday to Saturday from 10 am to 4 pm, Sunday noon to 4 pm (extended hours in summer).

Things to See Outstanding **Linlithgow Palace** (☎ 842896, HS), sits on the southern shore of Linlithgow Loch, up from the Cross. Begun by James I in 1425, it took nearly 200 years to complete and became a favoured royal residence. James V and Mary, Queen of Scots, were born here, Cromwell billeted his troops here in the 1650s and Bonnie Prince Charlie briefly visited in 1745. The central courtyard and the Great Hall are the most impressive of the remains. It opens April to September, Monday to Saturday, from 9.30 am to 6.30 pm, Sunday 2 to 6.30 pm (to 4.30 pm, October to March). Entry is £2.30/1.

Beside the palace is the Gothic **St Michael's Church**, built between 1497 and 1531, but curiously topped by an aluminium spire added in 1964.

The **Linlithgow Story** (☎ 670677), Annet House, 143 High St, is a small museum which tells the story of the Stewart monarchy and the town. It opens Easter to October, Monday and Wednesday to Saturday from 10 am to 4 pm, Sunday 1 to 4 pm; £1/60p (free Sunday).

Getting There & Away Buses (Nos 38, 38A, 38B and 138 from St Andrew Square) and trains between Edinburgh and Falkirk go through Linlithgow. Buses stop at the Cross and the train station is south of the centre. The M9 motorway passes north of the town.

Glasgow

• **pop 689,000** ☎ **0141**

Although Glasgow lacks the instantly inspiring beauty of Edinburgh, it's one of Britain's largest, liveliest and most interesting cities, with a legacy of appealing Victorian architecture and several distinguished suburbs of terraced squares and crescents. 'Glasgow – The Friendly City' say the billboards, and it's true, thanks mainly to the warmth, vibrancy and energy of its inhabitants.

In the early 1970s, the name Glasgow came to be synonymous with unemployment, economic depression and urban violence. It was known for the bloody confrontations that occurred between rival supporters of Protestant Rangers and Catholic Celtic football teams, and as the home of the Glasgow Kiss (a particularly unfriendly head butt). Over the following years, however, the city reinvented itself, rediscovering its rich cultural roots and proclaiming a new pride through a well orchestrated publicity campaign. By 1990, it had been elected European City of Culture and, in 1999, served as the UK's City of Architecture and Design. Currently, Glasgow is the third most popular destination in Britain for foreign tourists, after London and Edinburgh.

Although influenced by thousands of Irish immigrants, Glasgow is the most Scottish of cities, with a unique blend of friendliness, urban chaos, black humour and energy. In the late 20th century the city saw an incredible outburst of musical talent and produced such groups as Simple Minds, Tears for Fears, Deacon Blue, Aztec Camera, Wet Wet Wet and Texas, as well as comedians like Billy Connolly and Stanley Baxter.

It also boasts excellent art galleries and museums (including the famous Burrell Collection) – most of them free – as well as numerous good value restaurants, countless pubs and bars and a lively arts scene.

HIGHLIGHTS

- Gaze upon the beautifully displayed treasures of the Burrell Collection
- Marvel at the architecture of Charles Rennie Mackintosh
- Journey through a time warp at the Tenement House
- View the outstanding exhibits at the Art Gallery and Museum, Kelvingrove
- Visit the Scottish mainland's only cathedral to have survived the turbulent Reformation
- Jump headlong into the nightlife in the pubs and clubs

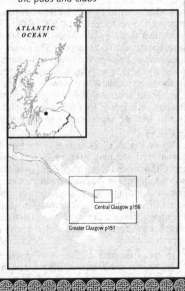

ATLANTIC OCEAN

Central Glasgow p156

Greater Glasgow p151

HISTORY

Glasgow grew up around the cathedral founded by St Mungo in the 6th century and, in 1451, the city became the site of the

University of Glasgow, the second university in Scotland. Unfortunately, with the exception of the cathedral, virtually nothing of the medieval city remains. It was swept away by the energetic people of a new age – the age of capitalism, the Industrial Revolution, and the British empire.

In the 18th century, much of the tobacco trade between Europe and the USA was routed through Glasgow and provided a great source of wealth. Other New World imports included rum and sugar. Even after the tobacco trade declined in the 19th century, the city continued to prosper as a centre of textile manufacturing, shipbuilding and the coal and steel industries.

The new industries created a huge demand for labour and peasants poured in from Ireland and the Highlands to crowd the city's tenements. In the mid-18th century the population had reached 17,500. By the end of that century, it had risen to 100,000. After 20 years, that figure had doubled and, by 1860, it was home to 400,000 people. The outward appearance of prosperity, however, was tempered by the dire working conditions in the factories, particularly for women and children. In the second half of the 19th century the city experienced four major cholera outbreaks and life expectancy was a mere 30 years.

While the workers suffered, the textile barons and shipping magnates prospered, and Glasgow could justifiably call itself the second city of the empire. Grand Victorian public buildings were constructed, and some of the wealthier citizens spent their fortunes amassing the large art collections which now form the basis of the city's superb galleries.

In the first half of the 20th century, Glasgow was the centre of Britain's munitions industry, supplying arms and ships for the two world wars. After those boom years, however, the port and heavy industries began to decline and by the early 1970s, the city looked doomed. Glasgow has always been proud of its predominantly working class nature but, unlike middle-class Edinburgh with its varied service industries, it

had few alternatives when recession hit and unemployment spiralled.

Certainly, there's now renewed confidence in the city but behind all the optimism, the standard of living remains low for the UK and life is tough for those affected by the relatively high unemployment, inadequate housing and generally poor diet. (In fact, the city has a reputation as the heart attack capital of the world. According to recent reports, Glasgow women are seven times more likely to die of a heart attack than their counterparts in Spain or China, and the record for men isn't much better.)

ORIENTATION

Glasgow's tourist sights are spread over a wide area. The city centre is built on a grid system on the north side of the River Clyde. The two train stations (Central and Queen St), the Buchanan Bus Station and the TIC are all within a couple of blocks of George Square, the main city square. Running along a ridge in the northern part of the city, Sauchiehall St (first syllable pronounced soch as in loch) has a pedestrian mall with numerous High St shops at its eastern end, and pubs and restaurants at the western end. Argyle St, running parallel to the river, and pedestrianised Buchanan St, at right angles to Argyle St, are important shopping streets. Merchant City is the commercial district, east of George Square.

The university and the youth hostel are near Kelvingrove Park, north-west of the city centre in an area known as the West End. Pollok Country Park and the Burrell Collection are in the South Side, south-west of the centre.

Motorways bore through the suburbs and the M8 sweeps round the western and northern edges of the centre. The airport lies 10 miles west of the centre.

INFORMATION

The *List*, available from newsagents (£1.90), is Glasgow's and Edinburgh's invaluable fortnightly guide to films, theatre, cabaret, music – the works. Also be sure to find a copy of the *Visitors' Transport Guide*

GREATER GLASGOW

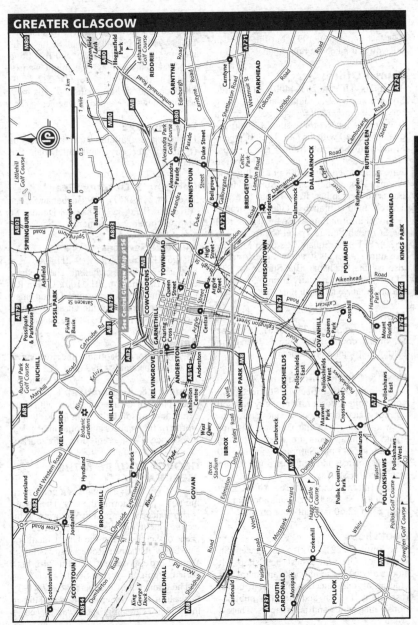

GLASGOW

Map (free) which provides a rundown of local transport options on a handy map. It was last updated in 1997, but the TIC can tell you if it has been reprinted.

Tourist Offices

The main TIC (☎ 204 4400), 11 George Square, has a £2 accommodation booking service and a *bureau de change*. There's a free orientation centre upstairs to help acquaint yourself with the city. The TIC opens Monday to Saturday from 9 am to 6 pm with extended opening hours until 7 pm in June and September, and 8 pm in July and August. It's also open on Sunday from Easter to September, from 10 am to 6 pm. There's another branch at Glasgow airport.

Travel information is also available from the St Enoch Square Travel Centre (☎ 226 4826), St Enoch Square. It's open Monday to Saturday, from 9.30 am to 5 pm. You can also try the Buchanan Bus Station (☎ 332 7133), which opens daily from 6.30 am (7 am on Sunday) to 10.30 pm.

Money

American Express (☎ 221 4366), 115 Hope St, opens commercial hours Monday to Friday, until noon on Saturday.

Post & Communications

At the main post office, 47 St Vincent St, you can collect poste restante, buy and sell currency, cash travellers cheques and withdraw directly from the German Savings Bank. Opening hours are weekdays from 8.30 am to 5.45 pm, Saturday 9 am to 5.30 pm. Post offices in some supermarkets are also open on Sunday.

The Internet Café (☎ 564 1052), 569 Sauchiehall St, has 10 terminals and charges from £2 to £2.50 per half-hour on line.

Bookshops

John Smith (☎ 221 7472), 57 St Vincent St, is one of Glasgow's best bookshops. It stocks a wide range of books and maps, including a good selection of foreign books (especially French and German publications), magazines and newspapers. There's

another branch (☎ 334 2769) at 252 Byres Rd near Glasgow University. Waterstone's (☎ 332 9105), 153 Sauchiehall St, has an Internet café and coffee shop, and five floors of just about anything you might want to read. The Borders superstore (☎ 222 7700), 98 Buchanan St, has a café and sells international newspapers and magazines.

Left Luggage

Lockers are available at Central Station (from £2 per day) and Buchanan Bus Station.

Camping & Outdoor Gear

Tiso's (☎ 248 4877), 129 Buchanan St, and Adventure 1 (☎ 353 3788), 38 Dundas St, both sell outdoor equipment.

Medical Services

Glasgow Royal Infirmary (☎ 211 4000) is at 84 Castle St, by the cathedral. The Southern General Hospital (☎ 201 1100), Govan Rd, is the main South Side hospital. Dental emergencies are handled at the Glasgow Dental Hospital (☎ 211 9600), 378 Sauchiehall St.

Emergency

As anywhere in Scotland, the free emergency numbers are ☎ 999 or ☎ 112.

Dangers & Annoyances

Keep clear of Orange marches, which are exhibitions of solidarity with the Protestant Northern Irish cause, and sometimes result in violence. These events aren't for tourists.

GEORGE SQUARE & THE MERCHANT CITY

The TIC on George Square is a good starting point for exploring the city. The square is surrounded by imposing Victorian architecture, including the old post office, the Bank of Scotland and the City Chambers. There are statues of Robert Burns, James Watt, Lord Clyde and, atop a 24m-high doric column, Sir Walter Scott.

The grand City Chambers (☎ 287 4195), the seat of local government, were built in the 1880s at the high point of the city's wealth. Their interior is even more extravagant than their exterior, and the chambers are sometimes used as a movie location to represent the Kremlin or the Vatican. There are free tours lasting 45 minutes from the main entrance, Monday to Friday, from 10.30 am and 2.30 pm.

A Walk Through the Merchant City

An interesting hour-long walk will take you from George Square to Glasgow Cathedral through The Merchant City, a planned 18th century civic development. The Tobacco Lords were the entrepreneurs who opened up European trade with the Americas, importing tobacco, rum and sugar in the 18th century and their profits went to build these warehouses, offices and gracious homes. The current redevelopment trend has turned the warehouses into apartments for Glaswegian yuppies, and stylish shopping malls such as the Italian Centre have sprung up to serve their retail needs.

Once you've seen the City Chambers, cross George Square and walk one block south down Queen St to the **Gallery of Modern Art** (☎ 229 1996). This four-floor colonnaded building, built in 1827, was once the Royal Exchange, where business transactions were negotiated. Further details on the gallery appear later in this chapter. The upmarket Rooftop Café (☎ 221 7484) opens for dinner, Thursday to Saturday; a two-course meal costs around £15.95, but there's a less expensive lunch menu.

The gallery faces Ingram St, which you follow east for two blocks. To the right, down Garth St, is **Trades House**, designed by Robert Adam in 1791 to house the trades guild. This is the only surviving building in Glasgow by this famous Scottish architect. A farther two blocks east along Ingram St brings you to **Hutchesons' Hall**. Built in 1805 to a design by David Hamilton, this elegant building is now maintained by the National Trust for Scotland. It's open Monday to Saturday from 10 am to 5 pm.

Retrace your steps one block and continue south down Glassford St past **The Warehouse**, a distinctive Art Nouveau building that now houses designer clothes shops. Turn right into Wilson St and first left along Virginia St, lined with the old warehouses of the Tobacco Lords. The **Tobacco Exchange** became the Sugar Exchange in 1820 and many of the old warehouses here have now been converted into flats.

Back on Wilson St, the bulky **Sheriff Court House** fills a whole block. It was originally built as Glasgow's town hall. Continue east past **Ingram Square**, another warehouse development, to the **City Halls**, now used for concerts. The city's markets were once held here. Turn right from Albion St into Blackfriars St. Emerging onto the High St, turn left and follow the street up to the cathedral.

Hutchesons' Hall, built in 1805, and now maintained by the National Trust for Scotland

GLASGOW

GLASGOW CATHEDRAL & PRECINCTS

The oldest part of the city is centred on Glasgow Cathedral, to the east of the modern centre. The area was given a facelift with the opening of St Mungo's Museum of Religious Life and Art. The money for the restoration of the cathedral was sensibly spent on updating the heating system rather than on giving the blackened exterior a high-pressure hose-down. Nearby, Provand's Lordship, the city's oldest house, completes a trio of interesting sights.

The crumbling tombs of the city's rich and famous crowd the recently renovated necropolis behind the cathedral.

It takes about 15 to 20 minutes to walk from George Square but numerous buses pass by. Nos 11, 12, 38 and 51 follow Cathedral St; the No 2 runs from Argyle St via High St.

Glasgow Cathedral

Glasgow Cathedral (☎ 552 6891), a shining example of pre-Reformation Gothic architecture, is the only mainland Scottish cathedral to have survived the Reformation. Most of the current building dates from the 15th century, and only the western towers were destroyed in the turmoil.

This has been hallowed ground for over 1500 years. The site was blessed for Christian burial in 397 by St Ninian. In the following century Kentigern, also known as St Mungo, accompanied the body of a holy man from Stirlingshire to be buried here. He stayed to found a monastic community, and built a simple church. The first building was consecrated in 1136, in the presence of King David I, but it burned down in 1197 and was rebuilt as the lower church.

The entry is through a side door into the **nave**, which is hung with regimental colours. The wooden roof above has been restored many times since its original construction but some of the timber dates from the 14th century. Much of the cathedral's stained glass is modern and to your left, you'll see Francis Spear's 1958 work *The Creation*, which fills the west window.

The cathedral is divided by the late 15th century stone choir screen, decorated with seven pairs of figures to represent the Seven Deadly Sins. Beyond is the **choir**. The four stained-glass panels of the east window, depicting the apostles and also by Francis Spear, are particularly effective. At the north-east corner is the entrance to the 15th century **upper chapter house**, where Glasgow University was founded. It's now used as a sacristy.

The most interesting part of the cathedral, **the lower church**, is reached by a stairway. Its forest of pillars creates a powerful atmosphere around St Mungo's tomb, the focus of a famous medieval pilgrimage that was believed to be as meritorious as a visit to Rome. Edward I paid three visits to the shrine in 1301.

The cathedral opens to visitors Monday to Saturday from 9.30 am to 6 pm, and 2 to 5 pm Sunday. In winter it closes at 4 pm daily. Sunday services are at 11 am and 6.30 pm.

St Mungo's Museum of Religious Life & Art

The award-winning St Mungo Museum (☎ 553 2557), near the cathedral, was opened in 1993. From its inception, it has been a highly controversial project as it's understandably challenging to select works of art outlining all the world's main religions – but the result is well worth it and is small enough not to be overwhelming.

The building may look like a bit of restored antiquity, but in fact it's just a few years old – a £6.5 million reconstruction of the bishop's palace that once stood here. A 10 minute video will provide an overall view before you delve into the exhibits. There are three galleries, representing religion as art, religious life and, on the top floor, religion in Scotland. In the main gallery Dali's *Christ of St John of the Cross* hangs beside statues of the Buddha and Hindu deities. Outside, you'll find Britain's only Zen garden.

The recommended restaurant downstairs provides both vegetarian and meat dishes.

Soup and a roll cost £1.25 and main dishes are £3.50.

The museum opens daily from 10 am to 5 pm (from 11 am on Sunday); entry is free.

Provand's Lordship

Across the road from the St Mungo Museum, Provand's Lordship (☎ 552 8819) is the oldest house in Glasgow. Built in 1471 as a manse for the chaplain of St Nicholas Hospital, it's said to have been visited by Mary Queen of Scots, James II and James IV. It's now a museum of various period displays connected with the house. These are as diverse as a 16th century room of one of the chaplains who lived here, and a 20th century sweet shop. Once the current conservation work is finished (around April 1999), Provand's Lordship will be open daily until 5 pm. Entry is free.

GALLERY OF MODERN ART

The Gallery of Modern Art (☎ 229 1996), Queen St, features contemporary paintings, ceramics, furniture and sculpture, including items from Scottish artists such as Peter Howson, Ken Currie and John Bellany. There are also permanent exhibits from overseas and occasional temporary exhibitions. The gallery opens daily from 10 am to 5 pm (from 11 am on Sunday); admission is free.

BURRELL COLLECTION

Glasgow's top attraction, the Burrell Collection (☎ 649 7151), was amassed by wealthy industrialist Sir William Burrell before it was donated to the city. It's now housed in a prize-winning museum in the Pollok Country Park, 3 miles south of the city centre. This idiosyncratic collection includes everything from Chinese porcelain and medieval furniture to paintings by Renoir and Cézanne. It's not so big as to be overwhelming, and the stamp of the collector lends an intriguing coherence.

The building was the result of a design competition in 1971. If it had not been run during a postal strike, necessitating an extension of the closing deadline, Barry Gasson's winning entry would not have been completed. From the outside, the building seems somewhat of a hybrid but the truly spectacular interior provides a fitting setting for an exquisite collection of tapestries, oriental porcelain, paintings and European stained glass. Floor-to-ceiling windows admit a flood of natural light, and the trees and landscape outside only enhance the effect created by the exhibits.

Carpeted floors maintain the silence to contemplate the beautifully displayed treasures. Carved-stone Romanesque doorways are incorporated into the structure so one actually walks through them. Some galleries are reconstructions of rooms from Hutton Castle, the Burrell residence. Even the public seating is of superb design and production quality.

The light and airy café on the lower ground floor includes the same floor-to-ceiling windows, hung with heraldic glass medallions. Meals are available in the adjacent restaurant. Weather permitting, you may prefer to save a good chunk of change (even a cup of coffee costs £1.10) and bring a picnic lunch.

The Burrell Collection opens from 10 am to 5 pm, Monday to Saturday, and from 11 am on Sunday. Admission is free, but parking costs a hefty £1.50. There are occasional guided tours. Numerous buses pass the park gates (including Nos 45, 48A and 57 from the centre); and there's a twice-hourly bus service between the gallery and the gates (a pleasant 10 minute walk). Alternatively, catch a train to Pollokshaws West from Central station (four per hour; the second station on the light blue line to the south, trains destined for East Kilbride or Kilmarnock).

Pollok House

Also in Pollok Country Park, and a 10 minute walk from the Burrell Collection, Pollok House (☎ 616 6410) contains a fine collection of Spanish paintings, including works by El Greco and Goya. The house is Georgian and parts have been redecorated with historically correct but bizarre-looking

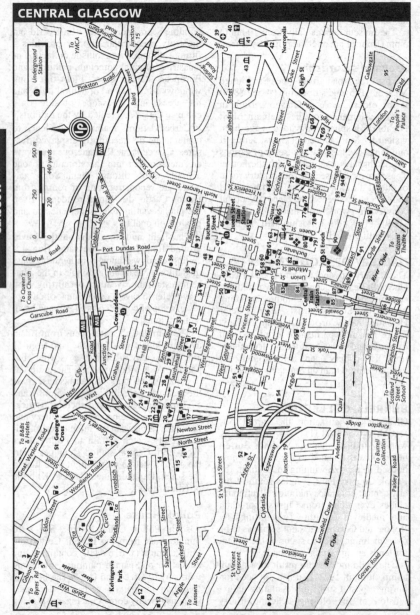

CENTRAL GLASGOW

PLACES TO STAY
7   Glasgow Backpackers Hostel
8   Glasgow Youth Hostel
9   Woodlands Houses
12 Alamo Guest House
13 Smith's Hotel
15 Berkeley Globetrotters
17 Charing Cross Tower Hotel
23 Baird Hall
24 McLay's Guest House
26 Willow Hotel & Hampton
     Court Hotel
27 Victorian House
42 Cathedral House Hotel
54 Glasgow Marriott

PLACES TO EAT
2   Joe's Garage
3   Stravaigin
5   Shalimar
11 Insomnia Café
16 Mitchell's Bistro & Bon
     Accord Pub
19 Loon Fung
20 Ristoro Ciao Italia
30 Bradford's Bakery
32 Willow Tearoom
34 Delifrance
47 Jade House
48 Blue Lagoon
49 Balbir's
52 The Buttery Restaurant
59 Yes
63 The Jenny
69 Café Gandolfi
86 Change at Jamaica

91 The Granary
93 Tivoli

PUBS
6   Uisge Beatha
10 Halt Bar
31 Brunswick Cellars
45 Sadie Frost's
50 Austin's
55 Waterloo Bar
57 Drum & Monkey
58 The Horse Shoe
68 Babbity Bowster
70 Blackfriars
75 The Court Bar
80 The Bank
82 Bar 10
83 Underworld
87 MacSorley's
92 Scotia Bar

OTHER
1   Hunterian Art Gallery
4   Hunterian Museum
14 Internet Café
18 King's Theatre
21 Royal Highland Fusiliers
     Museum
22 The Garage
25 Tenement House
28 Centre for Contemporary Arts
29 Glasgow School of Art
33 Glasgow Film Theatre
35 Victoria's
36 Theatre Royal
37 Glasgow Royal Concert Hall

38 Buchanan Bus Station
39 Glasgow Royal Infirmary
40 Glasgow Cathedral
41 St Mungo's Museum
43 Provand's Lordship
44 University of Strathclyde
     Campus Village Office
46 Adventure 1
51 King Tut's Wah Wah Hut
53 SECC
56 American Express Office
60 John Smith Bookshop
61 Post Office
62 Tiso's
64 Gallery of Modern Art
65 TIC
66 City Chambers
67 Hutchesons' Hall
71 City Halls
72 Sheriff Court House
73 Bennet's
74 The Warehouse
76 Polo Lounge, Café Del
     Monica's & Café Latte
77 Trades House
78 Tobacco Exchange
79 Archaos
81 Princes Square
84 Cathouse
85 Arches
88 St Enoch Travel Centre
89 QC's Bistro Bar & Glasgow
     Gay & Lesbian Centre
90 St Enoch Centre
94 Tron Theatre
95 The Barrows Market

GLASGOW

colour schemes. There's a tearoom in the old kitchens. The house, managed by the NTS, is open April to October, daily, from 10 am to 5 pm, and 11 am to 4 pm for the rest of the year. Admission costs £3/2 from April to October (free from November to March).

MACKINTOSH BUILDINGS

There are a number of superb Art Nouveau buildings designed by the Scottish architect and designer Charles Rennie Mackintosh (CRM). There are day tours of most of these buildings, from May to October (once or twice a month), at weekends, for £30 per

day. Contact the CRM Society (☎ 946 6600) for details.

Glasgow School of Art

Widely recognised as Mackintosh's greatest building, the Glasgow School of Art (☎ 353 4526), 167 Renfrew St, still houses the educational institution. It's hard not to be impressed by the thoroughness of the design; the architect's pencil seems to have shaped everything inside and outside the building. The interior design is strikingly austere, with simple colour combinations (often just black and cream) and those uncomfortable-looking high-backed chairs for which he is famous. The library, designed as an addition in 1907, is a masterpiece.

There are guided tours of the building Monday to Friday at 11 am and 2 pm, and on Saturday at 10.30 am (£3.50/2), but parts of the school may be closed to visitors if they're in use. The building is closed on Saturday afternoon and on Sunday.

Willow Tearoom

Located at 217 Sauchiehall St, the Willow Tearoom (☎ 332 0521) is more Mockintosh than Mackintosh – a reconstruction of the tearoom Mackintosh designed and furnished in 1904 for restaurateur Kate Cranston.

The restaurant closed in 1926 and the premises were then occupied by a series of retail businesses. Reconstruction took two years and the Willow opened as a tearoom again in 1980. Sauchiehall means 'lane of willows', hence the choice of a stylised willow motif.

Queues for light meals and tea (see Places to Eat later in this chapter) often extend into the gift shop and jeweller's downstairs.

Charles Rennie Mackintosh

The quirky, linear and geometric designs of this famous Scottish architect and designer have had almost as much influence on the city as have Gaudi's on Barcelona. Many of the buildings Mackintosh designed in Glasgow are now open to the public, and you'll see his tall, thin, Art Nouveau typeface repeatedly reproduced.

Born in 1868, he studied at the Glasgow School of Art. In 1896, when he was aged only 27, his design won a competition for the School of Art's new building. The first part was opened in 1899 and is considered to be the earliest example of Art Nouveau in Britain, and Mackintosh's supreme architectural achievement. This building demonstrates his skill in combining function and style.

Mackintosh applied himself to every facet of design, from whole façades to the smallest window fastener. As a furniture designer and decorative artist, he designed the interiors for Kate Cranston's chain of Glasgow tearooms between 1896 and 1911. The Willow Tearoom, 217 Sauchiehall St, has now been fully restored and reopened as a tearoom.

Although Mackintosh's genius was quickly recognised on the Continent (he contributed to a number of exhibitions in France, Germany and Austria), he did not receive the same encouragement in Scotland. His architectural career here lasted only until 1914 when he moved to England to concentrate on furniture design. He died in

An example of Mackintosh's innovative furniture design.

1928, but it's only in the last 30 years that Mackintosh's genius has been widely recognised. If you want to know more about the man and his work, contact the Charles Rennie Mackintosh Society (☎ 0141-946 6600, fax 0141-945 2321), Queen's Cross, 870 Garscube Rd, Glasgow, G20 7EL.

Queen's Cross Church

Now the headquarters of the CRM Society, Queen's Cross Church (☎ 946 6600), 870 Garscube Rd, is the only one of Mackintosh's church designs to be built. It's the wonderful simplicity of the design which is particularly inspiring.

There's an information centre, a small display and a gift shop. It's open to visitors Monday to Friday from 10 am to 5 pm, Saturday 10 am to 2 pm, and Sunday 2 to 5 pm. For adults, a donation is suggested; it's free for students.

Other Mackintoshiana

The principal rooms from CRM's house have been reconstructed as the **Mackintosh House**, with original furnishings, at the Hunterian Art Gallery.

At the Art Gallery and Museum in Kelvingrove Park, there's an interesting display of Mackintosh paintings, furniture and decorative art.

Scotland Street School (☎ 429 1202), 225 Scotland St, is an impressive Mackintosh building which is dominated by two glass-stair towers.

It's now a museum of education, which may sound dull but it's fascinating. There are reconstructions of classrooms from Victorian times, and the 1940s, 50s and 60s. It's open Monday to Saturday, from 10 am to 5 pm, and on Sunday from 2 pm. Admission is free.

Although designed in 1901 as an entry to a competition run by a German magazine, the **House for an Art Lover** (☎ 353 4770), Bellahouston Park, Dumbreck Rd, was not completed until 1996.

It has permanent Mackintosh displays and a café. It's open Saturday and Sunday, from 10 am to 5 pm; for weekday access details phone ☎ 353 4449. Admission is £3.50/2.50.

Twenty-three miles north-west of Glasgow at Helensburgh is the **Hill House** (☎ 01436-673900), Mackintosh's domestic masterpiece, now in the hands of the National Trust for Scotland. See Helensburgh in The Highlands chapter.

THE TENEMENT HOUSE

For an extraordinary time-capsule experience, visit the small apartment in the Tenement House (☎ 333 0183), 145 Buccleuch St. It gives an insight into middle-class city life in the late 19th/early 20th century, with box-beds, the original kitchen range and all the fixtures and fittings of the family who lived here for over 50 years.

It's an interesting place but surely the Toward family wouldn't have kept it quite so squeaky clean and orderly as the National Trust for Scotland manages to now.

Despite the additional exhibition area in the ground-floor flat, it can get crowded. The flat opens March to October daily from 2 to 5 pm. Entry is £3/2.

WEST END

In the West End you'll find Glasgow University, several museums and galleries, lots of restaurants and an extensive park, Kelvingrove Park. The area swarms with students during term time, but it's quieter during vacations.

Hunterian Museum & Art Gallery

Part of the university, and now housed in two separate buildings on either side of University Ave, when the Hunterian was opened in 1807 it was Scotland's first public museum. It houses the collection of William Hunter (1718-83), famous physician, medical teacher and one time student of the university.

The Hunterian Museum (☎ 330 4221), in the university building, comprises a disparate collection of artefacts including a notable coin collection, fossils and minerals, dinosaur eggs, Romano-British stone slabs and carvings, a display detailing the archaeological history of Scotland, and some of Captain Cook's curios from his voyages to the South Seas.

The Hunterian Art Gallery (☎ 330 5431) is nearby at 82 Hillhead St. Inside, behind a pair of imposing cast-aluminium doors by Edinburgh-born Paolozzi is the painting collection, opened in its new home in 1980.

The Scottish Colourists – Samuel Peploe, JD Fergusson, Francis Cadell – are well represented. There are also McTaggart's impressionistic Scottish landscapes, and a gem by Thomas Millie Dow. There's a special collection of James McNeill Whistler's limpid prints, drawings and paintings, but only the paintings are on permanent display. It's interesting to compare some of his own furniture and household goods to the contents of the Mackintosh House, the final section in the gallery.

Set up as a reconstruction of architect Charles Rennie Mackintosh's Glasgow home which had to be demolished, the style of the Mackintosh House is quite startling even today. You ascend from the gallery's sombre ground floor into the cool, white austere drawing room. There's something other-worldly about the very mannered style of the beaten silver panels, the long backed chairs, and the surface decorations echoing Celtic manuscript illuminations. The Northampton guest bedroom is impossibly elegant and dazzling, in blue and white stripes.

The Hunterian opens Monday to Saturday, from 9.30 am to 5 pm; the Mackintosh House is closed from 12.30 to 1.30 pm. Entrance is free. There's a coffee bar by the museum's entrance and the student refectory is next to the art gallery. Bus Nos 44 and 59 pass this way from the city centre (Hope St).

Kelvingrove Art Gallery & Museum

Opened in 1902, this grand Victorian cathedral of culture (☎ 357 3929) should not be missed, particularly for its excellent collection of Scottish and European art.

The impressive central hall is dominated at one end by organ pipes; recitals are an integral part of the museum program. An authentic museum smell emanates from the natural history of Scotland section, popular with school tours. Also downstairs there's a rather dowdy presentation of some interesting artefacts, including archaeological finds of prehistoric Scotland, European arms and armour, and silver.

The art gallery upstairs houses the city's art collection of 19th and 20th century works. Scottish painters of luminous landscapes and still lifes are comprehensively represented – Arthur Melville, McTaggart, Cadell, Joseph Crawhall; and, among the moderns, Eduardo Paolozzi, Bruce McLean, David Hockney and Jasper Johns. Other paintings include Rembrandt's wonderful *Man in Armour*, and works by Botticelli, Monet, Van Gogh and Picasso.

Grandly set back from the road in Kelvingrove Park, just west of Kelvin Way, the art gallery and museum are open daily from 10 am to 5 pm (from 11 am on Sunday); entrance is free. Any bus heading for Dumbarton Rd passes this way, such as Nos 6, 6A, 57, 64 and 64A; Kelvin Hall is the nearest underground station. There's an inexpensive café here.

Museum of Transport

Across Argyle St from the Art Gallery and Museum is a surprisingly interesting and very comprehensive **Museum of Transport** (☎ 287 2720). Exhibits include an excellent reproduction of a 1938 Glasgow street scene, a display of cars made in Scotland, plus assorted railway locos, trams, bikes and model ships. One of the model ships is the unique circular ship, the *Livadia*. There's also a display about the Clyde shipyards. The museum opens daily from 10 am to 5 pm (from 11 am on Sunday); entrance is free.

OTHER THINGS TO SEE

On Glasgow Green, the city's oldest park, **The People's Palace** (☎ 554 0223) was built in the late 19th century as a cultural centre for Glasgow's East End. It's now a splendid museum of social history, telling the story of the city from 1175 to the present. The adjoining Winter Gardens are also worth seeing. It's open daily from 10 am (11 am on Sunday) until 5 pm, with free admission.

The Royal Highland Fusiliers Museum (☎ 332 0961), 518 Sauchiehall St, charts the history of this and previous regiments from 1678 to the present. Exhibits include uniforms, medals, pictures and other militaria.

Barrisdale Bay, Knoydart

Lochranza Castle, Isle of Arran

Fishing boat at St Abbs, Borders

Standing stones on Machrie Moor, Isle of Arran

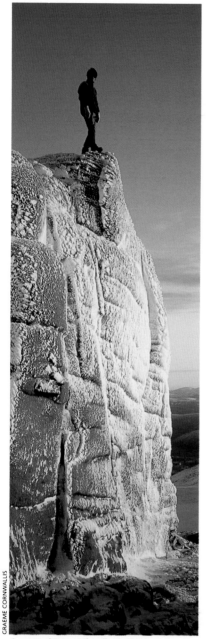

Summit of Beinn Mheadhoin, Cairngorms

Dunnottar Castle, Aberdeenshire

Balmoral Castle, the Queen's summer retreat

Crail Harbour, Fife

Wrought ironwork within the museum was designed by Mackintosh. It's open weekdays, from 9 am to 4.30 pm (until 4 pm on Friday), and weekends by appointment. Entrance is free.

Fossil Grove (☎ 287 2000), Victoria Park, Dumbarton Rd, has sections of 350-million-year-old fossilised trees, lying as they were found. Information boards provide explanations for this Site of Special Scientific Interest. The grove opens daily, April to September, from 10 am to 5 pm (from 11 am on Sunday); admission is free. To get there, take bus Nos 44, 44C or 44D from the city centre to Victoria Park Drive North.

Holmwood House (☎ 637 2129, NTS), 61-63 Netherlee Rd, Cathcart, is an interesting building designed by Alexander 'Greek' Thomson and built in 1857-58. Despite ongoing renovations, it's well worth a visit. Look out for sun symbols downstairs and stars upstairs in this attractive house with its adaptation of classical Greek architecture. Phone in advance for opening dates and times (usually daily 1.30 to 5.30 pm); admission is £2.40/1.60. To get to Cathcart train station, take a Neilston-bound train (twice hourly from Central station) or bus Nos 44 and 46 from the city centre. Then you should follow Rhannan Rd for about half a mile to Holmwood House.

The Scottish National Football Museum (☎ 287 2746) is currently in a room at the Museum of Transport, but it will move to the Scottish national football stadium, Hampden Park, in September 1999. Plans include temporary and permanent exhibits describing the history of the game in Scotland and the influence of Scots on the world game. You'll be able to view a press box and changing rooms. A café, library and archive will be available. Opening times will be at least 10 am to 5 pm daily (from 11 am on Sunday), with late opening some evenings. There will be a moderate admission charge. Hampden is off Aikenhead Rd, Mount Florida, in the South Side. To get there, take a train to Mount Florida station (trains bound for Neilston or Newton, four

per hour) or take bus No 12, 12A, 19 or 74 from Stockwell St.

The Barrows (pronounced barras), Glasgow's flea market on Gallowgate, shouldn't be missed. There are almost 1000 stalls and people come here just for a wander as much as for shopping, which gives the place a holiday air. It takes place only on Saturday and Sunday. The Barrows is notorious for designer frauds, so be cautious. Watch your wallet too.

WALKS & CYCLE ROUTES

There are numerous green spaces within the city. **Pollok Country Park** surrounds the Burrell Collection with numerous woodland trails. Nearer the centre of the city, the Kelvin Walkway follows the River Kelvin through Kelvingrove Park, the Botanic Gardens and on to Dawsholm Park.

There are several long-distance pedestrian/cycle routes that originate in Glasgow and follow off-road routes for most of the distance. The TIC has a range of maps and leaflets detailing these routes, most of which start from Bell's Bridge (by the SECC). For the latest information on the expanding National Cycle Network, contact Sustrans on ☎ 0117-929 0888.

The Glasgow-Loch Lomond Route traverses residential and industrial areas, following a disused railway to Clydebank, the Forth and Clyde canal towpath to Bowling, then a disused railway to Dumbarton, reaching Loch Lomond via the towpath by the River Leven. There's an extension to this route all the way to Inverness, from Balloch via Aberfoyle, Loch Vennachar, Callander and Strathyre to link with the Glen Ogle Trail, Killin, Pitlochry and Aviemore (the entire route should be open by 2000).

The Glasgow-Greenock/Gourock Route runs via Paisley, this first section partly on roads.

From Johnstone to Greenock the route follows a disused railway line; the final section to Gourock is yet to open. Sculpture from the Sustrans public arts project brightens parts of the way.

The Glasgow-Irvine, Ardrossan and West Kilbride Cycle Way runs via Paisley, then off-road as far as Glengarnock. From here to Kilwinning it follows minor roads, then the route is partly off-road. Ferries to the Isle of Arran, popular with cyclists, leave from Ardrossan. A planned extension via Ayr, Maybole and Glentrool leads to the Solway coast and Carlisle.

By 2000, the new Glasgow to Edinburgh Route should be open. It will partly follow the Clyde walkway and a disused railway line. Also, in the future, a cycle route should be completed to Callander via Bridge of Allan.

The long-distance footpath known as the West Highland Way begins in Milngavie, 8 miles north of Glasgow, and runs for 95 miles to Fort William. (See the Activities chapter).

ORGANISED TOURS

From the main TIC, 1½-hour guided walks (£4/3) through the city centre leave Monday to Friday at 6 pm and on Sunday at 10.30 am, from May to September. There's also a 1½ hour cathedral walk (£4/3) at 2.15 pm on Wednesday and Sunday.

Mercat Tours (☎ 772 0022) runs 1½-hour guided walking tours, leaving from the TIC daily at 7 pm year-round and also at 9 pm from April to October, for £5/4. The latter, known as the *Gruesome Glasgow Horror Walking Tour*, includes a night visit to the cathedral and graveyard, and requires some nerve.

In the summer, the *Waverley* (☎ 221 8152), the world's last ocean-going paddle steamer, cruises the Firth of Clyde from the Waverley Terminal. It serves several towns and the islands of Bute, Great Cumbrae and Arran.

SPECIAL EVENTS

Not to be outdone by Edinburgh, Glasgow has developed several festivals of its own, starting each January with a two-week Celtic music festival (☎ 332 6633).

Maydaze, in early May, is a new arts and dance festival; call Performing Arts on

☎ 287 5429 for details. The West End Festival of music and the arts (☎ 341 0844) runs for two weeks in June and it's currently Glasgow's biggest festival. The excellent International Jazz Festival (☎ 400 5000) is held in July. Glasgay! (☎ 553 1511) is a gay performing arts festival, held every two years around October/November. The next will be held in 1999.

Other festivals include the Scottish Proms (classical music, ☎ 332 6633) in mid-June and the World Pipe Band Championships (☎ 221 5414) in mid-August, with over 100 pipe bands.

PLACES TO STAY

Finding somewhere decent in July and August can be difficult – for a B&B, get into town reasonably early and use the TIC's booking service. Unfortunately, Glasgow's B&Bs are expensive by Scottish standards – you may have to pay up to £20. At weekends many of the expensive business hotels slash their prices by up to 50%, making them great value for tourists.

Hostels & Colleges

Glasgow Youth Hostel (☎ 332 3004, 7 Park Terrace) was once a hotel. It has mainly four-bed rooms, many with *en suite* facilities, as well as four doubles. In summer, it's advisable to make a booking. It's open all day and the nightly charge is £12.50/10.95, including a continental breakfast. Between March and October, three-course dinners are available for £4.40. From Central station take bus No 44 or 59 and ask for the first stop on Woodlands Rd.

Berkeley Globetrotters (☎ 221 7880, 63 Berkeley St) has beds from £7.50 (£6.50 if you have your own bedding) in dorms, £9.50 in twin rooms. Phone ahead for bookings. Berkeley St is a western continuation of Bath St (one block south of Sauchiehall St). The hostel's just past the Mitchell Library.

Near the SYHA hostel, the *Glasgow Backpackers Hostel* (☎ 332 9099, Kelvin Lodge, 8 Park Circus) is one of the university's halls of residence, so it's only open

July through September. Beds are from £8.90. This is an Independent Backpackers Hostel, and very popular since it's the best in the city. Nearby **Woodlands Houses** (☎ 332 2386, 4, 5 and 12A Woodlands Terrace) provide backpacker accommodation for around £10. They're also only open in the summer.

The **University of Glasgow** (☎ 330 5385) has a range of B&B accommodation at £21 per head or £127.50 per week, and self-catering at £12.50 or £75 per week mid-March to mid-April, and July, August and September.

The **University of Strathclyde** (☎ 553 4148) also opens its halls of residence to tourists mid-June to mid-September. In the **Campus Village** (☎ 552 0626, 24 hours), opposite Glasgow Cathedral, backpacker accommodation costs £9.50 (sleeping bag required). There's also a bed-only rate starting at £14, and en suite single B&B costs £36. The Campus Village office opens 24 hours, but phone ahead to make arrangements. Next to the office, there's a coin operated laundry. If you don't mind staying farther out of town, the university's cheapest B&B accommodation is at **Jordanhill Campus** (76 Southbrae Drive). Comfortable rooms are £19.50/29, and bus No 44 from Central station goes to the college gates. The university's impressive Art Deco **Baird Hall** (460 Sauchiehall St) is in a great location and offers some B&B accommodation year-round for £23.50/39. These B&B rates are also available mid-June to mid-September at the **Clyde Hall** (318 Clyde St) and the Campus Village.

The **YMCA Glasgow Aparthotel** (☎ 558 6166, David Naismith Court, 33 Petershill Drive), Springburn, is a characterless tower block north of the M8. With continental breakfast the nightly charge is £17/28 or £107.10/176.40 per week.

Camping

Craigendmuir Caravan Park (☎ 779 4159, Campsie View), Stepps, is the nearest, but it's still a 15 minute walk from Stepps station. It takes vans and tents for £6.50 (two people).

B&Bs & Hotels

City Centre McLay's Guest House (☎ 332 4796) is labyrinthine, but brilliantly located at 264 Renfrew St, which is behind Sauchiehall St. Considering the location, you can't quibble at £21 for a single room without bathroom, or £25 with. There are doubles for £38, or £44 with bath.

If you can't get in there try the **Victorian House** (☎ 332 0129, 212 Renfrew St) just down from the School of Art. It's a large guesthouse; prices are £23/38 with shared bathroom, £29/48 attached. There are several other similarly priced places along this street, including the **Willow Hotel** (☎ 332 2332, 228 Renfrew St). The **Hampton Court Hotel** (☎ 332 6623, 230 Renfrew St) is slightly cheaper. Singles without bath are £17, with bath they're £25; doubles are £40, with bath.

Babbity Bowster (☎ 552 5055, 16 Black-friars St) is a very lively pub/restaurant (see Entertainment later in this chapter) with six bedrooms. Singles/doubles with attached bathrooms cost £45/65. It's a great place to stay but forget it if you like to turn in early with a nice cup of cocoa.

The **Charing Cross Tower Hotel** (☎ 221 1000, 10 Elmbank Gardens) in the tower above Charing Cross train station offers room-only rates of £44.50/59.50 for singles/doubles with attached bath. At weekends, prices drop to £34.50/50. A full Scottish buffet breakfast costs £6.95.

The **Glasgow Marriott** (☎ 226 5577, 500 Argyle St) is a very comfortable city centre hotel. Rooms cost £89 to £145 per person during the week, and start at £59 at the weekend.

East There's a batch of reasonable-value B&Bs located to the east of the Necropolis. **Brown's Guest House** (☎ 554 6797, 2 Onslow Drive) has rooms from £15/26. **Craigpark Guest House** (☎ 554 4160, 33 Circus Drive) charges from £15/26. **Seton**

Guest House (☎ 556 7654, 6 Seton Terrace) has singles/doubles from £16.50/29.

One of the best places to stay in Glasgow is the small *Cathedral House Hotel* (☎ 552 3519, 28 Cathedral Square). Housed in a Victorian baronial-style building complete with turrets, it's very close to the cathedral and easily accessible from the M8. There's a pleasant café-bar, and in Glasgow's only Icelandic restaurant, diners cook at the table on hot rocks. The eight well-appointed rooms cost £49/69, all with bath.

West End Many of the places to stay in this area are situated on or around Great Western Rd. There are several B&Bs on Hillhead St (just south of Great Western Rd and near Byres Rd), including *Chez Nous Guest House* (☎ 334 2977, 33 Hillhead St), with rooms from £18.50/37 to £25/50 and *Iona Guest House* (☎ 334 2346, 39 Hillhead St), which is smaller and much the same price.

Kelvin View Guest House (☎ 339 8257, 411 North Woodside Rd) is just north of Great Western Rd and the M8. Rooms here are from £17/32; some have attached bathroom. There are several other similarly priced B&Bs on this road.

The highly recommended *Kirklee Hotel* (☎ 334 5555, 11 Kensington Gate) is more upmarket and you'll probably be treated as well as the plants in the window boxes – which are very well treated indeed. Rooms with attached shower/bath cost from £45/59.

Just off Great Western Rd, a little nearer the city centre, is the comfortable *Terrace House Hotel* (☎ 337 3377, 14 Belhaven Terrace). There are 13 rooms, all with attached bathrooms. It costs £47/60 during the week and £39/50 at weekends.

In the same area, the *Town House* (☎ 357 0862, 4 Hughenden Terrace) is similar to these last two places. It's very well run and an excellent choice. Rooms charges are from £58/68.

There are a number of places just south of Kelvingrove Park. The *Alamo Guest House* (☎ 339 2395, 46 Gray St), with 10

rooms from £18/32, is good value. *Smith's Hotel* (☎ 339 6363, 963 Sauchiehall St) charges £19/34 for its budget rooms.

Probably the best hotel in Glasgow is *One Devonshire Gardens* (☎ 339 2001, 1 Devonshire Gardens) just off Great Western Rd. Sumptuously decorated, and occupying three classical terrace houses, the atmosphere is that of a luxurious country house. There are 27 rooms, each very well appointed, from £140/165. From Friday to Sunday, prices are £125 per person. As one might expect, there's an excellent restaurant here, too.

South of the Clyde On and around Pollokshaws Rd, on the way to Pollok Country Park and the Burrell Collection, there are several places to stay in this quiet suburb. *Regent Guest House* (☎ 422 1199, 44 Regent Park Square) has B&B accommodation from £20 per person. Some rooms have attached bath. *Reidholm Guest House* (☎ 423 1855, 36 Regent Park Square), farther down the terrace, is about the same price.

On the other side of Pollokshaws Rd, just south of Queen's Park, *Boswell Hotel* (☎ 632 9812, 27 Mansionhouse Rd), off Langside Ave, can be an entertaining place to stay. The Boswell is better known as a watering hole, with its three bars and live jazz or rhythm and blues on occasion. Singles/doubles are £42.50/60 during the week, £35/50 at weekends; all with attached bath/showers.

North of Pollok Country Park, in the Bellahouston area between the M8 and M77, there's a couple of small B&Bs. *Mr Bristow's* (☎ 427 0129, 56 Dumbreck Rd) costs from £25/34 a single/double and opens year-round. *Mrs Ross's* (☎ 427 0194, 3 Beech Ave) has rooms from £25/40 with shower.

PLACES TO EAT

Twenty-five years ago, when the pubs in Scotland closed at 10 pm, Glaswegians went to restaurants to take advantage of extended licensing hours, not for the food. Things are very different now and Glasgow not only has an excellent range of places to eat but many are also very moderately priced.

The West End probably has the greatest range of restaurants, everything from Glasgow's most famous place to eat, the upmarket Ubiquitous Chip, to cheap cafés where they really do serve chips with everything. In the city centre, however, and along Sauchiehall St, there's also no shortage of places to eat.

If you're on a budget, have your main meal at lunchtime – the set lunches offered by many restaurants are usually very good value at £3 to £5.

West End

The main restaurant/pub area in the West End is about three-quarters of a mile west of the YH, around Byres Rd. The nearest underground station is Hillhead.

Café Antipasti (☎ 337 2737, 337 Byres Rd) is a pleasant and busy place with good food too. Lunch pasta dishes are £3 to £3.50; evening dishes (pizza, pasta etc) are £4.45 to £8. Just off Byres Rd, on the east side, Ashton Lane is packed with places to eat. Cheapest is the *Grosvenor Café (☎ 339 1848, 35 Ashton Lane)* where you can get soup, filled rolls and hot meals all day. Try the pizza with fried egg for £1.10; evening specials are under £4. This is a popular student hangout. *Ashoka (☎ 357 5904, 19 Ashton Lane)* is an Indian restaurant with a daily two-course pre-theatre menu for £7.95.

Some of Glasgow's top restaurants are also on Ashton Lane. The *Ubiquitous Chip (☎ 334 5007, 12 Ashton Lane)* has earned a solid reputation for its excellent Scottish cuisine, fresh seafood and game, and for the length of its wine list. A three-course dinner with coffee will set you back £24. Set among potted plants of arboreal proportions this is an excellent place for a night out. There's a cheaper restaurant here, *Upstairs at the Chip*, where two courses at lunchtime will cost less than £10. *Mitchells (☎ 339 2220, 35 Ashton Lane)* is an informal bistro with some excellent Scottish dishes. Main

courses range from £8 to £12 and a two-course pre-theatre meal costs £8.

Back on Byres Rd, the *University Café (☎ 339 5217, 87 Byres Rd)* is a university institution. It's very cheap, with all meals under £4; there's fish and chips and salad (£3.70), excellent pizza and superb home-made ice-cream.

On the west side of Byres Rd, directly across from Ashton Lane, is Ruthven Lane where, among the wacky shops, there are a number of interesting places to eat. At *Back Alley (☎ 334 7165, 8 Ruthven Lane)* students get a 10% discount. Mexican and Indian main courses are normally £7 to £9 and there are vegetarian options. It does Thai green coconut curry with shark for £8.95. The *Puppet Theatre (☎ 339 8444, 11 Ruthven Lane)* is a classy and expensive place featuring Scottish cuisine. Dinner is £27.95 for three courses; lunch £12.95 for two courses. Down the lane is *Di Maggio's (☎ 334 8560, 61 Ruthven Lane)*, good for pizzas and pasta from £5 to £7 (with vegetarian options).

Those staying in the vicinity of Kelvingrove Park will find a scattering of restaurants on or around Gibson St and Great Western Rd. The cheapest place is *Joe's Garage (☎ 339 5407, 52 Bank St)* at the junction with Gibson St. It's open daily to midnight and a three-course lunch is only £2.45. *Shalimar (☎ 339 6453, 23 Gibson St)* is a large Indian restaurant which offers a four-course buffet dinner for £8.95, £9.95 at weekends.

Stravaigin (☎ 334 2665, 28 Gibson St) is highly recommended. A two-course meal downstairs is around £16, but there's a cheaper menu upstairs. The chilli con carne (£7.95), Thai green curry with chicken (£4.95) and rack of blackfaced lamb (£13.95) are particularly good.

The vegetarian *Bay Tree Café (☎ 334 5898, 403 Great Western Rd)* is excellent value. Filling main dishes cost less than £4, salads are generous, and there's a good range of hot drinks. The café is famous for its all-day Sunday brunch, served from 11 am to 8 pm, including vegetarian burger, tattie scone, mushrooms, beans and tomato (£3.50). Felafel with pitta bread and dip costs £2.45. Open daily, except Monday, it closes at 9 pm (8 pm on Sunday). If you're in a hurry, the café also serves takeaways.

Insomnia Café (☎ *564 1700, 38 Woodlands Rd*) has never closed since it first opened in October 1995. There are sandwiches from £1.15, a wide range of meals (main courses are £4 to £6.25), herbal teas and coffees in Scotland's first 24 hour café.

Near the Kelvingrove Art Gallery, friendly Dutch-run *Janssens* (☎ *334 9682, 1355 Argyle St*) serves good lunches, and everything from adventurous sandwiches to full meals. Main courses are around £6 to £11, but pizzas start at £4. There's a specials blackboard and vegetarian choices. Not too far away, there's the *Snaffle Bit* (☎ *339 7163, 975 Sauchiehall St*). It's a popular place for a bar meal such as home-made soup or steak pie.

City Centre

There are a number of good choices elsewhere on Sauchiehall St. *Ristoro Ciao Italia* (☎ *332 4565, 441 Sauchiehall St*) is an efficient Italian restaurant where you should be able to eat and drink for around £10. Nearby, *Loon Fung* (☎ *332 1240, 417 Sauchiehall*) is one of the best Chinese places in town. There are set dinners from £17, a three-course lunch is £6.30, and a four-course pre-theatre dinner (Thursday to Saturday) costs £9.95.

There's a pleasant café with sandwiches (£4.95), and salads and main courses (£5 to £6.25) at the *Centre for Contemporary Arts* (☎ *332 7521, 346 Sauchiehall St*).

The main branch of Glasgow's well known bakery chain, *Bradford's* (*245 Sauchiehall St*), has a good tearoom upstairs where it also offers light meals (£4 to £5). We can't recommend the sausage rolls.

The *Willow Tearoom* (☎ *332 0521, 217 Sauchiehall St*), above a jewellery shop, was designed as a tearoom by Charles Rennie Mackintosh in 1903. Last orders are at 4.15 pm, and for lunch and tea the queues can be long. Avoid them by arriving when it opens

at 9 am (noon on Sunday) and splash out on a superior breakfast of smoked salmon, scrambled eggs and toast (£5.10). There's another branch at 97 Buchanan St.

Continuing east along Sauchiehall St, there's a branch of the pâtisserie chain, *Delifrance* (☎ *353 2700, 119 Sauchiehall St*). The filled baguettes (from £1.85) are good, but the tartelettes are pricey at £1.30.

Blue Lagoon, on the corner of Bath St and West Nile St, does takeaway fish and chips and chicken and chips for only £1.95.

Jade House (☎ *332 1932, 7 Bath St*) is a very pleasant Chinese restaurant. Daily, except Sunday, three-course lunches cost £4.50 and three-course dinners are £7.50. The à la carte menu is available all week. Vegetarian and carry out meals are available.

Balbir's (☎ *331 1980, 51 West Regent St*) originally opened as the Balti Bar, Glasgow's first balti restaurant. It's still good value with a daily three-course pre-theatre menu costing only £6.75.

At Princes Square, the stylish shopping centre on Buchanan St, one floor is given over to restaurants and foodstalls ranging from Caribbean to Chinese. There are more upmarket options here, too. Nearby, there's *The Jenny* (☎ *204 4988, 18 Royal Exchange Square*). This tearoom and bistro has a pavement café in summer, and it's highly recommended. Try the savoury buns (£4.45 to £5.85), two-in-one pies (£5.25), or a special (for around £4 to £6).

Yes (☎ *221 8044, 22 West Nile St*) is a stylish new restaurant, bar and brasserie that's building up a great reputation. It has an express lunch menu (all dishes served in under 15 minutes), with soup and a baguette for £2.45 and main courses for £5 to £6. In the evening, you can enjoy a three-course meal in the brasserie for £10.95 while listening to live music.

Near the St Enoch Centre is *The Granary* (☎ *226 3770, 82 Howard St*), a pleasant and inexpensive place. It's mainly vegetarian but also has a few non-veg choices. Main courses are £3 to £4. *Aulds on the terrace* is a coffee shop at the St Enoch Centre. It's popular with shoppers and does a wide range of snacks (sandwiches, toasties, baked potatoes, salads etc) for under £4.

Tivoli (☎ 552 1690, 39 Stockwell St) is a café with takeaways including filled rolls from 60p and fish and chips for £2.90. Try its excellent ice-cream – banana splits are £2.75.

In the Merchant City, near the City Halls, is *Café Gandolfi (☎ 552 6813, 64 Albion St)*. Once part of the old cheese market, it's now an excellent friendly bistro and upmarket coffee shop – very much the place to be seen. Main courses run from £4 to £12; smoked venison with gratin dauphinois is £8.90.

One of the best restaurants in the city is the *Buttery (☎ 221 8188, 652 Argyle St)*, just west of the M8. The menu is Scottish, a three-course dinner will cost around £30, and it's closed on Sunday. Downstairs is the cheaper bistro, the *Belfry (☎ 221 0630)*; reservations are advised. A two-course pre-theatre dinner (served from 6.30 to 7.30 pm) costs £9.95.

At 157 North St, near the Mitchell Library, is *Mitchell's (☎ 204 4312)*, an excellent bistro. Lunch main courses are £5 to £11, evening ones are £7.50 to £12. A three-course pre-theatre meal (5 to 7 pm) costs £10.95.

ENTERTAINMENT

Some of the best nightlife in Scotland is to be found in the pubs and clubs of Glasgow. Most pubs also do food, although many stop serving around 8 pm.

For the latest information, get a copy of the *List*. Also look out for the freebie magazine, *city live!*, which has a monthly listing of Glasgow's lively live music scene (www .glasgow.gov.uk/pav).

If it's a wee bit of Scottish dancing you're after, rather than a night in the pubs or clubs, go to the *Riverside (☎ 248 3144)*, Fox St (off Clyde St), on Friday or Saturday evening for the ceilidh. Doors open at 8 pm and the band starts at 9 pm. It's good clean fun for £5.

Note that owing to an odd law currently in force in Glasgow you may not be allowed entrance to a club after 1 am. Check with the clubs recommended in this section for the current regulations.

Football is taken seriously in Scotland. The reputation of violence at matches has now been replaced by mainly good behaviour, if a trifle rowdy.

Pubs

West End The *Halt Bar (☎ 564 1527, 160 Woodlands Rd)* is a popular university pub that hasn't yet been tarted up. It serves toasties, rolls and soup up to 9 or 10 pm. There's live music (free) most nights, a great atmosphere, and it's open until midnight on Friday and Saturday, 11 pm on other nights.

Farther along Woodlands Rd there's the *Uisge Beatha (☎ 564 1598, 246 Woodlands Rd)*, which keeps the same hours. The name's Gaelic for whisky (literally, Water of Life). It's a friendly place with eclectic décor and four bar areas.

Bar Oz (☎ 334 0884, 499 Great Western Rd) is an Australian theme pub that offers burgers (£2.95 to £3.25), the Oz meat pie for £3.25, and, to quench a thirst caused by the heat in there, a good range of bottled beers, lagers and wines from Down Under. There's an Australian quiz night on Tuesday and a live pop-rock band on Thursday. Big screen Australian and New Zealand sporting events are shown daily (10 am to 2 pm). Indoor barbecues are occasionally held!

There are numerous pubs on or around Byres Rd. *Curlers (☎ 338 6511, 256 Byres Rd)* is very popular with students who come for the bargain three-course set lunch (£3.25) and stay on for the live jazz (midweek). There's also live folk music every Thursday to Saturday from 8 pm, and student bands play every Tuesday from 8 pm. *Brel's (☎ 342 4966, 37 Ashton Lane)* is a new trendy bar. There's also *Cul de Sac (☎ 334 4749, 44 Ashton Lane)*, which has inexpensive meals from £3.45 to £5. The *Ubiquitous Chip (12 Ashton Lane)* also has a bar.

City Centre By the Union St exit of Central station is the basement *Underworld (☎ 221 5020)*, opened in 1996. It's a wacky, stylish but not too pretentious place with a

GLASGOW

restaurant area serving Tex-Mex food. Main courses are around £6 to £7.

Bar 10 (☎ *221 8353, 10 Mitchell Lane*) is a stylish and popular café bar off Buchanan St. It was designed by Ben Kelly who was responsible for Manchester's famous Dry Bar and Hacienda. It does soup and bread for £2.50 and pasta dishes for £3.95.

The subterranean ***Brunswick Cellars*** (☎ *572 0016, 239 Sauchiehall St*) is a popular bar that also does cheap lunches (main courses £4 to £5). The lunches are excellent value, and between 3 and 8 pm it serves drinks for £1 to £1.20 per pint.

The ***Scotia Bar*** (☎ *552 8681, 112 Stockwell St*) is Glasgow's oldest pub, boasting a history that goes back to 1792. It serves real ales and bar lunches. There's live folk music on Wednesday evenings and blues on Sunday afternoons.

Babbity Bowster (☎ *552 5055, 16 Blackfriars St*) is a popular Merchant City pub with a good range of real ales, excellent pub grub from £4 to £6 and live folk music on Saturday and Sunday. There's also a small hotel here, and a restaurant noted for its Scottish cuisine with à la carte main courses from £8 to £11.50.

The ***Horse Shoe*** (☎ *221 3051, 17 Drury St*) may have one of the longest bars in Europe, but its more important attraction is what's served over it – real ale and good food that's also good value. A three-course lunch is only £2.40; evening meals in the upstairs lounge are only a little dearer. The pub's been here for over 100 years and it's largely unchanged.

By Mitchell's is the traditional ***Bon Accord*** (☎ *248 4427, 153 North St*) with 14 real ales and 18 malt whiskies. There's also great pub grub – baked potatoes are £2.45 to £2.65, and doorsteps (large toasted sandwiches) cost £2.25.

There are lots of city centre pubs that do live music, including ***The Bank*** (☎ *248 4455, 35 Queen St*); ***Blackfriars*** (☎ *552 5924, 36 Bell St*); the ***Drum and Monkey*** (☎ *221 6636, 93 St Vincent St*); and ***MacSorley's*** (☎ *572 0199, 42 Jamaica St*).

Nightclubs

Glasgow's club scene rivals that of London and Manchester, but it changes so quickly it's difficult to make recommendations. The following places, however, seem to remain popular. Check the *List* and ask around for the latest places.

Glaswegians don't start hitting the clubs until after the pubs have closed, so many clubs will offer discounted entry and cheaper drinks if you get there before 10 or 11 pm. Most also usually give discounts for students. Don't arrive in trainers (runners or sneakers) or you'll be turned away from most places.

Off Jamaica St and under Central station, ***Arches*** (☎ *221 9736*) is the place to go at weekends – Slam Un-cut on Friday (£6, £5 student, 11 pm to 3.30 am), various others (Love Boutique, Colours, Cool Lemon, Inside Out, £10 to £15) on Saturday.

King Tut's Wah Wah Hut (☎ *221 5279, 272 St Vincent St*) has live music most nights from local, national and, occasionally, international bands. Ticket prices range from £3.50 to £10.50, and tickets for the bigger events should be bought in advance. The downstairs bar opens every day.

Archaos (☎ *204 3189, 25 Queen St*) is currently very popular. It has three floors with Indie, rave, chart, dance and house music. Over 18s should go after 10 pm.

The Cathouse (☎ *248 6606, 15 Union St*) is Glasgow's premier hard rock nightclub, open five nights. It occasionally has live music.

The ***Garage*** (☎ *332 1120, 490 Sauchiehall St*) appeals to 18 to 25-year-olds and is popular with students every night of the week. It plays disco music from the 70s onwards.

The Tunnel (☎ *204 1000, 84 Mitchell St*) is a stylish club in the West End. The gents' loos are famous for their designer waterworks. This is one Glasgow attraction women might have to miss out on!

Victoria's (☎ *332 1444, 98 Sauchiehall St*) is a large glitzy nightclub with two discos (music from the 60s to the 90s), a second floor piano bar with a resident cabaret, and a cabaret room featuring Scotland's foremost artistes. The average age is over 30, but there's a good mix of young and older people. You may see some of the country's well known personalities in here! Victoria's was Scottish Nightclub of the Year 1995, 1996 and 1997; it held the British title in 1996. The club opens Wednesday to Sunday and admission costs £7.95 to £11.95, depending on the day. This includes access to all rooms and a hot and cold buffet. Entrance to the discos only costs £3 to £7.

There are eight gay cafés and pubs, and one club, including *Austins (183 Hope St)*;

The Court Bar (69 Hutcheson St); the *Waterloo Bar (306 Argyle St)*; *Sadie Frost's* (☎ 332 8005, 8 West George St); the *Polo Lounge* (☎ 553 1221, 84 Wilson St), popular with women; *Café Latte (63 Virginia St)*, open daily, 9 to 1 am; *QC's Bistro Bar* (☎ 204 5418), at the Glasgow Gay and Lesbian Centre (☎ 221 7203); and the funkier *Café Del Monica's (68 Virginia St)*, which serves food from noon to 10 pm. *Bennet's* (☎ 552 5761, 80 Glassford St) is currently the only gay club, popular with men in their 20s.

On Friday and Saturday head for *Change at Jamaica* (☎ 429 4422, 11 Clyde Place)

The Glesca Patois

Glasgow enjoys a rich local dialect and knowledge of the vernacular might make your visit there a wee bit more interesting.

For many the pub is a focal point of social life. Order a 'half and a half', and you'll get a whisky and a half pint of beer. Seasoned drinkers may refer to their whisky as a 'wee goldie', or a 'nippy sweetie'. A pint of heavy will get you dark draught beer. A 'heavy bevvy' on the other hand will get you a major hangover with a 'loupin' heid' (headache), the 'dry boke' (nausea) and/or feeling 'awfy no weel' (very under the weather) the next day.

There may be some football supporters in the pub. The 'Bhoys' (Celtic football club) wear green colours and are traditionally supported by the 'Tims' (Catholics). The 'Gers' (Rangers football club) wear blue and are the 'Huns' (Protestant) team.

Football can be a touchy subject in Glasgow. Tell anyone who asks that you're a 'Jags' (Partick Thistle) supporter and you're on neutral ground. Billy Connolly, the comedian, who grew up in Partick, claims that he always thought the full team name was 'Partick Thistle Nil'. Enough said.

When males spot a 'wee stoater' (good-looking young woman) in the bar, they might be inclined to try their 'patter' (witty chat) on her. Impress her, and they might get a 'lumber' (pick-up). Inane conversation about the weather, 'the nights are fair drawin' in' (the days are getting shorter), or 'it's stoatin' doon ootside' (it's raining very heavily), will not impress, and almost certainly result in a 'KB' (knock-back, rejection). Should her boyfriend, 'the Big Yin', arrive unexpectedly, and offer to 'mollocate', 'wanner' or 'stiffen' the would-be lothario, or alternatively to give him his 'heid in your hauns' (head in your hands), then violence is probably imminent.

At that point it's best to 'shoot the crow' (go) before a 'stooshie' (brawl) develops, and in future, to give that particular pub the 'body swerve' (a wide berth).

However, Glaswegians are very friendly to travellers. You may be addressed as 'Jimmy' or 'Hen', depending on your sex. If you refer to their city as 'Glesca', and never 'Glasgie', they may even mistake you for a local.

John McKenna

where breakfasts are served from 10 pm to 5 am, Friday and Saturday. A full Scottish breakfast costs £4.95 (it also does weekday lunches, and evening meals may be up and running Monday to Saturday). This café is just south of the river, under the railway bridge, and has a lively party atmosphere after the clubs have closed.

Concerts, Theatre & Film
For tickets phone the Ticket Centre on ☎ 227 5511.

The *Theatre Royal (☎ 332 3321, 282 Hope St)* is the home of Scottish Opera, and the Scottish Ballet often performs here. The Royal Scottish National Orchestra plays at the modern *Glasgow Royal Concert Hall (☎ 332 6633, 2 Sauchiehall St)*.

The *King's Theatre (☎ 287 5511, 294 Bath St)* hosts musicals, variety shows, pantomimes, and occasional comedies. Ticket prices range from £8 to £25.

Rock and pop bands on the international circuit usually play at the *SECC (☎ 248 3000)* – the Scottish Exhibition and Conference Centre – which is a modern aircraft hangar of a place by the river. Some bands choose the *Barrowland Ballroom (☎ 552 4601, 244 Gallowgate)*, a vast dance hall in the East End that's far funkier.

The *Citizens' Theatre (☎ 429 0022, Gorbals St)* is one of the top theatres in Scotland and it's well worth trying to catch a performance here. Ticket prices for Citizen's own productions are £8/2; for visiting companies, prices range from around £5 to £10 (concessions half-price). The *Tron Theatre (☎ 552 4267, 63 Trongate)* stages contemporary Scottish and international performances. There's a good café here.

The *Centre for Contemporary Arts (☎ 332 0522, 350 Sauchiehall St)* is an interesting centre for the visual and performing arts – it also has a pleasant café. A couple of blocks east, the two-screen *Glasgow Film Theatre (☎ 332 8128, 12 Rose St)*, off Sauchiehall St, screens new releases, classics and popular re-runs (from £3.25/2 to £4.25/3). In the same area, the five-screen *ABC Film Centre (☎ 332 1592,*

326 Sauchiehall St), shows films for £3.20 to £4 (concessions £3).

SPECTATOR SPORT
Celtic Football Club (☎ 551 8653), Celtic Park, Parkhead (in the East End), has a 60,000-seat stadium with a restaurant. Celtic has overcome financial and on-field difficulties and is again a strong force in Scottish football.

Rangers Football Club (☎ 427 8800), Ibrox Stadium, 150 Edmiston Dr (in the South Side), has had several controversial players in recent times. The restaurant, however, has a good reputation; snacks are also available in the stadium during matches. It's possible to arrange a tour of the Trophy Room with any one of the players; just turn up and ask. Rangers' 52,000-seat stadium has entry charges starting at £12/8 for league games, rising to £18/14 for European games. Celtic's charges are similar.

GETTING THERE & AWAY
Glasgow is 405 miles from London, 97 from Carlisle, 42 from Edinburgh and 166 from Inverness.

Air
Glasgow International Airport (☎ 887 1111), 10 miles west of the city, handles domestic traffic, and international flights. Ryanair (☎ 0541-569569) flies from Prestwick airport, 30 miles south-west of Glasgow, to London Stansted airport (one hour, one to three flights per week), for £19 one way, including free rail travel to Glasgow Central station. The coach link from Stanstead to London Victoria coach station is an extra £5 return.

Bus
All long-distance buses arrive and depart from Buchanan Bus Station.

Buses from London are very competitive. Silver Choice (☎ 333 1400) is currently the best deal at £13/25 for a single/return. Departures are daily at 11 pm from both Victoria Coach Station in London and Buchanan Bus Station in Glasgow, and the

Hampden Park – Scotland's Field of Dreams

Scotland's National Football Stadium is most unusual since it's home to an amateur football club, Queen's Park, founded in 1867 as Scotland's first football club.

Always shy of professionalism, Queen's Park didn't join the Scottish League until 1900. In 1903, it moved to its newly built Hampden Stadium, which has since been modified and upgraded several times. Initially, the stadium could hold 40,000 standing and 4000 seated spectators. Its main use has been for international matches, particularly against England, and Scottish Cup finals, passionate sporting contests that have spawned legendary characters. The 1937 Scotland-England game drew an incredible 149,547 spectators, the highest ever official football match attendance in Britain.

When the latest refurbishment is completed, the stadium will include the new Scottish National Football Museum and Hampden may become one of the biggest visitor attractions in Glasgow.

run takes around eight hours. The service is very popular so you'll need to book.

National Express (☎ 0990-808080) also leaves from there and has four or five daily services for £18/28. The best option is to catch the 8 am bus from London, so that you arrive in good time to organise accommodation. There's one daily direct bus from Heathrow airport.

There are numerous links with other English cities. National Express services include: three or four daily buses from Birmingham (5½ hours, £28.75/30); one from Cambridge (nine hours, £33.50/35.50); numerous from Carlisle (two hours, £11.50/12.50); two from Newcastle (four hours, £17.50/18.25); and one from York (6½ hours, £20.20/21.25).

National Express/Scottish Citylink (☎ 0990-505050) has buses to most major towns in Scotland. There are numerous services to Edinburgh, every 15 minutes during the day, taking 1¼ hours with singles/returns from £4.50/5 (off peak). Around 18 buses per day run to Stirling (45 minutes, £3/4), 12 to Inverness (from 3½ hours, £11.50/15.50), three or four to Oban (three hours, £10/17), 18 to Aberdeen (3¼ to four hours, £13.30/22), four or five to Fort William (three hours, £10/17) and three to Portree on Skye (6¼ to seven hours,

£17/24). There's a twice daily summer service (mid-May to mid-October) to Stranraer, connecting with the ferry to Belfast in Northern Ireland (six hours). Singles, midweek returns and standard returns are £32/42/46.

Scottish Highway Express (☎ 01698-860231) runs 23 to 27 services daily to Edinburgh (1¼ hours) for only £2/3.50 single/return. A 10-journey ticket costs £14.

Martin's Coaches (☎ 01397-712579) runs once to Fort William each weekday (three hours, £8.90/12, £6.50/8.50 for students). There are additional journeys on Friday evening (northbound) and Sunday evening (southbound).

Fife Scottish (☎ 01592-261461) runs buses to Anstruther (three hours, £5.50, six per day), St Andrews (2¼ hours, £5, hourly) and Dundee (2½ hours, £5, hourly) via Glenrothes.

Walkers should check out Midland Bluebird (☎ 01324-613777), which runs hourly buses to Milngavie (30 minutes, £1.45), the start of the West Highland Way.

Train

As a general rule, Central Station serves southern Scotland, England and Wales, and Queen St serves the north and east. There are buses every 10 minutes between them

(40p, free with a through train ticket). There are up to seven direct trains a day from London's Euston station; they're not cheap, but they're much quicker (five to six hours) and more comfortable than the bus. There are also up to seven direct services from London King's Cross. Fares change name and price rapidly, but there are usually a few seats with return fares in the £30 to £40 range. At the time of writing, the best fare was Virgin Value at £30 return.

ScotRail has the West Highland line heading north to Oban and Fort William (see those sections in The Highlands chapter) and other direct links to Dundee (£18.50), Aberdeen (£35.10) and Inverness (£28.90). There are numerous trains to Edinburgh (50 minutes, £7.10 single). Train travellers are advised to purchase a Freedom of Scotland travelpass or a Highland Rover pass (see the Getting Around chapter).

For all rail inquiries call ☎ 0345-484950.

Car

There are numerous car rental companies; the big names have offices at the airport. Melvilles Motors (☎ 632 5757), 192 Battlefield Rd, charges £26.40 per day for a Micra, Punto or Corsa. Arnold Clark (☎ 848 0202), at the airport, has Renault Clios for only £18 per day.

Cabervans (☎ 01475-638775), Caberfeidh, Cloch Rd, Gourock, has motorhomes for rent from around £300 per week in winter, or £540 per week in summer, plus a collision damage waiver of £10 per day. You can be picked up from Glasgow, Prestwick or Edinburgh airports or Gourock train station.

GETTING AROUND

The Roundabout Glasgow ticket (£3.40/ 1.70) covers all underground and train transport in the city for a day; the Roundabout Glasgow Plus ticket (£6.50/3.25) also includes the Discovering Glasgow hop on hop off tourist buses that run along the main sightseeing routes. The three-day version of Roundabout Glasgow Plus costs £13/6.50.

To/From the Airport

There are buses every 30 minutes (every 15 minutes in summer) from the airport to Buchanan Bus Station; they take 25 minutes and cost £2.50. Buses continue to Edinburgh (£6.50 from the airport). A taxi would cost about £13.

Bus

Bus services are frequent. You can buy tickets when you board buses, but on most you have to have exact change. Routes are shown on the *Visitors Transport Guide Map* (see under Information earlier in this section). For short trips in the city, fares are 65p. After midnight there are limited night bus services around the city leaving from George Square. They depart at 12.30 am on weekdays; and 12.30, 1.45, and 3 am at weekends.

In summer, Discovering Glasgow (☎ 204 0444) runs tourist buses every 20 minutes along the main sightseeing routes, starting at George Square.

From mid-September to Easter there are four buses per day. You get on and off as you wish and fares are £6.50/5 for a day ticket. Guide Friday (☎ 0131-556 2244) is similar with a slightly longer route.

Train

There's an extensive suburban network; tickets should be bought before travel if the station is staffed, or from the conductor if it isn't.

There's also an underground line that serves 15 stations in the centre, west and south of the city (65p). It runs Monday to Saturday from around 6.30 am to around 10.30 pm, and on Sunday from 11 am to 5.45 pm. An Underground Heritage Trail Pass (£2) gives unlimited travel on the system for a day.

Taxi

There's no shortage. If you order a taxi from Glasgow Wide Taxis (☎ 332 6666 or ☎ 332 7070) by phone, you can pay by credit card. There's also the option of Croft Radio Cars on ☎ 633 2222.

Bicycle

West End Cycles (☎ 357 1344), 16 Chancellor St, is at the southern end of Byres Rd and rents mountain bikes for £12 per day or £50 per week. Helmets and locks are an extra £2 per day each. Two IDs and a £50 deposit are required.

Around Glasgow

Glasgow is surrounded by a grim hinterland of post-industrial communities. Industrial archaeologists could have a field day here and some might see a perverse beauty in the endless suburbs of grey council house architecture. But it's here, possibly, that the Glasgow area's gritty black sense of humour is engendered.

PAISLEY

• pop 78,000   ☎ 0141

This is the town that gave its name to the well-known fabric design of swirling stylised teardrops or pinecones called the Paisley Pattern. Now really a suburb west of Glasgow, Paisley grew up around the abbey. By the 19th century the town was a major producer of printed cotton and woollen cloth.

The famous design was, in fact, copied from shawls brought back from India. At one time, Paisley was the largest producer of cotton thread in the world; the Coats family of threadmakers have enjoyed a long association with the town.

Information

The helpful TIC (☎ 889 0711) is currently in the Lagoon Leisure Centre, Christie St, but may move to Gilmour St. Walk down Gilmour St from the train station, turn left into Gauze St and you'll see the leisure centre across the road and on your right at the busy intersection with Mill St. It's open from 9 am to 5 pm weekdays and, from June to October, including Saturday, 9 am to 6 pm.

Fernie Guided Tours of Paisley (☎ 561 8078) runs two-hour walking tours starting at the abbey, Monday to Saturday, from 10.45 am and 1.30 pm, for £5/4.

Walking Tour

Start your walking tour at Gilmour St train station and follow Gilmour St towards The Cross (keep the taxi stance on your right). Turn left into Gauze St, cross the river, and you'll see **Paisley Abbey** (☎ 889 7654), in Abbey Close, on your right. The abbey was founded in 1163 by Walter Fitzallan, the first High Steward of Scotland and ancestor of the Stuart dynasty. It was badly damaged by fire during the Wars of Independence in 1306, but rebuilt soon after. Most of the nave is 14th or 15th century. The building was a ruin from the 16th century, until the 19th century restoration, completed in 1928. There are two royal tombs in the abbey, excellent stained glass windows, and the 10th century Celtic **Barochan Cross**. It's open Monday to Saturday, from 10 am to 3.30 pm; admission is free.

On the other side of Abbey Close, you'll see the grand **Town Hall**. From the abbey, turn right along Abbey Close, then left into the High St.

At the western end of the High St, there's the **University of Paisley** and the **Museum and Art Gallery** (☎ 889 3151), with a large display of Paisley shawls and an interesting outline of the history of the Paisley Pattern. It also has collections of local and natural history, ceramics, and 19th century Scottish art. It's open Monday to Saturday from 10 am to 5 pm; entry is free.

From the museum, continue along the High St into Wellmeadow St, with the **Thomas Coats Memorial Church** on your right.

Turn right into West Brae and Oakshaw St West for the **Coats Observatory** (☎ 889 2013). There are interesting displays about astronomy, earthquake recording, weather and climate, all continuously monitored here since 1882.

The observatory opens Monday, Tuesday and Thursday, from 2 to 8 pm, and Wednesday, Thursday and Saturday from 10 to 5 pm. Admission is free.

Retrace your steps to the High St, past the museum, and turn right down Storrie St, taking the second left into George St, then left again into George Place. Here, you'll find the **Sma' Shot Cottages** (☎ 889 1708), an 18th century weaver's cottage and a 19th century artisan's house, both with period furniture and other items of historic interest. There's also a tea room with home baking. The cottages are open April to September, Wednesday and Saturday, from 1 to 5 pm; admission is free.

From the cottages, turn left up Shuttle St, then right along New St, to **Paisley Arts Centre** (☎ 887 1010), in a converted church dating from 1738. It has a theatre, bar and bistro. Continue past the arts centre, turn left into Causeyside St, and you'll return to Gilmour St.

Places to Stay & Eat

There's not much point in staying overnight in Paisley, being so close to Glasgow. However, there are several good guest houses, including the luxurious *Myfarrclan* (☎ 884 8285, 146 Corsebar Rd) with B&B from £40/60 for a single/double. *Gleniffer House* (☎ 848 5544, Glenpatrick Rd) is a 200-year-old building with B&B from £18 per person.

There are lots of inexpensive places to eat in central Paisley, including the *Bankhouse* (☎ 848 7108, 7 Gilmour St). It's a pub with all main courses under £3.

Caprice (☎ 889 9432, 11 Gilmour St) does three-course lunches on weekdays for £3.90. *O'Neill's* (☎ 847 5401, 27 New St) is an Irish theme pub with sandwiches from £2.25 and main courses from £3.75 to £6.25. Late at night, it gets a bit wild in there.

Café India (☎ 887 6877, 8 New St) has five-course buffets, Sunday to Thursday, from 7 to 10 pm, for £9.95.

Getting There & Away

Trains leave Glasgow's Central station up to eight times each hour for Paisley's Gilmour St station (£1.85 single, £2.30 off-peak day return). There are frequent buses from Central Rd.

KILBRACHAN

Kilbrachan is just off the A737 Glasgow to Irvine road and about 5 miles west of Paisley.

At The Cross, you'll find the interesting **weaver's cottage** (☎ 01505-705588, NTS) dating from 1723, with a rare cruck roof which supported the original thatch. Originally two cottages, the weavers living here produced Paisley shawls, muslin and tartan for buyers from Paisley. There's a video presentation, 18th and 19th century furnishings, and demonstrations of handloom weaving (Friday to Sunday). The loom is nearly 200 years old.

The cottage is open from Easter to 30 September, daily (and weekends in October) from 1.30 to 5.30 pm; admission costs £2/1.30. For a pleasant snack, try *Bobbins Tea Room* (25 Steeple St), just across the road from the cottage. Home-made soup and bread is £1.70 and chilli con carne is just £2.95.

The best way to get to Kilbrachan is by Ariva (☎ 0141-848 6313) bus No 36 which runs frequently from Union St in Glasgow (£1.50 each way).

DUMBARTON

- **pop 22,634**   ☎ 01389

This town was the ancient capital of the Britons of Strathclyde, but time has passed it by. Dumbarton stands at the gateway to Loch Lomond and the Highlands, where the River Clyde becomes the Firth of Clyde, 14 miles west of Glasgow. It was important both as a strategic and trading centre around 1500 years ago.

On top of spectacular **Dumbarton Rock**, there's **Dumbarton Castle** (☎ 732167), now mostly a modern barracks. It's open to visitors, daily to 6.30 pm for most of the year. Admission costs £1.50/1. The **Scottish Maritime Museum** (☎ 763444), Castle St, has a working experimental ship-model tank and a tearoom (£1.50/1).

Places to eat are generally fish and chip shops, and Chinese and Indian restaurants. There's also a McDonald's and a Safeway just off the main Glasgow Rd.

Trains to Dumbarton Central run twice an hour from Helensburgh and Balloch; and four times an hour from Glasgow (30 minutes, £2.50 single, £3.10 off-peak return).

FIRTH OF CLYDE

The ghosts of once great shipyards still line the banks of the Clyde west of Glasgow. Ten miles downstream from the city, the impressive Erskine Bridge links the north and south banks.

The only place of any interest at all along the coast west of here is Greenock, although there are a couple of items of interest in the otherwise unprepossessing town of **Port Glasgow**. You could stop to see the replica of the *Comet*, Greenock Rd, Europe's first commercial steamship, launched here in 1812. There's also **Newark Castle** (☎ 01475-741858), a fine 16th century house, open April to September, with standard Historic Scotland hours. Admission costs £1.80/1.30.

GREENOCK
- pop 50,013 ☎ 01475

James Watt, who perfected the steam engine, was born in this large town in 1736, which is 27 miles from Glasgow. There are several things to see and the Tall Ships Race will be coming to Greenock in July 1999. The Greenock Cut is a good walk over the hills above the town – it follows an old aqueduct. The circular route from Overton is about 5 miles long and takes about 2½ hours.

Information & Orientation

The TIC (☎ 722007) is at 7 Clyde Square, near the High St and behind the Town Hall. It's open all year. Ask for its *Greenock Cut* and *Greenock town trails* leaflets.

Most things of interest in Greenock are near the High St, where the A78 to Largs branches off the end of the A8 Glasgow road. The central train station is close to the A8, near the waterfront at Customhouse Quay. The Tesco supermarket is on Dalrymple St and the post office is on Nicolson St.

Museums

In the **McLean Museum and Art Gallery** (☎ 723741), 15 Kelly St, displays chart the history of steam power and Clyde shipping. It's open Monday to Saturday, from 10 am to 5 pm; admission is free.

The **Custom House Museum** (☎ 726331), on the quay, traces the interesting history of the Customs and Excise service. Robert Burns and Adam Smith were former employees. The Custom House was built in 1818 and is well worth a visit; it's open Monday to Friday, from 10 am to 4 pm, with free admission.

Places to Stay & Eat

Fairly central and down on the waterfront, *James Watt College* (☎ 731360, Ardmore Hall, Customhouse Way) has 168 single rooms with B&B for £17 to £22 per person. Evening meals are available for an extra £6. The *Tontine Hotel* (☎ 723316, 6 Ardgowan Square) is just off the A8 near the Clyde Port Container Terminal, with well appointed rooms for £60 to £65 single, £80 to £90 double.

The finest hotel in the area is the *Gleddoch House Hotel* (☎ 540711) at Langbank, situated 6 miles east of Greenock. B&B in this sumptuous establishment costs £95 for a single, £140 for a double, and £175 for a suite with four-poster bed. There are also weekend breaks available from £140 per person for two or three nights, which includes four-course dinners. Since the dinner normally costs £32.50 per sitting, this represents great value. The oldest bottle of wine in Scotland, an 1870 Chateau Leoville-barton 2eme Cru, will set you back a cool £1500!

In central Greenock, there are lots of restaurants, cafés and pubs on West Blackhall St, including *Burger King* and *Paccino's Diner & takeaway*; the latter does baked potatoes from £1.75.

Bennick's (49 West Blackhall St) is a brasserie that does good bar meals (three courses for £8).

Farther along, *Aldo's (☎ 725358, 121 West Blackhall St)* does three-course Italian

GLASGOW

Shipbuilding on the Clyde

One of the earliest permanent Lower Clyde shipyards was established in 1711 by John Scott at Greenock. Initial construction was for small-scale local trade but, by the end of the 18th century, large ocean-going vessels were being built. As the market expanded, shipyards also opened at Dumbarton and Port Glasgow.

The *Comet*, Europe's first steamship, was launched at Port Glasgow in 1812 and, soon afterwards, other local yards became involved in the lucrative steamship-building trade. By the 1830s and 40s, the Clyde had secured its position as world-leader in shipbuilding with the development of iron-hulled ships, which were 25% cheaper to run than wooden-hulled ones. Steel hulls came into use by the 1880s, allowing construction of larger ships with the latest and best engines.

In 1899, John Brown & Co, a Sheffield steelmaker, took over a Clydebank yard and by 1907 had become part of the world's largest shipbuilding conglomerate, producing ocean-going liners. Output from the Clyde shipyards steadily increased up to WWI. Yarrow & Co set up a warship-building yard further upriver at Scotstoun. With the advent of WWI, there was huge demand for new shipping from both the Royal Navy and Merchant Navy.

During and after the war, many small companies disappeared and shipbuilding giants like Lithgows Ltd took their place. The depression years of the 1920s and 30s saw many yards mothballed or closed. The *Queen Mary* sat unfinished at John Brown's yard for over two years, but was finally launched in 1934. Another boom followed during WWII – the Mulberry harbour used in the Normandy landings was built on the Clyde.

After the war, the market was in good shape, but yard owners were reluctant to invest in new plant. When they did eventually invest, it was for the wrong type of shipping (passenger liners were going out of fashion), and many yards went into liquidation in the 1960s. In 1972, Upper Clyde Shipbuilders was liquidated, causing complete chaos, a sit-in and a bad headache for Ted Heath's government

Lithgow's, Scott's and Yarrow's managed to survive by manufacturing oil tankers, submarines, cargo ships and naval vessels. Scott-Lithgow, formed from an amalgamation in 1967, attempted to diversify into oil-rig manufacture in the early 1980s, but the company ran into serious difficulties and had to be rescued by Trafalgar House. The rescue failed and the yard was closed, creating further unemployment and misery.

In 1985, Yarrow Shipbuilders Ltd was sold to GEC, and another old name disappeared from the scene. Now the great shipyards of the Clyde are mostly derelict and empty. The remains of a once mighty industry includes Govan Shipbuilders (Kvaerner Govan Ltd) in Glasgow, Ferguson Shipbuilders in Port Glasgow, and several specialised marine subcontractors.

meals for £4.75. There's also a Chinese and an Indian restaurant on the same street.

Getting There & Away

There are three trains an hour from Glasgow Central (£3.40), and hourly buses. The Glasgow to Greenock pedestrian/cycle route follows an old railway track for 10 miles (see the Glasgow section).

GOUROCK
* **pop 11,692**   ☎ **01475**

Gourock is a run-down seaside resort 3 miles west of Greenock. There is, however, a good walk up to Lyle Hill, where there's a Free French memorial and a great view over the Firth of Clyde. Cruises around the firth are run by CalMac (☎ 650100), May to September; it costs £10 return (£5 senior) to

Brodick on Arran, to Tighnabruaich, or Tarbert on Loch Fyne. Clyde Marine (☎ 721281) runs similar cruises.

Places to Stay & Eat

Kempock St, near the transport hub of the train station and ferry terminal, has banks, grocery stores and various cheap takeaway outlets. *Lorenzo's* does haggis and chips for only £1.50. *Taj Mahal (☎ 633268, 89 Kempock St)* does Monday and Tuesday evening buffets with a choice of seven starters, seven main courses and five desserts plus tea and coffee – eat as much as you like for £9.95. *Cathay Princess (☎ 632541, 25 Kempock Place)* is more upmarket, with a four-course meal for £17.

For accommodation, you'd be best to head for Glasgow or Dunoon. The only reasonable hotel in Gourock is the *Stakis Gourock (☎ 634671, Cloch Rd)* near the Western Ferries terminal. It does singles/doubles from £99.50/120.

Getting There & Away

CalMac ferries (☎ 650100) leave frequently every day for Dunoon (20 minutes, £2.45, cars £6.25) on Argyll's Cowal peninsula. Clyde Marine (☎ 721281) runs a passenger-only service to Kilcreggan (12 minutes, £1.55, 13 per day) and Helensburgh (40 minutes, £1.55, four per day), Monday to Saturday. Western Ferries (☎ 01369-704452) has a half-hourly service to Dunoon (20 minutes, £2.40, cars £7) from McInroy's Point, 2 miles from the train station, but the Citylink buses start here.

Gourock train station is next to the CalMac terminal; there are frequent trains to Glasgow central (£3.70).

Scottish Citylink (☎ 0990-505050) runs hourly buses to Glasgow (£2.50) from McInroy's Point via the Shore St Health Centre, by the train station.

WEMYSS BAY

• pop 1715

Eight miles south of Gourock is Wemyss Bay (pronounced weemz), where you can jump off a train and onto a ferry for Rothesay on the Isle of Bute (see the Argyll & Bute section in The Highlands chapter). One of the few places to eat is the *Wemyss Bay Hotel*, but the welcome may be less than warm. The only other place to eat near the pier is a fish and chip shop opposite the Victorian train station. This appealing structure, opened in 1865, is one of the finest of its age. Trains to Glasgow run hourly (£3.80). CalMac ferries (01700-502707), which run frequently, cost £2.95 a single and £11.45 for a car.

Southern Scotland

Southern Scotland is a large, beautiful region, although in many ways it's something of a 'no man's land'. Historically, it was the buffer between the rambunctious and imperialist English and the equally unruly Scots.

Although today's inhabitants are proudly and indisputably Scottish, they are unique – like but unlike the Scots farther to the north, like but unlike the northern English to the south. This duality is perhaps not incompatible with the fact that this region was home to the two men – Robert Burns and Sir Walter Scott – who, in the late 18th and early 19th centuries, did most to reinvent and popularise Scottishness.

The Romans attempted to draw a clean line across the map with Hadrian's Wall, leaving the Celtic Picts to their own devices. The great Anglo-Saxon kingdoms of Bernicia and Northumbria, however, dominated the east and the south-west and succeeded in driving many Celts farther north. Another wave of Anglo-Saxons arrived from northern England after 1066, bringing with them a language which evolved into Lowlands Scots – like but unlike English, as Robert Burns so vividly illustrated.

The Norman invasion of England led to war with the Scots, although in times of peace, especially in the south, the aristocracy intermarried, leading to complicated land holdings on both sides of the border. The wars of Scottish independence fought at the end of the 13th century and the beginning of the 14th took a terrible toll on southern Scotland. And although the Scots succeeded in consolidating their independence, and great monastic estates were established, the south was still periodically trampled on by opposing armies.

Worse still, large parts of today's Borders and Dumfries & Galloway regions were neglected – neither the English nor the Scottish had any real interest in bringing

HIGHLIGHTS

- Cycle through the scenic Tweed Valley
- Visit the old buildings and *wynds* of attractive Jedburgh
- Stroll among the heather of the Eildon Hills
- View beautiful Dryburgh Abbey
- Experience the captivating atmosphere of Traquair House
- Survey the lochs and pine-covered mountains of Galloway Forest Park
- Sample the floral delights of magnificent Castle Kennedy Gardens
- Walk among the varied flora and fauna of the Southern Upland Way
- Take the plunge at the St Abbs & Eyemouth Voluntary Marine Reserve

Map Index

ATLANTIC OCEAN

EDINBURGH

Peebles p194

Kelso p187

Arran p203

Ayr p208

Dumfries p214

Stranraer p222

ENGLAND

stability to their enemy's border. There were periods of relative calm when great monasteries were constructed (and reconstructed), but the Debateable Lands, as they were known, were virtually ungoverned and ungovernable from the late 13th to the mid-17th century. The great families with their complex blood feuds fought and robbed the English, the Scots and each other. This continuous state of guerrilla warfare, it's been argued, had an indelible effect on the region and its people.

Following the 1707 union, peace allowed a new surge of development. The Borders, partly thanks to the abbeys, had traditionally been an important wool growing and processing region, and during the 19th century the knitting and weaving industries that survive today were created.

The countryside varies from gentle open fields in the east, to beautiful hilly countryside flanking the River Tweed, to the high Glenken and Galloway hills in the west. The region is certainly not undiscovered by tourists – it's too obvious a stopover for those heading to/from Glasgow and Edinburgh. However, it's easy to escape the crowds, particularly in the south-west. Outside the main roads there's little traffic, which makes for good cycling.

ORIENTATION

Southern Scotland can be divided into four quarters. The southern uplands divide the region into northern and southern halves. In the north-west, the former region of Strathclyde is now divided into North & South Lanarkshire, and North, South & East Ayrshire, plus smaller unitary authorities around Glasgow. The Lothians are in the north-east (linked with Edinburgh). The Borders, in the south-east, also look to Edinburgh, and there are good bus links with that city. With the exception of the main routes to Stranraer (for Northern Ireland ferries), Dumfries & Galloway, in the south-west, is quite isolated.

Ayrshire was the birthplace of Scotland's national poet, Robert Burns, though it's the least spectacular part of the region. The Isle of Arran, in the Firth of Clyde, is noted for its magnificent scenery. In Dumfries & Galloway the coast and mountains approach the grandeur of the north. The Borders have beautiful countryside, particularly around the River Tweed, and pleasant towns built around monastic ruins. The Lothians, most of which are easily accessible on day trips from Edinburgh, have some wild, bleak hills and a beautiful coastline to the east.

INFORMATION

Every small town has an excellent TIC with free accommodation booking services (BABA for £3) and an excellent range of brochures. Southwaite TIC (☎ 01697-473445/46), on the M6 south of Carlisle, has a lot of information on Southern Scotland; it's open April to September, daily, from 10 am to 6 pm; October to March, weekdays, from 10 am to 5 pm, Saturday 10 am to 2 pm. There's another useful TIC, the Gretna Gateway to Scotland (☎ 01461-338500), on the A74.

The TICs have information on car touring routes, including the Burns Trail, from near Ayr where he was born to Dumfries where he died; the Solway Coast Heritage Trail, from Gretna Green around the beautiful coast to Ayr; and the Scottish Borders Woollen Trail, taking in the mills and mill shops.

SYHA hostels are scarce and, in general, not very accessible unless you have a car. The exceptions are at Melrose, Minnigaff (near Newton Stewart) and Ayr. There are also SYHA hostels at Kendoon, Wanlockhead, Broadmeadows, Kirk Yetholm (near Kelso), Abbey St Bathan's and Coldingham Bay.

WALKS

The region's most famous walk is the 212-mile **Southern Upland Way**, Britain's first official coast-to-coast footpath. Another long-distance walk is the 100-mile **St Cuthbert's Way**, inspired by the travels of St Cuthbert, which crosses some superb scenery. In Galloway, the **Pilgrims Way** follows a 25-mile trail from Glenluce

SOUTHERN

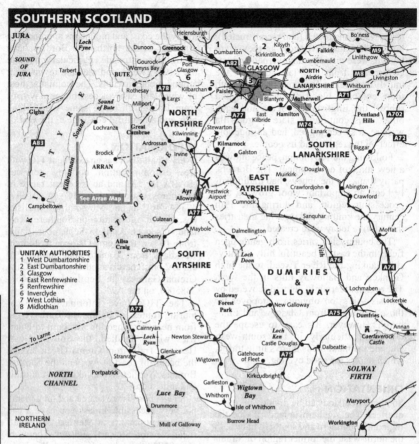

SOUTHERN SCOTLAND

UNITARY AUTHORITIES
1 West Dumbartonshire
2 East Dumbartonshire
3 Glasgow
4 East Renfrewshire
5 Renfrewshire
6 Inverclyde
7 West Lothian
8 Midlothian

Abbey to the Isle of Whithorn. See the Activities chapter.

Numerous circular walks can be made around the small towns, especially in the Tweed Valley; the TICs have information.

CYCLE ROUTES

With the exception of the main north-south A-roads and the A75 to Stranraer, traffic is sparse, which, along with the beauty of the countryside, makes this ideal cycling country. Bear in mind the prevailing winds

are from the south-west. Local TICs have information on possible routes.

The **Tweed Cycle Way** is a waymarked route running 62 miles along the beautiful Tweed Valley following minor roads from Biggar to Peebles (13 miles); to Melrose (16 miles); to Coldstream (19 miles); and to Berwick-upon-Tweed (14 miles). Jedburgh TIC has information.

Another interesting route is outlined in the *Scottish Border Cycle Way*, although this isn't waymarked. This route runs all of

210 miles from Portpatrick to Berwick-upon-Tweed – via Three Lochs, Talnotry, Castle Douglas, Dumfries, Ruthwell, Gretna Green, Newcastleton, Hawick, Jedburgh and Coldstream. Contact Jedburgh TIC for information. Another route is in the guide *Four Abbeys Cycle Route*, a 55-mile circular tour taking in Melrose, Dryburgh, Kelso and Jedburgh.

A decent map will reveal numerous other possibilities. The Tweed Valley is hard to ignore, but the Galloway Hills (north of

Newton Stewart) and coastal routes to Whithorn (south of Newton Stewart) are also excellent.

GETTING AROUND

Bus

Bus transport is excellent around Ayrshire, the Borders and the Lothians, reasonable on the main north-south routes and the A75 to Stranraer, but limited elsewhere in Dumfries & Galloway. The relevant inquiry lines and the telephone numbers for the major operators are given in the following sections. Various explorer tickets are available. These can be bought from bus drivers or bus stations, and are nearly always your best-value option if you're travelling reasonably extensively.

Train

Train services are limited. There are stations at Berwick-upon-Tweed (in Northumberland on the English side of the border, but the natural jumping-off point for the Tweed Valley) on the main east-coast line; at Dumfries on the main west-coast line; throughout Ayrshire and at Stranraer, which are linked to Glasgow.

Borders Region

There's a tendency to think that the real Scotland starts north of Perth, but the castles, forests and glens of the Borders have a romance and beauty of their own. The region survived centuries of war and plunder and was romantically portrayed by Robert Burns and Sir Walter Scott.

Although parts, especially to the west, are wild and empty, the fertile valley of the River Tweed has been a wealthy region for 1000 years.

The population was largely concentrated in a small number of *burghs* (towns, from burh, meaning a defensive ring of forts), which also supported large and wealthy monastic communities. These provided an irresistible magnet during the border wars and they were destroyed and rebuilt numerous times.

SOUTHERN

The monasteries met their final fiery end in the mid-16th century, burnt by the English yet again, but this time English fire combined with the Scottish Reformation and they were never again rebuilt. The towns thrived once peace arrived and the traditional weavers provided the foundation for a major textile industry, which still survives.

If you pause here on your way north, you'll find the lovely Tweed Valley, rolling hills, castles, ruined abbeys and sheltered towns. This is excellent cycling and walking country.

The Borders Region lies between the Cheviot Hills along the English border, and the Pentland, Moorfoot and Lammermuir Hills, which form the border with Lothian and overlook the Firth of Forth. The most interesting country surrounds the River Tweed and its tributaries.

GETTING THERE & AROUND
Bus
There's a good network of local buses, co-ordinated by the Scottish Borders Council which publishes bus guides available from TICs.

Lowland (☎ 01896-752237) has numerous buses to Edinburgh, Galashiels, Melrose, Jedburgh and Berwick-upon-Tweed. Lowland's Waverley Wanderer ticket allows a day (£11.50) or week (£33.50) of unlimited travel around the Borders, and includes Edinburgh. Swan's Coaches (☎ 01289-306436) also has regular services from Berwick-upon-Tweed.

National Express (☎ 0990-808080) bus No 383 runs once a day between Chester and Edinburgh via Galashiels, Jedburgh and Melrose; bus No 394 from Newcastle to Edinburgh also visits these towns.

McEwan's Coaches (☎ 01387-710357) operates a Rail Link service (No 195) from Carlisle in Cumbria, England, to Galashiels via Hawick and Selkirk; there are six a day Monday to Saturday, three on Sunday (£15).

Train
The main railway line north from Berwick-upon-Tweed follows the east coast to Dunbar in East Lothian, but doesn't stop in the Borders. Get off at Berwick if you intend to explore the Tweed Valley.

COLDSTREAM
- **pop 1750**   ☎ 01890

Sitting on the banks of the River Tweed, which forms the border with England, Coldstream is a small, relatively uninspiring town with a winding, undulating main street. It's best known for giving its name to the Coldstream Guards.

The town is on the busy A697 road which links Newcastle upon Tyne in Northumberland with Edinburgh. The TIC (☎ 882607), in the Town Hall on High St, opens April to September, Monday to Saturday, from 10 am to 5 pm, Sunday to 1 pm; and October, Monday to Saturday, from 10 am to 4.30 pm (closed 12.30 to 1 pm).

Things to See
The history of the Coldstream Guards and the town is covered in **Coldstream Museum** (☎ 882630), off High St in quiet Market Square. It opens Easter to September, Monday to Saturday, from 10 am to 4 pm, Sunday 2 to 4 pm; October, Monday to Saturday, from 1 to 4 pm; entry is £1/50p.

Near the five-arched bridge across the river is an 18th century cottage, formerly the **Toll House**, where eloping couples were once united in 'irregular marriages'.

On the western edge of Coldstream is the 3000 acre **Hirsel Country Park**, seat of the Earls of Home. Hirsel House isn't open to the public, but you can visit the grounds year-round during daylight hours.

Four miles south-east of Coldstream, across the border near Branxton, is **Flodden Field**. There, in 1513, a Scots incursion under James IV was cut short when his army was routed by the English.

Places to Stay & Eat
Coldstream Caravan & Camping Site (☎ 883376) has a beautiful grassy site beside a small tributary of the River Tweed; it's £8 for a cyclist and tent. *Attadale* (☎ 883047) is a B&B in a terraced house on

Coldstream Guards

The Coldstream Guards were formed in 1650 in Berwick-upon-Tweed for duty in Scotland as part of Oliver Cromwell's 'New Model' army and were originally known as Colonel Monck's Regiment of Foot. The regiment took its present name from the town where it was stationed in 1659; its full title is the Coldstream Regiment of Foot Guards.

The regiment played a significant part in the restoration of the monarchy in 1660. It saw service at Waterloo against Napoleon, at Sebastopol during the Crimean War, in the Boer War, at the Somme and Ypres in WWI and at Dunkirk and Tobruk in WWII.

It remains the oldest regiment in continuous existence in the British army and is the only one directly descended from the New Model army. The regiment's emblem is the Star of the Order of the Garter, its regimental motto is *nulli secundus* (second to none) and its colonel-in-chief is the British monarch.

The regiment's emblem is the Star of the Order of the Garter.

Leet St, with three rooms from £15 per person. The 18th century *Garth House* (☎ 882477, 7 Market St) is more expensive with rooms for £18.50 per person.

The Georgian *Crown Hotel* (☎ 882558, Market Square), near the museum, is a family-run hotel with good-value bar meals. Singles/doubles cost £18/34 (£26/46 with attached bathroom). All rooms have an attached bathroom at *Castle Hotel* (☎ 882380, 11 High St) and go for £25 per person. It also does good bar meals and has a restaurant; lunch time mains cost around £4.50.

Getting There & Away

There are six buses daily Monday to Saturday between Kelso and Berwick-upon-Tweed via Coldstream. The main operator is Swan's Coaches (☎ 01289-306436).

DUNS & AROUND
* pop 2308   ☎ 01361

Duns is a quiet market town in the centre of Berwickshire. The original settlement stood on the slopes of nearby Duns Law from which it gets its name.

Limited tourist information is available from the Cherry Tree Tea Room, Market Square, open Monday to Saturday from 9 am to 4.45 pm, Sunday from 11 am.

Things to See

The **Jim Clark Room** (☎ 883960), 44 Newtown St, is a museum dedicated to the life of Jim Clark (1936-68), who lived (and is buried) at nearby Chirnside. A farmer by trade, he was twice world motor racing champion in the 1960s before being killed in a crash while practising. The museum opens Easter to October, Monday to Saturday from 10.30 am to 4.30 pm (closed 1 to 2 pm), Sunday 2 to 4.30 pm; entry is £1/50p.

You can get to **Duns Law** (218m, 714 feet) in Duns Castle Estate by following Castle St up from the square. There are good views of the Merse and Lammermuir Hills from the summit, where the **Covenanter's Stone** marks the Covenanting army's camp in 1639; a copy of the Covenant was later signed at Duns Castle.

The castle isn't open to the public but you can visit the 190 acre **nature reserve**,

SOUTHERN

John Duns Scotus

Duns is the birthplace of John Duns Scotus (1266-1308), a renowned mediaeval Franciscan scholar and theologian, who taught at the universities of Paris and Oxford. He opposed the theology of Thomas Aquinas and argued in favour of the primacy of the individual and that faith could come through an act of will. His teachings divided the Franciscans and Dominicans.

Following his death his ideas fell out of favour and became associated with dullness and stupidity. From this association was derived the modern word 'dunce'.

In the public park is a bronze statue of him, donated by the Franciscans on the 300th anniversary of his birth. Near Duns Castle a cairn marks his birthplace.

managed by the Scottish Wildlife Trust. There are nature trails and many species of bird, animal and plant life. The lake, with the unfortunate name of Hen Poo', is a wildfowl haunt.

Manderston House (☎ 883450), 2 miles east of Duns on the A6105 in 56 acres of beautiful gardens, is a classic Edwardian stately home. Among its features are impressive state rooms and a silver staircase. The house opens mid-May to September, Thursday and Sunday, from 2 to 5.30 pm; entry is £5/2.50.

Places to Stay & Eat

There are B&Bs in the streets radiating from Market Square. *Claymore* (☎ *883880, 8 Murray St*) has two rooms with shared facilities from £16.50, and offers evening meals. The *Black Bull Hotel* (☎ *883379, Black Bull St*) is a small hotel. It only has one single and two doubles, and charges from £17.50 per person. The pubs are the best places for meals. The Black Bull Hotel is one of the few serving evening meals; its food is standard but filling and mains cost around £4. You can get bar meals at the *Whip & Saddle (Market Square)*; it also serves good real ale.

Getting There & Away

Buses running between Kelso and Berwick-upon-Tweed (up to six a day, Monday to Saturday) stop at Duns.

LAMMERMUIR HILLS

North of Duns the ancient low-lying Lammermuir Hills with their extensive grouse moors, rolling farmland and wooded valleys run east-west along the border with East Lothian. The hills are popular with walkers and there are numerous trails including a section of the Southern Upland Way.

To the west, the way can be accessed at **Lauder** where it passes through the grounds of **Thirlestane Castle** (☎ 01578-722430), beside Leader Water just outside town off the A68. Thirlestane is one of Scotland's most fascinating castles. The massive original keep was built in the 13th century, but was refashioned and extended in the 16th century – with fairy-tale turrets and towers, but without compromising the scale and integrity of the building. Its chief architect was William Bruce who also restored the Palace of Holyroodhouse in Edinburgh. The most impressive feature is the intricate plasterwork ceilings. It's still a family home and as a visitor you feel almost as if you're prying.

It's open Easter, May, June and September on Sunday, Monday, Wednesday and Thursday; July and August, Sunday to Friday. The castle opens from 2 to 5 pm (from noon July and August); the grounds open from noon to 5 pm. Entry to the castle and grounds is £4, grounds only £1.50. Bus Nos 29 and 30 go to Lauder.

You can also get onto the Southern Upland Way from the tiny village of **Abbey St Bathan's** in the secluded, bucolic Whiteadder Valley off the B6355. From there the final 10-mile section of the trail heads north-east to Cockburnspath beside the coast.

THE COAST

Following the A1107 off the A1, the short Borders coastline offers some attractive scenery, rich flora and fauna and a number of activities including cliff-top walks and scuba diving. The main settlement, Eyemouth, is a good base from which to explore the area.

Eyemouth
* pop 3480   ☎ 018907

Eyemouth, 5 miles north of the Scotland-England border at the mouth of the river from which it gets its name, is a busy fishing port and popular holiday destination.

David I promoted herring fishing here back in the 12th century and in the 18th century fishermen supplemented their income through the lucrative smuggling trade. The community suffered its greatest catastrophe in October 1881, when a storm destroyed the coastal fishing fleet killing 189 fishermen, 129 of whom were from Eyemouth.

Information The TIC (☎ 50678) is in Eyemouth Museum on Manse Rd near the harbour. It opens April to June and September, Monday to Saturday, from 10 am 5 pm, Sunday 1 to 3 pm; extended hours in July and August, shorter hours in October.

The Bank of Scotland and the Royal Bank of Scotland have ATMs, and there's a laundrette on Church St. Wednesday is early closing day.

Things to See & Do Open the same hours as the TIC, Eyemouth Museum (☎ 50678) has displays on local history particularly relating to the town's fishing heritage. The centrepiece is the large tapestry commemorating the 1881 fishing disaster. Entry is £1.75/1.25.

If you're interested in **walking**, get a copy of the brochure *Walks in and around Eyemouth*, available from the TIC, which describes a number of short walks. One of the most scenic is the 4-mile cliff-top path south to Burnmouth.

The clear, clean waters around Eyemouth form part of St Abbs & Eyemouth Voluntary Marine Reserve, one of the best cold water diving sites in Europe. The reserve is home to a wide variety of marine life including grey seals and porpoises. Eyemouth Diving Centre (☎ 51202), at Eyemouth Holiday Park on Fort Rd north of town, provides boat hire, equipment and courses.

Special Events The town is packed on the weekend in mid-June when the Eyemouth Seafood Festival takes place. Activities include cooking demonstrations, ceilidhs and folk dancing. The week-long Herring Queen Festival in late July is another calendar highlight.

Places to Stay & Eat *Eyemouth Holiday Park (☎ 51050, Fort Rd)*, overlooks the beach, and has camping sites from £8. There are a couple of B&Bs in town. The central *Hillcrest (☎ 50463, Coldingham Rd)* has a garden and rooms with shared bathroom for £16 per person. Similar is the friendly *Ebba House (☎ 50350, Upper Houndlaw)*.

Popular *Lough's Home Bakery (High St)* serves good bread, pies, cakes and pastries. One of the best places to eat is the *Old Bakehouse (☎ 50265)*, opposite the TIC, which serves snacks and meals all day (Eyemouth haddock is £4.95) plus delicious desserts. The pubs along the quay have suitably nautical names – the *Contented Sole*, the *Whale Hotel*, and the *Ship Hotel* – and serve freshly caught seafood.

Getting There & Away Monday to Friday, Lowland (☎ 01537-224141) bus Nos C4 and 12 each run once daily to/from Kelso via Duns; bus No 12 also goes south to Berwick-upon-Tweed (England) which has the nearest train station.

The scenic A1107 heads north to Coldingham and St Abbs before joining the A1 south of Cockburnspath.

South of Eyemouth
The small village of **Ayton**, 2 miles southwest of Eyemouth, is largely an 18th and 19th century creation. It's known for the restored 1846 red sandstone **Ayton Castle** (☎ 018907-81212). It's a family home and

SOUTHERN

isn't overly geared for tourism, only opening early May to mid-September, Sunday from 2 to 5 pm. Entry is £2/free.

Farther south, beyond the village of Foulden and about 3 miles west of the A1 along the B6461, is **Paxton House** (☎ 01289-386291), beside the River Tweed and surrounded by over 80 acres of parkland and gardens. It was built in 1758 by Patrick Home for his intended wife, the daughter of Prussia's Frederick the Great, though she stood him up. Designed by the Adam family – brothers John, James and Robert – it's acknowledged as one of the finest 18th century Palladian houses in Britain. It contains a large collection of Thomas Chippendale and Regency furniture, and its picture gallery houses paintings from the national galleries of Scotland.

In the grounds there are walking trails and a riverside museum on salmon fishing. The house opens Easter to October, daily, from 11 am to 5.30 pm, the grounds 10 am to sunset. Entry to house and grounds is £4/2, to grounds only, £2/1.

St Abb's Head & Coldingham Bay

About 3 miles north of Eyemouth, this picturesque area attracts anglers, scuba divers, birdwatchers and walkers.

The village of **Coldingham** is of little interest but from there the B6438 road takes you downhill to the harbour in the small fishing village of **St Abbs**, nestled about 90m below the cliffs. Offshore is the **St Abbs and Eyemouth Voluntary Marine Reserve** (see Eyemouth earlier). Divers can charter boats from D&J Charters (☎ 018907 -71377) or St Abbs Boat Charter (☎ 018907 -71681); the latter also does birdwatching trips.

Above the village is the 192 acre **St Abb's Head National Nature Reserve** (NTS) which has large colonies of guillemots, kittiwakes, herring gulls, fulmars, razorbills and some puffins. You get to the reserve by following the trail from beside the Northfield Farm car park and Head Start café on the road before you enter St Abbs.

Back in Coldingham, a signposted turn off to the right leads three-quarters of a mile down to quiet, away-from-it-all Coldingham Bay which has a sandy beach and cliff-top walking trails. For those interested in diving in the marine reserve, *Scoutscroft Holiday Centre* (☎ 018907-71338) rents equipment and offers courses, as well as having camping sites from £6.50. *Coldingham Youth Hostel* (☎ 018907-71298, The Mount) is on the cliff above the south side of the bay and has dorm beds for £6.10/4.95. It opens late March to early November. Several places offer B&B; opposite the entrance to the beach is *St Veda's House* (☎ 018907-71478), with rooms for £18/20 per person without/with bathroom; it also does evening meals.

Bus No 253 between Edinburgh and Berwick-upon-Tweed stops in Coldingham and St Abbs, as does bus No 235 which runs hourly from Eyemouth.

Cockburnspath

The 16th century Mercat Cross in Cockburnspath village square, about a mile inland from the coast, is the official eastern end/start of the Southern Upland Way.

KELSO
- pop 6045   ☎ 01573

Kelso is a prosperous market town, with a broad cobbled square flanked by Georgian buildings, at the hub of narrow cobbled streets. There's an interesting mix of architecture and the town has a lovely site at the junction of the Tweed and Teviot rivers. It's busy during the day, but dies completely in the evening. It's a real town, however, not a tourist trap.

Information

The TIC (☎ 223464), Town House, The Square, opens April to October; its core hours are Monday to Saturday from 10 am to 4.30 pm, but it opens extended hours June to September. Accommodation can be difficult to find during local festivals and markets held late June to mid-September; ring ahead.

Kelso Abbey

Kelso Abbey was built by Tironensians, an order founded at Tiron in Picardy, and brought to the Borders around 1113 by David I. Once one of the richest abbeys in southern Scotland, English raids in the 16th century reduced it to ruins. Today, there's little to see, although the abbey precincts are attractive and the nearby octagonal **Kelso Old Parish Church** (built in 1773) is intriguing. The abbey opens April to September, Monday to Saturday, from 9.30 am to 6 pm, Sunday 2 to 6 pm; October to March it closes at 4 pm; free.

Floors Castle

Floors Castle (☎ 223333) is an enormous mansion – Scotland's largest inhabited house – overlooking the Tweed about a mile west of Kelso. Built by William Adam in the 1720s, the original Georgian simplicity was 'improved' during the 1840s with the addition of rather ridiculous battlements and turrets. Floors makes no bones about being in the tourist business, and although the Roxburghe family is still in residence, there's no sense that this is a real house, and visitors are restricted to 10 rooms and a busy restaurant.

Floors opens Easter to late October, daily, from 10 am to 4.30 pm; £4.50/2.50. Follow Cobby Riverside Walk to reach the entrance to the castle grounds.

Walks

The **Pennine Way**, which starts its long journey at Edale in the Lake District, ends at Kirk Yetholm Youth Hostel, about 6 miles south-east of Kelso on the B6352. Less ambitious walkers should leave The Square by Roxburgh St, and take the signposted alley to **Cobby Riverside Walk**, a pleasant ramble along the river (past some expensive fishing

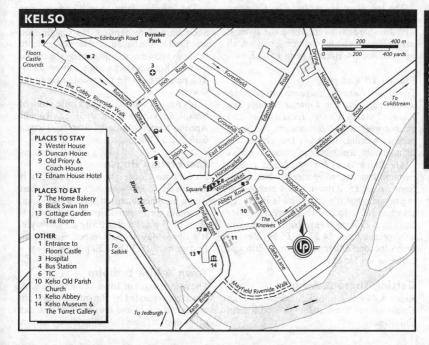

KELSO

Edinburgh Road — Poynder Park

Floors Castle Grounds

The Cobby Riverside Walk

Roxburgh Street

Bowmont Street

Inch Road

Forestfield

Drying House Lane

To Coldstream

Grovehill St

Edenside Road

Shedden Park Road

0   200   400 m
0   200   400 yards

Union St

East Bowmont St

Rose Lane

Horsemarket

Square

Woodmarket

Abbey Row

Abbotsford Grove

The Butts

River Tweed

Bridge Street

Maxwell Lane

The Knowes

To Selkirk

Coke Lane

Mayfield Riverside Walk

To Jedburgh

Kelso Bridge

PLACES TO STAY
2 Wester House
5 Duncan House
9 Old Priory & Coach House
12 Ednam House Hotel

PLACES TO EAT
7 The Home Bakery
8 Black Swan Inn
13 Cottage Garden Tea Room

OTHER
1 Entrance to Floors Castle
3 Hospital
4 Bus Station
6 TIC
10 Kelso Old Parish Church
11 Kelso Abbey
14 Kelso Museum & The Turret Gallery

SOUTHERN

spots) to Floors Castle (although you have to rejoin Roxburgh St to gain entry).

Special Events
The Kelso Borders Show and the Marches Ride both in July are two of the main events on Kelso's annual calendar.

Places to Stay
The nearest hostel is in Kirk Yetholm. In Kelso, *Wester House (☎ 225479, 155 Roxburgh St)* has a single at £12, and double rooms at £30, or £36 with attached bath. The attractively decorated *Old Priory & Coach House (☎ 223030, 12 Abbey Row)*, in the heart of Kelso, has eight rooms all with bathrooms from £18.50 per person.

Duncan House (☎ 225682, Chalkheugh Terrace) is an old house near the town centre, but with a view over the Tweed and Teviot rivers. There's a double, a twin and a family room, and private bathrooms. The rate is from £15.50 per person.

The top place is comfortable, Georgian *Ednam House Hotel (☎ 224168, Bridge St)* with fine gardens overlooking the river. It has a range of rooms, including singles, all with bathrooms. B&B is from £52/73.

Places to Eat
The *Home Bakery (Horsemarket)* sells delicious pastries. The *Cottage Garden Tea Room (7 Abbey Court)*, tucked away in a quiet corner near the museum, has some outdoor seating. It serves tea, coffee and light lunches; a ploughman's lunch is £3.50.

The *Black Swan Inn (☎ 224563, Horsemarket)* has decent, generous bar meals from around £5; it doesn't look prepossessing outside, but it's comfortable inside. (It also has B&B from £19 per person.) Bar lunches at *Ednam House Hotel* are reasonably priced from £4.50 to £5.50; dinners aren't too bad either with a main dish and coffee or tea for £11.50.

Getting There & Away
Kelso is 44 miles from Edinburgh, 18 from Galashiels, 11 from Jedburgh, and 9 from Coldstream.

The bus station is between Bowmont and Roxburgh Sts. See Coldstream for details on the bus service to Berwick-upon-Tweed. Lowland (☎ 224141) bus No 20 links Kelso, Jedburgh and Hawick; there are up to six Monday to Saturday, three on Sunday. It also has plenty of buses to/from Galashiels via Melrose.

AROUND KELSO
Bus No 65 between Melrose and Kelso stops in Smailholm village and passes about a mile from Mellerstain House.

Smailholm Tower
Perched on a rocky knoll above a small lake, the narrow stone Smailholm Tower (☎ 01573-460365, HS) provides one of the most evocative sights in the Borders and keeps the bloody uncertainties of its history alive. Although the displays inside are sparse, the panoramic view from the top is worth the climb.

The nearby farm, Sandyknowe, was owned by Walter Scott's grandfather. As Scott himself recognised, his imagination was fired by the ballads and stories he heard at Sandyknowe as a child, and by the ruined tower of his ancestors a stone's throw away. You pass through the farmyard to get to the tower.

It's 6 miles west of Kelso, a mile south of Smailholm village on the B6397, and opens April to September, daily, from 9.30 am to 6.30 pm; £1.80/75p.

Mellerstain House
Mellerstain House (☎ 01573-410225) is considered to be Scotland's finest Robert Adam designed mansion and, in particular, is famous for its ornate interiors. Completed in 1778 it has a classically elegant style. It's open May to September, Sunday to Friday, from 12.30 to 4.30 pm; £4/2.

Town & Kirk Yetholm
The twin villages of Town Yetholm and Kirk Yetholm, separated by Bowmont Water, are close to the England border about 6 miles south-east of Kelso. A hillwalking centre,

they are at the northern end of the **Pennine Way** and on **St Cuthbert's Way** between Melrose and Lindisfarne (Holy Island), Northumberland. *Kirk Yetholm Youth Hostel* (☎ 01573-420631), in a Georgian mansion, opens March to early November and charges £6.10/4.95 for a dorm bed.

Monday to Saturday, bus No 81 runs up to six times daily to/from Kelso. There's no Sunday service.

MELROSE

• pop 2276   ☎ 01896

Melrose is the most charming of the Border towns, lying at the foot of the three heather-covered Eildon Hills. It's spic-and-span, with a classic market square, some attractive parks and rugby ovals (Melrose is the birthplace of Rugby Sevens), and one of the great abbey ruins. However, urban sprawl from Galashiels is lapping at its western edges.

Information

The TIC (☎ 822555), Abbey House, Abbey St, opens April to October. Its core hours are Monday to Saturday from 10 am to 5 pm, Sunday 10 am to 1 pm, but opens for extended hours May to August. The post office is around the corner on Buccleuch St.

Melrose Abbey

Founded by David I in 1136 for Cistercians from Rievaulx in Yorkshire, the red sandstone abbey was repeatedly destroyed by the English in the 14th century. It was rebuilt by Robert the Bruce whose heart is buried here. The ruins date from the 14th and 15th centuries and were repaired by Sir Walter Scott in the 19th. They are pure Gothic and are famous for their decorative stonework – see if you can glimpse the pig gargoyle playing the bagpipes on the roof. The adjoining museum isn't particularly interesting.

The abbey (☎ 822562, HS) opens April to September, daily, from 9.30 am to 6.30 pm; October to March, Monday to Saturday, from 9.30 am to 4.30 pm, Sunday 2 to 4.30 pm; £2.80/1.

Next to the abbey are the sheltered **Priorwood Gardens** (☎ 822493, NTS), which feature plants used for dried flower arrangements (£1 donation requested).

Trimontium Exhibition

This small but interesting exhibition (☎ 822651), Market Square, tells the story of the Roman 'three hills' fort at nearby Newstead and the archaeological digs. You can also follow a guided Trimontium Walk to the Roman sites around Melrose. The exhibition opens daily April to October, from 10.30 am to 4 pm; £1.30/80p.

Walks

There are many attractive walks in the **Eildon Hills**, which you get to from a footpath off Dingleton Rd (the B6359), south of town, or via the trail along the River Tweed. The *Eildon Hills Walk* booklet is available from the TIC. St Cuthbert's Way starts in the Eildon Hills, while the coast-to-coast Southern Upland Way passes through Melrose (see the Activities chapter).

Special Events

In mid-April, rugby followers fill the town to see the week-long Melrose Rugby Sevens competition.

Places to Stay

Hostel *Melrose Youth Hostel* (☎ 822521) is in a large Georgian mansion on the edge of town. From the market square, follow the signposting for the A68. It's open Easter to September and dorm beds cost £7.75/6.50.

B&Bs & Hotels Melrose B&Bs and hotels aren't cheap by Scottish standards, but they are of a high standard; this wouldn't be a bad place to treat yourself. There aren't many, so consider booking.

Friendly *Birch House* (☎ 822391, High St) is a large, open place with a double and a twin for £16 per person; breakfasts are substantial including a choice of fresh fruit. *Orchard House* (☎ 822005, High St) is comfortable with a double and twin for £17 per person; it's open April to October.

Near the abbey, *Braidwood* (☎ 822488, Buccleuch St) is an excellent B&B with high-standard facilities and a nice warm welcome. There's a single, double and twin, and rates are from £18 per person.

Burts Hotel (☎ 822285), Market Square, dates from the late 18th century and offers upmarket B&B from £41 per person. Opposite, *Bon Accord Hotel* (☎ 822645, Market Square) is a small comfortable hotel where rooms cost £42/68 with bathroom attached.

Places to Eat

There's excellent pub food in town. The *Kings Arms* has substantial mains for £5 to £9; poached salmon steak is £8.95. *Burts Hotel* (Market Square) has good food (mains cost £4 to £8) as does the *Bon Accord Hotel* (☎ 822645) opposite. All provide vegetarian options.

The acclaimed *Melrose Station Restaurant* (☎ 822546, Palma Place) opens for lunches Wednesday to Sunday, for evening meals Wednesday to Saturday. You'll need to book for evening meals. Lunches are cheaper with Bombay potato curry for £5.75.

Getting There & Away

Bus Lowland has numerous, regular bus links to Galashiels, Kelso and Jedburgh. Bus No 62 runs regularly to Peebles, while bus No 65 to Kelso travels via the village of Smailholm and close to Mellerstain House (see the Around Kelso section earlier in this chapter).

Car & Motorcycle Melrose is about 38 miles south of Edinburgh via either the A7 or A68 which meet here. Jedburgh is 12 miles south-east along the A68. For Kelso, about 12 miles east, head south on the A68, then left (east) onto the A699.

AROUND MELROSE
Dryburgh Abbey

The most beautiful and most complete of the border abbeys is Dryburgh, partly because the neighbouring town of Dryburgh no longer exists (another victim of the wars), and partly because it has a lovely site in a sheltered valley by the River Tweed. The abbey belonged to the Premonstraten-

sians, a religious order founded in France, and was built from about 1150.

The pink-stoned ruins were chosen as the burial place for Sir Walter Scott and later for Earl Haig, the Allied commander during WWI. There are some beautiful picnic spots.

The abbey (☎ 01835-822381, HS) is 5 miles south-east of Melrose on the B6404, which passes famous **Scott's View** overlooking the valley. It's open April to September, Monday to Saturday, from 9.30 am to 6.30 pm, Sunday 2 to 6.30 pm, closing two hours earlier October to March; £2.30/1. Bus No 67 passes nearby.

Abbotsford

The home of Sir Walter Scott is definitely not an architectural masterpiece – the best one can say is that it's disjointed – but it's in a beautiful setting, and is quite fascinating. There's an extraordinary collection of the great man's possessions. It's well worth visiting. It's open late March to October, Monday to Saturday, from 10 am to 5 pm, Sunday 2 to 5 pm (Sunday from 10 am June to September); £3.50/1.80.

The house (☎ 01896-752043) is about 3 miles west of Melrose between the Tweed and B6360. Frequent buses run between Galashiels and Melrose; alight at the Tweedbank traffic island and walk 15 minutes.

GALASHIELS
• pop 13,766   ☎ 01896

Galashiels is a busy, unprepossessing mill town strung along the A6091, 3 miles west of Melrose. It's something of a transport hub and there's quite a bit of accommodation available, but there are few pressing reasons to stay. Except for the Pavilion cinema and one or two pubs and restaurants the town virtually closes down by 6 pm.

The TIC (☎ 755551), 3 St John St, opens April to September, Monday to Saturday from 10 am to 5 pm, Sunday 1 to 3 pm (extended hours in July and August); and October, Monday to Saturday.

Lowland (☎ 758484) is the main operator with frequent buses to/from Edinburgh, Melrose, Hawick, Kelso and Peebles.

SELKIRK
- **pop 5952** ☎ **01750**

Selkirk is an unusual little town that climbs a steep ridge above Ettrick Water, a tributary of the Tweed. Mills came to the area in the early 1800s, but it's now a quiet place (much quieter than Galashiels or the textile centre of Hawick). There's a statue of Sir Walter Scott at one end of High St, one of Mungo Park the explorer, at the other.

The TIC (☎ 720054), Market Square, opens April to October, Monday to Saturday from 10 am to 5 pm, Sunday 2 to 4 pm (extended hours July and August). Halliwell's House dates from 1712 and is the oldest building in Selkirk.

Things to See

Adjoining the TIC and open the same hours, **Halliwell's House Museum and Robson Gallery** (☎ 20096), Market Square, has an interesting display on local history and a program of temporary exhibitions. Also on Market Square, the 1804 **Sir Walter Scott's Court Room** (☎ 20096), where the great man served as sheriff of Selkirk County, houses an exhibition on his life and writings. It's open Easter to October, Monday to Saturday from 10 am to 4 pm, Sunday 2 to 4 pm; free.

You can see glass blowing at **Selkirk Glass** (☎ 20954), on the A7 north of the centre, weekdays from 9 am to 4.30 pm; free.

Places to Stay & Eat

Victoria Park Camping & Caravan Site (☎ 20897), pleasantly positioned beside Ettrick Water, has tent sites for £6.50. It's open April to October. There are some reasonably priced B&Bs including the friendly *Colenso* (☎ 22408, 40 Heatherlie Terrace) with a couple of rooms for £15 per person. *County Hotel* (☎ 721233, 3-5 High St) has *en suite* singles/doubles for £30/50 and good bar meals; beef and Guinness pie is £4.50.

The *Court House Coffee Shop* on Market Square is well known for its high teas; sandwiches cost £1.30. Alternatively, you can get delicious pies, pastries and Bannock bread from the nearby *Selkirk Bannock Shop*.

Getting There & Away

Buses leave from Market Square. Lowland bus No 95 runs frequently between Hawick, Selkirk, Galashiels and Edinburgh. The A7 road heads north to Galashiels and south to Hawick.

JEDBURGH
- **pop 4090** ☎ **01835**

Jedburgh, on the northern slopes of the Cheviot Hills, is the most visited of the Borders towns and has a number of interesting sights, which it has capitalised on with efficiency. It has a tendency to look like a film set, but it's an attractive town and many of the old buildings and wynds have been intelligently restored.

Information

The large, efficient TIC (☎ 863435), Murray's Green, opens March to May and October, Monday to Saturday from 10 am to 5 pm, Sunday noon to 5 pm; extended hours June to September; November to March it opens Monday to Saturday, from 10 am to 5 pm.

The post office is on High St. Early closing day is Thursday.

Jedburgh Abbey

Jedburgh Abbey, founded in 1138 by David I as a priory for Augustinian canons, dominates the town. It was the site for a royal wedding and a coronation, but it suffered the usual cycle of sacking and rebuilding. In fact, the red sandstone ruins are roofless, but comparatively complete.

The abbey (☎ 863925, HS) opens daily April to September, from 9.30 am to 6.30 pm; October to March, Monday to Saturday, from 9.30 am to 4.30 pm, Sunday 2 to 4.30 pm; £2.80/1.

Mary Queen of Scots House

Mary reputedly stayed here briefly in 1566 after her famous ride to visit the injured Earl of Bothwell, her future husband, at Hermitage Castle. The displays are interesting enough and evoke the sad saga of Mary's life, but they're sparse and the text engraved on the glass panels is hard to read. Nevertheless, it's a beautiful 16th century tower house, and worth a visit.

The house (☎ 863331) opens March and November, Monday to Saturday from 10.30 am to 3.30 pm, Sunday 1 to 4 pm; April to October, Monday to Saturday, from 10 am to 4.30 pm, Sunday from noon (June to August daily); £2/1.

Jedburgh Castle Jail & Museum

The former jail (☎ 863254) at the top of steep Castlegate south of the centre is worth the walk. It was built in the 1820s on the site of the castle that had been destroyed by the Scots in 1409 to prevent the perfidious English using it.

The displays in the cell blocks give a good depiction of prison life and the exhibition in the jailer's house does the same for Jedburgh's history.

It's open Easter to October, Monday to Saturday, from 10.30 am to 4.30 pm, Sunday 1 to 4 pm. Entry is £1.25/1.

Special Events

For two weeks in late June/early July the Jethart Callant Festival commemorates the perilous time when people rode out on horseback checking for English incursions.

Places to Stay

Camping At *Elliot Park Camping & Caravanning Club Park* (☎ 863393, *Edinburgh Rd)*, about a mile north of the centre, sites are £6.90.

B&Bs & Hotels *Castlegate Restaurant* (☎ 862552, 1 Abbey Close) on the corner of High St near the abbey has large clean rooms from a reasonable £15 per person. *Kenmore Bank* (☎ 862369, Oxnam Rd) overlooks the abbey and is good value. The twins, doubles and family rooms all have bathrooms and the cost is from £18 per person.

The very comfortable *Glenfriar's Hotel* (☎ 862000, Friarsgate) has two singles, two twins and two doubles all with bathrooms, for £35/64.

Places to Eat

Castlegate Restaurant has a traditional menu, with dishes like steak and kidney pie. It's a good place for either a full meal (you can bring your own wine or beer) or just a cup of tea.

The *Pheasant Lounge Bar* (☎ 862708, 61 High St) has a good range of bar meals around £5 to £7, including some interesting offerings like breast of pheasant with lemon and apple sauce. Vegetarian dishes are £5.25. At the bottom of High St, the *Wayfarer* (☎ 863503, 51 High St) has substantial meals like poached salmon (£7.10) and a good-value three-course evening menu for £9.95.

Getting There & Away

Bus Jedburgh has good bus connections around the Borders. Lowland (☎ 01896-752237 in Galashiels) is the main operator. There are many connections to Hawick, Galashiels and Kelso. Bus No 23 runs to/from Berwick-upon-Tweed via Kelso and Coldstream. Bus Nos 29 and 30 run three times daily Edinburgh to Jedburgh in each direction.

Car & Motorcycle Edinburgh is 45 miles north of Jedburgh along the A68. For Kelso (11 miles) take the A68 north then turn right (east) onto the A698. For Melrose (12 miles) and Galashiels (17 miles) continue farther north along the A68, then turn left (west) onto the A72.

HAWICK

- **pop 15,720**   ☎ 01450

Straddling the River Teviot, Hawick (pronounced hoick), the largest town in the Borders, has long been a major knitwear and hosiery production centre. Most people come to shop at the numerous factory outlets that dot the town. A list is available from the TIC (☎ 372547), 1 Tower Knowe, High St, in Drumlanrig's Tower.

The TIC opens March to October, Monday to Saturday, from 10 am to 5 pm, Sunday noon to 5 pm, longer hours April to September. The rest of the year it opens Monday to Saturday, from 10 am to 5 pm.

Dawn over Loch Coruisk, River Scavaig, Isle of Skye

GARETH McCORMACK

GRAEME CORNWALLIS

Am Basteir and Sgurr a'Fhionn Choire, Cuillin Hills, Isle of Skye

GRAEME CORNWALLIS

Warrior's grave, Isle of Islay

PAT YALE

Sheep are a major road hazard on Lewis, Outer Hebrides

GRAEME CORNWALLIS

Derelict cottage, Isle of Lewis, Outer Hebrides

In the same building and open the same hours **Drumlanrig's Tower Visitor Centre** (☎ 373457) tells the story of cross-border warfare from the 16th century. Entry is £2/1. Over the river in 107 acre Wilton Lodge Park, **Hawick Museum and Scott Art Gallery** (☎ 373457) has an interesting collection of mostly 19th century manufacturing and domestic memorabilia. It's open April to September, weekdays, from 10 am to 5 pm (closed noon to 1 pm), weekends 2 to 4 pm. Entry is £1.25/75p.

Lowland bus No 115 runs services to Melrose and Galashiels, while bus No 95 connects Hawick with Galashiels, Selkirk and Edinburgh.

HERMITAGE CASTLE

Hermitage Castle is a massive collection of stone with a heavy cubist beauty; it sits isolated beside a rushing stream surrounded by bleak, empty moorland. Dating from the 13th century, but substantially rebuilt in the 15th, it embodies the brutal history of the Borders; the stones themselves almost speak of the past. It was Sir Walter Scott's favourite castle.

It's probably best known as the home of the Earl of Bothwell, and the spot where Mary Queen of Scots rode in 1566 to see him after he had been wounded in a border raid.

It's also where, in 1338, Sir William Douglas imprisoned his enemy Sir Alexander Ramsay and deliberately starved him to death. Ramsay survived for 17 days by eating grain that trickled into his pit (which can still be seen) from the granary above. The castle is said to be haunted and it certainly has something of a spooky feel about it especially when dark clouds gather.

The castle (☎ 013873-76222, HS) opens April to September, daily, from 9.30 am to 6.30 pm; October to March, Monday to Wednesday and Saturday from 9.30 am to 4.30 pm, Thursday 9.30 am to 1 pm, Sunday 2 to 4.30 pm; £1.50/75p.

It's about 12 miles south of Hawick on the B6357 and can be reached by Telford's (☎ 031873-75677) bus No 128.

PEEBLES
• **pop 7080**   ☎ **01721**

Peebles is a prosperous little town set among rolling wooded hills on the banks of the River Tweed. Although it's not particularly notable, there's a broad, attractive High St, and it makes a pleasant base from which to tour the Tweed Valley.

The TIC (☎ 720138), High St, has complex opening hours but generally opens April to October, Monday to Saturday from 10 am to 5 pm, Sunday 10 am to 2 pm (extended hours in July and August); the rest of the year, Monday to Saturday, from 9.30 am to 12.30 pm, 1.30 to 4.30 pm.

Tweeddale Museum & Gallery

On High St, the museum (☎ 724820) is in the Chambers Institute which was given to the town by publisher William Chambers in 1859. It houses an interesting collection of displays including copies of the frieze taken from the Parthenon in Athens by Lord Elgin and the 19th century Alexander Frieze. It opens Easter to October, weekdays from 10 am to noon and 2 to 5 pm, weekends 10 am to 1 pm and 2 to 4 pm; November to March it opens weekdays only. Entry is free.

Neidpath Castle

Neidpath Castle (☎ 720333) is a tower house perched on a bluff above the River Tweed. It's in a lovely spot with good views from the parapets, although there's little to see inside.

The castle opens Easter to September, Monday to Saturday, from 9.30 am to 6.30 pm, Sunday 2 to 6.30 pm; £2.50/1. It's a mile west of the centre on the A72, but can be reached by following the walking trail along the river.

Places to Stay & Eat

Rosetta Caravan & Camping Park (☎ 720770, Rosetta Rd) is about half a mile north of the centre along High St. It's open April to October and sites are £8.75.

Rowanbrae (☎ 720630, Northgate) has only two rooms but it's very comfortable. B&B costs £16 per person.

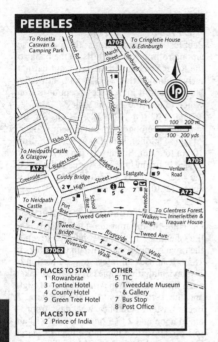

PEEBLES

To Rosetta Caravan & Camping Park
Dovecot Rd
March Street
A703 To Cringletie House & Edinburgh
Edinburgh Road
Cuddyside
Dean Park
Echo St
To Neidpath Castle & Glasgow
A72
Biggies Knowe
Greenside
Northgate
Bridgegate
Eastgate
Cuddy Bridge
A703
Venlaw Road
High Street
Tweeddale
A72
To Neidpath Castle
Port Brae
School Brae
River
Tweed Green
To Glentress Forest, Innerleithen & Traquair House
Walkers Haugh
Tweed Bridge
Riverside
Tweed Ave
Riverside
B7062
Tweed Walk
Walk

0   100   200 m
0   100   200 yds

PLACES TO STAY	OTHER
1 Rowanbrae	5 TIC
3 Tontine Hotel	6 Tweeddale Museum
4 County Hotel	& Gallery
9 Green Tree Hotel	7 Bus Stop
	8 Post Office
PLACES TO EAT	
2 Prince of India	

The well-organised, tidy *Green Tree Hotel* (☎ *720582, 41 Eastgate*) provides a range of rooms, including singles, most with bathrooms. Rates are £23 to £28 per person.

The *County Hotel* (☎ *720595, 35 High St*) is a downbeat but good pub, often with live music in the evening. It has some B&B rooms (£19 per person), decent bar meals from around £5 and a more expensive restaurant.

Two miles from Peebles on the A703, *Cringletie House* (☎ *730233*) is a comfortable country house hotel with an excellent restaurant. Rooms are from £55 per person. There are set lunches for £16, set dinners for £28.

Prince of India Restaurant (☎ *724455, 88 High St*) specialises in North Indian food and has four-course set lunches for £5.95. The *Tontine Hotel*, opposite, does decent,
good-value bar meals; steak and vegetable pie is £4.90.

Getting There & Away
Bus The bus stop is beside the post office on Eastgate. Lowland (☎ 720181) bus No 95 runs hourly to Edinburgh, Galashiels and Melrose. Bus No C1 leaves once daily at 10.15 am for Selkirk and Galashiels.

Bicycle Scottish Border Trails (☎ 720336), Glentress, organises bicycle tours – both on and off road. It also hires mountain bikes from £16 per day and tourers from £10. Pre-booking is recommended.

Car & Motorcycle The A703 heads north to Edinburgh, while the A72 heads east to Innerleithen and Galashiels, west to Biggar.

AROUND PEEBLES
Traquair House
Traquair (pronounced trarwkweer) is one of Britain's great houses; there are many that are more aesthetically pleasing, but this one has a powerful, ethereal beauty – and an exploration is like time travel.

Parts of the building are believed to have been constructed long before the first official record of its existence in 1107. The massive tower house was gradually expanded over the next 500 years, but has remained virtually unchanged since 1642.

Since the 15th century the house has belonged to various branches of the Stuart family and the family's unwavering Catholicism and loyalty to the Stuart cause is largely why development ceased when it did. The family's estate, wealth and influence was gradually whittled away after the Reformation, and there was neither the opportunity, nor, one suspects, the will, to make any changes.

One of the most fascinating rooms is the concealed priest's room where priests secretly lived and gave mass – up to 1829 when the Catholic Emancipation Act was finally passed. Other beautiful time-worn rooms hold fascinating relics, including the cradle used by Mary for her son, James VI of Scotland (who was also James I of England), and many letters written by the Stuart pretenders to their supporters.

In addition to the house, there's a garden maze, an art gallery, a small brewery producing Bear Ale, and an active craft community. The Scottish Beer and Jazz Festival takes place here in late May.

Traquair House (☎ 01896-830323) opens June to August, daily, from 10.30 am to 5.30 pm; April, May and September, daily, from 12.30 to 5.30 pm; and in October, Friday to Sunday, from 12.30 to 5.30 pm. Entry is £4.50/2.25.

It's 1½ miles south of Innerleithen, about 6 miles south-east of Peebles. Lowland (☎ 01721-720181) bus No 62 runs regularly to Innerleithen and Peebles from Edinburgh. Bus No C1 goes once daily to Traquair from Peebles.

Lanarkshire

South and east of Glasgow are the large satellite towns of East Kilbride, Hamilton, Motherwell and Coatbridge. Farther upstream, the Clyde passes through central Lanarkshire, once an important coal mining district and still important for its fruit farms. Plums from the area around Crossford and strawberries from Kirkfieldbank are particularly tasty.

BLANTYRE
- pop 18,531 ☎ 01698

This town's most famous son was David Livingstone, the epitome of the Victorian missionary-explorer, who opened up central Africa to European religion. Born in the one-roomed tenement, in 1813, that now forms part of the David Livingstone Centre, he worked by day in the local cotton mill from the age of 10, educated himself at night, and took a medical degree in 1840 before setting off for Africa.

The interesting **David Livingstone Centre** (☎ 823140), 165 Station Rd, tells the story of his life from a youngster in Blantyre to his later days as a missionary and explorer, his battle against slave traders, and his

famous meeting with Stanley. It's down by the River Clyde and is open daily from 10 am to 5 pm (Sunday from 12.30 pm only); tickets cost £2.95/1.95. There's an African theme café here serving reasonably priced snacks and meals.

It's a 20 to 30 minute walk down the river to **Bothwell Castle** (☎ 816894, HS), regarded as the finest 13th century castle in Scotland. Built of red sandstone, the substantial ruins, much fought over during the Wars of Independence, include a massive circular keep standing above the river. It's open April to September, daily 9.30 am to 6.30 pm. For the rest of the year it's open daily from 9.30 am to 4.30 pm (from 2.30 pm on Sunday) but closed on Thursday afternoon and Friday all day. Entry is £1.80/1.30.

It's best to come by train (20 minutes from Glasgow Central, two per hour) since the David Livingstone Centre is a short walk from Blantyre station. Fares are £1.90 single, £2.40 off-peak return, £3 peak return. The buses stop on Main St, a 15 minute walk away.

HAMILTON
- pop 51,511 ☎ 01698

Less than 2 miles from the centre of Hamilton, there's **Chatelherault** (☎ 426213), a country park with woodland trails, and an excellent restored hunting lodge and kennels dating from 1732. The visitor centre is open all year, daily, from 10 am to 5 pm (from noon on Sunday). The lodge is open daily, except Friday, from 10 am to 4.30 pm (from noon on Sunday); admission is free. **Cadzow Castle**, in the grounds, was completed in 1550. Trains from Glasgow Central to Hamilton Central (two stops beyond Blantyre) run twice hourly (£2.25 single, £2.70 off-peak return), then catch a bus to the park (destinations Ferniegair or Larkhall).

Hamilton Mausoleum (☎ 283981) is the burial vault of the Hamilton family. It's a most unusual circular building, with a 15-second echo. Tours are available on Wednesday, Saturday and Sunday at 3 pm for £1.05; telephone for further details.

LANARK & NEW LANARK
• pop 9000   ☎ 01555

Below the market town of Lanark, in an attractive gorge by the River Clyde, are the excellent restored mill-buildings and warehouses of New Lanark. This was once the largest cotton spinning complex in Britain but it was better known for the pioneering social experiments of Robert Owen, who managed the mill from 1800. An enlightened capitalist, he provided his workers with housing, a co-operative store (that was the inspiration for the modern co-operative movement), a school with adult education classes, and a social centre he called The New Institute for the Formation of Character.

In 1297, the great Scots patriot William Wallace killed Hazelrigg, the Sheriff of Lanark, precipitating the Wars of Independence. Nowadays, there's a Wallace Society in the town.

Orientation & Information

The TIC (☎ 661661), Horsemarket, Ladyacre Rd, Lanark, is near the bus and train stations and it's open all year. The 20 minute walk down to New Lanark is worth it for the views, but there's a daily bus service from the train station (hourly, but two-hourly on Monday to Saturday afternoons). Returning to Lanark, currently the last bus leaves New Lanark at 5.03 pm, but the service may improve.

Kirkfieldbank is by the River Clyde just downstream from New Lanark, about 1½ miles from Lanark on the A72.

There are two banks with ATMs on the High St and the post office is on the Edinburgh road (St Leonards St). The Lanark Health Centre is at ☎ 665522.

If you need a taxi, call Clydewide on ☎ 663221.

Things to See

There's a Visitor Centre (☎ 661345) in New Lanark, and £3.75/2.50 gets you entry to Robert Owen's house, a restored millworker's house, the Annie McLeod Experience (a high-tech audio-visual ride where the spirit of a 10-year-old mill girl recalls life

here in 1820) and the 1920s-style village store. It's open daily from 11 am to 5 pm. There are craft shops in the restored buildings and good-value woollens on sale.

Probably the best way to get the feel of this impressive place is to wander round the outside of the buildings and then walk up to the Falls of Clyde through the nature reserve. Visit the Falls of Clyde Wildlife Centre (☎ 665262) by the river in New Lanark first. It's open Easter to October on weekdays from 11 am to 5 pm and weekends 1 to 5 pm, the rest of the year at weekends only (closed January); admission to the centre costs £1/50p, but the reserve is free. Walk for a couple of miles to the power station, then half a mile to the beautiful Cora Linn (waterfalls) and, beyond them, Bonnington Linn.

About halfway between Lanark and Biggar, by the A73, there's the Discover Carmichael Visitor Centre (☎ 01899-308169), with an interesting wax model collection of historical and modern figures. On site, there's a brand-new windmill for electrical requirements and a restaurant serving meals for around £4 to £7. The centre is open March to December, daily, from 9.30 am to 5.30 pm; admission is £3.25/1.95. Lanark to Biggar buses (☎ 870344) pass this way, four to 15 times daily.

Places to Stay

Clyde Valley Caravan Park (☎ 663951), by the River Clyde at Kirkfieldbank, is open April to October, and charges £6 per tent.

The New Lanark Youth Hostel (☎ 666710, Wee Row), very pleasantly located near the river, was opened in 1994. Nightly charges are £9.75/8.50 with continental breakfast, and it's open year-round. The recently opened New Lanark Mill Hotel (☎ 667200) has singles/doubles from £40/60, all with bath. The bar and restaurant do soup and snacks for under £5, and three-course lunches and dinners for around £9 and £16 respectively.

If you want to stay in Lanark, the TIC has a free accommodation list for the area. There are numerous B&Bs, including Mrs

Buchanan's (☎ 661002, 5 Hardacres), who charges from £16 per person, and *Mrs Allen's (☎ 662540, 9 Cleghorn Rd)* with rooms from £20/34 a single/double.

Places to Eat

In the New Lanark Visitor Centre there's the *Mill Pantry* for snacks and light meals; try the hotel bar and restaurant for something more substantial. If you're staying in Kirkfieldbank, the *Tavern (☎ 662537, 200 Riverside Rd)* does pub grub.

In Lanark, the *Crown Tavern (☎ 662465, 17 Hope St)* does good bar meals. *Caesar's (☎ 666041, 3 High St)*, opposite St Nicholas' Church, has pizza and pasta dishes for £5.45 to £6.50, and steaks for £10.65 to £12.55. The *East India Company (☎ 663827, 32 Wellgate)*, again near the church, is a good choice. Its main courses range from £4.70 to £8.95; a three-course weekday lunch costs £4.50. *Mr A's Café (☎ 663797, 90 High St)* has toasties for £1.70 and all main courses are under £5. *Valerio's* fish and chips is near the bus station and the TIC. Self-caterers can stock up at the large *Somerfield* supermarket, conveniently situated by the TIC.

Getting There & Away

Lanark is 25 miles south-east of Glasgow. Hourly trains run daily between Glasgow Central and Lanark (£3.70).

BIGGAR

• pop 1900   ☎ 01899

Biggar is a pleasant town in a rural setting dominated by Tinto Hill (712m, 2335 feet). The hill is a straightforward ascent by its northern ridge from Thankerton. Biggar had a recent face-lift with the renovation of its main street. The town is well worth a visit – it probably has more museums and attractions per inhabitant than anywhere else of its size!

Information

There's a seasonal TIC (☎ 221066) at 155 High St. The post office and Royal Bank ATM are also on the High St. The Health Centre is at ☎ 220383.

Things to See

The Biggar Museums Trust (☎ 221050) looks after four major museums in the town. **Moat Park Heritage Centre**, Kirkstyle, in a renovated church, covers the history of the area with geological and archaeological displays. There are also natural and folk history exhibits, including a 6.7-sq-metre patchwork. The centre is open Easter to October, daily, from 10 am to 5 pm (from 2 pm on Sunday); admission costs £2.40/1.90. The **Greenhill Covenanter's House**, Burnbrae, is a reconstructed farmhouse with 17th century furnishings and artefacts relating to local Covenanters. It's open May to October, daily, from 2 to 5 pm, and charges £1/70p. **Gladstone Court**, North Back Rd, is an indoor street museum showing historic shops. It's open May to October, daily, from 10 am to 5 pm (from 2 pm on Sunday) and charges £1.80/1.30. The **Gasworks Museum** is the only coal-fired gasworks left in Scotland, originally opened in 1839. Now it's open June to September, daily, from 2 to 5 pm; admission costs £1/50p.

The **International Purves Puppets** (☎ 220631), Broughton Rd, has miniature Victorian puppets and bizarre modern ones over 1m high that glow in the dark. There are several ultraviolet displays, but you don't need your sunglasses. Guided tours are conducted in English and French. The puppet theatre is open all year, Monday to Saturday, from 10 am to 5 pm. From Easter to September, it's also open on Sunday, from 2 to 5 pm. Admission costs £4.40 (£3.30 for children).

Places to Stay and Eat

Campers can stay in the *YMCA Camp Site (☎ 850228)* at Wiston, 1½ miles south of Tinto Hill. It's open all year and costs £4 to £7 for two people with car and tent.

Mayfield House (☎ 220544, Edinburgh Rd) is an excellent B&B with tariff from only £18 per head. There's also a B&B at Thankerton, 4 miles from Biggar, and near Tinto Hill – *Elmwood (☎ 308740, 32 Sherifflats Rd)* – charging from £12 to £15 per person.

SOUTHERN

The *Elphinstone Hotel (☎ 220044, 145 High St)* has singles/doubles for £29/49. There's a bar where snacks such as toasties and baked potatoes cost £2 to £3 and main courses run from £5 to £14. The *Hartree Country House Hotel (☎ 221027)* is a well-appointed place complete with turret and battlements. It's set in seven acres of grounds about 1½ miles from Biggar (take the A702 towards Abington, then turn left); rooms cost from £50/65. Its restaurant, open for dinner only, has main courses from £8 to £14.

There are a couple of supermarkets on the High St. You'll find six restaurants, cafés and takeaways on the High St. The *Clootie Dumpling (☎ 221363, 152 High St)* does home baking and coffees, the *China Moon takeaway (154 High St)* is OK, but the *Taj Mahal (☎ 220801, 101 High St)* is the best.

Getting There & Away

Biggar is 33 miles south-east of Glasgow. Buses to Edinburgh (Stagecoach, ☎ 01387-253496) run five to seven times daily. There are four to 15 times daily runs to Lanark (Stokes & Sons, ☎ 01555-870344). There are Monday to Saturday postbus services (☎ 01463-256200) from Biggar to Tweedsmuir, Abington and Wanlockhead.

ABINGTON & CRAWFORD

At **Abington**, 35 miles south of Glasgow by the M74 (to be renamed the M6), there's a 24 hour motorway service station with a TIC (☎ 01864-502436), open daily all year, from at least 10 am to 5 pm. Turn off the motorway here for **Wanlockhead** and **Crawfordjohn**. In Abington village you'll find a general store, post office, tearoom and Royal Bank, but note that the nearest ATM is at the Happendon Services, farther north up the M74 (M6). Crawfordjohn has a **Heritage Venture** (☎ 01864-504265) with Covenanter's relics, wildlife and agricultural displays etc. The venture is open May to September, weekends, from 2 to 5 pm, and other times by arrangement. The admission charge is £1.

The *Crawford Arms Hotel (☎ 01864-502267)* does accommodation and bar meals and the *Merlindale Café* in Crawford does all-day breakfasts for £4. The *Coalbrook Arms (☎ 504239)*, in Crawfordjohn, does good bar meals.

Crawford Caravan and Camping Site (☎ 502258, Carlisle Rd), open April to October, has pitches for £3.50 to £5. The best place to stay in the area is *Holmlands Country House (☎ 01864-502753)*, with B&B from £22 to £35 per person. It's in a pleasant secluded spot, sheltered from the motorway.

Stagecoach (☎ 01387-253496) runs about seven buses a day between Dumfries and Edinburgh, via Abington. Stokes (☎ 01555-870344) does a weekday service from Lanark to Abington via Leadhills, but the times are awkward. There's a Monday to Saturday postbus service (☎ 01463-256200) from Abington and Crawfordjohn to Biggar and Wanlockhead.

DOUGLAS

The main road (A70) gives a rather negative impression of this interesting place. Douglas has close ties to Scottish history, begun during the Wars of Independence when the Good Sir James Douglas fought alongside Robert the Bruce.

With the almost total destruction of the grand Douglas family castle by fire in 1755, the village slipped into obscurity.

Turn off the A70 at the Douglas Arms Hotel and follow Main St to the **Douglas Heritage Museum** (☎ 01555-851536), previously the dower house for Douglas Castle, later converted into a chapel. It contains Cameronian military memorabilia and a mock-up of an old shop. It's open Easter to September, weekends, from 2 to 5 pm, and other times by arrangement. Admission is free.

St Bride's Chapel

Close by the heritage museum is the excellent St Bride's Chapel. The 14th century choir and nave were restored in 1880.

They contain three Douglas family wall-tombs, including one for the Good Sir James, who was killed in Spain in 1330 while taking the Bruce's heart to the Holy Land. Look out for the lead-encased hearts of the Good Sir James and Archibald, 5th Earl of Angus, on the floor of the chapel. The superb 16th century clock tower has the oldest working clock in Scotland (1565). Admission to the chapel is free; to get the key, call on Mrs Cowan, 2 Clyde Rd, behind the Crosskeys Inn.

Walks

There's an interesting walk up to the **Hagshaw Wind Farm** about a mile north-west of the village. Follow the minor road to Douglas West, then head up to the farm from the old schoolhouse. There are about 50 gigantic three-blade fans up there.

Places to Stay & Eat

For B&B, try the friendly *Springhill House* (☎ 01555-851727), off the Ayr Rd, with B&B for £19 per person. Behind the petrol station near the Douglas Arms Hotel is *Country Refreshments* (☎ 01555-851043), open daily to 11 pm. It does good fish and chips (£2.80), burgers and pizzas, both sit-in and takeaway.

Getting There & Away

Douglas is about 7 miles north-west of Abington. Stokes (☎ 01555-870344) runs hourly bus services to Lanark while another service goes to Muirkirk, with connections for Cumnock and Ayr.

Ayrshire

The rolling hills and farmland of Ayrshire are best known for being the birthplace and home of poet Robert Burns.

These rich pastures were once also famous for the Ayrshire breed of dairy cattle, since largely replaced by Friesians. Parts of the coast comprise attractive sandy beaches and low cliffs overlooking the mountainous island of Arran.

There are famous golf courses at Troon and Turnberry. It was at Prestwick Golf Club that the major golf tournament, the British Open Championship, was initiated in 1860.

NORTH AYRSHIRE
Largs
* **pop 10,000** ☎ 01475

Largs is a pleasant town facing the Isle of Great Cumbrae. There's a TIC (☎ 673765) on the Promenade; it's open all year. The Main St, with banks, cafés, and cheap eating places, is fairly short, running inland from the TIC and CalMac ferry terminal to just past the train and bus stations. The post office is just off the Main St, on Aitken St.

Things to See The main attraction in Largs is the award-winning **Vikingar!** (☎ 689777), Greenock Rd, a multimedia exhibition describing Viking influence in Scotland, until its demise at the Battle of Largs in 1263. To get there, follow the A78 coast road northwards from the TIC; you can't miss it, it's the only place with a longship outside. Vikingar is open daily from 10.30 am to 5 pm; entrance costs £3.50/2.50.

Largs Old Kirk (Skelmorlie Aisle), Bellman's Close, just off the High St, is well worth a visit. It has an unusual painted barrel-vaulted ceiling depicting the seasons, and an elaborately carved stone tomb. The church is open daily, from 2 to 5 pm, and admission is free.

Hunterston Visitor Centre (☎ 0800-838557) is 9 miles south of Largs, with displays explaining the production of nuclear electricity. Free tea, coffee and soft drinks are available. Perhaps Scottish Nuclear is trying to improve its image. It's open all year, daily, from 9.30 am to 4.30 pm (from October to February it opens at 1 pm at weekends); tours are on weekdays at 10.30 am, and daily at 1.30 and 3.30 pm.

Walks There's a good walk for a couple of miles into the hills east of Largs, starting from the Main St, left into Aitken St, then right up Gateside St and Flatt Rd, past the school. Follow the path high above the Gogo Water as far as Greeto Bridge and the waterfalls. You can climb up steeper slopes to the mast, at 300m, for great views of the Firth of Clyde and the town. Allow two to three hours.

Places to Stay & Eat There's a fine selection of places to eat in Largs. *Toby's Bar* (☎ *687183, 67 Gallowgate*) does really good, cheap bar meals, with soup and a roll at £1.15, and a chicken and chips basket supper (5 to 8 pm) for only £2.

The well known *Nardini's café* (☎ *674555, Esplanade*) does great ice cream, but the prices are astronomical. The *Baker's Oven* (*76 Main St*) does breakfast for £1.49. One of the best places in the area is 6 miles south of Largs – *Fins Seafood Restaurant* (☎ *568989*), Fairlie – which does smoked mussels, salmon and trout.

Brisbane House Hotel (☎ *687200, 14 Greenock Rd*) does tasty bar meals (most main courses from £5 to £8). There's also a good restaurant with à la carte main courses from £10, four-course meals (plus coffee) for £19.95, and a four-course seafood menu for £29.95 including coffee and a half-bottle of wine. All rooms are *en suite*, £55 to £65 single, £80 to £95 double.

Glendarroch (☎ *676305, 24 Irvine Rd*) is a central B&B; its rooms, all with shower, range from £15 to £21 per head.

There's also the *Old Rectory* (☎ *674405, Aubery Crescent*) with singles/doubles from £18/32.

Largs Tourist Hostel (☎ *672851, 110 Irvine Rd*) is open all year and has dorm beds for £8. You'll find it about a mile south of the town centre, at the A78/A760 junction.

There's a large *Safeway* supermarket beyond the south end of Main St, just off Irvine Rd.

Getting There & Away Largs is 32 miles west of Glasgow, by road. There are hourly trains to Largs from Glasgow Central (one hour, £4.50). Buses run to Ardrossan, Ayr, Glasgow, Greenock and Irvine (Stagecoach A1 Service, ☎ 01294-607007).

Isle of Great Cumbrae
• pop 1200   ☎ 01475

Included here because it's reached from North Ayrshire, the island is administered as part of Argyll & Bute. There's actually nothing very great about it – it's only 4 miles long – but it's bigger than privately owned Little Cumbrae island just to the south.

A frequent 15 minute CalMac ferry ride links the town of Largs with Great Cumbrae (£2.85 return, £12.30 for a car). Buses meet the ferries for the 3½-mile journey to slightly seedy **Millport**, which has two sandy beaches. The town boasts Europe's smallest cathedral **The Cathedral of the Isles** (☎ 530353), open daily, and the interesting **Robertson Museum and Aquarium** (☎ 530581), where admission costs £1.50/1. A short way along the coast from the aquarium is the remarkable rock feature called **The Lion. The Museum of the Cumbraes** is due to reopen in 1999 in **The Garrison**, pre-

Ayrshire Cattle

This hardy type of dairy cattle originated from cross-breeding in the 18th century and proved to be a great success, giving high milk yields even when feed was poor. Ayrshires are the only British-developed breed of dairy cattle.

By the early 19th century, Ayrshires were paramount in Britain. Large numbers of these variously-coloured cattle were exported to Canada, the US, Russia, Finland and Kenya. However, due to recent changes in the nature of dairy farming, the larger Friesian breed has overtaken the Ayrshire in popularity.

viously the excise and militia HQ. There's a seasonal TIC (☎ 530753), 28 Stuart St (at the waterfront), and several bike hire places including Mapes (☎ 530444), 3 Guildford St (£2.40 for two hours). Rural parts of the island are distinctly more pleasant than Millport; the narrow Inner Circle Rd is a good cycle route. Ask the TIC for maps of cycle routes.

On the main street around the bay you'll find a post office, VG supermarket, bank (with ATM), two fish and chip shops and a couple of cafés. For meals, try the *Newton* pub *(☎ 530920, 1 Glasgow St)* with main courses from £3.50. It also does cheap snacks, a wide variety of pizzas, and takeaways. *Minstrel's Wine Bar & Restaurant (3 Cardiff St)* has a good range of bar meals and vegetarian choices, £4 to £9. For B&B, try *Denmark Cottage (☎ 530958, 8 Ferry Rd)* where rooms cost from £14 per person. The *College of the Holy Spirit (☎ 530353)*, at the cathedral, does B&B single/double from £17/30. Dinner is an extra £11.

Irvine

• pop 35,000   ☎ 01294

In the early 1990s, Irvine Development Corporation flattened a large area and redeveloped it as **Irvine Harbourside**, an interesting place with brand-new 19th century-style buildings, not far from the town centre and train station. The cobbled street **Linthouse Vennel** is lined with impressive and very expensive-looking buildings. The all-year TIC (☎ 383886), New St, is near the train station. Ask the TIC for information on the town's Burns Trail. There are Asda and Tesco supermarkets in the Irvine Centre; banks with ATMs and the post office are on the High St.

Things to See & Do The **Scottish Maritime Museum** (☎ 278283) Gottries Rd, Harbourside, has various ships you can clamber about on and you can also see a restored shipyard worker's flat. It's open April to October, daily, from 10 am to 5 pm. There are regular guided tours throughout the day which visit sections not normally

open to the public. The Puffer café on site does snacks and daily specials. Admission to the museum costs £2/1 (£4 for a family ticket).

The **Magnum Leisure Centre** (☎ 278381), Harbourside, is open daily to 10 pm. The centre is Scotland's largest and has swimming (with flumes), ice rinks, football, squash, bowls, cinema, theatre, inexpensive café, and lots more. Swimming and ice skating charges start at £1.80.

Dundonald Castle (☎ 01563-850201) is 4 miles south-east of Irvine. It was the first home of the Stuart Kings, built by Robert II in the 1370s, and reckoned to be the third most important castle in Scotland, after Edinburgh and Stirling.

Historic Scotland has spent more than £1 million on recent renovations. There's a tearoom on site. The castle opens April to September, daily, from 1 to 4 pm; entry costs £1.50/75p. Stagecoach A1 Service (☎ 01294-607007) runs two buses each hour between Irvine Cross and Kilmarnock, via Dundonald village.

Places to Stay & Eat For accommodation at Harbourside, try the new *Harbourside Hotel (☎ 275515, 86 Montgomery St)*; £25 single, £36 double. The *Laurels (☎ 278405, 29 West Rd)* is conveniently located near the Irvine Centre. B&B there costs only £14 to £15 single/double.

The *Ship Inn (☎ 279722)*, near the Magnum Centre at 120 Harbour St, is the oldest pub in Irvine, built in 1597. Bar meals start at £4.45 and are excellent value. For similarly priced bar meals and live folk music, try *Marina Inn (☎ 274079, 110 Harbour St)*. The *Harbour Chippy (Gottries Rd)* does good fish and chips (£2.40).

Getting There & Away Irvine is 26 miles from Glasgow. Trains run to Glasgow Central half-hourly (35 minutes, £4 single, £5.10 off-peak return). In the other direction they go to Ayr. Buses depart from the High St (Irvine Cross) for Ayr, Glasgow, Greenock, Kilmarnock and Largs (Stagecoach A1 Service, ☎ 01294-607007).

SOUTHERN

Ardrossan

- **pop 11,000   ☎ 01294**

The main reason for coming here is to catch a CalMac ferry to Arran. Trains leave Glasgow Central (one hour, £4.10) five times a day to connect with ferries.

Ardrossan is a very run down area; there are several cheap but mostly uninspiring places to eat on the main street (Glasgow St) and in neighbouring Princes St. On Glasgow St there's a post office, grocer and general store. In Princes St there's a bank with an ATM. *Lainey's Café (Princes St)* does good sausage rolls for only 55p. The *Sangeet Indian Restaurant (☎ 601191, 51 Glasgow Rd)* does cheap takeaways, and three-course meals for only £5.95 on Thursday to Sunday evenings.

If you need B&B in town, try *Edenmore Guest House (☎ 462306, 47 Parkhouse Rd)*, just off the main A78 road. Singles cost from £16.50, doubles from £30.

ISLE OF ARRAN

- **pop 4800   ☎ 01770**

'Scotland in miniature' they call it, and parts of this island certainly are reminiscent of other areas of the country. There are challenging walks in the mountainous northern part of the island, often compared to the Highlands. The landscape in the south is gentler and similar to the rest of southern Scotland.

Since Arran is easily accessible from Glasgow and the south of the country, being only an hour's ferry ride from Ardrossan, it's very popular. Despite its popularity the 20-mile-long island seems to be big enough to absorb everyone. The bucket and spade brigade fill the southern resorts, cyclists take to the island's circular road and hikers tackle the hills, the highest (at 874m, 2867 feet) being Goat Fell. With seven golf courses, Arran is also popular with golfers.

Orientation & Information

The ferry from Ardrossan docks at Brodick, the island's main town. To the south, Lamlash is actually the capital, and, like nearby Whiting Bay, a popular seaside resort. From the village of Lochranza in the north there's a ferry link to Claonaig on the Kintyre peninsula.

Near Brodick pier, the TIC (☎ 302140) is open June through September, daily from 9 am to 7.30 pm (10 am to 5 pm on Sunday) and for shorter hours at other times of the year. The hospital (☎ 600777) is in Lamlash. There's a laundry by the Collins Good Food Shop (next to the River Cloy); a 30 minute wash costs £2.

The week-long Arran Folk Festival takes place in early June. Phone ☎ 302341 for information. There's also a weekend jazz festival in May.

Arran is known for its local cheeses, and Arran mustard is also worth buying. Watch out for the woollens, though. Real Aran (one 'r') sweaters come from the Irish island of Aran, not this one.

Western Buses (☎ 302000) runs full or half-day tours for £6/4 or £5/3. The full-day tours run May to September, departing from Brodick pier daily at 11 am. Half-day tours run in July and August, departing from Brodick pier Monday to Friday at 2 pm.

Check out the Internet at www.arran .uk.com for information about the island.

Things to See

The town of **Brodick** isn't particularly interesting, but it's in a pleasant location. There are several hotels, B&Bs, gift shops, a Co-op supermarket, and banks with ATMs. Taking the road 1½ miles north, you'll come to the small **Heritage Museum** (☎ 302636), with an early 20th century-style furnished cottage, an old blacksmith's workshop, local archaeology and geology exhibits, and a yearly special exhibition. It's open April to October, daily, from 11 am to 4 pm (June to August, 10 am to 5 pm); admission costs £2/1.25.

Brodick Castle (☎ 302202) and park is 2½ miles north of town. This ancient seat of the Dukes of Hamilton is now in the hands of the NTS, and has an excellent restaurant. It's an interesting stately home, with rather more of a lived-in feel than some NTS properties. The kitchens and scullery, complete

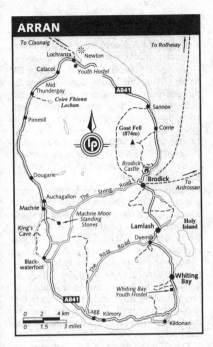

ARRAN

To Claonaig
Lochranza
Newton
To Rothesay
Catacol
Youth Hostel
Mid Thundergay
Coire Fhionn Lochan
A841
Sannox
Pirnmill
Goat Fell (874m)
Corrie
Dougarie
Brodick Castle
Brodick
To Ardrossan
Auchagallon
The String Road
Machrie
Machrie Moor Standing Stones
Lamlash
Holy Island
King's Cave
Dyemill
Blackwaterfoot
The Ross Road
Whiting Bay
Whiting Bay Youth Hostel
A841
Lagg Kilmory
Kildonan

0 — 2 — 4 km
0 — 1.5 — 3 miles

beach and great views of the mountains, the road cuts inland.

Lochranza is a village in a small bay at the north of the island. In summer there's a ferry link to the Kintyre peninsula from here. There's also a shop and post office, youth hostel, camping ground, several B&Bs and a couple of hotels. On a promontory stand the ruins of the 13th century **Lochranza Castle**, said to be the inspiration for the castle in *The Black Island*, Hergé's Tintin adventure. The key is available from Lochranza Stores (admission free). Also in Lochranza is Scotland's newest distillery, Isle of Arran Distillers (☎ 830264), opened in 1995. Tours run daily from 10 am to 5 pm (£3.50). The village has a boat race, and fiddlers rallies and other music events in summer. Two miles beyond Lochranza, the whitewashed cottages of **Catacol**, known as the Twelve Apostles, were built to house people cleared from land set aside for sheep and deer. Summer sunsets are wonderful here.

On the west side of the island, reached by the String Rd across the centre (or the coast road), are the **Machrie Moor standing stones**, upright sandstone slabs erected around 6000 years ago. It's an eerie place, and these are the most impressive of the six stone circles on the island. To get there you'll need an OS map; walk along the 1½-mile track from the coast road, starting from the Historic Scotland sign just north of Machrie village. There's another group at nearby **Auchagallon**, surrounding a Bronze Age burial cairn.

Blackwaterfoot is the largest village on the west coast; it has a shop/post office and two hotels. From here, you can walk to **King's Cave** via Drumadoon Farm – Arran is one of several islands that lays claim to a cave where Robert the Bruce had his famous arachnid encounter. This walk could be combined with a visit to the Machrie standing stones.

The landscape in the southern part of the island is much gentler; the road drops into little wooded valleys, and it's particularly lovely around **Lagg**. Walk from Lagg post

with displays of peculiar kitchen devices, are well worth a look. The grounds, now a country park with various trails among the rhododendrons, have an attractive walled garden. The house is open April to October from 11.30 to 4.30 pm; entry to the castle and park is £4.80/3.20. The park is open year-round, daily from 9.30 am to sunset (£2.40/1.60 for the park only).

As you go round Brodick Bay, look out for seals which are often seen on the rocks around Merkland Point. Two types live in these waters, the Atlantic grey and the common seal. They're actually quite easy to tell apart – the common seal has a face like a dog; the Atlantic grey seal has a Roman nose.

The coast road continues to the small pretty village of **Corrie** where there's a shop and hotel, and one of the tracks up Goat Fell starts here. After **Sannox**, with a sandy office to **Torrylin Cairn** (10 minutes each way), a chambered tomb over 4000 years old, where at least eight bodies were found. At **Kilmory**, you can visit the **Torrylin Creamery** (☎ 870240), open daily, except Saturday, from 10 am to 4 pm (admission free). There are displays about cheese making. In the shop, you can buy a tasty one-pound Arran Dunlop cheese for £3.20. At **East Bennan**, there's **Southbank Farm Park** (☎ 820221), with lots of beasts, including those wonderful hairy Highland cattle. **Kildonan** has pleasant sandy beaches, two hotels, a camp site and an ivy-clad ruined castle.

In **Whiting Bay** you'll find a youth hostel, village shop, post office and craft shops. There are lots of hotels; most of them serve meals. In the Whiting Bay Village Hall, on Wednesday evenings in summer, there's an audio-visual presentation *Discovering Arran*, £2.50.

Just north of Whiting Bay is **Holy Island**, owned by the Samye Ling Tibetan Centre (Dumfriesshire) and used as a retreat, but day visits are allowed. One ferry runs from Whiting Bay (☎ 700382, May to September, 15 minutes, £6, three daily), the other goes from Lamlash (☎ 0860-235086, 30 minutes, £6, five daily). No dogs, alcohol or fires are allowed on the island. There's a good walk to the top of the hill (314m, 1030 feet), a two to three-hour round trip.

Lamlash is a sailing centre with hotels, restaurants, cafés, grocery stores, and a post office. The bay was used as a safe anchorage by the Navy during WWI and WWII.

Walks & Cycle Routes

The walk up **Goat Fell** takes five to six hours for the round trip and, if the weather's good, there are superb views from the 874m-high summit. It can, however, be very cold and windy up here so come well prepared. There are paths from Brodick Castle and Corrie. From the high point of the road between Sannox and Lochranza, you can head southwards (avoiding the forestry) and walk up a pleasant ridge to **Caisteal Abhail** (859m, 2818 feet). The

view is magnificent from the top. Don't be tempted to follow the east ridge to Ceum na Caillich (Witch's Step) – it involves moderate rock climbing and it's quite exposed.

However, you can go southwards to **Cir Mhór** (798m, 2617 feet), scramble over its pointed summit, continue down its east ridge to a pass, then descend steeply into Glen Sannox. Only attempt this route in good weather; allow six hours. For both routes, carry OS map No 69 and a compass. Note that there's deer stalking on Caisteal Abhail from late August to late October; ask locally for advice.

Another good walk on a marked path goes up to **Coire Fhionn Lochan** from Mid Thundergay; it takes about an hour to reach the loch. You can continue up to the top of **Beinn Bhreac** (711m, 2332 feet), taking another 1½ hours from the loch.

More moderate walks include the trail through **Glen Sannox** from the village of Sannox up the burn, a two hour return trip. From Whiting Bay Youth Hostel there are easy one hour walks through the forest to the **Giant's Graves** and **Glenashdale Falls**, and back.

The 50-mile circuit on the coastal road is popular with cyclists and has few serious hills – more in the south than the north. Traffic isn't too bad, except at the height of the season.

Places to Stay

Camping Camping without the permission of the landowner isn't allowed, but there are several camping grounds (open April to October). When choosing a site note that midges can be a major pain in sheltered spots.

Two miles from Brodick, you can camp at *Glen Rosa Farm* (☎ 302380), from £4 for a tent and two people. *Middleton Camping* (☎ 600251), at Lamlash, charges £2.50 per person and £1.50 per tent. In Kildonan, *Breadalbane Lodge* (☎ 820210) charges campers £3.50 each, including use of the showers; it's very pleasantly located and the breeze here keeps the midges away. There's also camping at the *Kildonan Hotel*

(☎ *820207*) for £4 per head, including use of excellent new facilities. *Lochranza Golf* (☎ *830273*), in Lochranza, costs from £8 for a tent and two people.

Hostels Located in the north of the island, *Lochranza Youth Hostel* (☎ *830631*) is an excellent place to stay. It's a self-catering hostel open all year, except January. The nightly charge is £7.75/6.50. In the south there's *Whiting Bay Youth Hostel* (☎ *700339*), £6.10/4.95, open March to October. Right at the southern tip of Arran, the *Kildonan Hotel Bunkhouse* (☎ *820207*), Kildonan, charges £7. Currently, there's no kitchen. At Shiskine, near Blackwaterfoot, *Burncliff* (☎ *860245*) has dorm beds for £8, B&B for £10 per person and dinner for an extra £5. It's a friendly place, and Emmanuelle speaks French.

B&Bs & Hotels – Brodick It's best to get out of Brodick to some of the smaller villages, although there are numerous places to stay here.

Near the pier, the *Douglas Hotel* (☎ *302155*) charges from £20 to £30 per person, and is convenient if you're catching an early ferry. Some rooms have attached baths. Along Shore Rd, guesthouses include *Tigh-na-Mara* (☎ *302538*) which charges from £18 per person; and *Belvedere* (☎ *302397*) on Alma Rd, where rooms are from £16. *Pirate's Cove* (☎ *302438*), 3 miles north of Brodick, charges only £14 a single/double (with shared bath). Half a mile from the centre of Brodick *Rosaburn Lodge* (☎ *302383*) is a comfortable B&B with three rooms for £24 to £28, all with attached baths.

B&Bs & Hotels – Glen Cloy The island's best hotel is also its oldest building – it has a glass window dating from 1650. The *Kilmichael Country House Hotel* (☎ *302219*), in Glen Cloy, a mile outside Brodick, is a tastefully decorated hideaway. It's a small, elegant hotel with six rooms from £60 to £65 for a single, £78 to £124 for a double. There's an excellent restaurant here, with three-course dinners for £24.50.

B&Bs & Hotels – Corrie & Sannox The *Corrie Hotel* (☎ *810273*) has rooms from £21/42 with shared bathroom, £26/52 with bathroom attached. It serves bar meals and there's a beer garden in summer. The seafront *Blackrock Guest House* (☎ *810282*) opens from March to October and offers B&B from £19 per person in rooms with shared baths. *Sannox House* (☎ *810230*), Sannox, is a fine place with *en suite* singles from £17.50 and doubles from £46; dinner costs an extra £10.

B&Bs & Hotels – Lochranza This is a great place to stay. Apart from the youth hostel here, there's *Benvaren* (☎ *830647*), overlooking the bay and near the ferry slipway, with rooms from £18 to £20 per person. *Castlekirk* (☎ *830202*), a converted church opposite the castle, has two rooms for £18 per person and an in-house darkroom for photographers (phone for information on art courses run here). *Kincardine Lodge Guest House* (☎ *830267*) charges £18 to £20 per person and some rooms have attached baths. *Lochranza Hotel* (☎ *830223*) has singles/doubles for £32/52. The best place to stay here is *Apple Lodge* (☎ *830229*), with three double rooms for £50 to £60 and excellent dinners for £15.50 (residents only). You'll be well looked after in very comfortable surroundings.

B&Bs & Hotels – Blackwaterfoot The *Kinloch Hotel* (☎ *860444*) does B&B for £46 per person and dinner is an extra £13. The hotel has good leisure facilities (handy on a wet day), including a 15m swimming pool (£2.25 for nonresidents), sauna, squash court and multi-gym. *Morvern Guesthouse* (☎ *860254*), in the same building as the shop and post office, charges £16 to £20 a single/double.

B&Bs & Hotels – Kilmory & Lagg *Kilmory House* (☎ *870342*) is a converted 17th century flax mill with three rooms from £15 per person and dinner for an extra £10. Nearby at Lagg, there's the *Lagg Country House Hotel* (☎ *870255*). Although

SOUTHERN

it boasts a lovely location it's not currently recommended.

B&Bs & Hotels – Kildonan Kildonan is a very peaceful spot. The friendly *Breadalbane Hotel (☎ 820284)* has holiday flats with bedrooms, bathroom and kitchen, sleeping four to six people. It charges from £80 to £200 per week depending on the season, and outside the high season it may let a flat for less than a week. B&B is available for £25 per person. *Drimla Lodge (☎ 820296)* has rooms with attached shower from £22 to £30 per person.

B&Bs & Hotels – Whiting Bay Swiss-owned *Argentine House Hotel (☎ 700662, Shore Rd)* has singles from £17 to £71 and doubles from £44 to £78, all with attached bath. It has a recommended restaurant with a mid-European theme; a three-course meal costs £19. French, German and Italian are spoken here. There's a good B&B, *Rowallan (☎ 700377, School Rd)*, charging from £16 per head.

Places to Eat

The award-winning *Creelers Seafood Restaurant (☎ 302810)* is 1½ miles north of Brodick by the Arran Aromatics shopping centre. It's a bistro-style place with some outside seating, open daily, except Monday. The imaginative menu includes main dishes from around £6 to £16. There's also a shop here selling seafood and smoked foods. You can stock up on local cheeses from the cheese shop opposite, or have a snack in the *Home Farm Kitchen* with home baking, and baked potatoes from £1.85.

Back in Brodick, *Stalkers Eating House (☎ 302579)*, along the waterfront, does good-value meals. Home-made steak pie is £5.50, jacket potatoes are from £1.50, and there are solid British puddings like fruit crumble and sherry trifle. *Duncan's Bar* at the Kingsley Hotel on Shore Rd does good pub grub. The *Ormidale Hotel (☎ 302293)*, in Glen Cloy, is similar, with main courses for £5 to £10, and occasional live music. The *Ferry Fry*, by the pier, does toasties for 95p and good takeaway fish and chips for £2.80.

For a meal in Lochranza, try the *Lochranza Hotel (☎ 830223)*. The bar meals start at £4.75, but snacks are cheaper; check out the daily specials on the whiteboard. The three-course set restaurant meal is good value at £14; à la carte is also available. Two miles from Lochranza, the bar at the *Catacol Bay Hotel (☎ 830231)* does excellent bar food, with main courses from £4.50 to £7. The restaurant does a Sunday afternoon buffet for £8.50 and you can eat as much as you like. In summer, there are often ceilidhs and live music.

In Kildonan, the *Breadalbane Hotel (☎ 820284)* does great home-made bar food (main courses £3.25 to £10). The *Kildonan Hotel* is similar, but you can also have lobster salad, caught by the proprietor, for £8.50.

The *Coffee Pot (☎ 700382)*, Whiting Bay, has coffee pots from around the world, and a good selection of home baking and meals for around £5 to £6. The *Cameronia Hotel (☎ 700254)*, Whiting Bay, serves real ales; bar snacks start at £1.50, and main courses are £3.75 to £8.50. *Glenisle Hotel (☎ 600559)* is a good restaurant in Lamlash, with lunch main courses from £3.75 to £4.50 and two course dinners for only £12. *Carraig Mhor (☎ 600453, Shore Rd, Lamlash)* is recommended for its seafood.

Getting There & Away

CalMac (☎ 302166) runs a daily car ferry between Ardrossan and Brodick (four to six per day, 55 minutes, £3.95, from £22 for a car); summer services between Claonaig and Lochranza (10 per day, 30 minutes, £3.65, from £16.65 for a car); and summer services on Monday, Wednesday and Friday between Brodick, Largs and the Isle of Bute (one each way, two hours, £4.35, £22 for a car).

If you're going to visit several islands it's worth planning your route in advance. CalMac has a wide range of tickets including Island Hopscotch fares that work out cheaper than buying several single tickets.

Getting Around

The island's efficient bus services are operated by Western Buses (☎ 302000) and Royal Mail (01463-256200). There are four to six buses a day from Brodick Pier to Lochranza (40 minutes, £1.55). Buses for Blackwaterfoot run via Lochranza, the String Rd, or Whiting Bay (£1.55). Four to eight buses per day run from Brodick to Lamlash and Whiting Bay (30 minutes, £1.45). A Daycard costs £3. For a taxi phone ☎ 302274 in Brodick or ☎ 600725 in Lamlash.

In Brodick there are several places to rent bikes, including Mini Golf Cycle Hire (☎ 302272) on Shore Rd with bikes for around £9 per day. Whiting Bay Hires (☎ 700382) has 18-speed mountain bikes for £8 per day. You can also rent three-speeds from Sandy Kerr (☎ 830676) near Lochranza Youth Hostel for £4.50 per day or £15 per week.

EAST AYRSHIRE

There's not much to see in this county apart from depressed towns and farmland. However, near the eastern border with Lanarkshire and by the A71 Irvine to Edinburgh road, there's **Loudoun Hill**, a trachyte volcanic remnant with extensive views. It's a great place for a picnic and you can watch the rock climbers too. The **Pulpit Rock** is a great climb, moderate in standard, but you'll need experience and equipment before attempting it. In 1297, William Wallace and his men ambushed a party of English troops in the narrow valley below the hill – the first successful skirmish for the Scots.

In **Kilmarnock**, there's the excellent **Dean Castle** (☎ 01563-522702), a 15 minute walk along Glasgow Rd from the bus and train stations. Ask the Kilmarnock to Glasgow bus driver to drop you at Dean Rd (Western Buses, ☎ 01563-525192, half-hourly). Trains run to Kilmarnock from Glasgow Central (hourly, £3.50). The castle, restored in the first half of the 20th century, has a virtually windowless 14th century keep and an adjacent 15th century palace with a superb collection of medieval arms, armour, tapestries and musical instruments. The grounds are a good place for a picnic or you could eat at the visitor centre *restaurant*, where snacks and meals cost under £4. The castle opens daily, from noon to 5 pm (weekends only in winter), and admission costs £2.50/1.25 (including a guided tour).

SOUTH AYRSHIRE
Ayr

- **pop 49,500   ☎ 01292**

Ayr's long sandy beach has made it a popular family seaside resort since Victorian times. It's also known for its racecourse, the top course in Scotland, with more racing days than any other in Britain. The Scottish Grand National is held here in April. Ayr is the largest town on this coast and makes a convenient base for a tour of Burns territory.

Information The TIC (☎ 288688) is opposite the train station on Burns Statue Square. It's open September to June, Monday to Saturday, from 9.15 am to 5 pm, and Sunday 11 am to 5 pm (possibly closed at weekends, November to March). In July and August, the TIC opens Monday to Saturday, from 9.15 am to 6 pm, and Sunday, 10 am to 5 pm.

There are banks with ATMs on High St, and the post office is on Sandgate. Ayr Hospital (☎ 610555) is south of town, by the Dalmellington road. For a taxi, call Central Taxis on ☎ 267655.

Things to See Things to see in Ayr are mainly Burns related. The bard was baptised in the **Auld Kirk** (old church) off the High St. Several of his poems are set here in Ayr; in *Twa Brigs*, Ayr's old and new bridges argue with one another. The **Auld Brig** was built in 1491 and spans the river just down from the church. In Burns' poem *Tam o'Shanter*, Tam spends a boozy evening in the pub that now bears his name, at 230 High St.

St John's Tower, Montgomerie Terrace, is the only remnant of a church where a parliament was held in 1315, the year after the celebrated victory at Bannockburn. John

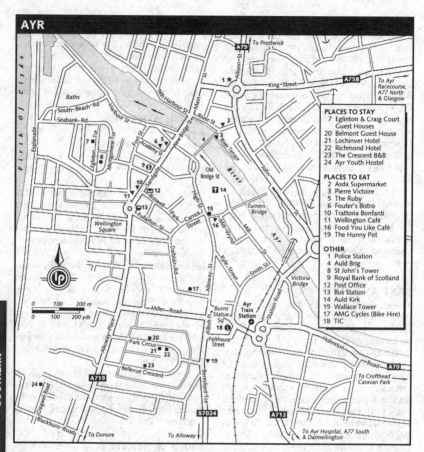

AYR

PLACES TO STAY
7 Eglinton & Craig Court
  Guest Houses
20 Belmont Guest House
21 Lochinver Hotel
22 Richmond Hotel
23 The Crescent B&B
24 Ayr Youth Hostel

PLACES TO EAT
2 Asda Supermarket
3 Pierre Victoire
5 The Ruby
6 Fouter's Bistro
10 Trattoria Bonfanti
11 Wellington Café
16 Food You Like Café
19 The Hunny Pot

OTHER
1 Police Station
4 Auld Brig
8 St John's Tower
9 Royal Bank of Scotland
12 Post Office
13 Bus Station
14 Auld Kirk
15 Wallace Tower
17 AMG Cycles (Bike Hire)
18 TIC

Knox's son-in-law was the minister here, and Mary, Queen of Scots, stayed overnight in 1563. The key is available during office hours from Parks & Environment, South Ayrshire Council, Burns Statue Square. Admission is free, but there's a £2 key deposit.

Cycle Routes With not too many steep hills, the area is well suited to cyclists. See the Glasgow section for the cycle way from that city. Ask the TIC for its useful leaflet.

From Ayr, you could cycle to Alloway and spend a couple of hours seeing the Burns sights before continuing via Maybole to Culzean. You could either camp here after seeing Culzean Castle, or cycle back along the coast road to Ayr, a round trip of about 22 miles.

In Ayr, AMG Cycles (☎ 287580), 55 Dalblair Rd, rents bikes for £10 per day (24 hour hire). Weekend rental is only £17.

Places to Stay The *Ayr Youth Hostel* (☎ 262322, 5 Craigweil Rd) is housed in a magnificent turreted mansion by the beach and is less than a mile south of the train and bus stations. It's open from March through October; the nightly charge is £7.75/6.50 for seniors/juniors.

There's a smart caravan park in town but it doesn't take campers. *Crofthead Caravan Park* (☎ 263516) is 2 miles east of Ayr near the A70. It charges from £5.50 for a small tent and two people (plus £1 per car).

There are numerous B&Bs and hotels. *Eglinton Guest House* (☎ 264623, 23 Eglinton Terrace) is a short walk west of the bus station and has rooms for £16/30 single/double. Just across the street is the recommended *Craig Court Guest House* (☎ 261028, 22 Eglinton Terrace) at £17/32.

A five to 10 minute walk from the station brings you to a crescent of upmarket B&Bs and small hotels. On Park Circus, *Belmont Guest House* (☎ 265588, 15 Park Circus) has *en suite* rooms for £19/36. *Lochinver Hotel* (☎ 265086, 32 Park Circus) is a homely sort of place and charges from £15.50 per person. The *Richmond Hotel* (☎ 265153, 38 Park Circus) is a small, friendly and efficient place with rooms from £25/36.

Park Circus continues into Bellevue Crescent and there are several other places to stay along here. The *Crescent* (☎ 287329, 26 Bellevue Crescent) is an excellent small hotel. Room tariffs are £25 to £30 single, £40 to £50 double (all with attached bath).

Places to Eat Supplies can be bought in the huge *Tesco* supermarket on Whitletts Rd, by Ayr Racecourse, and there's an *Asda* supermarket on Wallace St, near the river. For the best fish and chips in Ayr (£2.80), try the *Wellington Café (102 Sandgate)* near the bus station. You can sit-in or carryout. *Food You Like Café* (☎ 619998) at the corner of Mill Wynd does breakfast for 99p and main courses for under £3.50. The *Hunny Pot* (☎ 263239, 37 Beresford Terrace), a short walk from the TIC, is a pleasant place serving good teas and light meals (£4 to £5) from 9 am to 10 pm, 10.30 am to 9 pm on Sunday. There's a branch of

the French-style chain *Pierre Victoire* (☎ 282087, 4 River Terrace) where the set three-course lunch costs £5.90.

The *Ruby* (☎ 267131, 22 New Bridge St) is a good Chinese restaurant specialising in seafood. It also does takeaways. *Trattoria Bonfanti* (☎ 266577, 64 Sandgate) does good Italian food. Pasta dishes start at £5, and pizzas cost from £4.25.

The best place in town is *Fouters Bistro Restaurant* (☎ 261391, 2A Academy St) opposite the town hall. It specialises in Ayrshire produce and local seafood. Main dishes are £9.50 to £14, and there's a cheaper bistro menu. It's closed on Sunday and Monday.

Getting There & Away Ayr is 33 miles from Glasgow. There are at least two trains an hour from Glasgow Central to Ayr (50 minutes, £4.80) and some trains continue south to Stranraer (1½ hours from Ayr, £13.70). The main bus operator in the area is Western Buses (☎ 613500) – its hourly X77 service from Glasgow to Girvan/Stranraer via Ayr costs £3 (Glasgow to Ayr). It also runs buses from Ayr to Glasgow, Greenock, Irvine, Kilmarnock, Largs, Muirkirk and Newton Stewart.

Alloway

Three miles south of Ayr, Alloway is where Robert Burns was born in 1759. Even if you're not a fan it's still worth a visit, since the Burns-related exhibitions also give a very good impression of life in Ayrshire in the late 18th century. All the sights are within easy walking distance of each other and come under the umbrella title **Burns National Heritage Park**.

The **Burns Cottage and Museum** (☎ 01292-441215) stands by the main road from Ayr. Born in the little box bed in this cramped thatched cottage, the poet spent the first seven years of his life here. There's a good museum of Burnsiana by the cottage exhibiting everything from his writing compendium to a piece of wood from his coffin. Light meals are available in the tearoom. The museum opens April to

October, daily, from 9 am to 6 pm; from November to March, Monday to Saturday, from 10 am to 4 pm, and Sunday noon to 4 pm. Entry is £2.50/1.25; the ticket also permits entry to the Burns Monument and Gardens. You can also get a combined ticket to include the Tam o'Shanter Experience for £4.25/2 (£10 family).

From here you can visit the ruins of **Alloway Auld Kirk**, the setting for part of *Tam o'Shanter*. Burns' father, William Burnes (his son dropped the 'e' from his name) is buried in the kirkyard.

The nearby **Tam o'Shanter Experience** (☎ 01292-443700) has audio-visual displays (£2.50/1.25), a restaurant, and a bookshop/giftshop. It's open April to October, daily, from 9 am to 6 pm (closing at 5 pm the rest of the year). The restaurant here does excellent home-made soup. The **Burns Monument and Gardens** (opening hours as for the Burns Cottage) are nearby. The monument was built in 1823 and affords a view of the 13th century **Brig o'Doon**. There are also statues of Burns' drinking cronies in the gardens.

Brig O'Doon House (☎ 01292-442466) has a brasserie doing three-course dinners for around £15. Conveniently located, as its name suggests, rooms are £80/100. *Northpark House Hotel* (☎ 01292-442336) is off the road to Ayr. It's a small, luxurious hotel with a fine restaurant; room rates are from £60/80.

There are hourly buses daily, except Sunday, between Alloway and Ayr until 5.50 pm (Western Buses, ☎ 613500, service 57, £1.50 return). Otherwise, rent a bike and cycle here.

Culzean Castle & Country Park

Well worth seeing, Culzean (pronounced cullane), 12 miles south of Ayr, is one of the most impressive of Scotland's great stately homes. Perched dramatically on the edge of the cliffs, this 18th century mansion was designed by Robert Adam to replace the castle built here in the 16th century.

The original castle belonged to the Kennedy clan, who, after a feud in the 16th century, divided into the Kennedys of Culzean and Cassillis, and the Kennedys of Bargany. Because of the American connection (Eisenhower was an occasional visitor) most people wrongly assume that the Culzean Kennedys are closely related to JFK. Culzean Castle was given to the National Trust for Scotland (NTS) in 1945.

Robert Adam, clearly the most influential architect of his time, was renowned for his meticulous attention to detail and the elegant classical embellishments with which he decorated his ceilings and fireplaces. The beautiful oval staircase here is regarded as one of his finest achievements.

On the 1st floor, the opulence of the circular saloon contrasts splendidly with the views of the wild sea below. The other rooms on this floor are also interesting and Lord Cassillis' bedroom is said to be haunted by a lady in green, mourning a lost baby. Even the bathrooms are palatial, the dressing room beside the state bedroom being equipped with a state-of-the-art shower that directs jets of water from almost every angle.

Set in a 563 acre park combining woodland, coast and gardens, there's much more to see than just the castle. An interesting exhibition in the Gas House explains how gas was produced here for the castle. There's also a visitor centre, ice house, swan pond and aviary.

Culzean Castle (☎ 01655-760269) is the NTS's most visited property and it can get quite crowded on summer weekends. It's open April to October, from 10.30 am to 5.30 pm. The park opens year-round from 9.30 am to sunset. Entry is £6.50/4.40 (£17 for a family ticket), or £3.50/2.40 if you only want to visit the park.

It's possible to stay in the castle from April to October, but gracious living doesn't come cheap. A night for two in the Eisenhower suite costs £300 and the cheapest rooms are £100/150 for a single/double. If you're not in that league there's a *Camping and Caravanning Club* (☎ 01655-760627) site in the park. It costs £4 per person plus £4 for nonmembers, per night.

Robert Burns

Best remembered for penning the words of *Auld Lang Syne*, Robert Burns is Scotland's most famous poet, and a popular hero whose birthday (25 January) is celebrated as Burns Night by Scots around the world.

He was born in 1759 in Alloway. Although his mother was illiterate and his parents poor farmers, they sent him to the local school where he soon showed an aptitude for literature and a fondness for the folk song. He began to write his own songs and satires, some of which he distributed privately. When the problems of his arduous farming life were compounded by the threat of prosecution from the father of Jean Armour, with whom he'd had an affair, he decided to emigrate to Jamaica. He gave up his share of the family farm and published his poems to raise money for the journey.

The poems were so well reviewed in Edinburgh that Burns decided to remain in Scotland and devote himself to writing. He went to Edinburgh in 1787 to publish a second edition, but the financial rewards were not enough to live on and he had to take a job as a customs officer in Dumfriesshire. He contributed many songs to collections published by Johnson and Thomson in Edinburgh, and a third edition of his poems was published in 1793. Burns died in Dumfries in 1796, aged 37, after a heart attack.

While some dispute Burns' claim to true literary genius, he was certainly an accomplished poet and songwriter, and has been compared to Chaucer for his verse tale *Tam o'Shanter*. Burns wrote in Lallans, the Scottish Lowland dialect of English that is not very accessible to the Sassenach, or foreigner; perhaps this is part of his appeal. He was also very much a man of the people, satirising the upper classes and the church for their hypocrisy.

Many of the local landmarks mentioned in *Tam o'Shanter* can still be visited. Farmer Tam, riding home after a hard night's drinking in a pub in Ayr, sees witches dancing in Alloway churchyard. He calls out to the one pretty witch but is pursued by them all and has to reach the other side of the Doon river to be safe. He just manages to cross the Brig o'Doon, but his mare loses her tail to the witches.

The Burns connection in Southern Scotland is milked for all it's worth and TICs have a *Burns Heritage Trail* leaflet leading you to every place that can claim some link with the bard. There's a Burns festival in early June. There was a major jamboree in 1996, the bicentenary of his death.

Maybole is the nearest train station but since it's 4 miles away it's best to come by bus from Ayr (11 per day, except Sunday, 30 minutes, £1.95). The bus passes the park gates but it's still a 20 minute walk through the grounds to the castle.

Turnberry

To play the world-famous golf course here you usually must stay at the luxurious *Turnberry Hotel* (☎ 01655-331000). Singles cost £158 to £250, while doubles are £184 to £340. If you can afford that, dinner in the award-winning restaurant is a snip at £45.

Ailsa Craig & Girvan

From much of South Ayrshire, curiously-shaped Ailsa Craig can be seen, looking like a giant bread roll floating out to sea. It's now a bird sanctuary and taking a cruise from Girvan on the MV *Glorious* (☎ 01465-713219) is normally about as close as you'll get to the gannets that crowd this 340m-high (1115 feet) rocky outcrop. It's possible to land if the sea is reasonably calm; a four hour trip costs £9/6 per adult/child, while a six hour trip costs £10 per person. A minimum of eight people is required, with at least one week's notice.

Girvan isn't terribly exciting, but it has all tourist services, including a seasonal TIC (☎ 01465-714950), on Bridge St.

Mr Chips (21 Bridge St) does good fish suppers. For a pleasant bar meal, try the *Hamilton Arms Hotel* (☎ 01465-712182, 12 Bridge St).

Trains run approximately hourly (with only three trains on Sunday) from Girvan to Ayr (£2.95) and Glasgow (£6.10). Girvan to Stranraer trains run three to seven times daily. The X77 bus service goes through Girvan (see the Ayr section).

Dumfries & Galloway

The tourist board bills this region as Scotland's surprising south-west, and it will surprise you if you expect beautiful scenery to be confined to the Highlands. Only the local architecture disappoints. Otherwise it has many of the features for which Scotland is famous – mountains (which reach over 610m, 2000 feet), rolling hills, lochs and a rugged coastline.

This is, however, one of the forgotten corners of Britain, and away from the main transport routes west to Stranraer and north to Glasgow, traffic and people are sparse.

Dumfries & Galloway lies south of the Southern Uplands. Warmed by the Gulf Stream, this is the mildest corner of Scotland, a phenomenon that has allowed the development of some famous gardens. This is excellent cycling and walking country, and is crossed by the coast-to-coast Southern Upland Way (see the Activities chapter).

Many notable historic and prehistoric attractions are linked by the Solway Coast Heritage Trail from Gretna in the east to the Mull of Galloway in the west (information from TICs). Caerlaverock Castle, Threave Castle, and Whithorn Cathedral and Priory are just three. Kirkcudbright is a beautiful town, and makes a good base.

This stretch of coastline on the northern side of the wedge-shaped Solway Firth offers sheltered bays, mudflats, salt marshes and some forested hills. Don't let its beauty beguile you too much; the Solway Firth is tidal and when the tide's out you can walk out a long way, but when it turns it comes in very fast.

Stranraer in the far west is the ferry port to Larne in Northern Ireland and is the shortest link between Britain and Ireland.

Ailsa Craig

Ailsa Craig (340m, 1115 feet) is an eroded granite and basalt volcanic remnant sitting in the Firth of Clyde, roughly halfway between Glasgow and Belfast, hence its endearing epithet 'Paddy's Milestone'. This small island is roughly circular and less than a mile in diameter. It's known to bird-watchers as the world's second largest gannet colony – around 10,000 pairs breed annually on the island's sheer cliffs.

The unusual blue-tinted granite from Ailsa Craig has been used by geologists to trace the movements of the great Ice Age ice sheet, and bits of the rock have been found as far afield as Wales. More recently, the rock has been quarried to make curling stones. Visitors can still see quarry workers' cottages and a narrow-guage railway running from the jetty to the quarry.

GETTING THERE & AROUND

Dumfries & Galloway council has a travel information line (☎ 0345-090510), Monday to Friday from 9 am to 5 pm, with information on public transport.

Bus

National Express (☎ 0990-808080) has long-distance coaches from London, Birmingham (via Manchester and Carlisle), and Glasgow/Edinburgh to Stranraer. These coaches service the main towns and villages along the A75 (including Dumfries, Kirkcudbright and Newton Stewart). Stagecoach Western (☎ 01387-253496) and MacEwan's (☎ 01387-710357) provide a variety of local bus services. Sometimes different bus companies have services along the same route but charge different prices, so ring the travel information line above to check.

The Day Discoverer (£5, children £2) is a useful day ticket valid on most buses in the region and on Stagecoach Cumberland in Cumbria.

Train

Two lines from Carlisle to Glasgow cross the region, via Dumfries and Moffat respectively. The line from Glasgow to Stranraer runs via Ayr. Call ☎ 0345-484950.

DUMFRIES

- **pop 31,000   ☎ 01387**

Dumfries is a large town on the River Nith with a strategic position that placed it smack in the path of a number of vengeful English armies. As a result, although it has existed since Roman times, the oldest standing building dates from the 17th century.

It has escaped modern mass tourism, although it was the home of Robert Burns from 1791 to his death in 1796, and there are several important Burns-related museums. The centre is uninspiring, but there are some pleasant 19th century districts built in the area's characteristic red sandstone.

Orientation & Information

Most of the attractions and facilities are on the eastern side of the river. The bus station is situated by the new bridge; the train station is a 10 minute walk north-east. The TIC (☎ 253862), 64 Whitesands opposite the car park by the river, opens daily June to September from 9.30 am to 6 pm; to 5 pm the rest of the year. You can book National Express/Citylink buses here.

Early closing day is Thursday.

Burnsiana

On Burns St, **Burns House** (☎ 255297) is a place of pilgrimage for Burns enthusiasts; it's here the poet spent the last years of his life and there are some interesting relics, and original letters and manuscripts. It's open April to September, Monday to Saturday, from 10 am to 5 pm, Sunday 2 to 5 pm; October to March, Tuesday to Saturday, from 10 am to 1 pm and 2 to 5 pm; free.

The **Robert Burns Centre** (☎ 264808), Mill Rd, is an award-winning museum on the banks of the river in an old mill. It tells the story of Burns and Dumfries in the 1790s. There's also a café/gallery. It's open April to September, Monday to Saturday, from 10 am to 8 pm, Sunday 2 to 5 pm; October to March, Tuesday to Saturday, from 10 am to 1 pm and 2 to 5 pm; free (£1.20/60p for the audio-visual presentation).

Burns' **mausoleum** is in the graveyard at St Michael's Kirk. At the top of High St is a **statue** of the bard.

Places to Stay

There are some good-value B&Bs near the train station, in a quiet and pleasant suburb. *Cairndoon* (☎ 256991), 14 Newall Terrace, has spacious, comfortable rooms with TVs and a delightfully warm welcome. On Lovers Walk, try the *Fulwood Hotel* (☎ 252262, 30 Lovers Walk) with singles/doubles for £18/32, or *Torbay Lodge Guest House* (☎ 253922) with comfortable rooms from £16 per person.

Several options are on Lauriknowe including *Edenbank Hotel* (☎ 252759, 17 Lauriknowe), a short walk from the town centre. It's a small, family-run, renovated hotel with a range of rooms including two singles, all with bathrooms, for £45/58.

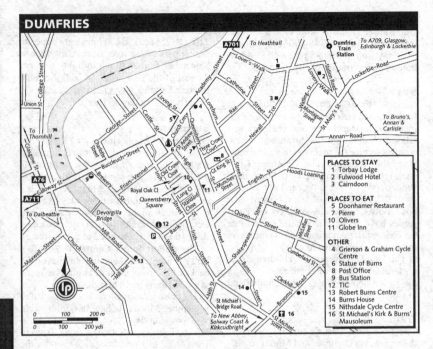

DUMFRIES

To A709, Glasgow,
Edinburgh & Lockerbie

To Heathhall

Dumfries
Train
Station

Lockerbie—Road

To Bruno's,
Annan &
Carlisle

Annan—Road

To
Thornhill

To
Dalbeattie

Devorgilla
Bridge

Queensberry
Square

Royal Oak Cl

To New Abbey,
Solway Coast &
Kirkcudbright

St Michael's
Bridge Road

PLACES TO STAY
1 Torbay Lodge
2 Fulwood Hotel
3 Cairndoon

PLACES TO EAT
5 Doonhamer Restaurant
7 Pierre
10 Olivers
11 Globe Inn

OTHER
4 Grierson & Graham Cycle
  Centre
6 Statue of Burns
8 Post Office
9 Bus Station
12 TIC
13 Robert Burns Centre
14 Burns House
15 Nithsdale Cycle Centre
16 St Michael's Kirk & Burns'
  Mausoleum

0	100	200 m
0	100	200 yds

Places to Eat

Olivers, on pedestrianised High St, has a range of good-value baked goods, sandwiches and baked potatoes. *Doonhamer Restaurant (17 Church Crescent)* serves snacks and hot meals from fish and chips to pizza (£3.25) and pasta (£4.10) including vegetarian dishes.

The set lunch menu at *Pierre (☎ 265888, 113 Queensbury Rd)* is excellent value at £4.95. It also does good-quality seafood; fresh halibut is £7.90.

The Italian *Bruno's (☎ 255757, 3 Balmoral Rd)* is one of the best places to eat. Lasagne della casa is £4.95. Next door is the recommended takeaway place, the *Balmoral Fish & Chicken Bar*, run by the same family.

The *Globe Inn (56 High St)*, a traditional pub said to be Burns' favourite watering hole, has bar meals and a restaurant.

Getting There & Away

Bus National Express bus No 920 runs three times daily between London and Belfast, via Birmingham, Manchester, Carlisle, Dumfries, the towns along the A75, and Stranraer. There are also regular local buses to Kirkcudbright and towns along the A75 to Stranraer (three hours, £3.50). Stagecoach Western has two buses daily (No 100) to/from Edinburgh.

Train Dumfries is on a line that leaves the main west-coast line at Gretna, and from Dumfries runs north-west along Nithsdale to join the Glasgow-Stranraer line at Kilmarnock. You can join the service at Carlisle or Glasgow; Monday to Saturday there are frequent trains between Carlisle and Dumfries (35 minutes, £6.40), and half a dozen between Dumfries and Glasgow

(1½ hours, £16.40); there's a reduced service on Sunday.

Car & Motorcycle Edinburgh is 75 miles north-east of Dumfries on the A76 and A702. Glasgow is 75 miles north-west and can be reached either via Kilmarnock on the A76/77 or on the A701 and A74 (M74). Stranraer is 75 miles west on the A75 via Castle Douglas and Newton Stewart.

Getting Around
Taxi Try Hastings Taxi (☎ 252664).

Bicycle Grierson & Graham (☎ 259483), 10 Academy St, and the Nithsdale Cycle Centre (☎ 254870), 46 Brooms Rd, hire bikes, with rates from £6 for three hours.

CAERLAVEROCK CASTLE
The ruins of Caerlaverock Castle (☎ 01387-770244, HS), on a beautiful stretch of the Solway coast south-east of Dumfries, are among the loveliest in Britain. Surrounded by a moat, lawns and stands of trees, the unusual pink-stoned triangular castle looks impregnable. In fact it fell several times. The current castle dates from the late 13th century. Inside, there's an extraordinary Scottish Renaissance façade to apartments that were built in 1634.

It's open April to September, daily, from 9.30 am to 6.30 pm; October to March, Monday to Saturday, from 9.30 am to 4.30 pm, Sunday 2 to 4.30 pm; £2.30/1. Monday to Saturday, the castle can be reached from Dumfries by Stagecoach Western's bus No 371. By car take the B725 south.

It's worth combining a visit to the castle with one to **Caerlaverock Wildlife and Wetlands Centre** (open daily from 10 am to 5 pm; £4.25/2.50) a mile away. It protects 1350 acres of salt marsh and mudflats, the habitat for numerous birds, including the barnacle goose.

SOUTH OF DUMFRIES
South of Dumfries the Solway Coastal Trail follows the A710 loop with side trips on minor roads to Rockcliffe and Kippford

before going inland to Dalbeattie then following the A711 to Kirkcudbright.

McEwan's (☎ 01387-710357) bus No 372 from Dumfries stops in New Abbey, Kirkbean, Rockcliffe, Kippford and Dalbeattie; from there bus No 505 continues to Kirkcudbright.

New Abbey & Around
This small picturesque village 7 miles south of Dumfries contains the remains of the red sandstone, 13th century Cistercian **Sweetheart Abbey** (☎ 01387-850397, HS). The abbey was founded by Devorgilla de Balliol in honour of her dead husband (with whom she had founded Balliol College, Oxford). On his death she had his heart embalmed and carried it with her till she died 22 years later. She and the heart are buried in the presbytery – hence the name. The abbey opens April to September, daily, from 9.30 am to 6.30 pm; October to March, Monday to Wednesday and Saturday from 9.30 am to 4.30 pm, Thursday to 1 pm, Sunday 2 to 4.30 pm; entry is £1.20/50p.

In wooded grounds just north of the village, **Shambellie House Museum of Costume** (☎ 01387-850375) is a branch of the National Museums of Scotland and displays a selection of Georgian to Edwardian clothes and furniture. It's open April to October, daily, from 11 am to 5 pm; £2.50/1.

About 1½ miles south there's a turn-off to Ardwall Farm. From the car park a forested, sometimes muddy track climbs 1¼ miles up **Criffel** hill (569m, 1866 feet); at the top are fine views of the Dumfries countryside and across the Solway Firth to Cumbria.

In the village square facing each other, the *Abbey Arms Hotel (☎ 01387-850489)* and *Criffel Inn (☎ 01387-850305)* both offer B&B. Comfortable singles/doubles cost £28/46 at the Abbey Arms which also has good bar meals from £3.50. The Criffel Inn is cheaper with rooms from £20 per person.

Kirkbean
About a mile south-east of this village in the private estate of **Arbigland**, there's a cottage

on a hillside overlooking the Solway Firth which was the birthplace of John Paul Jones (1747-92), father of the US navy. The **John Paul Jones Cottage** (☎ 01387-880613) is now a museum and includes a small exhibition, audio-visual display and video on his remarkable life. It opens April to September, Tuesday to Sunday, from 10 am to 5 pm (daily in July and August); £2/1. The **gardens** of the estate are also open to the public (May to September).

Rockcliffe & Kippford

The A710 continues through undulating farmland interspersed with the by now familiar yellow gorse past wide **Sandyhills Bay** to Colvend. From there a side road takes you to the sleepy villages of Rockcliffe and Kippford beside the River Urr estuary.

Rockcliffe is on a beautiful, rocky cove from the northern end of which (near the toilet block) there's a short footpath to the **Mote of Mark** (NTS), a hilltop stronghold inhabited by Celts in the 5th to 7th centuries. The footpath is part of the 30 minute **Jubilee Path** (NTS) along the rugged coastline to Kippford, which was built to commemorate Queen Victoria's jubilee.

Off the coast, **Rough Island** (NTS) is a 20 acre bird sanctuary which, except during May and June when the birds are nesting, can be reached at low tide by foot over the sand flats. Kippford is a popular sailing centre.

Dalbeattie & Around

Most buildings in this small commercial centre are made from granite mined at the local quarry (which also provided the stone for the Bank of England in London). From Dalbeattie you can either follow the scenic coast road to Kirkcudbright or head inland on the A745 to Castle Douglas. Off the B794, 2 miles north of town, the **Motte of Urr** is a 12th century, Norman motte-and-bailey castle, one of Scotland's largest.

About 4 miles south, off the Kirkcudbright road, is the 15th century **Orchardton Tower**, the only circular tower house in Scotland.

CASTLE DOUGLAS & AROUND
• pop 3500   ☎ 01556

Castle Douglas is an open, attractive little town that was laid out in the 18th century by Sir William Douglas, who had made a fortune in the Americas. Beside the town is the small but beautiful **Carlingwark Loch**. The TIC (☎ 502611), in a small park on King St, opens daily April to June and September to October from 10 am to 4.30 pm, July and August to 6 pm.

Threave Garden

Threave Garden (☎ 502575, NTS), a mile west off the A75, houses the NTS horticultural school and is noted for its spectacular spring daffodil display, though it's colourful in summer and autumn too. The visitor centre opens April to late October, daily, from 9.30 am to 5.30 pm; the garden opens all year, daily, from 9.30 am to sunset; £4.

Threave Castle

Two miles farther west, Threave Castle (☎ 0831-168512, HS) is an impressively grim tower on a small island in the middle of the lovely River Dee. Built in the late 14th century it became a principal stronghold of the Black Douglases. It's now basically a shell, having been badly damaged by the Covenanters in the 1640s, but it's a romantic ruin nonetheless.

It's a 10 minute walk from the car park to the ferry landing where you ring a bell for the custodian to take you across to the island in a small boat. The castle opens April to September, daily, from 9.30 am to 6.30 pm; £1.80/75p, including the ferry.

Loch Ken

Loch Ken, stretching for 9 miles north-west of Castle Douglas beside the A713, is an important outdoor recreational area. The range of watersports include windsurfing, sailing, canoeing, water-skiing and fishing. Galloway Sailing Centre (☎ 01644-420626), on the east bank north of Parton village, provides equipment, training and accommodation. There are also walking trails and a rich variety of birdlife. The RSPB has a nature reserve on the west bank at Hansol.

Places to Stay

Lochside Caravan & Camping Site (☎ *502949)* is an attractive spot alongside Carlingwark Loch; there are sites for vans and tents from £7.10. On the eastern shore of Loch Ken, *Galloway Sailing Centre* (☎ *01644-420626)* offers backpacker accommodation year-round; dorms are £7.50.

Craigvar House (☎ *503515, 60 St Andrew St)* is an agreeable B&B, with rooms from £20 per person. *Douglas Arms Hotel* (☎ *502231, King St)* has good food, and a range of comfortable rooms, most with bathrooms. Rates are from £35/65 a single/double.

Getting There & Away

MacEwan's bus No 501 between Dumfries and Kirkcudbright calls frequently Monday to Saturday (only three times Sunday). Bus No 520 runs along the A713 connecting Castle Douglas with New Galloway and Ayr.

Getting Around

Ace Cycles (☎ 504542), 11 Church St, hires touring and mountain bikes for £10 for 24 hours.

KIRKCUDBRIGHT
• pop 3500   ☎ 01557

Kirkcudbright's dignified streets of 17th and 18th century merchants' houses and its interesting harbour make it an ideal base to explore the beautiful southern coast. The lovely surrounding countryside has a distinctive hummocky topography, much of it covered in gorse – it's almost as if the hills have been heaped up to make a golf course. With its architecture and setting it's not hard to see why Kirkcudbright (pronounced kirk-coobree) has been something of an artists' colony since the late 19th century.

Orientation & Information

The town is on the east bank of the River Dee at the northern end of Kirkcudbright Bay. Everything in town is within easy walking distance. The TIC (☎ 330494), Harbour Square, opens Easter to October, daily, from 10 am to 5 pm. There are some useful brochures giving walks and road tours in the surrounding district.

Early closing day is Thursday.

Things to See & Do

The sights are fairly modest, but provide an excuse for exploring the town, and they do have charm.

McLellan's Castle (☎ 331856, HS), near the harbour and TIC, is a large ruin built in the late 16th century, by Thomas MacLellan, then provost of Kirkcudbright, as his town residence. It's open April to September, Monday to Saturday, from 9.30 am to 6.30 pm, Sunday 2 to 6.30 pm; £1.20/50p. Nearby, the 17th century **Broughton House** (☎ 330437) contains Hornel Art Gallery, a reminder of the town's 19th century artist's colony, featuring paintings by EA Hornel, one of the 'Glasgow Boys' group of painters. Behind the house is a beautiful Japanese-style garden. The house and garden open daily April to October, from 1 to 5 pm; £2.40/60p.

Tolbooth Arts Centre (☎ 331556), High St, as well as catering to today's local artists has an exhibition on the town's art history. It's open all year Monday to Saturday from 11 am to 4 pm, plus Sunday 2 to 5 pm June to September; £1.50/free. The **Stewartry Museum** (☎ 331643), St Mary St, is a particularly interesting local museum, with a wide-ranging collection of exhibits (same hours and entry fee as Tolbooth Arts Centre).

Daily, April to September there are one-hour **cruises** (☎ 331888) on Kirkcudbright Bay from the harbour on board the *Lady Angela* for £5.50/3.50.

Places to Stay & Eat

Silvercraigs Caravan & Camping Site (☎ *330123)* overlooks the town and has great views. There are sites from £6.60.

Parkview (☎ *330056, 22 Millburn St)* is a small blue-painted B&B charging £17 per person with shared bathroom. **Gladstone House** (☎ *331734, 48 High St)* offers up-market B&B to nonsmokers from £30/50 a single/double in an attractively decorated Georgian house.

The large, well-run **Royal Hotel** (☎ *331213, St Cuthbert St)* offers rooms with bathrooms for £22.50/38. It has good-value bar meals, including an all-you-can-eat buffet for £4.95 noon to 2.30 pm. The **Selkirk Arms Hotel** (☎ *330402, High St)* has well-equipped rooms, all with bathrooms, for £47.50/75. It also has good bar meals, plus a more expensive dining room.

The best place to eat is the **Auld Alliance** (☎ *330569, 5 Castle St)*, open daily for dinner only. The restaurant's name is a reference to the political alliance between Scotland and France, but here it means a combination of local fresh Scots produce (such as small scallops known as queenies) and French cooking and wine. Main dishes range from £5.90 to £14; booking is advised.

Getting There & Away

Bus Nos X75 and 500 run regularly to Dumfries (£2.50) and Stranraer (£4.90), via Newton Stewart and Castle Douglas. Kirkcudbright is 25 miles west of Dumfries on the A711 or A75; it's 50 miles east of Stranraer on the A75.

GATEHOUSE OF FLEET
• pop 900   ☎ 01557

Completely off the beaten track, Gatehouse of Fleet is an attractive little town, on the banks of the Water of Fleet surrounded by partly wooded hills. The TIC (☎ 814212), High St, opens daily Easter to October, from 10 am to 4.30 pm.

One mile south-west on the A75, well-preserved **Cardoness Castle** (☎ 814427, HS) was the home of the McCulloch clan. It's a classic 15th century tower house with great views from the top. It's open April to September, Monday to Saturday, from 9.30 am to 6.30 pm, Sunday 2 to 6.30 pm (shorter hours the rest of the year); £1.80/75p. **Mill on the Fleet Museum** (☎ 814099), High St, in a converted 18th century cotton mill with

a working water wheel, traces the history of the local industry. It opens daily Easter to October from 10 am to 5.30 pm; £4/2.

Simple, cosy rooms at the **Bobbin Guest House** *(36 High St)*, cost £20/35 or £25/45 with bath. There's a small coffee shop in the back through the archway. **Bank O' Fleet Hotel** (☎ *814302, 47 High St)* has B&B rooms with bathroom from £23.50 per person and good bar meals; savoury mince and tatties are £4.25.

Bus Nos X75 and 500 between Dumfries and Stranraer stop here.

NEW GALLOWAY & AROUND
• pop 290   ☎ 01644

New Galloway is a quaint little town in the Glenkens valley north of Loch Ken. There's nothing much in the town itself but it's surrounded by beautiful countryside, in which you feel as if you're on a high plateau, surrounded by tumbling short-pitched hills. There's a sense of space unusual in Britain.

Tourist information is available from The Smithy restaurant at the bottom of High St.

Galloway Forest Park

South and west of town is 300-sq-mile Galloway Forest Park, with numerous lochs and great whale-backed, heather and pine-covered mountains. The highest point is Merrick (842m, 2764 feet). The park is crisscrossed by some superb signposted walking trails, from gentle strolls to long-distance paths, including the Southern Upland Way.

The 19-mile A712 (Queen's Way) between New Galloway and Newton Stewart slices through the southern section of the park.

On the shore of **Clatteringshaws Loch** is Clatteringshaws Forest Wildlife Centre (☎ 420285) with an exhibition on the area's flora and fauna (open April to October, daily, from 10 am to 5 pm; free). From the centre you can walk to a replica of a Romano-British homestead and to Bruce's Stone, where Robert Bruce is said to have rested after defeating the English at the Battle of Rapploch Moss (1307).

The Auld Alliance

The Auld Alliance was the name given to an agreement between Scotland and France which would become the world's longest-standing political alliance between two countries. It's usually dated from 1295, with the treaty between John Balliol and Philip IV, and was renewed regularly over the next three centuries. As part of the alliance an army of 6000 Scots fought for Joan of Arc against the English at the Siege of Orleans in 1429.

Support in Scotland for the alliance began to wane when backers of the Scottish Reformation looked to England for guidance and it declined further when James VI of Scotland became James I of England.

The alliance allowed Scots and French dual nationality and this was recognised in French law until 1908.

Walkers and cyclists head for **Glen Trool** in the park's west accessed by the forest road east from Bargrennan off the A714 north of Newton Stewart. The road winds and climbs up to Loch Trool from where there are magnificent views. Glen Trool Visitor Centre (☎ 01671-840302) opens weekdays April to October, from 10.30 am to 5.30 pm. There are trails around the lake, south to Kirroughtree Forest and 3 miles north up to Merrick. Another Bruce's Stone beside the lake commemorates Robert Bruce's victory at the Battle of Glentrool (1307).

Dalry

Dalry or, to give it its full name, St John's Town of Dalry, is a charming village hugging the hillside about 3 miles north off the A713. It's on the Water of Ken and gives access to the Southern Upland Way.

Places to Stay & Eat

The closest hostel is *Kendoon Youth Hostel* (☎ 460680), about 8 miles north of New

Galloway beside the B7000. It's open late March to early October and dorm beds cost £4.65/3.85 (including bed linen). Bus No 520 stops about a mile away.

On High St, the refurbished *Kenmure Arms* (☎ 420240) does B&B from £16.50 per person, while opposite, the smaller *Leamington Hotel* (☎ 420327) has rooms with bathrooms from £15 to £24 per person. Both have bar meals.

At the bottom of High St, the *Smithy* (☎ 420269) has two rooms with B&B for £16 per person. There's a good restaurant/café with sandwiches for £1.50 and steak meals for £9.55.

Getting There & Away

MacEwan's (☎ 01387-710357) bus No 521 runs twice weekly (Wednesday and Saturday) to Dumfries. Bus No 520 connects New Galloway with Castle Douglas six times daily, Monday to Saturday (once on Sunday); three continue north to Ayr.

NEWTON STEWART
- **pop 3200**   ☎ 01672

Newton Stewart is surrounded by beautiful wooded countryside, and set on the west bank of the River Cree. On the east bank across the bridge is the older, smaller settlement of Minnigaff. The TIC (☎ 402431), Dashwood Square, opens April and October, daily, from 10 am to 4.30 pm; to 5 pm in May, June and September; to 6 pm in July and August.

Newton Stewart is a centre for **hiking** and **fishing**. Many hikers head for Galloway Forest Park. Creebridge House Hotel rents fishing gear and arranges permits.

Places to Stay

Creebridge Caravan Park (☎ 402324), under 300m from the bridge, charges £2.30 for a tent plus £2 per person. In Minnigaff, *Minnigaff Youth Hostel* (☎ 402211) opens April to September and charges £6.10/4.95 for dorm beds.

Also located in Minnigaff, beside the river, is the friendly *Flowerbank Guest House* (☎ 402629, Millcroft Rd). There are seven rooms and B&B starts from £16.50 per person (it's £20 in a room with bathroom attached).

Creebridge House Hotel (☎ 402121) is a magnificent, refurbished, 18th century mansion built for the Earl of Galloway. There's a good restaurant, and huntin', shootin' and fishin'. The rooms are tastefully decorated and all have bathrooms; prices range from £42/72 to £48/84.

Getting There & Away

Bus Newton Stewart is served by buses that run between Stranraer and Dumfries, including bus No 920 (National Express) and bus Nos X75 and 500 (various operators, at least two a day). Bus No 356 goes to Glen Trool village seven times daily, four on Sunday.

Newton Stewart is also a starting point for buses south to Wigtown and Whithorn.

Car & Motorcycle Newton Stewart is on the A75 between Dumfries and Stranraer. The A714 heads north-west to South Ayrshire where it joins the A77 south of Girvan. The A714 heads south of town to Wigtown and Whithorn.

THE MACHARS

South of Newton Stewart, the Galloway Hills give way to the serene, rich-green, softly rolling pastures of the triangular peninsula known as The Machars. The south has many early Christian sites and the 25-mile **Pilgrims Way** (see the Activities chapter).

Stagecoach Western (☎ 01776-704484) bus No 415 runs regularly between Newton Stewart and the Isle of Whithorn.

Wigtown & Around
* **pop 1000**   ☎ 01988
Surrounded by attractive countryside, Wigtown has expansive views overlooking Wigtown Bay and north to the Galloway Hills. There's little in the town, but it does have a slightly decrepit charm.

Wigtown Bay is a nature reserve with large areas of mudflats and salt marsh that attract thousands of birds. There's a bird-watching hide down on the shore by the **Martyr's Stake**. The 'stake' is a pillar commemorating the spot where in 1685 two female Covenanters were left to drown for their religious beliefs. Four miles west of Wigtown off the B733, the well-preserved, recumbent **Torehousekie Stone Circle** dates from the 2nd millennium BC.

At one time economically run down, the town's revival has begun with the decision to make it Scotland's first 'Booktown'. Over the next few years new bookshops will be set up, offering the widest selection of books in Scotland. In the meantime you can browse in the **Old Bank Bookshop and Gallery**, 7 South Main St.

Craigmount Guest House (☎ 402291), on the edge of town, has a range of rooms overlooking the bay, including one single and two with private bathrooms. B&B is from £17 per person. ***County Hotel*** *(South Main St)* has bar meals; high tea is £5.50.

Garlieston

You can't get more off the beaten track. There's a neat little harbour with a ring of 18th century cottages running round behind a bowling green. A coastal path leads south to the ruins of **Cruggleton Castle**. The ***Harbour Inn*** (☎ 01988-600685) is a basic pub with great views and accommodation in five rooms from £16 per person.

Whithorn
* **pop 1000**   ☎ 01988
Whithorn has a broad, attractive main street virtually closed at both ends – designed to enclose a medieval market. Hard hit economically, the town has virtually no facilities – a couple of shops and pubs – but it's worth visiting because of its fascinating history.

In 397, while the Romans were still in Britain, St Ninian established the first Christian mission beyond Hadrian's Wall in Whithorn (predating St Columba on Iona by 166 years). After his death Whithorn became the focus of an important medieval pilgrimage and Whithorn Cathedral was built to house his remains.

Today, its ruins are the centrepoint of the **Whithorn Visitor Centre and Dig** (☎ 500508). In the visitor centre, on George St, there are exhibitions and an audio-visual display. You can also visit excavations of the substantial remains of the monastic settlement behind the visitor centre. Beside the excavations is the Priory Museum with some important finds and early Christian sculpture; the Latinus Stone (circa 450 AD) is reputedly Scotland's oldest Christian artefact. Opening hours are April to October, daily, from 10.30 am to 5 pm; £2.70/1.50.

Isle of Whithorn

The Isle of Whithorn, once an island but now part of a peninsula, is a curious, raggedy sort of place with an attractive natural harbour. **St Ninian's Chapel**, probably built for pilgrims who landed nearby, is on the windswept, evocative, rocky headland. Around Burrow Head to the south-west, but accessed from a path off the A747 before you enter the Isle of Whithorn, is **St Ninian's Cave** where he went to pray.

The 300-year-old **Dunbar House** *(☎ 01988-500336, Tonderghie Rd)*, overlooking the harbour, has B&B in large rooms for £18 per person. On the quayside, the **Steam Packet Inn Hotel** *(☎ 01988-500334)* has popular bar meals that are excellent value; most mains cost around £5.

Glenluce

From the Isle of Whithorn the A747 heads north-west beside the coastal plain of **Luce Bay**, before turning inland to meet the A75 near Glenluce. It's a pretty, quiet, little village that stretches along steep Main St. A couple of miles north, signposted off the A75, is **Glenluce Abbey** (☎ 01581-300541, HS), in a tranquil valley near the Water of Luce. It was a Cistercian abbey founded in 1190 by Roland, Earl of Galloway; the chapter house and complex water-supply system are the most interesting of the remains. It's open April to October, daily,

from 9.30 am to 6.30 pm; weekends only the rest of the year. Entry is £1.50/75p.

Bus Nos 430 and 500 run to Castle Kennedy, Stranraer and Newton Stewart.

STRANRAER & CAIRNRYAN
• pop 10,700 ☎ 01776

Although a little run-down, Stranraer is rather more pleasant than the average ferry port. There's no pressing reason to stay, unless you're catching a ferry. Make for the south coast (maybe nearby Portpatrick) or Glasgow.

Orientation & Information

In Stranraer, the bus and train stations, accommodation and TIC are close to the Stena Sealink and SeaCat terminals. The TIC (☎ 702595), 28 Harbour St, opens April to June, September and October, Monday to Saturday from 9.30 am to 5 pm, Sunday 10 am to 4 pm; July and August, daily, from 9.15 am to 6 pm; the rest of the year, Monday to Saturday, from 10 am to 4 pm.

Early closing day is Wednesday.

Things to See

Worth a quick visit, **St John's Castle** was built in 1510 by the Adairs of Kihilt, a powerful local family. Government troops were garrisoned here during the suppression of the Covenanters in the 1680s and it was used as a prison in the 19th century. Displays and a video trace its history. It's open Easter to mid-September, Monday to Saturday, from 10 am to 1 pm, 2 to 5 pm; entry £1/50p.

Better than its external appearance might indicate, the two-storey **Stranraer Museum** (☎ 705088), George St, houses exhibits on local history downstairs; upstairs a room is devoted to the explorers Sir John Ross and his nephew James. The museum opens Monday to Saturday, from 10 am to 5 pm; free.

Places to Stay

Aird Donald Caravan Park (☎ 702025, London Rd) is the nearest camping ground which takes both vans and tents. Sites are from £7.

Harbour Guest House (☎ 704626, *Market St)* is on the harbour front near the town centre. Rooms cost £17 per person. There's a string of standard places along Agnew Crescent facing the harbour, including the low-key *Aislie View Guest House* (☎ 705792, 8 Agnew Crescent) which has good views of Loch Ryan and B&B from £15 per person.

Jan-Da-Mar Guest House (☎ 706194, 1 *Ivy Place, London Rd)* is conveniently located, and has a range of rooms (some with bathrooms). Singles/doubles are from £18/32.

The most luxurious hotel in Stranraer is *North West Castle Hotel* (☎ 704413), formerly the home of Arctic explorer Sir John Ross. It's expensive, but good, with singles/doubles from £52/74.

If you fancy a night in a lighthouse, *Corsewall Lighthouse Hotel* (☎ 853220) is an unusual place to stay, 10 miles north of Stranraer at Corsewall Point. Rooms are from £45/70, all with bathroom attached; one room is specially equipped for disabled travellers.

Places to Eat

There are reasonable pizzas and other fast food at two places in George/Charlotte St. *Petrucci's*, opposite St John's Tower, has pizzas from £2.25, and *Romano's* does a special of fish, chips, peas and tea for £4.25. Another option is *Star Fish Restaurant (14 Charlotte St)* with Scotch pie for £2.50; it's open daily until midnight. *Arches Restaurant (Hanover St)* is a bright, popular café with main dishes from £4.95.

The best restaurant is at *North West Castle Hotel* (☎ 704413), where a set four-course dinner costs £21, including a vegetarian choice.

Getting There & Away

Boat See the Getting There & Away chapter for details on services to Northern Ireland. There are three alternatives: P&O (☎ 0990-980777) ferries from Cairnryan to Larne; Stena Line (☎ 0990-707070) ferries from Stranraer to Larne and Belfast; and

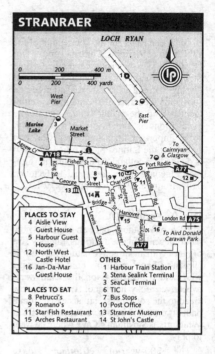

STRANRAER

PLACES TO STAY
4 Aislie View Guest House
5 Harbour Guest House
12 North West Castle Hotel
16 Jan-Da-Mar Guest House

PLACES TO EAT
8 Petrucci's
9 Romano's
11 Star Fish Restaurant
15 Arches Restaurant

OTHER
1 Harbour Train Station
2 Stena Sealink Terminal
3 SeaCat Terminal
6 TIC
7 Bus Stops
10 Post Office
13 Stranraer Museum
14 St John's Castle

fast SeaCat (☎ 0990-523523) catamarans from Stranraer to Belfast.

The Cairnryan to Larne service is used mainly by motorists and hauliers. Cairnryan is 5 miles north of Stranraer on the northern side of Loch Ryan. Bus No 303 runs there from Stranraer four times daily Monday to Saturday. For a taxi (around £4) phone Central Taxis (☎ 704999).

Stena Line ferries for Larne connect directly with rail and bus services. The train station is on the ferry pier. The SeaCat terminal is just south of the ferry pier.

Bus National Express bus No 920 runs three times daily between London and Belfast, via Birmingham, Manchester, Carlisle, Dumfries, the towns along the A75 and Stranraer. Stagecoach Western runs hourly buses to Glasgow (three hours, £7). There are also regular local buses to

Kirkcudbright and the towns along the A75, like Newton Stewart (£1.95) and Dumfries.

Train There are up to four trains daily between Stranraer and Belfast (Donegall Quay) via Larne (nine hours); and regular services to Glasgow (£19.50, 2½ hours). Call ☎ 0345-484950.

Car & Motorcycle It's 120 miles to Edinburgh; take the A75 east to Dumfries (75 miles), then the A701 north. Glasgow is 80 miles north on the coastal A77.

AROUND STRANRAER
Castle Kennedy Gardens
Magnificent Castle Kennedy Gardens (☎ 01776-702024), 3 miles east of Stranraer, are among the most famous in Scotland. They cover 75 acres and are set on a peninsula between two lochs and two castles (Castle Kennedy, burnt in 1716, and Lochinch Castle, built in 1864). The landscaping was undertaken in 1730 by the Earl of Stair, who used unoccupied soldiers to do the work. The gardens open April to September, daily, from 10 am to 5 pm; £2/1. Bus Nos 430 and 500 stop here.

Loch Ryan
Loch Ryan isn't a lake but a large, narrow inlet that provides a natural shelter from the rough waters of the Irish Sea. It's especially noted for its **birdwatching** opportunities (autumn is the best time) at the mudflats of Wig Bay on the western shore and at rocky Corsewall Point on the northern tip of the peninsula. Wig Bay is also a popular **sailing** centre.

PORTPATRICK
• **pop 600**   ☎ 01776
Portpatrick is a charming port on the rugged western coast of the Rhinns (or Rhins) of Galloway peninsula. Until the mid-19th century it was the main port for Northern Ireland, so it's quite substantial. It's now a coastguard station and a quiet holiday resort.

It's also a good base from which to explore the south of the peninsula and the

starting point for the **Southern Upland Way** (see the Activities chapter). You can follow part of the way to Stranraer (9 miles). It's a cliff-top walk, followed by sections of farmland and heather moor. Start at the way's information shelter at the northern end of the harbour. The walk is waymarked until a half-mile south of Stranraer, where you get the first good views of the town.

There are **fishing** trips from Portpatrick on the *Cornubia* for £8 for half a day; call Mr Tyerman (☎ 810468).

Places to Stay & Eat
On the hillside above the village are several caravan and camping parks. *Galloway Point Holiday Park (☎ 810561)* has the most number of sites (from £6 for a tent), but there's more space at *Castle Bay Caravan Park (☎ 810462)*, which charges £5. Both have great views.

There is a good variety of places to stay on North Crescent which curves around the harbour. *Knowe Guest House & Tea Room (☎ 810441, 1 North Crescent)* is a charming place overlooking the harbour; B&B with private bathrooms is £17 per person. *Ard Choille Guest House (☎ 810313, 1 Blair Terrace)* has doubles, including one with a private bathroom. Rates start at £15 per person.

Formerly the customs house, *Harbour House Hotel (☎ 810456, 53 Main St)* is a popular pub with a range of rooms, some with bathrooms; £24 per person.

At the bottom of Main St is the friendly *Port Pantry* which offers sandwiches (£1.50) and cakes (from 60p) and freshly ground Colombian coffee. Most pubs serve meals.

Getting There & Away
Stagecoach Western bus No 367 runs regularly Monday to Saturday to Stranraer.

SOUTH OF PORTPATRICK
From Portpatrick, the road south to the Mull of Galloway passes through prime agricultural land, where cattle and sheep graze on a thick carpet of grass (average annual rainfall is about 40 inches). The coastal scenery

varies from rugged cliffs to tiny harbours and sandy beaches. The warm waters of the Gulf Stream give the peninsula the mildest climate in Scotland and frosts on the coast are rare.

This mildness is demonstrated at **Logan Botanic Garden** (☎ 01776-860231), a mile north of Port Logan, where an array of sub-tropical flora includes tree ferns and cabbage palms. The garden is an outpost of the Royal Botanic Garden in Edinburgh; and there's a free self-guided audio tour. The garden opens March to October, daily, from 9.30 to 6 pm; £3/1.

Farther south, **Drummore** is a fishing village on the east coast. From there it's another 5 miles to the **Mull of Galloway**, a narrow, rocky, bleak and windy headland, Scotland's most southerly point. The RSPB nature reserve (☎ 01671-402861) here is home to thousands of seabirds.

ANNANDALE & ESKDALE

These valleys, in Dumfries & Galloway's east, form part of two major routes that cut across Scotland's south. From Carlisle in England the traffic-packed A74(M) heads north-westward to Glasgow, while the A7 runs north-eastward to Edinburgh. Most people rush through, but away from the highways the roads are quiet and there are a few places worth visiting. Placid enough now, this area saw some of the bloodiest fighting between the Scots and English.

Gretna Green
- **pop 3150**   ☎ 01461

There's little reason to visit this village, though people who do so are drawn by its romantic associations. Differences in Scottish and English law once meant that it was easier to marry in Scotland and many young runaway couples from the south came here to wed.

Today's Gretna Green is basically a tourist trap, but such is the power of the name that about 4000 weddings are performed here annually.

The helpful TIC (☎ 337834), Headless Cross, opens daily May and June from 10

am to 4.30 pm; July and August to 6 pm; April, September and October to 4.30 pm. Travel information is also available from the Gretna Gateway service area (☎ 338500) on the A74(M).

Opposite the TIC, the **Old Blacksmith's Shop** (☎ 338441) is mainly just that, although it does have a visitor centre with a small exhibition on Gretna Green's history. It's open daily May and June from 10 am to 5 pm; July and August 10 am to 6 pm; April, September and October from 10 am to 4.30 pm; £1.50/free.

Stagecoach Western bus No 79 runs to Dumfries.

Ecclefechan
- **pop 880**   ☎ 01576

Nearly 10 miles north of Gretna Green, Ecclefechan – a quiet village in spite of being close to the A74(M) – was the birthplace of Thomas Carlyle (1795-1881), writer, historian, social reformer and one of the great thinkers of Victorian Britain. The artisan's house where he was born is now a museum. **Carlyle's Birthplace** (☎ 300666, NTS) is set up to reflect 19th century domestic life and contains a collection of portraits and Carlyle memorabilia. It's open May to September, Friday to Monday, from 1.30 to 5.30 pm; entry is £2/1.30.

Cressfield Caravan Park (☎ 300702), close to the village, has tent sites for £5, or

Gretna Green Weddings

Under Scottish law people could (and still can) tie the knot at the age of 16 without parental consent. Furthermore, until 1940 they only needed to declare their mutual commitment in front of two witnesses to be considered married. At one time anyone could perform a legal marriage ceremony and in Gretna Green it was often the local blacksmith. Gretna Green's location on a major thoroughfare close to the border, made it the most popular venue.

£6 with a car. *Carlyle House* (☎ *300322*), opposite Carlyle's Birthplace, has B&B in large rooms with shared bathroom for £13. Beside the caravan park, the refurbished, sandstone *Cressfield Country House Hotel* (☎ *300277*), with good views over the valley, has comfortable singles/doubles for £41/52. It also does good substantial meals, including vegetarian, and mains are around £4.95.

Ecclefechan is served by bus No 382 to Lockerbie and Moffat.

Lockerbie

Red sandstone buildings line the main street of this small country town. Its peace was shattered in 1988 when pieces from a Pan-Am passenger jet fell on the town after a bomb blew up the aircraft; 207 people were killed including 11 townsfolk.

Little evidence of the event remains, but the townspeople have created a small garden of remembrance in Dryfesdale Cemetery about a mile west on the Dumfries road.

Bus No 81 runs frequently to Dumfries, bus No 382 to Moffat. There are also numerous trains to Edinburgh, Glasgow, Dundee, Aberdeen and south to England.

Moffat & Around
* pop 1990   ☎ 01683

Moffat lies in wild, hilly country near the upper reaches of Annandale. The former spa town is now a centre for the local woollen industry, symbolised by the bronze ram statue on High St. If you have your own transport it's a good base from which to explore the Lowther Hills and the western Borders.

Information The TIC (☎ 220620), Churchgate, opens April, May and October, Monday to Saturday, from 10 am to 5 pm, Sunday 11 am to 5 pm; June to September, Monday to Saturday, from 9.30 am to 6 pm, Sunday 11 am to 6 pm. The post office and bus stop are on High St. Wednesday is half-day closing, though many shops and services don't observe this during summer.

Things to See & Do The town has a couple of small attractions. At **Moffat Woollen Mill** (☎ 220134), beside the TIC, you can see a working weaving exhibition and trace your Scottish ancestry. It opens daily April to October, from 9 am to 5.30 pm (to 5 pm the rest of the year). Nearby, **Moffat Museum** (☎ 220868), in a former bakery, tells the town's history (open May to September, Thursday to Tuesday, from 10.30 am to 1 pm, 2.30 to 5 pm; £1/20p).

There are short **walks** down by the River Annan; follow the 'Waterside Walks' sign from High St. About 5 miles north of Moffat off the A701, you can walk into the **Devil's Beef Tub**, a deep, dark and mist-shrouded valley once used by Border reivers (raiders) to hide their stolen cattle. It was also used as a hide-out by Covenanters as were the hills around the **Grey Mare's Tail** (NTS), a 60m (200 feet) waterfall 10 miles north-east of Moffat on the A708. There's a trail to the waterfall and farther to Loch Skeen and up to the summit of White Coomb (822m, 2696 feet). This is also a popular **birdwatching** spot.

Places to Stay & Eat There are plenty of accommodation choices. Large *Hammerland's Farm Camping Ground* (☎ 220436), off the A708 just east of town, has laundry and showers and sites for £7. The moderately priced *Ram Lodge Guest House* (☎ 220594, *High St*) offers rooms only for £12.50 per person, or £15 with breakfast. A short walk north of the centre in quiet Beechgrove, flower-decked *Buchan Guest House* (☎ 220378) has B&B for £20/36 a single/double.

There are several good bakeries on High St and Well St; and a couple of good cafés on High St including *Rumblin' Tum*, where jacket potatoes are £2.50, and *Adamson's Coffee House*. The pubs all provide bar meals. For pure indulgence the *Moffat Toffee Shop* (*High St*) serves home-made fudge (and malt whisky).

Getting There & Away There are frequent buses to Edinburgh (bus Nos X73,

SOUTHERN

199), Glasgow (bus Nos X73, X74) and Dumfries (bus Nos X74, 114, 199). Bus No 382 runs regularly to Lockerbie and Gretna Green. Travelling west to Selkirk in the Borders by bus is limited to the Lowland (☎ 01573-224141) 'Harrier', which only runs Tuesday and Thursday between July and September.

There are several scenic roads out of Moffat: the A701 south-west to Dumfries, the A701 north to Edinburgh and the A708 north-east to Selkirk.

Langholm
• pop 2500   ☎ 013873

The waters of three rivers – the Esk, Ewes and Wauchope – meet at Langholm, which with its solid, granite streets is the centre of Scotland's tweed industry. Hugh MacDiarmid (1892-1978), poet, co-founder of the SNP and sometime member of the Communist Party, was born (and is buried) here. This is clan Armstrong country. Several years after he landed on the moon (1969), US astronaut, Neil Armstrong, came to Langholm and was given the freedom of the town.

The TIC (☎ 80976), north of the centre by the Esk, opens April, May and September, Monday to Saturday, from 10.30 am to 4.30 pm; June to August, daily, from 10 am to 5 pm. As well as getting information, you can buy some feed to give to the ducks outside.

The **Clan Armstrong Museum and Centre**, Langholm Castle, is probably only of real interest to those bearing that surname. It's open Easter to September, Tuesday to Sunday, from 1.30 to 4.30 pm; £1/50p. Most people come for the **fishing**, and low-key **walking** in the surrounding moors and woodlands (details from the TIC).

Ewes Water Caravan & Camping Park (☎ 80386), with tent sites for £3, and *Whitshiels Caravan Park* (☎ 80494), £4, are two small camping grounds close to Langholm. For B&Bs, try the central *Border House* (☎ 80376, 28 High St) where all rooms are *en suite* and cost £15.50 per person. Nearby, the white-painted *Reivers Rest Hotel* (☎ 81343, 81 High St) provides B&B and *en suite* rooms for £27/49 a single/double.

Langholm is on the bus No 195 route between Carlisle and Galashiels (up to six times daily), while bus No 112 has regular connections with Lockerbie and Eskdalemuir (no Sunday service). From Langholm the A7 heads north to Edinburgh and south to Carlisle. If you're driving to the Borders, an interesting route is the minor road off the A7 just north of town that runs across empty moorland to Liddlesdale and Newcastleton.

Eskdalemuir
Surrounded by wooded hills, Eskdalemuir is a remote village 14 miles north-west of Langholm. About 1½ miles north of the village is the **Samye Ling Tibetan Centre** (☎ 013873-73232), the first Tibetan Buddhist monastery in the west (1968). The colourful prayer flags and the red and gold of the Samye Temple contrast starkly with the grey, green landscape. The temple was built in 1988 and the centre offers meditation courses including weekend workshops for which basic accommodation is available.

Those staying here are asked to give two hours a day to help in the kitchen, garden, farm etc. The temple is open to casual visitors, for whom there's also a small café. Bus No 112 from Langholm stops at the centre.

Central & North-Eastern Scotland

The Highland line, the massive geological fault which divides the Highlands from the Lowlands, runs across the central section of Scotland, making this possibly the most scenically varied region in the country. To the south are undulating hills and agricultural plains; to the north, the wild, treeless Highland peaks.

The town of Stirling, 26 miles north-east of Glasgow, has witnessed many of the great battles in the Scottish struggle against English domination. Stirling's spectacular castle, dramatically perched on a rock as is Edinburgh's castle, was for centuries of paramount strategic importance, controlling the main routes in the area.

On the western side of central Scotland, less than 20 miles north of Glasgow, are the famous 'bonnie, bonnie banks' of Loch Lomond, straddling the Highland line (see also The Highlands chapter). Tourists have been visiting the Trossachs (the lochs and hills just east of Loch Lomond) for over 150 years – Queen Victoria among them. Having set her heart on adding a Highland residence to her list of royal properties, she toured the area, eventually purchasing the Balmoral estate in Aberdeenshire.

In the south-east of this area, Fife lies between the Firths (estuaries) of Forth and Tay. The attractive seaside town of St Andrews was once the ecclesiastical centre of the country, but is now better known for its university and as the home of golf. Near the eastern extremity of Fife, Crail is the most beautiful of a series of fishing villages.

Perth is on the direct routes from Edinburgh and Glasgow to Inverness. It was once the capital of Scotland, but it's now just a busy town. Both Dunkeld and Pitlochry, to the north, are appealing (though touristy) places which are useful as walking bases. Frequent buses and trains service this route.

HIGHLIGHTS

- Visit Scotland's grandest castle at Stirling
- Stroll down the hallowed fairways of St Andrews
- Surround yourself with the finery of upper-class Highland life at Blair Castle
- Treat yourself to an Antarctic experience at Discovery Point, Dundee
- Discover the haunted crypt and chapel of Glamis Castle
- Take off from Milngavie on the world-famous West Highland Way
- Sample the delights of the Malt Whisky Trail

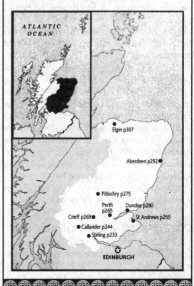

(sidebar tab) CENTRAL & NORTH-EASTERN

Following the coast to Aberdeen from Perth or St Andrews, you quickly reach Dundee, one of Scotland's largest cities. Despite its excellent location, it has not recovered from modern development and the loss of its jute and shipbuilding industries. It's worth pausing in Dundee to visit Captain Scott's Antarctic ship, *Discovery*, moored near the Tay Bridge.

The eastern Highlands is a great elbow of land that juts into the North Sea between Perth and the Firth of Tay in the south, and Inverness and the Moray Firth in the north. There are excellent hill walks in the Grampians, and the sub-arctic Cairngorm plateaus are as bleak and demanding as any Scottish mountains. The coastline, especially from Stonehaven to Buckie, is particularly attractive. The valley of the Dee – Royal Deeside, thanks to the Queen's residence at Balmoral – has sublime scenery. Braemar, in upper Deeside, is surrounded by good walking country, and every September hosts Scotland's most important Highland Games, the Braemar Gathering.

The largest city in the north-east is prosperous Aberdeen, a lively and attractive place fattened on the proceeds of a long history of sea trade and currently through the North Sea oil industry, for which it's the onshore base.

The small fishing villages of the north coast are little-visited, but some are very pretty. Gardenstown is built on steep slopes which plunge dramatically into the sea. Farther west along this coast, experiments with alternative lifestyles continue at the Findhorn Foundation, an international spiritual community that welcomes outsiders with a range of eclectic courses. Further spiritual guidance is provided in neighbouring Speyside, where whisky distilleries welcome visitors with tours and drams.

ORIENTATION & INFORMATION

This section of the country comprises the administrative regions of Stirling, Clackmannanshire, Fife, Perth & Kinross, Dundee, Angus, Aberdeen, Aberdeenshire, and Moray.

The larger towns and cities are almost all by the coast, but Stirling and Perth are located quite far inland at the tidal limits of the major rivers Forth and Tay, respectively. The main mountain range is the Grampians, lying north of the River Tay and rising to over 1000m (3280 feet). The Cairngorms, which extend into the Highland region, reach over 1200m (3936 feet) and include Scotland's second highest mountain, Ben Macdui (1309m, 4296 feet).

' There are TICs in all the main tourist centres, many open seven days a week in summer. Smaller TICs close completely from October to Easter. Most TICs make a charge for booking local accommodation, usually around £1 or £2; they usually ask only for a 10% advance.

The following tourist boards distribute useful accommodation brochures: Argyll, the Isles, Loch Lomond, Stirling and Trossachs Tourist Board (☎ 01786-470945, information@scottish.heartlands.org); Kingdom of Fife Tourist Board (☎ 01592-750066); Perthshire Tourist Board (☎ 01738-627958); Angus & Dundee Tourist Board (☎ 01382-434277, arbroath@sol .co.uk); and Aberdeen & Grampian Tourist Board (☎ 01224-288800).

WALKS & CYCLE ROUTES

The West Highland Way, possibly the finest long-distance walk in Scotland, follows the edge of Stirling region from Milngavie (near Glasgow) to Tyndrum, and on to Fort William in the Highland region. See the Activities chapter.

There's some superb hill walking in the Highland areas of central and north-eastern Scotland, with many hills over the magic figure of 3000 feet (914m).

The northern part of Stirling region, most of Perth & Kinross, and the Angus glens are mountainous areas which boast several excellent centres for walking holidays, including Killin (in the Stirling region), Pitlochry (in Perth & Kinross), and Kirriemuir (in Angus). Braemar is an excellent base in Aberdeenshire – there are challenging walks from here through the Cairngorms to

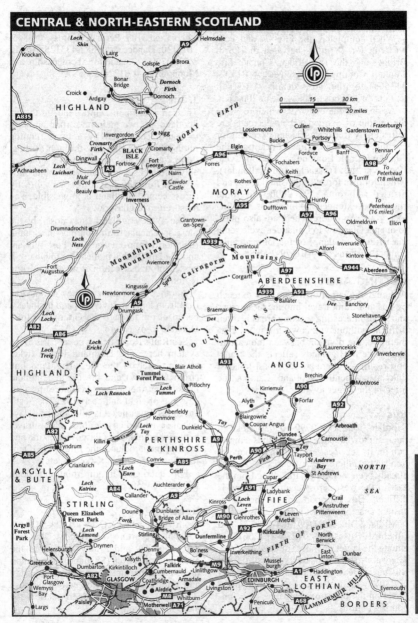

CENTRAL & NORTH-EASTERN SCOTLAND

Loch Shin · Krockan · Helmsdale · A9 · Lairg · Golspie · Brora · Bonar Bridge · Croick · Ardgay · Dornoch Firth · Dornoch · Tain · HIGHLAND · A835 · Invergordon · Nigg · Lossiemouth · Cullen · Whitehills · Gardenstown · Fraserburgh · MORAY FIRTH · Elgin · Buckie · Portsoy · Pennan · Cromarty Firth · BLACK ISLE · Cromarty · A96 · Fochabers · Fordyce · Banff · A98 · Dingwall · Fort George · Forres · Keith · To Peterhead (18 miles) · Achnasheen · Loch Luichart · Fortrose · Nairn · MORAY · Rothes · Huntly · Turriff · Muir of Ord · Cawdor Castle · A95 · Dufftown · A97 · A96 · To Peterhead (16 miles) · Beauly · Inverness · Oldmeldrum · Ellon · Grantown-on-Spey · A939 · Inverurie · Drumnadrochit · Tomintoul · Alford · Kintore · A944 · Aberdeen · Loch Ness · Monadhliath Mountains · Aviemore · Cairngorm Mountains · Corgarff · ABERDEENSHIRE · A97 · Fort Augustus · Kingussie · Newtonmore · A939 · A93 · Ballater · Dee · Banchory · Loch Lochy · A9 · Drumgask · Braemar · Dee · Stonehaven · A82 · A86 · Loch Ericht · Loch Treig · GRAMPIAN MOUNTAINS · North Esk · Laurencekirk · A92 · Inverbervie · Blair Atholl · A93 · ANGUS · Tummel Forest Park · Pitlochry · Brechin · A90 · Montrose · HIGHLAND · Loch Rannoch · Loch Tummel · Kirriemuir · A92 · Aberfeldy · Alyth · Forfar · Kenmore · Dunkeld · Blairgowrie · Arbroath · A82 · Loch Tay · Tay · Coupar Angus · Carnoustie · Killin · PERTHSHIRE & KINROSS · A9 · Dundee · Tyndrum · Firth of Tay · A85 · Comrie · A85 · Perth · A90 · Tayport · St Andrews Bay · NORTH · ARGYLL & BUTE · Crianlarich · Loch Earn · Crieff · Cupar · St Andrews · SEA · Loch Katrine · A84 · Auchterarder · A91 · Ladybank · Callander · A9 · Kinross · FIFE · Crail · STIRLING · Doune · Loch Leven · Anstruther · Pittenweem · Queen Elizabeth Forest Park · Dunblane · Glenrothes · Leven · Argyll Forest Park · Loch Lomond · Forth · Bridge of Allan · A92 · Methil · Helensburgh · Drymen · Stirling · Dunfermline · Kirkcaldy · Greenock · Dumbarton · Denny · Bo'ness · Inverkeithing · FIRTH OF FORTH · North Berwick · Port Glasgow · Kilsyth · Falkirk · M9 · Linlithgow · Musselburgh · Dunbar · Wemyss Bay · Kirkintilloch · Cumbernauld · East Linton · GLASGOW · Coatbridge · Armadale · EDINBURGH · Haddington · A1 · Largs · Paisley · Airdrie · M8 · Motherwell · A71 · Whitburn · Livingston · Dalkeith · EAST LOTHIAN · Eyemouth · Penicuik · A68 · LAMMERMUIR HILLS · BORDERS

0 15 30 km
0 10 20 miles

Aviemore, via the Lairig Ghru or the less-frequented Lairig an Laoigh.

When completed, the Fife Coastal Path will run for 78 miles between the Forth Bridges and the Tay Bridge. Contact Fife Council Community Services (☎ 01592-413664) for the latest details. TICs sell leaflets on sections of the walk for 20p each.

Aside from the busy A9, which roars up the middle of Scotland, the side roads are refreshingly free of traffic and excellent for cycling. There's an official cycle trail, the Glasgow, Loch Lomond and Killin Cycle Way (via the Trossachs and Callander), which follows forest trails, small roads and disused rail routes. By 2000, this route should be extended to Inverness via Pitlochry and Aviemore. There are also plans to open a Glasgow to Callander cycle route via Bridge of Allan. For the latest details, contact Sustrans on ☎ 01179-290888.

GETTING AROUND

Although the larger towns are easy to reach by bus and train, travel into the Grampians and other interesting walking areas is often difficult without your own transport. Furthermore, the division between the eastern and western Highlands reflects the transport realities – there are few coast-to-coast links across central Scotland. Cars can be hired in the larger towns.

Bus

Scottish Citylink (☎ 0990-505050) links all the main towns in the area; Perth is a major hub for its services. Away from the population centres, there are few buses and, as has already been mentioned, travelling from the east to the west across central Scotland is difficult. Bus transport around the north-eastern coast, however, is fairly reasonable.

Midland Bluebird (☎ 01324-613777) and Bluebird Buses (☎ 01224-212266) are among the larger operators of local services. There are some day passes, such as Midland Bluebird's Heart of Scotland Explorer ticket (£7.30), which also gives you half-price travel on the buses of companies in neighbouring regions.

For information on local buses in Stirling, phone ☎ 01324-613777; Fife, ☎ 01592-414141 ext 3103; Perth & Kinross, ☎ 0845-3011130; Dundee, ☎ 01382-433125; Angus, ☎ 01307-461775; and for Aberdeenshire and Moray buses ☎ 01224-664581.

Train

The rail system in central and north-east Scotland has two main lines running north to south, connected by a third running north-east from Glasgow through Stirling, Perth, Dundee and Aberdeen. It's a reasonably efficient service, but has a major flaw – travel from the east to the west directly across central Scotland is impossible. You must return to Glasgow.

The West Highland line, possibly the most spectacular train journey in Britain, runs north from Glasgow to Fort William and Mallaig (with a branch line to Oban); it passes through a section of western Stirling region.

Another scenic train journey in this area runs from Perth to Inverness and includes a beautiful run through the Grampians from Dunkeld to Aviemore.

ScotRail's Rover tickets cover parts of the system here. The Highland Rover ticket allows travel on the West Highland line (from Glasgow) and the North Highland lines (from Aberdeen or Aviemore) for four days out of eight and costs £42. The Festival Cities Rover ticket is valid for three days out of seven and costs £26; it allows travel between Edinburgh, Glasgow, Falkirk and Stirling and it includes the Fife circle (Dunfermline, Glenrothes, Kirkcaldy etc).

For detailed rail information phone ☎ 0345-484950.

Boat

From Aberdeen, P&O (☎ 01224-572615) has daily departures on Monday, Wednesday, Thursday and Friday leaving in the evening for Lerwick (Shetland). In summer, there are departures at noon on Tuesday and Saturday to Lerwick via Stromness (Orkney). See the Aberdeen section for more information.

Stirling Region

The administrative district of Stirling includes countryside on both sides of the Highland line: agricultural and industrial Lowlands to the south and the bare peaks of the Highlands to the north. Stirling and Clackmannanshire were formerly known as Central region, a name appropriate not only for the region's location, but for the fact that this area has played a pivotal role in Scotland's history. More than any other part of Scotland, this area has had the closest association with Scotland's struggle to maintain its freedom from England.

Stirling region's administrative capital is also known as Stirling, and it has a superb castle placed on a high rock at the most strategically important spot in the country – at the head of the Firth of Forth and the main route into the Highlands.

Loch Lomond lies on the western edge of the region (see Argyll & Bute in The Highlands chapter). The Trossachs, Rob Roy country, is another busy tourist destination, currently receiving even more attention following the success of the movie about this Scots hero. The mountainous north of the region sees far fewer visitors; public transport here is patchy in parts, nonexistent in others.

GETTING AROUND

For local transport information in the Stirling administrative region, phone Stirling Council's public transport unit on ☎ 01786-442707. Midland Bluebird (☎ 01324-613777) is the main operator. Its Heart of Scotland Explorer ticket (£7.30) gives you one day's travel on all its services in the Stirling region, West Lothian and Kincardine, and half-price travel in Fife, Lothian and Strathclyde.

The Trossachs Trundler (☎ 01877-330969) is a useful summer bus service circling Aberfoyle, Callander and the pier on Loch Katrine. Some Day Rover tickets (eg from Glasgow) are valid on this bus; connecting fares from Stirling (with Midland Bluebird) are available.

Stirling town is the rail hub but the lines skirt around the edge of this region, so you'll be relying on buses if you don't have your own transport. For train inquiries, phone ☎ 0345-484950.

The West Highland Way runs along the western edge of the region, from Glasgow to Fort William (see the Activities chapter). There are numerous other walks in the area. *Walk Loch Lomond & the Trossachs* is a useful guide published by Bartholomew and is available from TICs.

The Glasgow to Killin Cycle Way crosses the region from the centre of Glasgow via Balloch on the southern tip of Loch Lomond, Aberfoyle and Callander in the Trossachs, Loch Earn, Killin and Loch Tay. There are detours through Queen Elizabeth Forest Park and round Loch Katrine. It's a good route for walkers as well as cyclists because it follows forest trails, old railway routes and canal towpaths. A brochure showing the route is available from TICs.

STIRLING
- pop 37,000   ☎ 01786

The royal burgh of Stirling is such a strategic site that there's been a fortress here since prehistoric times. It was said that whoever held Stirling controlled the country, and Stirling has witnessed many of the struggles of the Scots against the English.

The castle is perched high on a rock and dominates the town. It's one of the most interesting castles in the country to visit, better even than Edinburgh Castle.

Two miles north of Stirling, and visible for miles around, the Wallace Monument commemorates William Wallace.

Mel Gibson's movie *Braveheart* recently revived interest in this hero of the wars of independence against England. You can climb this Victorian tower for a panoramic view of no less than seven battlegrounds – one of them at Stirling Bridge, where Wallace defeated the English in 1297.

A more famous battlefield is 2 miles south-east of Stirling at Bannockburn, where, in 1314, Robert the Bruce and his small army of determined Scots (outnumbered four to one) routed Edward II's English force and reclaimed Stirling Castle. This victory turned the tide of fortune sufficiently to favour the Scots for the following 400 years, in the long and bitter struggle against the prevalent threat of English domination. Although you can fit the main sights of Stirling into a day trip from Edinburgh or Glasgow, it's a very pleasant place to stay. There's an excellent youth hostel near the castle, and the town lays on Highland Games, a military parade, and numerous other activities in the summer.

Orientation

The largely pedestrianised old town slopes up from the train station and nearby bus station to the castle, which sits 250 feet above the plain atop the plug of an extinct volcano.

Stirling University's modern campus is to the north, by Bridge of Allan.

Information

The TIC (☎ 475019), 41 Dumbarton Rd, opens daily in July and August, from 9 am to 7.30 pm (6.30 pm on Sunday), and shorter hours for the rest of the year. It's closed on Sunday from October to April. As well as guided walks of the town, the TIC has details of the popular ghost walks (£5/3) that take place from Tuesday to Saturday at 7.30 and 9.30 pm.

The town puts on an entertaining program of events in summer, including ceilidhs at the guildhall on Monday evening and pipe bands on the castle esplanade on Tuesday. The medieval markets may be reinstated in future.

There are also 'living history' plays performed in and around the castle. The main post office, and banks with ATMs, can be found on Barnton St and Murray Place, respectively.

Medical Services The general hospital is Stirling Royal Infirmary (☎ 434000), Livilands Rd, south of the town centre.

Stirling Castle & Argyll's Lodging

The location, architecture and historical significance of Stirling Castle combine to make it one of the grandest of all Scottish castles. It commands superb views across the surrounding plains.

There has been a fortress of some kind here for several thousand years, but the current building dates from the late 14th to the 16th centuries, when it was a residence of the Stuart monarchs. James II murdered the Earl of Douglas in the castle and threw his body from a window (1452). The Great Hall and Gatehouse were built by James IV. The spectacular palace was constructed in the reign of James V (1540-42); French masons were responsible for the stonework. James VI remodelled the Chapel Royal and was the last King of Scots to live here.

A £20 million program of improvements at the castle is expected to be in progress until the end of the 20th century, but enough of the castle is kept accessible to make a visit worthwhile. During the work, a skeleton was discovered hidden in a wall of the castle. There's a visitor centre on the castle esplanade, with an audiovisual introduction to Stirling, including the history and architecture of the castle. The castle's 16th century kitchens, with a reconstruction of medieval conditions, are also very interesting.

In the King's Old Building is the museum of the Argyll and Sutherland Highlanders, which traces the history of this famous regiment from 1794 to the present.

Argyll's Lodging is the most impressive 17th century town house in Scotland and you'll find it by the castle, at the top of Castle Wynd. Parts of the Lodging date from the early 16th century. This spectacular mansion, complete with turrets, has recently opened to visitors after extensive renovations.

Stirling Castle and Argyll's Lodging (☎ 450000, HS) are open daily from April to September, from 9.30 am to 5.15 pm (last entry); in winter last entry is an hour earlier. Joint admission costs £4.50/3.50 (children £1.20). Entry to the visitor centre is free. There's a car park next to the castle (£2 for three hours).

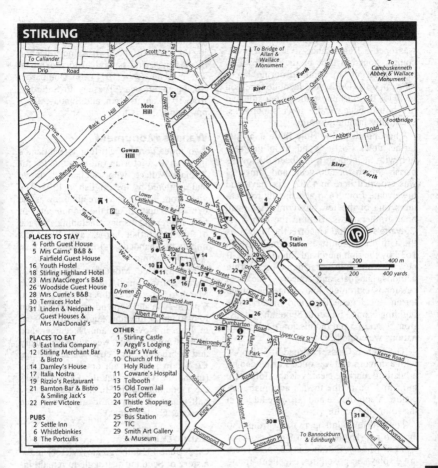

STIRLING

PLACES TO STAY
4 Forth Guest House
5 Mrs Cairns' B&B & Fairfield Guest House
16 Youth Hostel
18 Stirling Highland Hotel
23 Mrs MacGregor's B&B
26 Woodside Guest House
28 Mrs Currie's B&B
30 Terraces Hotel
31 Linden & Neidpath Guest Houses & Mrs MacDonald's

PLACES TO EAT
3 East India Company
12 Stirling Merchant Bar & Bistro
14 Darnley's House
17 Italia Nostra
19 Rizzio's Restaurant
21 Barnton Bar & Bistro & Smiling Jack's
22 Pierre Victoire

PUBS
2 Settle Inn
6 Whistlebinkies
8 The Portcullis

OTHER
1 Stirling Castle
7 Argyll's Lodging
9 Mar's Wark
10 Church of the Holy Rude
11 Cowane's Hospital
13 Tolbooth
15 Old Town Jail
20 Post Office
24 Thistle Shopping Centre
25 Bus Station
27 TIC
29 Smith Art Gallery & Museum

Old Town

Below the castle is the old town, which grew from the time Stirling became a royal burgh, around 1124. In the 15th and 16th centuries, when the Stuart monarchs held court in Stirling, rich merchants built their houses here.

Stirling has the best surviving town wall in Scotland and it can be followed on the **Back Walk**. It was built around 1547 when Henry VIII of England began what became known as 'Rough Wooing' – attacking the town in order to force Mary Queen of Scots to marry his son in order to unite the kingdoms. The walk follows the line of the wall from Dumbarton Rd (near the TIC) to the castle, continuing around Castle Rock and back to the old town. There are great views from the path, and you could make a short detour to Gowan Hill to see the **Beheading Stone**, where Murdoch, Duke of Albany and former Regent of Scotland, was executed in 1425. It's now encased in iron bars to keep ritual axe murderers away.

CENTRAL & NORTH-EASTERN

Mar's Wark, on Castle Wynd at the head of the old town, is the ornate façade of what was once a Renaissance-style town house commissioned in 1569 by the wealthy Earl of Mar, Regent of Scotland during James VI's minority. During the Jacobite rebellion in 1715, the Earl chose the losing side and his house became the town's barracks, eventually falling into ruin.

The **Church of the Holy Rude** is a little farther down Castle Wynd, at its intersection with St John St. It has been the town's parish church for 500 years and James VI was crowned here in 1567. The nave and tower date from 1456 and the church features one of the few surviving medieval, open-timber roofs. Behind the church is **Cowane's hospital** (incorrectly known as the Guildhall), built as an almshouse in 1637 by the rich merchant John Cowane. It now has multiple uses including hosting ceilidhs, banquets and concerts. The local curator is extremely knowledgeable about tartan, local genealogy and history. The building is open Easter to September, daily, from 9 am to 5 pm (admission free but donations welcomed).

The **Mercat Cross**, in Broad St, is topped with a unicorn and was once surrounded by a bustling market. Nearby is the **Tolbooth**, built in 1705 as the town's administrative centre. A courthouse and jail were added in the following century.

The **Old Town Jail** opens daily, from 9.30 am to 6 pm (last admission 5 pm; closes at 4 pm in winter). Entrance is £2.75/2. There are displays on prison life, excellent 'living history' performances, and a good view from the roof.

At the end of Broad St is **Darnley's House**, where Mary Queen of Scots' second husband, Lord Darnley, is said to have stayed. It has a rare architectural feature: the barrel-vaulted ground floor has no connection with the upper floors.

The floodlit **Thief's Hole**, an old dungeon in the town wall, contains two realistic dummies. Access is down a spiral staircase next to John Menzies in the Thistle Centre, open the same hours as the centre.

Smith Art Gallery & Museum

You'll find excellent displays here, covering the history of the town, a fine collection of paintings, and natural history exhibits. The museum (☎ 471917), on Dumbarton Rd, opens all year, Tuesday to Saturday, from 10.30 am to 5 pm, and Sunday, 2 to 5 pm. Admission is free.

Wallace Monument

Two miles north of Stirling is Scotland's impressive Victorian monument to Sir William Wallace, who was hanged, drawn and quartered by the English in 1305. The view from the top is as breathtaking as the 67m climb up to it, and the monument contains interesting displays including a parade of other Scottish heroes and Wallace's mighty two-handed sword. Clearly the man was no weakling.

The Wallace Monument (☎ 472140) opens daily from 10 am to 5 pm from March to May (and October); from 10 am to 6 pm in June and September; from 9.30 am to 6.30 pm in July and August; from 10 am to 4 pm in November and December; and from 10 am to 4 pm at weekends in January and February. Entry costs £3/2 (students £2.75). In summer, an open-top tour bus (phone the TIC for details; £5.50/4) links the monument with Stirling Castle every half-hour, but you could also walk (see Walks & Cycle Routes).

Bannockburn

On 24 June 1314, the greatest victory in the history of Scotland's struggle to remain independent took place at the Battle of Bannockburn.

At the Bannockburn Heritage Centre (☎ 812664), owned by the NTS, the story is told with audiovisual displays. Outside is the Borestone site, said to have been Robert the Bruce's command post before the battle. There's also his grim-looking statue, dressed in full battle gear and mounted on a charger.

The site never closes but the heritage centre opens daily from April to October, from 10 am to 5.30 pm; the last audiovisual show is at 5 pm. In March, November and

William Wallace, Scottish Patriot

William Wallace was born in 1270 as the second son of Sir Malcolm Wallace of Elderslie, near Paisley. Little-known before 1296, he was then catapulted into fame and a place in history as a highly successful guerrilla commander who harassed the English invaders for many years.

Driven to avenge the barbarous rule of his distant relative, the English king Edward Plantagenet (Edward I, Hammer of the Scots), Wallace secured his first victory in September 1296 by defeating a troop of about 100 English soldiers at the battle of Loudoun Hill in Ayrshire. In May 1297, Wallace summarily executed Sir William de Hazelrigg, the English-imposed Sheriff of Lanark, for killing Marion Wallace, his wife. By September, an English army met Wallace and his friends head-on at Stirling Bridge; a large party of English crossed the bridge and were routed after being cut-off by the Scots.

Wallace was knighted by Robert the Bruce and proclaimed Guardian of Scotland in March 1298. However, disaster struck in July, when Edward's superior force defeated the Scots at the Battle of Falkirk. Wallace resigned as Guardian, went into hiding, and travelled throughout Europe to drum-up support for the Scottish cause. Many of the Scots nobility were prepared to side with Edward, and Wallace was betrayed after his return to Scotland in 1305.

Sir William Wallace was tried for treason at Westminster (although he had never recognised Edward as his overlord), and he was cruelly hanged, beheaded and disembowelled at Smithfield, London. A memorial plaque is incorporated in the wall of St Bartholomew's Hospital at West Smithfield.

A highly recommended albeit fictionalised account of Wallace's exploits is *The Wallace*, by Nigel Tranter.

December it's open daily from 11 am to 3 pm. Entry is £2.30/1.50.

Cambuskenneth Abbey

The only substantial remnant of this Augustinian abbey, founded in 1147, is the belfry. In medieval times, Cambuskenneth became one of the richest abbeys in the country, and its high status is supported by the fact that Robert the Bruce held his parliament here in 1326, and James III and his queen are both buried here. The abbey is a mile from both Stirling Castle and the Wallace Monument. It's open at all times; entry is free.

Walks & Cycle Routes

The best way to reach the Wallace Monument is on foot or by bike; it takes about 45 minutes to walk there. Cross the railway line on Seaforth Place, continue straight ahead into Shore Rd and Abbey Rd. There's a footbridge over the River Forth to Cambuskenneth, where you can visit the ruins of the abbey. The Wallace Monument is

The March to Independence

SNP leader Alex Salmond

Every year on the Saturday nearest 24 June (the day in 1314 when the Scots inflicted their greatest defeat on the English at Bannockburn), there's a commemorative march from the north end of Stirling, through the town, and southwards as far as the Bannockburn Heritage Centre. The march ends at Bruce's statue and is followed by an address from the leader of the Scottish National Party (SNP), currently Alex Salmond, MP for Banff & Buchan. While some people finish the day with a family picnic on the grass of Bannockburn field, others adjourn to the nearby 1314 Inn, a great place for a pint, a bar meal, and heated political discussions.

located just a mile north of here; follow Ladysneuk Rd and turn left at the junction with Alloa Rd.

Organised Tours

From late May to September, an open-top hop on hop off bus tour runs daily between the castle and the Wallace Monument; there are two buses every hour. A day ticket costs £5.50/4 (£2 for children). Check details with the TIC or call ☎ 0131-556 2244.

Places to Stay

Camping *Witches Craig Caravan Park* (☎ 474947) is on the edge of the Ochil Hills in Blairlogie, 3 miles east of Stirling by the A91. Tent pitches cost from £4.

Hostels The façade of a 19th century church conceals *Stirling Youth Hostel* (☎ 473442), which is in a perfect location in the old part of town in St John St. Open year-round, it's a superb modern hostel with 126 beds in small dorms; the overnight charge of £11.50/9.95 includes continental breakfast (there's a £1 supplement in July and August). The hostel has a less attractive annexe in Union St, open in summer only.

Stirling Holiday Campus (☎ 467140), on the edge of Bridge of Allan, 3 miles north of the town, lets student rooms in the summer from £18. There are only single rooms – 1030 of them – and there's also a pub, golf course and cinema on the landscaped site.

B&Bs & Hotels There's a clutch of B&Bs on Linden Ave (just off Burghmuir Rd), which is fairly close to the bus station and less than a half-mile from the train station. *Linden Guest House* (☎ 448850, 22 Linden Ave) charges from £15 to £22 per person. *Neidpath Guest House* (☎ 474840, 24 Linden Ave) offers B&B for £15. *Mrs MacDonald's* (☎ 473418, 28 Linden Ave) charges £15 to £17 per person.

Just across the road from the TIC is *Woodside Guest House* (☎ 475470, 4 Back Walk) where B&B costs from £20/38 in rooms with bathroom attached. Equally close to the TIC, *Mrs Curry's* (☎ 451002, 1 Albert Place) has three rooms and charges around £18.

Conveniently located in the centre of town, *Mrs MacGregor's* (☎ 471082, 27 King St) does B&B from £18/30. Dinner is available for £7 extra.

On the other side of town, a short walk north of the train station, is the excellent *Forth Guest House* (☎ 471020, 23 Forth Place), just off Seaforth Rd. It's a small Georgian terrace house with a tiny rose-filled front garden and five comfortable rooms, all with bath attached. B&B costs from £19.50 per person and evening meals are available for £13.

Mrs Cairns' (☎ 479228, 12 Princes St) is conveniently located just an easy walk from the train station. There are two single and two twin rooms here; B&B costs from £18 per person in a room with bath attached. *Fairfield Guest House* (☎ 472685, 14 Princes St) has six rooms, five with attached bathroom, from £20/40.

The friendly *Terraces Hotel* (☎ 472268, 4 Melville Terrace) is popular with businesspeople and rooms cost £55/72 for a single/double. It's an efficient hotel with good food and real ales too.

The smartest hotel in town is the *Stirling Highland Hotel* (☎ 475444), a sympathetic refurbishment of the old high school located on Spittal St. B&B costs £95/123 in summer, but there are special offers available. Special B&B packages for over 60s cost from £51 per person.

Places to Eat

You'll find shops selling groceries in the Thistle Shopping Centre and surrounding streets.

There are good views from the restaurant at *Stirling Castle* but it's rather overpriced. Down the hill from the castle, beyond the end of Broad St, is the *Darnley Coffee House* (☎ 474468, 18 Bow St), which is a conveniently located pit stop for home baking and speciality coffees as you walk around the old town.

The *Barnton Bar & Bistro* (☎ 461698, 3½ Barnton St), opposite the GPO, is a very popular student hang-out serving excellent all-day breakfasts. Open daily and until 1 am at weekends, it's a great place to eat or drink. You'll get large servings of good food here; soup and snacks cost from £1.45 to £3.95.

Smiling Jack's Tex Mex (☎ 462809, 17 Barnton St) does chicken nachos for £4.30 and enchiladas from £6.10.

Italia Nostra (☎ 473208, 25 Baker St) is a busy Italian place that also does takeaways. If you haven't yet eaten at a branch of *Pierre Victoire* (☎ 448171, 41 Friars St), there's one here. (You might not get the chance since the company went into receivership in July 1998.) The £5.90 three-course set lunch is reasonable value, but take your own cushion – the wooden chairs are a bit hard.

The *East India Company* (☎ 471330, 7 Viewfield Place) is a very good Indian restaurant and takeaway. There's a cheaper balti bar upstairs.

Rizzio's Restaurant (☎ 475444) is in a corner of the Stirling Highland Hotel on Spittal St. For only £3.95 you can eat as much pizza and pasta as you like at lunchtime and from 5.30 to 6.30 pm, a remarkable offer from such an expensive hotel. The restaurant is named after Mary Queen of Scots' Italian secretary, David Rizzio, who was murdered on the orders of the Earl of Bothwell after he suspected an affair.

Close to the castle is the *Stirling Merchant Bar Bistro* (☎ 473929, 39 Broad St), which was formerly the town's bathhouse. It now serves contemporary Scottish cuisine and specialist ales and wines. It's open daily to midnight (11 pm in winter). *Hermann's* (☎ 450632, 32 St John's St) is round the corner at the Tolbooth. It's an excellent Scottish-Austrian restaurant; a two-course set lunch costs £7.95, and a Wiener schnitzel £12.95.

Melville's (☎ 472268), the restaurant at the Terraces Hotel, is popular with the locals. Good value bar meals start at £3.75. A steak with brandy and cream sauce is £12.50.

Entertainment

The *Portcullis* (☎ 472290, Castle Wynd) is the best pub in Stirling. You'll find it just below the castle, and excellent bar meals are served all day. There's a large range of malt whiskies, too.

There are two pubs farther down St Mary's Wynd: *Whistlebinkies*, and the very popular *Settle Inn* – established in 1733, and the oldest pub in Stirling. The *Barnton Bar & Bistro* (see Places to Eat) is another popular place for a drink.

Getting There & Away

Stirling is 26 miles north-east of Glasgow, 35 miles from Edinburgh and 420 miles from London.

Bus Scottish Citylink (☎ 0990-505050) has a number of routes, usually hourly, from Glasgow (45 minutes, £3). Some buses continue to Aberdeen via Perth and Dundee; others go to Inverness. Stirling to Aberdeen takes 3½ hours and costs £12.80; you may need to change at Dundee. Buses from Stirling to Inverness take 3¾ hours (£10.30) and you'll almost certainly have to change at Perth. A once-daily service runs from Edinburgh to Fort William via Stirling (with connections to Oban or Skye); fares to Edinburgh, Oban, Fort William, and Portree are £5.30, £10.50, £11 and £18.50, respectively.

Local buses are operated by Midland Bluebird (☎ 01324-613777). Midland also runs hourly to Edinburgh (two hours, £4.35).

Train ScotRail (☎ 0345-484950) runs services to Edinburgh (50 minutes, £4.70) twice an hour most of the day from Monday to Saturday, and hourly on Sunday. Not all services are direct. There are services twice an hour from Glasgow (40 minutes, £3.70) and frequent services to Perth (35 minutes, £7.10), Dundee (one hour, £10.90) and Aberdeen (2¼ hours, £29).

Car For car hire contact Arnold Clark (☎ 478686), Kerse Rd. Cheapest is a Nissan Micra at £16 per day.

Getting Around

Bus It's easy enough to walk around the central part of the town. From the train station to the castle is about three-quarters of a mile. Check with the TIC to see if the shuttle bus has been reinstated if you want to save your feet on this uphill walk. It previously ran every 20 minutes from 9.30 am to 5 pm.

Taxi Woodside Taxis (☎ 450005) can organise sightseeing trips for up to eight people at around £18 per hour.

AROUND STIRLING
Bridge of Allan
• pop 4607   ☎ 01786

This former spa town, just 2½ miles north of Stirling, is a pleasant place to visit.

Things to See & Do The old **Victorian bath-houses** on Mine Rd, built in 1861, have been turned into an upmarket restaurant. One of the most intriguing structures in the town is the **ornamental clock** in the main thoroughfare, Henderson St. The **Holy Trinity Church** at 12 Keir St dates from 1860 and is noted for its stained glass windows, unusual roof structure and Charles Rennie Mackintosh furniture. It's open to visitors from June to September, Saturday only, from 10 am to 4 pm; admission is free.

The factory shop **Village Glass** (☎ 832137), Queens Lane (just off Henderson St), sells unusual glassware gifts from £2 to £50; realistic-looking glass sweets are £3.50 each and solid glass writing pens cost £17.95. You can also watch the glassblowers at work, so you'll appreciate the skill which goes into making the products. The shop opens all year, on weekdays from 9 am to 5 pm and on Saturday from 10 am to 4 pm.

Places to Stay & Eat There are plenty of B&Bs in the £16 to £20 price range including: *Lorraine* (☎ 832042, 10 Chalton Rd); *Mrs Hogg's* (☎ 834797, 52 Henderson St); *Benmore* (☎ 833018, 8 Fountain Rd); and the *Gables* (☎ 833155, 9 Kenilworth Rd).

Former Glasgow Rangers footballer Terry Butcher will welcome you to the *Old Manor Hotel* (☎ 832169, 129 Henderson St). Comfortable singles/doubles start at £35/80. The food here is recommended; bar meals start at £6.25, and à la carte restaurant meals begin at £9.75. The *Royal Hotel*

(☎ 832284, 55 Henderson St) has pleasant rooms for £85/97.50. Bar meals are around £12 for three courses; a three-course table d'hôte dinner in the brasserie costs £10.50.

There are cheaper alternatives on Henderson St, including *Bayne's Bakery*; the *Coffee Pot*, for soup and snacks, and traditional afternoon teas for £4.25; and the *Allan Water Café*, famous for its huge portions – homemade soup and a roll is only £1.25 and a large haddock and chips is £5.20.

Getting There & Away You can walk to Bridge of Allan from Stirling in just over an hour. Local buses stop in Henderson St. Trains to Dunblane, Stirling, Glasgow and Edinburgh depart frequently from the station at the west end of Henderson St. For Stirling, you'll pay £1 each way.

Dunblane

* pop 6970   ☎ 01786

The name Dunblane will for many years be associated with the horrific massacre that took place in the primary school in March 1996. Five miles north of Stirling, the town straddles the banks of the Allan Water.

It was founded in 602 by St Blane, who lived in a beehive cell at the nearby old dun (fort). There's a seasonal TIC (☎ 824428) on Stirling Rd.

Things to See The main attraction is Dunblane Cathedral, which is a simple, elegant, sandstone building – a superb example of Gothic style. The lower parts of the walls date from Norman times, the rest is mainly 13th to 15th century. The roof of the nave collapsed in the 16th century, however the cathedral was saved from ruin by a major restoration project in the 1890s. It's open daily from 9.30 am to 6.30 pm (closing at 4.30 pm from October to March, and closed Thursday afternoon and Friday in winter).

The small cathedral museum, in barrel-vaulted rooms dating from 1624, is situated on the square and relates the history of both cathedral and town. The museum opens May to October, daily except Sunday, from

10 am to 12.30 pm and 2 to 4.30 pm. Admission is free.

Places to Stay & Eat Accommodation in Dunblane isn't particularly cheap and you have better choices in Stirling or Bridge of Allan. There are several places to eat with snacks from around £1 and main courses from about £3.50 to £8, including the *Allan Café (33 High St)*, the *Dunblane Hotel (☎ 822178, 10 Stirling Rd)* and the *Village Bar & Bistro* across the street. There's a good range of takeaway outlets, including Chinese, fish and chips, and a pizzeria. However, one of the nicest places in town is the friendly *Choices Delicatessen & Coffee Shop (21 High St)* where you can get light meals, soup and snacks.

Getting There & Away You can walk to Bridge of Allan from Dunblane along the Darn Rd, an ancient path used by the monks, in about an hour. Alternatively, there are local buses from Stirling. There are Scottish Citylink buses (☎ 0990-505050) to Stirling, Glasgow, Perth etc, once every hour or two, stopping at the police station on Perth Rd (near the TIC and Cathedral). Trains to Stirling (£1.80), and Glasgow or Edinburgh, are more frequent – roughly three per hour, fewer on Sunday.

Doune

* pop 1212   ☎ 01786

Seven miles north-west of Stirling, Doune is now a quiet rural town. In former times it was known for its drover's market, and was also famous as a centre for the manufacture of sporrans and pistols.

Things to See & Do The main street is dominated by a red sandstone church and tower, and there are some interesting houses in George St, just downhill from the Mercat Cross.

Doune Castle (☎ 841742) is one of the best preserved 14th century castles in Scotland, having remained largely unchanged since it was built for the Duke of Albany. It was a favourite royal hunting lodge, but was also of great strategic importance because it controlled the route between the Lowlands and Highlands, and Mary Queen of Scots stayed here. There are great views from the castle walls, and the lofty gatehouse is very impressive, rising nearly 30m. The castle opens standard HS hours (but in winter it's closed Thursday afternoon and all day Friday); entry is £2.30/1.75 (£1 for children).

A mile west from the castle (by the A84, towards Callander) is the **Doune Motor Museum** (☎ 841203), the Earl of Moray's collection of 50 vehicles, including the second-oldest Rolls-Royce in the world and Scotland's only production model racing car, the JP Special. There's a restaurant on site. From April to November the museum opens daily from 10 am to 5 pm (last admission 4.30 pm); entry is £3.50/2.50.

Two miles south of Doune (by the A84, towards Stirling), there's the **Blair Drummond Safari Park** (☎ 841456), with a collection of African and other animals. A safari bus is available for visitors without suitable transport. There's a restaurant in the park. You'll find the park open between late March and early October, daily from 10 am to 5.30 pm (last admission 4.30 pm). The entry charge of £8/4 covers most attractions.

Places to Stay & Eat There's a *Life Style* store in the Main St. The *Red Lion Hotel (☎ 842066, Balkerach St)* dates from 1692 and has three rooms for £18 to £25 per person. Bar meals cost £3.95 to £8.50. The *Highland Hotel (Main St)* also does pub grub.

Getting There & Away There are Midland Bluebird (☎ 01324-613777) buses every hour or two to Doune from Stirling (£2.40), via Blair Drummond (less frequent on Sunday).

DOLLAR
• pop 4199   ☎ 01259

About 11 miles east of Stirling, in the foothills of the Ochil Hills that run north-east into Perth & Kinross, is the small town of Dollar. **Castle Campbell** (☎ 742408) is a

20 minute walk up **Dollar Glen**, into the wooded hills above the town. It's a spooky, old stronghold of the Dukes of Argyll and stands between two ravines; you can clearly see why it was known as Castle Gloom. There's been a fortress of some kind on this site from the 11th century, but the present structure dates from the 15th century. The castle was sacked by Cromwell in 1654, but the tower is well preserved. You'll find a tearoom at the castle; soup is £1. Opening hours and charges are as for Doune Castle.

There are regular Midland Bluebird (☎ 01324-613777) buses to Dollar from Stirling; other services run from Alloa. From Kinross, the Rennie's (☎ 01383-620600) R5 service runs three times daily on Wednesday and Friday only.

ALLOA
• pop 11,384   ☎ 01259

Alloa is a large town 6 miles east of Stirling. **Alloa Tower** (☎ 211701), Alloa Park, is a short walk from the town centre, conveniently signposted. The 24m-high tower dates from before 1497 and it's one of the most interesting NTS properties. The Italianate staircase and dome are superb. There's also a well and pit dungeon, furnishings, and paintings belonging to the Mar family. Views from the parapet walk are spectacular.

The tower is open at Easter and May to September, daily, from 1.30 to 5.30 pm (last admission at 5 pm); entry costs £2.40/1.60. Midland Bluebird (☎ 01324-613777) runs buses to Clackmannan, Dollar, Stirling and Glasgow.

CLACKMANNAN
• pop 3410   ☎ 01259

This village lies 2 miles south-east of Alloa and has several interesting sights. In Main St, the **Clackmannan stone** sits on top of a large shaft – it's sacred to the pagan deity Mannan and it clearly predates Christian times.

The adjacent 17th century **Cross** is engraved with the Bruce coat of arms; the lower part is heavily worn due to prisoners' chains. Also adjacent is the **Tolbooth**, built in 1592 for £284, which served as a court and prison. **Clackmannan Tower**, uphill from the church and about 450m from Main St, was a residence of the Bruce family from 1365 to 1772. The widow of the last laird is said to have knighted Robert Burns in the tower, with the sword of Robert the Bruce, in 1787. The five storey tower has structural problems due to subsidence and it isn't open to the public, but it's well worth a visit.

Midland Bluebird (☎ 01324-613777) bus No 15 runs to Falkirk, Kincardine and Alloa from Main St.

FALKIRK
* **pop 33,351**   ☎ **01324**

Downstream from Stirling the southern side of the River Forth is a heavily industrialised built-up area not exactly noted for its scenic beauty, but there are interesting historical buildings in the area.

Falkirk is a large town about 10 miles south-east of Stirling. The main shopping street, High St, is pedestrianised. There's a TIC (☎ 620244) nearby, at 2 Glebe St; ask for their *Town Heritage Trail* leaflet. A mile east of the centre, and only a 10 minute walk from the bus and train stations, is the vast mansion **Callendar House** (☎ 503770), complete with turrets and extensive grounds.

Originally a 14th century keep, the building was greatly extended by a rich 18th century merchant, William Forbes, and his descendants. There are several exhibitions, galleries, a working Georgian kitchen (where food is prepared) and a tea shop. The house opens all year, Monday to Saturday, from 10 am to 5 pm, and from April to September, also on Sunday, 2 to 5 pm; admission costs £1.80/90p.

Midland Bluebird (☎ 613777) runs regular buses to Stirling (£2.50) and Edinburgh (£3.40). ScotRail (☎ 0345-484950) services go to Stirling, Dunblane, Perth, Glasgow (£4.20) and Edinburgh (£3.70) from Falkirk Grahamston station. Half-hourly Glasgow-Edinburgh express trains stop at Falkirk High.

THE CAMPSIES & STRATHBLANE
The Campsie Fells, commonly called the Campsies, reach nearly 600m (1968 feet) and lie about 10 miles north of Glasgow. The plain of the River Forth lies to the north; Strathblane and Loch Lomond lie to the west.

One of several villages around the Campsies, attractive **Killearn** is known for its 31m-high obelisk, raised in honour of George Buchanan, James VI's tutor. Eight miles to the east, **Fintry** is another pretty village, on the banks of the Endrick Water, which has an impressive 28m waterfall, the **Loup of Fintry**. In the west, nearer to Loch Lomond and lying on the West Highland Way, is **Drymen**, also with lots of character. There's a seasonal TIC in Drymen Library (☎ 01360-660068), at The Square.

Walks
One of the best walks in the area is the ascent of spectacular Dumgoyne hill (427m, 1400 feet) from Glengoyne distillery, about 2 miles south of Killearn. Walk up the track which heads uphill from the A81, about 90m north of the distillery. You'll pass through trees; go through the gate on the right and head through the field for the gap between two blocks of trees. A steep path beyond this leads up towards the rocky summit of this eroded volcanic remnant (easier on its north and west sides). It's possible to continue, with easier walking, to the highest point on the Campsies, Earl's Seat (578m, 1896 feet). Allow at least one hour for the ascent of Dumgoyne. It will take another hour to Earl's Seat, and 1½ hours to return from there to the distillery.

Just on the other side of Strathblane there's The Whangie, an impressive rock formation on the side of Auchineden Hill. A good path leads to the rocks from the Queen's View car park on the A809 Glasgow (Bearsden) to Drymen road; it takes about 45 minutes to hike each way.

Places to Stay & Eat
About a mile east of Fintry, *Craigton Farm (☎ 01360-860426, Denny Rd)* does B&B

CENTRAL & NORTH-EASTERN

from £15 a double. In Fintry village, you'll find the *Coffee Pot (☎ 01360-860226, Main St)* which serves home baking and lunches daily.

The 17th century former drovers' hostel, the *Clachan Hotel (☎ 01360-860237)* is situated by Fintry church on the Lennoxtown road. It has rooms with attached bath from £24 to £30 per person, and you can get a bar meal here.

In Drymen, there's a good choice of B&Bs and hotels. *Mrs Lander's (☎ 01360-660273, 17 Stirling Rd)* will be quite secure as her husband is an inventor of burglar alarms! B&B here costs from £18/32 single/double. Believe it or not, *Mrs Crooks (☎ 01360-660793, 13 Stirling Rd)* also does B&B, with two rooms starting at £20/36. The top hotel in the village is the *Buchanan Arms (☎ 01360-660588)*, with *en suite* rooms from £50/80, and a sport and leisure club with swimming pool, sauna etc.

You'll find a *Spar* supermarket and the *Drymen Tandoori* on The Square. However, the best place to eat is the *Clachan Inn (☎ 01360-660824)*, also on The Square. It's Scotland's oldest registered inn (opened in 1734) and in 1997 was voted second best in Scotland for bar food. The extensive menu includes steaks, burgers, salads and vegetarian choices. Try the deep-fried lobster tails at £7.50.

Getting There & Away

Midland Bluebird (☎ 01324-613777) runs up to five buses daily from Glasgow to Drymen (£3.10) via Queen's View (The Whangie). The hourly No 10 bus from Glasgow to Stirling goes via Dumgoyne and Balfron; connect for Aberfoyle (£4.60) at Balfron. Fintry is served by two postbuses (☎ 01463-256200); one runs from Denny at 9.55 am, except Sunday (take a local bus from Stirling to Denny), while the other runs twice on weekdays from Balfron, once on Saturday.

THE TROSSACHS

The narrow glen between Loch Katrine and Loch Achray is named the Trossachs, but it's now used to describe a wider scenic area around the southern border of the Highlands.

As all the tourist literature repeatedly informs you, this is Rob Roy country. Rob Roy Macgregor (1671-1734) was the wild leader of one of the wildest of Scotland's clans, Clan Gregor. Although he claimed direct descent from a 10th century King of Scots and rights to the lands the clan occupied, these Macgregor lands stood between powerful neighbours. Rob Roy became notorious for his daring raids into the Lowlands, to carry off cattle and sheep, but these escapades led to the outlawing of the clan – hence their sobriquet, 'Children of the Mist'. He also achieved a reputation as a champion of the poor. Rob Roy is buried in the churchyard at Balquhidder, by Loch Voil.

Actor Liam Neeson was just the most recent of Rob Roy's popularists – Sir Walter Scott's historical novel *Rob Roy* brought tourists to the region in the 19th century. Loch Katrine was the inspiration for Scott's *Lady of the Lake* and, since the early 20th century, the SS *Sir Walter Scott* has been taking visitors cruising on the loch. The main centres in the area are Aberfoyle and Callander. During the summer months, a vintage bus, the Trossachs Trundler, links these two places with Loch Katrine.

Aberfoyle

• pop 990   ☎ 01877

Known as the southern gateway to the Trossachs, Aberfoyle is on the eastern edge of the Queen Elizabeth Forest Park, which stretches across to the hills beside Loch Lomond. The village makes a good base for walks and cycle rides in the area, but it can be very busy with tourists in summer.

Three miles east is one of Scotland's two lakes, the Lake of Menteith. The substantial ruins of the priory (☎ 385294) where Mary Queen of Scots was kept safe as a child, during Henry VIII's 'Rough Wooing', are on Inchmahome Island.

A ferry takes visitors from the village to the priory. It's open April to September, Monday to Saturday from 9.30 am to 6.30

pm, and on Sunday from 2 to 6.30 pm; admission costs £2.80/2.10, including the ferry.

The TIC (☎ 382352), Main St, opens April to October. About half a mile north of Aberfoyle, on the A821, is the Queen Elizabeth Forest Park Visitors Centre (☎ 382258), which has audio-visual displays, exhibitions, and information about the numerous walks and cycle routes in and around the park. It's open from Easter to October, daily, and November weekends, from 10 am to 6 pm; car parking costs £1.

Walks & Cycle Routes Waymarked trails start from the Visitors Centre on the hills above the town.

There's an excellent 20-mile circular cycle route that links with the ferry (☎ 376316) along Loch Katrine. From Aberfoyle, join the Glasgow-Killin Cycle Way on the forest trail, or take the A821 over Duke's Pass.

Following the southern shore of Loch Achray, you reach the pier on Loch Katrine; from April to October, departures are daily at 11 am (not Saturday). The ferry should drop you at Stronachlachar (£3.25/1.70 single), at the western end (note that afternoon sailings do not stop here). From Stronachlachar, follow the B829 via Loch Ard to Aberfoyle.

Places to Stay & Eat *Cobleland Campsite (☎ 382392)* is off the A81, 2 miles south of Aberfoyle; camping is £4.20 per adult.

In Aberfoyle, *Mrs Oldham's (☎ 382845, Mayfield, Main St)* offers B&B from just £15 to £17 per person, with attached bath. Overlooking the village, by the A821 to the Duke's Pass, *Mrs More's (☎ 382470, Keith House, Trossachs Rd)* charges similar rates. In the middle of the village, the *Forth Inn (☎ 382372, Main St)* does B&B for £27/46 in rooms with bath attached. Bar meals are available all day, from £4.25 to £9.

There's also the *Old Coach Inn (☎ 382822, Main St)*. Good bar meals start at £4.75, but the service can be slow. For cheaper coffee and snacks on or just off the Main St, try the *Coffee Shop* (baked potatoes from £1.60) or the *Scottish Wool Centre coffee shop*.

The best place to eat in Aberfoyle is the pleasant *Covenanters Inn (☎ 382347)*, with a great location on a hillock just south of the River Forth, only a short walk from Main St. There also are rooms from £35 to £40 per person.

Getting There & Away Midland Bluebird (☎ 01324-613777) has up to five buses a day from Stirling (£3.40) and up to three connecting services per day from Glasgow (£4.60) via Balfron.

Royal Mail runs a postbus (☎ 01463-256200) on weekday afternoons from Aberfoyle to Callander via Port of Menteith (30 minutes). Another postbus does a round trip, Monday to Saturday, from Aberfoyle to Inversnaid on Loch Lomond, giving access to the West Highland Way. The Trossachs Trundler (☎ 330969) has a day ticket that includes Aberfoyle, Callander, Port of Menteith and Stirling for £8.10/5.40.

Getting Around Bicycles can be hired from Trossachs Cycle Hire (☎ 382614), from £7.50 for a half day.

Callander
- **pop 2429**   ☎ **01877**

Fourteen miles north-west of Stirling, Callander is a tourist town that bills itself as the eastern gateway to the Trossachs. It has been pulling in the tourists for over 150 years, and tartan and fudge shops now line the long main drag.

The **Rob Roy and Trossachs Visitor Centre** (☎ 330342) in an old church in the central square is also the TIC. The audiovisual Rob Roy show runs daily from May to September, from 9.30 am to around 9 pm (7 pm on Monday, Wednesday and Friday), and 10 am to 5 pm for the rest of the year; entry is £2.50/1.75.

There's a swimming pool in the new McLaren Community Leisure Centre (£2/1).

There are two banks near the TIC.

Walks The impressive Bracklinn Falls are reached by track and footpath from Bracklinn Rd (30 minutes each way from the car park). Also off Bracklinn Rd, a woodland trail leads up to Callander Crags, with great views over the surroundings; a round trip takes 1½ hours.

Places to Stay & Eat There are numerous places to stay. *Keltie Bridge Caravan Park* (☎ 330811) at the eastern end of Callander and just off the A84 has upgraded facilities and tent space from £5.50. *Trossachs Backpackers* (☎ 331200) is about a mile along Invertrossachs Rd, which runs on the south side of the river draining Loch Vennachar; beds are £10 to £12, including sheets and breakfast. Bike rental is available.

Mrs Callaghan (☎ 331062, *Auchyle, Stirling Rd*) has a fully equipped holiday flat, with central heating. It sleeps four

people and costs only £135 to £205 per week.

Ben A'an Guest House (☎ *330317, 158 Main St*) has five rooms and charges £16 to £18 per person. *Arden House Guest House* (☎ *330235, Bracklinn Rd*) is just north of the town; B&B costs £20 to £23 per person. It's an excellent place to stay and it was used as the setting for the TV series *Doctor Finlay's Casebook*. Evening meals are available for £10. The *Roman Camp Hotel* (☎ *330003*) is beautifully located by the River Teith; it's an upmarket place dating from 1625 with a very good restaurant and there's even a tiny chapel for weddings. Rooms cost from £45 to £85 per person.

Most places to eat are on the Main St; you'll find a *Co-op* foodstore and lots of places doing meals and snacks for under £5. The best fish and chip shop is the *Tasty Fry* (*6 Main St*), opposite the post office at the west end of town. A little farther west, the

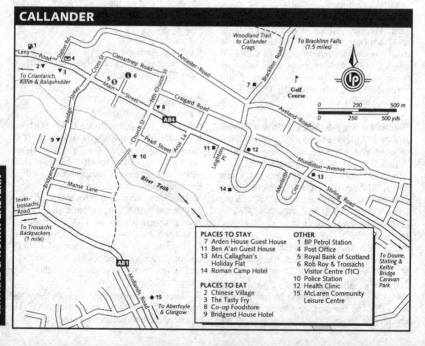

CALLANDER

PLACES TO STAY
7 Arden House Guest House
11 Ben A'an Guest House
13 Mrs Callaghan's Holiday Flat
14 Roman Camp Hotel

PLACES TO EAT
2 Chinese Village
3 The Tasty Fry
8 Co-op Foodstore
9 Bridgend House Hotel

OTHER
1 BP Petrol Station
4 Post Office
5 Royal Bank of Scotland
6 Rob Roy & Trossachs Visitor Centre (TIC)
10 Police Station
12 Health Clinic
15 McLaren Community Leisure Centre

Chinese Village Restaurant & Takeaway (☎ *331221, 10 Leny Rd*) does good take-aways from £4.50. Good bar meals are available from £4.50 at the mock-Tudor **Bridgend House Hotel** (☎ *330130)*, just across the river and by the A81 Aberfoyle road.

Entertainment In summer, on Monday, Wednesday and Friday evenings, the TIC (☎ 330342) organises Scottish evenings, with fiddlers, ceilidhs etc. Ticket prices vary from around £2.50 to £5, and concessions are available.

Getting There & Away Midland Bluebird (☎ 01324-613777) operates buses from Stirling (45 minutes, £2.90) and, on schooldays, Killin (£3.40). There's also a once daily Scottish Citylink bus (☎ 0990-505050) from Callander to Edinburgh (£7) and Fort William (£10) via Crianlarich, with connections to Oban and Skye.

Royal Mail runs a postbus (☎ 01463-256200) from Callander to Trossachs Pier. It departs daily except Sunday at 9.15 am, and connects with the 11 am weekday sailing of the SS *Sir Walter Scott* on Loch Katrine (see the upcoming Loch Katrine section). On weekday afternoons, the postbus runs from Callander to Aberfoyle (one hour) and returns via Port of Menteith.

The Trossachs Trundler calls at Callander and reaches the pier on Loch Katrine 35 minutes later.

Loch Katrine & Loch Achray

This rugged area, 6 miles north of Aberfoyle and 10 miles west of Callander, is the heart of the Trossachs. From April to September, the SS *Sir Walter Scott* sails along Loch Katrine from Trossachs Pier at the eastern tip of the loch. For bookings, phone ☎ 01877-376316; tickets are £4.95/3.25.

Walks There are two good walks starting from Loch Achray. The path to the rocky cone called Ben A'an (460m, 1509 feet) begins at a car park near the old Trossachs Hotel (now a timeshare development). It's

easy to follow but you'll take over an hour to get to the top.

On the other side of the Trossachs lies rugged Ben Venue (727m, 2385 feet); there's a path all the way to the summit. Start walking from Loch Achray Hotel, follow the Achray Water westwards to Loch Katrine, then turn left and ascend the steep flanks of Ben Venue. There are great views of both Highlands and Lowlands from the top. Allow four to five hours for the round trip.

BALQUHIDDER & BREADALBANE

This mountainous and sparsely populated area in the northern part of the Stirling administrative region has only a few villages but it's steeped in clan history and there are lots of good hillwalks.

Balquhidder

Things to See & Do In this small village (pronounced balwhidder), 2 miles off the main A84 Callander to Crianlarich road, there's a churchyard with **Rob Roy's grave**. His wife and two of his sons are also interred here. In the church, there's the 8th century **St Angus' stone** and a 17th century church bell. In nearby Stronvar House, the **Bygones Museum and Balquhidder Visitor Centre** (☎ 01877-384688) has various collections and includes the Clan Ferguson Centre. It's open daily from March to October, from 10.30 am to 5 pm.

The minor road continues along pretty Loch Voil to Inverlochlarig, where you can climb **Stob Binnein** (1165m, 3821 feet) by its south ridge. Stob Binnein is one of the highest mountains in the area, and it has a most unusual shape, like a cone with its top chopped off.

Places to Stay & Eat At the junction with the A84, the **Kings House Hotel** (☎ 01877-384646) was built in 1779 for £40, at the request of the drovers. Nowadays, B&B costs £29/48 in more salubrious surroundings. Bar meals start at £2.95 and there's a good vegetarian choice. About a mile north on the A84 and located at the old Balquhidder train station, the **Golden Larches** (☎ 01567-830262) is a pleasant restaurant with a cheery atmosphere. Situated nearby is the **Balquhidder Braes Caravan Park** (☎ 830293) which charges from £4 per tent.

Getting There & Away Midland Bluebird (☎ 01324-613777) runs buses between Callander and Killin (schooldays only) which stop at the Kings House Hotel. On Saturday, there's a postbus (☎ 01463-256200) which operates from Tyndrum, Crianlarich and Killin to Callander (and back again); it also stops at the Kings House Hotel. The once daily Scottish Citylink bus (☎ 0990-505050) from Edinburgh to Fort William also stops here.

Crianlarich & Tyndrum
* ☎ 01838

These villages are little more than service junctions on the main A82 road, although they're both in good hiking country and on the West Highland Way. At Crianlarich, there's a train station; tiny Tyndrum, just 5 miles along the road, is blessed with two stations and a useful TIC (☎ 400246) in the car park of the Invervey Hotel.

Tyndrum has attracted attention in recent years after the discovery of gold-bearing rock in the hills. Commercial exploitation is currently on a fairly low-key basis.

Walks The West Highland Way can be walked at any time of year.

In summer, hillwalkers can climb the popular An Caisteal (995m, 3264 feet). Start at the layby near Keilator farm, 1½ miles south of Crianlarich on the A82; a boggy path leads through a tunnel under the railway to a footbridge over the River Falloch. Follow the track towards Coire Earb for about 10 minutes, then head uphill on your right (no path). After 1½ hours, you'll gain the north ridge (Sròn Gharbh), which gives an easy and pleasant route to the top. Return the same way, or easily via Stob Glas and Derrydarroch farm. Allow around five hours return and carry OS map

50, a compass, and all appropriate high-level walking gear, food and drink.

Another popular climb is to the top of Ben More (1174m, 3851 feet). This unrelenting ascent starts at Benmore Farm, 2 miles east of Crianlarich on the A85. A track zig-zags up the first 150m, then you should head directly up the north-west shoulder. There are wonderful views from the summit. I've had some interesting days up here, including a near miss from lightning in August 1996! You'll need OS map 51. Six hours should see you up and down (return the same way).

The best walk in the Tyndrum area is to the top of magnificent Ben Lui (1130m, 3706 feet). If you're fit, you can include Beinn Dubhchraig (978m, 3208 feet) and Ben Oss (1029m, 3375 feet). Use OS map 50 to plan your route.

Start from Tyndrum Lower station, follow the track to Cononish farm, then keep to the riverbank as far as Coire Laoigh, between Ben Lui and Ben Oss. The south-east ridge is straightforward all the way to the top. Descend the same way, and allow seven hours (for Ben Lui alone). There are several other routes on the mountain, including the excellent north-east ridge, which should be climbed in hard winter conditions with ice-axe and crampons.

Places to Stay & Eat Near Crianlarich Station, on Station Rd, is **Crianlarich Youth Hostel** (☎ 300260), open all year except most of January. Beds cost £7.75/6.50. B&Bs in the village tend to be a bit expensive; one of the cheapest is **Craigbank Guest House** (☎ 300279), with doubles for £16 to £18 per person. The **Mace** supermarket also has the village's post office.

The **Rod & Reel** (☎ 300271), Crianlarich, serves snacks, baked potatoes (£3.40), and bar meals from £4.20 to £9.50. It has a cheaper takeaway service with fish and chips for £2.80 and burgers for £1.80. Packed lunches for hungry walkers cost £2.20. A little farther east on the Glen Dochart road (A85), the **Ben More Lodge Hotel** (☎ 300210) does B&B for £39/58.

Snacks and sandwiches start from £1.95, bar meals start at £4.50, and a full-blown three-course table d'hôte dinner is £15.

Three miles from Crianlarich (and 2 miles from Tyndrum), *Auchtertyre Farm* (☎ *400251)* has four five-bed heated wigwams for £8 per person. Camping with access to all facilities is only £3 per person.

The *Pine Trees Leisure Park* (☎ *400243)*, Tyndrum, has camping for £3 per person, and a bunkhouse for £8.50. Swimming in the pool costs £2 per hour. Breakfast is available at the attached *West Highlander Restaurant* (☎ *400314)*, from £2.45. The food here is rather good; soup and a roll is £1.85, and main courses sell for £3.95 to £8.95. The *Little Chef* is notable for its slow service and standard food and prices. Self-caterers can stock-up at *Brodie's*, the village grocer's and post office.

Getting There & Away Scottish Citylink (☎ 0990-505050) runs several buses daily to Glasgow, Oban, Fort William and Skye, from both villages.

A postbus service (☎ 01463-256200) links Crianlarich, Tyndrum and Killin twice on each weekday, once on Saturday, and not at all on Sunday. On Saturday, the postbus makes a return trip to Callander (1½ hours).

ScotRail (☎ 0345-484950) runs train services from both villages to Fort William, Oban and Glasgow. Journey times and fares from Crianlarich are 1¾ hours (£12.20), one hour (£7.20), and 1¾ hours (£11.10), respectively.

Killin
- pop 580   ☎ 01567

In the north-eastern corner of the region, just west of Loch Tay, Killin is a pleasant village to use as a base for exploring the hills and glens of the surrounding area.

Information The TIC (☎ 820254) is in the Breadalbane Folklore Centre (see Things to See), by the River Dochart. It's open March to October until 5 pm (June to September, until 6 pm).

Killin hosts an annual Highland Games

(entry £3), usually in early August. There's also a folk festival, in mid-June, with free session bands in pubs. Phone ☎ 820224 for details of these events.

The Outdoor Centre (☎ 820652), Main St, is a shop which sells and hires all sorts of equipment, including ice-axes and crampons (£3.50 each, per day), canoes (£22 per day), and mountain bikes (£13/9 per day/half day).

The village has a post office and a Bank of Scotland ATM.

Things to See Killin is a popular destination for tourists who come to see the pretty **Falls of Dochart**, in the centre of the village. The **Clan MacNab burial ground** lies on an island in the river, crossed by the main road and just downstream from the falls; ask the TIC for the gate key. The **Breadalbane Folklore Centre** is in an old mill overlooking the falls. St Fillan, a 7th century missionary, preached on this site and his sacred healing stones are kept in the centre. There are also displays about local and clan history, including the MacGregors and MacNabs. Opening hours are as for the TIC (see the information section); admission costs £1.50/1.

Nearly half a mile along the main street from the falls, by the Killin Hotel, there's an unusual-looking **church** dating from 1744. Inside, there's a remarkable seven-sided font which is over 2000 years old.

One mile from Killin on the Glen Lochay road, **Moirlanich Longhouse** (☎ 820988) is an excellent example of a mid-19th century byre. After restoration by the NTS, it's now open to the public from May to September, Wednesday and Sunday, 2 to 5 pm. Admission costs £1.50/1.

Walks & Cycle Routes Killin is at the northern end of the cycle way from Glasgow (see Getting Around at the start of the Stirling section).

Seven miles north-east of Killin, Ben Lawers (1214m, 3982 feet) rises above Loch Tay. There's an NTS Visitors' Centre

CENTRAL & NORTH-EASTERN

here and trails lead to the summit (see West Perthshire in the Perth & Kinross section).

Glen Lochay runs westwards from Killin into the hills of Mamlorn. You can take a mountain bike for about 11 miles up the glen, to just beyond Batavaime. The scenery is impressive and the hills aren't too difficult to climb. It's possible, on a nice summer day, to backpack over the top of Ben Challum (1025m, 3362 feet) and descend to Crianlarich, but it's very hard work. The passes on either side of this hill provide low-level alternatives. You'll need OS maps 50 and 51, and allow two days from Killin to Crianlarich (wild camping is possible in upper Glen Lochay from 20 October to 12 August, if you're discreet).

Places to Stay & Eat The *Shieling Accommodation (☎ 820334, Aberfeldy Rd)* has a pleasant woodland location outside the village; camping costs £6 to £7. It also has luxurious wooden chalets from £150 per week. At the northern end of the village, *Killin Youth Hostel (☎ 820546)*, open from March to October, charges £6.10/4.95.

There are numerous B&Bs and hotels. At the *Falls O'Dochart Cottage (☎ 820363)*, in the middle of the village, there's B&B for £15 per person; dinner is £8. *Fairview House (☎ 820667, Main St)* does B&B for £16 per person (without bath), or £18 (with bath).

The *Coach House (☎ 820349)* has rooms from £26 to £32 per person. It serves great pub food from £4.50, including salmon, duck and venison. Scottish folk bands play here on Friday nights in summer; there's also a 'Folk Club' (free admission) every second Sunday, from 4 pm. The *Clachaig Hotel (☎ 820270)* overlooks the falls; most rooms have attached bath and cost around £21 per person. It's also a good place for a meal or a drink, with bar meals all day from £3.95 to £5.75 and à la carte (evenings only) from £8.95.

You'll find cheaper places to eat along the Main St, including *Costcutter* and *Co-op* supermarkets. The *Tarmachan Teashop* does snacks, sandwiches and salads from

£1.50 to £4.25. In the car park at the village hall, there's a van selling chicken and chips, burgers etc.

Getting There & Away Midland Bluebird (☎ 01324-613777) operates a service on school days only from Stirling (1¼ hours, £4.75) via Callander.

There's a postbus (☎ 01463-256200) between Killin and Callander, once daily except Sunday (one hour). This bus also runs to Crianlarich and Tyndrum, twice on weekdays and once on Saturday. A postbus runs along the pretty south Loch Tay road, as far as Ardtalnaig, then back to Killin (once daily except Sunday). There's no bus from Pitlochry to Killin, but there's a daily (except Sunday) postbus service between Aberfeldy and Killin (three hours to Killin, 1¾ hours to Aberfeldy).

Fife

This region between the Firths of Forth and Tay refers to itself as the Kingdom of Fife – it was home to Scottish kings for 500 years. Despite its integration with the rest of Scotland, it has managed to maintain an individual Lowland identity quite separate from the rest of the country. As they still say outside the region, 'It takes a long spoon to sup with a Fifer'.

To the west, the Lomond Hills rise to over 500m; the eastern section is much flatter. Apart from a few notable exceptions inland, including Falkland Palace, most attractions in Fife are around the coast. As far as visitors are concerned, the focus of the region is undoubtedly St Andrews – an ancient university town and ecclesiastical centre that's also world famous as the home of golf. To the south, along the coastline of the East Neuk, are picturesque fishing villages. This coast is pleasant walking country, and at Anstruther there's the interesting Scottish Fisheries Museum.

GETTING AROUND

If you're driving from the Forth Road Bridge to St Andrews, a slower but much more scenic route than the M90/A91 is along the signposted Fife Tourist Route, via the coast.

For information about buses in the region, phone Fife Council on ☎ 01592-474238. The council produces a useful map-guide, *Getting Around Fife*, available from TICs, or phone the council on ☎ 01592-414141 ext 3103. Fife Scottish (☎ 01334-474238), part of the Stagecoach group, is the main bus operator.

Trains are less useful in Fife than in some regions, as the rails no longer run as far as St Andrews; the nearest station is at Leuchars, 5 miles from the town. For rail information, phone ☎ 0345-484950.

WEST FIFE
Culross
• pop 460   ☎ 01383

Around the 17th century, Culross (pronounced cooross) was a busy little community, trading in salt and coal. Now it's the best preserved example of a Scottish burgh, and the National Trust for Scotland owns 20 of the buildings, including the palace, which it bought in 1932. It's a picturesque village with small red-tiled, whitewashed buildings lining the cobbled streets.

Culross has a long history. As the birthplace of St Mungo, the patron saint of Glasgow, it was an important religious centre from the 6th century. The burgh developed as a trading centre under the businesslike laird George Bruce (a descendant of Robert the Bruce), whose mining techniques involved digging long tunnels under the sea to reach coal. A vigorous sea trade developed between Culross and the Forth ports and Holland. From the proceeds, Bruce built the palace, completed in 1611. When a storm flooded the tunnels and mining became impossible, the town switched to making linen and shoes.

The NTS Visitors Centre (☎ 880359), in the lower part of the Town House, has an exhibition on the history of Culross. You can visit **Culross Palace**, more a large house than a palace, which features extraordinary decorative, painted woodwork, barrel-vaulted

ceilings, and an interior largely unchanged since the early 17th century. The **Town House** and the **Study**, also early 17th century, are open to the public, but the other NTS properties can only be viewed from the outside. Ruined **Culross Abbey**, founded by the Cistercians in 1217, is on the hill; the choir of the abbey church is now the parish church. The pulpit is 17th century and originally had two levels. In the north-east corner of the north transept there's an unusual sight – statues of eight children kneeling in front of their parents' memorial.

Culross is 12 miles west of the Forth Road Bridge, off the A985. The palace is open from April to September, from 11 am to 5 pm with last admission at 4 pm (the Town House and Study are open from 1.30 to 5 pm, and October weekends from 11 am to 5 pm); admission costs £4.20/2.80.

The NTS tearoom is recommended as a good place for soup and a snack. You can get B&B at the 17th century *St Mungo's Cottage (☎ 882102, Low Causeway)* for £30 double (without shower) or £40 double (with shower).

Fife Scottish (☎ 621249) bus Nos 14 and 14A run hourly, daily, between Glasgow, Stirling, Culross and Dunfermline.

Dunfermline
• pop 52,000   ☎ 01383

Six Scottish kings, including Robert the Bruce, are buried at Dunfermline Abbey. Once the country's capital, Dunfermline is now a large regional centre surrounded by suburbs that are not particularly attractive, but the abbey's worth a visit and the pedestrianised High St is fairly pleasant.

Information The TIC (☎ 720999), 13 Maygate, close to High St and the abbey, opens Easter to October. There's also an all-year TIC (☎ 417759) about 5 miles from Dunfermline, in the Queensferry Lodge Hotel at the north end of the Forth Road Bridge.

The post office is in Pilmuir St, and the bus station is nearby. You'll find banks with ATMs in High St.

Things to See Queen Margaret founded a Benedictine priory on the hill here in the 11th century, and later her son King David I built **Dunfermline Abbey** on the site. After Margaret's canonisation in 1250, the abbey grew into a major pilgrimage centre, eclipsing the island of Iona (off Mull) as the favourite royal burial ground. Most of the abbey, having fallen into ruins, has now been absorbed into the parish church, but the wonderful Norman nave, with its ornate columns, remains. Robert the Bruce is buried in the choir. Next to the abbey are the ruins of **Dunfermline Palace**, rebuilt from the abbey guesthouse in the 16th century for James VI. It was the birthplace of Charles I, the last Scottish king born on Scottish soil. Both buildings (☎ 739026) are open daily (closed Thursday afternoon and Friday in winter), standard HS hours. The amission charge is £1.80/1.30, and the buildings are within walking distance of the train and bus stations.

The award-winning **Abbot House Heritage Centre** (☎ 733266), Maygate, also next to the abbey, dates from the 15th century. Now restored, it has interesting displays about the history of Scotland, the abbey, and Dunfermline. There's also a coffee shop serving excellent home baking and snacks. The centre opens all year, daily, from 10 am to 5 pm; admission is £3/2.

St Margaret's Cave, not far from the abbey and 80 steps down from the Bruce St car park, was used by Queen Margaret for prayer and meditation. It later became a shrine in her memory. It's open from Easter to September, from 11 am to 4 pm; admission is free.

Another famous former inhabitant of Dunfermline was Andrew Carnegie, who was born in a weaver's cottage in 1835, now a museum. He emigrated to America in 1848 and by the late 19th century had accumulated enormous wealth, $350 million of which he gave away. Dunfermline benefited by his purchase of Pittencrieff Park, beside the palace. The **Andrew Carnegie Museum** (☎ 724302), Moodie St, opens daily from April to October, from 11 am to

5 pm (afternoon only on Sunday), June to August from 10 am, and 2 to 4 pm in winter; entry costs £1.50/75p for adults, and children are free.

Places to Stay & Eat Right in the centre of town, *Pilmuir St Guest House* (☎ 725809, 80 Pilmuir St), does B&B from only £14 per person; you'll pay £20 per person for attached bath. Evening meals are available, from £5. The *Davaar House Hotel* (☎ 736463, 126 Grieve St) charges £48/65 for *en suite* single/double rooms. The restaurant (closed Sunday) is recommended; a three-course meal is around £14.

There's a *Safeway* supermarket and a *Bakers Oven* in the central Kingsgate shopping centre. The *snack bar* in the bus station has baked potatoes from £1.10 and toasties from £1.20. Nearby, on Carnegie Drive, there are several restaurants, a café, a fish and chip shop, and a nightclub. The nicest place is *Café Rene* which does two-course lunches and coffee for £5.95.

Spectator Sport Four miles north of the town centre, just off the A823, the **Knockhill Racing Circuit** (☎ 723337) stages major car and motorcycle racing events between April and December, usually on Sunday. Admission prices are in the range £4/2 to £20/10.

Getting There & Away Dunfermline is a major transport hub, with frequent buses to Stirling (£4.70), Edinburgh (30 minutes, £2.45), Dundee (1½ hours, £4.85), and Kirkcaldy (30 minutes, £2.20). Scottish Citylink (☎ 0990-505050) runs hourly buses to Edinburgh (£3) and Perth (£3.80). For Dunfermline bus station, phone ☎ 621249. The town's a half-hour train ride from Edinburgh (£3), and there's one direct train an hour.

SOUTH COAST
Aberdour
• pop 1800   ☎ 01383
It's worth stopping in this popular seaside town to see **Aberdour Castle** (☎ 860519). It

was built by the Douglas family in 1342 and the original tower was extended by the Morton family in the 16th and 17th centuries. They abandoned the castle in 1725 after it was gutted by fire, but the east wing was rebuilt and is still in use. An impressive feature of the castle is its attractive walled garden, where there's a fine beehive-shaped 16th century dovecot (pronounced doocot in Scotland). **St Fillan's Church**, by the castle, was founded in 1123 but the current building is mostly 17th century (restored in 1920). The castle opens standard HS hours (but it's closed on Thursday afternoon and on Friday in winter); admission costs £1.80/1.30 (children 75p).

The best place to eat in Aberdour is the **Aberdour Hotel** (☎ 860325, High St) where main courses, with a good vegetarian selection, start at £4.45, and real ales are served. Single/double B&B costs £41.50/58; all rooms have attached bath. Down at the lovely Silversands beach, the **Beach House Restaurant** (☎ 860882) serves two-course lunches and coffee for £4.95.

The stationmaster at the award-winning train station was given an honour himself – an OBE. Hopefully the trains are on time; there are hourly departures for Kirkcaldy (£2.50) and Edinburgh (£3.20).

Bus No 57 runs approximately every two hours to Edinburgh (£2.60), daily; there are two No 7 buses each hour to Dunfermline (£1.85).

Burntisland & Kinghorn
• **pop 8940 (combined)**   ☎ 01592

The Royal Burgh of Burntisland was captured by Cromwell in 1651. By the early 20th century, it was over-run with holidaymakers. Today it's a dreary run-down place, though Kinghorn is a bit better. Just south of Kinghorn, near Pettycur, there's a monument which commemorates where King Alexander III fell to his death in 1286, precipitating the contest for the throne, English invasion, and the Wars of Independence.

Both towns have the usual selection of takeaway outlets. About halfway between them, the **Kingswood Hotel** (☎ 872329,

Kinghorn Rd), Burntisland, has an excellent restaurant with bar meals from £4.95 to £15. The three-course table d'hôte dinners cost £20.

Trains run hourly to Kirkcaldy and Edinburgh from either town. Buses run three times an hour to Kirkcaldy (hourly on Sunday); the fare from Kinghorn is 85p.

Kirkcaldy
• **pop 49,570**   ☎ 01592

Another town worth stopping in if you're passing through, Kirkcaldy (pronounced kir-koddy) sprawls along the edge of the sea for several miles. The political economist, Adam Smith, was born here and, in the second half of the 19th century, Kirkcaldy was the world's largest manufacturer of linoleum. It has an attractive promenade with spectacular pounding surf on windy days, and an interesting museum and art gallery.

The TIC (☎ 267775), just off High St at 19 Whytecauseway, opens year-round. The pedestrianised part of High St has the Mercat Cross Shopping Centre and banks with ATMs.

Things to See Just a short walk from the train and bus stations, in the War Memorial Gardens, you'll find the **Kirkcaldy Museum and Art Gallery** (☎ 412860). As well as covering the town's history, there's an impressive collection of Scottish paintings from the 18th to 20th centuries and temporary exhibitions on a wide range of topics. It's open all year, daily, from 10.30 am to 5 pm (afternoon only on Sunday); entry is free.

After looking round the museum, you could walk along the Esplanade to Ravenscraig Park, where ruinous **Ravenscraig Castle**, built in 1460 and one of the earliest castles to be defended by artillery, stands on a plinth of coloured sandstone. Two miles north of Kirkcaldy, in Dysart, is the **McDouall Stuart Museum** (☎ 260732), Rectory Lane, the birthplace of the engineer and explorer who, in 1862, became the first person to cross Australia from the south coast to the north. It's open from June to August, from 2 to 5 pm; entry is free. Bus Nos K7 and K8 from Kirkcaldy centre pass this way twice every hour.

Places to Stay & Eat *Invertiel House* (☎ 264849, 21 Pratt St) is just south of the centre, by Beveridge Park. It's a comfortable place with B&B from £17 per person. Just uphill from the harbour, *Mrs Brown's* (☎ 264656, 32 Glebe Park) charges around £15 per person.

There are lots of places to eat in the High St, including the usual local bakers and Chinese and Indian takeaways. *LA Valente*, at the southern end, does good fish suppers for £2.60 and baked potatoes from £1.40. The *Wheatsheaf Inn* (☎ 263564, 5 Tolbooth St), just off High St, does bar lunches from £2.75 to £3.95. It's a pleasant place and it's the second oldest building in town.

Getting There & Away A major transport hub, numerous buses run from Hill St bus station (☎ 642394), two blocks inland from the Esplanade. Journey times and fares are: St Andrews (one hour, £3.30), Anstruther (70 minutes, £3.60), Dunfermline (30 minutes, £2.20) and Edinburgh (one hour, £3.20).

Kirkcaldy is on the main Edinburgh to Dundee and Aberdeen rail line. There are two to four trains an hour to Edinburgh (shortest journey time 30 minutes, £4.50).

CENTRAL FIFE
Falkland
• pop 1120   ☎ 01337

Below the soft ridges of the Lomond Hills in the centre of Fife is the Royal Burgh of Falkland, an attractive conservation village surrounded by rich farmland. It's a very pleasant place to stay and it's known for the superb 16th century **Falkland Palace**, a country residence of the Stuart monarchs.

Mary Queen of Scots is said to have spent the happiest days of her life 'playing the country girl in the woods and parks' at Falkland. Built between 1501 and 1541 to replace a castle dating from the 12th century, French and Scottish craftspeople were employed to create a masterpiece of Scottish Gothic architecture. The king's bedchamber and the chapel, which has a beautiful painted ceiling, have both been restored; you can also look around the gardens and the keeper's apartments in the gatehouse.

The wild boar that the royals hunted, and the Fife forest that was their hunting ground, have now disappeared. One feature of this royal leisure centre still exists: the oldest royal tennis court in Britain, built in 1539 for James V, is in the grounds and is still in use. Although the palace belongs to the current Queen, it's administered by the NTS.

Falkland Palace (☎ 857397) opens April to October, Monday to Saturday from 11 am to 5.30 pm, and on Sunday from 1.30 to 5.30 pm, with last admission at 4.30 pm. Entry costs £4.80/3.20.

Walks A narrow road runs from Falkland to Leslie over the pass between East and West Lomond. It takes about one hour to walk from Falkland to the pass, then a further 45 minutes or so on a good path to the 522m (1712 feet) summit of West Lomond. You can also include East Lomond (420m, 1378 feet) in your route; the 2000-year-old hill fort at the top is now reduced to a series of ramparts. The views from the tops are wonderful on a clear day.

Places to Stay & Eat *Falkland Youth Hostel* (☎ 857710, Back Wynd) opens from mid-March to early October and beds are £4.65/3.85. Opposite the palace, there's B&B at *Ladieburn Cottage* (☎ 857016, High St) with two en suite rooms costing from £20/36 to £25/40 for single/double occupancy. Evening meals are £7.

The *Covenanter Hotel* (☎ 857224) is also opposite the palace; rooms are £39/48, all with attached bath. It serves bistro and restaurant meals.

An excellent place for soup and home baking is the quaint 17th century cottage *Kind Kyttock's Kitchen* (☎ 857477, Cross Wynd), open daily except Monday.

Getting There & Away Falkland is 11 miles north of Kirkcaldy. There are three buses daily (except Sunday) to Kinross, and buses roughly every two hours (daily) from Perth (£2.75), Kirkcaldy (£2.05) and Cupar. The nearest train station is 5 miles away, at Markinch on the Edinburgh to Dundee line, with an hourly service.

Cupar & Around
* pop 7610   ☎ 01334

Cupar is a pleasant market town and the capital of the region. There are banks with ATMs in St Catherine's St. Places of interest to tourists are at Ceres, a pretty village 3 miles south-east of Cupar, with pantiled roofs, a Georgian church, and the shortest High St in Scotland.

Things to See The **Hill of Tarvit Mansionhouse**, 2½ miles south of Cupar and a mile from Ceres, was rebuilt for Frederick Sharp in 1906 by Scottish architect Sir Robert Lorimer. Sharp was a wealthy Dundee jute manufacturer who bought the house as a showcase for his valuable collection of furniture, Dutch paintings, Flemish tapestries and Chinese porcelain. There's also an on-site tearoom. A 15 minute walk takes you to the top of the Hill of Tarvit, which has an excellent panoramic view. An NTS property, the house and garden (☎ 653127) opens daily from May to September and October weekends, from 1.30 to 5.30 pm (last admission at 4.45 pm). Entry is £3.70/2.50.

In Ceres' High St, you'll find the **Fife Folk Museum**, in the historic 17th century weigh-house and other buildings. There's a wide-ranging collection of folk history exhibits, agricultural tools and a heritage trail. It's open at Easter and from mid-May to October, Saturday to Thursday, 2 to 5 pm. Admission costs £2/1.50.

Places to Stay & Eat *Mrs Gardner* (☎ 656378, 20 Drumryan Place), Cupar, charges £16 per person for B&B.

In Cupar town centre, you'll find two supermarkets, two bakeries, fish and chip shops, and the obligatory Asian restaurants and takeaways. *McPhail's Tearoom & Gallery*, Bonnygate, serves soup, snacks and meals from £1.55 to £4.50. *Ostler's Close Restaurant* (☎ 655574), in a lane called Temperance Close (off Bonnygate), is a trifle expensive with three-course lunches around £18. There are various bars (some may be best avoided), including the *Drookit Dug* (translation: the soaking wet dog).

The *Ceres Inn* (☎ 828305, The Cross) serves bar meals and Sunday high teas. There's also the option of a *Chinese takeaway (3 Main St)*.

Getting There & Away Cupar is a busy transport centre with direct bus services to St Andrews (20 minutes, £1.70), Dundee and Edinburgh.

The Kirkcaldy to Dundee bus passes through Ceres and Cupar roughly every two hours, but almost hourly on Saturday and only twice on Sunday. Service 64 runs from Cupar to St Andrews via Ceres, every two hours (not Sunday). There's also a daily (except Sunday) postbus (☎ 01463-256200) linking Cupar, Ceres and Peat Inn.

Cupar is on the rail line between Edinburgh and Dundee; there's roughly one train an hour in each direction (one train every two hours on Sunday).

ST ANDREWS
* pop 13,900   ☎ 01334

St Andrews is a beautiful, unusual seaside town – a concoction of medieval ruins, obsessive golfers, windy coastal scenery, tourist glitz and a schizophrenic university which sees wealthy English undergraduates rubbing shoulders with Scottish theology students.

Although St Andrews was once the ecclesiastical capital of Scotland, both its cathedral and castle are now in ruins.

For most people, the town is the home of golf and a mecca for the sport's aficionados. It's the headquarters of the game's governing body, the Royal and Ancient Golf Club, and the location of the world's most famous golf course, the Old Course.

CENTRAL & NORTH-EASTERN

History

St Andrews is said to have been founded by the Greek monk, St Regulus, in the 4th century. He brought important relics from Greece, including some of the bones of St Andrew, who became Scotland's patron saint.

The town soon grew into a major pilgrimage centre for the shrine of the saint. The Augustinian Church of St Rule was built in 1127 (only the tower remains); the adjacent cathedral was built in 1160. St Andrews developed into the ecclesiastical capital of the country and, around 1200, the castle was constructed (part fortress, part residence) for the bishop.

The university was founded in 1410, the first in Scotland. James I received part of his education here, as did James III. By the mid-16th century there were three colleges: St Salvator's, St Leonard's and St Mary's.

Although golf was being played here by the 15th century, the Old Course dates from the following century. The Royal and Ancient Golf Club was founded in 1754, and the imposing clubhouse was built a hundred years later. The British Open Championship, which was first held in 1860 in Prestwick on the west coast near Glasgow, has taken place regularly at St Andrews since 1873.

Orientation

St Andrews preserves its medieval plan of parallel streets with small closes leading off them. The most important parts of the old town, lying to the east of the bus station, are easily explored on foot. The main streets for shops are Market and South Sts, running east-west. Like Cambridge and Oxford, St Andrews has no campus – most university buildings are integrated into the central part of the town. There's a small harbour near the cathedral, and two sandy beaches: East Sands extends south from the harbour and the wider West Sands is north of the town.

Information

The TIC (☎ 472021), 70 Market St, opens all year. From early May to mid-October,

it's open Monday to Saturday, from 9.30 am to 6 pm (closing at 8 pm in July and August), and on Sunday from 11 am to 4 pm (closing at 6 pm from June to August). The rest of the year it's open daily, except Sunday, from 9 am to 5 pm. It makes bookings for the theatre and the Edinburgh Tattoo, and sells NTS passes.

You'll find the four main banks (with ATMs) near the Holy Trinity Church, South St. Shops have half-day closing on Thursday, but in summer many stay open. Parking requires a voucher, which is on sale in many shops.

The St Andrews Memorial Hospital (☎ 472327) is on Abbey Walk, south of Abbey St.

Walking Tour

The best place to start a walking tour is St Andrews Museum (☎ 477706), in Kinburn Park on Doubledykes Rd, near the bus station. Displays chart the history of the town from its founding by St Regulus through its growth as an ecclesiastical, academic and sporting centre. Much more interesting than some local history museums, it's open April to September, daily from 10 am to 5 pm, and for the rest of the year for shorter hours; there's no entry charge.

Turn left out of the museum driveway and follow Doubledykes Rd back to the roundabout on City Rd. Turn right, then left into South St. You pass through West Port, formerly Southgait Port, the main entrance to the old city. It was built in 1589 and based on Netherbow Port in Edinburgh. Walking down South St, you pass Louden's Close on the right, a good example of the closes built according to the city's medieval street plan. Continuing along South St, the apse of the 16th century Blackfriars Chapel stands in front of Madras College.

Opposite the Victorian town hall is Holy Trinity, the town's parish church, built in 1410. On the same side of the street as the town hall is St Mary's College, founded in 1537; beside it is the university library. The oak tree in the courtyard is over 250 years old.

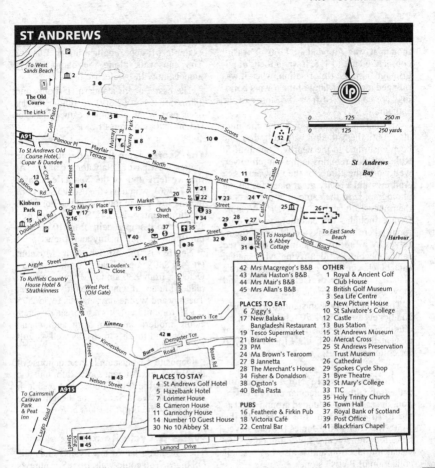

ST ANDREWS

To West
Sands Beach

The Old
Course

The Links

A91

To St Andrews Old
Course Hotel,
Cupar & Dundee

Station   Rd

Kinburn
Park

To Rufflets Country
House Hotel &
Strathkinness

St Andrews
Bay

St Andrews
Bay

0   125   250 m
0   125   250 yards

West Port
(Old Gate)

Louden's
Close

To Hospital
& Abbey
Cottage

To East Sands
Beach

Harbour

Kinness

Burn

Kinnessburn Road

Boase Rd

Nelson Street

A915

To Cairnsmill
Caravan
Park
& Peat
Inn

Laigh o Moray
Rd

King
Street

Lamond Drive

42 Mrs Macgregor's B&B
43 Maria Haston's B&B
44 Mrs Mair's B&B
45 Mrs Allan's B&B

PLACES TO EAT
6 Ziggy's
17 New Balaka
      Bangladeshi Restaurant
19 Tesco Supermarket
21 Brambles
23 PM
24 Ma Brown's Tearoom
27 B Jannetta
28 The Merchant's House
34 Fisher & Donaldson
38 Ogston's
40 Bella Pasta

PUBS
16 Featherie & Firkin Pub
18 Victoria Café
22 Central Bar

PLACES TO STAY
4 St Andrews Golf Hotel
5 Hazelbank Hotel
7 Lorimer House
8 Cameron House
11 Gannochy House
14 Number 10 Guest House
30 No 10 Abbey St

OTHER
1 Royal & Ancient Golf
     Club House
2 British Golf Museum
3 Sea Life Centre
9 New Picture House
10 St Salvator's College
12 Castle
13 Bus Station
15 St Andrews Museum
20 Mercat Cross
25 St Andrews Preservation
     Trust Museum
26 Cathedral
29 Spokes Cycle Shop
31 Byre Theatre
32 St Mary's College
33 TIC
35 Holy Trinity Church
36 Town Hall
37 Royal Bank of Scotland
39 Post Office
41 Blackfriars Chapel

Cross over to cobbled Market St, one street parallel to South St, via Church St. Street markets are held around the **Mercat Cross**, although the cross is now a fountain. The TIC is nearby, at No 70. Turn right out of the TIC and follow Market St down to the junction with South Castle St, turn left, and then right into North St. On the right is **St Andrews Preservation Trust Museum** (☎ 477629), an old merchant's house and a museum of local social and commercial history. Opening times are at Easter, June to

September, and 30 November, daily from 2 to 5 pm; admission is free. It's interesting to note that St Andrews did not retain its medieval character by accident. In the mid-19th century, the provost (mayor) Hugh Lyon Playfair implemented plans for sympathetic civic improvements making sure that they didn't involve the destruction of old buildings.

St Andrews Cathedral At the eastern end of North St is the ruined west end of what was once the largest and one of the most magnificent cathedrals in the country. Although it was founded in 1160, it wasn't consecrated until 1318. It was a focus of pilgrimage until the Reformation, when it was pillaged in 1559. Many of the town's buildings are constructed from the stones of the cathedral.

St Andrew's bones lay under the high altar; until the cathedral was built, they had been enshrined in the nearby Church of St Rule. All that remains is the church tower, well worth the climb for the view across St Andrews and a really great place for taking photographs. In the same area are parts of the ruined 13th century priory. The Visitors Centre includes the calefactory, the only room where the monks could warm themselves by a fire; masons' marks on the red sandstone blocks, identifying who shaped each block, can still be clearly seen. There's also a collection of Celtic crosses and gravestones found on the site.

The cathedral is open standard HS hours, and tickets are £3.50/2.70 (child £1.25), including entry to the castle. If you only want to visit the cathedral, it's £1.80/1.30 (75p for children).

St Andrews Castle Not far from the cathedral, with a spectacular cliff-top location, the castle was founded around 1200 as the fortified home of the bishop. In the 1450s the young king James II often stayed here. A visitors centre gives a good audiovisual introduction and it also has a small collection of Pictish stones.

In 1654, part of the castle was pulled down to provide building materials for rebuilding the harbour wall and pier. Enough survives to give you an idea of what each of the chambers was used for. After the execution of Protestant reformers in 1545, other reformers retaliated by murdering Cardinal Beaton and taking over the castle. The cardinal's body was hung from a window in the Fore Tower before being tossed into the bottle-shaped dungeon. The reformers then spent almost a year besieged in the castle; one of the most interesting things to see here is the complex of siege tunnels, said to be the best surviving example of siege engineering in Europe. You can walk along the damp, mossy tunnels, now lit by electric light.

The castle opens standard HS hours and admission costs £2.30/1.75 (children £1), or as part of the combined cathedral ticket (£3.50/2.70, children £1.25).

The Scores From the castle, follow The Scores west past St Salvator's College. At the western end is the **Sea Life Centre** (☎ 474786), which has the usual displays of marine life and an interesting sea-horse exhibition; entry is £4.25/3.75 (children £3.25) and it's open daily from 10 am to 6 pm (9 am to 7 pm in July and August).

Nearby is the **British Golf Museum** (☎ 478880), open daily from April to October, from 9.30 am to 5.30 pm, and with reduced hours in winter when it's closed on Tuesday and Wednesday; entry is £3.75/2.75 (£1.50 for children). It's a surprisingly interesting modern museum with audiovisual displays and touch screens, as well as golf memorabilia.

Opposite the museum is the clubhouse of the Royal and Ancient Golf Club. Outside the club is the Old Course, and beside it stretch the West Sands, the beach made famous by the film *Chariots of Fire*.

Walks & Cycle Routes

The TIC has a list of local walks and sells OS maps. You could walk from St Andrews to Crail along the coast, but it's about 15 miles and you'd have to take care not to get caught by the tide; this section of the Fife Coastal Path is yet to be opened. There are some excellent shorter walks along the southern part of the East Neuk coast (see the upcoming East Neuk section).

Since there are few steep hills in eastern Fife, cycling is pleasant and there are some good rides along quiet side roads. Kellie Castle and the Hill of Tarvit mansion are within easy cycling distance. The narrow and busy coast road from St Andrews to

Crail isn't advised for cycling due to dangerous bends and no verges in places.

Organised Tours

Guided walks of the town are run in summer (the University Tour, ☎ 462245) or all year (the Witches Tour, ☎ 655057).

The Witches Tour (£5/4) runs regularly on Thursday and Sunday at 8 pm (Sunday in winter, at 6.30 pm) and at other times by arrangement (minimum two people, but six required on Saturday). This 1¼ hour tour details the history and folklore of the town in an unusual fashion! There's also the Fishwives Tale, a 1½ hour tour from April to September on weekdays at 2.30 pm (£4.50/3). The Saints & Sinners evening tour (£6) covers the Reformation – phone (☎ 655057) for details.

Places to Stay

Camping & Halls of Residence Between April and October, you can camp at *Cairnsmill Caravan Park (☎ 473604, Largo Rd)* for £3.50 (one person) or £6.50 (two

people). It's about a mile from St Andrews on the A915.

There's no hostel or bunkhouse, but there's one 9 miles away near Anstruther (see the upcoming East Neuk section). Between June and September, however, you can stay for £10, room only but including sheets, at the university's *Gannochy House (☎ 464870, North St)*, next to Younger Hall. There are 40 single rooms but there's no kitchen. You must check in between 2 and 6 pm (telephone first at other times), and check out by 9.30 am.

B&Bs & Guesthouses The cheapest B&Bs in St Andrews are south of the centre, within five to 15 minutes walk. *Maria Haston's (☎ 473227, 8 Nelson St)* is one of the closest and excellent value at £12 to £13 per person. Closer to the centre, *Mrs Macgregor's (☎ 474282, 8 Dempster Terrace)* has just one room with three single beds for £16 per person.

Farther south, on King St, there's *Mrs Allan's (☎ 476326, 2 King St)* which has rooms from £15 to £18, and *Mrs Mair's*

Playing the Old Course

Golf has been played at St Andrews since the 15th century, and by 1457 was apparently so popular that James II had to place a ban on it because it was interfering with his troops' archery practice.

Everyone knows that St Andrews is the home of golf, but few people realise that anyone can play on the Old Course, the world's most famous golf course. Although it lies beside the exclusive, all-male Royal and Ancient Golf Club, the Old Course is a public course, and is not owned by the club.

However, getting a tee-off time is something of a lottery. Unless you book months in advance, the only chance you have of playing here is by entering a ballot before 2 pm on the day before you wish to play. Be warned that applications by ballot are normally heavily oversubscribed, and green fees are a mere £72. There's no play allowed on Sunday. You must present a handicap certificate or letter of introduction from your club to the St Andrews Links Trust (☎ 01334-466666; linkstrust@standrews.org.uk). If you want to make a booking yourself, write a year in advance (for summer and autumn reservations) to The Secretary, St Andrews Links Trust, Pilmour Cottage, St Andrews, Fife, KY16 9SF.

If your number doesn't come up, there are five other public courses in the area, none with quite the cachet of the Old Course, but all of them significantly cheaper. Fees are as follows: New £31, Jubilee £29, Eden £21, Strathtyrum £16 and Balgove £7.

(☎ 472709, 10 King St) from £18/32 single/ double; both are open year-round. You can check out nearby Largo Rd, which has lots of B&B signs in summer.

No 10 Abbey St (☎ 474094) is a bigger place with one single and two twin rooms. It's near the Byre Theatre and charges from £14 to £22.50 per person. The 18th century *Abbey Cottage* (☎ 473727, Abbey Walk), just south of Abbey St, has pet doves and hens. B&B here is £18 to £20 (double).

Almost every house on Murray Park and Murray Place is a B&B. The area couldn't be more convenient but prices are on the high side – most places charge around £22 per person. Rooms tend to have bathrooms attached. During summer, you need to book in advance, but at other times it's probably best to knock on a few doors and pick what you like. *Lorimer House* (☎ 476599, 19 Murray Park) opens year-round and charges from £18 to £28 per person. *Cameron House* (☎ 472306, 11 Murray Park) offers B&B from £19 to £26 in comfortable single or double rooms.

Number 10 Guest House (☎ 474601, 10 Hope St) is a good place to stay. There are 10 rooms, all with bathroom attached, from £22 to £28 per person.

Hotels Facing the bay, The Scores is lined with expensive hotels. *Hazelbank Hotel* (☎ 472466, 28 The Scores) has rooms from £25 to £85 per person. *St Andrews Golf Hotel* (☎ 472611, 40 The Scores) is an excellent upmarket hotel less than 200m from the Old Course. Prices start from £78/130 for a single/double, with cheaper two-night deals. The hotel has a bar and an excellent restaurant.

Just under 2 miles from the town centre, *Rufflets Country House Hotel* (☎ 472594, Strathkinness Low Rd) is a high-class hotel with a recommended restaurant. B&B and dinner ranges from £75 to £90 per person, depending on the season.

If money's really no object, stay at the *St Andrews Old Course Hotel* (☎ 474371), the imposing building by the golf course, at the western end of town. Rooms at this luxurious establishment range from £195/244 to £360. There are resident golf pros and a team of therapists and beauticians providing massage for both body and ego. If you're planning to drop in out of the sky, it's worth noting that you need prior permission to use the helipad.

Places to Eat

If you're on a very tight budget, *PM*, on the corner of Market and Union Sts, does breakfast, burgers and fish and chips from £1.85 to £3.10. For more upmarket snacks, head for *Fisher & Donaldson*, which sells Selkirk bannocks (rich fruit bread), cream cakes and a wonderful range of pastries. *Tesco (138 Market St)* is a good centrally located supermarket.

Ma Brown's Tearoom (24 North St) is the place to go for coffee, cream tea or a light lunch. One of the busiest places at lunchtime is *Brambles* (☎ 475380, 5 College St), which has excellent salads (£2 to £5.25) and a huge selection of vegetarian dishes. A three-course set dinner costs £17.95. The *Merchant's House* (☎ 472595, 49 South St) is in a venerable building. It serves delicious home-made soup (£1.50) and excellent home baking; it's open from 10 am to 5.30 pm.

Bella Pasta (☎ 476268, 39 Bell St) does reasonable Italian food for the standard prices. The *New Balaka Bangladeshi Restaurant* (☎ 474825, 3 Alexandra Place) is recommended for curries. A three-course meal here costs around £15.

Ziggy's (☎ 473686, 6 Murray Place) is popular with students. Hamburgers start at £3.95, and a range of steaks, Mexican dishes and seafood is priced from £7.45. *Ogston's* (☎ 473473, 116 South St) is a trendy café, bar and bistro. Its eclectic evening menu, available in the conservatory restaurant, has main courses from around £5 to £12.

Apart from the pricey restaurant at the *St Andrews Old Course Hotel* (see Places to Stay), you need a car to reach the best restaurants in the area. For the recommended *Peat Inn* (☎ 840206), go 5 miles along the A915 then turn right on the B940 for 1½ miles. It's open from Tuesday to Saturday for lunch and dinner and meals are prepared by David Wilson, one of Scotland's leading chefs. Four-course table d'hôte lunches are £18.50; set dinners, including excellent fresh seafood, cost £28 per person, excluding wine. There's another good restaurant at Anstruther (see the upcoming Anstruther section).

Finally, don't leave town without sampling one of the 52 varieties of ice cream or sorbet from *B Jannetta (31 South St)*. Don't confuse this main branch with the smaller shop at the other end of South St. This is a St Andrews institution. Most popular flavour? Vanilla. Weirdest? Irn Bru!

Entertainment

Check the local *What's On* guide, published weekly and available from the TIC.

The St Andrews Living History Programme presents free medieval plays on weekends in July and August. They're usually held in Church Square, at the cathedral or the castle. Contact the TIC for details.

In July and August, the Royal Scottish Country Dance Society holds dances and will show novices the steps. Contact the TIC for information. There are also other country dances in summer.

The *Byre Theatre (☎ 476288, Abbey St)* started life as a cow shed. Originally built in 1970, it's being completely rebuilt on the same site and should be open again by 2000. The quality of performances, both touring and local, is often high. Until the re-opening, the theatre company is performing in local halls – contact the TIC for details.

The two-screen *New Picture House (☎ 473509)* shows current films.

St Andrews has a good supply of pubs, representing its varied population. The *Central Bar (Market St)* is all polished brass and polished accents, full of rich students from south of the border. The *Featherie & Firkin (5 Alexandra Place)* has live music on Thursday and Friday; it also serves bar meals. The *Victoria Café (St*

Mary's Place) is popular with all types of students and serves Mexican food for around £4.25. There's a good bar at the *St Andrews Golf Hotel*.

Getting There & Away

St Andrews is 55 miles north of Edinburgh and 13 miles south of Dundee.

Bus Fife Scottish (☎ 474238) runs a half-hourly bus service from St Andrew's Square, Edinburgh, via Kirkcaldy, to St Andrews (two hours, £5; £3.40 for students). Buses to Dundee (30 minutes, £2) and Cupar (20 minutes, £1.70) also have a half-hourly frequency. Service No 23 to Stirling runs six times daily, except Sunday. Other destinations include Crail (30 minutes, £1.80) and Anstruther (40 minutes, £1.80).

Train The nearest station to St Andrews is Leuchars (one hour from Edinburgh, £6.80), 5 miles away, on the Edinburgh-Dundee-Aberdeen line. There are three direct trains to London daily. Bus Nos X59 and X60 leave Leuchars every half-hour (not Sunday) to St Andrews; bus No 95 departs hourly every day; and bus No 94 departs roughly every two hours (not Sunday).

Car Ian Cowe Coachworks (☎ 472543), 76 Argyle St, rents Fiat Puntos for £27 per day.

Getting Around

Taxi Try Golf City Taxis (☎ 477788) at 13 Argyle St. A taxi between Leuchars train station and the town centre costs around £7.

Bicycle You can rent bikes at Spokes (☎ 477835), 77 South St; mountain bikes and hybrids cost from £8.50 per day.

AROUND ST ANDREWS
Kellie Castle

Kellie is a magnificent example of Lowland Scottish domestic architecture and is well worth a visit. It's set in a beautiful garden, and many of the rooms contain superb plasterwork. The original part of the building dates from 1360; it was enlarged to its present dimensions around 1606. Robert Lorimer worked on the castle in the 1870s, when it was not in good shape, and it was bought by the NTS in 1970.

Kellie Castle (☎ 01333-720271) is 3 miles north-west of Pittenweem on the B9171. It's open daily at Easter and from May to September, 1.30 to 5.30 pm, and in October at weekends, 1.30 to 5.30 pm (last entry is at 4.45 pm). The admission cost is £3.70/2.50.

Fife Scottish (☎ 01333-426038) runs bus Nos 61A/B from St Andrews to Arncroach, past the castle gates, four times daily except Sunday (one hour).

Scotland's Secret Bunker

Three miles north of Anstruther is a fascinating attraction – what would have been one of Britain's underground command centres and a home for Scots leaders if nuclear or civil war had broken out. Hidden 30m underground, and surrounded by nearly 5m of reinforced concrete, are the operation rooms, communication centre, café and dormitories. A 25 minute audiovisual display, shown at 11.30 am and 2.30 pm, explains how it would have been used.

The bunker (☎ 01333-310301) is at Troy Wood, 5 miles south of St Andrews, by the B9131 road to Anstruther. It's open from Easter to October daily from 10 am to 5 pm; entry costs £5.95/4.95 (£3.25 for children).

Fife Scottish (☎ 01333-426038) runs nine buses daily (except Sunday) between St Andrews and Arncroach, Earlsferry or Leven, via Troy Wood and Anstruther.

EAST NEUK

The section of the south Fife coast that stretches from Leven east to the point at Fife Ness is known as the East Neuk. There are several picturesque fishing villages and some good coastal walks in the area.

Crail
• pop 1290   ☎ 01333

One of the prettiest of the East Neuk villages, Crail has a much-photographed

harbour surrounded by white cottages with red pantiled roofs. There are far fewer fishing boats in the harbour now than there once were, but you can still buy fresh lobster and shellfish here.

The TIC (☎ 450869), 62 Marketgait (at the museum), opens Easter to September. The Royal Bank, in High St, has an ATM.

Guided walks run in July and August on Sunday at 2.30 pm. Phone ☎ 450869 for details.

Things to See The village's history and involvement with the fishing industry are outlined in the **Crail Museum** (☎ 450310), 62 Marketgait. It's open at Easter, weekends and holidays, then June to September, Monday to Saturday from 10 am to 1 pm and 2 to 5 pm, and Sunday afternoons only (admission is free).

The 16th century **tolbooth**, also in Marketgait, is now the library and town hall. Also worth looking for are the 13th century **collegiate church** and the **Mercat Cross**, topped with a unicorn. Follow **Castle Walk** for the best views of the harbour.

Places to Stay & Eat The centrally located *Caiplie Guest House (☎ 450564, 53 High St)* does B&B from £16 to £22 per person and excellent three-course dinners for £12.50. The *Marine Hotel (☎ 450207)* charges £30 to £37.50 per person and all rooms have attached bath; good bar meals cost £4.95 to £8.25.

There are also two coffee shops, a bakers, and an *Alldays* supermarket in High St.

Getting There & Away Crail is 10 miles from St Andrews. The Fife Scottish (☎ 01333 426038) No 95 bus between Leven, Anstruther, Crail, St Andrews and Dundee passes through Crail hourly every day (30 minutes, £1.80 to St Andrews).

Anstruther
• pop 3270   ☎ 01333

A large former fishing village, 9 miles south of St Andrews, Anstruther is worth visiting for the **Scottish Fisheries Museum**

(☎ 310628) by the harbour. Displays include a cottage belonging to a fishing family, and the history of the herring and whaling industries that were once the mainstay of the local economy. The museum has a coffee shop. It's open April to October, daily from 10 am to 5.30 pm (11 am to 5 pm on Sunday), and with shorter hours for the rest of the year. Admission costs £3.50/2.50.

From the harbour there are sea angling trips or visits to the **Isle of May**, a nature reserve only a mile long. You can make reservations for both at the kiosk (☎ 310103) near the museum. A three hour fishing trip costs £10, including bait and rod. The five hour excursion to the Isle of May sails daily (except Friday) from May to September for £12/10 (£5 for children); the crossing takes just under an hour. Between April and July, the cliffs are packed with breeding kittiwakes, razorbills, guillemots, shags and around 40,000 puffins. Inland, there are remains of the 12th century **St Adrian's Chapel**, dedicated to a monk who was murdered on the island by Danes in 875.

The helpful TIC (☎ 311073) is by the Fisheries Museum. It's open April to October, daily from 10 am to 5 pm (noon to 5 pm on Sunday). There are banks with ATMs in the town centre.

Places to Stay & Eat The rather scruffy 22-bed *Bunkhouse* (☎ 310768) in West Pitkierie is 1½ miles out of Anstruther by the B9131 to St Andrews. Beds cost £6.50; it's best to book ahead in summer.

Just uphill from the museum, *Mrs Smith* (☎ 310042, 2 Union Place) charges £15 to £17 for B&B. The *Spindrift* (☎ 310573, Pittenweem Rd) is a very comfortable guesthouse a short walk from the village centre. All rooms have bathroom attached and cost from £26.50 per person.

On Shore St, there's a *Co-op* foodstore. *Caspian Fast Food* and the *Anstruther Fish Restaurant*, also on Shore St, both do cheap takeaways from around £2. The *Sun Tavern* (Shore St) has soup for only £1,

baked potatoes from £2.50, and main courses for around £4.

The *Craw's Nest* (☎ 310691) is in Bankwell Rd, off Pittenweem Rd on the western side of the village. Rooms are £45/84 and bar meals cost £6.25 to £8.50. The *Cellar Restaurant* (☎ 310378, 24 East Green), just behind the museum, is famous for its seafood – crabs, lobster, scallops, langoustine, monkfish, turbot etc. Advance bookings are essential. Lunch main courses start at £6.50 and there's a three-course set dinner for £28.50.

Getting There & Away The hourly Fife Scottish (☎ 426038) bus No 95 runs daily from Dundee to Leven via St Andrews, Crail, Anstruther (harbour), St Monans and Elie. There are also four daily buses (except Sunday) to Kellie Castle and nine daily (except Sunday) to West Pitkierie, Troy Wood and St Andrews (40 minutes, £1.80). The X27 service connecting Anstruther with Kirkcaldy (70 minutes, £3.60) and Glasgow (three hours, £5.50) runs every two hours (only twice on Sunday).

Pittenweem

• pop 1640   ☎ 01333

This is now the main fishing port on the East Neuk coast, and there are lively fish sales from 8 am at the harbour. The village name means 'place of the cave', referring to **St Fillan's cave** in Cove Wynd, which was used as a chapel by this 7th century missionary. The saint reputedly possessed miraculous powers – apparently, when he wrote his sermons in the dark cave, his arm would illuminate his work by emitting a luminous glow. The key is available from The Gingerbread Horse café (☎ 311495), 9 High St (usually open 10 am to 5 pm).

Kellie Lodging, High St, is a small and intriguing restored 16th century town house.

The *Anchor Inn* (☎ 311326, 42 Charles St) charges £20 per person for B&B. Bar meals and high teas (£4.75) are available.

Bus details (except times and fares) are as for Anstruther.

St Monans

• pop 1360 ☎ 01333

This ancient fishing village is situated just over a mile west of Pittenweem and is named after a local cave-dwelling saint who most probably was killed by pirates.

You can get fresh fish at several retail outlets at the Nethergate Industrial Estate, off the road to Elie; try Unit 5 first.

Things to See In streets near the attractive **harbour** there are lots of houses with crow-stepped gables, forestairs and red pantiled roofs.

The **parish church**, at the west end of the village, was constructed in 1362 on orders from a grateful King David II, who was rescued by villagers from shipwreck in the Firth of Forth.

From the church, follow the coast path westwards for half a mile to the ruins of 15th century **Newark Castle**. There's not much left of the castle, but there's an adjacent 16th century **beehive dovecot**, which housed pigeons that were intended for human consumption in winter.

Just east of the village, by the coast path to Pittenweem, there's a recently renovated 18th century **windmill**, with displays about the local coal and salt industries (now defunct); admission is free.

Places to Stay & Eat *Inverforth* *(☎ 730205, 20 Braehead)*, overlooking the harbour, charges £16 to £18 per person for B&B. The *Cabin (☎ 730327, West End)*, near the church, is an expensive restaurant specialising in seafood, but it has vegetarian choices. A three-course dinner here costs around £20. Just over 2 miles west of St Monans, in the village of Elie, the *Ship Inn (☎ 330246, The Toft)*, by the harbour, is a pleasant and popular place with main courses from £6.

Getting There & Away Bus details for St Monans (except times and fares) are as for Anstruther.

Perth & Kinross

This area includes most of the former region of Tayside – the area covered by the River Tay and its tributaries. It contains, in miniature, as many variations in terrain as Scotland itself, from the bleak expanse of Rannoch Moor in the west to the rich farmland of the Carse of Gowrie between Perth and Dundee.

From 838, Scotland's monarchs were crowned at Scone, just outside Perth. Mary Queen of Scots was imprisoned in Loch Leven Castle, and at Killiecrankie the Jacobites defeated the government forces.

The county town of Perth, built on the banks of the Tay, has a medieval church and many fine Georgian buildings. West of Perth there's attractive Strath Earn, with small towns and villages including the wealthy former resort of Crieff. Blairgowrie lies north of Perth, in an area known for fruit growing.

The Highland line cuts across this region – in the north and north-west along the rounded, heathery Grampians. North of Blairgowrie, the twisty road to Braemar follows Glen Shee and crosses the Cairnwell Pass, Britain's highest main-road pass.

Flowing out of Loch Tay, in West Perthshire, the River Tay runs eastwards through hills and woods towards Dunkeld, where there's a cathedral on the riverbank. Queen Victoria, when looking for a place to buy, was quite taken by the Pitlochry area, particularly the view over Loch Tummel. North of Pitlochry, at Blair Atholl, is Blair Castle, ancestral seat of the Dukes of Atholl.

GETTING AROUND

The A9, Scotland's busiest road, cuts across the centre of this region through Perth and Pitlochry. It's the fast route into the Highlands and to Inverness – watch out for speed traps.

Perth is the main public transport hub. Phone Perth & Kinross Council's Public Transport Traveline on ☎ 0845-3011130, Monday to Friday from 8.30 am to 5 pm.

Bus operators include: Scottish Citylink (☎ 0990-505050), Stagecoach (☎ 01738-629339), Strathtay Scottish (☎ 01382-228054) and Fife Scottish (☎ 01334-474238). For detailed rail information phone ☎ 0345-484950.

Trains run alongside the A9, destined for Inverness. The other main line connects Perth with Stirling (in the south) and Dundee (in the east).

KINROSS & LOCH LEVEN
- **pop 4032**   ☎ **01577**

Kinross lies in the extreme south of Perth & Kinross region, on the western shore of Loch Leven. It's the largest loch in the Lowlands, known for its extensive bird life.

Helpful Kinross Services TIC (☎ 863680), by Junction 6 of the M90, opens all year (closed Sunday in winter). All four banks in town have ATMs.

Things to See Loch Leven Castle (☎ 01786-450000), on an island in the loch, served as a fortress and prison from the late 14th century. Its most famous captive was Mary Queen of Scots, who spent almost a year incarcerated here from 1567. Her infamous charms bewitched Willie Douglas, who managed to get hold of the cell keys to release her, then row her across to the shore. The castle is now roofless but basically intact. It's open standard HS hours (April to September) and admission costs £2.80/2.10, including the ferry trip from Kinross.

About 2 miles from Kinross, just outside Milnathort on the A911 to Leslie, there's the intriguing **Burleigh Castle**. This red-sandstone tower house, built around 1500, has an extraordinary-shaped and still-roofed tower. King James IV was a frequent guest here. You can get the key from the farm opposite the castle. It's open from April to September, daily, from 9 am to 6.30 pm (from 2 pm on Sunday); admission is free.

Places to Stay & Eat *Gallowhill Farm Caravan Park* (☎ 862364), open from April to October, is 2 miles from Kinross, near the A91. Camping charges start at £4.

B&B at the *Roxburghe Guest House* (☎ 862498, 126 High St), Kinross, costs from £15 to £20 per person (double). Four miles from the M90 (Junction 6), near Milnathort, there's comfortable *Warroch Lodge* (☎ 863779). B&B costs £18 per person and evening meals are available for £9.

The recommended *Kirklands Hotel* (☎ 863313, 20 High St), Kinross, has nine *en suite* rooms for £39/78. Bar meals cost from £3.95 to £8.50, but there's a good three-course lunch deal for £4.75.

The *Coffee Kitchen* (High St), Kinross, does home-made soup and a roll for £1.20. The *Central Café* does takeaway fish and chips for £2.90, but there's a better 'chippy' in Milnathort.

Getting There & Away Scottish Citylink has an hourly service between Perth (30 minutes, £2.50) and Edinburgh (50 minutes, £3.80) via Kinross, also stopping at Milnathort and Dunfermline. There are three buses daily (except Sunday) to Falkland and a twice-weekly service to Dollar.

PERTH
- **pop 42,086**   ☎ **01738**

In *The Fair Maid of Perth*, Sir Walter Scott extolled the virtues of this county town. 'Perth, so eminent for the beauty of its situation, is a place of great antiquity,' he wrote. This is all still true and the town was recently voted the best place to live in Britain, for quality of life.

Perth's rise in importance derives from Scone (pronounced scoon), 2 miles north of the town. In 838, Kenneth MacAlpin became the first king of a united Scotland and brought the Stone of Destiny, on which all kings were ceremonially invested, to Scone. An important abbey grew up on the site. From this time on, all Scottish kings were invested here, even after Edward I of England stole the sacred talisman, carting it off to London's Westminster Abbey in 1296. In 1996 Prime Minister John Major persuaded the Queen to promise to return it to Scotland, but it went to Edinburgh Castle rather than Scone.

Built on the banks of the River Tay, Perth grew into a major trading centre, known for weaving, dyeing and glove-making. It was originally called St John's Toun, hence the name of the local football team, St Johnstone. From the 12th century, Perth was Scotland's capital, and in 1437 James I was murdered here. There were four important monasteries in the area and the town was a target for the Reformation movement in Scotland.

Perth is now a busy market town and centre of service industries. It's the focal point for this agricultural region and there are world-famous cattle auctions of the valuable Aberdeen Angus breed. The bull sales in February draw international buyers.

The top attraction in the area is Scone Palace, but the town itself has a number of interesting things to see, including an excellent art gallery, housing the work of local artist JD Fergusson.

Orientation & Information

Most of the town lies on the western bank of the Tay; Scone Palace and some of the B&Bs are on the eastern bank. There are two large parks: North Inch, the scene of the infamous 'Battle of the Clans' in 1396, and South Inch. The bus and train stations are next to each other, near the north-western corner of South Inch.

The TIC (☎ 638353), 45 High St, opens daily from April to October, and from Monday to Saturday for the rest of the year. In July and August, the TIC is open Monday to Saturday from 9 am to 8 pm, and Sunday 11 am to 6 pm. Opening hours are shorter at other times. Buy tickets here for the hop-on, hop-off bus service (£5/3.50, children £2) that takes in Scone Palace. Ask for details about the walk up Kinnoull Hill. The TIC may relocate to Lower City Mills in 1999 or 2000.

There are banks with ATMs on High St, between the TIC and the river. For outdoor equipment visit Mountain Man Supplies (☎ 632368) 133 South St.

Perth Royal Infirmary (☎ 623311), Taymount Terrace, is west of the town centre.

Walking Tour

From the TIC, walk one block south to St John's Kirk. Founded in 1126, and surrounded by cobbled streets, this is still the centrepiece of the town. In 1559, John Knox preached a powerful sermon here that helped begin the Reformation, resulting in the destruction of monasteries, including the one at Scone. The kirk was restored in the 1920s. Opening times are posted by the west door.

Four blocks south is the Round House, the old waterworks building on the edge of South Inch that now houses the JD Fergusson Gallery (☎ 441944). This artist, one of the group known as the Scottish colourists, was noticeably influenced by French styles after spending much of his life in France in the early part of this century. The gallery is well worth seeing; it's open Monday to Saturday, from 10 am to 5 pm (entrance is free).

Two blocks north of the High St is the Museum and Art Gallery (☎ 632488), 78 George St, which charts local history. There are displays of Perth art glass, an impressive silver collection and natural history displays. It's open the same hours as the Fergusson Gallery.

Nearby, on Curfew Row, is the Fair Maid's House, the house chosen by Sir Walter Scott as home for Catherine Glover, the romantic heroine in his novel *The Fair Maid of Perth*. The novel was set in the 14th century, but this house dates from the 16th, when it was a meeting hall for the town's glove manufacturers.

South-west of the Fair Maid's House, Lower City Mills (☎ 627958), West Mill St, is a restored and working Victorian oatmeal mill, open from April to October, Monday to Saturday, from 10 am to 5 pm. Admission costs £1.50/75p. In the north of the town, Balhousie Castle houses the Black Watch Museum (☎ 621281), charting the military campaigns since 1740 of Scotland's foremost regiment. It's open May to September, daily except Sunday, from 10 am to 4.30 pm. The rest of the year, it's open on weekdays from 10 am to 3.30 pm. Admission is free.

Scone Palace

Two miles north of Perth and just off the A93 near Old Scone, Scone Palace, the home of the Earl and Countess of Mansfield, should not be missed. It was built in 1580 in the grounds of a former abbey; the abbey was destroyed in 1559 by a crowd inflamed by John Knox's sermon in St John's Kirk. With the destruction of the abbey buildings, the land passed to the Gowrie family and then to the Murrays.

In 1803, the palace was enlarged, and it now houses a superb collection of French furniture, including Marie Antoinette's writing table. Displays of 16th century needle work include bed hangings worked by Mary Queen of Scots. In the library is a valuable collection of 18th and 19th century porcelain. The palace is surrounded by parkland, including rare pine trees.

Scone Palace (☎ 552300) opens Easter to October, daily from 9.30 am to 5.15 pm (last entry is at 4.45 pm). Admission costs £5.20/3 for the house and grounds (half-price for the grounds only). The hop-on, hop-off bus (contact the TIC for tickets) goes this way, as does bus No 58.

Places to Stay

The excellent *Perth Youth Hostel* (☎ 623658, 107 Glasgow Rd) opens in late February and closes at the end of October. Beds cost £7.75/6.50.

The main B&B areas are along Glasgow Rd, Dunkeld Rd, Dundee Rd and Pitcullen Crescent. *Iona Guest House* (☎ 627261, 2 Pitcullen Crescent) charges from £17/34, all with private showers. At *Achnacarry Guest House* (☎ 621421, 3 Pitcullen Crescent) you'll pay from £19.50 to £26 per person. Somewhat cheaper is the *Darroch Guest House* (☎ 636893), also on Pitcullen Crescent, which costs from £15/30 and has some *en suite* rooms. *Pitcullen Guest*

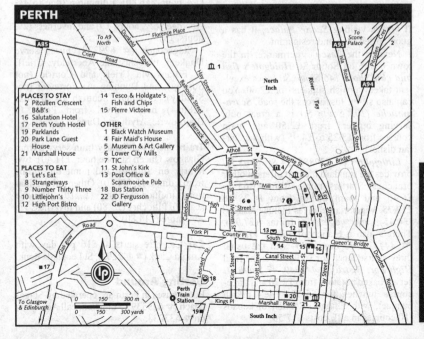

PERTH

PLACES TO STAY
2 Pitcullen Crescent B&B's
16 Salutation Hotel
17 Perth Youth Hostel
19 Parklands
20 Park Lane Guest House
21 Marshall House

PLACES TO EAT
3 Let's Eat
8 Strangeways
9 Number Thirty Three
10 Littlejohn's
12 High Port Bistro

14 Tesco & Holdgate's Fish and Chips
15 Pierre Victoire

OTHER
1 Black Watch Museum
4 Fair Maid's House
5 Museum & Art Gallery
6 Lower City Mills
7 TIC
11 St John's Kirk
13 Post Office & Scaramouche Pub
18 Bus Station
22 JD Fergusson Gallery

House (☎ 626506, 17 Pitcullen Crescent) charges from £20 per person.

Closer to the centre, there are several B&Bs along Marshall Place, overlooking South Inch. *Marshall House (☎ 442886, 6 Marshall Place)* has three double/twin rooms with private showers and charges £15 per person. The very comfortable *Park Lane Guest House (☎ 637218, 17 Marshall Place)* offers B&B at around £23 per person.

The *Salutation Hotel (☎ 630066, 34 South St)* first opened in 1699 and was reputedly used as a headquarters by Bonnie Prince Charlie during the Jacobite rebellion of 1745. Rooms cost up to £95 but if business is slack at weekends it sometimes offers dinner B&B for as little as £30 per person.

Parklands (☎ 622451, St Leonard's Bank), former home of Lord Provosts (mayors), is one of the most luxurious places to stay. It's a small hotel and all rooms have bath attached, one with a spa. B&B starts at £37.50/70.

Places to Eat

If you're visiting *Scone Palace*, it has a good coffee shop and restaurant.

Next to the *Tesco* supermarket in the town centre on South St, *Holdgate's fish and chip shop (146 South St)*, does excellent takeaway fish suppers for £2.60. You can also sit-in. Just across the road, *Scaramouche (103 South St)* is a great pub, serving burgers from £2.50 and main courses from £3.25 to £4.95 (with vegetarian dishes).

Littlejohn's (☎ 639888, 24 St John's St) provides the standard menu it offers at other branches. Starters range from £1.65 to £6.45 and main dishes from £4.25 to £12.75. Vegetarian choices include lasagne (£4.45), and vegetable fajitas (£7.95). There's also a branch of *Pierre Victoire (☎ 444222, 38 South St)* with the usual three-course lunch for £5.90. Over the road *High Port Bistro (☎ 444049, 47 South St)* serves baked potatoes from £2.70 and three-course lunches for £5.50. The Turkish banquet, with a huge selection of kebabs (10 courses in all), costs £17.50.

In County Place and South St there are about a dozen Italian, Chinese, Turkish and Indian restaurants.

Strangeways (☎ 628866, 24 George St) is a bistro that's open daily. It's a good place to have a drink in the evening, but stops serving food at 5 pm; two-course bar lunches cost £4.

Number Thirty Three (☎ 633771, 33 George St) has a good oyster bar and restaurant specialising in seafood. Popular menu items include Mary's seafood soup, and sticky toffee pudding with butterscotch sauce, both £2.95. A three-course meal will set you back around £21.

The best place in town for a special meal is the award-winning *Let's Eat (☎ 643377, 77 Kinnoul St)*. It's a very pleasant bistro with main courses in the £10 to £12 range.

Getting There & Away

Bus Scottish Citylink (☎ 0990-505050) operates regular buses from Perth to Glasgow (1½ hours, £6.80), Edinburgh (one to 1½ hours, £4.50), Dundee (35 minutes, £3), Aberdeen (2½ hours, £9) and Inverness (2½ hours, £9).

Stagecoach (☎ 629339) buses serve Dunkeld, Pitlochry and Aberfeldy; Crieff; St Fillans via Crieff and Comrie (not Sunday); and Dunning via Forteviot (not Sunday). Strathtay Scottish (☎ 01382-228054) buses travel from Perth to Blairgowrie, Alyth and Dundee.

Train There's an hourly train service from Glasgow Queen St (one hour, £11.40), two hourly on Sunday, and numerous trains from Edinburgh (£9.10). Other rail destinations include Stirling (£7.10), Dundee (£4.30), Pitlochry (£7.80) and Inverness via Aviemore (£14.80).

Car Car hire starts at £16 per day with Arnold Clark (☎ 442202), St Leonards Bank.

Getting Around

Local buses in Perth are operated by Stagecoach (☎ 629339). For a taxi, call Ace Taxis on ☎ 633033.

STRATHEARN

West of Perth, the wide *strath* (valley) of the River Earn was once a great forest where medieval kings hunted. The Earn, named after a Celtic goddess, runs from St Fillans (named after the mystic who lived on an island in Loch Earn), through Comrie and Crieff and eventually into the Tay near Bridge of Earn. The whole area is known as Strathearn, a very attractive region of undulating farmland, hills and lochs. The Highlands begin in the western section of Strathearn and the so-called Highland line runs through Comrie and Crieff, and on through Angus (via Kirriemuir and Edzell) to Stonehaven.

Dunning

- pop 1000   ☎ 01764

Historic Dunning nestles at the foot of the Ochil Hills on the south side of Strathearn, about 8 miles south-west of Perth. The area was always of strategic importance. The Battle of Duncrub was fought nearby in 965 and, in 1716, retreating Jacobites burned the village after their defeat at Sherriffmuir. Dunning is dominated by the 12th century Norman tower of **St Serfs church**, but most of the building dates from 1810. The 9th century **Dupplin Cross**, one of the earliest Christian stone crosses in Scotland, will soon be moved from its current location near Forteviot (3 miles from Dunning) to the new museum in Chambers St, Edinburgh; it will then be sent to St Serfs church, by 2003. About a mile west of Dunning, by the B8062, there's a strange **cross** commemorating the burning of a witch in 1657.

The *Kirkstyle Inn (☎ 684248, Kirkstyle Square)* does excellent bar and restaurant meals, including a vegetarian dish, for around £8 to £10. The *Pan Haggerty (☎ 684604, Tron Square)* is popular with locals and serves home baking, bistro meals, and takeaway fish and chips.

Stagecoach bus No 17 runs from Perth to Forteviot and Dunning seven times daily, except Sunday (40 minutes, £2.20). Docherty's Midland Coaches (☎ 662218)

No 18 bus departs for Auchterarder (two to six times each weekday) and Crieff (two or three times each weekday). The No 166 bus runs from Dunning to Auchterarder four times daily (except Sunday); three journeys continue to Stirling (45 minutes).

Auchterarder

- pop 2932   ☎ 01764

Four miles west of Dunning and overlooked by the Ochil Hills, Auchterarder is a small town in a rich agricultural area. There's a TIC (☎ 663450), 90 High St, open all year, with an interesting **heritage centre** detailing wide-ranging aspects of local history. **Whitelaw's antique shop**, 118 High St, almost doubles-up as a museum of 18th and 19th century furniture.

The town is probably best known for the internationally famous hotel on its outskirts. *Gleneagles Hotel (☎ 662231)* is a splendid place with three golf courses (including a championship course), a swimming pool, jacuzzi, sauna, gym, and tennis and squash courts. Room charges, including full use of the leisure facilities, range from £140/260 for single/double to £1250 for the Royal Lochnagar Suite (complete with antiques, silk-lined walls and hand-woven carpets). The hotel even has its own train station, 50 minutes (£8.80) from Glasgow, and there's complimentary transport between the station and hotel. However, if you can afford to stay here, you can afford the limousine from Glasgow airport (£130).

A cheaper alternative is B&B at *Mamore (☎ 662036, 10 The Grove)*, just off the B8062 to Crieff, which charges £15 to £17.50 per person.

Top Shop (168 High St) does freshly baked pizza and reasonable fish and chips, and *Gleneagles Bakery (162 High St)* is good for bread and pastries. *Sheray Punjab (97 High St)* does good, large portions and a takeaway service. The pleasant *Old Tudor Bistro (☎ 664092, 151 High St)* does great burgers and meals.

Docherty's Midland Coaches (☎ 662218) operates buses from Auchterarder to Dunning, Crieff, Stirling (two to four daily), and Perth (three to eight daily, 30 minutes, £1.80).

Crieff & Around
• pop 6359 ☎ 01764

Attractively located on the edge of the Highlands, Crieff has been a popular resort town since Victorian times. Until 1770 it was the scene of a large cattle fair; some vendors would come from as far away as Skye – swimming the cattle across to the mainland.

Information The all-year TIC (☎ 652578) is in the High St clock tower, part of the town hall. The four banks all have ATMs. Crieff Hospital (☎ 653173) is just off King St. Needy travellers should note that the public toilets on James Square charge 20p.

Things to See There are several interesting things around Crieff. **Glenturret Distillery** (☎ 656565) is about a mile from the centre of town. Its visitors centre opens daily from 9.30 am to 6 pm (afternoon only on Sunday); the last tour is at 4.30 pm. Opening hours are shorter in January and February. It's all fairly touristy but a free dram is included in the price of £3.50/3.

Innerpeffray Library (☎ 652819), about 4 miles south-east of Crieff on the B8062, is Scotland's first lending library (founded in 1680). There's a huge collection of rare, interesting and ancient books, some of them 500 years old. The library building, and the early **16th century chapel and graveyard** next door are very interesting too. A **Roman road** runs nearby. The library's open from April to September, Monday to Saturday (closed Thursday), from 10 am to 12.45 pm and 2 to 4.45 pm (Sunday, 2 to 4 pm), closing at 4 pm the rest of the year (open in January and December by appointment). Admission costs £2.50/50p, including a guided tour. The chapel opens daily. There's a tearoom at the library.

At Muthill, 3 miles south of Crieff, you'll find the excellent **Old Church**. The church is now just a series of ruined arches, but the attached **bell tower** (originally free standing) is still roofed. This extraordinary tower, with unusual arched belfry windows, is one of the oldest complete structures in Scotland: it dates from around 1225 to 1250. The key to the grounds is available from Cunningham's Newsagent, across the road (admission is free).

Places to Stay Crieff has a large selection of B&Bs and hotels. The nearest budget accommodation is 5 miles away, near Comrie (see the upcoming Upper Strathearn section). However, there's year-round camping at **Crieff Holiday Village** (☎ 653513), by the A85 just west of the town, for around £6 per tent.

Ambleside (☎ 652798, Burrell Square), centrally located, is a pleasant B&B which charges £15/30 a single/double. One of the best places in town is **Merlindale** (☎ 655205, Perth Rd), a luxurious Georgian house with three en suite rooms for only £20 per person, and a fourth room with a jacuzzi.

Most of the hotels are on Perth Rd or Comrie Rd, but the most well-known is **Crieff Hydro** (☎ 655555), on the hill at the north side of town. The hydro, owned by the Church of Scotland, has one of the highest occupancy rates in Scotland. There's a wide range of leisure facilities and good food is served. B&B costs from £44 to £66 per person.

Places to Eat There are lots of places to eat in both King St and High St. For self-catering, there's a **Costcutter** supermarket (39 High St). The **Central Fish Bar** (King St) serves salmon suppers for £3. At the **Strathearn Hotel** (☎ 652089, King St) bar snacks start at £1.25 and meals cost from £3.95 to £9.85. **Harts Bistro** (☎ 654407, 1 West High St) does pasta, bread and salad for £3.95; main courses are around £6.

The **Gallery Restaurant** (☎ 653249, Hill St) serves Mexican and Greek dishes; burritos are £8.95. Other quality restaurants include the **Hydro** (see Places to Stay) and wood-panelled **Satchmo's** (☎ 656575, 32 High St), opposite the TIC, where a two-course lunch is only £5.75. Satchmo's holds jazz nights in summer.

Getting There & Away Stagecoach (☎ 01738-629339) buses link Crieff with Perth, hourly (less frequently on Sunday, 45 minutes, £2.20). Other buses run to Comrie and St Fillans (hourly, not on Sunday), and Stirling (four to six daily). Docherty's Midland Coaches (☎ 662218) runs between Crieff, Auchterarder (three to five on weekdays) and Dunning (two or three direct buses on weekdays).

Stagecoach operates a special 'Tourist Trail' vintage bus in July and August on Monday, Wednesday and Saturday. It runs from Crieff to Dunkeld, but the £6.95 fare is valid between any two points across the trail, including St Fillans, Comrie, Stirling, Perth, Pitlochry and Aberfeldy.

Getting Around Most of the weekday Stagecoach buses to Auchterarder run via Muthill; others go via Innerpeffray (once on Tuesday and Thursday only). The Crieff to Stirling bus goes via Muthill. Bikes can

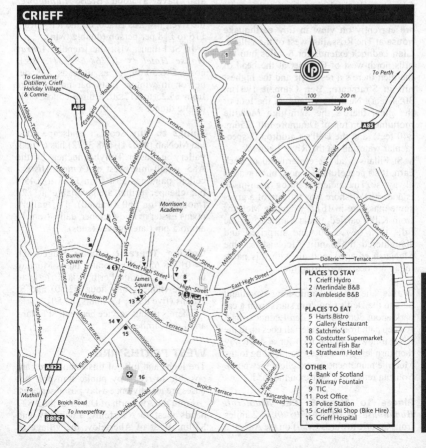

CRIEFF

PLACES TO STAY
1 Crieff Hydro
2 Merlindale B&B
3 Ambleside B&B

PLACES TO EAT
5 Harts Bistro
7 Gallery Restaurant
8 Satchmo's
10 Costcutter Supermarket
12 Central Fish Bar
14 Strathearn Hotel

OTHER
4 Bank of Scotland
6 Murray Fountain
9 TIC
11 Post Office
13 Police Station
15 Crieff Ski Shop (Bike Hire)
16 Crieff Hospital

CENTRAL & NORTH-EASTERN

be hired from Crieff Ski Shop (☎ 654667), 66 Commissioner St, for £12 per day.

Upper Strathearn

The Highland villages of **Comrie** and **St Fillans**, in upper Strathearn, are surrounded by craggy scenery, forests and bare mountaintops where deer and mountain hares live in abundance. Comrie is 24 miles west of Perth and St Fillans is about 5 miles farther west.

Things to See Comrie is near several geological faults and small earthquakes occur frequently. In the 19th century, the world's first seismometers were set up here; replicas are currently on view in tiny **earthquake house** at The Ross, just west of the village. **Glen Lednock** extends for 6 miles into the hills north-west of Comrie; at the head of the glen there's a reservoir and the highest hill in Strathearn, Ben Chonzie (931m, 3054 feet). Near the village, at the foot of the glen, there's the 22m-high **Melville monument** on top of Dunmore hill (256m, 840 feet), and the **Deil's Cauldron**, a spectacular waterfall on the River Lednock.

St Fillans is at the eastern end of **Loch Earn**. It's a peaceful place now, but it wasn't always so. The ancient **crannog** (man-made island) just offshore was the site of a gruesome massacre in 1612, when the McNabs from Killin carried a boat 8 miles over the hills then rowed out and surprised and slaughtered the bandit McNeishes. One McNeish escaped, and all with this name today are descended from him.

Walks The pleasant mile-long woodland hike to the Deil's Cauldron starts from a car park about 50m up the Glen Lednock road. A steep path from the waterfall goes up to the road; follow it up the glen for a short way then turn left onto a steep trail leading to the Melville monument, an excellent viewpoint. You can return to Comrie on the road.

Places to Stay & Eat *Braincroft Bunkhouse* (☎ 01764-670140) is 2 miles from Comrie towards Crieff on the A85. It's

open all year and has beds for £7 to £9 per person.

Comfortable *Comrie Hotel* (☎ 01764-670239, Drummond St) charges from £27 per person for B&B. Jacket potatoes start at £2.95 and bar meals range from £4.95 to £12.50. The more luxurious *Royal Hotel* (☎ 01764-679200, Melville Square), Comrie, has superb rooms with attached bath and four-poster beds. Rates start at £75/130. Bar lunches are inexpensive (£3.95 to £4.95), but you'll pay around £18 for à la carte.

The bright and cheery *Carrick Coffee House* serves soup and snacks. The owners also have a good B&B, *Landgower* (☎ 01764-679990), Dalginross – south of the river, towards Braco, on the left – from £16 to £18 per person (double/twin).

In St Fillans, visit the friendly *Achray House Hotel* (☎ 01764-685231). B&B costs £46.50/69, or as little as £18 per person in winter. Tasty bar meals range from £5.25 to £12.50; a three-course table d'hôte dinner is £17.50.

Things to Buy Scottish landscape artist Ian McNab (☎ 0141-638 3072) has a small gallery at Easter Tullybannocher, by the A85, a half-mile west of Comrie. His excellent paintings cost from £135 to £450, but cheaper prints are available at £28 (mounted) or £60 (framed). The gallery opens Easter to mid-October, daily, from 11 am to 5 pm (later at weekends).

Getting There & Away Stagecoach (☎ 01738-629339) operates buses Monday to Saturday from Perth, via Crieff, to Comrie (hourly, one hour, £2.80) and St Fillans (five daily, 1¼ hours, £3.50).

There's no bus service between St Fillans and Lochearnhead.

WEST PERTHSHIRE

The lochs and hills of this remote area are possible to reach by public transport but buses are usually once a day postal services.

From the A9, north of Dunkeld, the A827 heads west to Aberfeldy, Loch Tay and Killin. West of Aberfeldy, the village of

Fortingall, at the foot of beautiful Glen Lyon, is famous as the birthplace of Pontius Pilate. A little farther north, the Rannoch area is renowned for its beauty and the almost perfectly shaped hill, Schiehallion.

Aberfeldy
• **pop 1956**   ☎ **01887**

This small town has the unique distinction of sitting at the exact geographic centre of Scotland.

Potential visitors should note that the streets can be rowdy with low-life after dark, but there was high-profile policing during my last visit.

The TIC (☎ 820276), in an old church on The Square, opens all year; there's a plan of the town on the wall. Two banks have ATMs; the cottage hospital (☎ 820314) is on Old Crieff Rd.

Things to See The B846 to Tummel Bridge crosses the River Tay in Aberfeldy by a fine **Wade bridge**; construction was begun in 1733 by General Wade as part of his pacification of the Highlands project.

The **Aberfeldy water mill** (☎ 820803), Mill St, was built in 1825 and restored in 1983. Stone-ground oatmeal is produced here by water-power and two stones, each weighing 1½ tonnes. The mill's open from Easter to October, Monday to Saturday, from 10 am to 5 pm (noon to 5 pm on Sunday); admission costs £1.80/1.62.

Castle Menzies (☎ 820982), 1½ miles west of town by the B846 at Weem, is the impressive restored 16th century seat of the Chief of the Clan Menzies. There's a small clan museum and a tearoom at the castle. It's open from April to October, daily from 10.30 am to 5 pm (from 2 pm on Sunday); last admission is at 4.30 pm (£3/2.50).

Places to Stay & Eat On the east side of town, *Aberfeldy Caravan Park (☎ 820662)* opens April to October and charges £4.20 for one person in a tent (plus £1 per car). At the west end, by the A827 and the river, *Dunollie House (☎ 820298, Taybridge Drive)* has hostel beds from £5 to £8.25.

Mavisbank (☎ 820223, Taybridge Drive) has two rooms with shared bath for £16 to £17 per person. *Tigh'n Eilean Guest House (☎ 820109, Taybridge Drive)* is an excellent place with *en suite* rooms for £18 to £24 per person. The grand-looking *Palace Hotel (☎ 820359, Breadalbane Terrace)* charges £25 to £46 per person for B&B. Baked potatoes start at £3.50, bar meals range from £4.95 to £9.75, and excellent high teas are £7.25.

Self-caterers can visit the *Co-op* on The Square. The *Plaice in The Square* (really) is a clean fish and chip shop – haddock and chips is £2.90. *Food for Thought*, Bridge End, does soup, toasties and other snacks from £1.60. Several bars do pub grub, including the *Black Watch Inn (Bank St)*. On Dunkeld St, the Chinese takeaway is considerably cheaper than the Indian.

Getting There & Away Stagecoach (☎ 01738-629339) runs buses from Aberfeldy to Pitlochry (45 minutes, £2.50), Dunkeld (1¼ hours, £2.50) and Perth (around 1¾ hours, £3.75) up to 10 times daily (except Sunday). Strathtay Scottish (☎ 01382-228054) has a twice daily service (except Sunday) between Aberfeldy and Blairgowrie, via Dunkeld. A postbus service (☎ 01463-256200) goes to Killin (three hours) via Kenmore, and another goes to the top of Glen Lyon, at Lubreoch, via Fortingall (both once daily except Sunday). Elizabeth Yule Transport (☎ 01796-472290) operates from Aberfeldy to Kinloch Rannoch on schooldays (£2.20).

Loch Tay
The greater part of Ben Lawers (1214m, 3982 feet), Scotland's ninth tallest peak, crouches like a lion over Loch Tay. It's in the care of the NTS and there's a visitors centre (admission £1) high on the slopes of the mountain; the access road continues over a wild pass to Glen Lyon. A trail leads to the summit from the centre, but a more interesting seven hour route is up Lawers Burn from Machuim Farm, just north of Lawers village. You can walk around the

ridges via Meall Garbh to the summit, but you should take a good map (OS sheet 51).

Attractive **Kenmore**, at the eastern end and outlet of Loch Tay, is about 6 miles west of Aberfeldy. The short main street is dominated by a church with a clock-tower, and a spectacular archway – the entrance to privately owned Taymouth Castle. The opening of the salmon-fishing season is always celebrated with style on 15 January in Kenmore. Just a quarter of a mile along the south Loch Tay road from the village, the **Scottish Crannog Centre** (☎ 01887-830583) has a reconstruction of an artificial Iron Age island-house. There are interesting demonstrations of Iron Age skills, including starting a fire using only two pieces of wood and dry kindling. It's open from April to October, daily, from 10 am to 5 pm (closing at 6 pm from July to September, last entry 5 pm); admission costs £2.80/1.80.

The ***Kenmore Hotel*** (*☎ 01887-830205*) claims to be Scotland's oldest inn, and dates from 1572. Look out for the Burns poem on the wall, written here in 1787. The gents toilets are distinctly unusual! Top-floor rooms, such as 'The Square', also have great character; B&B ranges from £30/50 to £45/80 and a suite costs £90 (double only). In the bar, filled baguettes start at £2.95 and bar meals cost from £5.50 to £15.50.

The ***Ben Lawers Hotel*** (*☎ 01567-820436*), Lawers, charges from £15 to £24 per person for B&B. Dinner is available for £10 to £15 extra.

The Aberfeldy to Killin postbus passes through Kenmore and Lawers once daily, except Sunday.

Fortingall & Glen Lyon

Fortingall is one of the prettiest villages in Scotland, with 19th century thatched cottages in a very tranquil setting. In the churchyard, there's a **3000-year-old yew**, probably the oldest tree in Europe. This tree was already ancient when the Romans camped on the meadows by the River Lyon.

Glen Lyon is one of Scotland's most wonderful glens. The long single track road ensures few visitors penetrate its remote

upper reaches, where capercaillie live in patches of Scots pine forest. Just 3 miles upstream from Fortingall, opposite Chesthill, there's a **Roman bridge** crossing the Allt Dà-ghob, where there's a waterfall. You can see the bridge from the Glen Lyon road.

Highly recommended for B&B, ***Fendoch*** (*☎ 01887-830322*), Fortingall, charges from £15 to £17; all rooms have attached bath. You can have dinner here or at the ***Fortingall Hotel*** (*☎ 01887-830367*), where delicious bar meals start at £3.75. Try the local venison braised in red wine and port, with mushrooms, for £7.50. Part of the hotel dates from 1300. There are some very nice rooms on the first floor, eg room No 8; B&B starts at £30/48.

The Aberfeldy to Glenlyon postbus (☎ 01463-256200) runs via Fortingall once daily, except Sunday.

Strathtummel & Loch Rannoch

There are comparatively few sites of interest, but there's lots of great scenery in this area. A visit in autumn is recommended, when the birch trees are at their finest. In winter, Tummel Bridge is often one of the coldest places in Scotland.

Queen's View Visitor Centre (☎ 01796-473123), at the eastern end and outlet of Loch Tummel, has a magnificent outlook towards Schiehallion and displays and audio-visual programs about the area. Al-

---

Crannogs

Usually built in a loch for defensive purposes, a crannog (from the Gaelic word crann, meaning tree) consists of an artificial rock island with timber posts and struts supporting a hut above high-water level. Crannogs were used on many lochs, including Lochs Awe, Earn and Tay, from prehistoric times up to the 18th century. Some crannogs had curious underwater causeways which could zig-zag or have traps, making night-time assaults without a boat extremely difficult.

though Queen Victoria probably visited in 1866, it's thought that the viewpoint is named after Queen Isabella, wife of Robert the Bruce. The centre opens April to October, daily, from 10 am to 5.30 pm; there's a £1 parking charge.

Kinloch Rannoch is a pleasant village with a grocer's shop and post office. It's a good base for local walks or a cycle trip around **Loch Rannoch**. There's an interesting **clan trail** around the loch, with roadside notice boards about local clans. Beyond the west end of the loch, you enter bleak Rannoch Moor, which extends all the way to Glen Coe. The rivers and lochs on the moor are good for fishing.

Walks You can walk up the popular peak Schiehallion (1083m, 3552 feet) from Braes of Foss (five hours return). There's a path up to the summit ridge, then it's very rocky and can be unpleasant in bad weather. Take all the usual precautions: map (OS sheet No 51), compass, food, water, and good boots and waterproofs. The near-perfect shape of this hill allowed physicists to use its gravitational attraction on a pendulum to estimate the gravitational constant, G, and hence calculate the mass of the Earth.

Places to Stay & Eat The *Kilvrecht* (☎ 01350-727284) camp site is secluded and situated 3½ miles from Kinloch Rannoch on the south Loch Rannoch road. It's open from March to October; tent pitches are from £3 per night.

Vegetarian B&B is available at *Glenrannoch House* (☎ 01882-632307), just off the south Loch Rannoch road, for £18 to £20 per person (dinner is £14 extra). Alternatively, try *Bunrannoch House* (☎ 01882-632407), a former shooting-lodge where B&B is £20 per person and three-course set dinners are £18.50. Rather cheaper is the *Bunrannoch Hotel* (☎ 01882-632367), in the centre of the village, where bar meals are around £4 to £8. If you get as far as Rannoch Station (16 miles west of Kinloch Rannoch), the *Moor of Rannoch Hotel* (☎ 01882-633238) does excellent à la carte

meals for about £10; B&B is £23 to £25 per person.

Getting There & Away On schooldays only, Elizabeth Yule Transport (☎ 01796-472290) operates from Kinloch Rannoch to Aberfeldy (70 minutes, £2.20), passing within 2½ miles of Braes of Foss. The Kinloch Rannoch to Pitlochry service runs one to three times daily, except Sunday (one hour, £2.20).

The Pitlochry to Rannoch Station postbus (☎ 01796-472386) has a once daily service (except Sunday and public holidays) via Kinloch Rannoch and both sides of the loch.

ScotRail (☎ 0345-484950) runs trains from Rannoch Station, north to Fort William and Mallaig, south to Glasgow.

PERTH TO AVIEMORE

There are a number of major sights strung out along the A9, the main route north to Aviemore in the Highlands. Frequent buses and trains run along this route; most stop at the places described in this section.

Dunkeld & Birnam
• pop 1050   ☎ 01350

Fifteen miles north of Perth, Dunkeld is an attractive village on the Highland line with some excellent walks in the surrounding wooded area. Dunkeld TIC (☎ 727688), The Cross, opens all year.

Things to See & Do Dunkeld Cathedral must be among the most beautifully sited cathedrals in the country. Half of it is still in use as a church, the rest is in ruins. The oldest part of the original church is the choir, completed in 1350. The 15th century tower is also still standing. The cathedral was damaged during the Reformation and burnt in the Battle of Dunkeld in 1689. From April to September, it's open standard HS hours; admission is free.

On High and Cathedral Sts is a collection of 20 artisans' houses restored by the NTS. Across the bridge is Birnam, made famous by *Macbeth*, but there's not much left of Birnam Wood.

Good local walks include the Hermitage Woodland Walk, starting from a car park by the A9, a mile west of Dunkeld. The well-marked trail follows the River Braan to the Black Linn Falls, where the Duke of Atholl built a folly, **Ossian's Hall**, in 1758.

The **Loch of Lowes Visitor Centre** (☎ 727337), 2 miles east of Dunkeld off the A923, has wildlife displays and an excellent birdwatching hide with binoculars provided. A pair of ospreys breeds here. It's open from April to September, daily, from 10 am to 5 pm; admission is free (though a donation is advised).

Places to Stay & Eat *Wester Caputh Independent Hostel (☎ 01738-710617)* has just opened at Caputh, 5 miles east of Dunkeld, by the A984 Coupar Angus road. There are 14 beds for £8 (with your own sleeping bag); free pick-up at Birnam or Dunkeld is available. This lively place runs music evenings and guests frequently attend traditional music sessions in Dunkeld at *MacLean's Real Music Bar (Tay Terrace)*.

Teroan (☎ 727220, High St), Dunkeld, and *Torlee (☎ 728891, Perth Rd)*, Birnam, both charge around £14 per person for B&B. The *Birnam House Hotel (☎ 727462, Perth Rd)*, Birnam, is a grand-looking place with crow-stepped gables and four-poster beds; *en suite* B&B is from £35/50. The bar meals here are recommended. The *Tappit Hen (7 Atholl St)* serves coffee, cakes, sandwiches (around £2) and ploughman's lunches (£3.25 to £4.25). You can get fish and chips at the *Osprey (Atholl St)*.

Getting There & Away Scottish Citylink (☎ 0990-505050) buses between Glasgow/Edinburgh and Inverness stop at the train station (by Birnam) four or five times daily. Birnam to Perth or Pitlochry takes 20 minutes (£3.80 and £3.30, respectively). Trains (☎ 0345-484950) to Inverness or Perth run six to eight times daily.

Stagecoach (☎ 01738-629339) buses from Perth to Pitlochry and Aberfeldy all stop in Dunkeld. Strathtay Scottish (☎ 01382-228054) have a twice daily service (except Sunday) between Blairgowrie and Aberfeldy, via Dunkeld.

See Crieff earlier in this chapter for details of the Stagecoach 'Tourist Trail' bus.

Pitlochry
• pop 2439   ☎ 01796

Despite the tourist shops, Pitlochry is a pleasant town and makes a useful base for exploring the area; there are good transport connections if you don't have your own wheels.

The TIC (☎ 472215), 22 Atholl Rd, opens daily (except Sunday in winter). From late May to mid-September, its opening hours are from 9 am to 8 pm. You'll find an ATM at the Bank of Scotland, Atholl Rd.

Things to See If you haven't yet been on a tour of a whisky distillery, Pitlochry has two. **Bell's Blair Athol Distillery** (☎ 472234) is at the southern end of the town; admission costs £3 (with a voucher redeemable against purchases). The **Edradour** (☎ 472095) is Scotland's smallest distillery, 2½ miles east of Pitlochry; admission is free.

When the power station was built on the River Tummel, a **fish ladder** was constructed to allow salmon to swim up to their spawning grounds. It's at the south-western end of the town, and you can walk up to the observation chamber from the Pitlochry Festival Theatre to watch the fish, from April to October, daily, from 10 am to 5.30 pm. May and June are the best months.

Walks The TIC sells the useful publication *Pitlochry Walks* (50p), which lists four short and four long local walks.

The Edradour walk (2 miles) goes past the distillery and the Black Spout waterfall. An 8½-mile hike goes round Loch Faskally, past the theatre and fish ladder, and up to the Pass of Killiecrankie (see the following section). A 7-mile hike takes you to Blair Castle; you could catch the bus back, but check times with the TIC before you go. There's a steep 3-mile round trip to 400m-high Craigower, a viewpoint above Pitlochry. For a more spectacular view, tackle Ben Vrackie (841m, 2758 feet), a steep 6-mile walk from Moulin (on the A924).

Places to Stay Pitlochry is packed with places to stay, but anything central tends to be a bit pricey. *Pitlochry Youth Hostel* (☎ 472308, Knockard Rd) overlooks the town centre and has great views. It's open year-round and beds cost £7.75/6.50. Laundry facilities are available.

The cheapest B&Bs are in Moulin, just over a mile to the north on the A924. At

Craig Dubh Cottage (☎ 472058, Manse Rd), B&B costs around £14 per person; there's one double with bath attached for £30. Also on Manse Rd is *Lavalette* (☎ 472364), which is similarly priced.

There are plenty of places to stay along Atholl Rd, which runs through the centre of the town. *Craig Urrard Hotel* (☎ 472346, 10 Atholl Rd) charges from £20 to £28 per person. The luxurious *Acarsaid Hotel* (☎ 472389, 8 Atholl Rd) has 19 rooms, all with attached bath, from £25 to £40 per person. Dinner costs about £14 extra.

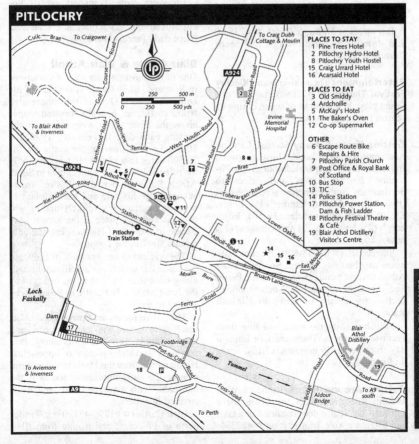

PITLOCHRY

PLACES TO STAY
1 Pine Trees Hotel
2 Pitlochry Hydro Hotel
8 Pitlochry Youth Hostel
15 Craig Urrard Hotel
16 Acarsaid Hotel

PLACES TO EAT
3 Old Smiddy
4 Ardchoille
5 McKay's Hotel
11 The Baker's Oven
12 Co-op Supermarket

OTHER
6 Escape Route Bike Repairs & Hire
7 Pitlochry Parish Church
9 Post Office & Royal Bank of Scotland
10 Bus Stop
13 TIC
14 Police Station
17 Pitlochry Power Station, Dam & Fish Ladder
18 Pitlochry Festival Theatre & Café
19 Blair Athol Distillery Visitor's Centre

CENTRAL & NORTH-EASTERN

The *Pitlochry Hydro Hotel* (☎ 472666, *Knockard Rd)* has singles/doubles from £55/100. The best hotel in town is the *Pine Trees* (☎ 472121, *Strathview Terrace)* with rooms from £71/78.

Places to Eat On Atholl Rd, try the hot pies for 49p at the *Baker's Oven*, or the takeaway fish and chips for £2.70 at *Ardchoille*. There's a *Co-op* supermarket if you're self-catering. The café at the *Festival Theatre* is recommended.

The *Old Smiddy* (☎ 472356, *154 Atholl Rd)* is also worthwhile. It boasts braised pheasant flambéed in brandy for £9.95, and there are vegetarian choices available.

Bar meals at *McKay's Hotel* (☎ 473888, *138 Atholl Rd)* include haggis and neeps (turnip) at £5.30.

Entertainment The well-known **Pitlochry Festival Theatre** (☎ 472680) stages a different play six nights out of seven during its season from May to October.

Getting There & Away Scottish Citylink runs approximately hourly buses between Inverness and Glasgow/Edinburgh via Pitlochry. Journey times and prices to destinations from Pitlochry are: Inverness (two hours, £7), Aviemore (1¼ hours, £5.50), Perth (40 minutes, £4.50), Edinburgh (2¾ hours, £6.30) and Glasgow (2¼ hours, £6.80).

Stagecoach (☎ 01738-629339) runs daily buses to Aberfeldy (except Sunday), Blair Atholl (except Sunday), Dunkeld and Perth. See the Strathtummel & Loch Rannoch section for details of buses to Kinloch Rannoch.

Pitlochry is on the main rail line from Perth to Inverness. There are five trains a day from Perth (30 minutes, £7.10), fewer on Sunday.

Getting Around Escape Route, 8 West Moulin Rd, hires bikes for £14/8 for a full/half-day. It also does repairs. For a taxi, call Elizabeth Yule Transport on ☎ 472290.

Pass of Killiecrankie

The first skirmish of the Jacobite rebellion took place in 1689 in this beautiful, rugged gorge, 3½ miles north of Pitlochry. Highland soldiers led by Jacobite Bonnie Dundee routed government troops led by General Mackay, but Bonnie Dundee was killed. One of the government soldiers is said to have jumped across the gap, now known as Soldier's Leap, to evade capture. An NTS Visitors Centre has a display on the battle and local natural history. The centre opens April to October, daily, from 10 am to 5.30 pm; admission costs £1.

Elizabeth Yule Transport (☎ 01796-472290) runs between Pitlochry and Blair Atholl/Calvine via Killiecrankie at least twice daily (except Sunday).

Blair Castle & Blair Atholl

One of the most popular tourist attractions in Scotland, Blair Castle is the seat of the Duke of Atholl. Outside this impressive white castle, set beneath forested slopes above the River Garry, a piper pipes in the crowds each day. In February 1996, the 10th duke died, leaving the castle and its 70,000 acres to a charitable trust and only the title to his heir, a distant cousin in South Africa. Since the new duke has refused to acknowledge his title and has no plans to move to Scotland it's unlikely that he will take his cousin's place at the annual May parade of the Atholl Highlanders, the only private army in the country.

The original tower was built in 1269, but the castle has undergone significant remodelling since then. In 1746 it was besieged by the Jacobites, the last castle in Britain to be subject to siege.

Thirty-two rooms are open to the public, and they're packed with paintings, arms and armour, china, lace and embroidery, presenting a wonderful picture of upper-class Highland life from the 1500s to the present. One of the most impressive rooms is the ballroom, with a wooden roof and walls covered in antlers.

Blair Castle (☎ 01796-481207) is 7 miles north of Pitlochry, and a mile from Blair

Atholl village. It's open daily from April to October, from 10 am to 6 pm (last entry 5 pm); tickets cost £5.50/4.50 (family tickets are £17), and there's also a £2 parking charge. There's a restaurant and a tearoom at the castle.

The other attractions in Blair Atholl village include a working **water mill** (☎ 01796-481321) dating from 1613. You can hire bikes from Atholl Mountain Bikes (☎ 01796-481646) for £10/6 for a full/half-day. It has a leaflet listing cycle routes in the area, including a 16-mile ride along an estate road up Glen Tilt, a 12-mile ride around Bruar Falls and Old Struan, or a 6-mile ride to Killiecrankie Pass and back.

The *Atholl Arms* (☎ 01796-481205) is a pub near the station and B&B is £32.50 per person.

Elizabeth Yule Transport (☎ 01796-472290) runs a service two to four times daily between Pitlochry and Blair Atholl (20 minutes, £1.10). Some buses go directly to the castle. There's a train station in the village, but not all trains stop here.

For a continuation of this route, see The Cairngorms section in The Highlands chapter.

BLAIRGOWRIE & GLENSHEE
• pop 8000   ☎ 01250

Blairgowrie and Braemar are the main accommodation centres for the Glenshee ski resort, although there's a small settlement 5 miles south of the ski runs at Spittal of Glenshee.

There's a TIC (☎ 872960), 26 Wellmeadow (the central square), Blairgowrie, which opens all year. You'll find two banks with ATMs in Allan St, just off Wellmeadow.

Glenshee Ski Resort Glenshee ski resort (☎ 875800), on the border of Perthshire and Aberdeenshire, has 38 pistes and it's one of Scotland's largest skiing areas. The chair lift (£3.70 return) can whisk you up to 910m, near the top of The Cairnwell (933m, 3060 feet). It's open daily from May to mid-September, and whenever there's enough snow in winter. A combination of instruc-

tion, hire and lift passes starts at £73 for five days and is available from Glenshee Ski Centre (☎ 01339-741320).

Other Things to See There's not much to see in Blairgowrie, but **Keathbank Mill** (☎ 872025), off the A93 Braemar road, is worth a look. You'll see Scotland's largest working water wheel, a steam engine dating from 1862, a model railway, a heraldry museum and woodcarving displays. It's open from Easter to September, daily, from 10.30 am to 5 pm; admission costs £2.95/1.75.

About 3 miles south of Blairgowrie, by the A93 to Perth, there's a curious attraction – the **Meikleour beech hedge**, planted in 1746. At 30m, it's the world's highest hedge. It must be difficult to trim.

Alyth is an interesting village about 5 miles east of Blairgowrie. Ask the TIC for the *Walk Old Alyth* leaflet; there are lots of old buildings to see, including church ruins dating from 1296. **Alyth Museum** (☎ 01738-632488), in Commercial St, covers local history. It's open from May to September, Wednesday to Sunday, from 1 to 5 pm (admission is free).

Places to Stay & Eat For year-round B&B, try *Dunmore* (☎ 874451, Newton St), Blairgowrie, which costs from £15 to £16.50 per person. The *Angus Hotel* (☎ 872455, 46 Wellmeadow) does B&B from £37.50 per person, but winter special rates can be as low as £30 for dinner, B&B. The bar meals here are good and cost from £4.50 to £8.95. *Cargill's Bistro* (☎ 876735, Lower Mill St) does excellent snacks (soup and a roll, £1.45) and meals from £5.50 to £10.50.

There are several supermarkets, including *Kwik Save*, by Wellmeadow. Of several takeaway places, the *Balti of Bengal* (☎ 876076, 46 High St) is one of the best, with three-course weekday lunches only £3.95. Best of all is the *Alyth Fish & Chip Shop*, Alyth, where a tasty haddock and chips is £2.85.

The *Losset Inn* is by the A926, just west of Alyth. It's a drovers inn, dating from 1760. Home-made bar meals here are mostly under £5 and some are as cheap as £3. Camping in the adjacent field costs only £4 for two people.

In Glenshee, you could try the **Blackwater Inn** (☎ 882234), Blackwater, where B&B costs around £18 per person and dinner is £10 extra. The **Compass Christian Centre** (☎ 885209, Glenshee Lodge) charges around £13.50 per person for B&B, and only £5 more for dinner.

The **Spittal of Glenshee Hotel** (☎ 885215) is a large place offering B&B in rooms with attached bath from £17.50 to £27 per person. The hotel has a good bar and a bunkhouse for £12.50 per person (without cooking facilities). The grand **Dalmunzie House Hotel** (☎ 885224), Spittal of Glenshee, boasts the highest nine-hole golf course in Britain and is set in a 6000 acre estate, 1½ miles off the main road. B&B costs from £50/78.

Getting There & Away Strathtay Scottish (☎ 01382-228054) operates a service from Perth to Blairgowrie (50 minutes, £2.05), hourly from Monday to Saturday, and six times a day on Sunday. This bus also runs from Blairgowrie to Dundee (one hour, £2.25), with the same frequency.

The only service from Blairgowrie to the Glenshee area is the postbus (☎ 872766) to Spittal of Glenshee (no Sunday service). A small postbus serves the ski resort from Ballater and Braemar, once daily except Sunday.

Dundee & Angus

Formerly part of the region of Tayside, Dundee and Angus are now two separate unitary authorities.

Dundee was once a whaling port and the centre of the thriving jute industry. It's now a victim of 20th century decline and chronic unemployment, but has several interesting attractions for visitors, including Captain Scott's ship *Discovery*.

Robert the Bruce signed a declaration of independence from England at Arbroath Abbey in 1320. Although a ruin, much of the abbey still stands. The main draw in Angus is Glamis Castle of *Macbeth* fame. Angus is an attractive county of peaceful glens and wide straths running down to the sea. The area was part of the Pictish kingdom in the 7th and 8th centuries; there are still interesting Pictish symbol stones at Aberlemno.

GETTING AROUND

Angus Council publish an annual *Public Transport Map & Guide*, available from TICs. For information on buses within the Dundee and Broughty Ferry area phone ☎ 01382-433125 (Dundee City Council, Transportation Division); for Angus, call the Transport Team, ☎ 01307-461775. For services throughout Dundee and Angus, contact Strathtay Scottish (☎ 01382-228054); its Day Rover ticket, covering all services, is £4.80.

Postbus services run up the Angus Glens. From Blairgowrie, a postbus runs up Glen Isla; Glen Prosen and Glen Clova are reached from Kirriemuir.

The rail inquiry line is ☎ 0345-484950.

DUNDEE
• pop 177,540 ☎ 01382

Poor Dundee. This grey city is an unfortunate example of the worst of 1960s and 70s town planning – ugly blocks of flats and office buildings joined by unsightly concrete walkways. Once there were more millionaires per head in Dundee than anywhere else in Britain. Today it's Dole City, with one of the highest unemployment rates in Scotland.

In 1993, the city decided to stake all its tourist fortunes on one main attraction – Captain Scott's polar research ship *Discovery* – but the city's main asset is its people. Despite the feeling of desolation here, the vigour that remains in the city is in the hearts of the Dundonians, who are among the friendliest, most welcoming and most entertaining people you'll meet anywhere in the country.

It's worth staying here a while. Dundee's hotels and restaurants are good value, there are some great drinking places and 4 miles east of the city is the seaside suburb of Broughty Ferry.

History

Dundee first began to grow in importance as a result of trade links with Flanders and the Baltic ports. It was awarded the first of its royal charters by King William in the late 12th century.

In its chequered history, Dundee was captured by Edward I, besieged by Henry VIII and destroyed by Cromwellian forces in the 17th century. It became the second most important trading city in Scotland (after Edinburgh).

In the 19th century, Dundee was a major player in the shipbuilding and railway engineering industries. Linen and wool gave way to jute, and since whale oil was used in the production of jute, whaling developed alongside. At one time, there were as many as 43,000 people employed in the textile industry, but as the jute workers became redundant, light engineering, electronics and food processing provided employment.

Dundee is often called the city of the three 'Js' – jute, jam and journalism. No jute is produced here anymore, and when the famous Keiller jam factory was taken over in 1988, production was transferred to England. There is still journalism, and DC Thomson, best known for its comics (such as the *Beano*), is the city's largest employer.

Orientation

Most people approach the city from the Tay Road Bridge or along the A90 from Perth. From the A90, turn onto Riverside Drive for the city centre. The train station and *Discovery* are near the bridge; the bus station is a short walk to the north, just off Seagate.

Four miles to the east of Dundee is Broughty Ferry, Dundee's seaside resort. Regular buses run to the resort and it's a very pleasant place to stay.

Information

The very helpful TIC (☎ 434664), 4 City Square, opens May to September, Monday to Saturday, from 9 am to 6 pm, and Sunday 10 am to 4 pm; from October to April, it's open Monday to Saturday only, from 9 am to 5 pm. As well as the usual bed-booking facility (£1 for local bookings), it sells Scottish Citylink and National Express tickets. Pick up a copy of *What's On*, free from the TIC.

Guided walks are available with a minimum charge of £10 per hour per group (minimum four people) – a heritage and industrial walk, a maritime walk, and other possibilities can be catered for. For details, call ☎ 532754.

You'll find banks with ATMs in High St and Murraygate.

Medical Services Dundee Royal Infirmary (☎ 660111) is on Barrack Rd.

Discovery Point

Make an effort to see Dundee's much-publicised visitor attraction, centred on Captain Scott's famous polar expedition vessel, the research ship *Discovery*.

The ship was constructed here in 1900, and was built with a hull at least two feet thick to survive the Antarctic pack ice. Scott sailed for the Antarctic in 1901 and, in a not uneventful voyage, spent two winters trapped in the ice.

After viewing the interesting exhibitions and audiovisual displays in the main building, you go on board the ship to see the cabins used by Scott and his crew. The complex (☎ 201245) is on the bank of the Firth of Tay, near the Tay Road Bridge. It's open daily from 10 am to 5 pm (to 4 pm daily from November to March). Admission costs £4.50/3.45; the joint ticket with the Verdant Works costs £8/6.

HM Frigate Unicorn

Unlike the *Discovery*, Dundee's other floating tourist sight retains the atmosphere of an old ship. Built as a warship in 1824, the *Unicorn* is the oldest British-built warship still afloat – perhaps because it never saw action. By the mid-19th century, sailing ships were outclassed by steam and the *Unicorn* served as storage for gunpowder, then later as a training vessel. When it was proposed to break up the historic ship for scrap in the 1960s, a preservation society was formed.

Wandering around the four decks gives you an excellent impression of what it must have been like for the crew forced to live in such cramped conditions. The *Unicorn* (☎ 200900) is berthed in Victoria Dock, just east of the Tay Bridge. Open daily from 10 am to 5 pm (from November to February, weekdays only, 10 am to 4 pm), tickets are £3/2, including a guided tour (also available in French and German).

Other Things to See

The **McManus Galleries** (☎ 432020), Albert Square, is a solid Victorian Gothic building, designed by Gilbert Scott, containing the city's art collection and museum. The exhibits are well displayed and interesting, and include the history of the city from the Iron Age. There's an impressive display of Scottish Victorian paintings, furniture and silver. Look out for the display on William McGonagall, Scotland's worst poet, whose lines about the Tay Rail Bridge disaster are memorably awful. The galleries are open

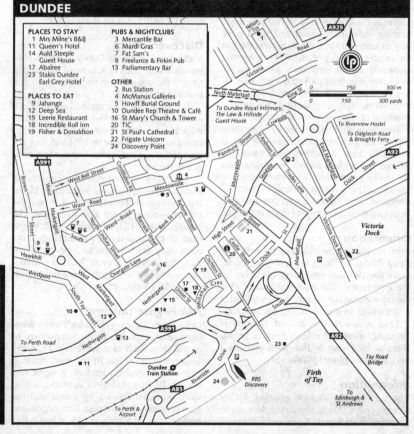

DUNDEE

PLACES TO STAY
1 Mrs Milne's B&B
11 Queen's Hotel
14 Auld Steeple Guest House
17 Abalree
23 Stakis Dundee Earl Grey Hotel

PLACES TO EAT
9 Jahangir
12 Deep Sea
15 Leerie Restaurant
18 Incredible Roll Inn
19 Fisher & Donaldson

PUBS & NIGHTCLUBS
3 Mercantile Bar
6 Mardi Gras
7 Fat Sam's
8 Freelance & Firkin Pub
13 Parliamentary Bar

OTHER
2 Bus Station
4 McManus Galleries
5 Howff Burial Ground
10 Dundee Rep Theatre & Café
16 St Mary's Church & Tower
20 TIC
21 St Paul's Cathedral
22 Frigate Unicorn
24 Discovery Point

Monday to Saturday from 10 am to 5 pm (from 11 am on Monday); admission is free.

Over the road is the **Howff Burial Ground**, a historic graveyard given to the people of Dundee by Mary Queen of Scots. The carved gravestones feature the signs and symbols of the old craft guilds and date back to the 16th century.

The **Verdant Works** (☎ 225282), West Henderson's Wynd, is a heritage centre in a restored jute works which details the history of the jute industry. It's open daily from 10 am to 5 pm (closing at 4 pm from November to March), except Sunday when it opens at 11 am; admission is £4.50/3.45, or a joint ticket with the *Discovery* costs £8/6.

It's worth the hike up to **The Law**, at 174m the highest point in the city. **Mills Observatory** (☎ 667138), at the summit, has a 10-inch telescope for public use. It's open evenings are from October to March, daily, 3 to 10 pm (admission is free). The Law is the remains of an ancient volcanic plug and there are great views of the city, the two Tay bridges, and across to Fife. The 1½-mile Tay road bridge was opened in 1966. The **railway bridge** is just over 2 miles long, still the longest in Europe. The part nearest Dundee was completed in 1887, replacing a section destroyed by a storm one dark night in 1879. Moments after the collapse, a train attempted to cross, and plunged into the firth, killing 75 people.

Broughty Ferry

This pleasant suburb is 4 miles east of Dundee. There's a long, sandy beach (though not exactly spotless) and a number of good places to eat and drink.

Claypotts Castle (☎ 01786-450000), built in the late 16th century, was once in the country but has now been absorbed into suburbia. Looking like a house perched on top of a castle, it's actually one of the most complete Z-plan tower houses. Phone for details of opening hours.

Broughty Castle Museum (☎ 776121) is in a reconstructed 16th century tower guarding the entrance to the Firth of Tay. It has an interesting display on the local whaling industry. Admission is free, but it's closed Friday.

Places to Stay

Hostels & Colleges *Riverview* (☎ 450565, 127 Broughty Ferry Rd) is a 10 minute walk east of the bus station. It's open all year; reservations are recommended since there are only 17 beds. You'll pay £10 per person (£12 with breakfast).

From 15 March to 10 April and 20 June to 30 September, you can stay in the halls of residence at the *University of Dundee* (☎ 344038) in West Park, 1½ miles from the centre. Single and twin rooms are available from £20/30.

B&Bs & Guesthouses *Abalree* (☎ 223867, 20 Union St) is a basic guesthouse but you couldn't be more central, and overnight B&B costs around £17/28. Just around the corner, and much more upmarket, is the *Auld Steeple Guest House* (☎ 200302, 94 Nethergate). It charges £22/36 for a single/double with attached bath, £18/34 without. In the north of the city, a 10 minute walk from the bus station, is *Mrs Milne's* (☎ 225354, 8 Nelson Terrace) which has B&B for around £14. *Hillside Guest House* (☎ 223443, 43 Constitution St), off Constitution Rd, charges from £20 to £30 per person.

In the east, *Errolbank Guest House* (☎ 462118, 9 Dalgleish Rd) charges from £17.50 to £25 per person. At the *Birks* (☎ 453393, 149 Arbroath Rd) B&B is available from £16/30.

There's a good range of places to stay in Broughty Ferry. *Auchenean* (☎ 774782, 177 Hamilton St) charges £17/34. Dinner is available from £6.50. It's a pleasant place, a five minute walk from the beach. *Hollies Orchard* (☎ 776403, 12 Castle Roy Rd) does *en suite* B&B for £25 per person.

Hotels On the western side of Dundee, just off the Perth Rd and about 1½ miles from the city centre, is the *Shaftesbury Hotel* (☎ 669216, 1 Hyndford St). It's a former jute baron's mansion, and an excellent place to stay; it's popular with businesspeople.

B&B costs from £44.50/58, but there are bargain midweek and weekend rates available. There's a good restaurant and the set dinner is £14.90.

The two main business hotels in the city centre are the *Queen's Hotel* (☎ *322515, 160 Nethergate)*, a grand Victorian hotel with B&B from £40/58; and the waterfront *Stakis Dundee Earl Grey Hotel* (☎ *229271)* by the Tay Bridge, which charges from £45 to £125.50 per person. The lowest rates apply at the weekend.

In Broughty Ferry, the friendly *Beach House Hotel* (☎ *776614, 22 Esplanade)* has five *en suite* rooms with B&B for around £38/48.

Places to Eat

There's a surprising number of interesting places to eat in Dundee, and prices are very competitive. Self-caterers should head for *Tesco*, just off Riverside Drive, near the train station. For a snack, the popular *Incredible Roll Inn* *(Whitehall Crescent)* is a good sandwich shop with 100 different types of hot and cold filled rolls, from 80p to £2.60. The *bus station cafeteria*, Seagate, does all main courses under £2.55.

The *Het Theatre Café* (☎ *206699)* is at the Dundee Rep Theatre on Tay Square. It's a European-style coffee-bar, open daily except Sunday, and a great place for coffee, a drink or a meal.

The *Deep Sea* *(81 Nethergate)* is the oldest fish and chip shop in Dundee, but it doesn't stay open late; haddock and chips is £3.40. Nearby, the *Leerie Restaurant* *(Unit 80, Nethergate Centre)* is very cheap, with main courses from £4 to £5.35. Rather more upmarket, *Fisher & Donaldson* *(12 Whitehall St)* is an excellent bakery/pâtisserie with a café attached.

It's worth going to *Jahangir* (☎ *202022, 1 Session St)* for the décor alone. This extraordinary Indian restaurant is painted pink on the outside; inside, it's pure Moghul Hollywood, with an over-the-top tent, and a fountain with goldfish and carp (they're not on the menu). The food's good and it also does takeaways, with chicken curries from

£4.10. It's open until 1 am at the weekends, midnight during the week.

There are lots of interesting places to eat along Perth Rd, although some of them are a fair walk from the centre. The best restaurant in Dundee, *Raffles Restaurant* (☎ *226344, 18 Perth Rd)* is not far, however, and main courses are £8 to £11.75.

The most interesting restaurant here is the *Agacan* (☎ *644227, 113 Perth Rd)*, part Turkish restaurant, part art gallery, and a great place to spend the evening.

In Broughty Ferry, *Visocchi's* *(40 Gray St)* is an Italian ice-cream shop and café that's an institution. *Gulistan Balti & Tandoori Restaurant* (☎ *738844, Queen St)* is in an old church hall near the train station; in the early evening (5 to 7 pm, not Saturday) it has a set menu for £7.95.

Entertainment

The *Dundee Rep Theatre* (☎ *223530, Tay Square)* hosts touring companies and also stages its own performances. Some of the Dundee Jazz and Blues Festival is held here in June.

The *Parliamentary Bar* (☎ *202658, 134 Nethergate)* is a large, stylish pub popular with students. There's live jazz on Saturday afternoon.

The *Mercantile Bar* (☎ *225500, 100 Commercial St)* is a lively city centre pub. The *Freelance & Firkin* (☎ *227080, 13 Brown St)* has journalism as its theme. It's housed in a converted school building and brews its own beer on the premises. There's live music on Saturday (pop/rock) and a disco on Friday – admission is free.

In Broughty Ferry, the beer's good at the *Fisherman's Tavern* *(12 Fort St)*. Another good place to drink is the *Ship Inn* *(121 Fisher St)* which also serves pub grub.

Dundee has several nightclubs. *Fat Sam's* (☎ *228181, 31 South Ward Rd)* is popular with students. Nearby, there's *Mardi Gras* (☎ *205551)*.

Getting There & Away

Dundee is 445 miles from London, 84 from Glasgow, 62 from Edinburgh, 67 from Aberdeen and 21 from Perth. If you're driving over the Tay Road Bridge from Fife, it's toll-free in that direction only.

Air The airport (☎ 643242), in Riverside Drive, close to the centre, has flights to Aberdeen, Edinburgh and Manchester.

Bus National Express (☎ 0990-808080) operates four services a day (two direct) to Dundee from London (10 hours direct, from £22), including one night service.

Scottish Citylink (☎ 0990-505050) has hourly buses from Edinburgh (two hours, £6.50) and Glasgow (2¼ hours, £7.80). On some services, you may have to change in Perth.

There are also hourly services to Perth (35 minutes, £3) and Aberdeen (two hours, £6.50). Some runs to Aberdeen go via Arbroath, others via Forfar. However, getting to the west coast is a major pain – you must go via Glasgow to reach either Fort William or Oban.

Strathtay Scottish (☎ 01382-228054) runs buses to Perth (hourly, one hour, £2.20), Blairgowrie (hourly, one hour, £2.25), Forfar (once or twice an hour, 40 minutes, £2.05), Kirriemuir (hourly, 70 minutes, £2.45), Brechin (13 daily, change at Forfar, 1¼ hours, £3.30) and Arbroath (every 30 minutes, one hour, £2.35).

Train For rail information phone ☎ 0345-484950. From Edinburgh (1¼ hours, £14) and Glasgow (1½ hours, £18.50) trains run at least once an hour, Monday to Saturday; hourly on Sunday to Edinburgh, every two hours on Sunday to Glasgow.

For Aberdeen (1¼ hours, £16.40), trains run via Arbroath and Stonehaven. There are around two trains an hour, fewer on Sunday.

Car Rental companies include Arnold Clark (☎ 225382), East Dock St, and Mitchell's Self Drive (☎ 223484), 90 Marketgait.

Getting Around
Bus Most city-centre buses pass along High St, stopping by St Mary's Church.

It's possible to catch a train to Broughty Ferry, but the buses (15 minutes, 80p) are much more frequent.

Taxi Phone Tele Taxis (☎ 889333) if you need a cab.

ARBROATH
• **pop 23,528** ☎ **01241**
Source of the famous Arbroath smokie (smoked haddock), this fishing port was established in the 12th century. Nowadays, the town is impoverished and unemployment is high, but it's still interesting for all that. There's an all-year TIC (☎ 872609) in Market Place and you'll find banks with ATMs at nearby Brothock Bridge.

For sea fishing trips, contact the skipper of the *Girl Katherine* (☎ 874510).

Things to See King William the Lion founded **Arbroath Abbey** (☎ 878756) in 1178, and he's buried here. It was at the

The Declaration of Arbroath

In April 1320, the Abbot of Arbroath (who was also Chancellor of Scotland) wrote a letter to Pope John XXII, countering English claims of suzerainty. This letter, also called the Declaration of Independence, was sealed by no less than eight earls and 31 barons and had been prompted by the pope's summons of four Scottish bishops the previous year on charges of rebellion. The Archbishop of York's claims of primacy over St Andrews (which the pope had accepted) were only part of the continuing English campaign to control Scotland, despite their disastrous defeat at Bannockburn only six years before.

Part of the text, originally written in Latin, reads: 'For so long as a hundred of us remain alive, we will yield in no least way to English dominion. For we fight, not for glory, nor riches, nor honour, but only for freedom, which no good man surrenders but with his life'.

abbey that Robert the Bruce signed Scotland's famous declaration of independence from England in 1320. Closed following the Dissolution, the fortified abbey fell into ruin, but enough survives to make this an impressive sight. There's a tall gable in the south transept, with a circular window that once held a shipping beacon, and parts of the nave and sacristy are intact. The Abbey is near the top of High St, near the TIC, and bus and rail stations. It's open standard HS times; tickets cost £1.80/1.30. There's a good booklet available for £1.95.

The **Signal Tower Museum** (☎ 875598), Ladyloan, covers local history, including the textile and fishing industries. It's open from Monday to Saturday, from 10 am to 5 pm, and (in July and August) Sunday, 2 to 5 pm; admission is free.

At **St Vigeans**, about a mile north of the town, there's an interesting red sandstone **church** perched on top of a conical hill. At the foot of the hill, you'll find the excellent museum of **Pictish & medieval sculptured stones**, which includes crosses and human and animal carvings. It's open from April to September, daily, from 9.30 am to 6.30 pm (from 2 pm on Sunday); admission is free. The key's kept at cottage No 7.

Three miles north-east of Arbroath, **Auchmithie** is a cliff-top village with a steep descent to an attractive stony beach, where there are several caves.

Places to Stay & Eat By the harbour there's *Harbour House Guest House* (☎ 878047, 4 Shore) charging from £15 to £18 per person for B&B. There are several other B&Bs in nearby Market St and Ladybridge St.

Café Rendezvous (1B Millgate), behind the Arbroath Herald building near the bus station, is incredibly cheap: soup and bread is just 95p, stovies and bread are £1, and all main courses are under £3.60. The *Old Brewhouse* (☎ 879945, 34 Reform St), near the bottom of High St, does good bar meals, which includes seafood dishes. *Santana* (☎ 872839, 43 High St) is an Italian restaurant with pasta dishes from £4.20 to £6.50.

Getting There & Away Scottish Citylink (☎ 0990-505050) buses run every two hours to Aberdeen (1½ hours, £6), via Montrose and Stonehaven. The Strathtay Scottish company (☎ 01382-228054) operates buses to Brechin (two tickets required, £1.80 and £1.20), changing at Montrose. Bus No 140 runs from Arbroath to Auchmithie roughly every two hours (but only twice on Sunday).

There are frequent buses to Dundee, but it's best to go by train along the scenic coastline (20 minutes, £3, two trains an hour).

GLAMIS CASTLE & VILLAGE

Looking every bit a Scottish castle, with turrets and battlements, Glamis (pronounced glamz) was the legendary setting for Shakespeare's *Macbeth*. The Grampians and an extensive park provide a spectacular backdrop for this family home of the Earls of Strathmore and Kinghorne. A royal residence since 1372, the Queen Mother (née Elizabeth Bowes-Lyon) spent her childhood here and Princess Margaret (the Queen's sister) was born at Glamis.

The five-storey, L-shaped castle was given to the Lyon family in 1372, but was significantly altered in the 17th century. Inside, the most impressive room is the drawing room, with its arched plasterwork ceiling. There's a display of armour and weaponry in the crypt (haunted) and frescoes in the chapel (also haunted). Duncan's Hall is where King Duncan was murdered in *Macbeth*. You can also look round the royal apartments, including the Queen Mother's bedroom.

Glamis Castle (☎ 01307-840393) is 12 miles north of Dundee. It's open daily from April to October, from 10.30 am to 5.30 pm (last entry 4.45 pm), and there's a restaurant on site. You're escorted round in a guided tour which takes an hour and leaves every 15 minutes. Tickets are £5.20/2.70.

The **Angus Folk Museum** (☎ 01307-840288, NTS) is just off The Square in Glamis village. In a row of 18th century cottages, you'll find a fine collection of domestic and agricultural relics. It's open from May to September, daily, from 11 am to 5 pm, and October weekends; admission is £2.40/1.60.

There are two to five buses a day from Dundee (35 minutes, £2.10) to Glamis (school), operated by Strathtay Buses (☎ 01382-228054); some runs continue to Kirriemuir. There's also a bus to Perth on the first Thursday of each month.

FORFAR & AROUND
* pop 12,652   ☎ 01307

Forfar, the county capital of Angus, isn't terribly exciting, but there are some excellent sites nearby. The TIC (☎ 467876), 40 East High St, opens April to September; ask for the *Town Trail* leaflet. Buses stop in East High St, by the Royal Bank. The bank has an ATM.

Things to See The ruins and early Romanesque square tower of **Restenneth Priory** are 1½ miles from Forfar (by the B9113), probably founded by David I. It's open at all times and admission is free. About 4 miles east of Forfar, there's the site of the **Battle of Nechtansmere**, where the Picts defeated invading Northumbrians in 685.

Five miles north-east of Forfar, by the B9134 at Aberlemno, there are some of Scotland's best **Pictish stones**; these are well worth going to see. Check with Historic Scotland (☎ 0131-668 8800) as they may be moved in the near future. There are several 7th to 9th century stones by the roadside with various symbols, including the z-rod and double disc.

In the churchyard at the bottom of the hill, there's a magnificent 8th century cross-slab displaying a Celtic cross, interlace decoration, entwined beasts and, on the reverse, a battle scene. See the boxed text 'Pictish Symbol Stones' on the next page. The stones are covered up from November to March; otherwise there's open access (admission is free). The adjacent **Aberlemno parish church** has a 12th or 13th century stone baptismal font.

Places to Stay & Eat Nearby Kirriemuir (see the next section) is a nicer place to stay

but, if you need B&B in Forfar, try *Mrs Horsburgh's* (☎ *468205, 34 Canmore St)*, off Castle St, where single/double rooms are from £12/20.

Cheap places to eat include five bakeries on East High St and Castle St; try a Forfar bridie (£1.20) at *Saddler's (35 East High St)*. There are the usual Chinese and Indian takeaways too. *Raffters Bar (116 Castle St)* does bar lunches from £2 to £4.50. *O'Hara's Bistro Bar (41 West High St)* does lunchtime snacks; evening main courses, from £7.95 to £13.95, include prime Angus steaks, and Mexican, balti and seafood dishes.

Getting There & Away Scottish Citylink (☎ 0990-505050) buses run three or four times daily to Dundee (30 minutes, £2.80), Brechin (20 minutes, £3.30) and Aberdeen (1½ hours, £6.50).

Strathtay Scottish (☎ 01382-228054) operates buses to Dundee (once or twice an hour, 40 minutes, £2.05), Kirriemuir (hourly, 25 minutes, £1.20), and Aberlemno and Brechin (once every hour or two, 15 and 30 minutes respectively).

KIRRIEMUIR
* pop 5306   ☎ 01575

The highly recommended conservation town of Kirriemuir is a very attractive place, with narrow winding streets and a great feeling of times past. Kirriemuir is a good base for exploring the Angus Glens (see the next section), and it's one of the cheapest places to eat in the country. The TIC (☎ 574097), Cumberland Close, opens April to September. There are two banks with ATMs on Bank St.

Things to See
The NTS property **Barrie's Birthplace** (☎ 572646), 9 Brechin Rd, is a two-storey house where JM Barrie, author of *Peter Pan*, was born in 1860. The upper floors are furnished in traditional style. There's also an outside wash-house and an exhibition about Barrie's work. It's open from May to September, Monday to Saturday, from 10 am to

5.30 pm (Sunday from 1.30), and on weekends in October. Admission costs £2/1.30.

By the town square there's **The Tolbooth**, dating from 1604, and previously used as a jail. The **Aviation Museum** (☎ 573233), Bellies Brae, has a large collection of WWII relics, both Allied and German. It's open daily, from 10 am to 5 pm; donations are welcomed.

Places to Stay & Eat
The *Airlie Arms Hotel* (☎ 572847, *St Malcolm's Wynd*) is in a medieval monastery which was converted into an inn after the Dissolution. The original arch-roofed refectory is now the function suite. Single/double B&B, all *en suite*, costs £26.50/43.

Bar meals range from £2.95 to £3.75, high teas are £5.95, and a three-course table

---

Pictish Symbol Stones

The Romans permanently occupied only the southern half of Britain up to 410. Caledonia, the section north of Edinburgh and Glasgow, was mostly left alone, especially after the mysterious disappearance of the Ninth Legion.

Caledonia was the homeland of the Picts, about whom little is known. In the 9th century they were culturally absorbed by the Scots, leaving a few archaeological remains and a scattering of Pictish place names beginning with Pit-. However, there are hundreds of mysterious standing stones decorated with intricate symbols, mainly in the north-east. The capital of the ancient Southern Pictish kingdom is said to have been at Forteviot in Strathearn, and Pictish symbol stones are to be found throughout this area and all the way up the eastern coast of Scotland into Sutherland and Caithness.

It's believed that the stones were set up to record Pictish lineages and alliances, but no-one is yet quite sure exactly how the system worked. The stones fall into three groups: Class I, the earliest, are rough blocks of stone, carved with any combination from a basic set of 28 symbols; Class II are decorated with a Celtic cross as well as with symbols; and Class III, dating from the end of the Pictish era (790-840), have only figures and a cross.

With your own transport, it's possible to follow a number of symbol-stone trails in the area. Starting at Dundee (visit the McManus Galleries first), drive north-east to Arbroath. On the outskirts of Arbroath is St Vigeans Museum which contains several interesting stones. Continue north along the A92 to Montrose, where there are more stones in the local museum. Along the A935, in Brechin Cathedral, is a good example of a Class III stone. From Brechin, take the B9134 to Aberlemno, where there are excellent examples of all three classes. Along the A94, at Meigle, there's a museum with one of the best collections of stones in the country.

For more information, it's worth getting a copy of *The Pictish Trail* by Anthony Jackson (Orkney Press), which lists 11 driving tours, or his more detailed *Symbol Stones of Scotland*, both available in TICs.

d'hôte dinner is £10.95. French is spoken here.

Cheaper B&B is available at *Crepto* (☎ *572746, Kinnordy Place*) for £16 to £17 per person. *Woodlands* (☎ *572582, 2 Lisden Gardens*) charges £18 to £20 per person.

Kirrie Food Bazaar (Reform St) does cheap takeaways for around £1 to £1.50. *Tin On (30 Roods)* does chicken chow mein for £3.50. There's a large *Tesco* supermarket across the street. The popular and amusingly named *Kilt & Clogs (High St)* does lunches for under £4.

Getting There & Away

Strathtay Scottish (☎ 01382-228054) operates hourly bus services to Dundee (every two hours on Sunday, 70 minutes, £2.45), Forfar (hourly, 25 minutes, £1.20), and Glamis (twice daily except Sunday, 20 minutes).

A postbus (☎ 01463-256200) runs from Kirriemuir to Glen Prosen (once daily except Sunday); another runs to Glen Clova (twice on weekdays, once on Saturday, £2.10 to Glendoll).

ANGUS GLENS

There are five major glens in the north of Angus: Glens Isla, Prosen, Clova, Lethnot and Esk.

Although each glen has its own peculiar character, they all have attractive scenery. Glen Clova and Glen Esk are clearly the most beautiful while Glen Lethnot is the least frequented.

Glen Isla

This glen, which runs roughly parallel with Glen Shee, has a number of scattered communities. At the foot of the glen, by Bridge of Craigisla, there's a pleasant waterfall, **Reekie Linn**.

The wild and mountainous upper reaches of Glen Isla include the Caenlochan National Nature Reserve.

A small postbus (☎ 01463-256200) operates from Blairgowrie to Auchavan at the head of the glen, once daily except Sunday.

Glen Prosen

Near the foot of the glen, 6 miles north of Kirriemuir, there's a good forest walk up to the **Airlie monument** on Tulloch Hill (380m, 1246 feet); start from the eastern road, about a mile beyond Dykehead.

From Glenprosen Lodge, at the top of the glen, the **Kilbo Path** leads over a pass between Mayar (928m, 3044 feet) and Driesh (947m, 3106 feet), descending to Glendoll Youth Hostel at the head of Glen Clova. Allow at least five hours, and wear appropriate mountain gear.

The Kirriemuir to Glen Prosen postbus runs once daily except Sunday.

Glen Clova

This long and beautiful glen stretches north from Kirriemuir and is dominated by craggy mountains at its head. Look out for the waterwheel by the Clova Hotel, and picturesque **Cortachy Castle** in the lower part of the glen, where Charles II stayed in the 17th century.

There are great hikes in the glen, including the **Loch Brandy** circuit from the hotel (four hours) and Mayar and Driesh from Glendoll Youth Hostel (six to seven hours); use OS map No 44.

You can also walk **Jock's Road** from the hostel to Braemar (five to seven hours), but this route climbs above 900m and it's not an easy option. The descent to Glen Callater is very steep and may require crampons in winter. You'll need OS map Nos 43 and 44.

Camping (☎ *01575-550233*) with basic facilities is available in summer by the bridge at Acharn (near the end of the road) for £3 per tent. *Glendoll Youth Hostel* (☎ *01575-550236*), at the end of the Glen Clova public road, opens late March to October and beds cost £6.10/4.95. The *Clova Hotel* (☎ *01575-550222*), 3½ miles down the road from the hostel, charges £28/56 for B&B. Bar meals cost from £3 to £6. There's also an all-year eight-bed bunkhouse for £3 per person. It has a kitchen, but no shower.

The Kirriemuir to Glen Clova postbus runs services twice on weekdays and once

CENTRAL & NORTH-EASTERN

on Saturday. The 8.30 am departure from Kirriemuir goes to the hostel (£2.10), but the 3.05 pm departure from Kirriemuir (not Saturday) only goes as far as Clova Hotel.

Glen Lethnot

At the foot of this glen, about 5 miles northwest of Brechin, there are the **Brown and White Caterthuns**. These two extraordinary Iron Age hill forts, defended by ramparts and ditches, are at 287m and 298m, respectively. From the road between them it's an easy walk to either fort, and they're both great viewpoints. If you don't have your own car, you'll have to walk from Brechin, or from Edzell (4 miles).

Two miles north of the forts, at Bridgend in Glen Lethnot, there's good B&B at the **Post House** (☎ 01356-660277) for only £12.50 per person, and dinner for £5.50 extra.

Glen Esk & Edzell

A pleasant planned village at the foot of Glen Esk and 6 miles north of Brechin, Edzell has an unusual stone-arched gateway over the public road, the **Dalhousie Arch**. One mile to the west, there's **Edzell Castle**, a 16th century L-plan tower house. It has an excellent garden, the 'pleasance', with sculptured wall panels. The castle's now roofless, but it's worth a visit; it's open standard HS hours, but closed Thursday afternoon and Friday in winter. Admission costs £2.30/1.75.

Ten miles up the glen from Edzell, **The Retreat** (☎ 01356-670254), or Glenesk Folk Museum, has an extensive local folk history collection and a tearoom. From June to October it's open daily, from 10 am to 6 pm (from Easter to May it's closed on Sunday). Tarfside village, 1½ miles beyond The Retreat, has a general store.

Four miles farther on, the public road ends at **Invermark Castle**, an impressive ruined tower guarding the southern approach to The Mounth, a hill track to Deeside. About three-quarters of a mile west of the castle, there's an old church by

Loch Lee. Beyond the loch, there are lots of beetling cliffs and waterfalls.

Inchcape (☎ *01356-647266, High St)*, Edzell, is a good B&B which charges £16/30. French is spoken here. Bar and restaurant meals are available at the **Glenesk Hotel** (☎ *01356-648319)*, while B&B is £52/84. In Glen Esk, pleasant B&B is available at the head of the glen from **House of Mark** (☎ *01356-670315)*, Invermark, for £20 per person. Dinner in this remote place is £14.

Strathtay Scottish (☎ 01382-228054) runs two to six daily buses from Brechin to Edzell (20 minutes, £1.10). There's no public transport from Edzell into the glen.

BRECHIN

• pop 7593   ☎ 01674

Brechin, on the River South Esk, is an interesting town with several things to see. There's a TIC (☎ 623050) in St Ninian's Place, east of High St. You'll find a bank with an ATM on Clerk St.

Things to See

There's been a church in Brechin since the 9th century, and a 32m-high free-standing **round tower** (one of only two in Scotland) was built around 1000. Its elevated doorway, 2m above the ground, has carvings of animals, clergy, and a crucifix. The adjacent **Brechin Cathedral**, Church Square, has been much altered throughout history. Nearby, High St is on a steep hill, and there are several interesting buildings.

Farther east, near the TIC, the **Brechin Museum** (☎ 622687), St Ninian's Square, has local historical relics. It's open the same hours as the attached library; admission is free.

The **Brechin Caledonian Railway** (☎ 810318), St Ninian's Square, runs steam trains to the NTS **House of Dun** (☎ 810264) from June to early September, Sunday only (six daily journeys); tickets are £4.50/2.50 return.

The house, a well-appointed Georgian mansion built in 1730, opens May to September, daily, from 1.30 to 5.30 pm (also

Loch Duich, Highlands

Climbers on Old Man of Stoer

Loch Ness and Castle Urquhart, Highlands

Eilean Donan Castle, Loch Duich, Highlands

open at Easter and October weekends); admission costs £3.70/2.50.

Places to Stay & Eat
Centrally located *Doniford (☎ 622361, 26 Airlie St)* offers excellent B&B for £18.50 to £19.50 per person, with dinner for £9.50. The *Northern Hotel (☎ 625505, 2 Clerk St)* charges £20/40 without attached bath, £35/55 with attached bath. Bar snacks start at £1.50 (toasties), and main courses are £3.25 to £5. A three-course set dinner is only £12.50.

On High St, there are the usual Chinese and Indian takeaways. The *Coffee Shop (St James Place)* has a huge snack menu; meals here cost under £4.20, and there's takeaway service.

Getting There & Away
Scottish Citylink (☎ 0990-505050) runs buses three or four times daily to Dundee (50 minutes, £5.30), Forfar (20 minutes, £3.30) and Aberdeen (one hour, £4.80). The bus stop is in Clerk St.

Strathtay Scottish (☎ 01382-228054) operates buses from South Esk St to Forfar (roughly once an hour, 30 minutes, £2.05), Edzell (two to six daily, 20 minutes, £1.10), and Aberlemno (once every hour or two, 15 minutes).

MW Nicoll's (☎ 01561-377262) bus service from South Esk St to Stonehaven runs two to five times daily (55 minutes).

Aberdeenshire & Moray

Known from 1974 to 1996 as Grampian region, the area is (not surprisingly) bound to the west and south by the Grampians. The largest place is prosperous Aberdeen – a tidy city of impressive and renowned granite architecture – which is still benefiting from the North Sea oil industry.

Aberdeenshire incorporates the valley of the grand River Dee, Royal Deeside – royal because Queen Victoria liked it so much that she bought Balmoral.

The royal family still spends part of every summer here, appearing at the well known Braemar Gathering.

Around the coast are the fertile plains immortalised by Lewis Grassic Gibbon in his trilogy, the *Scots Quair*, which was based on the life of a farming community early in the 20th century. The east coasters, and particularly the Aberdonians, have always had a reputation for being hard-working and thrifty. Certainly anyone living near, or making a living from, the North Sea would have to be tough.

There's a vigorous culture in the northeast, quite separate from the rest of Scotland. Much of it is expressed in lively anecdotal or poetic form (in dialect). The *bothy ballads* and bands which provided home entertainment among the workers on the big farms still get high billing on local radio and TV.

Along the northern coast of Banff and Moray are small fishing ports which have neat little streets looking out to sea. This coastline gets a lot of sun and not much rainfall, and the small non-touristy towns have a brisk, no-nonsense feel.

There are many castles in the characteristic Scottish baronial style in this area. In the north-west, and across the border in the Highlands, the biggest industry is the distilling of whisky – many distilleries offer tours followed by drams.

GETTING AROUND
For information on buses around Aberdeen phone ☎ 01224-664581. TICs and council offices stock the useful free publication *Aberdeen & Moray Transport Map*. Bluebird Buses (☎ 01224-212266) is the main bus company in the area. A Day Rover ticket (£8.50) covers all its services.

The only rail line runs from the south to Aberdeen and continues through Inverurie, Huntly and Elgin to Inverness. For rail information, phone ☎ 0345-484950.

There are some superb walks in the mountains in the south-western part of this region. TICs sell the very useful *Hillwalking in the Grampian Highlands* for £1.

ABERDEEN

- **pop 217,260** ☎ **01224**

Aberdeen is an extraordinary symphony in grey. Almost everything is built of grey granite, including the roads, which are paved with crushed granite. In the sunlight, especially after a shower of rain, the stone turns silver and shines like a fairytale, but with low, grey clouds and rain scudding in off the North Sea, it can be a bit depressing.

Aberdeen was a prosperous North Sea trading and fishing port centuries before oil was considered a valuable commodity. After the townspeople supported Robert the Bruce against the English at the Battle of Bannockburn in 1314, the king rewarded the town with land for which he had previously received rent. The money was diverted into the Common Good Fund, to be spent on town amenities, as it still is today. It finances the regimented floral ranks that have won the city numerous awards, and helps keep the place spotless. As a result, the inhabitants have been inculcated with an almost overbearing civic pride.

The name Aberdeen is a combination of two Pictish-Gaelic words, 'aber' and 'devana', meaning the meeting of two waters. The area was known to the Romans, and was raided by the Vikings when it was an increasingly important port, with trade conducted in wool, fish, hides and fur. By the 18th century, paper and rope-making, whaling and textile manufacture were the main industries; in the following century it was a major herring port.

Since the 1970s, Aberdeen has become the main onshore service port for one of the largest oilfields in the world. Unemployment rates, once among the highest in the country, dropped dramatically, but have since fluctuated with the rise and fall of the price of oil.

Aberdeen is certainly worth a visit. It's a very lively city – there are more bars than would seem even remotely viable. Start with over 200,000 Scots, add multinational oil workers and a large student population – the result: thriving nightlife.

Orientation

Aberdeen is built on a ridge that runs east-west to the north of the train and bus stations and the ferry quay. The bus and train stations are next to each other, off Guild St. Old Aberdeen and the university are to the north of this area. To the east lies a couple of miles of clean, sandy beach; at the southern end is Footdee (pronounced fittee), a fishing community at the mouth of the River Dee.

Information

The TIC (☎ 632727) is in St Nicholas House, Broad St. It's open daily from May to September, at least 9 am to 5 pm (with extended weekday opening to 7 pm in July and August; shorter hours on Sunday). Between October and May, it's closed on Sunday. As well as the usual bed-booking facility, there's a bureau de change.

There are two handy banks with ATMs on Union St at St Nicholas St.

Medical Services Aberdeen Royal Infirmary (☎ 681818), Foresterhill, is about a mile north-west of the west end of Union St.

The Harbour

The harbour has always been a busy place. From dawn until about 8 am, the fish market operates as it has for centuries.

Maritime Museum Situated in Provost Ross's House, the oldest building in the city, the Maritime Museum (☎ 337700) explains Aberdeen's relationship (almost exclusively commercial) with the sea. There are some interesting displays about shipbuilding and the whaling and fishing industries. Speedy Aberdeen clippers were a 19th century shipyard speciality which were attractive to British tea merchants for the transportation of emigrants to Australia and, on return, the import of tea, wool and exotic goods (opium, for instance). Opening hours are daily, from 10 am to 5 pm (from 11 am on Sunday). The admission cost is £3.50/2.50.

The City

Union St is the main thoroughfare in the city, lined with solid granite buildings, many of them Victorian. The oldest area is **Castlegate**, at the eastern end, where the castle stood. When it was captured from the English for Robert the Bruce, the password used by the townspeople was 'Bon Accord'. A street and shopping centre commemorate the password.

Provost Skene's House About 50m behind the TIC, surrounded by concrete and glass office blocks in what was once the worst slum in Aberdeen, is a late medieval, turreted town house occupied in the 17th century by the Provost (the Scots equivalent of a mayor) Sir George Skene. It was commandeered for a short time by the Duke of Cumberland and his English redcoat soldiers, and later it became a dosshouse. It would have been demolished in the 1940s but a successful long-running campaign to save it, supported by the present-day Queen Mother, led to its opening as a museum in 1953.

Typical of its kind, it has intimate, panelled rooms. The 1622 tempera-painted ceiling, with its religious symbolism, is unusual for having survived the depredations of the Reformation. It's a gem of its time, featuring earnest-looking angels, St Peter with cockerels crowing, and period-type soldiers. At the top of the house is an archaeology display and a gallery of local domestic artefacts.

Provost Skene's House (☎ 641086) opens Monday to Saturday, from 10 am to 5 pm; admission costs £2.50/1.50.

Marischal College Across the road from the TIC, this building used to house the science section of the University of Aberdeen. It was founded in 1593 by the 5th Earl Marischal. The present building is late Victorian Gothic, made peculiar by the use of granite. It's the kind of building you either love or hate, but cannot avoid being impressed by. There are plans to turn it into a hotel around 2000.

The **museum** (☎ 273131) is straight ahead through the main quadrangle and up the stairs. In one room, there's a lively depiction of north-east Scotland through its famous people, customs, architecture, trade and myths. The displays are organised thematically, so visitors can easily get a good picture of the complex and rich local culture.

The other gallery is set up as an anthropological overview of the world, incorporating objects from vastly different cultures. It's also arranged thematically (Polynesian wooden masks alongside gasmasks etc). There are the usual bizarre Victorian curios, an Indian kayak found in the local river estuary and some Inuit objects collected by whalers.

The museum is well worth visiting. Open Monday to Friday, from 10 am to 5 pm, and on Sunday afternoon; entry is free.

Tolbooth Museum Opened in 1995, this is a museum of civic history, housed in the Tolbooth built in the early 17th century to accommodate prisoners awaiting trial.

There are displays in the cells, narrow winding staircases and tales of escape recounted by an animated model of prisoner William Baird.

The museum (☎ 621167), Town House, Union St, opens April to September, daily, from 10 am to 5 pm (except Monday all day, and Sunday morning); tickets cost £2.50/1.50.

Aberdeen Art Gallery Behind the grand façade of the art gallery is a cool, white space exhibiting the work of young contemporary Scottish and English painters, such as Gwen Hardie, Stephen Conroy, Trevor Sutton and Tim Ollivier. There's also a Francis Bacon and a selection of modern textiles, ceramics and jewellery. There's evidently a vigorous school of applied arts in Aberdeen. There are also several Joan Eardley landscapes; she lived in a cottage on the cliffs near Stonehaven in the 1950s and 60s, and painted tempestuous

CENTRAL & NORTH-EASTERN

ABERDEEN

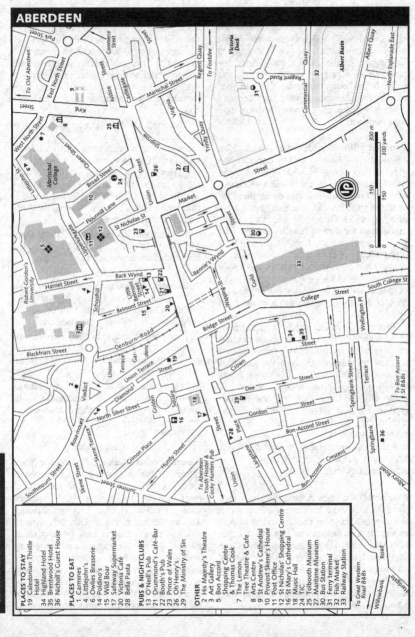

PLACES TO STAY
19 Caledonian Thistle Hotel
34 Highland Hotel
35 Brentwood Hotel
36 Nichol's Guest House

PLACES TO EAT
1 Carmines
4 Littlejohn's
6 Owlies Brasserie
14 Poldino's
15 Wild Boar
17 Safeway Supermarket
20 Victoria Café
28 Bella Pasta

PUBS & NIGHTCLUBS
13 O'Neill's Pub
21 Drummond's Café-Bar
22 Booth's Pub
23 Prince of Wales
26 Oh! Henry's
29 The Ministry of Sin

OTHER
2 His Majesty's Theatre
3 Art Gallery
5 Bon Accord
Shopping Centre
& Thomas Cook
7 The Lemon
Tree Theatre & Cafe
8 Arts Centre
9 St Andrew's Cathedral
10 Provost Skene's House
11 Post Office
12 St Nicholas' Shopping Centre
16 St Mary's Cathedral
18 Music Hall
24 TIC
25 Tolbooth Museum
27 Maritime Museum
30 Bus Station
31 Ferry terminal
32 Fish Market
33 Railway Station

oils of the North Sea and poignant portraits of slum children.

Among the Pre-Raphaelites upstairs is a collection of 92 small portraits of artists, many of them self-portraits of now forgotten painters. The collection was begun around 1880 by Alexander Macdonald, and the first portrait painted was of Millais.

Downstairs, a large, empty, white, circular room, with fish-scaled balustrades evoking the briny origins of Aberdeen's wealth, commemorates the 165 people who lost their lives in the Piper Alpha oil rig disaster in 1988.

The gallery (☎ 646333), Schoolhill, opens Monday to Saturday, from 10 am to 5 pm, and on Sunday from 2 to 5 pm.

Old Aberdeen

One and a half miles north of the city centre is the separate suburb of Old Aberdeen. The name is somewhat misleading, since the area around the harbour is actually older; it's called Alton in Gaelic, meaning village by the pool, and this was anglicised to Old Town. The university buildings and St Machar's Cathedral are at the centre of this peaceful area.

It was here that Bishop Elphinstone established King's College, Aberdeen's first university, in 1495. Earl Marischal founded the college in the city centre in 1593 but it was not until the 19th century that the two colleges were united as the University of Aberdeen. The 16th century **King's College Chapel** (☎ 272137) is easily recognisable by its crowned spire. Its interior is largely unchanged – the stained-glass windows and choir stalls are most impressive. It's open weekdays only, from 9 am to 4.30 pm (admission is free).

The **King's College Visitors Centre** (☎ 273702) houses a multimedia display on the university's history. It's open Monday to Saturday, from 10 am to 5 pm, and on Sunday afternoon, year-round; there's no admission charge.

The 15th century **St Machar's Cathedral** (☎ 485988), with its massive twin towers, is one of the few examples in the country of a fortified cathedral. According to legend, St Machar was ordered to establish a church where the river takes the shape of a bishop's crook, which it does just here. The cathedral is best known for its impressive heraldic ceiling, dating from 1520, which has 48 shields of kings, nobles, archbishops and bishops. It's open daily from 9 am to 5 pm; services on Sunday are at 11 am and 6 pm.

Places to Stay

Camping The nearest camping ground is *Hazelhead Caravan Park & Campsite* (☎ 321268), 4 miles west of the centre and near the A944, with pitches for £4.30 in a woodland setting. Phone for directions.

Hostels & Colleges *Aberdeen Youth Hostel* (☎ 646988, 8 Queen's Rd) is a mile west of the train station. It's open all year; beds cost £8.60/7.10 in small dormitories (£1 surcharge in July and August). Walk west along Union St and take the right fork along Albyn Place until you reach a roundabout; Queen's Rd continues on the western side.

During the university holidays, some colleges let rooms to visitors. The list of colleges offering accommodation changes from year to year – check with the TIC. *Robert Gordon's University* (☎ 262134, Woolmanhill Residence) has *en suite* single rooms for £15 per person (with cooking facilities). At King St there are 12 six-person self-catering flats costing £255 per week for six people, £215 per week for two people, or £61.43 for two nights (two people). The *Scottish Agricultural College* (☎ 711195, Craibstone Estate, Bucksburn) has rooms from £18 to £24 per person.

B&Bs & Hotels There are clusters of B&Bs on Bon Accord St and Springbank Terrace (both close to the centre), and Great Western Rd (the A93, a 25 minute walk). They're usually more expensive than the Scottish average and, with all the oil industry workers here, single rooms are at a premium. Prices tend to be lower at the weekend.

There's a choice of guesthouses in Bon Accord St. *Applewood Guest House* (☎ 580617, 154 Bon Accord St) charges from £18 to £24 per person for B&B. *Crynoch Guest House* (☎ 582743, 164 Bon Accord St) has singles/doubles for £19/34. The two guesthouses next door are both similarly priced: *Denmore Guest House* (☎ 587751, 166 Bon Accord St) and *Dunrovin Guest House* (☎ 586081, 168 Bon Accord St).

Nearby, *Nicoll's Guest House* (☎ 572867, 63 Springbank Terrace) is a recommended, friendly place with rooms at around £20/31 (£28/43 for rooms with bath attached). There are plenty of other alternatives in the area.

There are numerous places to stay along Great Western Rd. *Penny Meadow Private Hotel* (☎ 588037, 189 Great Western Rd) is a small, friendly place. Rooms with attached bath are from £30/40. The *Corner House Hotel* (☎ 313063, 385 Great Western Rd) is a solid, turreted building with off-street parking, and evening meals if required. It charges from £35/46 for an *en suite* single/double.

For nonsmokers only, *Strathisla Guest House* (☎ 321026, 408 Great Western Rd) is a comfortable place. All rooms have bath attached, and charges are around £25/40. *Klibreck Guest House* (☎ 316115, 410 Great Western Rd) charges from £20/30. *Aurora Guest House* (☎ 311602, 429 Great Western Rd) is another small, family run B&B. There are six rooms, from £20/34, all with shared bathroom.

Back in the centre of Aberdeen, the friendly *Brentwood Hotel* (☎ 595440, 101 Crown St) is very conveniently located and comfortable, but is often full during the week. Rooms cost from £69/77 for singles/doubles, about 50% less at weekends. The hotel has a good bar and restaurant.

Just a few doors away, the *Highland Hotel* (☎ 583685, 93 Crown St) offers B&B for £49/65 during the week, and £32.50/45 at weekends. There's also a good bar and restaurant here.

The *Atholl Hotel* (☎ 323505, Kings Gate), an elegant granite building on the western edge of the town, has an excellent reputation. Luxurious rooms range from £46/54 at weekends to £78/88 during the week.

A fine place to stay in the centre of town is the *Caledonian Thistle Hotel* (☎ 640233, Union Terrace). It has 80 rooms from £115/135, but cheaper rates are available.

Places to Eat

Aberdeen has an excellent range of places to eat, from branches of the big-name fast-food chains to expensive gourmet restaurants.

Self-Catering You'll find large supermarkets at Bridge of Dee and Bridge of Don. There's also a *Tesco Metro* in St Nicholas St (off Union St) and a *Safeway* near the Music Hall on Union St.

Takeaways & Cafés The *Ashvale Fish Restaurant* (☎ 596981, 42 Great Western Rd) is a fish and chip shop that's well known outside the city, having won several awards. Ask for mushy peas with your haddock and chips (from £3.10 to take away) – they don't taste as bad as they sound. The *New Dolphin* (3 Chapel St), just off Union St, isn't a Chinese takeaway, but it's an excellent fish and chip shop with a sit-in section. Haddock and chips is £3.20 and it's open to 3 am Thursday to Sunday.

Carmines (☎ 624145, 32 Union Terrace) does good inexpensive Italian food. Three-course lunches are only £3.90, and pizzas start at £3.50. It's only open from Monday to Saturday, noon to 5.30 pm.

The café at the *Lemon Tree* (☎ 621610), the theatre at 5 West North St, does excellent coffee, cakes and light meals. It's open Wednesday to Sunday from noon to 3 pm. The *Music Hall coffee shop* (☎ 632080, Union St) has a good reputation.

The *Victoria Café* (☎ 621381, 140 Union St) does snacks and sandwiches from £2. Just around the corner, the *Wild Boar* (☎ 625357, 19 Belmont St) is a popular, stylish bistro. Cake fanatics will have a great time here. Main courses range from £4.25 to £9.95, with vegetarian choices; couscous is £5.45.

Bar Meals The bar at the *Brentwood Hotel* (see Places to Stay) does great food. The eat-as-much-as-you-like hot buffet lunch is only £3.50 (not Sunday). The *Highland Hotel* (see Places to Stay) has a good seafood selection, including shark and shrimp for £9.50. Main courses start at £3.95.

O'Neill's Pub (9 Back Wynd) serves burgers from £2.95 and Irish stew for £4.35 – see the upcoming entertainment section.

Restaurants Cheery *Bella Pasta (☎ 575737, 261 Union St)* serves pasta dishes for £4.85 to £7.15. *Poldino's (☎ 647777, 7 Little Belmont St)* is an up-market Italian restaurant; pizza and pasta cost £6.60 to £7.30. It's open from Monday to Saturday for lunch and dinner.

Owlies Brasserie (☎ 649267, Littlejohn St) is highly recommended, good value and, consequently, very popular. It produces tasty food with unusual flavours – try the couscous Marocain (£3.85 at lunchtime, £7.20 in the evening). It also has a good range of vegetarian and vegan food.

There's a branch of the chain *Littlejohn's (☎ 635666, 46 School Hill)* with all the usual diversions, including a toy train. Re-training in hospitality would be better than gimmicks. There are burgers from £4.35, other main dishes (eg char-grilled chicken) from around £8.

For a splurge, there are a number of choices. The *Silver Darling Restaurant (☎ 576229)* is at the southern end of the Beach Esplanade on Pocra Quay, North Pier, Footdee. It's renowned for its seafood and superb location overlooking the entrance to the port; reservations are recommended. A three-course dinner here will cost at least £20. Another excellent place to eat is *Faradays Restaurant (☎ 869666, 2 Kirk Brae, Cults)*, 4 miles from the city centre. It's in a refurbished

electricity station and has interesting décor. The cuisine is a combination of traditional Scottish and French, with lots of fresh local ingredients. It's open Tuesday to Saturday.

Entertainment

Pubs Aberdeen is a great city for a pub crawl – it's more of a question of knowing where to stop than where to start. Note that many pubs don't serve food in the evening.

The *Prince of Wales (☎ 640597, 7 St Nicholas Lane)* is possibly the best known Aberdeen pub. Down an alley off Union St, it boasts the longest counter in the city, a great range of real ales and good-value pub grub at lunchtime. It can get very crowded. Located nearby, on Back Wynd, *Booth's (☎ 646475)* is a better place for a pub lunch, with a good range of traditional pies for £2.95 or £3.75.

Cocky Hunters (☎ 626720, 504 Union St), popular with professionals, is a great place with regular live music. *Drummond's Café-Bar (☎ 624642, Belmont St)* serves meals during the day, but it's more of a student pub in the evening.

O'Neill's Pub (☎ 621456, 9 Back Wynd) has a good selection of Irish beers, stout, whiskeys and poitín. It serves food (see Places to Eat) all day and there's live music (mainly Celtic) on evenings from Thursday to Saturday.

Nightclubs There are numerous nightclubs but note that most will not let you in if you're wearing trainers, and some will turn you away if you're wearing jeans.

The *Ministry of Sin (☎ 211661, Dee St)* is in a deconsecrated church. It attracts 20 to 35-year-olds and is a fairly good club. *Amadeus (☎ 572233, The Esplanade)* is quite impressive and holds up to 1700 people, but it's not a cool place. It's open from Thursday to Monday from 9 pm to 2 am, and admission varies from £1 to £6.

Oh'Henry's (☎ 586949, 20 Adelphi) is a club/bar that's open daily until 2 or 3 am. One of the wildest clubs is upstairs at *O'Neill's Pub (☎ 621456, 9 Back Wynd)*, open daily until 2 am. The £1 to £2.50 cover charge will admit you to pounding Irish rock, indie and alternative music. This place appeals to 18 to 25-year-olds.

Concerts, Theatre & Film A free listings guide, *What's on in Aberdeen*, is available from the TIC. There's also the bi-monthly *Aberdeen Arts & Recreation Listings*. You can book tickets for most plays and concerts on the Aberdeen Box Office line (☎ 641122), or just drop in – it's next to the Music Hall in Union St.

The city's main theatre is *His Majesty's* (☎ 637788, *Rosemount Viaduct*), which hosts everything from ballet and opera to musicals and pantomimes. The *Music Hall* (☎ 632080, *Union St*) is the main venue for classical music concerts. The *Arts Centre* (☎ 635208, *King St*) stages exhibitions at its gallery and drama in its theatre.

The *Lemon Tree* (☎ 642230, *5 West North St*) usually has an interesting program of dance, music or drama. It hosts festivals, has an excellent café, and often has rock, jazz and folk bands playing.

The nine-screen *Virgin Cinema Complex* (☎ 0541-550502 *for bookings, Queen's Links*) charges from £3.50 to £5.25 per film (a special cinema with reclining seats and drinks service costs up to £11).

Getting There & Away

Aberdeen is 507 miles from London, 129 from Edinburgh and 105 from Inverness.

Air Aberdeen airport is 6 miles north-west of the city centre. The presence of the oil industry ensures there are flights to numerous Scottish and UK destinations, including Orkney and Shetland, and international flights to the Netherlands and Norway.

For airport information, phone ☎ 722331. Bus Nos 27 and 27A run from the city centre to the airport, taking about 35 minutes.

Bus National Express (☎ 0990-808080) has daily buses from London, but it's a tedious 12 hour trip (from £24.50 one-way). Scottish Citylink (☎ 0990-505050) runs direct

services to Dundee (two hours, £6.50), Perth (2½ hours, £9), Edinburgh (four hours, £13), Stirling (3½ hours, £12.80) and Glasgow (4¼ hours, £13.30), plus other Scottish destinations.

Bluebird Buses (☎ 212266) is the major local bus operator. Bus No 10 runs hourly to Huntly (£5.50), Keith (£5.50), Elgin (£6.50), Nairn (£9.50) and Inverness (£9.50). Service No 201 runs every half-hour to Banchory (hourly on Sunday, £2.40), every hour to Ballater (less frequently on Sunday, £5.50), and five to eight times daily to Braemar (£5.50). You can also get to Ballater on bus No 210 (one to five daily runs).

Other local bus routes serve Stonehaven (£2.40), Alford (£4.50), Peterhead (£3.50), Fraserburgh (£4.25), Banff (£6), Buckie (£7.50) and lots of other places. From Aberdeen, you can travel around the coast to Elgin (possible in one day, better in two), then continue on bus No 10 to Inverness.

Train For rail information, phone ☎ 0345-484950. There are numerous trains from London's King's Cross (usually requiring changing train in Edinburgh). Direct trains (three per day) take an acceptable seven hours, although they're considerably more expensive than buses (up to £77.50, one way!).

Other destinations served from Aberdeen by rail include Edinburgh (2½ hours, £32), Glasgow (2¾ hours, £35.10), Stirling (2¼ hours, £29), Perth (1¾ hours, £19.50), Dundee (1¼ hours, £16.40) and Inverness (2¼ hours, £18.50).

Car Try Arnold Clark (☎ 249159), Girdleness Rd, with Nissan Micras for £16 per day or £80 per week. There's also Morrison Brothers (☎ 826300), Broadfield Rd, Bridge of Don.

Boat The passenger terminal is a short walk east of the train and bus stations. P&O (☎ 572615) has once daily evening departures from Monday to Friday leaving for Lerwick (Shetland). The trip takes approximately 14 or 20 hours (some sailings go via Orkney). A reclining seat costs £49/55 in the low/high season, one way (high season is June to August). Car fares start at £110/131.

From June to August, there are Tuesday and Saturday departures to Stromness (Orkney). The rest of the year, there's usually a Saturday departure (confirm with P&O); eight or 14 hours. Fares are £37/40 low/high season, but there are discounted mid-week fares. For a car, tickets start at £84/101.50.

Getting Around

Bus The *Aberdeen Passport* is available from the TIC and gives basic details of city bus services; for full details, you'll need the *Travel Guide to Aberdeen* (50p). For local bus information phone Grampian Busline on ☎ 650065. The most useful services are Nos 18, 19 and 24 from Union St to Great Western Rd, No 27 from the bus station to the youth hostel and Nos 20 and 26 for Old Aberdeen. If you're using the buses frequently, get a prepaid farecard (like a phonecard).

Taxi For a taxi, phone Mair's (☎ 724040). A trip to the airport costs £10 to £11.

Bicycle Mountain bikes can be rented from Alpine Bikes (☎ 211455), 64 Holburn St. It's open every day and charges £12/8 per full/half-day during the week, and £24 for the weekend (Friday evening to Monday morning).

DEESIDE & DONSIDE

The region around the rivers Dee and Don, eastwards from Braemar to the coast, is castle country, and includes the Queen's residence at Balmoral. There are more fanciful examples of Scottish baronial architecture here than anywhere else in Scotland. The TICs have information on a Castle Trail, but you really need private transport to follow it.

The River Dee, flowing through the southern part of this area, has its source in the Cairngorm mountains, to the west. The River Don follows a shorter, but almost parallel course. The best walking country in the region is around Braemar and Ballater, in upper Deeside.

Crathes Castle

By the A93, 16 miles west of Aberdeen, this excellent 16th century castle contains painted ceilings and original furnishings. The gardens include 300-year-old yew hedges which will interest topiarists. There's an on-site restaurant. Crathes Castle (☎ 01330-844525, NTS) opens April to October, daily, from 11 am to 5.30 pm (last admission is at 4.45 pm). Tickets cost £4.80/3.20 (castle and grounds), or £2/1.30 for the castle or grounds alone.

The castle is situated on the main Aberdeen-Banchory-Ballater bus route.

Ballater
• **pop 1260**   ☎ **01339**

This small town supplies nearby Balmoral Castle with provisions, hence the shops sporting 'By Royal Appointment' crests. Ballater is a pleasant place, but accommodation is fairly expensive and budget travellers head for Braemar.

The TIC (☎ 755306), Station Square, opens from Easter to October. There's a supermarket and a bank with an ATM on Bridge St.

Things to See & Do There's a parish church and clock tower (1798) in the central square. In **Dee Valley Confectioners** (☎ 755499), Station Square, hungry travellers can drool over the manufacture of Scottish 'sweeties'. It's open from April to October, Monday to Thursday, from 9 am to noon and 2 to 4.30 pm; admission is free and there are free samples.

Walks There are a few pleasant walks in the hills around Ballater. The woodland walk up Craigendarroch (400m, 1312 feet) takes just over an hour, but it's quite steep. Morven (871m, 2857 feet) is a more serious prospect, taking around six hours, but has good views from the top.

The best walk in the area goes to the summit of Lochnagar (1155m, 3788 feet) from Spittal of Glenmuick car park. It's not a difficult route, but care should be taken on the summit plateau – there are huge cliffs on the northern side. Follow the track westwards from the car park; after 2½ miles, a steep path leads up to the plateau. Allow at least six hours, and carry OS map No 44 along with a compass, food, water and appropriate equipment.

Places to Stay & Eat B&Bs include *Mrs Cowie's (☎ 755699, Celicall, 3 Braemar Rd)* for around £17/30 single/double. The *Alexandra Hotel (☎ 755376, 12 Bridge Square)* is a friendly and comfortable hotel offering B&B from £24 to £30 per person. Bar meals cost £4.50 to £9.80.

There are several other places with meals from £5 to £15. A cheaper alternative is the *Station Restaurant (☎ 755805, Station Square)* with home baking from £1.80 and inexpensive burgers for around £2.

Getting There & Away Bluebird Buses (☎ 755422) run almost every hour from Aberdeen (1¾ hours, £5.50); every two hours on Sunday. The service continues to Braemar.

Balmoral Castle

Eight miles west of Ballater, Balmoral was built for Queen Victoria in 1855 as a private residence for the royal family. The grounds and an exhibition of paintings, artwork and royal tartans in the ballroom are open; the rest of the castle is closed to the prying eyes of the public. On the edge of the estate is Crathie Church, which the royals visit when they're here.

Balmoral Castle (☎ 01339-742334) opens 28 April to 3 August, daily, from 10 am to 5 pm (closed on Sunday in April and May), and attracts large numbers of visitors. Admission costs £3/2.50. It's by the A93 and can be reached on the Aberdeen-Braemar bus (see the next section).

Braemar

• pop 410   ☎ 01339

Braemar is an attractive village surrounded by mountains. It makes an excellent walking base and there's winter skiing at Glenshee (see the earlier Blairgowrie & Glenshee section). In winter, Braemar is usually the coldest place in the country, and temperatures as low as minus 29°C have been recorded. During spells of severe cold, hungry deer wander the streets looking for a bite to eat.

There's a very helpful TIC (☎ 741600), The Mews, Mar Rd, open all year. It has lots of useful information on walks in the area. There's a bank with an ATM at the junction in the centre.

Things to See Just north of the village, turreted **Braemar Castle** (☎ 741219) dates from 1628 and it's well worth a visit. It was a government garrison after the 1745 Jacobite rebellion, then it became the home of

---

Braemar Gathering

There are Highland games in many towns and villages throughout the summer, but the best known is the Braemar Gathering which takes place on a 12-acre site on the first Saturday in September. It's a major occasion, annually organised by the Braemar Royal Highland Society since 1817. Events include highland dancing, pipers, tug-of-war, a hill race up Morrone, tossing the caber, hammer and stone throwing, and the long jump. International athletes are among those who take part.

These types of event took place informally in the Highlands for many centuries as tests of skill and strength, but they were formalised around 1820 due to rising pseudo-Highland romanticism caused by people like King George IV and Sir Walter Scott. Queen Victoria attended the Braemar Gathering in 1848, starting the tradition of royal patronage which continues to this day.

the Farquharson family. It's open from Easter to October, from 10 am to 6 pm, daily except Friday; entry costs £2/1.50.

The **Braemar Highland Heritage Centre** (☎ 741944), by the TIC, tells the story of the area with displays and video. It's open from April to October, daily, from 9 am to 6 pm (closed on Friday and closing at 5 pm for the rest of the year); admission is free.

Walks An easy walk from Braemar is up Creag Choinnich (538m, 1765 feet), a hill to the east of the town, above the A93. There are route markers and the walk takes about 1½ hours. For a longer walk (three hours) and superb views of the Cairngorms, climb Morrone (859m, 2818 feet), the mountain south-west of Braemar.

Special Events On the first Saturday in September, Braemar is invaded by 20,000 people, including the royal family, for the Braemar Gathering (Highland Games). Bookings are essential and tickets cost from £5/1 (field) to £17.50 (grandstand). Contact the TIC for current details.

Places to Stay & Eat *Braemar Youth Hostel* (☎ 741659), south of the centre and by the A93 to Perth, opens all year and charges £7.75/6.50. The *Braemar Bunkhouse* (☎ 741517, 15 Mar Rd), near the newsagent/chemist, has dorm accommodation from £7.

Craiglea (☎ 741641, Hillside Drive) charges around £18 per person, while *Wilderbank* (☎ 741651, Kindrochit Drive) charges a little less. *Schiehallion House* (☎ 741679, 10 Glenshee Rd) offers B&B for around £19 per person.

Callater Lodge Hotel (☎ 741275, 9 Glenshee Rd) is a small hotel set in its own grounds; most rooms have a bathroom attached and cost around £27 per person – evening meals are available for £13. The best place to stay is *Braemar Lodge* (☎ 741627, Glenshee Rd), a restored Victorian shooting lodge on the outskirts of the village. B&B costs from £25 to £36 per person.

The *Fife Arms Hotel* (☎ 741644, Mar Rd) is a great place with a daily carvery, and bar meals are £4.95 to £9.95. There's a special winter B&B rate of £17.50 per person; normal rates are £27.50/40 to £37.50/50. The *Invercauld Arms Hotel* is a reasonable place for a pint, but the food is *nouvelle cuisine*.

Cheaper alternatives include the fairly good *Braemar Takeaway (14 Invercauld Rd)* with fish and chips for £2.90. There's also an *Alldays* supermarket *(Mar Rd)*.

Getting There & Away It's a beautiful drive between Perth and Braemar but public transport is limited. From Aberdeen to Braemar (2¼ hours, £5.50) there are several buses a day operated by Bluebird Buses (☎ 01224-212266) which travel along the beautiful valley of the River Dee.

Inverey

Five miles west of Braemar is the little settlement of Inverey. Numerous mountain walks start from here, including the adventurous Lairig Ghru walk – 21 miles over the pass to Aviemore. The Cairngorm peaks of Cairn Gorm and Ben Macdui (see Aviemore in The Highlands chapter) are actually on or just this side of the regional border.

The Glen Luibeg circuit is a good day hike. Start from the **Linn of Dee**, a narrow gorge about 1½ miles west of Inverey. From the woodland car park less than 300m beyond the linn, follow the footpath and track to Derry Lodge and **Glen Luibeg**, where there are wonderful remnants of the ancient Caledonian pine forest. Continue westwards on a pleasant path, over a pass into Glen Dee, then follow the River Dee back to the linn. It's an easy 15-mile route from the linn (six hours). Another interesting circuit includes Glen Lui and Glen Quoich. The **Linn of Quoich** is a narrow slot which the river thunders through; don't try to jump it. Use OS map No 43 for both routes.

Inverey Youth Hostel (no telephone) opens mid-May to early October; beds cost £4.65/3.85. There's an afternoon postbus (not Sunday) from Braemar to the hostel, Linn of Dee and Linn of Quoich.

Strathdon

The A944, A97 and A939 run through Strathdon and many of the best castles in Aberdeenshire are near these roads. Beyond Inverurie, Kemnay and Alford (pronounced ah-ford) are the main villages.

Alford, 27 miles west of Aberdeen, is well worth a visit and makes a good day trip from the city. It has a TIC (☎ 01975-562052), open April to October, banks with ATMs, and a supermarket. Avoid detouring along a minor road from tiny Strathdon village: the sign indicates 'Lost'!

Castle Fraser This superb 16th century castle (☎ 01330-833463, NTS), 3 miles south of Kemnay, looks rather like a French château and it's reputedly the most photographed castle in Scotland. It's open at Easter and May to September, daily from 11 am to 5.30 pm (opening at 1.30 pm in May, June and September); £4.20/2.80.

Alford There's a huge, albeit slightly shabby, **heritage centre** (☎ 01975-562906) here with over 3000 domestic and agricultural displays (£1.50/50p). The **Grampian Transport Museum** (☎ 01975-562292) is a fascinating place with lots of cars, buses, steam engines, trams and some unique exhibits. It's open April to October, daily, from 10 am to 5 pm (£3/2). There's also a small **railway museum** at the TIC; the narrow-gauge **Alford Valley steam railway** runs daily from here in afternoons from June to August (£1.50).

Craigievar Castle The most spectacular of local castles, Craigievar (☎ 01339-883280, NTS), 9 miles south of Alford, has remained unchanged since completion in 1626. Turret fans will enjoy this place. It's open May to September, daily, from 1.30 to 5.30 pm (£5.80/3.90).

Kildrummy Castle Nine miles west of Alford, this interesting and extensive 13th

century ruin (☎ 01975-571331) was attacked and treacherously captured in 1306 while being defended by Sir Neil Bruce, a brother of Robert the Bruce. After the 1715 Jacobite rebellion, the Earl of Mar was exiled in France and his castle fell into ruin. It's open April to September, Monday to Saturday, from 9.30 am to 6.30 pm, and Sunday afternoon (£1.80/1.30, HS).

Corgarff Castle In the wild upper reaches of Strathdon, by the A939 to Tomintoul, you'll find this impressive tower house and star-shaped defensive curtain wall. Most of the castle dates from 1750 (it was a redcoat's barracks after the 1745 rebellion). Corgarff Castle (☎ 01975-651460) opens standard HS hours from April to September, and shorter hours the rest of the year; £2.30/1.75.

Lecht Ski Resort At the head of Strathdon, the A939 crosses the Lecht pass (637m, 2089 feet), where there's a small skiing area with lots of easy and intermediate runs. You can hire skis, boots and poles from the Good Brand knitwear shop (☎ 01975-651433), Corgarff, for £10 per day. At the slopes, equipment hire is £11, a day pass is £12 and a two hour ski lesson is £12; contact the Lecht Ski Company on ☎ 01975-651440.

Places to Stay & Eat – Alford For B&B, try *Dunvegan (☎ 01975-563077, 26 Gordon Rd)*, from £16 to £18 per person. *Salad Days (Main St)* serves takeaways, filled rolls from £1.85, and meals from £3.35 to £4.95. A mile away at Bridge of Alford, the pleasant *Forbes Arms Hotel (☎ 01975-562108)* has en suite rooms for £35/55 and bar meals from £5.25 to £9.

Places to Stay & Eat – Kildrummy At the A944/A97 junction, the popular *Mossat Restaurant (☎ 01975-571355)* has baked potatoes from £2.25 and main courses from £4.05. It closes at 5.30 pm. The luxurious *Kildrummy Castle Hotel (☎ 01975-571288)*, across the river from the castle, is

CENTRAL & NORTH-EASTERN

the best place to stay in Donside. B&B starts at £75/125 and the three-course table d'hôte menu is £15.50 (not available on Sunday).

Places to Stay & Eat – Corgarff *Jenny's Bothy* (☎ *01975-651449*) is an excellent all-year bunkhouse which charges £7 for a bed. Look out for the sign by the main road, then follow the old military road (drivable) for 1200m.

The *Good Brand tearoom* has toasties for £1.45, soup and a roll for £1.55, and baked potatoes from £2.95. It's open daily, but closes at 6 pm (5 pm in winter).

Getting There & Away Bluebird Buses (☎ 01224-212266) runs bus No 220 from Aberdeen to Strathdon village (via Alford; £5.50) twice daily except Sunday. Buses from Aberdeen to Alford run around once an hour, but there are only five runs on Sunday (1¼ hours, £4.50). You'll need your own transport, or try hitching, to reach Craigievar or Corgarff castles, and the Lecht.

NORTHERN ABERDEENSHIRE & INLAND MORAY

The direct, inland rail and road route from Aberdeen to Inverness cuts across rolling agricultural country that, thanks to a mild climate, produces everything from grain to flower bulbs. The grain is turned into that magical liquid known as malt whisky. You may be tempted by the **Malt Whisky Trail**, a 70-mile signposted tour which gives you an inside look and tastings at a number of famous distilleries (including Cardhu, Glenfiddich and The Glenlivet). TICs stock a leaflet covering the tour. See also Food and Drink in the Facts for the Visitor chapter.

Haddo House (☎ 01651-851440, NTS), 19 miles north of Aberdeen, was designed by William Adam in 1732. It's best described as a classic English stately home transplanted in Scotland. It's open at Easter and daily from May to September, 1.30 to 5.30 pm (admission £4.20/2.80). Bluebird

Buses (☎ 01224-212266) runs bus Nos 290/291 hourly (infrequent on Sunday) from Aberdeen to Tarvis/Methlick via the end of the Haddo House driveway (a mile-long walk). The fare is £3.

This is also castle country, and there's a *Castle Trail* leaflet to guide you round. **Fyvie Castle** (☎ 01651-891266), 8 miles south of Turriff, is a magnificent example of Scottish baronial architecture and there's a tearoom here. It's open April to September, daily from 1.30 to 5.30 pm, opening at 11 am in July and August (£4.20/2.80). Bluebird Buses runs bus No 305 hourly every day from Aberdeen to Banff and Elgin via Fyvie village, a mile from the castle. The fare is £4. There are numerous other castles, in various states of preservation.

Huntly
- **pop 4150**   ☎ **01466**

This small town, with an impressive ruined castle and a pleasant town square, is located in a strategically important position on a low-lying plain, along the main route from Aberdeen to Moray and Strathspey.

The TIC (☎ 792255), The Square, opens daily from Easter to October. There's a bank with an ATM, next to the TIC. For the hospital, ring ☎ 792114.

On the northern edge of town, 16th century **Huntly Castle** (☎ 793191), the former stronghold of the Gordons, is in a park on the banks of the River Deveron. Over the main door is a superb carving that includes the royal arms and the figures of Christ and St Michael. The castle opens standard HS hours (closed Thursday afternoon and Friday in winter); tickets are £2.30/1.75.

Glenburn (☎ *792798, 19 Castle St)* charges around £16 per person for B&B (with shared bath). The *Huntly Hotel* (☎ *792703, 18 The Square)* has single/double rooms from £25/35 to £35/50. In the bar, toasties start at £1.40, and main courses are £2.95 to £5.25.

The *Huntly Tandoori* (☎ *792667, 109 Gordon St)* serves curries from £4.95 and there's a 10% takeaway discount.

The Aberdeen to Inverness Bluebird bus (No 10) passes through Huntly hourly (1¼ hours, £5.50), and the town is on the rail line that follows the same route (£6.90). The bus fare to Elgin is £4.25.

Dufftown

* **pop 1700**   ☎ 01340

Founded only in 1817 by James Duff, 4th Earl of Fife, Dufftown is 14 miles west of Huntly. It's a good place to start the Malt Whisky Trail; there are seven working distilleries in Dufftown alone. Locals state that 'Rome's built on seven hills, Dufftown's built on seven stills'.

At the northern edge of town there's the **Glenfiddich Distillery Visitors Centre** (☎ 820373). Visitors are guided through the process of distilling, and can also see whisky being bottled here – the only Highland distillery where this is done on the premises. It's open all year, Monday to Saturday, from 9.30 am to 4.30 pm; also, Easter to October, on Sunday from noon to 4.30 pm. There's no entry charge – your free dram really is free.

The nearby 13th century ruins of **Balvenie Castle** (☎ 320121, HS) were built by Alexander 'Black' Comyn. It was transformed into a stately home after 1550 and was visited by Mary Queen of Scots in 1562. Note the moat and external latrine chutes. It's open from April to September, Monday to Saturday, from 9.30 am to 6.30 pm (and Sunday, 2 to 6.30 pm); £1.20/90p.

The TIC (☎ 01340-820501), in the clock-tower in the square, opens Easter to October; the attached **museum** has interesting local items.

***Davaar** (☎ 820464, Church St)* offers B&B for £14.50 to £17 per person. The *Fife Arms Hotel (☎ 820220, 2 The Square)* has rooms for £25/40. Bar snacks start at £1.50 and main courses (including ostrich and kangaroo) are from £5.

In the *Commercial Hotel (☎ 820313, 4 Church St)* there are ceilidhs from June to September, on Thursday at 8.30 pm (£2); there's also whisky tasting (£3.50) on Tuesday at 8 pm.

Bluebird Buses (☎ 01224-212266) links Dufftown to Elgin (No 336, hourly from Monday to Saturday, 50 minutes, £2.90), among other places.

Tomintoul

* **pop 320**   ☎ 01807

This high-altitude village (345m) lies on the A939, roughly mid-way between Strathdon and Grantown-on-Spey, and 6 miles from the Lecht ski rèsort (see Strathdon earlier). There's a TIC (☎ 580285) on The Square, open Easter to October.

Tomintoul Visitor Centre (☎ 673701), The Square, has displays on a range of local topics. It's open from late March to late October, Monday to Saturday, from 10 am to 5 pm (admission is free). Glenlivet estate have an **information centre** (☎ 580283) in Main St, which distributes free maps of walking and cycling trails.

Currently, the long-distance footpath, the Speyside Way, extends 45 miles from Tomintoul to Spey Bay, but there are plans to extend it to Aviemore. For information about the route, contact the Ranger Service on ☎ 01340-881266.

Tomintoul Youth Hostel (☎ 580282, Main St) is fairly good. It's open from mid-May to October and beds cost £4.65/3.85. There's also *Tomintoul Bunkhouse (☎ 01343-548105, The Square)* which opens all year and charges just £7. The *Glenavon Hotel (☎ 580218, The Square)* has rooms for £15 to £24 per person, and bar meals cost £4.50 to £8. There are various other places to eat, including the *Clockhouse (The Square)*. Two places sell groceries (including the post office).

Buses connect Tomintoul with Aberlour (on schooldays, with connection to Elgin), Elgin (Thursday only, 1¼ hours) and Keith via Dufftown (Tuesday only,1¼ hours). For details phone Roberts of Rothiemay on ☎ 01466-711213.

THE COAST

The Grampians meet the sea at Stonehaven, which is home to spectacular Dunnottar Castle. Continuing around the coast from

Aberdeen, there are long stretches of sand and, on the north coast, some magical fishing villages – like Pennan, where the film *Local Hero* was shot.

Stonehaven
• **pop 9310**   ☎ **01569**

Originally a small fishing village, 'Stane-hyve' became the county town of Kincardineshire in 1600. There's a TIC (☎ 762806) at 66 Allardice St. On Market Square, there's a supermarket and banks with ATMs. Stonehaven is situated on the busy bus and rail routes between Dundee and Aberdeen.

Dunnottar Castle The principal attraction in Stonehaven is definitely Dunnottar Castle (☎ 762173), on the coast 1½ miles to the south. It's pleasant to walk to the castle from town; the TIC has a walking leaflet. The castle ruins are spread out across a grassy promontory rising 150 feet above the sea – as dramatic a film set as any director could wish for. It was last used for Zeffirelli's *Hamlet*, starring Mel Gibson. The original fortress was built in the 9th century; the keep is the most substantial remnant, but the Drawing Room (restored in 1926) is more interesting. The castle must have supported quite a large community, judging by the extent of the ruins.

The castle opens Easter to September, Monday to Saturday from 9 am to 6 pm, and on Sunday (in summer) from 2 to 5 pm; November to March, Monday to Saturday, from 9 am to 5 pm. Entry is £3/1 and last admission is half an hour before closing.

Other Things to See Just west of the A90 bypass and only a mile from the town centre, there's the pretty hamlet of **Kirkton of Fetteresso**, where the cottages cluster around the ruin of a 17th century church.

At the harbour, **The Tolbooth**, built around 1600 by the Earl Marischal, is Stonehaven's oldest building. It's now a pricey restaurant and museum (open June to September). Nearby, parts of the **Mercat Cross** date from 1645.

Places to Stay & Eat If you want to stay, the TIC has a list of B&Bs. *Robertson's bakery and tearoom (68 Allardice St)* has soup and snacks from 50p (including the local favourite, hot butteries with butter, 50p). The *Royal Hotel (44 Allardice St)* serves bar meals with vegetarian options from £4.25 to £11.75.

Peterhead
• **pop 18,500**   ☎ **01779**

The remains of a once-great fishing industry are still based in this fairly dreary town. Only a few years ago, the high-tech trawlers operating from here were so productive that they supported a local Ferrari-driving fishing community with a high disposable income.

The **Peterhead Maritime Heritage** (☎ 473000), South Rd, is worth a visit. There's an audio-visual presentation on sealife and displays on whaling, fishing and the oil industry. It's open daily from 10 am to 6 pm (from noon on Sunday), with shorter winter hours; £2.50/1.50. The central **Arbuthnot Museum** (☎ 477778), St Peter St, has wide-ranging displays of local and arctic interest. It's open Monday to Saturday, from 10.30 am to 1.30 pm and 2.30 to 5 pm (closing at 1 pm on Wednesday).

The *Palace Hotel (☎ 474821, Prince St)* is a good hotel with *en suite* rooms from £35/49 (cheaper at weekends). In the bar, soup and a roll is £1.20, burgers start at £2.25, and main courses are from £4.60. *Carrick Guest House (☎ 470610, 16 Merchant St)* is cheaper with rates from £18 to £25 per person.

Bluebird Buses (☎ 01224-212266) run every half-hour from Aberdeen (hourly on Sunday); the fare is £3.50.

Fraserburgh
• **pop 13,000**   ☎ **01346**

This town, 42 miles north of Aberdeen, achieved burgh status in 1546, but prosperity has clearly moved elsewhere. However, the harbour can be interesting when crowded with boats. There's a TIC (☎ 518315) and a

CENTRAL & NORTH-EASTERN

supermarket on Saltoun Square, and you'll find banks with ATMs on Broad St.

The interesting **Scotland's Lighthouse Museum** (☎ 511022) is a recommended attraction with guided tours to the top of bizarre-looking Kinnaird Head lighthouse, a converted 16th century castle. It's open from Monday to Saturday from 10 am to 6 pm (opens on Sunday at 12.30 pm), closing at 4 pm from November to March; entry is £2.50/2.

Maggie's Hoosie (no ☎), 26 Shore St, Inverallochy, is 4 miles east of Fraserburgh. It's a traditional 'fish-wife's' cottage, with earth floor and original furnishings. It's open from April to September, Monday to Friday (except Tuesday), 10 am to noon and 2 to 4.30 pm (afternoons only at weekends); admission is free.

The pleasant *Saltoun Arms Hotel* (☎ 518282, Saltoun Square) has en suite rooms from £38/55 and offers cheap weekend breaks.

Bar lunches start at £2.95; suppers start at £4.95. B&B at *Clifton House* (☎ 518635, 131 Charlotte St) is only £16 per person. The cheapest place to eat is the *Fisherman's Mission* (Shore St), with main courses from £1.65 to £2.95.

Bluebird Buses (☎ 01224-212266) run regularly from Aberdeen (£4.25), and hourly from Peterhead (£2.50).

Buses to Banff (£4.75) are infrequent; the No 271 runs once on college days, departing at 3.55 pm. There are also two runs on Saturday.

Pennan

Nestling under red-sandstone cliffs, Pennan is a very attractive village with a small harbour. Whitewashed houses are built gable-end-on to the sea here – the waves break just metres away, on the other side of the road. The *Pennan Inn* (☎ 01346-561201) offers B&B for £40 per double room, and bar meals from £4.50. Bluebird Buses (☎ 01224-212266) run twice to Banff on Saturday only; they pick up and drop off past the junction with the main road, just over 350m from the village.

Gardenstown

• pop 800   ☎ 01261

Gardenstown (or Gamrie, pronounced game-ree) was founded by Alexander Garden in 1720. It's another fishing village, but it's unique in Scotland for being built on cliff ledges.

Drivers should beware of severe gradients and hairpin bends in the village. Parts of the village can only be reached on foot.

Brooms Restaurant (☎ 851629, Main St) serves snacks from £1.60 and main courses from £4.25. *Palace Farm* (☎ 851261), at the junction with the main road (B9031), charges around £18 per person for B&B.

Bluebird Buses (☎ 01224-212266) run every two or three hours to Banff from Monday to Friday.

Banff & Macduff

• pop 8170 (combined)   ☎ 01261

A popular seaside resort, the twin towns of Banff and Macduff are separated by Banff Bridge. Interesting Banff could be an attractive little town, but there's vandalism and neglect here. Nearby Macduff is still a busy fishing port.

The TIC (☎ 812419) is beside St Mary's car park (at the south end of High St), Banff. It's open from April to October, daily (and Sunday afternoon in July and August), and has an hour-long free Walkman tour (£1 deposit) to encourage you to look round the town. You'll find banks with ATMs in Castle St, Banff, and in Shore St, Macduff. There's a large supermarket near Banff Bridge.

Duff House This impressive Georgian baroque mansion (☎ 818181) is in Banff, situated just upstream from the bridge. It was designed by William Adam and completed in 1737. It's been a hotel, hospital and POW camp, however after recent refurbishment opened as an art gallery housing a collection of paintings from the National Gallery of Scotland. It's open daily from 10 am to 5 pm (closed from Monday to Wednesday from October to March); £3/2.

Macduff Marine Aquarium The aquarium (☎ 833369), 11 High Shore, is in a 400,000L open-air tank, complete with kelp reef and wave machine. Oddities include the local cuckoo wrasse – it looks more like a tropical fish. It's open all year, daily, from 9 am to 5 pm (late closing in summer, at 8 pm); £2.75/2.

Other Things to See On High St, **Banff Museum** (☎ 622906) has an award-winning nature display, local geology and history, and Banff silver. It's open from June to September, daily except Thursday, from 2 to 5.15 pm (admission is free). Just off Carmelite St, Banff, there's the medieval ruin of **St Mary's Kirk** and an interesting graveyard, sadly vandalised. Nearby, the **Market Arms Bar**, built in 1585, is the oldest continuously occupied building in Banff. In Low St, Banff, the **Townhouse** dates from 1797; the adjacent cannon was captured at Sebastopol.

Two miles west of Banff, the quiet, picturesque fishing village **Whitehills** has narrow lanes and rows of neatly painted cottages gable-end-on to the sea. The village church has an excellent **clock tower**.

Places to Stay & Eat In Macduff, the recommended *Knowes Hotel* (☎ 832229, 78 Market St) charges £25/42 for B&B. Bar meals start at £4.25. There are 54 courses on the à la carte menu, including lots of seafood (from £6.50).

In Banff, try the *Broken Fiddle (9 Strait Path)*, with snacks from £1.25 and basic main courses from £2.25 to £3.95. There's also the *County Hotel* (☎ 815353, High St), with bar meals for around £6 and lunch specials at £4.25; rooms are £25/40.

Bryvard Guest House (☎ 818090, Seafield St), on the A98 heading west, is a good B&B with rates from £15 per person. *Banff Links Caravan Park* (☎ 812228), open April to October, is at the west end of town. Tent pitches are £6.20.

Getting There & Away Bluebird Buses (☎ 01224-212266) runs an infrequent service to Fraserburgh (once on college days, twice on Saturday; £4.75). There are hourly buses to Aberdeen and Elgin (infrequent on Sunday evening; £6 to either place). The bus to Elgin runs via Whitehills.

Portsoy
- **pop 1800** ☎ 01261

In Portsoy there's an excellent 17th century harbour, two churches and lots of narrow streets with interesting architecture. The town is now a conservation area; it's well worth stopping here to soak up its atmosphere. Beautiful Portsoy marble was quarried near the harbour, and there's some in the Palace of Versailles.

Situated by the harbour, the *Shore Inn* (☎ 842831) has a great atmosphere. Bar meals are served and the roast Sunday lunch is £4.95. At the *Boyne Hotel* (☎ 842242, 2 North High St) B&B is £18 to £25 per person, and dinner is £5.

The hourly No 305 bus between Elgin and Banff stops in Portsoy.

Fordyce
This historic and well-preserved village lies 1½ miles south of the A98 and about 3 miles south-west of Portsoy. **St Tarquin's Church** dates back to at least 1272 and has extraordinary canopied tombs. There's also the four-storey 16th century **Fordyce Castle** (not open to the public). The **Joiner's Workshop Visitor Centre** also provides demonstrations; it's open Easter to September, Thursday to Monday, from 12.30 pm to 5 pm (admission is free).

There's a good B&B at *Academy House* (☎ 842743, School Rd), which has rates from £15 to £20 per person and dinner for around £10.

The hourly No 305 bus between Elgin and Banff can drop you off by the A98.

Fochabers
- **pop 1500** ☎ 01343

The last bridge over the River Spey, before it enters the sea, is in Fochabers. The town has a pleasant square with a church and clock tower dated 1798.

In a converted church, the **Fochabers Folk Museum** (☎ 821204), High St, has over 4000 exhibits, covering a wide range of subjects. It's worth a visit, but you'll need plenty time! It's open daily from 9.30 am to 6 pm (closing at 5 pm in winter).

West of the bridge, by the A96, **Baxters Visitor Centre** (☎ 820666) tells the story of this famous food-producing family from 1868, when it opened its first shop in Fochabers. You get a factory tour on weekdays, with cookery demonstrations. It's open daily, from 10 am to 5 pm (the last tour is at 4 pm, and 2 pm on Friday); admission is free.

Baxters *Spey Restaurant*, at the visitor centre, is a good place for a meal. Soup and a roll is £1.75 and the daily special is £3.50. For accommodation, there's a better choice in Elgin.

Bluebird Buses (☎ 01224-212266) run frequently from Aberdeen to Elgin and Inverness via Fochabers, passing the factory.

Elgin

* **pop 20,000** ☎ 01343

At the heart of Moray, Elgin has been the provincial capital for the past eight centuries, but in medieval times the town was much more important than it is now.

The TIC (☎ 542666), 17 High St, opens all year. The central part of High St is pedestrianised and quite pleasant; it has a good range of shops and banks with ATMs. The bus station, Alexandra Rd, is central, but the train station is south of the centre.

Elgin Cathedral This great cathedral (☎ 547171, HS), known as the 'lantern of the north', was consecrated in 1224. In 1390, it was burnt down by the infamous Wolf of Badenoch, the illegitimate son of Robert II, following excommunication by the bishop.

It was rebuilt, but ruined once more in the Reformation. Among the ruins, there's a particularly fine octagonal chapter house and a Pictish cross-slab.

The cathedral's open from April to September, Monday to Saturday from 9.30 am to 6.30 pm, and on Sunday from 2 to 6.30 pm; for the rest of the year it closes on Sunday at 4.30 pm and is closed on Thursday afternoon and all day Friday. Tickets cost £1.80/1.30, but a joint ticket with Spynie Palace is available (£2.80/2.10).

Spynie Palace The palace (☎ 546358, HS), 2 miles north of Elgin, was the residence of the medieval bishops of Moray until 1686. It's now a ruin, with good views over Spynie Loch. It's open from April to September, daily, from 9.30 am to 6.30 pm (opening on Sunday at 2 pm), and weekends only for the rest of the year closing at 4.30 pm. Admission prices are as for the cathedral.

Other Things to See Elgin Museum (☎ 543675), 1 High St, has renowned fossil and Pictish stone collections. There are also displays on archaeology, natural and social history.

It's open April to October, weekdays, from 10 am to 5 pm; Saturday from 11 am to 4 pm; and Sunday from 2 to 5 pm. Admission is £1.50/75p.

Pluscarden Abbey (☎ 890257), 6 miles south-west of Elgin, was restored in 1948 by Benedictine monks, who still run it today. There are guided tours, and services are open to the public. The abbey's open all year, daily, from 4.45 am to 8.30 pm; admission is free.

Places to Stay & Eat A few minutes walk from the centre of the town, *Mrs McMillan's* (☎ 541515, 14 South College St) has singles/doubles from £16 to £25 per person, with attached bath.

Southbank Guest House (☎ 547132, 36 Academy St) has 11 rooms and charges from £16 to £25 per person (evening meals are around £6).

Just west of the centre, *Rosemount* (☎ 542907, 3 Mayne Rd) offers comfortable *en suite* B&B in two rooms for £20 to £28 per person. *Mr Ross* (☎ 542035, 7 New Elgin Rd) just south of the train station, is a friendly chap and offers B&B for £15 per person.

The elegant *Mansefield House Hotel* (☎ 540883, Mayne Rd) charges from £55/65 for B&B.

You'll find *Ca'Dora's* fish and chip shop at 181 High St. *Qismat Tandoori* (☎ 541461, 202 High St) has a good reputation; business lunches (not Sunday) start at £2.95. For a bar meal from around £5 to £7, try the *Sunninghill Hotel* (☎ 547799, Hay St). The *Abbey Court Restaurant* (☎ 542849, 15 Greyfriars St) has an international menu with vegetarian dishes but also serves traditional Scottish meals, including seafood. Main courses at lunchtime are around £5; a three-course dinner costs from £10.50.

Getting There & Away Bluebird Buses (☎ 01224-212266) runs buses along the coast to Banff and Macduff (£6), south to Dufftown (£2.90), west to Inverness (£5.50), and south-east to Aberdeen (£6.50). A local

bus runs to Lossiemouth, passing near Spynie Palace. Trains run five to ten times daily from Elgin to Aberdeen (£12.20) and Inverness (£6.70).

Findhorn & Forres

Old and new hippies should check out the Findhorn Foundation (☎ 01309-690311), Forres, IV36 0TZ. The Foundation is an international spiritual community, founded in 1962. There are about 150 members and many more sympathetic souls who have moved into the vicinity.

With no formal creed, the community is dedicated to creating 'a deeper sense of the sacred in everyday life, and to dealing with work, relationships and our environment in new and more fulfilling ways'. In many ways it's very impressive, although it can become a bit outlandish. A recent course was entitled 'Towards Inner Peace and Planetary Wholeness'.

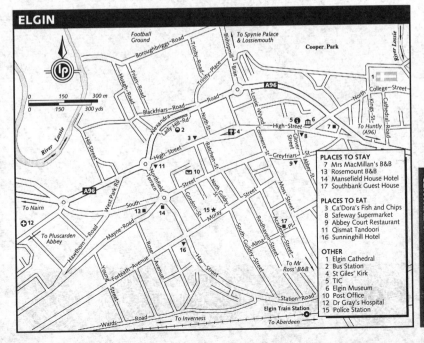

ELGIN

PLACES TO STAY
7 Mrs MacMillan's B&B
13 Rosemount B&B
14 Mansefield House Hotel
17 Southbank Guest House

PLACES TO EAT
3 Ca'Dora's Fish and Chips
8 Safeway Supermarket
9 Abbey Court Restaurant
11 Qismat Tandoori
16 Sunninghill Hotel

OTHER
1 Elgin Cathedral
2 Bus Station
4 St Giles' Kirk
5 TIC
6 Elgin Museum
10 Post Office
12 Dr Gray's Hospital
15 Police Station

CENTRAL & NORTH-EASTERN

There are daily tours at 2 pm in summer. The community is not particularly attractive itself – it started life in the Findhorn Bay Caravan Park and still occupies one end of the site.

It's possible to stay in the *caravan park* (☎ 01309-690203), with camping from £5 per tent. There are also week-long residential programs from £250 to £395.

Pleasant Findhorn village is about a mile north of the Findhorn Foundation and 4 miles north of Forres.

The *Kimberley Inn* (☎ 01309-690492), Findhorn, serves real ales and does good bar meals from £5.25. Forres, which is on the main bus and rail route between Inverness and Elgin, has lots of places to eat, including the *Central Fish Bar (106 High St)* and the trendy *Verdant Restaurant* (☎ 01309-674387, 22 Tolbooth St), with snacks from £1 and meals from £3.50 to £5.

The Highlands

Forget the castles, forget the towns and villages. The spectacular Highlands are all about mountains, sea, heather, moors, lochs – and wide, empty, exhilarating space. This is one of Europe's last great wildernesses, and it's more beautiful than you can imagine.

The Highlands is an imprecise term for the upland area which covers the far west and northern half of mainland Scotland. This chapter covers the administrative regions known as Argyll & Bute and Highland, excluding the Isle of Skye and the islands of the Inner Hebrides.

The east coast is dramatic, but it's the north and west, where the mountains and sea collide, that exhaust superlatives. Some of the most beautiful areas can only be reached by many miles of single track road, by boat or on foot. Make the effort and you'll be rewarded!

ORIENTATION & INFORMATION

The Great Glen, with a series of deep, narrow lochs (including mysterious Loch Ness), cuts across the country south-west to north-east, from Fort William to Inverness, neatly dividing the southern Highlands from the north.

Most population centres in the rugged, wild Highlands are dotted around the coast. Thurso in the far north-east is the gateway for Orkney. Ullapool and Gairloch are important transport centres in the north-west. East of Loch Ness are the Monadhliath and Cairngorm Mountains' arctic plateaus, divided by the valley of Strathspey, with Aviemore as the main resort. Ben Nevis dominates the town of Fort William in the west. Farther south, gloomy Glen Coe, famous for its massacre, guards the northern limit of Argyll & Bute. Oban, Inverary, Loch Lomond and Arrochar are the most significant destinations in Argyll.

Several island groups are linked to the Highlands, by bridge or ferry (see The Hebrides and Orkney & Shetland chapters).

HIGHLIGHTS

- Visit idyllic Plockton, a treat for *Hamish Macbeth* fans
- Stroll among Cromarty's 18th century gabled cottages
- Marvel at the soaring peaks of scenic Glen Shiel
- Survey spectacular scenery from the Fort William to Mallaig train
- Make the pretty coastal village of Ullapool your base for excellent hillwalking
- Gaze upon the seabird colonies and cliffs of Cape Wrath
- Discover the many moods of magical Glen Coe
- View photogenic Eilean Donan Castle and Loch Duich from Dornie

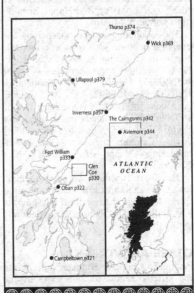

There are TICs in all the major centres in the Highlands but many smaller offices close during the low season; even those open all year usually have shorter winter opening hours. Almost all TICs charge £1 to £2 for accommodation bookings. The Highlands of Scotland Tourist Board (☎ 01997-421160, admin@host.co.uk; www.host.co.uk) publishes free accommodation guides for the Highlands north of Glencoe (including Skye). Argyll & Bute is similarly covered by Argyll, the Isles, Loch Lomond, Stirling & Trossachs Tourist Board (☎ 01786-470945, fax 01786-471301, information@scottish .heartlands.org).

An expanding Website of local information, including maps, is available at www .cali.co.uk/highexp/.

WALKING

The Highlands offer some of Scotland's finest walking country, whether it's along the coast, or to inland peaks and ridges like the Aonach Eagach, the Five Sisters of Kintail, An Teallach, Stac Pollaidh, Suilven (the Sugar Loaf) or Ben Hope (Britain's most northerly Munro).

The mountains can be treacherous and every year some walkers come unstuck. Nevisport Climbline is a voice/fax Highlands weather-report service – phone ☎ 0891-333 100601 for west Scotland or ☎ 0891-333 100602 for east Scotland. Avalanche information is available free on ☎ 0800-987988. A handy leaflet, *Enjoy the Scottish Hills in Safety*, offers basic safety advice. Campers should read the Mountaineering Council of Scotland's *Wild Camping* leaflet.

The West Highland Way is the main long-distance footpath and runs for 95 miles from Milngavie (just north of Glasgow) to Fort William. The route is almost entirely within this chapter.

OTHER ACTIVITIES

Fishing is a popular Highland activity but it's strictly regulated and some of the famous salmon fishing beats can be very expensive. Fishing for brown trout in lochs is more affordable. Local tourist offices can advise on permits and equipment and suggest the best locations.

For skiing and snowboarding, try Cairngorm (Aviemore) or Nevis Range (Fort William).

Thurso has some of Europe's best surf. Pony trekking, deer stalking, cycling and golf are other popular Highland activities.

GETTING AROUND

Aviemore, Inverness, Fort William, Mallaig and Oban are easily accessible by bus and train. Buses and trains also provide regular connections from Inverness up the east coast to Wick and Thurso, and from Inverness across the Highlands to Kyle of Lochalsh and Ullapool. Postbuses serve many remote communities. Although you can make your way around the north and west coasts from Thurso to Ullapool and on to Kyle of Lochalsh by public transport, consider hiring a car in Inverness or Fort William.

Bus

Wick, Thurso, Ullapool and Kyle of Lochalsh can all be reached by bus from Inverness, or from Edinburgh and Glasgow via Inverness or Fort William. See the Inverness and North & West Coast sections later in this chapter for more information.

There are several bus services specifically aimed at backpackers. Go Blue Banana (☎ 0131-556 2000) operates a hostel-to-hostel loop around Scotland with stops at Inverness, Kyle of Lochalsh and Fort William. Haggis Backpackers (☎ 0131-557 9393) has a similar service, including Oban. See the Getting Around chapter for details of both services. The Orkney Bus (☎ 01955-611353) operates an east-coast link from Inverness to Orkney via John o'Groats; for more details, see the Inverness section later in this chapter.

Train

The two Highland railway lines from Inverness – up the east coast to Wick and Thurso, and west to Kyle of Lochalsh – are justly famous.

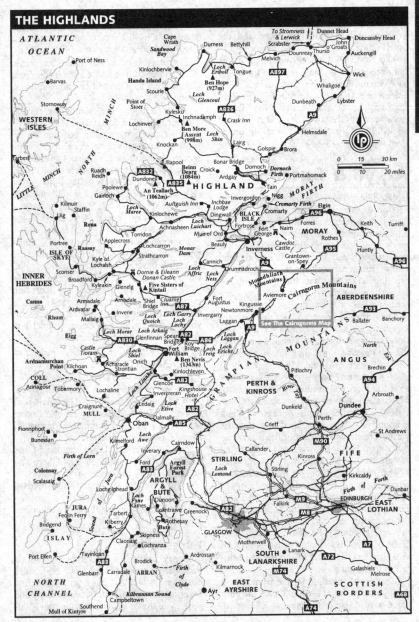

The West Highland line also follows a spectacular route from Glasgow to Fort William and Mallaig (for Skye and the Small Isles).

The North Highland Rover ticket offers unlimited travel on the lines from Inverness to Wick and Thurso, Kyle of Lochalsh, Aberdeen and Aviemore for four days in eight for £40. The similar West Highland Rover ticket covers Glasgow, Oban, Fort William and Mallaig, also for £40. For rail information phone ☎ 0345-484950.

Argyll & Bute

Created in 1996 to replace the northern section of the large region of Strathclyde, Argyll & Bute stretches from the tip of the Kintyre peninsula (subject of Paul McCartney's *Mull of Kintyre*) almost to Glen Coe, and east to Loch Lomond. It includes the Isle of Bute, parts of the West Highlands, and the islands of the Inner Hebrides – Islay, Jura, Colonsay, Mull, Coll and Tiree (see The Hebrides chapter).

This area is centred on the ancient kingdom of Dalriada, named by Irish settlers (known as the Scotti) who claimed it in the 6th century. From their headquarters at Dunadd, in the Moine Mhor (great bog) near Kilmartin, they gained ascendancy over the Picts and established the kingdom of Alba, which eventually became Scotland.

Just 20 miles from Glasgow, Loch Lomond is a very popular destination. Its western bank, where most of the tourist activity takes place, lies in Argyll & Bute; the eastern bank in Stirling.

The Firth of Clyde, to the south, is a complex system of long, deep fjords, or sea lochs, such as Loch Long and Loch Fyne. This pattern of glacial valleys, drowned by the incoming sea, continues all the way up the western coast of Scotland, creating hundreds of miles of indented coastline. It's an area that records some of the highest rainfall in the country.

Most people heading for the islands pass through the pleasant town of Oban, the only place of any size in the area, at least once.

GETTING AROUND

The main bus companies in the area are Scottish Citylink (☎ 0990-505050) and Oban & District Buses (☎ 01631-562856).

There are two railway lines, the scenic West Highland line and a branch line from Crianlarich to Oban. For rail inquiries, phone ☎ 0345-484950.

Most ferries to the islands are run by CalMac (☎ 01475-650100). Its Island Hopscotch tickets, which can be used on 15 route combinations, are valid for one month. They're better value than buying single tickets, but require advance planning. For example, the Wemyss Bay to Rothesay (Isle of Bute) and Colintraive to Rhubodach ticket costs £3.45 (£15.80 for a car), a saving of 9% on regular fares. Bicycles are carried free with a Hopscotch ticket.

For general inquiries about public transport in Argyll & Bute contact the Glasgow-based St Enoch Square Travel Centre (☎ 0141-226 4826).

The Argyll Tourist Route is a driving route marked with brown signposts. It runs from Tarbet on Loch Lomond through Inveraray, Lochgilphead, Oban, Connel and Ballachulish to Fort William.

ISLE OF BUTE
• pop 7354   ☎ 01700
The resort of **Rothesay** is Bute's only town, with all the usual facilities. The island sees around a million visitors a year and Rothesay is very busy in summer with crowds from Glasgow and Ayrshire.

The TIC (☎ 502151), 15 Victoria St, has long lists of B&Bs and hotels, but there's no youth hostel or camp site on the island. In late July there's a popular folk festival (☎ 504140) on Bute. There's also a jazz festival (☎ 841283) during the first weekend of May.

Things to See
Rothesay Castle is a substantial ruin with a water-filled moat (£1.80/1.30, HS). **Bute Museum** (☎ 505067) has a good collection covering the natural history, archaeology and geology of the island. It has an unusual 3500-

year-old lignite necklace. Botanists should enjoy the **Victorian Fernery** (☎ 504555) at Ascog (£2.50). Mock-Gothic **Mount Stuart House** (☎ 503877), belonging to the Marquess of Bute, is worth seeing. It's open May to mid-October daily, except Tuesday and Thursday, from 11 am to 4.30 pm; entry is £6/2.50.

In the southern part of Bute, you'll find the 12th century ruin of **St Blane's Chapel**, with a 10th century tombstone in the graveyard. There's a good walk from Kilchattan, via the coast (1½ hours). The main beach, with red sand, is at **Kilchattan Bay**.

Places to Stay & Eat

Two of the best cafés in Rothesay are the *Bay Café (11 Argyle St)* and the *XL Cafe Diner (Gallowgate)*. XL has 11 vegetarian choices on its extensive menu (main courses from £4.80 to £12.50). The *Black Bull* (☎ 502366), does good quality bar meals. Out of town, near Mt Stuart, *New Farm* (☎ 831646) does great home-made food from £4 for afternoon tea to £12.50 for a three-course meal. B&B here costs from £17.50 per person.

St Blane's Hotel (☎ 831224) is an unusual building with a pleasant location at Kilchattan Bay. Bar meals here start at £2.95 and B&B costs from £18.50 to £25.50 per head.

For permission to camp wild, call *Bute Estates* (☎ 502627).

Getting There & Away

Frequent CalMac ferries ply between Wemyss Bay and Rothesay (30 minutes, £2.95, £11.45 for a car). Another regular ferry crosses the short stretch of water between Rhubodach in the north of the island and Colintraive (five minutes, 85p, £6 for a car). On Monday, Wednesday and Friday in summer there's a ferry link with the Isle of Arran (two hours, £4.35, £22 for a car).

Western Buses (☎ 502076) runs several times weekly from Rothesay, west to Tighnabruaich, and east to Dunoon.

Getting Around

The Western Buses service around Bute is fairly good, but limited on Sunday. Buses link with ferries at Rothesay and run hourly to Mount Stuart House. A daycard costs £3.20.

Cycling on Bute is excellent – the roads are well-surfaced and fairly quiet. Hire a bike at the Mountain Bike Centre (☎ 502333), 24 East Princes St, Rothesay for £8 per day (£10 deposit) or at Mount Stuart House.

COWAL

Located north of Bute and between Loch Fyne and Loch Long, the Cowal peninsula has extensive forests and mountains almost 800m high (2624 feet). The northern section of the area is part of the Argyll Forest Park.

The area is traversed by several roads, some of them fairly narrow. The scenery around Loch Riddon, on the way to the village of Tighnabruaich, is particularly enchanting. The only town in the area is the uninviting Dunoon, on the Firth of Clyde, opposite Gourock.

Tighnabruaich

• pop 196   ☎ 01700

This pleasant little village is well worth a visit and has an excellent location by the Kyles of Bute. Ask at the SYHA hostel for information about local forest walks.

Tighnabruaich has a bank (without ATM), two shops, a post office, and bakery. High above the water, with a commanding view, is the whitewashed SYHA *Youth Hostel* (☎ 811622), with beds for £6.10/4.95. The *Royal Hotel* (☎ 811239) on the seafront charges from £25 to £35 per head for B&B. Excellent bar meals here cost from £3.45, with cheaper snacks from £1.85. A three-course set meal is £15. The *Burnside Cafe-Bistro* (☎ 811739) is a cheaper option, with main courses under £5.

Western Buses (☎ 502076) runs several times a week to Rothesay, with possible connections at Auchenbreck for Dunoon. There's also a weekday postbus (☎ 01463-256200) to Colintraive.

Dunoon

• **pop 8726**   ☎ 01369

If you stay in Dunoon, be careful after dark. The local economy took a downturn after the Americans pulled out of the nearby Holy Loch naval base, and there's little sign of improvement.

The town is served by two frequent ferry routes from Gourock. The CalMac sailing is best if you want to arrive in the town centre. See the Gourock section in the Glasgow chapter for details.

Dunoon has all facilities, including banks with ATMs on Argyll St, which runs parallel with the shore. There's a big Safeway supermarket on John St, just off Argyll St. You'll find the TIC (☎ 703785) on Alexandra Parade; it's open year-round. Dunoon will host the Gaelic music festival, The Mod, in 2000.

The new *Dunoon Hostel and Café* *(☎ 706665, Alexandra Parade)*, near the seafront and swimming pool, charges £10; turn right after leaving the CalMac ferry. *Pitcairlie House (☎ 704122, Alexandra Parade)* does B&B from £14 to £18 for a single/double, with shared bath. Dinner is about £6 extra. The prominent *Argyll Hotel (☎ 702059, Argyll St)* has *en suite* rooms from £25/40 for single/double. Bar meals here range from £3.50 to £11.

There's a *fish and chip shop* on Church St and several cheap eateries and carry-outs on Argyll St. *Chatters (☎ 706402, 58 John St)* does good evening meals with main courses from £6.50 to £11.95. It's closed on Sunday.

Western Buses (☎ 01700-502076) run several times a week to Rothesay, with possible connections at Auchenbreck for Tighnabruaich. On Saturday, a postbus (☎ 01463-256200) goes to Colintraive.

Highland Stores, at 156 Argyll St, has bicycle hire.

HELENSBURGH

• **pop 14,047**   ☎ 01436

For such a large place, there's comparatively little of interest, apart from the **Hill House** (☎ 673900) in Upper Colquhoun St. This NTS property is one of the best houses Charles Rennie Mackintosh designed and there's a tearoom in the kitchen. The house opens April to October, daily from 1.30 to 5 pm; entry costs £5.80/3.90.

The seasonal TIC (☎ 672642) is in the Clock Tower on the waterfront; there are supermarkets and banks (with ATMs) in the same area.

The *Pinewood Inn (☎ 672958, 47 East Clyde St)* is a pleasant place with lunch specials from £2.50 and main courses (with vegetarian options) for £5 to £10. *Bonners (☎ 677677, 41 West Clyde St)* does lunches for under £5 and two-course evening meals for £15. *Lido (7 West Clyde St)* is the best place for fish and chips.

B&Bs are fairly expensive but *Eastbank (☎ 673665, 10 Hanover St)* has three rooms from £17 per person.

Helensburgh has ferry connections with Gourock (see that section in the Glasgow chapter for details) and good train connections with Dumbarton and Glasgow (two trains per hour, 45 minutes, £3.40 to Glasgow).

LOCH LOMOND

After Loch Ness, this is perhaps the most famous of Scotland's lochs. Measuring 27½ sq miles, it's the largest single inland waterway in Britain. Its proximity to Glasgow (it's only 20 miles north-west) means that parts of the loch get quite crowded in summer. The main tourist focus, however, is on the western shore of the loch, along the A82, and at the southern end, around Balloch, which can be a nightmare of jet skis and motorboats. The eastern shore north of Rowardennan, which the West Highland Way follows, sees few visitors.

The loch was formed during the Ice Age by the action of glaciers, and lay at the junction of the three ancient Scottish kingdoms of Strathclyde, Dalriada and Pictland. Some of the 37 islands in the loch made perfect retreats for early Christians. The missionary St Mirrin spent some time on Inchmurrin, the largest island, which is named after him.

The loch crosses the Highland line and its character changes quite obviously as you move from south to north, with the most dramatic scenery in the north. The highest mountain in the area is Ben Lomond (974m, 3196 feet) on the eastern shore.

Orientation & Information

The loch is 22 miles long and up to 5 miles wide. The A82 is a major route north and sticks to the western shore through Tarbet and on to Crianlarich. The main thoroughfare on the eastern shore is just a walking trail, the West Highland Way, but it's reached by road from Drymen and Aberfoyle.

There are TICs at Balloch (☎ 01389-753533), Balloch Rd, open April to October; Drymen (☎ 01360-660068), in the library on the square, open May to September; and Tarbet (☎ 01301-702260), at the A82/A83 junction, open April to October.

Walks & Cycle Routes

The big walk is the West Highland Way, portions of which are accessible for shorter walks. See the Activities chapter.

From Rowardennan, you can tackle **Ben Lomond**, a popular five to six-hour round trip. The route starts at the car park by the Rowardennan Hotel, and you can return via the Ptarmigan (731m, 2398 feet) for good views of the loch.

Another good walk is **Ben Vorlich** (943m, 3093 feet), a good five to six-hour return trip from Ardlui station. From the underpass just south of the station, head uphill into Coire Creagach and bear right up to the ridge at 580m (1902 feet). Then follow the ridge to the double summit of the hill.

The main cycle route in the area is the Glasgow to Killin Cycle Way, which reaches the loch at Balloch. Most of the route is set back to the east of the loch, through the Queen Elizabeth Forest Park. Along the western shore, the A82 is very busy in summer, but there are short sections of the old road beside it that are quieter.

Boat Trips

The main centre for boat trips is Balloch, where two outfits, Sweeney's Cruises (☎ 01389-752376) and Mullen's Cruises

(☎ 01389-751481), offer a wide range of trips from £4.50/2 an hour for an adult/child. There's a daily 2½ hour cruise (£6.50/3) to the village of Luss, allowing 30 minutes ashore, departing at 2.30 pm. If this twee village looks like a film set, that's because it is. The village is popular with Scottish visitors hoping to catch a glimpse of the stars of the soap *Take the High Road*.

Cruise Loch Lomond (☎ 01301-702356) operates from Tarbet – its trips go to Inversnaid and Rob Roy MacGregor's cave. MacFarlane & Son (☎ 01360-870214) sails from Balmaha.

Places to Stay & Eat

Camping For campers, *Tullichewan Caravan Park (☎ 01389-759475)*, Balloch, costs £8 per tent and two people; the popular and well-located *Forestry Commission Cashel Campsite (☎ 01360-870234)* on the eastern shore at Rowardennan, costs £7.90, and has a café; and the *Ardlui Caravan Park (☎ 01301-704243)* costs £8 to pitch a tent – you can also rent boats here. Near the station in Ardlui, there's a *backpacker's camp site (☎ 01301-704244)* which charges £4 per tent.

Hostels One of the most impressive hostels in the country is *Loch Lomond Youth Hostel (☎ 01389-850226)*. It's in an imposing building set in beautiful grounds, 2 miles north of Balloch, near Arden. It's open all year and the overnight charge is £8.60/7.10 (£1 more in July and August). Book in advance in summer. And yes, it is haunted.

Rowardennan Youth Hostel (☎ 01360-870259) is across the loch, halfway up the eastern shore and by the water. It's also an activity centre, and opens late January to the end of October. Beds are £7.75/6.50. It's the perfect base for climbing Ben Lomond. Bar meals are available at the nearby *Rowardennan Hotel (☎ 01360-870273)* for £5 to £8.

There are weird-looking beehive-type huts on the West Highland Way at *Beinn Ghlas Farm wigwams (☎ 01301-704281)*,

Inverarnan, at the north end of the loch. A night here costs £7, and breakfast is £6 extra.

B&Bs & Hotels There are numerous B&Bs, centred on Balloch, Luss, Inverbeg and Tarbet. They tend to be rather expensive. However, *Mrs Gilfeather (☎ 01389-753215, 2 McLean Crescent)*, Balloch, does single and double B&B from £13.

The *Inverbeg Inn (☎ 01436-860678)* has singles/doubles from £45/76, all *en suite*. Its bar meals are OK, with most main courses between £5.75 and £7. The *Ardlui Hotel (☎ 01301-704243)* has rooms from £29 per person and bar meals start at £6.

There's one pub in this area you shouldn't miss. The *Drover's Inn (☎ 01301-704234)*, in Inverarnan at the northern end of the loch, has smoke-blackened walls, bare wooden floors, a grand hall filled with moth-eaten stuffed animals, and wee drams served by barmen in kilts. It's a great place for a serious drinking binge; and you can even stay here for £17 per person B&B.

Restaurants & Snack Bars Across the road from the Drover's Inn in Inverarnan, the cheery *Stagger Inn (☎ 01301-704274)* does good home-made snacks from £3 to £5.25, and main courses from £6.50.

In Balloch, the *Balloch Hotel (☎ 01389-752579)* does good bar meals. The *Princess Rose (☎ 01389-755873, Luss Rd)* is a good Chinese restaurant and it does takeaways.

There's a popular *milk bar* in Luss and a *snack bar* in Inveruglas.

Getting There & Away
Scottish Citylink (☎ 0990-505050) runs regular daily buses from Glasgow to Balloch (40 minutes, £3), but the bus stop is at a layby nearly a mile from the centre of the town; the buses continue up the west shore to Luss (55 minutes) and Tarbet (65 minutes).

Some buses go to Ardlui (1¼ hours, £6.30) and, north of the loch, Crianlarich.

There are two railway lines from Glasgow. One serves Balloch twice an hour (35 minutes, £2.90); the other is the West Highland line to Oban and Fort William (three daily), which follows the loch from Tarbet to Ardlui.

Getting Around
Ferry services run between Mid-Ross (a mile north of Arden) and Inchmurrin Island, but you need to have a reservation with the hotel on the island; Balmaha and the nature reserve on Inchcailloch Island (☎ 01877-386223); Inveruglas and Inversnaid (☎ 01877-386223); and Inverbeg and Rowardennan (☎ 01360-870273, three daily, £4).

ARROCHAR
• pop 635   ☎ 01301

Arrochar isn't much of a place, but it has a wonderful location, dominated by sharp peaks. Situated at the inner end of Loch Long, Arrochar is the starting point for walks to **The Cobbler** (884m), the **Arrochar Caves** and **Cruach Tairbeirt**.

The village has several hotels, shops, a bank and post office. You can hire a bike from Iain Paterson (☎ 702288) in Glen Croe.

Walks
To reach The Cobbler, start from the roadside car park at Succoth, just round the top of the loch. It's a steep hike up beside the woods, then it's easier as you trend leftwards towards the triple peaks. Once you pass the Shelter Stone, it's steep uphill work to the pass between the north and central peaks. Turn left for the central peak; scramble through the hole and along the ledge to reach the airy summit. This is a serious hill walk and you must be properly equipped. Allow five to six hours for the return trip.

The Arrochar Caves are about a mile north of Succoth. Follow the track past the houses, into the forest. Bear left on a rough path and head uphill to the caves. Take a torch (flashlight), but don't venture too far in, or you might not get out. The walk to the caves takes under an hour.

Forest Enterprise has marked a 2½ mile forest walk on the flanks of Cruach Tairbeirt. It starts at Arrochar and Tarbet train station and climbs fairly easily to a couple of good viewpoints. Follow the red markers and allow two hours.

Places to Stay & Eat
Most budget travellers head for *Ardgartan Youth Hostel* (☎ 702362), 2 miles from Arrochar at the foot of Glen Croe and open all year, except most of January (£7.75/6.50). There's also the *Ardgartan Caravan & Campsite* (☎ 702293), with a grocery store; camping costs from £7.

The *Pit Stop Diner* in Arrochar does fish and chips and cheap burgers (from £1.85). The *Arrochar Hotel* (☎ 702484) and the *Cobbler Hotel* (☎ 702238) both do bar meals from around £5. B&B at the Cobbler starts at £25 per person. An interesting option is the *Road Man's Cottage* (☎ 702557) in Glen Croe, with B&B from £14 to £15, and good dinners for £8.50.

Getting There & Away
Scottish Citylink (☎ 01990-505050) buses from Glasgow call at Arrochar and Ardgartan three to six times daily (1¼ hours, £4.50); they continue to Inverary and Campbeltown. ScotRail (☎ 0345-484950) runs two or three trains daily from Glasgow to Arrochar and Tarbet station (1¼ hours, £7.10) and on to Oban and Fort William.

INVERARAY
- **pop 704**　☎ 01499

On the shores of Loch Fyne, Inveraray is a picturesque, small town with some interesting attractions. It's an early planned town, built by the Duke of Argyll when he revamped his nearby castle in the 18th century. The TIC (☎ 302063) is on the street that runs along the loch and it's open all year. There's a Spar shop and two banks with ATMs. The Inverary Highland Games take place in mid-July.

Inveraray Castle
On the edge of the town, Inveraray Castle has been the seat of the chiefs of Clan Campbell, the Dukes of Argyll, since the 15th century. The current 18th century building includes whimsical turrets and fake battlements. Inside is the impressive armoury hall, which has walls patterned with an extensive collection of pole arms, dirks, muskets and Lochaber axes – more than 1000 of them. The dining and drawing rooms have ornate ceilings and there's a large collection of porcelain.

Near the castle, the **Combined Operations Museum** (☎ 500218) relates the part the town played in the training of Allied troops for the D-day landings.

The castle (☎ 302203) opens early April to mid-October daily, except Friday (but open on Friday in July and August), from 10 am to 1 pm and 2 to 5.45 pm (afternoon only on Sunday, and no lunch break in July and August). There's a tearoom. Entry is £4.50/3.50 (£2.50 for children); it's well worth visiting.

Inveraray Jail
The Georgian jail and courthouse, in the centre of the town, have been converted into an entertaining tourist attraction. You sit in on a trial, try out a cell and discover the meaning of 'picking oakum'. Chatty warders and attendants in 19th century costume accost visitors.

The jail (☎ 302381) opens daily from 9.30 am to 6 pm (last entry 5 pm); tickets are £4.30/2.75 (child £2.10).

Inverary Maritime Museum
The *Arctic Penguin*, a three-masted schooner built in 1911 and one of the world's last iron sailing ships, is now a 'unique maritime experience'. There are displays on the maritime history of the Clyde, piracy, and the Highland Clearances, archive videos, and activities for children. Open daily from 10 am to 6 pm (5 pm in winter), entry is £3/2 (£1.50 for children).

Places to Stay & Eat
Inveraray Youth Hostel (☎ 302454) is a modern building on Dalmally Rd. Open from mid-March to October, the overnight charge is £6.10/4.95.

There are several B&Bs around the town. *Mrs Campbell's* (☎ 302258, Main St West) opens April to October and charges from £15 per person. The *Old Rectory* (☎ 302280) has nine rooms, from £14/28 to £22/44, and opens year-round.

The *Argyll Hotel* (☎ 302466), formerly the Great Inn, looks out over the loch and offers pub meals from £4.50; B&B costs from £32.50 per person. The *George Hotel* (☎ 302111, Main St East) has a pub with stone walls, a flagstone floor, and log and peat fires. It does B&B from £22.50 to £27.50 per head and bar meals cost from £2.75 to £11.25.

The best place to eat in the area is the *Loch Fyne Oyster Bar* (☎ 600236), 6 miles north of Inveraray. It's open to 9 pm in summer. Half a dozen oysters are £4.90 and there's a good range of smoked fish and fresh seafood. Cheaper fish is sold in the attached shop.

Getting There & Away

There are six daily Citylink buses (three on Sunday) from Glasgow (1¾ hours, £5.80). Three of these buses (two on Sunday) continue to Lochgilphead and Campbeltown (two to 2½ hours, £6.50). The other three (one on Sunday) continue to Oban (1¼ hours, £5).

LOCHGILPHEAD

- **pop 2607**   ☎ **01546**

Lochgilphead isn't a particularly attractive place, but there's lots to see in the surrounding area including Kilmartin Glen. Nearby Ardrishaig has the 6-mile long **Crinan Canal** which takes small boats safely from the Sound of Jura to Loch Fyne.

The TIC (☎ 602344), Lochnell St, opens April to October. On Argyll St, there's a post office, Spar and Co-op. There are two banks with ATMs on Portalloch St, which runs parallel and close to the shore of Loch Gilp. There are various places to eat, including an Indian restaurant and a Chinese takeaway on Lochnell St. *Friendly Mac's Bistro (Argyll St)* serves snacks from £1.30, salads from £4.25, and main courses for around £5.

The *Stag Hotel* (☎ 602496, Argyll St) does all bar meals under £5.50, and B&B for £35/60. Ask for the upper-floor room with the turret and jacuzzi.

You can camp for £7.50 at the *Lochgilphead Caravan Park* (☎ 602003), a short walk west of the town centre. It has bikes for rent – useful for getting to Dunadd and around Kilmartin.

From Glasgow to Lochgilphead (2½ hours, £7.50), and on to Campbeltown, there are three daily Citylink buses (two on Sunday). There's also a daily (except Sunday) bus to Oban (1½ hours, £3.30).

KILMARTIN GLEN

This magical glen is at the centre of one of the most concentrated areas of prehistoric sites in Scotland. This is where Irish settlers founded Dalriada and formed the kingdom of Alba, which eventually united a large part of the country, so this part of mid-Argyll is seen as the cradle of modern Scotland.

The nearest TIC is at Lochgilphead, 8 miles south of Kilmartin – see the previous Lochgilphead section.

Things to See

The oldest monuments date from 5000 years ago and comprise a linear cemetery of burial cairns, running south of Kilmartin village for 1½ miles. There are also ritual monuments – two stone circles at Temple Wood, three-quarters of a mile south-west of Kilmartin. Four miles north of Lochgilphead, at Kilmichael Glassary, elaborate designs are cut into rock faces; their purpose is unknown.

The hill fort of Dunadd, 4 miles north of Lochgilphead, overlooks the boggy plain that's now the Moine Mhór Nature Reserve. It was chosen as the royal residence of the first kings of Dalriada, and this was probably where the Stone of Destiny, used in investiture ceremonies, was originally located. The faint rock carvings – an ogham inscription (an ancient script), a wild boar and two footprints – were probably used in some kind of inauguration ceremony.

There are some 10th century Celtic crosses in Kilmartin Church and lots of medieval graveslabs in the churchyard. Beside the church, **Kilmartin House** (☎ 01546-510278) is an interesting centre for archaeology and landscape interpretation with artefacts from local sites, reconstructions, prehistoric music, interactive displays, guided tours and a tearoom. The project was partly funded by midges – the curator exposed himself in Temple Wood on a warm summer's evening and was sponsored per midge bite! It's open March to December, daily from 10 am to 5.30 pm, and admission costs £3.90/1.20. Its Internet site is at www.kht.org.uk.

Just over a mile north of Kilmartin, are the extensive remains of the 16th century tower house **Carnassarie Castle**, built by the Bishop of the Isles. There's some excellent carved stonework and other architectural detail. Admission is free.

Places to Stay & Eat

There are several places to stay and eat in and around Kilmartin. At *Burndale (☎ 01546-510235)* there's B&B in an old manse from £16 to £20 per person. *Kilmartin Hotel (☎ 01546-510250)* charges £18 per person (£25 with bath) and has a restaurant and bar; there's folk music here some weekends. The *Cairn Restaurant (☎ 01546-510254)*, nearby, does good lunches and dinners. There's also the *Horseshoe Inn (☎ 01546-606369)*, which does bar meals all day, from £3 to £13. B&B here is £20 per head.

At Ardfern, adjacent to Craobh Haven marina and in an idyllic, peaceful location overlooking the Isles of Shuna and Luing, is *Lunga (☎ 01852-500237)*, a grand 17th century mansion. The hospitable laird offers B&B from £15.50 to £19.50 per person. There are also self-catering apartments on this 3000 acre estate. Lunga is about 10 miles north of Kilmartin.

Loch Melfort Hotel (☎ 01852-200233), Arduaine, is also 10 miles north of Kilmartin, but on the main road to Oban. B&B there costs from £50/75 for singles/doubles.

The bistro has an excellent menu; a three-course meal is around £11. Next door to the hotel is beautiful Arduaine Garden (£2.40/1.60, NTS).

Getting There & Away

For the 8 miles from Lochgilphead to Kilmartin there's only one daily bus in summer (not Sunday), leaving at 9.10 am (15 minutes, £1.50). From Oban to Kilmartin (1¼ hours, £3.30), the bus leaves at 1.45 pm.

KINTYRE

Forty miles long and 8 miles wide, the Kintyre peninsula is almost an island, with only a narrow strand to connect it to the wooded hills of Knapdale at Tarbert. Magnus Barefoot the Viking, who was allowed to claim as his own any island he had circumnavigated, made his men drag their longship across this strand to validate his claim in 1098.

Tarbert & Skipness
• pop 1507   ☎ 01880

Tarbert is the gateway to Kintyre. It's a pleasant and busy fishing village that also attracts the yachting crowd. There's a Co-op supermarket and two banks near the head of the harbour. The TIC (☎ 820429) is also by the harbour and it's open April to October.

Skipness is about 13 miles south of Tarbert (by road), on the east coast of Kintyre, and has a post office and general store. It's a pleasant and quiet spot with great views of Arran.

Things to See The **An Tairbeart Heritage Centre** (☎ 820190) is by the road to Campbeltown, at the southern edge of Tarbert. It has interpretative displays about local natural history and human interaction with the environment. You may see various wild birds on the mile-long woodland trail, including peregrine falcons, hen harriers and owls. The centre opens all year, daily, from 10 am to sunset; entry is £3/1.50.

Above Tarbert is a small crumbling castle built by Robert the Bruce for £511.

However, in Skipness there's the much better 13th century **Skipness Castle**, with a 16th century tower house which is still in good condition. **St Brendan's Chapel**, less than 300m from the castle, has some excellent carved graveslabs. All three places are open year-round and there's no entry charge.

Places to Stay & Eat The hotels do bar and restaurant meals and there are also cafés and a fish and chip shop. *An Tairbeart* has a good restaurant; a baked potato with an oyster is £2.50, and meals start at £5. On Harbour St, you'll find *Ca' Dora*, with toasties from £1.40, and the *Anchorage* (☎ 820881), where good local seafood, game and meat dishes are available (around £15 for three courses).

A little farther along the street, the *Islay Frigate Hotel* (☎ 820300) does B&B from £18/24 for singles/doubles and bar meals from £4.25. The more upmarket *Tarbert Hotel* (☎ 820264, Harbour St) does B&B for £30/44. Another B&B is *Southcliffe* (☎ 820604, Ladyleene Rd) with seven rooms from £16 per person.

In Skipness, the *Seafood Cabin* (☎ 760207) sits near a house between the village and the castle and serves takeaways, snacks and lunches during summer.

Mid-Kintyre

From Tayinloan, there are hourly ferries (20 minutes, £4.30 return), fewer on Sunday, to the **Isle of Gigha** (pronounced ghee-a, with a hard 'g'), a flat island 6 miles long by about a mile wide. It's known for the subtropical gardens of Achamore House (☎ 01583-505254), open daily from 9 am to dusk; entry is £2/1. Gigha cheese is sold in many parts of Argyll and is recommended, though not cheap. There are island walks and bikes can be rented from Gigha Stores (post office) or the Gigha Hotel (£5/10 for a half/full day). Several places do B&B: the *Post Office* (☎ 01583-505251) charges around £18 per person, with dinner for another £10. The *Gigha Hotel* (☎ 01583-505254) has rooms from £34 to £40 per

person. The good restaurant and bar do meals for around £6.

At Glenbarr, 6 miles south of Tayinloan, there's the **Glenbarr Abbey Visitor Centre** (☎ 01583-421247), an 18th century house with a large collection of clothes, thimbles, china, and a pair of gloves worn by Mary, Queen of Scots. The abbey opens Easter to October daily, except Tuesday, from 10 am to 5.30 pm. The laird himself will take you on a guided tour (£2.50/2).

On the east coast of Kintyre, opposite the Isle of Arran, there's the pretty village of **Carradale**, with a shop and post office. Drivers should take great care on the road to Carradale due to the severe bends and gradients. The **Network Heritage Centre** (☎ 01586-431296) in Carradale has an old school house, and fishing, farming and forestry displays. It's open from Easter to mid-October, Monday to Saturday, from 10.30 am to 5 pm, and Sunday 12.30 to 4 pm. There are several old ruins in the area, including the 12th century **Saddell Abbey** (4 miles south), and, in Carradale, **Airds Castle** and a **vitrified fort**. *Mains Farm* (☎ 01583-431216) does B&B from £15.50; dinner is £6 extra. You can also eat at the *Carradale Hotel* (☎ 01583-431223) where *en suite* rooms cost from £20 to £39 per person. You can camp at the pleasant *Carradale Bay Caravan Park* (☎ 01583-431665), which charges from £5.70.

Campbeltown
• pop 6076   ☎ 01586

Campbeltown is an unattractive place and feels very much the end of the road. With the closure of almost all the distilleries, Campbeltown was left to decay slowly. However, the new ferry to Ireland is bringing in the tourists, and things are beginning to brighten up for the town. Campbeltown is also linked by daily buses to Glasgow.

There are shops and banks (with ATMs), and an all-year TIC (☎ 01586-552056) by the quay.

Things to see include the **Springbank Distillery** (☎ 552085) – phone to make an appointment. The **Campbeltown Heritage**

Looking across the Mamores, Highlands

Walkers near the summit of Buachaille Etive Mór, Highlands

Puffin paradise, Sumburgh Head, Shetland

Jarlshof, Mainland, Shetland

Rough seas at Midhowe Broch, Rousay, Orkney

Centre (☎ 551400) covers most aspects of local life and is worth a visit. It's open April to October, daily, from noon to 5 pm (from 2 pm on Sunday); admission is £2/1.25. In the **museum** (☎ 552366), there's a jet necklace, among other items of archaeological interest. It's open Tuesday to Saturday; entry is free. The **cinema** (☎ 553657), opened in 1913, is the oldest purpose-built cinema still in operation in Scotland.

Just over 2 miles east of Campbeltown, on the **Isle of Davaar**, there's a cave with a painting of the crucifixion. You can reach the island at low water by following a shingle tombolo called The Dhorlinn, but make sure you're not caught by a rising tide. A narrow winding road, about 18 miles long, leads south of the town to the **Mull of Kintyre**, popularised by the song – and the mist does indeed often roll in. A lighthouse marks the spot closest to Ireland – only 12 miles across the water.

The Mull of Kintyre Music Festival (☎ 551053), held annually in late August in Campbeltown, is a popular event. It features traditional Scottish and Irish music; pub sessions are free.

The *Dhorlinn Café*, Longrow, is good for fish and chips. The best places for bar meals are the *White Hart Hotel (☎ 552440, Main St)* and the popular *Ardshiel Hotel (☎ 552133, Kilkerran Rd)*. At Ardshiel, main courses start at £5.25 with Kintyre salmon steak in prawn, cream and asparagus sauce for £10.50. It's excellent. It also does B&B for £28 per person. *Eagle Lodge (☎ 551359, 56 High St)* does B&B for £14 to £15 per head.

Getting There & Around

British Airways Express (☎ 0345-222111) flies twice each weekday from Glasgow to Machrihanish airport, 4 miles west of Campbeltown.

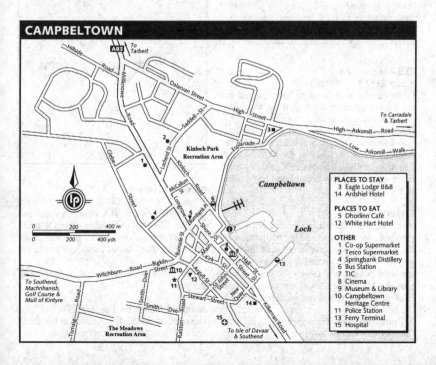

CAMPBELTOWN

PLACES TO STAY
3   Eagle Lodge B&B
14 Ardshiel Hotel

PLACES TO EAT
5   Dhorlinn Café
12 White Hart Hotel

OTHER
1   Co-op Supermarket
2   Tesco Supermarket
4   Springbank Distillery
6   Bus Station
7   TIC
8   Cinema
9   Museum & Library
10 Campbeltown
    Heritage Centre
11 Police Station
13 Ferry Terminal
15 Hospital

Scottish Citylink (☎ 0990-505050) runs three buses daily (two on Sunday) from Glasgow to Campbeltown (4½ hours, £10) via Tarbert, Kennacraig and Tayinloan.

A postbus (☎ 01463-256200) runs once daily, except Sunday, from Tarbert to Claonaig (Arran ferry) and Skipness.

There are CalMac ferry terminals at Tarbert (no ☎), for Portavadie on the east side of Loch Fyne (hourly in summer, 20 minutes, £2.40/11.65 per passenger/car); Kennacraig (☎ 01880-730253) for Islay; Claonaig (no ☎) near Skipness, for Arran; and Tayinloan (no ☎), for Gigha.

See Islay (in The Hebrides chapter), Arran (in the Southern Scotland chapter), and Gigha (earlier in this chapter) for details.

In 1997, the Argyll & Antrim Steam Packet Company (☎ 0345-523523) started a twice-daily ferry from Campbeltown to Ballycastle in Northern Ireland (three hours). It runs from May to early October; fares start at £24/17 for foot passengers (£15 for a child) and £126 for a car (with driver), but ask about special offers.

OBAN
• pop 8517   ☎ 01631

Oban can be inundated by visitors, but as the most important ferry port on the west coast, it manages to hold its own. By Highlands standards, it's quite a large town, but you can easily get around it on foot. There isn't a great deal to see or do, but it's on a beautiful bay, the harbour is interesting and there are some good coastal and hill walks in the vicinity.

Orientation

The bus, train and ferry terminals are all grouped conveniently together by the side of the harbour, on the southern edge of the bay. Argyll Square is situated one block east of the train station, and George St leads north past the North Pier. From the pier, Corran Esplanade runs round the northern edge of the bay.

From Tyndrum, the A85 brings you into the northern end of town.

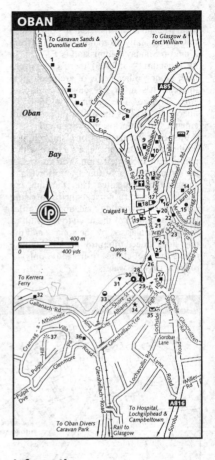

Information

Oban TIC (☎ 563122) is in the old church on Argyll Square. It's open in July and August, Monday to Saturday from 9 am to 9 pm, and on Sunday until 7 pm; May, June and September until at least 5.30 pm (5 pm on Sunday).

It's closed on Sunday during the rest of the year.

Medical Services The Argyll & the Isles Hospital (☎ 567500) is located at the south end of Oban, just off Soroba Rd.

OBAN

PLACES TO STAY
1 Barriemore Hotel
2 Glenrigh Private Hotel
3 Kilchrenan House
4 Oban Youth Hostel
6 Cuan B&B
8 Sand Villa Guest House
10 Oban Backpackers Lodge
13 Heatherfield House
14 Mrs Frost's B&B
18 Regent Hotel
22 Invercloy Guest House
25 Palace Hotel
27 Jeremy Inglis' B&B

32 Manor House
36 Maridon House

PLACES TO EAT
11 Coasters Pub
16 Studio Restaurant
20 China Restaurant
24 McTavish's Kitchens
31 Waterfront Restaurant & Caithness Glass

OTHER
5 St Columba's Cathedral
7 Swimming Pool
9 Gathering Restaurant & O'Donnell's Bar

12 St John's Cathedral
15 McCaig's Tower
17 Oban Cycles (Bike Hire)
19 Oban Inn
21 Oban Distillery
23 Jacobs Ladder
26 Oban & District Bus Office
28 Bus Stops
29 TIC & Exhibition Centre
30 Train Station
33 CalMac Ferry Terminal
34 Police Station
35 Main Post Office & Tesco Supermarket
37 Pulpit Hill Viewpoint

Things to See & Do

Crowning the hill above town is **McCaig's Tower**, built at the end of the 19th century. It was intended to be an art gallery, but was not completed and now looks like a version of Rome's colosseum.

There are good views over the bay from this peculiar structure and it's spectacularly floodlit at night. The tower is always open and there's no entry charge. There's an even better view from **Pulpit Hill**, to the south of the bay.

Since 1794, **Oban Distillery** (☎ 572004) has been producing Oban single malt whisky in the centre of the town. There are tours (£3) from Monday to Friday, year-round, and on Saturday from Easter to October. Even if you don't want to join the tour, it's still worth visiting the distillery for the small exhibition in the foyer.

You can watch glass-making in action at the **Caithness Glass Visitor Centre**, by the station on Railway Pier. It's open daily to 5 pm, including Sunday from April to October. Admission is free.

At Kilninver, 8 miles south of Oban, **World in Miniature** is a bit twee but considerable skill must have been involved in the construction of these miniature houses and tableaux. It's open Easter to October, daily from 10 am to 5 pm; entry is £1.80/1.30.

Walks & Cycle Routes

It's a very pleasant 20 minute walk north from the youth hostel along the coast to **Dunollie Castle**, built by the MacDougalls of Lorn in the 13th century. The castle was besieged unsuccessfully for a year during the 1715 Jacobite rebellion. It's now open all the time and very much a ruin. You could continue along this road to the beach at Ganavan Sands, 2½ miles from Oban.

Some of the best walking in the area is on the beautiful **Isle of Kerrera**. There's a 6-mile circuit of the island (two to three hours) which follows tracks or paths (use OS map No 49). At Lower Gylen there's a tearoom with dorm beds.

A TIC leaflet lists local bike rides. They include a 7-mile Gallanach circular tour, a 16-mile route to the Isle of Seil and routes to Connel, Glenlonan and Kilmore.

Organised Tours

On Sunday, Oban & District (☎ 562856), the local bus company, operates a range of half-day tours to Loch Etive, Inveraray, Glencoe, Kilmartin and the Sea Life Centre (10 miles to the north).

Day trips from Oban to Mull and Iona now use the CalMac ferry to Mull. Bowman & MacDougall's Tours (☎ 563221), 3 Stafford St, has a Mull and Iona tour for £16/10; a Mull, Iona, Staffa and Ulva tour

McCaig's Tower

A bizarre landmark on top of a hill over-looking Oban harbour, McCaig's tower is reminiscent of Rome's Colosseum. The reason for the design of the tower is unclear, and it certainly differs from the Colosseum in fundamental respects. Con-struction was ordered by local worthy John Stuart McCaig, an art critic, philosophical essayist and banker.

A planned 29m-high central tower was never built. Work was abandoned in 1900 when over £5000 had been spent – at least it kept the local stone masons gain-fully employed.

And that, ostensibly, was the reason for the oddness of the construction. McCaig's will directed that the 'windows' be filled with stone and bronze statues of McCaig family members but that never took place.

for £26/16; and a coach tour to Tobermory for £10.

Places to Stay

Camping The nearest camp site, 1½ miles south of town in pleasant Glenshellach, is the *Oban Divers Caravan Park (☎ 562755)*. *Gallanachmore Farm Caravan & Camping Park (☎ 562425)* is by the sea 2½ miles south of Oban on the road to Gal-lanach. Both sites charge around £6.

Hostels The popular *Oban Backpackers Lodge (☎ 562107, Breadalbane St)* charges from £8.90 (including sheets). From the train station and ferry terminal walk north to the end of George St, past the cinema, and veer right into Breadalbane St. It's a friendly place with a communal kitchen. Breakfast costs £1.40.

Oban Youth Hostel (☎ 562025) is on the Esplanade, north of the town centre, on the other side of the bay from the terminals. Beds are £8.60/7.10 (£1 more in July and

August) and it's open all year, except most of January.

On the Isle of Kerrera, *Gylen Bothy (☎ 570223)* has beds for £7. It's a fair hike from the ferry – phone to arrange a lift.

B&Bs & Hotels The cheapest B&B is *Jeremy Inglis' (☎ 565065)*, across the square from the TIC, at 21 Airds Crescent. Jeremy Inglis (alias Mr McTavish's Kitchens) charges only around £7 per person, including continental breakfast, so it gets booked up quickly. There are some double and family rooms.

Convenient for the ferry terminal is *Maridon House (☎ 562670)*, a large, blue house on Dunuaran Rd. There are 10 rooms and B&B ranges from £13 to £19 per person. Book in advance in summer.

The principal area for B&Bs and guest-houses is at the northern end of George St, along Dunollie Terrace and Breadalbane St. *Sand Villa Guest House (☎ 562803, Breadalbane St)* is an efficient place with 15 rooms (three with attached bathroom), charging from £12.50 to £20 per person. There are numerous other places in this area.

North of the town, Corran Esplanade is lined with more expensive guesthouses and small hotels, all facing seaward and most of-fering rooms with bathrooms attached. *Glenrigh Private Hotel (☎ 562991)* offers B&B from £23 per person. *Kilchrenan House (☎ 562663)*, near the youth hostel, is an excellent place to stay, charging from £23 to £32 per person. At the far end of the Es-planade is *Barriemore Hotel (☎ 566356)*, another recommended place, with B&B from £25 to £30 per person. It does an ex-cellent dinner.

High above the Esplanade, *Cuan (☎ 563994, Lismore Crescent)* has B&B from £12 to £14 per person.

There are a number of B&Bs below McCaig's Tower. *Mrs Frost's (☎ 566630, Largiemhor, Laurel Rd)* is the white build-ing that looks like a castle, nearest to the tower. There are superb views and great breakfasts, but only one single, a double and a twin. B&B is around £15 per person.

On Ardconnel Terrace, there are good views from *Invercloy Guest House (☎ 562058)*. It offers B&B from £12/24 to £22/44.

You'll find plenty more B&Bs along Soroba Rd and Glencruitten Rd.

The *Palace Hotel (☎ 562294)* is in the centre, on George St. B&B is from £16 to £25 per person and all rooms have bathroom attached.

Just north of the North Pier, on the Esplanade, the *Regent Hotel (☎ 562341)* is Oban's attempt at Art Deco. B&B in a room with bath attached costs £25 to £50 per person.

The top hotel is the *Manor House (☎ 562087)*, south around the bay, on Gallanach Rd. Built in 1780, this house was originally part of the estate of the Duke of Argyll. It's worth eating in the hotel's restaurant if you're staying here. B&B and dinner ranges from £47 to £92 per person. Also highly recommended is *Heatherfield House*, which has been described as a restaurant with rooms.

Places to Eat

There's no shortage of places to eat in Oban. Most are along the bay between the train station and the North Pier, and along George St.

You can't miss the highly publicised, central *McTavish's Kitchens (☎ 563064, George St)*. There's a self-service café with good home baking, and a Scottish show in the restaurant each night.

Opposite the Oban Distillery, the *China Restaurant (☎ 563575)* does takeaways and table-service and most of its menu items are under £6.

The *Studio Restaurant (☎ 562030, Craigard Rd)*, off George St, continues to deserve its good reputation. Local cuisine includes paté and oatcakes, roast Angus beef and Scottish cheeses. A three-course dinner costs £10.75 between 5 pm and 6.30 pm, then £11.95 until 10 pm.

North of the North Pier, along Corran Esplanade, is *Coasters Pub*, a popular place with cheap food such as fish and chips, and curries etc for under £6.

The *Waterfront Restaurant (☎ 563110)*, by the railway quay, is an excellent place for seafood. Main courses are between £10.25 and £16.50 (eg Scallops Tobermory with prawns in cream sauce, £12.75), but there's also a cheaper bar menu, with most dishes under £6.

The best place to eat is *Heatherfield House (☎ 562681, Albert Rd)*. There's a two-course set dinner in the nonsmoking dining room for £16.50; it bakes its own bread, cures its own hams, smokes its own salmon and all seafood is locally caught. There are also a few rooms here, from £43.50 to £50 per person including dinner, B&B.

Entertainment

The nightly Scottish show at *McTavish's Kitchens* packs 'em in from mid-May to the end of September. It starts at 8.30 pm and there's dancing, a live band and a piper. It costs £1.50/75p for adults/children if you also eat here, £3/1.50 if you don't; there are also set meals from £7.95 including the show.

The *Gathering Restaurant & O'Donnells Bar (☎ 564849, Breadalbane St)* has live entertainment, usually Celtic music, most nights. The pub opens from noon to 1 am; the restaurant specialises in steaks (prices up to £15), but the bar is cheaper with main courses around £4 to £5. If you're staying at a hostel, ask for a 10% discount.

The best pub is the *Oban Inn*, overlooking the harbour by the North Pier. It's a lively place which dates from 1790. It has a good range of single malt whiskies and the bar food includes wholetail breaded scampi (£4.95).

Getting There & Away

Oban is 123 miles from Edinburgh, 115 from Inverness, 93 from Glasgow and 50 from Fort William.

Bus Scottish Citylink (☎ 0990-505050) runs two to four buses a day to Oban from Glasgow (three hours, £10). Oban to Inveraray is a 1¼ hour journey (£5). Another service follows the coast via Appin to Fort William (1¾ hours; £6) and Inverness.

Train For rail inquiries, phone ☎ 0345-484950. Oban is at the end of a scenic branch line that leaves the West Highland line at Crianlarich. Up to three trains a day leave Glasgow for Oban (three hours, £17). There's a free *Window Gazer's Guide* available on the train.

To get to other parts of Scotland from Oban, the train's not much use. To reach Fort William requires a trip via Crianlarich round three sides of a rectangle – take the bus.

Boat Numerous CalMac (☎ 566688) boats link Oban with the Inner and Outer Hebrides. There are services to Mull (five to seven daily), Colonsay (three times a week), Coll and Tiree (daily except Thursday and Sunday), Barra and South Uist (five sailings per week). See the island entries for details.

There are also two to four services daily, except Sunday, to the nearby island of Lismore (five minutes, £2.15).

The passenger-only ferry from Gallanach (2 miles south of Oban) to Kerrera is run by Duncan MacEachan (☎ 01631-563665). It sails several times daily (five minutes, £2.50/1.50 return), and also on request – to call the ferry at Gallanach, you'll have to turn a white board around in order to show the black side.

Getting Around

Bus Oban & District (☎ 562856) is the local bus company and it has services up to McCaig's Tower and to the beach at Ganavan Sands.

Bicycle Oban Cycles (☎ 566996), Craigard Rd, rents out mountain bikes for £2/10 per hour/day.

LOCH ETIVE & APPIN

Loch Etive is one of Scotland's most beautiful sea lochs, extending for 17 miles from Connel to Kinlochetive, and flanked by some impressive mountains, including Ben

Cruachan (1126m, 3695 feet) and Ben Starav (1078m, 3537 feet).

Where the loch exits into the sea at **Connel**, there's an underwater rock ledge; at certain times of the tide, this causes **The Falls of Lora**.

Connel village (4 miles from Oban) has a store and several places to stay. The *Dunstaffnage Hotel (☎ 01631-710666)* does bar meals, from burgers at £3 to steaks at £13.50. Trains between Oban and Glasgow, and buses between Oban and Fort William or Glasgow, all stop here.

Dunstaffnage Castle (☎ 01631-562465) is by the main A85 road, 2 miles west of Connel and easily reached by bus from Oban. It was built on a rock plinth, around 1260, and captured by Robert the Bruce during the Wars of Independence in 1309. The nearby ruins of the 13th century **chapel** are slightly creepy – perhaps these skulls carved in the stonework are watching you?

Taynuilt is 6 miles east of Connel. Here you'll find the **Bonawe Iron Furnace** (☎ 01866-822432), the best preserved charcoal-burning ironworks in Scotland, dating from 1753. It's open April to September, Monday to Saturday, from 9.30 am to 6 pm, and from 2 pm on Sunday; entry costs £2.30/1.75. There are a couple of shops for groceries and the *Robin's Nest* tearoom for snacks and lunches.

The *Polfearn Hotel (☎ 01866-822251)*, has 14 rooms and charges from £20 per person. It has an extensive bar meal menu (from £5 to £14.50), including venison steaks and scallops. Citylink buses and trains to Oban stop at Taynuilt.

In the Benderloch area, north of Loch Etive, you'll find the 16th century **Barcaldine Castle** (☎ 01631-720598), 2 miles north of Ledaig and just off the main road. It's an interesting place, with secret stairways and a bottle dungeon. The castle is reputedly haunted by the ghost of the Blue Lady. It's open May to September, daily, from 11 am to 5.30 pm, or by appointment. Admission costs £2.95/2.65.

Glen Creran, at the head of Loch Creran, is a pleasant glen with several walks. North of Loch Creran, you come to **Appin**, with the villages of Portnacroish and Port Appin. At Portnacroish, there's a wonderful view of **Castle Stalker** on a tiny island just a few hundred metres offshore. Port Appin is a couple of miles off the main road – it's a pleasant spot, with an excellent seafood restaurant at the *Pierhouse Hotel* (☎ *01631-730400*). B&B here costs from £35 per person.

Citylink buses run three times daily (twice on Sunday) from Oban to Appin (45 minutes, £3.80) and on to Fort William.

LOCH AWE & GLEN ORCHY
Loch Awe
Loch Awe is one of Scotland's most beautiful lochs, with rolling forested hills around its southern end and spectacular mountains in the north. The loch lies between Oban and Inverary and it's the longest in Scotland at about 24 miles long – but it averages less than a mile wide.

At its northern end the loch widens out and there are several islands you can visit; **Inishail** has a ruined church and **Fraoch Eilean** has a broken down castle. For boat hire, contact Loch Awe Boats (☎ 01866-833256), Ardbrecknish. Motor boats cost £30 per day, and canoes and rowing boats are £15.

Loch Awe escapes to the sea through the narrow **Pass of Brander** where Robert the Bruce defeated the MacDougalls. In the pass, by the A85, you can visit **Cruachan Power Station** (☎ 01866-822618).

Electric buses take you more than half a mile inside **Ben Cruachan** allowing you to see the pump-storage hydro-electric scheme in action. It's open from April to November, daily, from 9.30 am to 5.30 pm (6 pm in July and August); entry is £3/2.50.

At the north end of Loch Awe stands the scenic ruin of 16th century **Kilchurn Castle**, one of Scotland's finest (closed in winter; admission free).

The *Tight Line* pub in Lochawe village does bar meals. In nearby **Dalmally**, there's a snack-bar, train station, post office, and shop. For a meal there, try the *Glenorchy*

Lodge Hotel (☎ *01838-200312*), with a good choice of main courses, mostly under £7. It has a few rooms with B&B for £30/50 a single/double.

Ben Cruachan Walk
Ben Cruachan can be climbed from the power station. A complete traverse of the ridge, mostly a walk with some scrambling, could take as long as nine hours. The quickest route follows the path from the power station, steeply uphill to the dam, then left around the reservoir to its head. From there, go westwards up to the pass below Meall Cuanail, then northwards up a steep boulderfield to the summit (six hours return, by the same route). This is no mere ramble – you must be well equipped with boots, food and water.

Glen Orchy
The A85 goes east from Dalmally up bleak Glen Lochay to Tyndrum, but it's much better to follow beautiful **Glen Orchy** to Bridge of Orchy and **Loch Tulla**, where there are lots of Munros. The A82 Glasgow to Fort William road passes Loch Tulla, but the western side is quiet, and you'll see remnants of the ancient **Caledonian pine forest** here.

You can camp wild by the bridge about 280m west of the *Inveroran Hotel*. The *Bridge of Orchy Hotel* (☎ *01838-400208*), by the A82, does singles/doubles from £35/50. It has a large bunkhouse without a kitchen (£8.50); breakfast is available at the hotel for £5 while bar meals range from £6 to £12.

Getting There & Around
Trains from Glasgow to Oban stop at Dalmally and Lochawe, while trains from Glasgow to Fort William stop at Bridge of Orchy. Citylink buses from Glasgow to Oban go via Dalmally, Lochawe and Cruachan Power Station. Bridge of Orchy is served by the Glasgow to Fort William bus.

Daily, except Sunday, there's a postbus run around the area; ring ☎ 01463-256200 for details.

Central West Highlands

This area extends northwards from Rannoch Moor and Appin, beyond Glen Coe and Fort William, and includes the southern reaches of the Great Glen. Its scenery is grand throughout, with high and wild mountains dominating the glens. Great expanses of moor alternate with lochs and patches of planted forest. Fort William, at the inner end of Loch Linnhe, is the only town in the area, but there's a fair number of villages. Roads follow the coast and run through the main glens and the railway from Glasgow cuts across Rannoch Moor to Lochaber district, the town of Fort William and the west coast village of Mallaig.

GLEN COE

Scotland's most famous glen was written into the history books in 1692 when Mac-Donalds were murdered by Campbells in what became known as the Massacre of Glen Coe. However, it's also one of the most beautiful glens, with steeply sloping sides and narrow-sided valleys that provided any cattle-rustling Highlanders with the perfect place to hide their stock. The glen is dominated by three massive, brooding spurs, known as the Three Sisters of Glencoe.

There are wonderful walks in this highly atmospheric glen, much of which is owned by the NTS, and there's also some excellent accommodation.

Glencoe Village
* pop 360   ☎ 01855

Standing by Loch Leven, at the entrance to the glen, the village is 16 miles from Fort William on the main Glasgow road. There's little to see in the village apart from the thatched **Glencoe Folk Museum**, which has a varied collection of stuff, from costumes and military memorabilia to domestic items and dairy equipment, as well as tools of the woodworking, blacksmithing and slate quarrying trades. It's open late May to September, Monday to Saturday, from 10 am to 5.30 pm. Admission costs £1/50p. McCubbin's store is useful if you need provisions, and there's a post office.

There's a NTS visitors centre and snack-bar (☎ 811307) 1½ miles from the village along the main A82 road into the glen. It's open daily April to October from 10 am to 5 pm, and 9.30 am to 5.30 pm from mid-May to August. It's worth paying the 50/30p entry fee to see the 14 minute video on the Glencoe Massacre, but the centre may close permanently within the next few years.

You can learn basic winter mountaineering skills with Paul Moore, Glencoe Guides (☎ 811402) for £100 per day (one to eight people). Paul also does guiding on hard winter climbs for more advanced parties.

Places to Stay & Eat You can camp at **Invercoe Caravans** (☎ 811210) where the view down Loch Leven is stunning. Sites cost from £8 to £12 per night, or you can rent a caravan by the week. The Brown family also runs the well-appointed **MacIain Cottages** opposite the camp site; a five bed cottage costs from £220 to £420 per week, and they're available year-round.

Glencoe Youth Hostel (☎ 811219) is 1½ miles from the village, on the old Glencoe road. It's very popular, particularly with climbers, so you'll need to book ahead. Open all year, the overnight charge is £7.75/6.50. Nearby, the **Leacantuim Farm Bunkhouse** (☎ 811256) has bunkhouse accommodation for £7.50, or £6 in the Alpine Barn. It also runs **Red Squirrel Campsite**, farther along this road, charging campers £3.50 each.

Two and a half miles from the village is the **Clachaig Inn** (☎ 811252); it's popular with climbers. It offers B&B in rooms with private bath from £18 to £32 a head. The ice-axe door-handle is decidedly quirky; the sign at reception 'No Hawkers or Campbells' even more so. There's a pub, good food (from £5.45 to £12) and live Scottish, Irish and blues music several times weekly. From January to March, slide lectures on mountain topics are held fortnightly (£5).

On the village outskirts, **Glencoe Guest House** (☎ 811244), Strathlachan, charges

The Glen Coe Massacre

The brutal murders that took place here in 1692 were particularly shameful, perpetrated as they were by one Highland clan on another (with whom they were lodging as guests).

In an attempt to quash remaining Jacobite loyalties among the Highland clans, the king (William III) had ordered that all chiefs take an oath of loyalty to him by the end of the year (1691). MacIain, the elderly chief of the MacDonalds of Glen Coe, was late in setting out to fulfil the king's demand, and going first to Fort William rather than Inverary made him later still.

The Secretary of State for Scotland, Sir John Dalrymple, declared that the MacDonalds should be punished as an example to other Highland clans, some of whom had not bothered to even take the oath. A company of 120 soldiers, mainly of the Campbell clan, were sent to the glen. Since their leader was related by marriage to MacIain, the troops were billeted in MacDonald homes. It was a long-standing tradition for clans to provide hospitality to passing travellers.

After they'd been guests for 12 days, the order came for the soldiers to put to death all MacDonalds under the age of 70. Some Campbells alerted the MacDonalds to their intended fate, while others turned on their hosts at 5 am on 13 February, shooting MacIain and 37 other men, women and children. Some died before they knew what was happening, while others fled into the snow, only to die of exposure.

The ruthless brutality of the incident caused a public uproar and after an inquiry several years later, Dalrymple lost his job. There's a monument to MacIain in Glencoe village and members of the MacDonald clan still gather here on 13 February each year.

£14 to £19 per person. Nearby, *An Darag* (☎ 811643) has rooms with bath for £15 to £18 a head. In the main street you can get B&B in several places, including the quaint cottage *Oakwood*.

Getting There & Away Highland Country Buses (☎ 01397-702373) runs six buses daily from Fort William to Glencoe (30 minutes). Scottish Citylink buses run to Glasgow (2½ hours, £8.80) and Fort William (£2.80).

Glencoe Ski Centre

About 1½ miles from the Kingshouse Hotel, on the other side of the A82, is the car park and base station for this ski centre, where commercial skiing in Scotland first started in 1956. At the base station there's a **Museum of Scottish Skiing and Climbing** (☎ 01855-851226); among the relics is the ice axe Chris Bonington used to climb

Everest. It's open May to September, daily, from 9 am to 5 pm. There's also an inexpensive café here, with snacks from £1.50 and main courses around £3.50.

The chair lift (☎ 01855-851226) operates daily in summer (late June to August), from 9.30 am to 5 pm; £3.75/2.50 return. In winter, a full day-pass including ski-tows costs £15.50/9.50, and the skiing is generally good. The chair lift is the easiest way to get to the 640m-high viewpoint and several good walks.

Kingshouse Hotel & Glen Etive

Scotland's oldest established inn, this isolated hotel (☎ 01855-851259) has been a landmark for so long that it now appears on maps, marked simply as 'Hotel'. It's on the West Highland Way at the east end of the glen, and hikers stop here to tuck into a plate of haggis, tatties and neeps and a refreshing drink in the bar (two courses for

GLEN COE

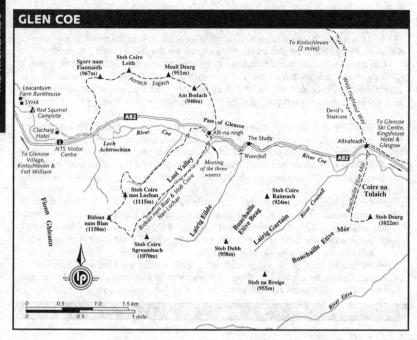

around £10). It's a good place to stay, with rooms from £23.50/52 plus £7 for breakfast.

Quiet **Glen Etive** runs south-west from the hotel and it's worth visiting for the beautiful scenery en route. Wild camping is possible. There's a Monday to Saturday postbus run (☎ 01463-256200) from Fort William to Glen Etive.

Walks

This is serious walking country and you'll need maps, warm clothes, and food and water. The NTS visitors centre stocks lots of useful information.

A great six hour hike leads through the Lost Valley to the top of **Bidean nam Bian** (1150m, 3774 feet). Cross the footbridge below Allt-na-reigh and follow the gorge up into the Lost Valley, continuing up to the rim, then along it, to the right, to the summit. You need to be very careful crossing to Stob Coire Nan Lochan as there are

steep scree slopes. Descend the west side of this ridge and round into Coire nan Lochan, where a path heads back to the road.

For something less strenuous, hike this route only as far as the **Lost Valley**, a hidden mountain sanctuary still haunted by the ghosts of murdered MacDonalds. Allow three hours for the return trip.

The **Aonach Eagach**, the glen's northern wall, is said to be the best ridge walk on the Scottish mainland, but it's difficult in places and you need a good head for heights. Some parts could almost be graded a rock climb. It's best done from east to west, and there's a path up the hillside north of Allt-na-reigh and down from Sgor nam Fiannaidh at the west end, towards Loch Achtriochtan. The more direct gully that leads to Clachaig Inn isn't a safe way down. It takes six to eight hours.

From Kingshouse Hotel, the view of **Buachaille Etive Mór** (1022m, 3352 feet), known as the 'Queen of Scottish Mountains', will give you a sense of *déjà vu*, as it appears in photographs and adverts all over the world. The walking route to the top starts at Altnafeadh, 2½ miles west of the hotel. It takes only four hours return, but it's not for casual hikers, as the higher part of the route leads up steep scree slopes in Coire na Tulaich. There's also a newly designated Munro at the far south-western end of the summit ridge.

There are several short, pleasant walks around **Glencoe Lochan**, near the village. To get there, turn left off the minor road to the youth hostel, just beyond the bridge over the River Coe. There are three walks (40 minutes to an hour), all detailed on a signboard at the car park. The artificial lochan was created by Lord Strathcona in 1895 for his homesick Canadian wife Isabella and is surrounded by a North American-style forest.

KINLOCHLEVEN
- **pop 1100**   ☎ **01855**

Kinlochleven is hemmed in by high mountains at the head of the beautiful fjord-like Loch Leven, about 7 miles east of Glencoe. The village has depended on the aluminium factory for its survival but, with the impending closure of the smelter and consequent threat of unemployment, the villagers are developing new ideas. There are hopes of turning Kinlochleven into Scotland's premier mountaineering centre as part of a multi-million pound redevelopment plan.

Things to See & Do
Kinlochleven Visitor Centre (☎ 831663), by the factory, tells the interesting story of the British Aluminium Company, the smelter (which opened in 1908), the Blackwater Reservoir and the hydro-electric scheme. It's in the same building as the public library and it's open variable hours. From mid-April to mid-October, the centre opens on weekdays from 10 am to 6 pm and on weekends from 11.30 am to 4.30 pm. Admission is free.

The West Highland Way passes through Kinlochleven. Most walkers decide to stay in the village before walking the last 14-mile section to Fort William. Other hikes in the area include moderate walks up the glen of the River Leven, with pleasant woods and the Grey Mares Tail waterfall, and harder mountain trips on the Mamores. Paths give access to the Mamores from the Mamore Lodge road.

Once you're up there, you can walk fairly easily around the ridges of **Na Gruagaichean** (1055m, 3460 feet), **Stob Coire a'Chairn** (981m, 3219 feet) and **Am Bodach** (1032m, 3386 feet). You must be well equipped though, and you'll need OS map No 41 and a compass.

Places to Stay & Eat
The village has a Co-op supermarket, a general store and a post office. There are several places to eat, including a cheap bakery and a fish and chip shop.

West Highland Lodge (☎ 831471, Hostel Brae) has dorm beds from £7, including sheets. *Grant's Garage (☎ 831666, Wades Rd)*, heading for North Ballachulish, has two heated wigwams for £7 per person. The *Tailrace Inn (☎ 831777)* does cheap snacks (from £1.50) and bar meals, with most dishes under £6. It has karaoke evenings in the bar, so you might prefer somewhere quieter.

The *MacDonald Hotel (☎ 831539)* does *en suite* B&B from £36/52 for single/double. It also serves pub grub from £3 to £10.50. There's a *camp site (☎ 831539)* behind the hotel which charges £3.75 per person, including shower.

There's a distinctly wacky hotel 200m above Kinlochleven called *Mamore Lodge (☎ 831213)*. The pine-panelled rooms and strange beds have an air of decrepitude about them. The meals are also a bit odd. B&B here costs £19 to £35 per head, and it's an interesting experience you will not forget in a hurry.

Getting There & Away
Highland Country Buses (☎ 01397-702373) has services from Fort William and Ballachulish to Kinlochleven six/eight times daily, except Sunday (50 minutes, £2.10).

GLEN COE TO FORT WILLIAM

From Glencoe, the B863 goes east to Kinlochleven and the A82 goes westwards to the old slate quarrying village of Ballachulish. There's a seasonal TIC situated here (☎ 01855-811296) with displays about the quarries.

Just across the A82 there's **Highland Mysteryworld** (☎ 01855-811660), a surprising place with a creepy atmosphere and highly professional actors. Highlights of the tour include the funny fachan and the stirring talk by the shennachie. It's open Easter to October daily, from 9.30 am to 6 pm (last admission 5.30 pm); £4.95/3.50. The on-site *Corag's café* does soup and a roll for £1.25. Near the TIC, *Strathassynt* (☎ 01855-811261) offers B&B from £25/34 and dinner for £10.

Two miles farther west, at South Ballachulish, the A828 goes west then south to Oban, while the A82 goes north over the **Ballachulish Bridge**, to meet the B863 after its circuit of Loch Leven. There are great views of the mountains from the bridge.

North Ballachulish merges with **Onich** and there are a number of hotels here with lovely lochside locations. *Creag Mhor* (☎ 01855-821379) has singles/doubles from £27.50/45. A set three-course lunch costs £5; main courses cost £5 to £10. For something even more stylish, there's the *Lodge on the Loch* (☎ 01855-821237) with luxurious singles/doubles from £44/88 and a good restaurant.

Beyond Onich, you'll reach **Inchree**, where accommodation includes *Inchree Bunkhouse* (☎ 01855-821287), with beds from £6 and a good *pub/restaurant* (☎ 01855-821393). A three-course meal here is around £13. It's easy to get to Inchree by bus as it's on the main route between Fort William and Glasgow or Oban.

Less than a mile to the north, there's the Corran ferry to Ardgour. Boats run at least once hourly across Loch Linnhe (five minutes, foot passengers free, cars £4.20). The *Nether Lochaber Hotel* (☎ 01855-821235), by the ferry, is another good place to eat, with pub grub for under £8.

Singles/doubles are £27.50 to £40 per person.

North of Corran, the A82 twists its way along Loch Linnhe to Fort William.

FORT WILLIAM

• pop 10,774 ☎ 01397

Fort William, which lies beside Loch Linnhe amid some of Britain's most magnificent mountain landscapes, has one of the finest settings in the country. Although insensitive civic planning compromised its appeal for many years, the pedestrianisation of the High St and the determination of its people have turned it into a rather pleasant little town. As a major tourist centre, it's easily accessed by rail and bus lines, and makes a great place to base yourself for exploring the mountains and glens of Lochaber. Magical Glen Nevis begins near the north end of the town and extends south and east below the slopes of Ben Nevis. 'The Ben' – Britain's highest mountain at 4406 feet – and neighbouring mountains are a magnet for hikers and climbers. The glen is also popular with movie-makers – part of Mel Gibson's Oscar-winning *Braveheart* was filmed here.

Orientation & Information

The town meanders along the edge of Loch Linnhe for several miles. The centre, with its small selection of shops, takeaways and pubs, is easy to get around on foot unless you're booked into a far-flung B&B.

The busy TIC (☎ 703781), in Cameron Square, has a good range of books and maps. For local walks, its series of *Great Walks* leaflets (30p), incorporating a map and basic information, are handy, but you'll need an OS map for more adventurous hikes, such as Ben Nevis. More information is available from the Glen Nevis Visitors Centre, Ionad Nibheis, 1½ miles up the glen from town (admission £1).

There are banks with ATMs in the High St. As you might expect, Fort William has well-stocked outdoor-equipment shops. Nevisport (☎ 704921), near the train station, has a marvellous range of books and maps for mountaineers. West Coast Outdoor Leisure (☎ 705777) is at the other end of the High St.

The Belford Hospital (☎ 702481) lies opposite the train station.

West Highland Museum

Beside the TIC, this museum (☎ 702169) is packed with Highland memorabilia. Of particular interest is the secret portrait of Bonnie Prince Charlie. After the Jacobite rebellions, all things Highland were banned, including pictures of the exiled leader. This picture looks like nothing more than a smear of paint until placed next to a curved mirror, when it reflects a credible likeness of the prince.

The museum opens all year from Monday to Saturday, until at least 4 pm (5 pm from May to September), and in July and August on Sunday afternoon. Admission costs £2/1.50.

Steam Train

The Jacobite (☎ 703791) steam train runs from Fort William to Mallaig at 10.35 am

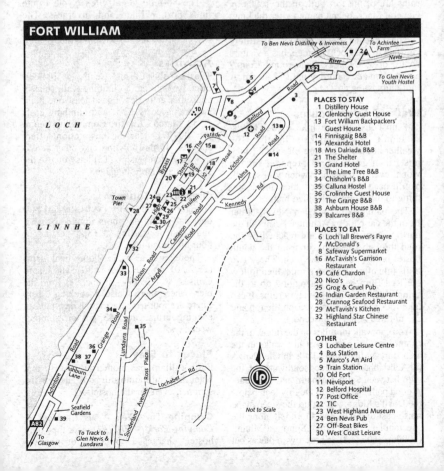

FORT WILLIAM

To Ben Nevis Distillery & Inverness
To Achintee Farm
River Nevis
A82
To Glen Nevis Youth Hostel
To Glen Nevis
LOCH
The Parade
Belford Road
Victoria Road
Alma Rd
Kennedy Rd
Bypass
High Street
Bank St
Fassifern Road
Cameron Road
Union Road
Argyll Road
Grange Road
Lundavra Road
Achintore Road
Ashburn Lane
Sunderland Avenue
Ross Place
Lochaber Rd
Town Pier
LINNHE
Seafield Gardens
A82
To Glasgow
To Track to Glen Nevis & Lundavra

Not to Scale

PLACES TO STAY
1 Distillery House
2 Glenlochy Guest House
13 Fort William Backpackers' Guest House
14 Finnisgaig B&B
15 Alexandra Hotel
18 Mrs Dalriada B&B
21 The Shelter
31 Grand Hotel
33 The Lime Tree B&B
34 Chisholm's B&B
35 Calluna Hostel
36 Crolinnhe Guest House
37 The Grange B&B
38 Ashburn House B&B
39 Balcarres B&B

PLACES TO EAT
6 Loch Iall Brewer's Fayre
7 McDonald's
8 Safeway Supermarket
16 McTavish's Garrison Restaurant
19 Café Chardon
20 Nico's
25 Grog & Gruel Pub
26 Indian Garden Restaurant
28 Crannog Seafood Restaurant
29 McTavish's Kitchen
32 Highland Star Chinese Restaurant

OTHER
3 Lochaber Leisure Centre
4 Bus Station
5 Marco's An Aird
9 Train Station
10 Old Fort
11 Nevisport
12 Belford Hospital
17 Post Office
22 TIC
23 West Highland Museum
24 Ben Nevis Pub
27 Off-Beat Bikes
30 West Coast Leisure

daily, except Saturday, from mid-June to late September. It leaves to return at 2.10 pm. The journey crosses the historic Glenfinnan viaduct, with great views down Loch Shiel. A day return costs £19.25.

Other Things to See

There's little left of the original **Fort William** from which the town takes its name, as it was pulled down in the 19th century to make way for the railway. It was originally built by General Monk in 1635 to control the Highlands, but the surviving ruins are of the fort built in the 1690s by General MacKay and named after the king, William III.

The local **Ben Nevis Distillery** (☎ 702476), at Lochy Bridge, has a visitors centre open weekdays year-round from 9 am to 5 pm and Saturday until 12.30 pm. A tour and tasting costs £2.

Walks & Cycle Routes

The most obvious local hike, up **Ben Nevis**, shouldn't be undertaken lightly. The weather at the top is more often bad (thick mist) than good, so go prepared for the worst, even if it's sunny when you set off. You'll need warm clothes, food and something to drink, and a detailed map.

The path begins in Glen Nevis, either from the car park by Achintee Farm (on the north side of the river and reached by the road through Claggan), or from the youth hostel on the road up the glen. These two trails join after less than a mile, then follow the Red Burn before zigzagging up to the summit and the old observatory ruins. It can take four to five hours to reach the top and 2½ to three hours to descend.

You can walk for miles on the ridges of the **Mamores**. One of the best hill walks in the area starts at the Lower Falls in Glen Nevis (at Achriabhach) and goes southwards up the glen between **Sgurr a'Mhaim** and **Stob Ban**. A good path takes you to the tiny loch below the **Devil's Ridge**; zigzag up the steep slope north-east of the loch and turn left along the spectacular ridge for Sgurr a'Mhaim (1099m, 3605 feet). It's narrow in places but

there's little real scrambling. From the top of Sgurr a'Mhaim you can easily descend to the car park at Achriabhach. The round trip takes about six hours.

There are very pleasant (and far less strenuous) walks along Glen Nevis, through the gorge at the east end to beautiful **Steall Meadows**, with its 100m-high waterfall. You could also walk part of the scenic West Highland Way from Fort William to Kinlochleven via Glen Nevis (14 miles) or even to Glencoe (21 miles to the junction with the A82).

The 80-mile Great Glen Cycle Route links Fort William and Inverness. The Forestry Commission's free leaflet gives details of this mainly off-road route.

Activities

The Lochaber Leisure Centre (☎ 704359) offers swimming, a climbing wall, squash, and other activities. For at least one hour, swimming costs £2/1, and climbing costs £2.50. Marco's An Aird Community Centre (☎ 700707), near the bus station, offers snooker, 10-pin bowling and other activities. Day membership (£2) lets you use the showers and store luggage.

Organised Tours

Glengarry Mini Tours (☎ 01809-501297) does half or full-day tours around Lochaber and Glencoe starting at £8.50 for a four hour afternoon tour.

There are also 1½-hour boat trips (£5/2.50) on the loch with Seal Island Cruises (☎ 703919) – it operates from the pier, where there's also a booking kiosk. There are four trips during the day, plus an evening cruise at 7.45 pm on summer weekdays.

Places to Stay

Fort William has numerous B&Bs and hotels but you should still book ahead in the summer, even for the hostels.

Camping The *Glen Nevis Caravan & Camping Park* (☎ 702191), near the youth hostel, charges £4.60/5.60 for one/two people. If you bring a car, there's an extra charge. The few seasonal camping grounds at Nevis Bridge are little more than fields with basic facilities.

Hostels The popular *Fort William Backpackers' Guest House* (☎ *700711, Alma Rd*) is a short walk from the train station and charges £8.90, including linen.

Three miles from Fort William, by the start of the path up Ben Nevis in Glen Nevis, the large *Glen Nevis Youth Hostel* (☎ *702336*) opens all year. The charge is £8.60/7.10 (£1 more in July and August). A good alternative is the *Ben Nevis Bunkhouse* (☎ *702240*), Achintee Farm, over the river from the Glen Nevis Visitor Centre. It costs £8 per person with linen. A new restaurant is planned.

The *Shelter* (☎ *703293, Fassifern Rd*), behind the TIC, has dorm beds for £8.90. A 15 minute walk from the town centre lies *Calluna* (☎ *700451*), a hostel run by well-known mountain guide Alan Kimber. Dormitory accommodation costs from £8. Phone for a free pick-up from town.

In Corpach, 4 miles along the Mallaig road north of Fort William, there's the *Smiddy Bunkhouse* (☎ *772467, Station Rd*), an independent hostel charging from £8.50. The attached activity centre organises mountaineering, kayaking and sailing trips.

B&Bs & Hotels Several B&Bs in and around Alma and Fassifern Rds are closest to the train and bus stations. Try *Finnisgaig* (☎ *702453, Alma Rd*) which charges from £14 per person for a double, or *Mrs Dalriada* (☎ *702533, 2 Caberfeidh, Fassifern Rd*) where B&B costs from £15 to £21 per person for a double. Achintore Rd, which runs south along the loch, is packed with B&Bs and hotels, but some seem large and characterless. More interesting is the B&B-cum-art gallery at the *Lime Tree* (☎ *701806*), which has beds for around £14 per person. The comfortable *Ashburn House* (☎ *706000*) has rooms with bath for £25 to £35 per person. Nearby, *Chisholm's*

(☎ *705548, 5 Grange Rd*) does B&B from £13 to £16 per person.

Several B&Bs just off Achintore Rd offer pleasant loch views, including *Balcarres* (☎ *702377*), which charges from £16 to £25.

On Grange Rd, parallel to Achintore Rd, there are two very comfortable guesthouses whose owners' attention to detail has earned them the top tourist-board rating. The excellent three-room *Grange* (☎ *705516*) and *Crolinnhe* (☎ *702709*) next door charge from £33 to £35 per person.

Glen Nevis offers several more places to stay, including *Achintee Farm* (☎ *702240*), which has B&B accommodation as well as the bunkhouse. Rooms cost from £16 to £22 per head.

The *Alexandra Hotel* (☎ *702241, The Parade*) is a large, traditional hotel with comfortable doubles with bath from £34.50 per person. The *Grand Hotel* (☎ *702928, High St*) is the other large, central hotel, with rooms from £25 per person.

Distillery House (☎ *700103*), at the old Glenlochy Distillery opposite the road into Glen Nevis, is thoroughly recommended. Rooms with private baths cost from £25/44 to £35/64 for *en suite* single/double. Evening meals are available for £15. Just across the road, *Glenlochy Guest House* (☎ *702909*), does B&B from £20/30.

The wonderfully grand five-star *Inverlochy Castle* (☎ *702177*), in 500 acre grounds 3 miles north of Fort William, is an opulent Victorian creation completed in 1865. It has everything you'd expect to find in a castle – crenellated battlements, stags' heads, log fires and a wide staircase. Luxurious single/double rooms cost from £180/250. Reservations are requisite.

Places to Eat

With the honourable exception of the popular *Crannog Seafood Restaurant*, Fort William is pretty much a culinary desert. For those on a tight budget, the *Safeway Coffee Shop* sells good value light meals, such as filled jacket potatoes from £2 and a cheap all-day breakfast. It's open until 8 or 9 pm on weekdays and Saturday, 6 pm on

Sunday. Just across the road, the *Loch Iall Brewer's Fayre* (☎ 703707) does a range of main courses from £4.35.

The *Nevisport Bar & Restaurant* (☎ 704921), in the outdoor-equipment shop, does cheap meals but the restaurant closes at 7.30 pm daily, except Sunday when it closes even earlier. Bar meals, including vegetarian options, start at £4 but they're fairly average.

Most other places to eat line the High St. *Nico's* fish and chip shop charges £3.40 for cod and chips and is recommended. The *Café Chardon*, upstairs in P Maclennan's store, has soup for £1.85, filled ciabatta sandwiches for £2.50 and focaccia Italian bread for £3.05.

McTavish's Kitchen (☎ 702406, High St) has the same menu and floor show (see under Entertainment) as the Oban branch. There's a self-service café downstairs. The popular *McTavish's Garrison Restaurant* (☎ 702406, High St), offers food only.

Indian Garden Restaurant (☎ 705011, 88 High St) is not too expensive, with two-course lunches for £5.95. It does takeaways for around £5, and stays open late.

You can also get takeaways from the town's only Chinese restaurant, the *Highland Star* (☎ 703905, 155 High St).

Another ethnic option is the Tex-Mex oriented *Grog & Gruel* (☎ 705078, 66 High St). Enchiladas, burritos and tacos, including vegetarian versions, are all around £7.

The best restaurant in town also has the best location. The *Crannog Seafood Restaurant* (☎ 705589) is on the pier, giving diners an uninterrupted view over the loch. A two-course set lunch is £7.50, and main courses cost from £10 to £15.

Up in Glen Nevis, and near the SYHA hostel, you can get a good meal at the pleasant *Glen Nevis Restaurant* (☎ 705459). Home baking and snacks during the day cost from £2 to £4 and evening main courses are £4.50 to £12.50. *Café Beag* (☎ 703601) has a gallery of local landscapes and is even nearer the hostel. It's cheaper, but with a more limited menu.

Entertainment

McTavish's Kitchen (☎ 702406) takes the pile 'em high, sell 'em cheap approach to Scottish cuisine and culture, but the music's good and it can be a lot of fun as long as you get into the spirit of things. Shows are staged nightly from 8.30 pm, with dancing, a live band and a piper. It costs £1.50/1 with a meal, £3/1.50 without, and set meals start at £8, including the show. A disco operates on Friday and Saturday from 10.30 pm (cover charge £3).

On the opposite side of the High St, the Jacobite Bar in *Ben Nevis* is a popular music venue and a good place for a drink or inexpensive meal (two courses from £3.50). The *Nevisport Bar*, in the Nevisport complex, beckons walkers and climbers with real ales and, on the second Saturday of each month, free blues, folk and jazz performances.

Getting There & Away

Fort William lies 146 miles from Edinburgh, 104 from Glasgow and 66 from Inverness. If you have a spare week, you may want to trek in on the 95-mile West Highland Way from just north of Glasgow (see the Activities chapter).

Bus Scottish Citylink (☎ 0990-505050) has four or five direct daily buses to Glasgow (three hours, £10), via Glencoe, with connections to London. Martin's Coaches (☎ 712579) runs once to Glasgow each weekday and on Sunday evening (three hours, £8.90, £6.50 for students). There are three direct daily Citylink buses between Fort William and Kyle of Lochalsh (two hours, £9). There also are two or three buses daily between Fort William and Oban (1¼ hours; £6). Several daily services run along Loch Ness to Inverness (two hours, £6.30) and two or three daily, except Sunday, run to and from Mallaig (1½ hours, £4.50), via Glenfinnan. Another useful Monday to Saturday service runs to Glencoe (30 minutes, £1.40).

Highland Country Buses (☎ 702373) runs six daily services to Kinlochleven (45 minutes, £2.10) via Inchree, Onich, Ballachulish and Glencoe.

Train For rail inquiries, phone ☎ 0345-484950. The spectacular West Highland line runs from Glasgow via Fort William to Mallaig. There's a particularly wonderful wild section across the bleak Rannoch Moor. There's no direct rail connection between Oban and Fort William; use the Citylink bus services to avoid backtracking to Crianlarich.

There are two or three trains daily from Glasgow to Fort William (3½ hours, £22.70), and one to four trains between Fort William and Mallaig (1½ hours, £7.20). The Highland Rover ticket (£42) allows unlimited travel on four days in eight consecutive days.

An overnight train connects Fort William and London Euston (from £79, including the sleeper), but you'll miss the views.

Car The TIC has a leaflet listing car hire companies. It's worth trying MacRae & Dick (☎ 702500), Road to the Isles Filling Station, Lochy Bridge.

Getting Around

Bus Highland Country Buses does the 10 minute run from the bus station up Glen Nevis to the youth hostel. They leave roughly hourly from 8 am to 11 pm, Monday to Saturday, June to September. The fare is £1.10. Buses to Corpach (15 minutes) are more frequent.

Taxi You can phone a taxi on ☎ 706070 or 704000.

Bicycle Off-Beat Bikes (☎ 704008), at 117 High St and at the Nevis Range base station, has mountain bikes for £8.50/12.50 for a half/full day. It also runs guided bike tours of the area for around £40 for up to 12 people, excluding bike hire.

ARDGOUR & ARDNAMURCHAN

West of Fort William lies Scotland's Empty Quarter – a rugged landscape of wild mountains, lonely coastlines and few roads, with a turbulent history. Nowadays, it's home to few people, mainly due to the 19th century

Highland Clearances, in which entire villages were evicted by zealous landlords who preferred sheep to tenants. As a result, the Gaelic culture was undermined in the region.

This part of the country is noted for its wildlife; the name Ardgour means 'height of the goats', but you can also see deer, pine martens, wildcats and eagles.

Glenmore Natural History Centre

The recommended Glenmore Natural History Centre (☎ 01972-500254), midway between Salen and Kilchoan, devised by local photographer Michael MacGregor, displays some of his finer work and brings you face to face with the flora and fauna of the Ardnamurchan peninsula. The Living Building is designed to attract local wildlife and you'll have a decent chance of observing pine martens, eel-like butterfish and local birdlife. Snacks and lunches are available in the tearoom. It's open daily April to October from 10.30 am (noon on Sunday) to 5.30 pm. Admission costs £2.50/1.50. Access is on the bus between Fort William and Kilchoan.

Ardnamurchan Lighthouse

The lighthouse (☎ 01972-510210) at stark Ardnamurchan Point, the westernmost bit of the British mainland, boasts a cluster of related attractions. The imposing 36m lighthouse dates from 1849 and the adjacent keepers' cottages, engine room and head keeper's house are all open to the public. Light meals are available at the attached Stables Café. Soup and a roll will set you back £1.80. The complex opens daily, April to October, from 10 am to 5 or 6 pm, depending on the season. Entry costs £2.50/1.20.

Corran & Clovullin

These two lochside villages sit at the bottom end of wild Glen Gour on a large glacial outwash deposit which nearly cuts Loch Linnhe in two. Several nearby tracks are good for afternoon strolls. Between them, they have a general store, tearoom, and a hotel, *The Inn at Ardgour* (☎ *01855-841225*), where B&B is, at most, £30 per person. Bar meals here are home-cooked and include seafood (around £6 to £12).

Access is on the Corran ferry or along a long single-track road from Kinlocheil.

Strontian

This attractive little village's greatest claim to fame is the fact that it lent its name to the element strontium, which was discovered in ore from the nearby lead mines in 1790. The *Ariundle Nature Reserve*, about 2 miles north of the village, offers a pleasant nature trail through the glen. In Strontian, you'll find two shops, a post office, and a TIC (☎ 01967-402131), open from April to October.

The *Glenview Caravan Park* (☎ *01967-402123*), immediately north of the village, charges £7 to £9.50 per tent. The *Strontian Hotel* (☎ *01967-402029*), which dates back to 1808, has single/double B&B accommodation from £25/40. Bar meals are available for £5 to £10.

Salen

Walkers wishing to explore the appealing surroundings of Salen, at the head of constricted Salen Bay, will find information on hikes at the *Salen Hotel* (☎ *01967-431661*). Here, single/double rooms with breakfast cost £28/46 and bar meals, including seafood, venison and rabbit dishes, cost from £5 to £12.50. Camping and meals are available at *Resipole Caravan Park* (☎ *01967-431235*), 2 miles east of the village. Tent camping starts at £8 for two people.

Acharacle & Castle Tioram

At one time, the village of Acharacle seemed destined for greatness as the western sea outlet of the Caledonian Canal, but the proposed extension via Glenfinnan and Loch Shiel was never completed. Today, the main reason to visit this traditional crofting community is the picturesque 13th century **Castle Tioram**

(whose name means 'dry land'), just 2½ miles to the north. It sits on a lovely island in Loch Moidart, connected to the mainland by a narrow strand which is submerged at high tide. It served as the headquarters of the chief of Clanranald MacDonald (sorry kids, no burgers here) but was severely damaged during the Jacobite rebellion of 1715 in hopes of discouraging a takeover by enemy Hanoverian troops. An ongoing restoration project hopes to return it to its former condition. Admission is free.

The village has a small shop, a post office and the *Burger Bite* takeaway. The central *Loch Shiel House Hotel* (☎ *01967-431224*) does single/double B&B for £32.50/50 and bar meals for under £7. At the *Clanranald Hotel* (☎ *01967-431202*), Mingarry, you'll find B&B accommodation from £20/30. The meals here are recommended.

Kilchoan

This scattered crofting village is best known for the scenic fortified tower of the ruined **Mingary Castle**, which serves as a stark reminder of medieval clan warfare. For information, visit the TIC (☎ 01972-510222), which opens Easter to October.

You'll find provisions at the incongruously named Ferry Stores, which is actually in the village, a mile from the pier. You can camp at the *Kilchoan House Hotel* (☎ 01972-510200) or get B&B for £27 per person. *Hill View* (☎ *01972-510322*), run by Ms Catherine MacPhail, offers B&B for £30 to £32 for a double. It lies in Achnaha, 4 miles up a back road north of the village, and affords ready access to some wild and interesting coastline on the north side of the peninsula.

Getting There & Away

Shiel Buses (☎ 01967-431272) has one daily service (except Sunday) between Fort William and Kilchoan (£5), via Corran (£2), Strontian (£2.70) and Acharacle (£3.70). It also runs buses from Fort William to Acharacle via Lochailort (£4.25).

For details on ferries between Kilchoan and Tobermory, see Getting There & Away under the Isle of Mull in The Hebrides chapter.

MORVERN PENINSULA

Although the eastern coast of the Morvern Peninsula has been despoiled by the Glensanda Superquarry, the inland route to Loch Aline passes through some very pleasant hillscapes.

Ardtornish is known as the home of Patrick Sellers, the rather unsavoury factor and landlord who cleared large numbers of clanspeople from the region in the early 19th century. (This was the sort of bloke who'd now greet hillwalkers with a shotgun.) For a look at the substantial stone keep at **Kinlochaline Castle**, Ardtornish, check the instructions on the door explaining how to find a key.

For supplies, go to Lochaline village, which has a store, post office and art gallery. In the late 1980s, the CalMac ferry to Mull ploughed into the fish farm cages at Lochaline, allowing the salmon to escape. For the local people, it seemed as if Christmas had come early, and their freezers were full for months.

The **Lochaline Hotel** (☎ 01967-421657), half a mile from the Mull ferry pier, has single/double B&B without bath for £23/35 and bar meals for around £6, but at lunchtime, it only serves snacks.

Getting There & Away

Shiel Buses (☎ 01967-431272) runs on schooldays to Fort William on Monday at 7.10 am and returns on Friday at 3.40 pm. For information on ferries to Fishnish on the Isle of Mull, see The Hebrides chapter.

ROAD TO THE ISLES

The scenic, 46-mile Road to the Isles (the A830) takes you from Fort William via Glenfinnan and on to Arisaig and Mallaig.

It's worth taking a half-mile detour from the main route at Banavie to see **Neptune's Staircase**, a flight of eight locks which raises the water in the Caledonian Canal by 20m. Thomas Telford's canal was built from 1803-22 to connect the east and west coast

of Scotland, from Inverness to Fort William. Three lochs make up 38 miles of the canal's total 60 miles and there are 29 locks.

Corpach

In Corpach, rock hounds shouldn't miss the award-winning **Treasures of the Earth** (☎ 01397-772283) exhibition. Particularly impressive are the large amethyst samples and the grossular garnet, which looks good enough to eat. It's open daily year-round (except most of January) from 10 am to 5 pm, with extended hours from July to September. Admission costs £3/2.75.

Glenfinnan

The NTS visitors centre (☎ 01397-722250) at **Glenfinnan** recounts the story of Prince Charles Edward Stuart, or Bonnie Prince Charlie, whose 1745 rising (rebellion) started here and ended 14 months later when he fled to France. A lookout tower offers fine views over Loch Shiel. The centre opens daily from 10 am to 1 pm and 2 to 5 pm from April to October, with extended hours in summer. Admission is £1.50/1. Another site of interest is the **Station Museum**, which contains relics of the West Highland line, from the opening of the Glenfinnan section in 1901 until the present day. It's open most days from 9.30 am to 4.30 pm, and entry costs 50/25p.

Arisaig & Morar

Arisaig is the only place between Mallaig and Fort William where you'll find a decent range of supplies. Between Arisaig and Morar, the road winds around attractive bays, as well as the beaches known as the **Silver Sands of Morar**. Morar village lies at the outlet of 330m deep **Loch Morar**, which is Britain's deepest body of fresh water. It's thought to contain its own monster, known as Morag.

Mallaig

- **pop 900**   ☎ 01687

The lively fishing village of Mallaig makes a nice stopover between Fort William and Skye or the Small Isles. The TIC (☎ 462170) opens April to October. For medical services, contact the doctor (☎ 462202).

In addition to its lively pub life, a main attraction in Mallaig is **Mallaig Marine World** (☎ 462292), an aquarium which keeps mainly local aquatic species. Summer opening hours are daily from 9 am to 9 pm (but it's open year-round until 5.30 pm), and admission costs £2.75/2.

The **Mallaig Heritage Centre**, open Tuesday to Saturday from 1 to 4 pm, provides insight into the archaeology and history of the region, including disturbing details on the Clearance of Knoydart and information on steam trains and the ongoing fishing industry. The admission charge is £1.80/1.20.

Minch Charters (☎ 462304), at Harbour Slipways, runs both whale and dolphin-

watching cruises several times weekly in summer. It charges around £40 for seven hours at sea.

Places to Stay & Eat

Glenfinnan The *Sleeping Car Bunkhouse* (☎ 01397-722295), housed in a railway carriage at the station, costs £7 per person. Another railway theme item is the *Railway Carriage Restaurant* (☎ 01397-722400), which serves snacks during the day and evening meals ranging from £5 to £10.

It isn't known whether Bonnie Prince Charlie actually stayed at the historic *Prince's House Hotel* (☎ 01397-722246) in 1745, but the building dates from 1658, so he was definitely aware of it. Until recently, the public bar had a hatch in the floor through which locals could fish while enjoying a pint. *En suite* single/double rooms with breakfast start at £45/85. The Stuart Room is recommended. Bar meals start at £5 and a four-course set meal costs £25, with coffee.

Lochailort The recently rebuilt *Lochailort Inn* (☎ 01687-470208) has rooms with bath and breakfast starting at £30 per person. In the attached bar, good value main courses start at £3.25.

Arisaig Try the *Arisaig Hotel* (☎ 01687-450210), where B&B costs £20 per person. Bar meals start at £4.40, or you can opt for a cheap takeaway. The nicer *Old Library* (☎ 01687-450651) has a recommended restaurant and offers rooms with private bath for £34 per person. You'll also find a number of seasonal *camping grounds* scattered north along the coast; most are open only in summer.

Mallaig Mallaig has several pleasant B&Bs. *Sheena's Backpacker's Lodge* (☎ 462764, Harbour View) has dorm beds from £6 to £8.50 and doubles for £11 per person. The *Marine Hotel* (☎ 462217) has single/double rooms from £25/48. Its highly recommended restaurant does à la carte chicken, venison, seafood and vegetarian

---

Highland Cattle

Kept for their quality beef, Highland cattle are Scotland's most distinctive bovine breed. They're fierce-looking but docile-natured, with long reddish-brown coats and vicious-looking horns.

Highland cattle were popular with 18th-century drovers who took them from their mountain fastnesses to the Lowland markets. Nowadays, they're popular with tourist photographers who are looking for interesting foreground!

meals from £7.50, as well as such specialities as pan-fried Minch scallops in cream and wine sauce for £9.25.

The *Harbour Shop & Cornerstone Cafe* (☎ 462229) at the harbour does light meals and snacks for £3 to £5, and main courses starting at £5. The *Cabin Seafood Restaurant* (☎ 462207) cooks up seafood specialities (and what else would you want in a fishing community?) for £5 to £10.

Getting There & Away

Scottish Citylink operates two or three buses daily, except Sunday, between Fort William and Mallaig (1½ hours, £4.50) from July to September. Shiel Buses (☎ 01967-431272) runs two buses daily, June to September (three per week the rest of the year), for £5.50.

The beautiful West Highland railway to and from Fort William (£7.20) operates four times daily from Monday to Saturday, and once on Sunday, with connections through to Glasgow. In July, one train each day is steam-operated.

Ferries run from Mallaig to the Small Isles and Skye year-round (Skye ferries take vehicles in the summer only). Arisaig Marine's MV *Shearwater* (☎ 01687-450224) connects Arisaig to the islands of Rum, Eigg and Muck. For details, see The Hebrides chapter.

The ferry service run by Bruce Watt Cruises (☎ 01687-462320) has two return trips from Mallaig to Inverie in Knoydart (£4 each way) on Monday, Wednesday and Friday at 10.15 am and 2.15 pm (the afternoon trip includes a quick return to Tarbet in upper Loch Nevis).

KNOYDART PENINSULA

Stuck solidly between heaven and hell (actually, the Lochs of Nevis, or 'heaven' and Hourn, or 'hell'), the Knoydart Peninsula is now a wilderness region thanks to depopulation in the 19th century Highland Clearances. As a result, walkers can tramp for days through wild country.

Inverie, with just 60 inhabitants, is the peninsula's only population centre, and is the only village in Scotland without access to the road system.

A favoured two-day hiking route leads from Kinloch Hourn to Inverie via Barrisdale. You may also enjoy spending an additional day at Barrisdale to climb the dramatic 1020m (3346 feet) peak **Ladhar Bheinn** (pronounced lar ven), which affords some of the west coast's finest views.

Places to Stay & Eat

The very basic *hostel* in Barrisdale (no ☎) has sleeping platforms for £2.50, or you can just camp outside.

In Inverie, there's a shop, post office and a pub which does meals. The atmospheric *Torry Shieling* hostel (☎ 01687-462669), three-quarters of a mile from the pier in Inverie, is a tad overpriced at £13, especially as you must provide your own sleeping bag. However, it's a great place to stay and meet people.

The alternative is the *Knoydart Hostel* (☎ 01687-462331), near Inverie House, a half-mile from the ferry landing. Beds cost £7.

A highly recommended place for dinner, B&B is the rustic *Skiary* (☎ 01809-511214), a mile from road's end at Kinloch Hourn. It costs £60 per person. You can either walk in on the Barrisdale track or arrange to be picked up by boat from Kinloch Hourn.

Getting There & Away

For ferry information see Mallaig earlier in this chapter. Len Morrison (☎ 01599-522352), Croftfoot, Arnisdale, runs a boat service from Arnisdale to Barrisdale, by arrangement. It's an open boat so trips only run in fair weather. Mr Morrison can take up to five passengers for £14 plus £2 per person, one way.

There's a postbus (☎ 01463-256228) between Invergarry and Kinloch Hourn on Monday, Wednesday and Friday (£2.90). It arrives/departs Kinloch Hourn at around 1 pm, but you should confirm in advance. This bus can only take two or three people with luggage.

The Cairngorms

The magnificent Cairngorms, Britain's second highest range and most popular skiing area, soars above forests of regenerating native Caledonian pine in the upper reaches of Strathspey (Speyside).

Far more attractive than the regimented Forestry Commission conifer plantations, these native woodlands are home to rare animals such as pine martens and wildcats. Red squirrels, ospreys and capercaillie also survive here, as does Britain's only herd of reindeer.

The Cairngorm summits provide Britain's only example of Alpine tundra vegetation, and are therefore inhabited by high-altitude species otherwise found farther north, such as snow buntings, ptarmigans and dotterels. What's more, even non-hikers can reach the high peaks, as the Cairngorm chair lift operates year-round.

Aviemore, which is popular with flocks of skiers, hikers and cyclists, is the main resort town. The top hiking routes include the 24-mile Lairig Ghru tramp through the peaks and right down to Braemar in the Grampians. If you prefer to avoid the crowds, the lovely but less dramatic Monadhliath (pronounced mona-lee-a) Range, west of the Spey, sees fewer tourists.

The 100-mile-long Spey, one of Scotland's top salmon rivers, attracts anglers from around the world. Pure mountain water from its tributaries provides a basic ingredient for whisky production, and some distilleries are open to the public. North of Grantown-on-Spey, the Spey joins the River Avon (pronounced ahn) and continues out of the Cairngorms into Moray. For information, including details on the popular Speyside whisky distilleries, see Aberdeenshire & Moray in the Central & North-Eastern Scotland chapter.

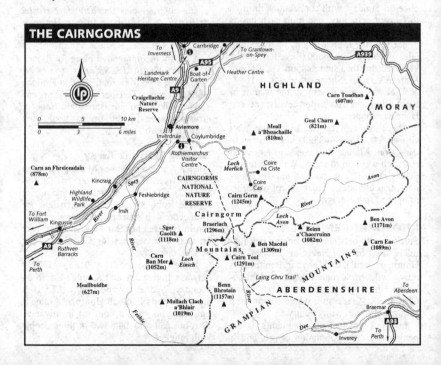

THE CAIRNGORMS

AVIEMORE

- pop 2421   ☎ 01479

In the early 1960s, Aviemore was still a sleepy Highland village of 200 inhabitants but today it looks more like a downmarket resort in the Rockies that can't quite invent itself in the swank image to which it aspires. Fortunately, winter visitors are spared the appalling kitsch that reigns through the summer, and even then you can eschew such recent additions as the Santa Claus Land children's theme park (one of several dire visitor attractions in Scotland) and head for the hills.

Orientation

Aviemore is just off the A9 bypass. With all the kitsch lined up along Grampian Rd you can hardly get lost.

The train station, banks and eateries are found along this road. The Cairngorm skiing/hiking area lies 8 miles east of Aviemore at the end of the Ski Rd, which passes through two large forest estates: Rothiemurchus and Glenmore.

Information

The busy TIC (☎ 810363), 500m south of the centre on Grampian Rd, opens year-round, with extended hours in July and August (Monday to Saturday until 7 pm and Sunday until 6 pm). The local accommodation guide is distributed free, but you'll pay a £1.50 charge for bookings through the TIC. It sells a good range of books and maps, including the yellow Ordnance Survey Outdoor Leisure Map *Aviemore & the Cairngorms*, which covers the whole area. Ernest Cross' *Walks in the Cairngorms* describes the main hikes.

Money Outside the Tesco supermarket, you'll find a cluster of ATMs. There's also a *bureau de change* at the TIC.

Outdoor Equipment Of the outdoor-equipment shops along Grampian Rd, you should try Ellis Brigham (☎ 810175) at No 9 which can organise both equipment hire and ski lessons.

Craigellachie Nature Reserve

Over the A9 from Aviemore, the Craigellachie Nature Reserve makes a great place for day hikes over steep hills, through natural birch forest.

Look out for the birds and other wildlife which shelter here including finches, jackdaws and peregrine falcons (which nest from April to July), and you may even spot a capercaillie.

Rothiemurchus Estate

The Rothiemurchus Estate, which takes in the villages of Inverdruie and Coylumbridge, extends from near Aviemore to the Cairngorm tops.

It's owned by a single family, the Grants (no connection with the whisky family), who manage the extensive Caledonian pine forest here, and lay on facilities for visitors. There's free access to 50 miles of footpaths including some particularly attractive trails through the forests and around Loch an Eilein. Visitors can also opt for ranger-guided walks, clay pigeon shooting instruction, Land Rover tours, and fishing for rainbow trout at the estate's fish farm or in the Spey.

The Rothiemurchus Estate Visitors Centre (☎ 810858), a mile from Aviemore along the Ski Rd, opens daily from 9 am to 5.30 pm. Pick up the free *Visitor Guide and Footpath Map*.

Glen More Forest Park

Around Loch Morlich, 7 miles from Aviemore, the Ski Rd passes through 5000 acres of pine and spruce that make up Glen More Forest Park.

Attractions include a pleasant sandy beach and a popular **watersports centre** (☎ 861221) offering canoeing, windsurfing, sailing and fishing. At the **Cairngorm Reindeer Centre** (☎ 861228), the warden will take you to see and feed the reindeer. Walks leave daily at 11 am (and 2.30 pm in summer); the cost is £4/3.

The visitors centre (☎ 861220), near the loch, has a *Glen More Forest Guide Map* detailing local walks.

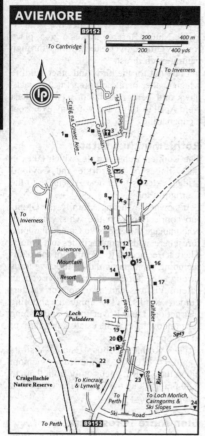

AVIEMORE

PLACES TO STAY
1   Craig na Gower Ave B&Bs
2   Balavoulin Hotel
11   Kila B&B
14   Cairngorm Hotel
16   Kinapol Guesthouse
17   Ardlogie Guesthouse
18   Four Seasons Hotel
22   Aviemore Youth Hostel

PLACES TO EAT
4   Winking Owl
6   Ski-ing Doo
8   Littlejohn's
10   Tesco Supermarket
12   Smiffy's Fish & Chips
13   Sheffield's Café Bar
19   Aviemore Tandoori
23   Old Bridge Inn
24   Rothiemurchus Estate Fish
   Farm Shop

OTHER
3   Church of Scotland
5   Post Office
7   Strathspey Steam Railway
   Station
9   Police Station
15   Train Station
20   TIC
21   Petrol Station

Activities

Walks To get straight to the best views, take the chair lift (☎ 861261) to the Cairngorm plateau. It starts from the car park at the end of the Ski Rd and ascends in two sections to the 1085m level, where you'll find Britain's highest café. It operates daily from 9.15 am to 5.15 pm and costs £5/3 return. Plans to replace the lift with a funicular railway have still not been finalised, and the controversy rumbles on.

From the top station, it's a relatively short climb to the summit of Cairn Gorm (1245m, 4084 feet). You can continue south to climb Ben Macdui (Britain's second highest peak at 1309m, 4296 feet), but this can take six to eight hours, including the chair-lift ride up.

The Lairig Ghru walk, which can take up to eight hours, is a demanding 24-mile route from Aviemore over the Lairig Ghru Pass to Braemar. If you're not doing the full route, it's still worth taking the six hour return hike up to the pass.

Hikers will need a lunch, plenty of liquids, a map, a compass and a wind and waterproof jacket. The weather can change almost instantly and snow, even in midsummer, isn't unknown.

Skiing Aviemore isn't Aspen or Val d'Isere, but with 28 runs and over 35km of pistes, it's Britain's biggest ski area, and when the snow is optimum and the sun is shining, you can close your eyes and imagine you're in the Alps. The season runs from January until the snow melts, which may be as late as the end of April. There are also several cross-country routes. Unfortunately, in recent years the region has received below average snowfall and the season has been pared down to as little as six weeks.

The ski area is about 9 miles from Aviemore centre and lifts start at the main Coire Cas car park, connected to the more distant Coire na Ciste car park by free shuttle bus. A Cairngorm Day Ticket costs £17/14.50 for adults and under 18s pay £8.50. Ski/snowboard rental costs £13/16 per day. The TIC distributes a free *Cairngorm Piste Map & Ride Guide* leaflet.

During the season the TIC displays relevant avalanche warnings. For reports on snow conditions, phone the Ski Hotline (☎ 0891-654655) or tune into Cairngorm Radio Ski FM on 96.6.

Fishing Fishing is a major sport, both on the Spey and in most of the lochs. Ask the TIC for information on beats and permits. At local shops, salmon and trout fishing permits cost £20 to £30 and around £12 per day, respectively. Alvie Estate (☎ 01540-651255) hires rods for £5 per day.

Organised Tours

Highland Discovery Tours (☎ 811478), 27 Corrour Rd, hires out a 16-seat mini-bus and guide. Day trips to Loch Ness and Skye cost £12 and £17, respectively.

Places to Stay

Camping The nearest camping ground is *Rothiemurchus Camping & Caravan Park* (☎ 812800) at Coylumbridge, 1½ miles along the Ski Rd. It charges from £6 per tent. The Forestry Commission's *Glenmore Camping & Caravan Park* (☎ 861271), 5 miles farther along the road near Loch Morlich, opens year-round (except November to mid-December) and charges £7.50 per site.

Hostels From late December to mid-November, the *Aviemore Youth Hostel* (☎ 810345, 25 Grampian Rd) offers up-market hostelling in a newly refurbished building near the TIC and the start of the Ski Rd. Beds cost £8.60/7.10 (with a £1 surcharge in July and August).

In Glen More Forest Park, 7 miles from Aviemore, the popular *Loch Morlich Youth Hostel* (☎ 861238) has a great location but pre-booking is essential. It's open year-round and charges £7.75/6.50. North of Loch Morlich and a mile from the Ski Rd, the *Badaguish Outdoor Centre* (☎ 861285) has dormitory accommodation from £5 to £8 and camping from £2.

B&Bs & Hotels – centre Off Grampian Rd on Craig na Gower Ave, 400m north of the train station, there's an enclave of B&Bs. Most offer single/double rooms with private baths for around £17/34. You could try *Mrs Sheffield's* (☎ 810698), in Dunroamin Cottage. *Karn House* (☎ 810849) charges start at £16 per person. *Kila* (☎ 810573, Grampian Rd), in the centre, opens year-round and charges from £18/32 for *en suite* single/double rooms.

On Dalfaber Rd are two larger guest-houses. *Kinapol Guest House* (☎ 810513) charges from £16/30 for singles/doubles and room only costs from £11 per person. *Ardlogie Guest House* (☎ 810747) has rooms with bath for £17 to £20.

The highly commended *Balavoulin Hotel* (☎ 810672, Grampian Rd) has eight well-equipped double rooms with bath for £18 to £22.50 per person.

In the centre on Grampian Rd is the recommended *Cairngorm Hotel* (☎ 810233), otherwise known as the Cairn, which charges £23 per person for B&B.

A mile out of town, on the Lynwilg road, is an excellent country-house hotel, *Lynwilg House* (☎ 811685). B&B costs £27 to £35 per person, or £45 to £57 for dinner, B&B to write home about.

B&Bs & Hotels – Ski Rd The excellent *Corrour House Hotel* (☎ 810220), 1½ miles from Aviemore with splendid views of the Lairig Ghru Pass, opens December to October and charges from £24 to £35 per person for rooms with attached bath.

In Inverdruie, the small *Avondruie Guest House* (☎ *810267)* charges from £19 per person for rooms with attached bath. Just beyond Inverdruie on Dell Mhor are several B&Bs. *Mrs Mackenzie* (☎ *810235, 1 Dell Mhor)*, *Mrs Bruce* (☎ *810230, 2 Dell Mhor)* and *Mrs Harris* (☎ *810405, 5 Dell Mhor)* all offer single/double B&B for around £15/28.

Perhaps the finest of the resort hotels is the *Stakis Coylumbridge* (☎ *811811)*, which enjoys an excellent location just outside Aviemore. Single/double rates start at £55/70.

Places to Eat

There's no shortage of places to eat, but few are particularly inviting. If you prefer to self-cater, Aviemore has an enormous Tesco supermarket. For smoked trout, venison, paté and other delicacies visit the *Rothiemurchus Fish Farm* shop (☎ *810703)*, a short way along the Ski Rd.

Near the TIC, the *Aviemore Tandoori Restaurant* (☎ *811199, 43 Grampian Rd)* does seven vegetarian choices from £7, other main courses from £6.75 and takeaways at a 10% discount. *Smiffy's Fish & Chip Restaurant*, nearer the station, does takeaways and a reasonable fry-up, with cod and chips at £2.25. The nearby *Sheffield's Café Bar* (☎ *811670)* opens daily from 9 am until 10 pm; the all-day breakfast costs £3.75 and bar meals start at £4.50.

Farther north along Grampian Rd, opposite the police station, there's a branch of *Littlejohn's* (☎ *811633)* serving steaks, pizzas, burgers, ribs, potato skins, vegetable fajitas etc in slightly wacky surroundings. Main dishes are from £4.25.

Over the road, the *Ski-ing Doo* (☎ *810392, 9 Grampian Rd)* conjures up images of schussing pigeons. It serves a range of steaks, including 10-ounce sirloins (£11.29) but thanks to BSE, the 16-ounce T-bone steaks were temporarily off the menu. Another (albeit less active) avian type, the *Winking Owl* (☎ *810646, Grampian Rd)* has a reasonable choice of pub food and great outdoor seating.

The highly recommended *Old Bridge Inn* (☎ *811137, Dalfaber Rd)*, near the youth hostel, does an excellent salmon and dill tart, among other innovative choices. All main courses cost £5.95.

There's a small *café* along the Ski Rd in Glen More Forest Park. The *snack bar and restaurant* at the ski resort day lodge in Coire Cas serves snacks, meals and drinks until 4.30 or 5 pm in the winter and until 11 pm in July and August.

Entertainment

Every Tuesday at 7 pm from Easter to the end of October, the *Old Bridge Inn* (☎ *811137)* hosts a Highland Evening. For £17.50 you get a four-course Scottish meal (including soup, haggis, salmon and the delicious Scottish pudding, cranachan), a piper, Highland dancers and live music. Advance booking is advisable.

The *Aviemore Mountain Resort* (☎ *810624)* is a large leisure complex, signposted from the centre, with ice rink, dry ski slope, cinema, bars and restaurants and a swimming pool. However, it's a bit of an eyesore and may soon be demolished.

Getting There & Away

Aviemore is 33 miles from Inverness, 62 from Fort William and 127 from Edinburgh.

Bus Buses stop on Grampian Rd; book at the TIC. Scottish Citylink (☎ 0990-505050) connects Aviemore with Inverness (45 minutes, £4), Kincraig (10 minutes, £2), Kingussie (20 minutes, £3), Newtonmore (30 minutes, £3.50), Dalwhinnie (45 minutes, £4.50), Pitlochry (1¼ hours, £5.50), Perth (two hours, £7.80), Glasgow (3½ hours, £9.80) and Edinburgh (3½ hours, £11.30). For Aberdeen, you must change to a Midland Bluebird bus at Inverness.

There's one direct daytime service to London's Victoria (11 hours, £39), another overnight service and an early morning service requiring a change in Glasgow. There are also overnight services to Heathrow and Gatwick airports. For details, call National Express (☎ 0990-808080).

Train There are direct train services to London (7½ hours, normally from £61, but bargain singles are £24 – believe it or not!), Glasgow/Edinburgh (3 hours, from £20) and Inverness (40 minutes, £8.80). For details phone ☎ 0345-484950.

Strathspey Steam Railway (☎ 810725) operates between Aviemore, Boat of Garten and Nethy Bridge, and work has begun on an extension to Grantown. The station is over the tracks from the main train station.

Car MacDonald's Self Drive (☎ 811444), 13 Muirton, rents cars from £30 a day and will deliver/collect from your hotel.

Getting Around

A Cairngorm Chairlift Company (☎ 861261) bus links Aviemore and Cairngorm, three to six times daily from late October to April (£2.20/1.10).

Several places in central Aviemore hire out mountain bikes. You can also hire bikes in Rothiemurchus Estate and Glen More Forest Park. Most charge £9 to £14 per day. Aviemore Mountain Bikes (☎ 811007), 45A Grampian Rd, organises guided bike tours.

AROUND AVIEMORE
Kincraig

Kincraig, 6 miles south-west of Aviemore, makes another good Cairngorm base. Run by the Royal Zoological Society of Scotland, the **Highland Wildlife Park** (☎ 01540-651270), just outside the village, features breeding stocks of local wildlife past and present. There's a drive-through safari park and several woodland walks offering most people their best opportunity to come face to face with an elusive wildcat or furiously displaying male capercaillie. Admission costs £5/10 for a car with two/four people. Visitors without cars are driven around by staff (£5/2.50 per person). It's

open daily April to October from 10 am to 6 pm (7 pm from June to August), the rest of the year from 10 am to 4 pm.

At Kincraig, the Spey widens into **Loch Insh**, home of the **Loch Insh Watersports Centre** (☎ 01540-651272) which offers canoeing, windsurfing, sailing, bike hire and fishing, as well as B&B accommodation from £16 a head in comfortable rooms with attached baths. Food here is good, especially after 6.30 pm when the lochside café metamorphoses into a restaurant.

Glen Feshie extends east into the Cairngorms. About 5 miles from Kincraig, *Glen Feshie Hostel* (☎ 01540-651323) is a friendly, independent 14-bed hostel that's popular with hikers. The overnight charge of £8 includes linen and a steaming bowl of porridge to start the day.

Carrbridge
• pop 543　　☎ 01479

At Carrbridge, 7 miles north-east of Aviemore, the **Landmark Highland Heritage Centre** (☎ 01479-841614), set in a forest of Scots pines, offers a few novel and worthwhile concepts, such as the raised Treetop Trail which allows you to view red squirrels, crossbills and crested tits. Most of it, however, seems rather tacky. It's open daily, year-round, with extended hours in the summer. Admission costs £5.95/4.20.

You'll find the ultimate in humpback bridges in the centre of the village. Built in 1717, it now looks decidedly unsafe but remains impressive with the thundering rapids below.

In September, the village hosts a Celtic music festival (☎ 841242) and a series of ceilidhs.

Places to Stay & Eat Carrbridge has a Spar store, an inexpensive *coffee shop*, and a couple of hotels.

The comfortable *Cairn Hotel* (☎ 841212) has single rooms for £17 and singles/doubles with bath for £26/44. Snacks start at £1 and bar meals are from £4.50.

On the left when heading for Inverness, you'll see the *Carrbridge Bunkhouse*

Hostel (☎ 841250), which has dorm beds for £6.50.

Getting There & Away Highland Country Buses (☎ 01463-233371) runs several buses daily (except Sunday) from Inverness to Grantown on Spey, via Carrbridge.

Boat of Garten
• pop 571   ☎ 01479

Eight miles north-east of Aviemore, Boat of Garten is known as the Osprey Village, since these rare birds of prey nest at the RSPB **Loch Garten Osprey Centre** (☎ 831694) in Abernethy Forest, 2 miles east of the village. RSPB volunteers guard the site throughout the nesting season to deter egg collectors. The hide opens to visitors from late April to August, daily, from 10 am to 6 pm. Admission for nonmembers is £2.

Boat of Garten has a general store and post office. You can stick up a tent at the *Campgrounds of Scotland (☎ 831652)* for £5.25. The *Boat Hotel (☎ 831258)* has very pleasant rooms from £25 to £40 per person, and bar meals here start at £5.25. West coast mussels steamed in wine and garlic are £5.95.

The best way to get here is on the Strathspey Steam Railway (☎ 810725) which runs at least five times daily from Aviemore – a ticket in 3rd class costs £4.60 return.

Dulnain Bridge & Skye of Curr
At the Heather Centre (☎ 01479-851359) in Skye of Curr, 2 miles south-west of Dulnain Bridge, you'll learn about the innumerable uses of heather over the centuries. It's open year-round and admission to the small exhibition costs 75p. However, the garden centre is free.

After taking a pleasant stroll around the garden centre, you may wish to sample one of 21 recipes for Scottish dumpling (rich fruit cake steamed in a *cloot* or linen cloth) in the adjacent *Clootie Dumpling Restaurant*; the Heather Centre Special comes with cream, ice cream, heather cream liqueur, chopped nuts and blackberry preserve for £3.20.

Nethy Bridge
• pop 675

This quiet village isn't particularly exciting, but is actually a very inviting place to simply sit and soak up the clean air and woodland atmosphere. You can stay in the novel *Aspen Lodge (☎ 01479-821042),* which is housed in an old police station. B&B starts at around £18 per person.

GRANTOWN-ON-SPEY
• pop 3241   ☎ 01479

This Georgian town on the Spey (pronounced granton), which attracts throngs of coach tourists in the summer, lies amid an angler's paradise. Most hotels can kit you up for a day of fishing or put you in touch with someone who can. The TIC (☎ 872773) at 54 High St opens daily from April to October. Other amenities include a bank, ATM, food shops and post office.

Places to Stay
Grantown's accommodation reflects its senior clientele, with plenty of comfortable upmarket hotels noted for their food. There are also budget options. The *Grantown-on-Spey Caravan Park (☎ 872474),* half a mile from the centre, charges £5 to £10 per vehicle. If you prefer a roof over your head, try the *Speyside Backpackers (☎ 872529, 16 The Square),* also known as the Stop-Over. It has dorm beds for £8.50 per person, but you need your own sleeping bag.

Crann-Tara Guest House (☎ 872197, High St) has singles and doubles from £16 with shared bath. The *Bank House (☎ 873256, 1 The Square),* in the Bank of Scotland, does B&B from £16 to £18 per person.

Ardconnel House (☎ 872104, Woodlands Terrace) is in a highly commended Victorian villa known for its French/Scottish cuisine and elegant atmosphere. Dinner, B&B costs from £42 to £49 per person, and all rooms have private baths. The similarly deluxe *Ravenscourt House Hotel (☎ 872286, Seafield Ave),* near the main square, has *en suite* accommodation for £35 to £45 per person.

Places to Eat

On the High St, you'll find huge portions of fish and chips at the *Royal Fish Bar* for £2.70. The nearby *Coffee House & Ice Cream Parlour* does snacks and the *Golden Grantown* Chinese takeaway is just two doors from the TIC. The *Ben Mhor Hotel* (☎ 872056), opposite the TIC, offers a pleasant atmosphere and bar meals from £4.50. You can also treat yourself to the acclaimed £17 meals at the French-run *Ardconnel House* (see Places to Stay); bookings are essential.

Getting There & Away

Highland Country Buses (☎ 01463-233371) runs six to eight buses daily, Monday to Saturday, between Grantown and Aviemore (35 minutes, £3.25). To or from Inverness, you can take the Highland Bus & Coach (01463-233371) service two or three times daily, except Sunday (1¼ hours, £3.40). Also, work is in progress to extend the Strathspey Steam Railway to Grantown-on-Spey.

KINGUSSIE

• pop 1461   ☎ 01540

The tranquil Speyside town of Kingussie (pronounced king-yewsie) is best known as the home of one of Scotland's finest folk museums. The TIC (☎ 661297), just off the High St in King St, opens daily from late May to September.

Highland Folk Museum

The Kingussie Highland Folk Museum (☎ 661307), in Duke St, comprises a collection of historical buildings and relics revealing all facets of Highland culture and lifestyles. The 18th century Pitmain Lodge holds displays of ceilidh musical instruments, costumes and washing utensils.

The village-like grounds also include a traditional thatch-roofed Isle of Lewis blackhouse, a water mill, a 19th century corrugated iron shed for smoking salmon, and assorted farm implements.

In summer, you can watch spinning, wood carving and peat-fire baking demonstrations. It's open March to September,

Monday to Saturday, from 10 am to 6 pm, Sunday 2 to 6 pm; £3/2.

Ruthven Barracks

Built in 1719 on the site of an earlier 13th century castle, Ruthven Barracks was one of four fortresses constructed after the first Jacobite rebellion of 1715 as part of a Hanoverian scheme to take control of the Highlands. Given the long-range views, the location makes perfect sense. The Barracks were last occupied by Jacobite troops awaiting the return of Bonnie Prince Charlie after the Battle of Culloden. Learning of his defeat and subsequent flight, they destroyed the barracks before taking to the glens. Admission is free and the ruins are floodlit at night.

Walks

The Monadhliath Range, north-west of Kingussie, attracts fewer hikers than the nearby Cairngorms, and makes an ideal destination for walkers seeking peace and solitude. However, during the deer-stalking season (August to October), you'll need to check with the TIC before setting out.

The recommended six hour circular walk to the 878m (2880 feet) summit of Carn an Fhreiceadain, above Kingussie, begins north of the village. It continues to Pitmain Lodge and along the Allt Mór river before climbing to the cairn on the summit. You can then follow the ridge east to the twin summits of Beinn Bhreac before returning to Kingussie via a more easterly track.

Places to Stay & Eat

The *Lairds Bothy Hostel* (☎ 661334, 68 High St) lies behind the Tipsy Laird pub. There are four family rooms and several eight-bed dorms which cost £8 per person. Alternatively, you can camp at the *Caravan Park* (☎ 661600) by the golf course, which costs from £6 per tent.

Mrs Jarratt (☎ 661430, St Helens, Ardbroilach Rd) has doubles from £20 per person. On the western outskirts friendly *Homewood Lodge* (☎ 661507, Newtonmore Rd) does three-star B&B for £18 to £20 per person. You'll have views just outside the front door.

The *Osprey Hotel* (☎ *661510)*, a stone townhouse on the corner of Ruthven Rd, charges £24 per person for B&B in a comfortable Victorian house with good home cooking. Excellent four-course table d'hôte dinners cost £22.

If you're feeling flush, *The Cross* (☎ *661166, Tweed Mill Brae, Ardbroilach Rd)* is one of the top hotel-restaurants (closed Tuesday) in the Highlands. Dinner, B&B costs from £85.

The quality and portions of the pub meals at the *Tipsy Laird (High St)* are great, in keeping with the friendliness of the staff. You get an excellent main meal for £5.95. The most promising of the High St cafés is *La Cafetière*, which does soup and home-made seed bread or herb scone and butter for £1.50, and toasties from £2.10.

Getting There & Away

Kingussie is 120 miles from Edinburgh, 75 from Perth and 40 from Inverness. Just to the north of town, the A9 heads south to Perth, leaving the Highland region via the bleak Pass of Drumochter.

It's also on the main Edinburgh/Glasgow to Inverness routes, so all trains and most Citylink buses stop here. Highland Country Buses runs an infrequent schooldays-only service between Aviemore, Kingussie, Newtonmore and Dalwhinnie. For rail information, phone ☎ 0345-484950.

NEWTONMORE
• pop 1172   ☎ 01540

It's hard to imagine a more relaxed place than Newtonmore, which is strung out along a single main street. The only time it has ever hit the news was during the severe winter of 1995-96 when the boiler at the Braeriach Hotel exploded, causing extensive damage.

In the main street, you'll find hotels, the post office, a bank with an ATM, a TIC, and the old-style MacRae Brothers licenced grocery shop, which still has counter service.

Clan MacPherson Museum

At the junction of the A86 and B9150 you'll find the Clan MacPherson Museum (☎ 673332) which reveals the histories of Clan MacPherson and Badenoch district. It's open May to October, from 10 am to 5 pm Monday to Saturday and 1 to 5 pm on Sunday (admission free).

Dalwhinnie Distillery

A short day excursion from Newtonmore will take you to the Dalwhinnie Distillery (☎ 01528-522208), 12 miles south, which claims to be Scotland's highest distillery. From March to December, it's open weekdays from 9.30 am to 4.30 pm; June to October, it's also open the same hours on Saturdays, and in July and August, also on Sundays from 12.30 to 4.30 pm. Tours cost £3 and include a £4 discount voucher.

Places to Stay & Eat

The main budget place is the *Newtonmore Independent Hostel* (☎ *673360)*, in the heart of town, which charges £8.50 for a bed without linen. It also runs a B&B costing from £16 to £20 per person.

The grand and turreted *Craigerne House Hotel* (☎ *673281, Golf Course Rd)* offers B&B for £22 to £28 per person.

The bar at the *Glen Hotel* (☎ *673203)*, at the main road junction, does snacks from £2 and bar meals from £4.25 in a cosy setting. The *Mains Hotel* (☎ *673206)*, over the road, exudes a similar ambience and puts on entertainment regularly.

Getting There & Away

From Kingussie, the A86 to Fort William leaves the A9 and follows a lovely route through Newtonmore to skirt Loch Laggan and Loch Moy, providing fine views of Ben Nevis.

A postbus (☎ 01463-256228) runs daily, except Sunday, between Newtonmore and Kinlochlaggan. All trains between Inverness and Edinburgh/Glasgow stop in Newtonmore, but only some of the Citylink buses call in here.

The Great Glen

The Great Glen is a natural fault line running across Scotland from Fort William to Inverness as a series of lochs – Linnhe, Lochy, Oich and Ness – linked by the Caledonian Canal. It has always been a communication (and invasion) route, and General George Wade built a military road along the south side of Loch Ness from 1724. The modern A82 road along the north side was completed in 1933.

The 80-mile Great Glen Cycle Route from Fort William to Inverness via Fort Augustus follows canal towpaths and gravel tracks through forests to avoid the busy roads where possible. The *Cycling in the Forest* leaflet, available from TICs or the Forestry Commission, gives details.

FORT WILLIAM TO FORT AUGUSTUS

For 33 miles inland from Fort William, the A82 to Fort Augustus provides access to some of the forested glens and narrow lochs of the Lochaber region.

Nevis Range

The Nevis Range ski area (☎ 01397-705825), 6 miles north of Fort William, skirts the slopes of Aonach Mór (1221m, 4006 feet). The gondola cable car to the top station at 655m (2148 feet) operates year-round, except November to Christmas, and costs £6.25/5.60 return. Lift tickets, including the gondola and all ski lifts cost £16.95 per day. The *Snowgoose Restaurant* does hearty inexpensive meals; soup and a roll costs £1.75. There are walking routes from the Snowgoose and through nearby Leanachan Forest. A new mountain bike route will run between the Snowgoose and the base station, where bikes can be rented for £8.50/12.50 for a half/full day.

Achnacarry & Loch Arkaig

The B8004 starts at Banavie and follows the Great Glen, with great views of Ben Nevis, to Gairlochy, where it turns eastward to the Commando Memorial. From Gairlochy, the B8005 turns north and follows the shore of Loch Lochy to the **Clan Cameron Museum** (☎ 01397-712480) at Achnacarry, which displays the history of the clan and its involvement with the Jacobite rebellions. Just to the west, lies the lovely Loch Arkaig. By the road, at the mouth of Gleann Cia-aig, there's a series of spectacular waterfalls. From the road end at the western end of the loch, it's possible to hike through the glens to Loch Nevis and Knoydart (taking two days, and you'll need a tent). There's no public transport beyond Achnacarry and hitching along the loch could be difficult.

Glen Spean & Glen Roy

These two glens are noted for their intriguing parallel 'roads', which follow natural terraces formed by the waters of an ice-dammed glacial lake during the last glacial period of the Ice Age. Whenever the dam burst or otherwise allowed water to spill out, the level dropped and formed a new terrace. The best viewpoint is 3 miles up Glen Roy – drive, cycle, or walk up the road.

The two main villages are Spean Bridge and Roy Bridge, both of which have post offices and shops.

Spean Bridge to Fort Augustus

North of the Commando Memorial, which commemorates the WWII military force who trained here, the A82 follows the south-eastern shore of Loch Lochy before crossing the canal by the Laggan Locks to run along the north-western shore of narrow Loch Oich. At the head of Loch Oich, the monument at the Well of the Seven Heads details the summary justice handed out to seven 16th century murderers by their victims' aggrieved family.

The only village between Spean Bridge and Fort Augustus is Invergarry, where there's a shop half a mile out on the A87.

Places to Stay & Eat

In Spean Bridge, there's no shortage of food or accommodation options. One of the best is the *Smiddy House Guest House*

(☎ 01397-712335) and its bistro. Rooms range from £18 to £23 per person. Ample bistro meals, including vegetarian choices, cost around £8. The place takes its name from the small 18th century smithy's house round the back.

The independent *Roybridge Inn Hostel (☎ 01397-712236)*, also known as the Grey Corrie Lodge, in Roybridge, charges £9 per person. The inn does bar meals for around £5 and laundry costs £2 per wash. Two miles away at Achluachrach is the recommended hostel, *Àite Cruinnichidh (☎ 01397-712315)*, with beds in a converted barn for £7, including linen. Phone for free pick-up from the station.

Five miles east of Roy Bridge there's *Station Lodge Bunkhouse (☎ 01397-732333)*, Tulloch Station, with beds (including linen) for £9. There's a kitchen but meals (including vegetarian dishes) are available.

At the Corrour train station on Rannoch Moor is the small *Corrour Station Bunkhouse (☎ 01397-732236)* which has 14 beds and charges £14.50 per person. A mile away lies the *Loch Ossian Youth Hostel (☎ 01397-732207)*. It's open late March to October and costs £4.65/3.85. Take your own supplies and a sleeping bag.

The *Loch Lochy Youth Hostel (☎ 01809-501239)*, at Laggan, just north of Loch Lochy, opens late March to October and charges £6.10/4.95. There's a grocery shop a mile away at The Well of the Seven Heads.

At Invergarry, the well-appointed *Invergarry Hotel (☎ 01809-501206)* has rooms with bath from £25 to £46 per person. It does good pub grub for around £6. Vegetarians will love the *Glendale Guest House (☎ 01809-501282)*, also in Invergarry, where all-vegetable B&B costs around £18.

Getting There & Away

Highland Country Buses (☎ 01397-702373) has services from Fort William to Achnacarry, Nevis Range, Spean Bridge and Roy Bridge. Scottish Citylink buses connect Fort William with Spean Bridge, Invergarry, Skye and Inverness. The railway from Fort William to Glasgow has stops at Spean Bridge and Roy Bridge. It leaves Glen Spean at Tulloch station and follows Loch Treig south to Rannoch Moor.

Courrour Station Bunkhouse and Loch Ossian Youth Hostel can only be reached by train, by bicycle, or on foot.

LOCH NESS

Dark, deep and narrow Loch Ness stretches 23 miles from Fort Augustus at its southern end nearly as far as Inverness. Its bitterly cold waters have been extensively explored for Nessie, the elusive Loch Ness monster, and although some visitors get lucky, most see only her cardboard cut-out form. Along the north-western shore runs the congested A82, while the more tranquil but extremely picturesque B862 follows the south-eastern

Don't Get Shirty

Scottish Highland clans are known for their fighting abilities, mainly due to their indulgence in internecine warfare prior to the Clearances.

Although most clan battles were little more than skirmishes, the curiously-named Battle of the Shirts was a more vigorous affair. On 3 July 1544, around 400 Frasers were engaged at the southern end of Loch Oich by an allied force of MacDonalds and Camerons which was almost double their strength. The two sides were prepared to fight to the last over a feud regarding who was chief of Clan Donald of Moidart.

Due to the great heat that day, the fighters stripped to their shirts, then proceeded to butcher each other on the beach and in the water. About 10 hours later, when there were only four Frasers and eight allies left alive, darkness (and, no doubt, weariness) brought a halt to this incredible affray. Amazingly, the allies claimed victory, but they didn't enjoy it for long since the king, James V, sent a punitive expedition to deal with them.

shore. A complete circuit of the loch is about 70 miles, and you'll have the best views travelling anti-clockwise.

Fort Augustus

• pop 600   ☎ 01320

Fort Augustus, at the junction of four of General Wade's military roads, was the headquarters for his road-building operations from 1724. Today it's overrun by monster-hunting tourists, but still manages to convey a rather haunting medieval ambience. Look out for the bizarre Loch Ness Monster bush by the canal!

The TIC (☎ 366367) in the car park opens Easter to October.

Fort Augustus Abbey Between 1729 and 1742, as part of his plan to pacify the Highlands, General George Wade built a fort at the point where the River Tarff joined Loch Ness. Although it was captured and later damaged by the retreating Jacobites, it remained occupied until 1854. In 1876 Benedictine monks took over the building and founded Fort Augustus Abbey. The abbey shut late in 1998. The adjoining Catholic boys' school was closed in 1994 and converted into the Heritage Centre which now has an uncertain future. As we went to press it opened daily from 9 am to 6 pm (admission £4/2).

Clansman Centre The Clansman Centre (☎ 366444), an exhibition of traditional and historical Highland ways, is staffed by young people who dress in period costumes and put on entertaining presentations in an old turf house, recounting old legends and demonstrating how a 17th century Highland family conducted its daily routine. It's open daily, March to October, from 10 am to 8 pm (winter hours are shorter). Admission costs £2.50/2.

Caledonian Canal Locks At Fort Augustus, boats using the Caledonian Canal are raised and lowered 13m by **five locks**. When the swing bridge is opened, however, it can cause long delays on the busy A82.

The promontory between the canal and the River Oich affords a fine view over Loch Ness. Tiny **Cherry Island**, on the Inverness side of Fort Augustus, was originally a *crannog* or artificial island settlement.

Organised Tours Cruises on Loch Ness on the *Catriona* (☎ 366233) operate April to October. The 50 minute trip costs £4.

Special Events There are Highland gatherings four times a year: late June, late July, mid-August and early September. Events include tossing the caber, throwing the hammer, falconry, sheep dog trials, piping competitions and traditional dancing.

Places to Stay & Eat Camping is available at the *Fort Augustus Caravan & Camping Park* (☎ 366618). It's just out of the village, on the right side of the Fort William road. The *Abbey* (☎ 366233) offers B&B from £16 per person; the attached *Abbot's Table* restaurant does everything from soup and a roll to main courses and it's highly recommended.

There's also a good choice of B&Bs for £13 to £19 per person: *Appin* (☎ 366541, Inverness Rd), *Greystone's* (☎ 366736, Station Rd), *Mrs Martin* (☎ 366344, Tullochard, Auchteraw Rd), *Ms McInnes* (☎ 366461, Auchteraw Rd) and *Mrs Service* (☎ 366291, Sonas).

The *Richmond House Hotel* (☎ 366719), in the centre, charges £20/22 per person without/with bath. Recommended bar meals cost from £5 to £12; haggis and clapshot is £5.50. You'll find more upmarket accommodation at the three-star *Lovat Arms Hotel* (☎ 366206), where *en suite* accommodation costs from £32 per person.

The *Coffee House* (☎ 366361) opposite the car park offers café-style food by day but becomes a restaurant in the evening. Near the canal the *Jac-O-Bite* tearoom and takeaway deserves a visit for its name alone. Filled rolls start at £1 and jacket potatoes cost from £2 to £3. The *Bothy Bite* (☎ 366710) is an alternative lunch spot with good canal views.

Getting There & Away Scottish Citylink runs five or six buses daily in each direction between Inverness and Fort William, stopping at Fort Augustus en route. To either town takes an hour and costs £5.80.

Getting Around You can hire bikes at Nessie Bike Hire (☎ 366305) for £8/12 per full/half day and at the Loch Ness Ferry Company (☎ 366233) for £10/6.

Drumnadrochit

- **pop 600**   ☎ **01456**

Exploitation of poor Nessie reaches fever pitch at Drumnadrochit where two Monster exhibitions vie for the tourist pound. The villages of Milton, Lewiston and Strone are virtually contiguous with Drumnadrochit while Urquhart Castle lies immediately south.

Monster Exhibitions The prominent **Official Loch Ness Monster Exhibition Centre** (☎ 450218) is the better of the two Nessie-theme exhibitions, featuring a 40 minute audiovisual presentation plus exhibits of equipment used in the various underwater monster hunts. In the summer, it's open daily, from 9.30 am to 6.30 pm, with shorter winter hours. Admission costs £4.50/3.50. Children over seven are charged £2.50; students must have ID. The nearby **Original Loch Ness Monster Centre** (☎ 450342) shows a marginal 30 minute Loch Ness video for £3.50/2.75. The video portion comes with multilingual headsets. It's open June to September daily from 8.30 am to 9.30 pm, with shorter hours the rest of the year.

Urquhart Castle The 13th and 14th century Urquhart Castle (☎ 450551, HS), one of Scotland's best known castles, was taken and lost by Edward I, held for David II against Edward III and fought over by everyone who passed this way. Not only was it repeatedly sacked, damaged and rebuilt over the centuries but the unfortunate inhabitants of the Great Glen were also regularly pillaged and robbed in the process.

Destruction and reconstruction followed so regularly that it's hard to trace the full story of the castle's development. By the 1600s it had become redundant, superseded by more palatial residences and more powerful fortresses at Fort William and Inverness. It was finally blown up in 1692 to prevent Jacobites using it and its remains perch dramatically on the edge of the loch, approached by a steep path from the roadside car park.

The castle was entered by a drawbridge which led into the gatehouse. The summit of the upper bailey at the southern end was probably used as a hillfort over 1000 years ago but by the 15th century the nether bailey at the northern end had become the focus of fortifications. The five-storey tower house at the extreme north end is the most impressive remaining fragment and offers wonderful loch views.

Summer hours are daily from 9.30 am to 6.30 pm and in winter it closes at 4.30 pm. Admission costs £3.50/2.80 and the guidebook costs £2.50 extra.

Loch Ness Monster

Although there's a tale of St Columba meeting Nessie (the Loch Ness Monster) in the 6th century, the craze has only really developed since 1933, when the A82 road was completed along the loch. The classic monster photograph of a dinosaur-like creature's long neck emerging from the water was taken in 1934, and the monster hunt was on. In recent years there have been sonar hunts, underwater cameras and computer studies, but unfortunately no monster has turned up. Sonar hunts, however, have located large moving objects near the bottom of the loch and it's believed that a rare form of plankton exists there. The loch is very deep and very murky, so underwater photography faces natural barriers. But keep your camera handy on the loch's banks – you could be the one to prove the monster does exist.

Organised Tours One-hour monster-hunting cruises aboard the *Nessie Hunter* (☎ 450395) operate from April to October, daily from 10.30 am to 5 pm and cost £8/5.

Places to Stay & Eat *Loch Ness Backpackers* (☎ 450807), East Lewiston, lies within walking distance of Drumnadrochit and Urquhart Castle. Dorm beds cost from £8.50. The *Loch Ness Youth Hostel* (☎ 01320-51274), 13 miles down the loch towards Glenmoriston, charges £6.10/4.95. In addition, Drumnadrochit boasts numerous B&Bs, but single rooms are in short supply. Try *Mrs MacDonald* (☎ 450382, *Maes Howe*), Balmacaan, with rooms for £14 per person; or *Mrs Witty* (☎ 450837, *The Haining*), Lower Balmacaan, who has three rooms with bath from £15 per person. Welcoming *Drumbuie Farm* (☎ 450634), on the right as you enter Drumnadrochit from Inverness, has comfortable rooms for £16 to £20. Dinner costs an additional £12. *Gillyflowers* (☎ 450641), in a renovated 18th century farmhouse, does single/double B&B from £18/28.

The *Glen Café* (☎ 450282) and the more expensive *Fiddler's Café Bar* (☎ 450678), which does traditional Scottish fare, are both near the village green. The restaurant at the *Drumnadrochit Hotel* (☎ 450218) is noted for its fine cuisine and service. Well-appointed rooms start at £24.50 per person.

Getting There & Away Citylink (☎ 0990-505050) has five or six daily services along the loch between Fort William and Inverness, via Drumnadrochit (30 minutes/1½ hours from Inverness/Fort William, £3.50/6.30). From July to September, there are four additional daily services between Urquhart Castle and Inverness. Highland Bus & Coach (☎ 01463-233371) operates four to six weekday bus services from Inverness to Cannich and Tomich, via Drumnadrochit.

Getting Around Fiddler's Café Bar (☎ 450678) hires good quality mountain bikes for £12/45 per day/week, all inclusive.

INVERNESS
• pop 41,800 ☎ 01463

Inverness has a great location on the Moray Firth at the northern end of the Great Glen. The town was probably founded by King David in the 12th century and is now the capital and transportation hub of the Highlands. In summer it overflows with visitors intent upon monster-hunting at nearby Loch Ness. However, it's worth spending some time strolling and birdwatching along the picturesque River Ness or cruising on the Moray Firth in search of its 100 or so bottlenose dolphins.

Orientation & Information
The River Ness, which links Loch Ness and the Moray Firth, flows through the heart of town. The bus and train stations and the hostels are all east of the river, within 10 minutes walk of each other. The TIC (☎ 234353) is beside the museum on Castle Wynd just off Bridge St, and you'll find a smaller tourist office at North Kessock on the A9 north.

Museum & Art Gallery
The Inverness Museum and Art Gallery (☎ 237114) contains wildlife dioramas, geological displays, period rooms with historic weapons, Pictish stones and a missable art gallery, along with a variety of short-term events and displays. It's entered through Castle Wynd, off Bridge St, and opens Monday to Saturday, from 9 am to 5 pm. Entry is free.

Inverness Castle
In the 11th century a timber castle probably stood to the east of the present castle site. In the 12th century it was replaced with a stone castle, which was then rebuilt in the 15th century. It was repaired in 1718 and expanded in 1725, only to be taken by the Jacobites in 1746 and blown up. The present rose-coloured structure was constructed between 1837 and 1847.

Today it serves as the local Sheriff's Court and most of the youths hanging around outside are waiting for their cases to be heard. The Drum Tower now houses the **Castle Garrison Encounter** (☎ 243363), which opens daily Monday to Saturday from Easter to late November (and on Sundays in July and August), from 10.30 am to 5.30 pm. For £3/2.70 you meet actors representing characters from the Hanoverian army of 1746. In front stands a statue of Highland heroine Flora McDonald, who helped the escaping Bonnie Prince Charlie.

Other Things to See

Thanks to Inverness' often violent history, few buildings of real age or historical significance have survived and much of the town dates from the completion of Telford's Caledonian Canal in 1822. Older structures include the 1593 **Abertarff House** and the 1668 **Dunbar's Hospital**, both in Church St. Inverness' **Mercat Cross** stands in front of the ornate **Town House**, the Gothic-style town hall. Across the river and south along the bank lie **St Andrew's Cathedral**, dating from 1866-69, and the **Eden Court Theatre**, which hosts regular art exhibits. It's also worth strolling to the **Ness Islands**, connected to the river banks by footbridges.

Organised Tours

Over Easter and from May to early October, Guide Friday (☎ 224000) runs hop-on hop-off bus tours of Inverness and the Culloden battlefield. An all-day ticket costs £6.50/5.

Guided walking tours of town leave from the Flora MacDonald statue on summer Sundays at 10.30 am; inquire at the TIC. The Inverness Terror Tour (☎ 716690) departs from the TIC blackboard at 7 pm nightly. During these 1¼ hour, £5.50/5 tours, visitors will be treated to tales of Inverness' horrific past, including ghosts, torture, witches, murders and hangings. They're led by an 18th century ghost in period costume.

Inverness Traction (☎ 239292) tours to Loch Ness leave from the TIC at 10.15 am daily and take in Fort Augustus Abbey, the Official Loch Ness Monster Exhibition and a loch cruise for £9.75/7.75 – about the same price as the regular bus fare! Gordon's (☎ 731202) runs alternative five-hour Loch Ness tours in a 12-seat mini-bus for £9.90/7.90. These can get quite entertaining.

From Tomnahurich Bridge, the *Jacobite Queen* (☎ 233999) cruises Loch Ness for £9/7 to £12/9. A one-way trip to Urquhart Castle, including entry, costs £9.50/8.

Moray Firth Cruises (☎ 717900) offers 1½ hour cruises to look for dolphins, seals and birdlife. Sightings aren't guaranteed but it's still enjoyable, especially on fine days. Follow the signs to Shore St Quay from the far end of Chapel St. Trips cost £10/8 and leave between 10.30 am to 4.30 pm (until 6 pm in July and August). Buses leave from the TIC 15 minutes before sailings.

From June to early September, John o'Groats Ferries (☎ 01955-611353) operates daily tours (13½ hours) from Inverness to Orkney for £40/20.

Highland Taxi Tours (☎ 220222) has a wide range of day tours to places as far afield as Skye and Deeside. Prices per car (with up to four people) range from £15 to £130.

Places to Stay

In peak season, either pre-book your accommodation or get an early start looking for something. The TIC charges £1.50 for local bookings.

Camping *Bught Camping Park* (☎ 236920) lies by the A82 at the southern edge of town and charges from £3 per site.

Hostels *Inverness Student Hostel* (☎ 236556, 8 Culduthel Rd) has the same owner as Edinburgh's High St Hostel – you can make phone bookings from there. It's friendly and homely with a great view and charges £8.50 in five to 10-bed dorms. It's a 10 minute walk from the train station, just past the castle.

Nearby *Bazpackers Backpackers Hotel* (☎ 717663, 4 Culduthel Rd) is a clean, new building with a wood-burner fire, small garden and more great views. Beds in six-bed dorms cost from £7.50, with linen; twins or doubles cost £12.

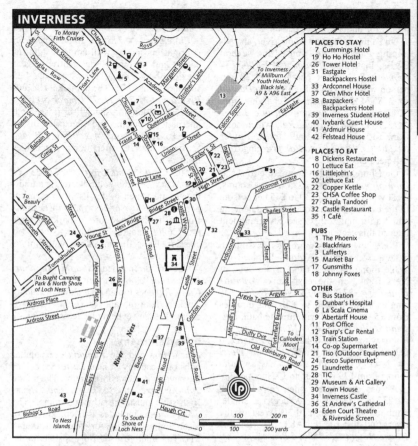

INVERNESS

PLACES TO STAY
7 Cummings Hotel
19 Ho Ho Hostel
26 Tower Hotel
31 Eastgate
   Backpackers Hostel
33 Ardconnel House
37 Glen Mhor Hotel
38 Bazpackers
   Backpackers Hotel
39 Inverness Student Hotel
40 Ivybank Guest House
41 Ardmuir House
42 Felstead House

PLACES TO EAT
8 Dickens Restaurant
10 Lettuce Eat
16 Littlejohn's
20 Lettuce Eat
22 Copper Kettle
23 CHSA Coffee Shop
27 Shapla Tandoori
32 Castle Restaurant
35 1 Café

PUBS
1 The Phoenix
2 Blackfriars
3 Laffertys
15 Market Bar
17 Gunsmiths
18 Johnny Foxes

OTHER
4 Bus Station
5 Dunbar's Hospital
6 La Scala Cinema
9 Abertarff House
11 Post Office
12 Sharp's Car Rental
13 Train Station
14 Co-op Supermarket
21 Tiso (Outdoor Equipment)
24 Tesco Supermarket
25 Laundrette
28 TIC
29 Museum & Art Gallery
30 Town House
34 Inverness Castle
36 St Andrew's Cathedral
43 Eden Court Theatre
   & Riverside Screen

The strangely named *Ho Ho Hostel* (☎ 221225, 23A High St) charges from £8.50. Also central, the *Eastgate Backpackers Hostel* (☎ 718756, 38 Eastgate) has dorm beds (with linen) for £8.90 and breakfast for £1.50.

The 166-bed *Inverness Millburn Youth Hostel* (☎ 231771, Victoria Drive) charges £11.50/9.95, with a continental breakfast (rates are £1 higher in July and August). Note that it has recently moved and some reckon it's now the best hostel in the

country. Booking is essential, especially over the Easter break and July and August.

B&Bs & Hotels Along Old Edinburgh Rd and on Ardconnel St there are lots of guesthouses and B&Bs. Rooms at the highly recommended *Ivybank Guest House* (☎ 232796, 28 Old Edinburgh Rd) cost £18 per person. *Ardconnel House* (☎ 240455, 21 Ardconnel St) is a four-star guest house with beds from £18. Just off Old Edinburgh Rd there's *Leinster Lodge Guest House*

(☎ 233311, 27 Southside Rd) which has rooms for under £20 per person.

On Kenneth St, west of the river, and adjoining Fairfield Rd, you'll find several B&Bs, including *Mardon* *(☎ 231005, 37 Kenneth St)*, which charges £14/20 per person without/with bath; *Mrs MacDonald* *(☎ 238774, 30 Kenneth St)*, charging from £14 to £18 per person; *Strome Lodge* *(☎ 221553, 41 Fairfield Rd)*, which costs from £12 to £18.50; and *Mrs M Phyfer* *(☎ 240309, 16 Fairfield Rd)*, charging £14 per person.

On Church St in the centre, the four-star *Cummings Hotel* *(☎ 232531)* has rooms, most with bath, from £30 to £45 per person. In the evenings it puts on Highland dancing and traditional songs (see Entertainment later in this section).

For a few pounds more, it's possible to have a river view in Ardross Terrace/Ness Walk, along the west bank of the river, or Ness Bank, on the east bank. *Ardmuir House* *(☎ 231151, 16 Ness Bank)* has singles from £32.50 to £38 and doubles from £53 to £64, all with private bath. *Felstead House* *(☎ 231634, 18 Ness Bank)* has rooms with or without bath from £20 to £30 per person. The larger *Glen Mhor Hotel* *(☎ 234308, 10 Ness Bank)* has *en suite* rooms from £29 right up to £72 per person.

Across the river, the *Tower Hotel* *(☎ 232765, 4 Ardross Terrace)* has single/double rooms from £30/50. West of the river, and just off the A82, the *Moyness House Hotel* *(☎ 233836, 6 Bruce Gardens)* offers B&B with bath for £26 to £34 per person and exceptional meals for £18.

Places to Eat

The museum has a small *coffee shop*, which opens Monday to Saturday, from 10 am to 4 pm. The *CHSA Coffee Shop* in Mealmarket Close serves soup and snacks. Pub-style food and snacks, including £1.50 soup and a roll, are found at the *Copper Kettle* *(☎ 233307, 50 Baron Taylor's St)*, above the Eagle Bar. It does main courses from £3.75 to £4.75. For takeaway sandwiches from 75p or jacket potatoes from £1.65, try

Lettuce Eat *(☎ 715064, 7 Lombard St or in Church St)*.

Littlejohn's *(☎ 713005, 28/30 Church St)* is bright and noisy, with amusing 'global' decor and a highly descriptive pasta-Mexican-burger menu. Pizzas start at £4.25 and burritos at £7.25. The upmarket *Dickens Restaurant* *(☎ 713111, 77 Church St)* has a good reputation and specialises in seafood, international cuisine and vegetarian dishes from £6. *Bella Pasta* *(☎ 230138, 1 Bridge St)*, below the TIC, offers Italian specialities from £4.85.

The *Castle Restaurant* *(☎ 230925, 41 Castle St)*, near the youth hostel, is a traditional café which prides itself on plentiful portions and low prices; main dishes cost from £3 to £8. The more upmarket *1 Café* *(☎ 226200)* nearby attempts to be a bit classier. Braised rump steak with onions cost around £9.

The recommended *Shapla Tandoori Restaurant & Takeaway* *(☎ 241919, 2 Castle Rd)* does Indian specialities, including chicken tikka masala for £6.95. The two-course Tuesday evening buffet is £12.95.

Entertainment

Blackfriars and the *Phoenix* are popular pubs on Academy St near *Laffertys*, one of the new-style themed Irish pubs. The trendy *Johnny Foxes* *(☎ 236577, 26 Bank St)*, has Irish-style music nightly in summer. The wacky menu includes ostrich, kangaroo, bison and cajun alligator steaks for around £11. The small *Market Bar*, upstairs in the *Old Market Inn (Market Hall)* is just off Church St and has live folk music nightly. *Gunsmiths (Union St)* also has live bands Tuesday to Saturday.

From June to September, Scottish Showtime at the *Cummings Hotel* *(☎ 232531, Church St)*, costs £12/11. Highland dancing and traditional singing are featured. The *Eden Court Theatre* *(☎ 221718, Ness Walk)*, has regular theatre performances. At the same location, *Riverside Screen* is Inverness' art-house cinema, showing both recent films and classics. *La Scala (Strother's Lane)* shows mainstream films.

Getting There & Away

Inverness is 155 miles from Edinburgh, 110 from Aberdeen and 135 from Dundee.

Air Inverness airport (☎ 232471) is at Dalcross, 8 miles from town. You can fly to Glasgow, Edinburgh, Stornoway and other centres.

Bus For Inverness bus station phone ☎ 233371. Citylink (☎ 0990-505050) has connections with lots of major centres in England, including London (13 hours, £24.50 single) via Perth and Glasgow. There are numerous buses to Glasgow (from 3½ hours, £11.50), and Edinburgh via Perth (four hours, £12.30). Buses to Aberdeen (three hours, £9.50) are run by Bluebird Buses (☎ 01224-212266).

In summer there are several buses daily to Ullapool (1½ hours, £7), connecting with the CalMac ferry to Stornoway on Lewis (not Sunday).

There are three to five daily Citylink services via Wick to Thurso and Scrabster (from three hours, £9) for the ferries to Orkney. The Citylink bus leaving Inverness at 1.30 pm connects at Wick with a Highland Country Buses service to John o'Groats. There are connecting ferries and buses from John o'Groats to Burwick and Kirkwall. There also are regular daily services along Loch Ness to Fort William (two hours, £6.30).

Citylink/Skye-Ways (☎ 01599-534328) operates three buses a day (two on Sunday) from Inverness to Kyle of Lochalsh and Portree, on Skye. The journey takes three hours and costs £10.50.

It's possible to head towards the northwest through Lairg. Inverness Traction (☎ 239292) has a Monday to Saturday service to Lairg (Sunday too in summer). In summer, daily buses run through to Durness. There's also a Monday to Saturday postbus service (☎ 256228), travelling Lairg-Tongue-Durness.

Train Phone ☎ 0345-484950 for Inverness rail inquiries. London to Inverness costs £61 on Inter-City trains and takes from eight hours (bargain singles on some GNER trains are only £24). There are direct trains from Aberdeen (£18.50), Edinburgh and Glasgow (both £28.90).

The line from Inverness to Kyle of Lochalsh offers one of the greatest scenic journeys in Britain. There are three trains a day (none on Sunday); it takes 2½ hours (£14.30). Some trains to Thurso (3¾ hours, £12.20) connect with the ferry to Orkney.

Car The TIC has a handy *Car Hire* leaflet. The big boys charge from around £33 per day or you could try Sharp's Reliable Wrecks (☎ 236694), 1st Floor, Highland Rail House, Station Square, for cheaper cars and vans from £19 per day.

Getting Around

To/From the Airport The twice-daily airport bus connects with Stornoway and London flights; it takes 20 minutes and costs £2.45. A taxi costs around £10.

Bus Inverness Traction (☎ 239292) and Highland Country Buses have services to places around Inverness including Nairn, Forres, the Culloden battlefield, Beauly, Dingwall and Lairg.

An Inverness Traction Day Rover Highland ticket costs £6.50/3.25, while a Highland Bus Day Rover ticket costs £6/3. The Highland Bus fare to Culloden is £1.30; to Cawdor it's £3.85.

Bicycle There are some great cycling opportunities out of Inverness and several rental outlets, including Wilder Ness (ask at Bazpackers Hostel) charging £7.50/10 for a half/full day, the Ho Ho Hostel and the Bught Camping Park.

Taxi Call Central Taxis on ☎ 222222.

AROUND INVERNESS

The area around the northern end of the Great Glen, Inverness and the Moray Firth has farmland along the coast, with forest and rolling heather-clad hills inland. In the more mountainous western part of the district there are several wild and beautiful glens, with plenty of wildlife to look out for. An autumn visit reveals the forests at their very best.

Beauly
- **pop 1800**   ☎ **01463**

In 1584, Mary Queen of Scots is said to have given this village its name when she exclaimed, in French, 'quel beau lieu' (what a beautiful place). Nothing much has changed – in 1995, Beauly won the Britain in Bloom contest. The red sandstone **Beauly Priory** was founded in 1230 and is now an impressive ruin; admission is £1/75p (get the key from the Priory Hotel). Beauly has supermarkets, banks with ATMs, and a couple of camping grounds. Quality gifts, crafts and knitwear are available at the Made in Scotland Shop (☎ 782821), on Station Rd.

The aptly named *Friary* does fish and chips for £3. On the other side of The Square, the *Beauly Tandoori* (☎ 782221) does curries for £6.50.

For B&B, try *Ellangowan* (☎ 782273, *Croyard Rd*) where rooms cost from £13 to £15 per person. The *Lovat Arms Hotel* (☎ 782313) charges £30/60 to £60/102 for singles/doubles. In its excellent restaurant, a four-course meal is £20; bar meals are also available from £5.25.

Inverness Traction (☎ 239292) operates hourly services daily from Dingwall and Inverness (only four run on Sunday).

Strathglass & Glen Affric

Strathglass extends about 18 miles inland from Beauly. Several long and narrow glens lead into the hills from Strathglass, including **Glen Affric**, one of the most beautiful glens in Scotland. All the glens have hydro-electric schemes, but Loch Affric is unaffected. The upper reaches of Glen Affric, owned by the NTS, offer lots of great walking, both in the glens and on the mountain ridges.

The only village in the area is **Cannich**, where there's a Spar shop and a post office.

Things to See & Do About 5 miles from Beauly, at Aigas, there's a **fish lift** where you can watch salmon taking advantage of a dam bypass. It's open mid-June to early October, Monday to Friday, from 10 am to 3 pm (you can see the fish lift from a nearby walkway).

The **Cluanie Park Falconry Centre** (☎ 01463-782415) does demonstrations with eagles, falcons, kites and owls; at the time of writing, its future was uncertain.

The impressive curving **Monar Dam** in Glen Strathfarrar was built in the 1940s; motorists can get a key for the private road up the glen, all the way to the dam (☎ 01463-761285).

Places to Stay & Eat In Cannich, *Glen Affric Backpackers* (☎ 01456-415263) has dorm beds for £5 and mountain bike hire at £5/10 for a half/full day. *Cannich Youth Hostel* (☎ 01456-415244) opens late March to October and charges £6.10/4.95 per bed. *Cougie Lodge* (☎ 01320-351354), Tomich (9 miles south-west of Cannich and 6 miles from the Tomich bus stop), has beds for £7.50, including sheets. An 11 mile walk west of Cougie Lodge brings you to the remote *Glen Affric Youth Hostel* (no ☎), where dorm beds cost £5.65/4.85. It's open late March to October.

One of the best hotels in the area is the *Mullardoch House Hotel* (☎ 01456-415460) in Glencannich, where *en suite* B&B costs from £39 to £61 per person. Bar meals cost from £4.25 to £11.

For a good bar meal, try the *Slaters Arms* (☎ 01456-415215), Cannich, where main courses and vegetarian options start at £4. Bar food is also recommended at the *Tomich Hotel* (☎ 01456-415399), Tomich. Rooms with attached bath are available from £20 to £35.

Getting There & Away Highland Bus & Coach (☎ 01463-233371) operates four to six weekday bus services from Inverness to Cannich (45 minutes, £4), via Drumnadrochit. Some runs extend as far as Tomich. There's also a Ross' Mini-bus service

(☎ 01463-761250) from Beauly, three days each week.

Black Isle

Actually a peninsula rather than an island, the Black Isle can be reached from Inverness by a short-cut across the **Kessock Bridge**. Stop at the *North Kessock Hotel* (☎ *01463-731208)* and enjoy a beer while watching the dolphins in the water under the bridge.

Fortrose & Rosemarkie You'll find the vaulted crypt of a 13th century chapter house and sacristy, and ruinous 14th century south aisle and chapel, at **Fortrose Cathedral**. A mile and a half away, at Chanonry Point, there's a lighthouse and you'll have a good chance of seeing dolphins. In Rosemarkie the **Groam House Museum** (☎ 01381-620961) has a superb collection of Pictish stones incised with designs like those on Celtic Irish stones. It's open over Easter and from May to September, Monday to Saturday from 10 am to 5 pm, and Sunday from 2 to 4.30 pm (2 to 4 pm at weekends in winter); admission is £1.50/50p.

The short but pleasant Fairy Glen walk starts at the north end of the High St (Bridge St), in Rosemarkie. The signposted trail leads you through gorges with waterfalls.

Both villages have shops, post offices and narrow, architecturally interesting streets. Fortrose has a bank with an ATM, and the *Royal Hotel (☎ 01381-620236)* has rooms from £20. Bar meals cost from £4 to £9. On the waterfront in Rosemarkie, the *Crofters (☎ 01381-620844)* does bar meals for around £4.50.

Cromarty At the peninsula's north-eastern end, the pretty village of Cromarty has many fascinating 18th century stone houses, with several offering B&B. The village has two stores, a post office, a bank (without ATM), and a pottery (☎ 01381-600226) which runs classes.

Cromarty has its own Web site located at www.cali.co.uk/highexp/Cromarty/.

The Cromarty Firth is famous for the huge offshore oil rigs which are built at Nigg (just a mile from Cromarty, on the other side), before being towed out to the North Sea. Dolphin Ecosse (☎ 01381-600323) runs boat trips to see bottlenose dolphins and other wildlife.

The 18th century **Cromarty Courthouse** (☎ 01381-600418) in Church St has a thoroughly interesting local-history museum, open April to October, daily from 10 am to 5 pm (shorter hours in winter). The £3/2 admission fee includes loan of headsets for a recorded tour of Cromarty's other historic buildings (available in French). Next to the Courthouse is **Hugh Miller's Cottage** (☎ 01381-600245, NTS). This well-known author's thatch-roofed former home opens daily May to September, from 11 am to 1 pm and 2 to 5 pm (afternoon only on Sunday); £2/1.30.

Mrs Robertson (☎ 01381-600488, 7 Church St) does B&B for £15 per head. You'll find the pleasant *Binnies Teashop* in the High St. The inviting *Thistles Restaurant (☎ 01381-600471, Church St)* has main courses from £8 to £11, but it's closed Sunday evening and Monday. There's also a good pub, the *Cromarty Arms (☎ 01381-600230)*, opposite the Courthouse. The pub has live music and bar meals cost from £3.75. Dinner, B&B is only £20 to £22 per person.

Getting There & Away The Cromarty to Nigg ferry is currently not operating, but that may change. Highland Bus & Coach (☎ 01463-233371) runs a daily service (except Sunday) from Inverness to Fortrose and Rosemarkie. Some buses continue to Cromarty (55 minutes, £4.40).

Culloden

Culloden is about 6 miles east of Inverness. The Battle of Culloden in 1746, the last fought on British soil, saw the defeat of Bonnie Prince Charlie and the slaughter of 1200 Highlanders in a 68 minute rout. The Duke of Cumberland won the label Butcher Cumberland for his brutal treatment of the defeated Scottish forces. The battle sounded the death knell of the old clan system, and the horrors of the Clearances (see the Dunrobin Castle section later in this chapter) soon followed. The sombre 122 acre moor where the conflict took place has scarcely changed in the ensuing 250 years. The site, with its many markers and memorials, is always open.

The visitors centre (☎ 01463-790607, NTS) offers a 15 minute audiovisual presentation on the battle. It's open in summer, daily from 9 am to 5.30 pm, with shorter hours in winter, and closed completely in January. Admission is £3/2.

Clava Cairns

Clearly signposted 1½ miles east of Culloden, the Clava Cairns are a picturesque group of cairns and stone circles dating from the late Neolithic period (around 4000 to 2000 BC). There's a superb railway viaduct nearby.

Fort George

Covering much of the headland is a magnificent and virtually unaltered 18th century artillery fortification, one of the best examples of its kind in Europe. It was completed in 1769 as a base for George II's army. The mile-plus walk around the ramparts offers fine views out to sea and back to the Great Glen. Given its size, you'll need several hours to look around.

There's a visitors centre (☎ 01667-462777, HS), open year-round, Monday to Saturday, from 9.30 am to 6.30 pm, and Sunday from 2 to 6.30 pm (closing on Sundays in winter at 4.30 pm). Admission costs £3/2.30.

Nairn

* pop 11,190   ☎ 01667

This pleasant seaside town is a popular resort but it's not terribly exciting. The main road from Inverness to Aberdeen (A96) goes through Nairn, but bypasses the High St, and you will not see the beach either. In the rather compact centre it's easy to find your way around, and there's a good selection of shops, hotels and restaurants.

The seasonal TIC (☎ 452763) is at 62 King St. You'll find banks with ATMs in the High St, the post office in Cawdor St, and a Safeway supermarket in King St (A96). Nairn has a swimming pool (☎ 453061) on Marine Rd and a cinema (☎ 456144) on King St.

In August, the Nairn Highland Games is a major event held on The Links. Admission is free.

Things to See & Do The small **Fishertown Museum** (☎ 458523) is on King St; the **Nairn Museum** (☎ 453177), 4 Wellington Rd, is threatened with closure.

Two miles east of Nairn at Auldearn, 17th century **Boath Doocot** is a circular pigeonhouse with displays about a nearby battle between royalists and Covenanters in 1645 (admission is £1/50p).

You can spend many pleasant hours wandering along the **East Beach**, which is one of the best in Scotland.

Places to Stay & Eat There's no hostel, but you can camp at the *Spindrift Caravan Park* (☎ 453992), Little Kildrummie (2 miles from town, along Moss-side Rd), from £4.50 per pitch.

For B&B, try the *Braighe* (☎ 453285, Albert St) which charges from £15 per person. In Auldearn, you can stay in the huge *Brightmony Farm House* (☎ 455550) for £15 single or double.

Most of the hotels have bars and restaurants. *Havelock House Hotel* (☎ 455500, Crescent Rd) was built by the Emir of Jaipur as his summer residence after he was exiled from India in 1757. You can still get a good curry in here for just £5. The *Windsor Hotel* (☎ 453108, 16 Albert St) has single/double rooms with attached bath for £35/67.50. Bar meals cost £4.25 to £12.50 and à la carte restaurant meals are around £10 to £18. The *Links Hotel* (☎ 453321) is a fine stone building at 1 Seafield St and costs from £30/50 for *en suite* singles/doubles. Highly recommended bar meals in the conservatory start at £6; three-course table d'hôte dinners cost £15.

The best place for a fish supper is *Friar Tucks (30 Harbour St)*. There are seven tearooms, three in the High St, and a really cheap one at the bus station. *Asher's Bakery (2 Bridge St)*, by the A96, is recommended for baked goods and snacks.

Getting There & Around Highland Country Buses (☎ 01463-233371) runs a twice-hourly service from Inverness to Nairn (30 minutes, £2.60). Bluebird Buses (☎ 01224-212266) runs hourly (less frequently on Sunday) from Inverness to Aberdeen via Nairn.

Nairn lies on the Inverness to Aberdeen railway line; there are five to seven trains daily (20 minutes, £3.10, from Inverness).

Bike hire is available at The Bike Shop (☎ 455416), 178 Harbour St.

Around Nairn

Cawdor Cawdor Castle (☎ 01667-404615), the 14th century home of the Thanes of Cawdor, was reputedly Macbeth's castle and the scene of Duncan's murder. The central tower dates from the 14th century but the wings were 17th century additions. It's open May to October, daily from 10 am to 5 pm; £5.20/4.20.

Cawdor Tavern (☎ 01667-404777) in the nearby village is worth a stop. Deciding what to drink can be difficult as it stocks over 100 varieties of whisky. There's also reasonable pub grub, with most specials under £7.

Highland Bus & Coach (☎ 01463-233371) runs a service every two or three hours from Inverness or Nairn to Cawdor village.

Brodie Castle Set in 175 acres of parkland, the castle (☎ 01309-641371, NTS) is 8 miles east of Nairn. Although the Brodies have been living here since 1160, the present structure dates from the 16th century. You can look round several rooms, some with wildly extravagant ceilings, and there's a large collection of paintings and furniture. Don't miss the huge Victorian kitchen beyond the small café.

The castle opens April to September from 11 am to 5.30 pm (1.30 to 5.30 pm on Sunday); £4.20/2.80. There are also woodland walks and an observation hide by the pond. Bluebird Bus No 10 runs every half-hour, taking three-quarters of an hour to reach Brodie from Inverness via Culloden and Nairn.

East Coast

The east coast starts to get interesting once you leave behind Invergordon's industrial development. Beyond this, great heather-covered hills heave themselves out of the wild North Sea, with pleasant little towns moored precariously at their edge. The scenery is particularly lovely around the Dornoch Firth and Kyle of Sutherland.

DINGWALL & STRATHPEFFER
Dingwall
• **pop 5000** ☎ **01349**
Located at the head of Cromarty Firth, Dingwall was the legendary birthplace of Macbeth. It's an unattractive place, but there are good shops which attract people from a large surrounding area. The shops, banks with ATMs, and post office, are mostly on the High St, which runs west from the train station.

Local military hero Sir Hector MacDonald features in the **Dingwall Museum** (☎ 865366) on High St (open May to September only) and in a monument which overlooks the town.

There are several takeaway outlets on High St. You can get a bar meal from £4.25 in the *National Hotel (☎ 862166)*.

Strathpeffer
• **pop 1385** ☎ **01997**
Five miles west of Dingwall, you'll find Strathpeffer, which is much more pleasant, but it can be busy in summer with coach parties. The village was a Victorian spa and there's still a **Sampling Pavilion** in the square where you can test the waters. In

summer, there's Highland dancing and bagpipe playing in the square. You'll find a Spar shop and a post office there.

Out on the road towards Dingwall, the **Highland Museum of Childhood** (☎ 421031) has a wide range of social history displays about childhood in the Highlands, from birth to school, toys, and child labour. It has a collection of dolls, toys, games and train sets. It's open from March to October, daily, from 10 am to 5 pm and 7 to 9 pm in July and August (from 1 pm on Sunday). Admission costs £1.50/1.

Strathpeffer Youth Hostel (☎ 421532) opens March to October and charges £6.10/4.95 for dorm beds. *Craigvar* (☎ 421622, The Square) is a deluxe B&B where rooms cost from £27/34. *Scoraig* (☎ 421847, 8 Kinnettas Square) is cheaper with B&B from £13 to £16 per person and dinner for £7. The *Brunstane Lodge Hotel* (☎ 421261) has rates from £32/60 and does good bar meals from £5. Four-course meals cost £17. The *Spar shop* has a cheap tearoom and takeaway; soup and a roll is £1.45.

Getting There & Away

Dingwall is on the railway route from Inverness to Kyle of Lochalsh and Thurso. There are four to seven trains daily to Inverness (£3.50).

Inverness Traction (☎ 01463-239292) operates an hourly service Monday to Saturday from Inverness to Dingwall and Strathpeffer.

It also runs hourly from Inverness to Dingwall via Beauly. Four buses per day go as far as Strathpeffer on Sunday. The Inverness to Gairloch and Durness buses, and some Inverness to Ullapool buses, run via Dingwall and Strathpeffer.

CROMARTY FIRTH

Sir Hector Munro, another military hero, commemorated his most notable victory, the capture of the Indian town of Negapatam in 1781, by erecting the Fyrish Monument, a replica of the town's gateway, high above nearby **Evanton**. Turn towards

Boath off the B9176; from the car park it's a 45 minute walk along the Jubilee Path.

Invergordon is the main centre for repairing North Sea oil rigs in the Cromarty Firth. There's an unemployment problem in the area due to the closure of the aluminium factory several years ago.

The church in **Nigg** village contains a fine Pictish carved stone. You can see it from Easter to October from 10 am to 4.30 pm, 5 pm on Sunday.

DORNOCH FIRTH
Tain
- **pop 4119**   ☎ **01862**

Tain's High St has the usual shops, post office and banks (the Royal Bank has an ATM). Turn down Castle Brae for the train station.

Things to See Tain was a centre for the management of the Clearances and has a curious 17th century **tolbooth**, originally court offices and a jail. St Duthac was born in Tain, died in Armagh (Ireland) in 1065, and is commemorated by the 11th to 12th century ruins of **St Duthac's Chapel**, as well as by St Duthus Church, which is now part of the **Tain Through Time** heritage centre (☎ 894089).

The centre describes the history of Tain as a place of pilgrimage and it's open daily April to October, from 10 am to 6 pm (noon to 4 pm, November, December and March, and at other times by arrangement) for £3.50/2.

You can ask for a tour of the **Highland Fine Cheeses** factory (☎ 892034).

Places to Stay & Eat The *Railway Hotel* (☎ 892069), Castle Brae, does B&B for £16 per person. The *St Duthus Hotel* (☎ 894007, Tower St), at the west end of High St, has rooms from £22 per person and bar meals start at £5.

The *Morangie Hotel* (☎ 892281, Morangie Rd) has singles/doubles with attached bath from £45/66. Set dinners are £18.70. Cheaper B&Bs are lined all along Morangie Rd.

Getting There & Away Citylink buses to Inverness and Thurso pass through Tain (fares are £4.80 and £8.80 respectively). There are three trains daily (two on summer Sundays) to Inverness and Thurso.

Portmahomack
• **pop 608**   ☎ **01862**

This small place used to be a busy fishing village, but it's now a quiet and relaxing place. The **Portmahomack Discovery Centre** (☎ 871790), in Tarbat Church, covers Pictish and early Christian archaeological finds. Nearby **Fearn Abbey** looks great when floodlit at night. Take a 3-mile trip out to **Tarbat Ness lighthouse**, where the sea is on three sides. Portmahomack has a shop and post office, and two hotels for bar meals.

For hostel accommodation, try the *Stables* (☎ 832219), Balintore, 8 miles south of Portmahomack and on the Moray Firth. It's open Easter to October and dorm beds cost £6.

The *Caledonian Hotel* (☎ 871560) charges from £28/46 for singles/doubles. You can also eat at the *Oyster Catcher Restaurant* (☎ 871560); seafood pancakes and other snacks start at £2, while evening meals cost £5.50 to £10. It also has B&B with sea views from £20/36.

Inverness Traction (☎ 01463-239292) operates local buses from Tain to Portmahomack and Balintore.

Ardgay & Around

The A9 crosses the Dornoch Firth by bridge and causeway near Tain. Alternatively, you can go around the inner end of the firth to Ardgay, where you'll find a train station, shop and a hotel. From there, a road leads 10 miles up Strathcarron to **Croick**, scene of notorious evictions during the 1845 Clearances. Refugee crofters from Glencalvie scratched their sad messages on the east windows of Croick Church.

Another detour from Ardgay along the Kyle of Sutherland leads to **Carbisdale Castle** (dating from 1914), which now houses Scotland's largest *Youth Hostel*

(☎ 01549-421232). It's open from March to October and charges £11.50/9.95 (£1 more in July and August).

Bonar Bridge bridges the head of the firth less than a mile from Ardgay. From there, the A949 continues eastwards to rejoin the A9 just before Dornoch, while the A836 goes north to **Lairg** (see The Interior section later in this chapter).

There are three buses daily (not Sunday) from Inverness to Lairg via Ardgay and Bonar Bridge. Trains between Inverness and Thurso stop at Ardgay and Culrain (three-quarters of a mile from Carbisdale Castle) two or three times daily.

DORNOCH
• **pop 1000**   ☎ **01862**

On the coast, 2 miles off the A9, Dornoch is a pleasant seaside town clustered around the 13th century **Dornoch Cathedral**. The original building was destroyed in 1570 during a clan feud. Despite some patching up, it wasn't completely rebuilt until 1835-37. The last witch to be burned in Scotland was set alight in Dornoch in 1722.

Nowadays, Dornoch is famous for its **championship golf course** (☎ 810283). There are less expensive courses at Golspie and Brora.

The all-year TIC (☎ 810400) is in the main square.

Dornoch has several camping grounds and plenty of B&Bs. If you want to stay in grand *Dornoch Castle* (☎ 810216), the 16th century former Bishop's Palace, expect to pay from £34 per person.

Sutherland House (☎ 811023) just off the square has cheap pub-style food (burgers from £4.50), or you can dine in style at Dornoch Castle for £22.

South of Dornoch, seals are often visible on the sand bars of **Dornoch Firth**. North of Dornoch the A9 crosses the head of **Loch Fleet** on the Mound, an embankment built by Telford in 1815-16. Look out for seals and wading birds here.

Citylink buses between Inverness and Thurso stop in Dornoch from three to five times daily.

Crofting & the Clearances

Many Highland settlements are described as crofting communities. The word croft comes from the Gaelic *croitean*, meaning a small enclosed field.

Until the early 19th century, Highland land was generally owned by clan chiefs, and their tenants farmed land on the 'run-rig' system. The land was divided into strips which were shared among the tenants. The strips were periodically shuffled around so no tenant was stuck with bad land or always enjoyed the good land. Unfortunately, it also meant they might end up with several widely scattered strips and with no incentive to improve them because they knew they would soon lose them. Accordingly, the system was changed and the land rented out to the tenants as small 'crofts', averaging about three acres. Each tenant then built their own house on their croft and the former tight cluster of homes became scattered. Crofters could also graze their animals on the common grazings, land which was jointly held by all the local crofters.

Crofting remained a precarious life. The small patch of land barely provided a living and each year the tenancy could be terminated and the crofter lose not only the croft but the house they had built on it. During the Highland Clearances, when many clan chiefs decided sheep farming was more profitable than collecting rent from poverty-stricken crofters, that was exactly what happened. The guidebook to Dunrobin Castle, seat of the Sutherland family, blithely notes that they 'proceeded to make large-scale improvements to Sutherland's communications, land and townships which involved the clearance of some 5000 people from their ancestral dwellings'. Crofting tenancies still exist but complex regulations now protect the crofters.

GOLSPIE

• pop 1647   ☎ 01408

This village is basically one uninteresting street with djacent residential areas. Apart from Dunrobin Castle, the only other item of interest is the statue of the first **Duke of Sutherland** on top of nearby Beinn a'Bhragaidh. There's talk of removing the statue (memories of the Clearances run deep).

Golspie has a couple of supermarkets, banks, a post office, and a hospital (☎ 633157). By the central car park, there's a useful notice board with a plan of the village. The SNH Sutherland area office is here and it stocks some interesting and well-produced booklets.

On Main St, there's a Chinese takeaway and a fish and chip shop. The ***Ben Bhraggie Hotel*** (☎ 633242), at the north end of Golspie, does bar meals, while ***Tulachard*** (☎ 633808, Fountain Rd) does B&B from £14 per person.

Dunrobin Castle

One mile north of Golspie, Dunrobin Castle (☎ 01408-633177), the largest house in the Highlands (187 rooms), dates back to around 1275. Additions were made in the mid-1600s and late 1700s, but most of what you see today was built in French style between 1845-50. One of the homes of the Earls and Dukes of Sutherland, it's richly furnished and offers an insight into their opulent lifestyle.

Judging by the numerous hunting trophies and animal skins, much family energy seems to have gone into hunting. The house also displays innumerable gifts from farm tenants (probably grateful that they hadn't been asked to join in the Sutherlands' clearance activities). Behind the house, magnificent formal gardens slope down to the sea and a summer house offers an eclectic museum of archaeological finds, natural-history exhibits and more big-game trophies.

The house opens April to October, Monday to Saturday, from 10.30 am to 4.30 pm, Sunday from noon, and June to September daily to 5.30 pm; £5/3.50.

Getting There & Away

Citylink buses between Inverness and Thurso stop in Golspie three to five times daily. Trains between Inverness and Thurso stop at Golspie two or three times daily.

BRORA & HELMSDALE

Between Dunrobin and Brora, the **Carn Liath Broch** is a well-preserved Iron Age fort.

Brora

• pop 1860   ☎ 01408

Located at the mouth of a river famed for its salmon, Brora has a fine beach, but parts of the village could do with improvement. The village has two small supermarkets, a bank and a post office. The golf course has a good reputation. The **Clynelish Distillery** (☎ 621444), opens March to October, weekdays, from 9.30 am to 4.30 pm and does tours for £2.

There are camp sites, plenty of B&Bs, and two good hotels. *Seaforth (☎ 621793)* has rooms from £13 to £16 per person. The *Royal Marine Hotel (☎ 621252)* has singles/doubles, with attached bath, from £50/80; its excellent leisure facilities include a swimming pool and a curling rink. River fishing is available for residents for £10 per day. Eight miles north-west, in delightful Strath Brora, *Sciberscross Lodge (☎ 641246)* charges £40 per person for B&B and £45 for a five-course dinner.

Cheaper snacks and meals can be found at the *Fountain Café (Rosslyn St)* and the *Golden Fry (☎ 621327)*, where there's a wide range available, from burgers to steaks (£4 to £9).

Helmsdale

• pop 861   ☎ 01431

Helmsdale, with its pretty harbour and salmon river, is a busy place in summer. The TIC (☎ 821640) is by the A9 on the south side of the village and it's open April to September. There are three stores, a bank, and a post office.

The excellent **Timespan Heritage Centre** (☎ 821327) has details of the 1869 Strath of Kildonan gold rush and a model of Barbara Cartland. It's open Easter to mid-October, Monday to Saturday from 9.30 am to 5 pm, Sunday from 2 to 5 pm (to 6 pm in July and August); entry costs £3/2.40.

Strathullie Crafts & Fishing Tackle (☎ 821343) can organise fishing on the river for around £20 per day, and rod hire is available at £15 per day. It also hires gold-prospecting kits (trowel, riddle and pan) for £2.50 per day, but you'll also need rubber boots, a shovel and lots of determination. Licences are free. Small quantities of gold are still found in the Kildonan Burn at Baile an Or (town of gold), about a mile from Kildonan train station.

There are several B&Bs, or a bed at *Helmsdale Youth Hostel (☎ 821577)* costs £4.65/3.85. It's open from mid-May to September, but book well ahead for July or August.

Barbara Cartland, queen of romantic novelists, has been holidaying in Helmsdale for 62 years. You're unlikely to spot her, but Nancy Sinclair, proprietor of the *La Mirage* fish and chip shop in Dunrobin St, is a dead ringer for Cartland – they share the same hairdresser.

Bar meals are available at the *Belgrave Arms Hotel (☎ 821242)* from £5, with cheaper snacks from £1.60. The *Bunillidh Restaurant (☎ 821457, 2 Dunrobin St)* serves seafood, venison and vegetarian meals for £4.50 to £10.

Getting There & Away

Buses and trains are the same as for Golspie; see earlier in this section.

HELMSDALE TO LATHERON

North of Helmsdale, the road climbs to a fine viewpoint at the **Ord of Caithness**. About 7 miles north of Helmsdale a 15 minute walk from the A9 takes you to **Badbea**, where the ruins of crofts are perched on the cliff top. **Berriedale** has a llama farm and, in early summer, puffin colonies inhabit the shoreline. The **Berriedale Braes** is a difficult section of the A9, with steep gradients, sand escape-pits, and hairpin bends.

Dunbeath, a pleasant village in a deep glen, has a couple of shops and a heritage centre (☎ 01593-731233), with displays about the history of Caithness, including crofting and fisheries. The centre opens daily, April to September, from 11 am to 5 pm, and admission costs £1.50/50p. The *Dunbeath Hotel (☎ 01593-731208)* does *en suite* B&B from £38/66, and excellent bar meals start at £5.

Just north of Dunbeath, the **Laidhay Croft Museum** (☎ 01593-731244), in a restored longhouse, recreates crofting life from the mid-1800s to WWII. Its tearoom serves home baking and soup. It's open daily April to October, from 10 am to 6 pm (£1/50p). At the **Clan Gunn Centre** (☎ 015932-731370) in Latheron you learn that it was really a Scot, not Christopher Columbus, who discovered America. It's open June to September, Monday to Saturday from 11 am to 5 pm; Sunday in July and August from 2 to 5 pm; £1.20/75p.

CELTIC SITES

There are several Celtic sites between Dunbeath and Wick. Turn north on the A895 at Latheron, and at Achavanich, wedged between Loch Rangag and Loch Stemster, double back on the road to Lybster to the 40 or so **Achavanich Standing Stones**.

Just beyond Lybster, a turn-off leads to the **Grey Cairns of Camster**, 5 miles north of the A9. Dating from between 4000 and 2500 BC, these burial chambers are hidden in long, low mounds rising from an evocatively desolate stretch of moor.

The Long Cairn measures 200 feet by 70 feet. You can enter the main chamber but must crawl into the well-preserved Round Cairn. The Round Cairn has a corbelled ceiling. Afterwards you can continue 7 miles north on this remote road to approach Wick on the A882.

The **Hill o'Many Stanes**, just beyond the Camster turn-off, is a curious, fan-shaped arrangement of 22 rows of small stones probably dating from around 2000 BC. Nearer to Wick at Ulbster (Whaligoe), the **Cairn o'Get** is a quarter-mile off the A9, and then a 2-mile walk. Steps lead down to small, picturesque **Whaligoe** harbour, directly opposite the Cairn o'Get.

Getting There & Away

Citylink buses between Inverness and Thurso run via Dunbeath, Latheron and Ulbster three to five times daily. Dunnet's Motors (☎ 01955-631202) runs three or four times daily from Wick to Ulbster, Latheron, Dunbeath and Berriedale.

WICK

• **pop 8000**   ☎ **01955**

Wick, with its boarded-up buildings, hasn't always been so dismal. A century ago, it was the world's largest herring fishing port, its harbour crammed with fishing boats and larger ships to carry barrels of salted herring abroad, and thousands of seasonal workers streaming into town to pack the catch. After WWI, the herring began to disappear, and by WWII the town had died.

Wick's massive harbour was the work of the engineer and canal pioneer Thomas Telford, who also designed Pulteneytown, the model town commissioned by the engagingly named British Society for Extending the Fisheries and Improving the Sea Coasts of the Kingdom. A failed attempt to add a breakwater was the work of Thomas Stevenson, father of author Robert Louis Stevenson.

Information

The TIC (☎ 602596), open all year, is in Whitechapel Rd, the road leading to the Safeway supermarket car park off High St.

For Caithness General Hospital, call ☎ 605050.

Wick Heritage Centre

The town's award-winning local museum (☎ 605393) in Bank Row deserves all the

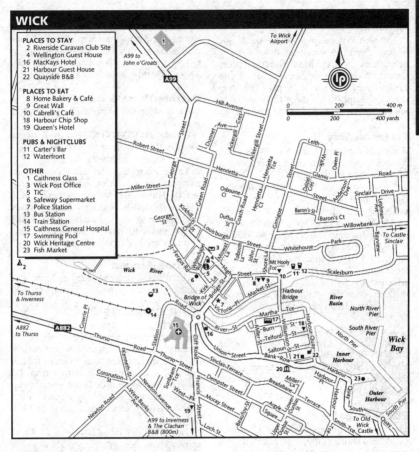

WICK

PLACES TO STAY
2 Riverside Caravan Club Site
4 Wellington Guest House
16 MacKays Hotel
21 Harbour Guest House
22 Quayside B&B

PLACES TO EAT
8 Home Bakery & Café
9 Great Wall
10 Cabrelli's Café
18 Harbour Chip Shop
19 Queen's Hotel

PUBS & NIGHTCLUBS
11 Carter's Bar
12 Waterfront

OTHER
1 Caithness Glass
3 Wick Post Office
5 TIC
6 Safeway Supermarket
7 Police Station
13 Bus Station
14 Train Station
15 Caithness General Hospital
17 Swimming Pool
20 Wick Heritage Centre
23 Fish Market

praise heaped upon it. It tracks the rise and fall of the herring industry, and displays everything from fishing equipment to complete herring fishing boats.

The Johnston photographic collection is the museum's star exhibit. From 1863 to 1977, three generations of Johnstons photographed everything that happened around Wick, and the 70,000 photographs are an amazing portrait of the town's life. The museum even displays Johnston's photo studio; prints of superb early photos are for sale.

It's open May to September, Monday to Saturday from 10 am to 5 pm; the admission charge is £2/50p.

Other Things to See

A path leads a mile south of town to the 12th century ruins of **Old Wick Castle**, with the spectacular rock formations of the **Brough** and the **Brig**, or **Gote o'Trams**, a little farther south. In good weather, it's a fine coastal walk to the castle, but take care on the final approach. Three miles north-east of Wick there's the magnificently located cliff-top ruin of **Castle Sinclair**.

Just past Wick airport, on the north side of town, you can watch the glass-blowing operations in **Caithness Glass Visitors Centre** (☎ 602286), year-round, Monday to Friday from 9 am to 4.30 pm. The shop stays open until 5 pm daily (opening at 11 am on Sunday from Easter to December).

Places to Stay

Riverside Caravan Club Site (☎ *605420, Riverside Drive)*, close to the centre, charges from £3.55 to £7.50 per tent.

For a central B&B, try the *Wellington Guest House* (☎ *603287, 41 High St)*, right behind the TIC. It has singles/doubles with attached bath for £25/40. Close to the waterfront, the *Harbour Guest House* (☎ *603276, 6 Rose St)* has singles/doubles from £18/32. By the A9 at the southern edge of town, there's the *Clachan* (☎ *605384, South Rd)*, which charges from £22/36 and is recommended. *Quayside* (☎ *603229, 25 Harbour Quay)* costs £14.50 per person and dinner is £6.95 extra.

The best hotel in Wick is *MacKays Hotel* (☎ *602323)*, with *en suite* singles/doubles for £45/70 and four-course dinners for £18.50. The 2.75m-long Ebenezer Place, the shortest street in Britain, runs past one end of the hotel.

Places to Eat

There's a *Harbour Chip Shop* (*Harbour Quay)* and another chippy near the TIC, but most places are along High St and its continuation, The Shore. On High St, there's the *Home Bakery*, with snacks (from 40p) and baked potatoes from £1. Just along the street, you'll find the *Great Wall Chinese Takeaway*. *Cabrelli's Café* (*134 High St)* does good pasta dishes from £3 and other main courses from £2.50. *Carter's Bar* (☎ *603700, 2 The Shore)* does pub-style food all day, and it's popular with young people. The *Waterfront* (☎ *602550)*, is a cavernous disco/nightclub (£5 cover charge on Saturday when there's live music); the restaurant is best avoided.

The pleasant *Queen's Hotel* (☎ *602992, 16 Francis St)*, by the A9, has an extensive bar meal and restaurant menu (from £5), including wild boar (£10.95), wood pigeon (£7.95), and roast hen pheasant (£8.95). There are also rooms from £20 per head.

Getting There & Away

Wick is 280 miles from Edinburgh and 125 from Inverness.

Gill Air (☎ 603914) and British Airways Express fly to Wick from Aberdeen, Edinburgh, Orkney and Shetland.

There are regular bus and train services from Inverness to Wick and on to Thurso; see the Inverness section earlier in this chapter for details. Highland Country Buses runs the connecting service to John o'Groats for the passenger ferry to Burwick, Orkney. The Citylink bus fare to Thurso is £2.

Getting Around

Richard's Garage (☎ 604123) on Francis St rents cars and bicycles.

JOHN O'GROATS

- **pop 512**   ☎ **01955**

Sadly, the coast most people see at the country's north-east tip is not particularly dramatic, and modern John o'Groats is little more than a ramshackle tourist trap. Its name comes from Jan de Groot, one of three brothers commissioned by James IV to operate a ferry service to Orkney in 1496 for just 4p.

Two miles east of John o'Groats is **Duncansby Head**, home to many seabirds at the start of summer. A path leads to **Duncansby Stacks**, spectacular natural rock formations soaring over 60m above the sea. There are a series of narrow inlets and deep coves on this wonderful stretch of coast.

The TIC (☎ 611373) opens April to October. There are also shops, a post office, a fish and chip shop and a crafts complex.

Places to Stay & Eat

Three miles west of John o'Groats at Canisbay, the *John o'Groats Youth Hostel* (☎ *611424)* opens late March to October and costs £6.10/4.95. There are several B&Bs in

John o'Groats and nearby Canisbay, and a couple of camping grounds. The *Caberfeidh Guest House* (☎ *611219*) at the junction in John o'Groats charges from £14 for B&B. The big *John o'Groats House Hotel* (☎ *611203*) has a reasonable restaurant, and the adjacent *Groats Inn* serves pizzas.

Getting There & Away

Highland Country Buses (☎ 01847-893123) operates two to seven daily buses to John o'Groats from Wick (£2.10) from Monday to Saturday, and on Sunday from mid-May. Harrold Coaches (☎ 01955-631295) operates the Thurso to John o'Groats service which runs several times daily, except Sunday (£2.30).

From May to September the MV *Pentland Venture* (☎ 01955-611353) shuttles across to Orkney. The single fare to Burwick is £15/7.50 and day tours around Orkney cost £30/15.

See the Inverness section earlier in this chapter for details of the John o'Groats Ferries bus, which takes you straight to the islands from Inverness.

DUNNET HEAD

Let's put a misconception to rest. Contrary to popular belief, John o'Groats is not the mainland's most northerly point, an honour which goes to Dunnet Head, a few miles to the west. The head is marked by a lighthouse that dates from 1832.

The tricky Pentland Firth, the strait between Orkney and the mainland, stretches from Duncansby Head to Dunnet Head. *Dunnet Head Tearoom* (☎ *01847-851774*) offers economically priced food, including meals for vegetarians, and B&B from £13 a head.

Just past Dunnet Head and a magnificent stretch of sandy beach, there's a turning to the tiny harbour at **Castlehill** where a heritage trail explains the evolution of the local flagstone industry.

THE INTERIOR

It's easy to think of northern Scotland as a coastline and forget the interior Highlands,

even though they loom in the backdrop throughout the region.

Access into this bleak but inspiring high country is provided by only a few roads, some single track.

From Lairg, single-track roads run north to Tongue, Laxford Bridge (between Durness and Kylesku) and Ledmore (between Kylesku and Ullapool).

The A836 from Lairg to Tongue passes Ben Klibreck (961m, 3152 feet) and Ben Loyal (764m, 2506 feet). Ben Hope (927m, 3041 feet) lies just to the west, at the head of Loch Hope.

Lairg

• pop 904   ☎ 01549

From June to September, just south of Lairg, at the southern end of Loch Shin, you can watch salmon leaping the **Falls of Shin** on their way upstream to spawn.

Lairg is the only village in the area; it has a seasonal TIC (☎ 402160) and visitors centre, shops, a bank (with ATM), post office and camp site.

The *Nip Inn* (☎ *402243, Main St*) does bar meals from £5.50 to £12 and B&B with attached bath is charged at £21 to £25 per person.

The *Shin Fry* does fish and chips. Nine miles east of Lairg at Rogart train station, you can get hostel accommodation at *Rogart Railway Carriages* (☎ *01408-641343*). It's open March to November and charges £8.50 for a bed.

The small and remote *Crask Inn* (☎ *411241*), 13 miles north of Lairg on the A836, is notorious for being the coldest place in Scotland. In December 1995 a record low of -30°C was recorded here. Rooms with bath are £15 to £18 per person, and dinner is £8.

Getting There & Around

Trains between Inverness and Thurso stop at Lairg and Rogart two or three times daily.

Inverness Traction buses (☎ 01463-239292) run from Inverness to Lairg via Tain from Monday to Saturday. Postbus services (☎ 01463-256228) connect Lairg to the coast.

North & West Coast

From just beyond Thurso, the coast round to Ullapool is mind-blowing. Everything is massive – vast, empty spaces, enormous lochs and snowcapped mountains. Ullapool is the most northerly village of any significance and there's more brilliant scenery round to Gairloch, along the incomparable Loch Maree and down to Kyle of Lochalsh (a short hop from Skye). From here you're back in the land of the tour bus; civilisation (and main roads) can be quite a shock after all the empty space.

Local tourist offices have excellent information leaflets about the coast route. Look for *Scotland's North Coast* (John o' Groats to Durness), *The North Coast Trail* (Melvich to Tongue) and *The North West Highland Explorer* (Durness to Lochcarron).

Banks and petrol stations are few and far between in this corner of Scotland, so check your funds and fuel before setting out.

GETTING AROUND

Public transport in the north-west is very patchy. Getting to Thurso or Kyle of Lochalsh by bus or train is easy, but it can be difficult to follow the coast between these places.

In July and August, Highland Country Buses (☎ 01847-893123) runs a once daily bus from Thurso to Durness, leaving Thurso at 11.30 am (2¾ hours, £7.05). At other times of year, there are Monday to Saturday services from Thurso to Bettyhill (Highland Country Buses; Rapson's, ☎ 01408-621245). On Tuesday, Friday and Saturday, you can get from Thurso (depart 10.55 am; Rapson's) to Tongue (changing to the postbus at Melvich, depart 12.56 pm), arriving at 4.20 pm. To get to Durness, there's a postbus (☎ 01463-256228) from Tongue at 10 am, Monday to Saturday, arriving in Durness at 10.45 am.

The alternative is to come up from Inverness via Lairg. There are trains (daily, including Sunday in summer), and Inverness Traction buses (☎ 01463-239292) to Lairg, but no buses on Sunday. From May to early October, there's a Heatherhopper service once daily, Monday to Saturday, between Lairg and Ullapool, connecting with the Inverness-Ullapool-Durness service at Ledmore Junction.

Monday to Saturday postbus services (☎ 01463-256228) operate the Lairg-Tongue-Durness and Lairg-Kinlochbervie-Durness routes and from Lairg to Lochinver. There are also services around the coast from Elphin to Scourie, Drumbeg to Lochinver, Shieldaig to Kishorn via Applecross, and Shieldaig to Torridon and Strathcarron, but always with gaps between villages.

There are regular bus services between Inverness and Ullapool. The once daily (except Sunday) service from Inverness to Gairloch runs via Kinlochewe and Achnasheen on Tuesday, Thursday and Friday or via Dundonnell on Monday, Wednesday and Saturday (Westerbus, ☎ 01445-712255). The route via Dundonnell provides the only link between Ullapool and Gairloch (via Braemore Junction); a postbus service only runs as far as Laide (from Braemore Junction). The Achnasheen-Kinlochewe-Torridon postbus can be used in conjunction with the Westerbus, taking you from Gairloch to Kinlochewe and Torridon (at least one day after the Ullapool to Gairloch leg).

From Torridon, the MacLennan bus service (☎ 01520-755239) goes to Strathcarron where you return to sanity and bin all your bus timetables! From Strathcarron, trains run two to four times daily to Inverness (£12.20) and Kyle of Lochalsh.

Renting a car or hitching are, perhaps, better options.

THURSO & SCRABSTER
• pop 9000   ☎ 01847

The most northerly town on the mainland, Thurso is a fairly large, fairly bleak place looking across the Pentland Firth to Hoy, in Orkney. Medieval Thurso was Scotland's major port for trade with Scandinavia. Today, ferries cross from Scrabster, 2½ miles west of Thurso, to Orkney. The ferry aside, Scrabster is little more than a collection of BP oil storage containers.

Information

The TIC (☎ 892371), Riverside Rd, opens April to October, daily in summer. The doctor's surgery is in Janet St (☎ 892027).

Things to See & Do

There's a **Heritage Museum** (☎ 892459) in Thurso Town Hall, with Pictish and Christian carved stones, fossils, and a reconstruction of a croft interior. There's also a display on Sir John Sinclair, who planned the 'new town' of Thurso at the end of the 1700s. It's open June to September, Monday to Saturday, from 10 am to 1 pm and 2 to 5 pm. The ruins of **Old St Peter's Kirk** date mainly from the 17th century, but the original church on the site was founded around 1220 by Gilbert Murray, the Bishop of Caithness. The small round building over the **Meadow Well** marks the site of a former well.

Thurso is an unlikely surfing centre, but the nearby coast has arguably the best and most regular surf in Britain. There's an excellent right-hand reef break on the east side of town, directly in front of Lord Caithness' castle, and another shallow reef break 5 miles west at Brimms Ness.

If the weather's bad, there's **Viking Bowl** (☎ 895050), a six-lane bowling alley and cinema, on Ormlie Rd. Prices for bowling start at £1.55/1.25. The swimming pool (☎ 893260) on Millbank Rd charges £1.35/75p for a dip.

North of Scrabster harbour, there's a fine cliff walk along Holborn Head. Take care in windy weather.

Places to Stay

Ormlie Lodge (☎ 896888, Ormlie Rd) opens all year and charges £6/8 for dorm beds without/with sheets. In July and August *Thurso Youth Club (☎ 892964, Old Mill)*, Millbank, has basic dorm accommodation for £8 including linen; phone ahead to check though. *Thurso Camping Site*

(☎ 607771) is by the coast, on the edge of Thurso towards Scrabster; it charges from £7.25 per tent.

Thurso has many moderately priced B&Bs and the TIC charges £1.50 for local bookings. *Pathecia (☎ 894751, 3 Janet St)* costs £17 per person, with another £1 to use the spa bath. *Kerrera (☎ 895127, 12 Rose St)* charges from £16/30 for singles/doubles. Pleasant *Murray House (☎ 895759, 1 Campbell St)* does B&B from £16/30 to £22/40. Also central on Princes St is the large *Pentland Hotel (☎ 893202)*, with rooms with attached bath from £30/54. The attached restaurant has an adventurous menu (£9 to £14). The *Royal Hotel (☎ 893191, Traill St)* has *en suite* singles from £30 to £50, and doubles from £50 to £90.

Places to Eat

Basic cafés include *Reid's Bakery* in the pedestrian mall and *Johnston of Thurso (10 Traill St)*. For takeaways, try *Robin's Fish & Chips (15a Princes St)* or the *Empire Chinese takeaway*, across the road (sweet and sour pork with rice, £5.30). The *Stewart Pavilion* at the camp site does excellent value meals. For a cheap bar meal, try the *Central Hotel (☎ 893129)*; snacks start at £1.45, and main courses are £3.90 to £5.50.

The *Redwood Restaurant (☎ 894588, Grove Lane)*, opposite the Co-op supermarket, does takeaways from £3.80 and bar meals from £4.40. It has evening entertainment and ceilidhs on Monday, Tuesday and Wednesday in summer.

In Scrabster, you can eat at the very cheap *Fisherman's Mission (☎ 892402)*; light meals start at £1.65. It's a Christian organisation, so it's closed on Sunday.

Getting There & Away

Thurso is 290 miles from Edinburgh, 130 from Inverness and 21 from Wick. From Inverness, Citylink buses operate via Wick to Thurso (3½ hours, £9); they stop at the post office in Sir George's St. Highland Country Buses (☎ 893123) operates the Wick-Thurso-Dounreay route.

THE HIGHLANDS

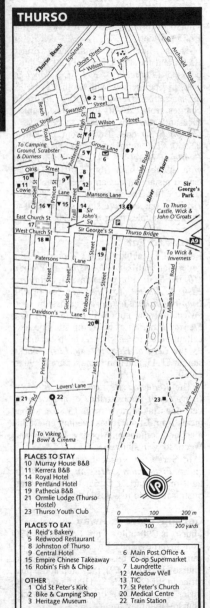

THURSO

PLACES TO STAY
10 Murray House B&B
11 Kerrera B&B
14 Royal Hotel
18 Pentland Hotel
21 Pathecia B&B
21 Ormlie Lodge (Thurso Hostel)
23 Thurso Youth Club

PLACES TO EAT
4 Reid's Bakery
5 Redwood Restaurant
8 Johnston of Thurso
9 Central Hotel
15 Empire Chinese Takeaway
16 Robin's Fish & Chips

OTHER
1 Old St Peter's Kirk
2 Bike & Camping Shop
3 Heritage Museum

6 Main Post Office & Co-op Supermarket
7 Laundrette
12 Meadow Well
13 TIC
17 St Peter's Church
20 Medical Centre
22 Train Station

There are two or three train services daily in summer (3½ hours, £12.20), but space for bicycles is limited so book ahead.

Getting Around
It's a 2-mile walk from Thurso train station to the ferry port at Scrabster, or there are buses from Olrig St for 90p. The Bike & Camping Shop (☎ 896124), The Arcade, 34 High St, rents mountain bikes for £8.50/45 per day/week. William Dunnet & Co (☎ 893101) and Northern Motors (☎ 892777) rent cars.

THURSO TO DURNESS
It's 80 winding and often spectacular coastal miles from Thurso to Durness.

Dounreay & Melvich
On the coast 10 miles west of Thurso, there's the interesting **Dounreay nuclear power station** visitors centre (☎ 01847-802572), open daily June to September, from 10 am to 4 pm (admission free). Just beyond Dounreay, **Reay** has a camp site, fine beaches, and an interesting little harbour dating from 1830. **Melvich** overlooks a fine beach and there are great views from **Strathy Point** – from the coast road, it's a 2-mile drive, then a 15 minute walk. The *Melvich Hotel (☎ 01641-531206)* does B&B from £30/50 and you can get a bar meal here.

Bettyhill
• pop 553   ☎ 01641
Bettyhill is a crofting community named after Elizabeth, Countess of Sutherland, who kicked her tenants off their land at Strathnaver to make way for more profitable sheep, then resettled the tenants here.

Bettyhill has a seasonal TIC (☎ 521342), a shop and post office.

The **Strathnaver Museum** (☎ 521418), in an old church in Bettyhill, tells the sad story of the Strathnaver Clearances. The museum contains memorabilia of Clan Mackay and various items of crofting equipment. It's open April to October, Monday to Saturday from 10 am to 1 pm and 2 to 5 pm (and at other times by arrangement). The entry charge is £1.90/1.20. There's a late 8th century Pictish cross-slab in the graveyard behind the museum.

Dunveaden (☎ 521273) charges £16 per person for B&B and from £2 per person for camping. In the *Bettyhill Hotel* (☎ 521352) B&B is from £14 per person; there's home baking and bar meals. From Bettyhill the B871 turns south for Helmsdale, through **Strathnaver**, where the Clearances took place.

Coldbackie & Tongue
• pop 445   ☎ 01847

The wonderful beach at Coldbackie is overlooked by the Watch Hill viewpoint. Only 2 miles farther on is Tongue, with the 14th century ruins of Castle Varrich, once a Mackay stronghold. Tongue has a shop, post office, bank and BP petrol.

You'll find several B&Bs in Tongue, including *Mrs MacIntosh* (☎ 611251, 77 Dalcharn), who charges from £13 per person. The excellent *Ben Loyal Hotel* (☎ 611216) has rooms from £25 per person and bar meals for £4.25 to £8. Down by the causeway, the *Tongue Youth Hostel* (☎ 611301) has a spectacular location looking up and down the Kyle of Tongue (a kyle is a narrow strait) for an overnight cost of £6.10/4.95.

Tongue to Durness

From Tongue it's 37 miles to Durness – you can take the causeway across the **Kyle of Tongue** or the beautiful old road which goes around the head of the kyle. A detour to **Melness** and **Port Vasgo** may be rewarded with the sight of seals on the beach. The atmospheric *Craggan Hotel* (☎ 01847-601278), Melness, does great bar meals, with an adventurous menu.

Continuing west, the road crosses a desolate moor past **Moine House** (built as a shelter for travellers in 1830, but now a ruin) to the northern end of **Loch Hope**. A 10-mile detour south along the loch leads to **Dun Dornaigil**, a well-preserved broch in the shadow of **Ben Hope** (927m, 3042 feet).

If you'd like to bag this Munro, it's a three to four-hour round trip along the route from the car park, which is 2 miles before the broch, near a large barn.

Beyond Loch Hope on the main road, **Heilam** has stunning views out over **Loch Eriboll**, Britain's deepest sea inlet and a shelter for ships during WWII.

DURNESS
• pop 300   ☎ 01971

Durness is one of the best located Scottish villages. When the sun shines, the effects of blinding white sand, the call of sea birds and the lime-coloured seas combine in a magical way. Perhaps this magic inspired John Lennon, who had many happy holidays here.

Information

The TIC (☎ 511259) and visitors centre opens April to October, and has slide shows at the Village Hall and guided walks in summer. The visitors centre has folk and natural history and geological displays.

Durness has two stores (Mace is recommended), petrol, a health centre (☎ 511273), and a travelling bank once a week.

Things to See & Do

A mile east of the village centre there's a path down to **Smoo Cave** from near the hostel. The vast cave entrance stands at the end of an inlet, or *geo*, and a river cascades through its roof then flows out to sea. There's evidence the cave was inhabited around 6000 years ago. You can take a boat trip (£2.50/1.25) into the floodlit cave, although after heavy rain the waterfall can make it impossible to get past.

Durness has several beautiful beaches, starting at Rispond to the east. One of the best is Sangobeg, but there's also a 'secret beach' just to the east, which can't be seen from the road. The sea offers some superb scuba-diving sites complete with wrecks, caves, seals and whales.

A disused radar station at **Balnakeil**, less than a mile up a minor road from Durness, has been turned into a scruffy hippy craft village. At the end of the road, there's the interesting ruined **Balnakeil Church**, dating from 1619. Have a look for the graveslab with carved skull and crossbones. There's also a mass grave with the remains of people from a ship which sank with all hands off **Faraid Head** in 1849. The austere **Balnakeil Farm**, overlooking the church, has a room panelled with wood salvaged from a 1688 Spanish Armada wreck (not open to the public). Walk north along the beach to reach Faraid Head, where puffin colonies can be seen in early summer.

Places to Stay & Eat
Durness Youth Hostel (☎ *511244)* is at Smoo, on the east side of the village. It's open mid-March to early October and costs £4.65/3.85. It's fairly basic but it now has showers. *Sango Sands Caravan Park* (☎ *511222)* has camping sites and the *Oasis Café*, one of the few places to eat in Durness. The pub food is unexceptional (£3.60 to £10.25). *Smoo Cave Hotel* (☎ *511227)* does *en suite* B&B from £15.50 per person and pub grub, including a vegetarian selection, for around £6.50. Durness also has several B&Bs, like *Morven* (☎ *511252)* or *Puffin Cottage* (☎ *511208)* from £16 per person. Friendly *Smoo Falls* (☎ *511228)* is opposite the hostel and charges from £15 to £20 per person.

DURNESS TO ULLAPOOL
It's 69 miles from Durness to Ullapool, with plenty of side trips and diversions to make along the way.

Cape Wrath
The cape is crowned by a lighthouse (dating from 1827) and stands close to the seabird colonies on Clo Mor Cliffs, the highest sea cliffs on the mainland. Getting to Cape Wrath involves a ferry ride (☎ 01971-511376) across the Kyle of Durness (£2.25 return) and a connecting minibus (☎ 01971-511287) for the 11 miles to the cape (40 minutes one way, £6 return). The services operate from May to September daily, and up to eight times a day in July and August.

South of Cape Wrath, **Sandwood Bay** boasts one of Britain's most isolated beaches. It's guarded at one end by the spectacular rock pinnacle **Am Buachaille**. Sandwood Bay is about 2 miles north of the end of a track from Blairmore (approach from Kinlochbervie), or you could walk south from the cape (allow eight hours) and on to Blairmore. **Sandwood House** is a creepy place reputedly haunted by the ghost of a 17th century shipwrecked sailor.

Kinlochbervie
- **pop 464**   ☎ **01971**
For such a small place, you'll be amazed to learn that, until recently, Kinlochbervie was one of Scotland's premier fish-landing ports. Fish is sold in the evening and it's possible to get incredible bargains if there are a few spare fish lying about. However, it can be a bit difficult trying to eat a gigantic cod before it goes bad.

The village has a well-stocked Mace supermarket.

Camping is available at *Oldshoremore camp site* (☎ *521281)*, less than 2 miles from Kinlochbervie. B&B at *Braeside* (☎ *521325)* costs from £16 to £17 per person. The popular and well-appointed *Kinlochbervie Hotel* (☎ *521275)* has singles/doubles for £55/90, all with attached bath. Regular ceilidhs are held here, and bistro meals cost from £4.25 to £6.75. It also does B&B in the adjacent bunkhouse for £12 per person.

Handa Island & Scourie
Boats go out to Handa Island's important seabird sanctuary from Tarbet for around £6 return (ask locally for details). You may see skuas and puffins, as well as seals. The **Old Man of Stoer** can be seen across Eddrachillis Bay and there are impressive stacks on Handa, too.

Scourie is a pretty crofting community with a well-known herd of Highland cattle. The village has a Mace supermarket and post office, petrol, camp site (on Harbour Rd), and several B&Bs. The *Scourie Hotel* (☎ *01971-502396)* has rooms from £33/56 to £45/80, and does bar meals. The attractive *Eddrachilles Hotel* (☎ *01971-502080*) offers B&B from £34 to £50 per person in lovely surroundings. Lunchtime bar snacks start at around £2, and a three-course table d'hôte dinner in its excellent restaurant costs £11.60.

Kylesku & Loch Glencoul

Kylesku is known for its sweeping modern bridge over Loch a'Chàirn Bhàin. Cruises on Loch Glencoul pass seal colonies and the 213m (700 feet) drop of **Eas a'Chual Aluinn**, Britain's highest waterfall. In summer, the MV *Statesman* (☎ 01571-844446) runs two-hour trips at 11 am and 2 pm (also 4 pm in July and August) from Kylesku Old Ferry Pier for £9/3. While you wait, you can enjoy a pint and a snack or meal in the *Kylesku Hotel* (☎ *01971-502231*) overlooking the pier.

It's a fine three hour, 6-mile (round trip) walk to the top of the falls, starting from beside Loch na Gainmhich at the top of the climb out of Kylesku towards Ullapool. The OS Landranger No 15 map shows the route.

There's a small hostel at *Kylesku Lodges* (☎ *01971-502003*). It's open from Easter to October and costs from £9 to £10, including sheets.

The Old Man of Stoer

It's roughly a 30-mile detour off the main A894 to the Point of Stoer and the Rhu Stoer Lighthouse (1870) and back to the main road again. Along the coast road you need to be prepared for single-track roads, blind bends and summits ... and sheep. The rewards are spectacular views, pretty villages and excellent beaches. From the lighthouse, it's a good one hour cliff walk to the Old Man of Stoer, a spectacular sea stack (tower of rock rising from the sea).

There are more good beaches between Stoer and Lochinver, including one at Achmelvich, where there's a camp site and hostel. The *Achmelvich Youth Hostel* (☎ *01571-844480*) opens late March to early October and charges £4.65/3.85. It's about 1½ miles from the Lochinver-

Drumbeg postbus route, and 4 miles from Lochinver.

Lochinver & Assynt
• ☎ 01571

Lochinver The popular little fishing port of Lochinver (pop 560) has a TIC and visitors centre (☎ 844330), open April to October, a camping ground and a nearby hostel at Achmelvich. Lochinver Stores stocks groceries. There's also a post office, bank (without an ATM), Esso petrol, and a doctor (☎ 844755).

There are numerous B&Bs, including *Mrs Munro* (☎ *844257, Ardglas*), who charges from £14 to £16 per person. The sprawling waterfront *Culag Hotel* (☎ *844270*), has beds from £25 and rather pricey bar meals. The *Lochinver Larder & Riverside Bistro* (☎ *844356*) has interesting local food, especially fish, to eat in or takeaway. Alternatively, the noisy *Caberfeidh Restaurant* (☎ *844321*) serves snacks from £1 and main courses (including seafood and vegetarian) from £7.

Inverkirkaig Two miles south of Lochinver on the narrow road to Achiltibuie there's a pleasant bay and a great walk along the river for 2 miles to the Falls of Kirkaig. *Achins Bookshop & Coffee Shop* (☎ *844262*) is at the start of the trail and you can browse or enjoy a snack there.

Loch Assynt The Lochinver-Lairg road (A837) meets the Durness road (A894) at **Skiag Bridge**, by Loch Assynt and about 10 miles east of Lochinver. Half a mile south of here, by the loch, there's the ruin of the late 15th century MacLeod stronghold, **Ardvreck Castle**. The Marquis of Montrose was betrayed here in 1650, after fleeing the disastrous battle at Culrain near Bonar Bridge. There are wonderful summer sunsets over the castle and the loch.

Hills of Assynt The spectacularly shaped hills of Assynt are popular with walkers and include peaks like Suilven (731m, 2398 feet), Quinag (808m, 2650 feet), Ben More

Assynt (998m, 3275 feet) and Canisp (846m, 2775 feet). Remember to check locally regarding access during the deer stalking season, from August to October. The *Assynt Field Centre* (☎ *822218)*, in Inchnadamph on the Lochinver-Lairg road, has 50 beds from £8.50 to £10 and doubles for £13 to £14.50. It's an ideal base for climbing Ben More Assynt, a seven hour round trip via the caves in Gleann Dubh and the northern ridge of Conival (988m, 3240 feet). The nearby *Inchnadamph Hotel* (☎ *822202)* is a rather homely but old-fashioned place catering for fishing and deer stalking clients; B&B costs around £30 to £40. It does bar meals for nonresidents.

Knockan & Inverpolly Nature Reserve

There's an SNH information centre (☎ 01854-666234) and geological and nature trails at Knockan, on the A835 Ledmore Junction to Ullapool road, beside Inverpolly Nature Reserve. The centre has interesting displays, including bear and lynx bones.

Check out the Knockan Studio (☎ 01854-666261), an excellent craft and jewellery centre which uses Scottish gold and stones. There's another craft shop farther north, at Ledmore Junction, which sells hand-knitted sweaters for around £50.

The nature reserve has numerous glacial lochs and the three peaks of Cul Mor (849m, 2785 feet), Stac Pollaidh (613m, 2011 feet) and Cul Beag (769m, 2522 feet). Stac Pollaidh is one of the most exciting walks in the area, with some good scrambling on its narrow sandstone crest. It takes just three hours return from the car park on Loch Lurgainn.

Farther south along the A835, there are good views of Isle Martin from just before Ardmair and then of the Summer Isles, Loch Broom and Ullapool.

Achiltibuie

• pop 290   ☎ 01854

Reached by a circuitous route around Loch Lurgainn or south from Lochinver via In-

verkirkaig, Achiltibuie has a great situation, sheltered from the west by the wonderfully named Summer Isles. In the village, there's a post office and general store.

Things to See & Do The Hydroponicum (☎ 622202) grows tropical fruit, vegetables and flowers, without soil. It also has an attached café, where hydroponically made soup (and a home-baked roll) costs £2. From April to September, tours operate on the hour from 10 am to 5 pm, and cost £4/3.25. About 4 miles north of Achiltibuie, at Altandhu, the Smokehouse (☎ 622353) smokes all sorts of things, from chicken and duck to salmon. You can watch the food being prepared, from Easter to October, Monday to Saturday, from 9.30 am to 5 pm; admission is free.

Boat trips operate to the Summer Isles from Achiltibuie (Summer Isles Cruises, ☎ 622200). The 3½-hour trips cost £10/5, and you get one hour ashore on Tanera Mor, where the post office issues its own stamps.

The coastal path from Achiltibuie to Strath Kanaird isn't an easy route and is best avoided.

Places to Stay & Eat The basic 20-bed *Achininver Youth Hostel* (☎ *622254)* is at the south end of Achiltibuie. It's open from mid-May to early October and charges £4.65/3.85. The *Summer Isles Hotel* (☎ *622282)* has singles/doubles from £48/72. It serves snacks and bar meals all day, and is well-known for its excellent though expensive evening meals and wine list.

Getting There & Away Spa Coaches (☎ 01997-421311) operates Monday to Saturday buses from Reiff, Badenscallie (half a mile from the hostel) and Achiltibuie to Ullapool, once or twice daily, except Sunday.

ULLAPOOL

• pop 1000   ☎ 01854

Ullapool is a pretty fishing village from where ferries sail to Stornoway on the Isle of Lewis. Small though it is, Ullapool is the

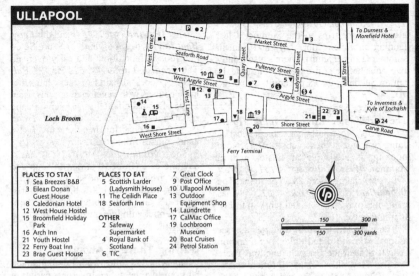

ULLAPOOL

PLACES TO STAY	PLACES TO EAT	7 Great Clock
1 Sea Breezes B&B	5 Scottish Larder	9 Post Office
3 Eilean Donan	(Ladysmith House)	10 Ullapool Museum
Guest House	11 The Ceilidh Place	13 Outdoor
8 Caledonian Hotel	18 Seaforth Inn	Equipment Shop
12 West House Hostel		14 Laundrette
15 Broomfield Holiday	**OTHER**	17 CalMac Office
Park	2 Safeway	19 Lochbroom
16 Arch Inn	Supermarket	Museum
21 Youth Hostel	4 Royal Bank of	20 Boat Cruises
22 Ferry Boat Inn	Scotland	24 Petrol Station
23 Brae Guest House	6 TIC	

biggest settlement in Wester Ross. Although it's a long way around the coast in either direction, Ullapool is only 59 miles from Inverness via the A835 along beautiful Loch Broom.

Information
The TIC (☎ 612135) at 6 Argyle St opens from April to November (daily from May to September), and at some other times. The only bank is the Royal Bank of Scotland in Ladysmith St. The Ullapool Bookshop opposite the Seaforth Inn on Quay St is excellent and has lots of books on Scottish topics. For outdoor equipment, try the shop opposite the museum (recently taken over by Mountain Man Supplies of Perth). The new Safeway supermarket is next to the large car park north of Seaforth Rd.

Things to See
The **Ullapool Museum and Visitor Centre** (☎ 612987), in a converted church in West Argyle St, opens April to October, Monday to Saturday from 9.30 am to 5.30 pm (also 7.30 to 9.30 pm in July and August); from noon to 4 pm in winter. Entry costs £2/1.50.

If you require details of the tiny **Lochbroom Museum** on Quay St, ring ☎ 612356 or contact the TIC.

Walks
There's a good low level walk up the track beside the Ullapool River to Loch Achall (two hours return) or farther, to East Rhidorroch Lodge, a round trip of 16 miles (six hours).

Ullapool is a great centre for hillwalking. Even if you don't have a car, the regular buses to Inverness on the A835 can be used, giving access to Beinn Dearg (1084m, 3556 feet), and The Fannichs, a range south of the road.

There are only a few paths in the area – the good one up Gleann na Sguaib heads for Beinn Dearg from Inverlael at the inner end of Loch Broom. Another way of approaching this rough and wild mountain is from the south, from the top of Loch Glascarnoch (no path). The walk will take about eight hours, whatever your route. Make sure that you're well equipped, and remember to carry OS map No 20.

Organised Tours

The MV *Summer Queen* (☎ 612472) operates four-hour trips to the Summer Isles, landing on Tanera Mor, daily at 10 am in summer (£14 per adult). There's also a daily two hour nature cruise at 2.15 pm (and 11 am on Sunday), for £8 per adult.

Places to Stay

The harbourside *Ullapool Youth Hostel* (☎ 612254) opens all year, except most of January. Dorm beds cost £7.75/6.50; booking is advisable at Easter and in summer. *West House* (☎ 613126, West Argyle St) charges from £8.50 per bunk. The *Broomfield Holiday Park* (☎ 612664) has camping from £5 (hiker and tent) up to £10 (car and tent).

There are lots of B&Bs and guesthouses along Seaforth Rd and Pulteney St, and on Argyle St near the Quay St junction. There are also a few places in the Morefield estate, just off the A835 at the north end of the village. The *Arch Inn* (☎ 612454, 11 West Shore St) has rooms from £18 to £27 per person. Also right on the waterfront, the *Brae Guest House* (☎ 612421, Shore St) has rooms with and without bath from £19 per person.

The friendly *Eilean Donan Guest House* (☎ 612524, 14 Market St) has rooms from £15 per person. Nearby, *Ladysmith House* (☎ 612185, 24 Pulteney St) charges from £14 per person. At *Sea Breezes* (☎ 612520, 2 West Terrace), singles/doubles cost from £16/30.

The *Ferry Boat Inn* (☎ 612103, Shore St) has pleasant hotel rooms with views up the loch for £31/58. The big *Caledonian Hotel* (☎ 612306, Quay St) offers rooms with bath from £30 to £47 a single, and £50 to £84 a double. The *Morefield Hotel* (☎ 612161), in the Morefield estate at the north end of the village, charges from £25 to £50 per person for B&B in *en suite* rooms.

Places to Eat

Upstairs at the junction of Quay and Shore Sts, the *Seaforth Inn* (☎ 612122) does good fish and chips; takeaways from the hatch downstairs (not the Quayplaice!) are £2.90.

The *Arch Inn* (☎ 612454) and the *Ferry Boat Inn* (☎ 612366), both in Shore St, do pub food at lunch time and early evening. The *Scottish Larder* (☎ 612185, 24 Pulteney St) does all sorts of pies, and other main courses with vegetarian options, from £4.95. For excellent but pricier bar and restaurant meals, the *Morefield Hotel* (☎ 612161) does full menus, with 'fishy' main courses from £6.50.

The *Ceilidh Place* (☎ 612103) has a daytime café (from 10 am) with soup and snacks from £1.95 and a much pricier evening restaurant (it's a bit of a tourist trap). It's also Ullapool's main entertainment centre, with live music most nights in summer.

Getting There & Away

Ullapool is 215 miles from Edinburgh and 60 from Inverness. See Inverness earlier in this chapter for bus information. See The Hebrides chapter for details of the ferry to Stornoway on Lewis.

Getting Around

Bikes can be rented from the West House hostel for £10/6.50 per day/half-day.

ULLAPOOL TO THE EAST COAST

The A835 goes south from Ullapool to Braemore Junction, then continues over the wild Dirrie More to the Glascarnoch dam, with great views of Beinn Dearg on the way. This section is sometimes closed by snow in winter.

Just below the dam, there's the friendly *Aultguish Inn Bunkhouse* (☎ 01997-455254) with hostel beds for £6 (no kitchen) and B&B in rooms with attached bath for £21. Meals are available in the welcoming bar.

Farther down the road, below the bulk of Ben Wyvis (1046m, 3433 feet), there's the *Inchbae Lodge Hotel* (☎ 01997-455269), which charges from £33/56 for B&B. Excellent bar meals, with vegetarian dishes, start at £4.25; the five-course set dinner changes daily and costs £28. There's also a selection of real ales in the bar. Hiking opportunities from the lodge include Ben Wyvis, but some of the tracks through the forestry can be extremely wet. Allow five hours return from Garbat, just a mile down the road from the lodge. Use OS map No 20 and carry plenty food and water (there's no water on the hill).

Five miles south of Inchbae, there's a junction where the A832 goes west to Gairloch through pleasant **Strath Braan**. You may be able to get a tour of **Loch Luichart power station**; call ☎ 0345-200150 for details. The A835 continues south-east, past **Garve** village and Loch Garve to **Contin**, where there's a Spar shop, a camp site, B&Bs and a couple of good hotels. The *Achilty Hotel (☎ 01997-421355)* does B&B with attached bath from £22.50 to £40.50. You can get bar meals here. The *Coul House Hotel (☎ 01997-421487)* is an excellent country mansion up a half-mile private drive from Contin; it's quite expensive but has bar meals for under £8.

From Contin, it's only 2 miles to Strathpeffer (see the Dingwall & Strathpeffer section earlier in this chapter).

The Inverness to Ullapool buses follow this route. Trains from Inverness to Kyle of Lochalsh stop at Garve.

ULLAPOOL TO KYLE OF LOCHALSH

Although it's less than 50 miles as the crow flies from Ullapool to Kyle of Lochalsh, it's more like 150 miles along the circuitous coastal road, with fine views of beaches and bays backed by mountains all along the way.

Falls of Measach

The A832 doubles back to the coast from the A835, 12 miles from Ullapool. Just before the junction, the Falls of Measach ('ugly' in Gaelic) spill 45m into the spectacularly deep and narrow Corrieshalloch Gorge.

You can cross from side to side on a wobbly suspension bridge. The gorge is of great botanical and geological interest and there's an informative notice board giving details.

Dundonnell
• ☎ 01854

Between Braemore and Poolewe there are relatively few houses but lots of great scenery. An Teallach (1062m, 3484 feet) at Dundonnell is a magnificent mountain, and the highest summit can be reached by a path starting less than 500m south-east of the Dundonnell Hotel (six hours return). The traverse of the ridge to Sail Liath is a more serious proposition, with lots of scrambling in precarious places, and difficult route finding. Carry OS map No 19, food and water. Make sure you're well equipped; it's amazing how quickly the weather can turn foul here.

The *Badrallach Bothy (☎ 633281)*, 7 miles from the main road at Badrallach, has basic accommodation from £3 to £4.50 per night, and camping from £4.50. *Sail Mhor Croft* hostel (☎ 633224), by the main road at Camasnagaul, has dorm beds for £7.75. The *Dundonnell Hotel (☎ 633204)* has adventurous menus and B&B with attached bath costs from £30 to £55 per person. Bar meals cost from £6 to £11 and three-course table d'hôte dinners are £20.95.

There's also the small basic *Northern Lights Campsite* just before Badcaul. You'll find a well stocked shop at Badcaul, just off the main road.

Gruinard Island, in the large Gruinard Bay, west of Dundonnell, was contaminated with anthrax spores after testing of biological weapons in WWII. After extensive treatment with formaldehyde, the island was declared safe.

Inverewe Gardens

At Poolewe on Loch Ewe, the subtropical Inverewe Gardens (☎ 01445-781200, NTS) are a testament to the warming influence of the Gulf Stream. The gardens were founded by Osgood Mackenzie in 1862 – a barren, windswept peninsula was gradually transformed into a luxuriant, colourful 64 acre garden. They're open all year, daily from 9.30 am to sunset; admission costs £4.80/3.20. There's a pleasant restaurant for soup and sandwich lunches.

Gairloch
• pop 1061   ☎ 01445

Gairloch is a group of villages around the inner end of a loch of the same name. The TIC (☎ 712130) is at the car park in Auchtercairn, where a road branches off to the main centre at Strath. It's normally open all year. There are shops and takeaways in Strath and Auchtercairn, a petrol station in Auchtercairn, and a bank (with an ATM) between Auchtercairn and Charlestown.

Things to See The Heritage Museum (☎ 712287) tells of life in the West Highlands, complete with a typical crofting cottage, schoolroom and shop. It's open Easter to October, Monday to Saturday from 10 am to 5 pm (£1.50/50p).

Places to Stay & Eat For accommodation, there are several camp sites, including *Gairloch Holiday Park* (☎ 712373) in Strath, which charges from £4 for a tent. *Sands Bunkhouse* (☎ 712083), Auchtercairn, is behind the Gairloch Sands Hotel and near the junction at Wildcat Stores. It has 45 beds (£7.50), kitchen facilities, and it's open all year. Three miles west of Gairloch, on the road to Melvaig, *Carn Dearg Youth Hostel* (☎ 712219) costs £6.10/4.95. Half a mile farther on, there's another camp site by a sandy beach. At the end of the road, 13 miles from Gairloch, you can stay at the *Ruadh Reidh Lighthouse* hostel (☎ 771263) for £7.50 including sheets, or from £14 for B&B; it also does good meals for £10, by reservation. There are buses from Gairloch as far as Melvaig one to three times daily (except Sunday), then it's a 3-mile hike along the road to the lighthouse (Westerbus, ☎ 712255).

B&B accommodation is available throughout Gairloch from £13 to £21 per person. Try *Mrs Gibson* (☎ 712085, 13 Strath), from £13 to £16 per person, or *Ho-risdale House* (☎ 712151, Strath), from £16 to £19. The *Myrtle Bank Hotel* (☎ 712004), has rooms with attached bathroom from £36 to £42 per person. You'll get an excellent bar or restaurant meal here; bar meals start at £4.75. The Italian-run *Millcroft Hotel* (☎ 712376) has rooms with bath from £24 to £36 per person, and excellent meals (including pizzas) start at £4.

Loch Maree & Victoria Falls
The A832 runs alongside craggy Loch Maree, sprinkled with islands and a series of peaks along the north shore culminating in 980m-high Slioch (3215 feet).

The Victoria Falls (commemorating Queen Victoria's 1877 visit) tumble down to the loch between Slattadale and Talladale. Look for the 'Hydro Power' signs to find it.

Kinlochewe to Torridon
Kinlochewe & Around Check out the SNH Beinn Eighe Visitors Centre, with details on local geography, geology, ecology, and walking routes.

The village is a good base for outdoor activities. You'll find an outdoor-equipment shop, petrol, and a shop/post office which runs a café in summer. There's a basic camp site a half-mile north of the village (£2).

The *Kinlochewe Hotel* (☎ 01445-760253) has a bunkhouse for £7 and B&B without/with bath for £18.50/25 per person. Bar meals with large helpings start at £5. There are a couple of cheaper B&Bs down the Torridon road charging about £16.

East of Kinlochewe, the single-track A832 continues to Achnasheen, where there's a train station. The friendly olde-worlde hunting lodge, *Ledgowan Lodge Hotel* (☎ 01445-720252), has a huge aquarium and does B&B from £29.50 per person.

Torridon & Around Westwards, the A896 follows Glen Torridon, overlooked by the multiple peaks of Beinn Eighe (1010m, 3313 feet) and Liathach (1055m, 3461 feet). The road reaches the sea at Torridon, where an NTS countryside centre (☎ 01445-

791221), open May to September, offers information on walks in the rugged area. There's a **deer museum** nearby.

Torridon village has a shop and several B&Bs. The *Torridon Youth Hostel* (☎ 01445-791284) charges £7.75/6.50, and there's an adjacent camp site. Up in Glen Torridon, *Glen Cottage* may have bunkhouse accommodation available – check locally.

The beautiful *Loch Torridon Hotel* (☎ 01445-791242), complete with clock tower, is one of the nicest places to stay in Scotland; *en suite* B&B costs from £50 to £125 per person. A superb four-course table d'hôte dinner will set you back £35, but there's bar food at the nearby Ben Damph Lodge from £4. The A896 continues westwards to lovely **Shieldaig**, which boasts an attractive main street of whitewashed houses. In Shieldaig there's a shop, post office, basic camp site, and a hotel at which you can get reasonable bar meals.

Applecross & Loch Carron

Applecross A long side trip abandons the A896 to follow the coast road to the remote seaside village of Applecross, which has a good grocery store and petrol. The scenery around here is fantastic.

The *Applecross Hotel* (☎ 01520-744262) reputedly does the best pub grub in the West Highlands. Main courses cost from £4 to £8. There's also a garden centre (☎ 01520-744268) with a tearoom and camp site. Turning inland from Applecross, the road climbs to the Bealach na Ba pass (626m, 2053 feet), then drops steeply to rejoin the A896. This winding, precipitous road can be closed in winter. There's a once-daily (except Sunday) postbus service from Applecross to Torridon.

The A896 continues to **Kishorn**, where there are spectacular views westwards to the steep sandstone Applecross hills. You can eat at the *Kishorn Seafood & Snack Bar* (☎ 01520-733240); its queen scallops (50p each) and home-made soup (£1.40) are rather good. A half-pound of squat lobster in garlic butter costs £3.95 and is worth every penny.

Lochcarron The next place is the village of Lochcarron, a veritable metropolis with two supermarkets, a bank (with an ATM!), a post office, two hotels, two tearooms (*Brambles* does takeaways), petrol and a nine-hole golf course. The TIC (☎ 01520-722357) opens from April to October. Two miles along the road to **Strome**, you'll find Lochcarron Weavers, where you can watch tartan being made (free).

Lochcarron is a good base for hillwalking, with lots of spectacular peaks and good trails in the area. Ask the TIC or the hotels for details.

There are lots of B&Bs in Lochcarron, including the *Bank House* (☎ 01520-722332, Main St), in the same building as the Bank of Scotland, and the former manager's home. Rooms cost from £15 to £18 per person for a double. Single/double B&B is also available at *Corrack* (☎ 01520-722647, Main St) for £15/27.

If you like fresh seafood, you should know that the proprietor of the *Rockvilla Hotel* (☎ 01520-722379, Main St) dives for his own scallops. Double rooms are available here for £22 to £30 per person, and bar meals are around £4 to £6. You can also eat in the restaurant where scallops thermidor costs £8.50.

Three miles away, at the top of Loch Carron, you'll reach the A890; southwards leads to Plockton, Kyle of Lochalsh, and Skye.

At **Strathcarron**, you'll find a train station and the cosy, friendly *Strathcarron Hotel* (☎ 01520-722227), where single /double rooms are charged at £29.50/49. Good pub grub starts at £1.50 for soup and snacks and main courses in the restaurant start at £8. Free camping is available, and you can use the hotel facilities.

PLOCKTON
* **pop 400**   ☎ 01599

From Stromeferry (no ferry!), there are two routes to Kyle of Lochalsh, from where ferries used to cross to Skye. The coastal route detours via idyllic Plockton, once a clearing centre for those displaced in the

Clearances. This is a really delightful place to stay with its main street lined with palms and whitewashed houses, each with a seagull perched on its chimneystack gazing out to sea.

Recently the steady flow of visitors has been augmented with viewers of the popular TV series *Hamish MacBeth* coming in search of scenes from the stories.

Plockton has a grocery store, post office and train station.

Organised Tours

From May to September, Leisure Marine (☎ 544306) runs one hour seal and otter-watching cruises for £3.50/2 a head. Sea Trek Marine (☎ 544356) operates similar tours, with hourly departures through the day.

Places to Stay & Eat

Plockton Station Bunkhouse (☎ 544235) opens all year and charges £10, including sheets. There are several pleasant places to stay in Harbour St; try *An Caladh* (☎ 544356, 25 Harbour St) with beds at £16. Right by the sea, the *Sheiling* (☎ 544282) charges about the same.

Craig Highland Farm (☎ 544205) is a delightful conservation centre, about 2 miles east of Plockton, with beds from £15 a head, and excellent self-catering cottages from £100 per week. There are lots of animals around and if you don't want to stay you can still visit for £1.50/1.

Plockton Hotel (☎ 544274, Harbour St) isn't the village's prettiest building but its pub food is popular; fish dishes start at about £6.

Good home-made food is available at *Off The Rails* (☎ 544423, Plockton Station); during the day you can get things like baked potatoes for £2.30; in the evening, meals such as 'haggis, neeps and tatties' cost around £5 to £7.

The best food of all is to be had at the *Haven Hotel* (☎ 544223) where four-course meals cost £24. B&B in this four-star hotel costs only £35 to £37 per person.

KYLE OF LOCHALSH
- **pop 800**   ☎ 01599

Until the Skye Bridge opened, Kyle of Lochalsh was the main jumping off point for trips to Skye. Now, however, its many B&B owners have to watch most of their trade whizzing past without stopping. The TIC (☎ 534276), beside the main seafront car park, opens from April to October and stocks information on Skye. In the village, you'll find two small supermarkets, two banks with ATMs, a post office and a swimming pool (£2).

Places to Stay & Eat

For dorm accommodation, try *Cuchulainn's* (☎ 534492, Station Rd) which costs from £8. *Ms Hornsby* (☎ 534196, 23 Wemyss Pl) does B&B for £12 per person. Two miles north of the village, the *Old Schoolhouse* is a luxurious B&B with *en suite* singles/doubles from £30/38 to £35/52. Its excellent restaurant caters for vegetarians.

The *Gateway Café* does good takeaway fish and chips for £2.85. The *Seagreen Restaurant & Bookshop* (☎ 534388, Plockton Rd), less than a mile from Kyle, has wonderful wholefood; oysters baked with butter and lemon are 95p each, and the oak-smoked seafood platter is £6.95. Alternatively you could try the pricier *Seafood Restaurant* (☎ 534813) in Kyle Station. Lunch main courses start at £5 and dinners start at £9.50.

Getting There & Away

Kyle can be reached by bus and train from Inverness (see Getting There & Away under Inverness earlier in this chapter), and by direct Citylink buses from Glasgow (five hours, £14.80). Citylink continues across the bridge to Kyleakin (80p) and on to Portree (one hour, £5.80) and Uig (1½ hours, £6.80), for ferries to Tarbert on Harris and Lochmaddy on North Uist.

The 82-mile train ride between Inverness and Kyle of Lochalsh (2½ hours, £14.30) is one of Scotland's most scenic. From May to September you can enjoy the view from the observation saloon, or the view and a meal from the dining car.

KYLE TO THE GREAT GLEN

It's 55 miles via the A87 from Kyle to Invergarry, which is between Fort William and Fort Augustus on Loch Oich (see The Great Glen section earlier in this chapter).

Dornie
* ☎ 01599

This quiet village at the junction of Loch Long, Loch Duich and Loch Alsh has a general store and post office.

Eilean Donan Castle Photogenically sited at the entrance to Loch Duich, Eilean Donan Castle (☎ 555202) is Scotland's best looking castle, and you get an excellent new exhibition and history display panels inside for your £3/2. It was ruined in 1719 after Spanish Jacobite forces were defeated at the Battle of Glenshiel, and was rebuilt between 1912 and 1932. It's open late March to October, daily from 10 am to 5.30 pm.

Places to Stay & Eat Hostel accommodation is available at the four-bed *Bunkhouse B&B Dornie* (☎ 555264) from £7.50, including breakfast. There are several B&Bs in and around the village. The recommended *Dornie Hotel* (☎ 555205) charges £25 to £32 per person for B&B. Good bar meals, with vegetarian choices, are mostly under £8. You can also eat at *Jenny J's* (☎ 555362); soup and a roll is £1.95, and main courses start at £6.25.

Getting There & Away Citylink buses from Fort William and Inverness to Portree stop opposite the castle and by the bridge at Dornie.

Glen Shiel & Glenelg

The TIC at Shiel Bridge opens from April to October.

Things to See & Do From Eilean Donan Castle, the A87 follows Loch Duich into spectacular Glen Shiel, with 1000m-high

peaks (over 3000 feet) soaring up on both sides of the road.

There are several good walks in the area, including the low-level route from Morvich to Glen Affric Youth Hostel via spectacular Gleann Lichd (four hours one way). A traverse of the **Five Sisters of Kintail** is a classic and none-too-easy expedition; start a mile east of the Glen Shiel battle site and finish at Shiel Bridge (eight to 10 hours).

Turn off the main road at Shiel Bridge for the **Bealach Ratagain**, a pass with great views of the Five Sisters, and continue past Glenelg to see two fine ruined Iron Age **brochs**, Dun Telve and Dun Troddan. Dun Telve still stands to a height of 10m, making it the second best-preserved broch in Scotland, after Mousa in Shetland.

From Glenelg round to the road-end at **Arnisdale** the scenery becomes even more spectacular, with great views across Loch Hourn to Knoydart. Gavin Maxwell wrote his famous book *Ring of Bright Water* while living at Sandaig, on the coast south of Glenelg.

Places to Stay & Eat You can camp at *Morvich* (☎ 01599-511354) or *Shiel Bridge* (☎ 01599-511211). By Loch Duich, at Ratagan, there's also the good *Ratagan Youth Hostel* (☎ 01599-511243) which charges £7.75/6.50.

There's a shop and the *Five Sisters Restaurant* (☎ 01599-511307) at the BP petrol station in Shiel Bridge; main courses are £4.25 to £5.75, including vegetarian dishes.

The much-improved *Kintail Lodge Hotel* (☎ 01599-511275), Shiel Bridge, has singles/doubles from £29.50/55. Bar meals cost from £6 to £12 and a three-course set restaurant meal is £19.50.

There's a shop in Glenelg. Don't miss the wacky *Glenelg Inn* (☎ 01599-522273) with its flagstone floors and tasty bar meals.

Getting There & Away Citylink buses between Fort William, Inverness and Skye operate along the A87. There's a postbus

(☎ 01463-256228) operating once daily, except Sunday, from Kyle of Lochalsh to Arnisdale via Shiel Bridge and Glenelg. For details of the ferry from Glenelg to Skye, see The Hebrides chapter. For details of the ferry service between Arnisdale and Barrisdale (in Knoydart), see Knoydart Peninsula earlier in this chapter.

Cluanie Inn

Beyond the top of Glen Shiel, the A87 passes the remote but welcoming *Cluanie*

Inn (☎ 01320-340238). Singles/doubles start at £29.50/71; there's even a four-poster bed, jacuzzi, sauna and multi-gym in here. Bar meals for hungry walkers are around £6 or £7.

From the inn, you can walk along several mountain ridges, bagging Munros till your heart's content (check locally about the deer stalking, August to October). There's a low-level route through to Glen Affric Youth Hostel (three hours), but it gets very wet at certain times of year.

The Hebrides

The islands of western Scotland offer some of the best scenery in the world. From beautiful silver-sand beaches to craggy mountain tops, there's a huge range of spectacular vistas. Soft light is the most attractive feature and the seemingly endless summer sunsets appeal to all. The best time for a visit is from spring to early summer, when the weather's usually at its best, the midges haven't hatched, and a pleasing freshness pervades the air.

This chapter covers sections of three different unitary authorities. The Southern Inner Hebrides are part of Argyll and Bute, the Small Isles and Skye are governed by Highland Council, and the Outer Hebrides come under the Western Isles.

The Isle of Islay is famous for its distilleries, while Jura is best known for its 'Paps' (breast-shaped hills). Colonsay is a secluded island; Seil and Luing have an interesting industrial heritage; and Lismore is a good place to explore by bicycle. Accessible from the town of Oban, the Isle of Mull has virtually everything, from picturesque villages and castles to whale watching and mountain walking. Just off Mull's western coast is beautiful Iona, where St Columba founded his monastery in the 6th century. Nearby Staffa has incredible rock architecture and, farther west, the rather flat Isles of Coll and Tiree beckon with their miles of unspoilt beaches.

The Small Isles are reached from Mallaig. Each is different – Muck is flat and sandy, Eigg is hilly with one rock peak, Rum (Rhum) has a high mountain ridge, and Canna has interesting history and a great position near the Cuillin of Skye.

The Isle of Skye is great for walking and climbing; there are also castles, lots of wildlife, and an attractive capital, Portree. Raasay is much quieter, and good for walking.

Scenery in the Outer Hebrides includes bleak moors on Lewis, wonderful beaches,

HIGHLIGHTS

- Treat yourself to some of the local *uisge beatha* on Islay
- View the marvellous mountain scenery of Mull
- Hike the spectacular Paps of wild and lonely Jura
- Cycle around the quiet and scenic Firth of Lorn island of Lismore
- Discover the geological gems of Staffa
- Relish excellent windsurfing conditions off Tiree
- Survey the coastal scenery of Skye's Trotternish Peninsula
- Marvel at the mysterious Callanish Standing Stones on Lewis

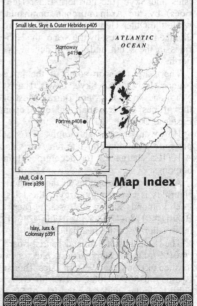

Map Index

Small Isles, Skye & Outer Hebrides p405

Stornoway p419

ATLANTIC OCEAN

Portree p408

Mull, Coll & Tiree p398

Islay, Jura & Colonsay p391

rocky mountains in Harris, and the maze of lochs on North Uist. Listen for corncrakes and curlews on the machair (grass and wild-flower-covered dunes). From the sea around Mingulay and St Kilda you can look at the birdcliffs and stacks and, if you're lucky with the weather, you may be able to go ashore.

In the islands, you'll find many Gaelic speakers, mainly on Islay, Skye and the Outer Hebrides. In Harris, Lewis and Raasay, the Sabbath is strongly observed. Take care not to upset local sensitivities, whatever your views. Although many areas are still traditional crofting communities without glitzy 'visitor attractions', things are changing, particularly on Skye, where tourism has really taken off in the last 10 years.

ORIENTATION & INFORMATION

The Hebrides extend along most of the western seaboard of Scotland. The southern Inner Hebrides are divided from the Small Isles and Skye (the northern Inner Hebrides) by the Ardnamurchan peninsula, while the Outer Hebrides, to the west, are divided from the rest by the Sea of the Hebrides in the south and The Minch in the north.

There are TICs on some of the large islands (Islay, Mull, Skye, Lewis, Harris, North and South Uist, and Barra). Most of the offices are seasonal and only open Easter to October.

However, in summer months, TICs at ports are often open for late ferry arrivals. All TICs charge £2 for accommodation bookings.

Accommodation options in the Southern Hebrides is covered by Argyll, the Isles, Loch Lomond, Stirling & Trossachs Tourist Board (☎ 01786-470945, fax 01786-471301, information@scottish.heartlands.org).

The Highlands of Scotland Tourist Board (☎ 01997-421160, admin@host.co.uk, www .host.co.uk) and the Western Isles Tourist Board (☎ 01851-703088, www.witb .co.uk) publish similar guides for the Isle of Skye and the Outer Hebrides, respectively.

WALKS

There are lots of great walks in the islands, from easy coastal rambles to ridge scrambling. The rugged landscapes of Jura, Rum, the Cuillin of Skye, and Harris, provide challenging ground for even the most serious walker.

Although parts of the Cuillin Ridge involve serious rock climbing (with no easy alternative), there's plenty for the casual rambler to do in the area. See also Walking in The Highlands chapter.

GETTING THERE & AWAY

Highland Council publishes four useful *Public Transport Travel Guides* (updated biannually) and a *Public Transport Map* (updated every two years). TICs sell them for 95p and 20p each, respectively.

Air

Flights to the islands are run by British Airways Express (☎ 0345-222111). You can fly from Glasgow International Airport to Islay, Tiree, Barra, Benbecula and Stornoway (Lewis). There are flights from Barra to Benbecula and Stornoway, and from Stornoway to Inverness. See individual entries for further details.

Bus

Scottish Citylink (☎ 0990-505050) runs buses to ports, linking with ferries. Buses to Campbeltown connect with Islay ferries at Kennacraig, while buses to Oban link with ferries to most of the Southern Hebrides, and Barra and South Uist in the Outer Hebrides. Citylink buses also run from Inverness to Oban. There are buses from Fort William to Mallaig which connect with sailings to Skye (connections to the Small Isles are better by train). The Glasgow/Portree/Uig bus connects with ferries to Raasay at Sconser (Skye); and with sailings to North Uist and Harris at Uig. The Citylink bus from Inverness to Ullapool meets ferries to Stornoway.

Shiel Buses (☎ 01967-431272) runs from Fort William to Mallaig, and Kilchoan (Ardnamurchan), to link with onward ferries.

Haggis Backpackers (☎ 0131-557 9393) and Go Blue Banana (☎ 0131-556 2000) run hop on hop off backpacker buses throughout the Highlands, and include Skye. See The Highlands chapter for details.

Train

ScotRail trains (☎ 0345-484950) run from Glasgow to Oban, Fort William to Mallaig, and Inverness to Kyle of Lochalsh. The Oban and Mallaig trains connect well with ferries. From Kyle of Lochalsh, it's a short hop over the bridge to Skye.

Boat

Caledonian MacBrayne (CalMac, ☎ 01475-650100), The Ferry Terminal, Gourock, PA19 1QP, sails regularly to the main islands from Kennacraig, Oban, Lochaline, Kilchoan, Mallaig and Ullapool; and from Sconser and Uig on Skye. Its Island Hopscotch tickets are better value than buying single fares and they're valid for a month. The Mull and Morvern Hopscotch ticket takes you from Oban to Craignure on Mull, then from Fishnish to Lochaline (£4.70 passenger, £29 car), a saving of about 10% compared to normal fares. Island Rover Passes give unlimited travel on all CalMac routes for 8 or 15 days; they're worthwhile if you're visiting a lot of islands. For car ferry reservations, phone ☎ 0990-650000 (www.calmac.co.uk).

Argyll and Bute Council (☎ 01631-562125) runs a passenger service to Lismore from Port Appin. To get to Jura, you have to go to Islay first, then go by Western Ferries (☎ 0141-332 9766) from Port Askaig to Feolin. The passenger-only ferry from Oban to Kerrera is run by Duncan MacEachan (☎ 01631-563665).

See the individual entries for full details.

GETTING AROUND

You should get a copy of the Highland Council's *Public Transport Travel Guide – Skye and Western Isles* for comprehensive public transport information.

Bus

Bus services on the islands can be rather infrequent. Services on Mull, Lewis and the Uists are a little better than on some other islands, and connect with ferries. Skye has a reasonable bus service along main routes. Always check details locally before travelling since changes do occur.

Boat

CalMac (☎ 01475-650100) provides inter-island services on the following routes: Eigg, Rum and Canna; Skye and Raasay; Barra and South Uist; and North Uist and Harris.

THE HEBRIDES

Argyll and Bute Council (☎ 01631-562125) operates a passenger service from Ellanbeich (Seil) to Easdale, and a vehicle ferry from Seil to Luing.

Other operators link Barra and Eriskay with South Uist.

Some remote islands can only be reached by charters or tours. The most popular destinations are Staffa, the Treshnish Isles, Mingulay, the Shiant Isles, and St Kilda.

Hitching

Hitching is a possibility when there's no bus, but you may have to wait a long time for a lift, especially on Sunday. Skye is usually quite good for lifts. On some of the quieter islands, you'd be quicker to walk.

Bicycle

This is a good option on small quiet islands or on the Outer Hebrides, where the bike is a great way to get around. There are some steep hills on Skye and Harris but elsewhere it's reasonably flat. The wind could be a problem, though.

Southern Inner Hebrides

Islay (pronounced eye-la) is the most southerly island in the Hebrides, famous for its whisky. Gaelic is spoken by many of the inhabitants. Beside Islay is the wild and beautiful Isle of Jura, where George Orwell wrote *1984*. Jura is definitely walker's territory and you'll see lots of interesting wildlife here. There are ferry links to Islay from the Kintyre peninsula on the mainland and, in summer, from the Isle of Colonsay. Jura and Islay are connected by a short ferry trip.

Colonsay, Seil and Luing are interesting islands, all easily reached from Oban. Colonsay has deserted beaches and varied wildlife. Seil and Luing were quarried for slate and have attractive villages with old slateworkers' cottages.

Ferries leave Oban for the popular Isle of Mull (nothing to do with the Mull of Kintyre). It's a great place to hike, with one

peak over the magical figure of 3000 feet (914m) – Ben More. There are two interesting castles, Torosay and Duart, near the eastern port of Craignure, and a narrow-gauge railway. The pretty fishing port of Tobermory is in the north of the island.

A five minute ferry trip to the west of Mull is the tiny Isle of Iona, where St Columba arrived from Ireland in the 6th century. Boat trips leave for the uninhabited Isle of Staffa, where the incredible fluted pillars of Fingal's Cave inspired Mendelssohn to compose the *Hebridean Symphony*.

Ferries run from Oban to the islands of Coll and Tiree. North from Oban they sail to Lismore; south they link Colonsay and, in summer, Islay. Coll is noted for its beaches, bird life, and solitude. The more densely populated Isle of Tiree is a very windy place, great for surfing off the sandy beaches. Lismore and Colonsay are as quiet as Coll. Colonsay has interesting historical relics, while Lismore is good for cycling.

ISLE OF ISLAY
* pop 3538   ☎ 01496

The most southerly of the islands of the Inner Hebrides, Islay is best known for its single malt whiskies, which have a highly distinctive smoky flavour. There are six distilleries, some of which welcome visitors with guided tours. The creamery at Port Charlotte makes excellent cheese – try it, and take some home with you.

With a list of over 250 recorded species, Islay also attracts birdwatchers. It's an important wintering ground for thousands of white-fronted and barnacle geese. As well as the whisky and the wildfowl, there are miles of sandy beaches and some good walks. There's great scenery and pleasant walking around the beach at Machir Bay, Kilchoman.

However, the path from Ardtalla to Storakaig, shown on Ordnance Survey map No 60, is virtually nonexistent and this route isn't recommended.

Since it's farther from the Scottish mainland than Arran or Mull, Islay receives far fewer visitors. It's definitely worth the trip.

Orientation & Information

Port Askaig is the ferry terminal opposite Jura; it has a grocery store, post office, hotel, and two distilleries (Caol Ila and Bunnahabhainn). CalMac ferries call in here, but a few more boats per week leave from Port Ellen.

Port Ellen is a larger place, with a hotel, several shops, post office and bank (no ATM). The village is slightly scruffy and could do with a tidy up. Ferries to the mainland leave from the pier. There are three distilleries nearby: Laphroaig, Lagavulin and Ardbeg.

Islay Airport lies midway between Port Ellen and Bowmore, 5 miles from both. The airport is near one of the best beaches on Islay, The Strand, on Laggan Bay.

At the southern end of Laggan Bay, 4 miles from Port Ellen, there's a good restaurant and backpacker's hostel at Kintra (pronounced kintraw).

The pleasant village of Bowmore is the island's capital. It's 10 miles from both Port Askaig and Port Ellen, and on the island's western coast. The Co-op supermarket, Main St, is open daily. The Spar on Shore St is open daily and closes late. There are two banks – the Royal Bank of Scotland, The Square, has an ATM. Bicycles are for hire at the post office, near the church.

Eleven miles from Bowmore, around the top of Loch Indaal, there's the attractive village of Port Charlotte. You'll find a Spar shop, post office, youth hostel, museum and wildlife centre here. Another 6 miles to the west, the road ends at Portnahaven, another pretty village, with a row of wacky houses, all different. Queen's University, Belfast, has been studying wave energy here.

The TIC (☎ 810254) is in Bowmore, at The Square, and it's open from March to October. For the hospital in Bowmore, ring ☎ 810219.

THE HEBRIDES

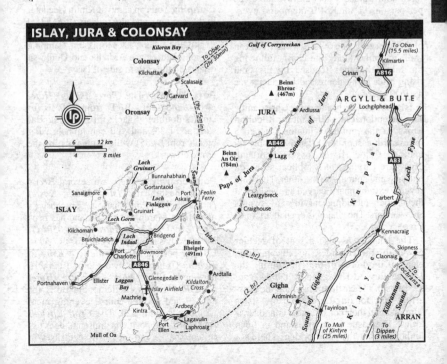

Things to See & Do

The **Caol Ila Distillery** (☎ 840207), opened in 1846, is just a half mile walk north of Port Askaig. There are guided tours on weekdays, all year, by appointment. It costs £2 per person, and you get a £3 voucher redeemable against whisky purchased. The distillery is in a wonderful location, with great views across to Jura.

Islay has a long history, which is related at the **Museum of Islay Life** (☎ 850358) in Port Charlotte. The museum has around 10,000 items covering just about every feasible topic. It's open Easter to October, Monday to Saturday from 10 am to 5 pm, Sunday 2 to 4.30 pm (£1.60/1.10).

North of Port Charlotte, there's an interesting **RSPB information centre** (☎ 850505) at the Gruinart nature reserve. It's open all year, daily, from 10 am to 5 pm (4 pm November to March); admission free. Two to three-hour guided walks are available (£2 per person, £1 for RSPB members) every Thursday at 10 am and Tuesday in August at 6 pm. The beach at **Killinallan**, north-east of the reserve, is one of Islay's best. You can walk for miles along the coast, following the **raised beaches** (caused by the land rising after being depressed by glacier ice during the Ice age).

Islay was an early focus for Christianity. The exceptional late 8th century **Kildalton Cross**, at the roofless Kildalton Chapel, 5 miles north-east of Port Ellen, is the only remaining Celtic High Cross in Scotland. There are carvings of a biblical scene on one side and animals on the other. There are several extraordinary carved graveslabs at the chapel, including carvings of swords and warriors. The chapel is open at all times (free).

The island was also a seat of secular power for the Hebrides, and the meeting place of the Lords of the Isles during the 14th century. At **Finlaggan** (☎ 840644) are the ruins of the castle from which the powerful MacDonald Lords of the Isles administered their considerable island territories. The castle is on an island in Loch Finlaggan, but there's a bridge. There's a good information centre here, open by appointment, or May to August from 2 to 5.30 pm (except Wednesday), with more restricted hours in other months. Contact the TIC or Finlaggan for details.

At Bowmore, the **Round Church** was built in 1767 in this curious shape to ensure that the devil had no corners to hide in. It's open to visitors, daily from 9 am to 6 pm. **Bowmore Distillery** (☎ 810441), School St, has a friendly visitors centre, and tours run May to September, weekdays at 10.30 and 11.30 am, 2 and 3 pm, and Saturday at 10.30 am. From October to April, tours are on weekdays at 10.30 am and 2 pm. The charge (£2/1) includes a dram and is redeemable against purchases. If the weather's bad, there's always the nearby **Mactaggart Leisure Centre** (☎ 810767). It has a 25m pool (£1.90/1.10 adult/child).

Places to Stay & Eat

Camping You can camp at Kintra (see later in this section), and at *Craigens (☎ 850256)* on the eastern side of Loch Gruinart (£2 to £2.50). Elsewhere, ask permission. Camping is prohibited on the Ardtalla and Dunlossit estates on the eastern side of Islay.

Port Askaig The *Port Askaig Hotel (☎ 840245)* does B&B from £30/36 for singles/doubles. Snacks in the Snug Bar start at £1.25, and you can munch a bar meal (from £4.55) while contemplating the erotic artwork.

Port Charlotte There are several B&Bs and a hostel, the *Islay Youth Hostel (☎ 850385)*, in Port Charlotte. The hostel's open from March to October and has beds for £6.10/4.95. *Mrs Halsall's (☎ 850431, Nerabus)* has rooms with bath for £17.50 to £20 per person. *Mrs Hastie's (☎ 850432, Tigh-na-Greing)* has two rooms from £16 per head. The *Port Charlotte Hotel (☎ 850360)* does single/double B&B for £45/79 and a three-course evening meal will cost around £20. The *Croft Kitchen (☎ 850230)*, opposite the museum, does excellent snacks and meals. It specialises in seafood and main courses range from £4.50 to £17.

Kintra & the Airport *Kintra Bunk Barns* (☎ *302051, Kintra Farm)*, Kintra Beach, open from April to September, has 23 beds for £6.50 (plus £2 if you need bedding). It also does farmhouse B&B from £18 per person, and camping is available (from £4.80). In summer, the *Granary restaurant* at Kintra serves snacks and meals. Situated near the airport, *Glenmachrie Farmhouse* (☎ *302560)* has five rooms, all with bath, for £28 per person. Excellent meals cost £20 (residents only).

The airport has a *café*, but the *Heather Hen Tearoom* (☎ *302147)* has a better reputation for snacks and meals. One of the best places on Islay for a bar meal is the *Machrie Hotel* (☎ *302310)*, about 2 miles south of the airport.

Port Ellen The pleasant *Trout Fly Guest House* (☎ *302204)* has rooms from £16.50 per person; evening meals are £10.50 (residents only). You can also get a meal at the *White Hart Hotel* (☎ *302311)*, with main courses and vegetarian dishes from £5 to £12. The hotel has live music weekly in summer. The *Davaar Café* does good takeaways; fish and chips is £2.80. Snacks start at 95p and all main courses are under £5.

Bowmore The *Harbour Inn* (☎ *810330, The Square)* has a good restaurant that serves seafood, game and beef; main courses start around £9, but there are vegetarian options from £6. B&B is £35/55 for a single/double. The *Lochside Hotel* (☎ *810244, 19 Shore St)* does good bar snacks from £3.50 and main courses from £4 to £12. The hotel bar has around 400 malts on offer, including a 29-year-old Black Bowmore (50% ABV) for £150 per 35ml! It runs speciality malt whisky weekends from £125 per person, including three nights dinner, B&B and whisky tours etc. *Tiree* (☎ *810633)* and *Lambeth House* (☎ *810597)*, both on Jamieson St, offer B&B for £16.

Getting There & Away

British Airways Express (☎ 0345-222111) flies from Glasgow to Islay twice on weekdays and once on Saturday (from £60/78 one way/return).

CalMac (☎ 302209) runs ferries from Kennacraig to Port Ellen (2¼ hours; £6.45, £34.50 for a car) and Port Askaig (two hours; same fare). They operate daily, except Wednesday when there's only a ferry to Port Askaig, and on Sunday when there's only a ferry to Port Ellen. On Wednesday in summer, there's a ferry between Colonsay and Port Askaig (£3.15, £17.25 for a car).

Getting Around

A bus service operates between Ardbeg, Port Ellen, Bowmore, Port Charlotte, Portnahaven and Port Askaig. There's only one bus on Sunday. The timetable is so complex, you're likely to miss your bus while trying to figure it out. Contact the TIC for a copy.

Taxis are available in both Bowmore (☎ 810313) and Port Ellen (☎ 302155).

Mountain bike hire is available at Bowmore Post Office (☎ 810366 or ☎ 810653) for £10/50 per day/week.

ISLE OF JURA
• pop 196   ☎ 01496

Jura is a magnificently wild and lonely island and one can quite understand why George Orwell chose it as a writer's retreat. He spent several months in Barnhill, a house in the north of the island. It's a wonderful place to walk – in fact there's really nothing else to do here, apart from having a look around Craighouse, the island's only village. There's a shop in the village (Jura Stores) and The Isle of Jura Distillery (☎ 820240), which is open by appointment (free). The mountain scenery is superb and the distinctive shapes of the Paps of Jura are visible from miles around.

North of the island, between Scarba and Jura, is the epicentre of a great tide race known as the Corryvreckan whirlpool. Caused by the tide running out more slowly on the landward side of the islands, it can be heard roaring on a still day. Stags have been known to swim it and quite small boats can slip through. It's most impressive an hour after low tide. There's an even more impressive tide race north of Scarba, between Scarba and Lunga, called Bealach a'Choin Ghlais or the 'Pass of the Grey Dogs'; this one runs like a waterfall at certain times.

Walks

The Paps of Jura provide a tough hill walk that requires good navigational skills and takes around eight hours, although the record for the Paps of Jura fell race is just three hours!

Look out for adders – the island is infested with them, but they are shy snakes that will move away as you approach.

A good place to start is by the bridge over the Corran River, north of Leargybreck. The first pap you reach is Beinn a'Chaolais (734m, 2408 feet), the second is Beinn an Oir (784m, 2572 feet) and the third is Beinn Shiantaidh (755m, 2476 feet). Most people also climb Corra Bheinn (569m, 1866 feet), before joining the path that crosses the island from Glenbatrick, to return to the road.

It's possible to follow the coast from Feolin Ferry all the way to the northern tip of Jura, but it's a gruelling endurance test and only suitable for a very fit, well equipped and experienced party. It's about 40 miles one way and takes at least five days. Camping will be necessary. You're likely to encounter raised beaches; unbridged rivers; lots of wildlife, including wild goats; extreme tussocks; caves with rooms, ladders and beds; and a range of other experiences. There's not much chance of seeing anyone else. You'll never forget Jura afterwards.

Places to Stay & Eat

In Craighouse, there's B&B from £17 to £19 per person at *Gwen Boardman's* (☎ 820379, 7 Woodside). The *Jura Hotel* (☎ 820243) is a great place to stay and the place to drink on Jura. It charges from £30 per person; try to get the rooms at the front for the views. There's pub grub (main

courses £4 to £10), and set three-course meals are £16.95. There's also *Antlers Tearoom* (☎ 820395) for snacks and teas during the day.

Getting There & Away

You reach Jura via Islay. Western Ferries (☎ 840681) shuttles between Port Askaig and Feolin (five minutes, 80/35p), roughly hourly from Monday to Saturday, and less often on Sunday. The ferry also takes cars (£5.75 single).

Getting Around

Charles MacLean (☎ 820314 or ☎ 820221) runs a bus service five or six days a week between Feolin and Craighouse. One or two of the runs go as far as Inverlussa, in the north of the island.

ISLE OF COLONSAY
* pop 106   ☎ 01951

North of Islay, Colonsay is one of the most remote isles of the Inner Hebrides. It's an unspoilt island of varied landscapes which has a good sunshine record and receives only half the rainfall of the Argyll mainland. As well as cliffs and a rocky coastline, there are several beaches of white sand, the most spectacular being Kiloran Bay. Along the western coast are several stony raised beaches.

The island is of particular interest to ornithologists, with more than 150 species of birds recorded, including golden eagles. Botanists will appreciate the subtropical gardens of Colonsay House, known for their rhododendrons. Grey seals are often seen around the coast and wild goats inhabit some of the neighbouring islets.

There are standing stones at various places, such as Kilchattan and Garvard. Some of the caves near Kiloran Bay may have been inhabited 6000 years ago.

At low tide (full or new moon), you have three to four hours to walk across the strand and visit Oronsay, a small island to the south, where the ruins of a priory date from the 14th century. There's a spectacular stone cross at the entrance, and a large collection of 15th and 16th century carved tombstones in the Prior's House.

The ferry pier is at the main village, Scalasaig. You'll find a grocery shop/post office (Rutherford's) and a hotel there. For a doctor, call ☎ 200328.

Places to Stay & Eat

There are few places to stay, none of them cheap, and camping isn't allowed. For B&B, there's *Seaview* (☎ 200315) on the rugged western coast at Kilchattan, charging £22 per person and £15 extra for dinner.

The *Isle of Colonsay Hotel* (☎ 200316) is open from March to October and is the only hotel on the island. Most people stay on a dinner B&B basis; rates are around £60 per person, including bicycle hire. Bar meals are £3 to £4 for lunch and £6 for supper.

The *Pantry* (☎ 200325) serves meals and snacks throughout summer and on the days the ferry calls.

Getting There & Away

CalMac has ferries to Colonsay from Oban on Monday, Wednesday and Friday (2¼ hours; £9.30, £44 for a car), and from Islay's Port Askaig on Wednesday in summer (1¼ hours; £3.15, £17.25 for a car) and Kennacraig on the Kintyre peninsula (3½ hours; £9.30, £44 for a car). From April to September, a Wednesday day trip from Oban to Colonsay allows you about five hours on the island.

Getting Around

Bike hire is available from A McConnel (☎ 200355). On Tuesday, Wednesday and Saturday, there's a postbus service (☎ 01463-256200) around the island – it also goes to Oronsay with times dependent on tides.

ISLE OF SEIL
• pop 506   ☎ 01852

The small island of Seil is best known for its connection to the mainland – the **Bridge over the Atlantic**, designed by Thomas Telford and opened in 1793. The bridge has one stone arch and spans the narrowest part of the tidal Clachan Sound.

After several centuries of slate quarrying, the industry collapsed in 1881 when the sea got into the pit. The flooded quarry can still be seen. The pretty conservation village of **Ellanbeich** with its whitewashed cottages is now home to an artist community. Ellanbeich is 4 miles from the Clachan bridge; it has a post office and grocery store.

Just offshore from Ellanbeich is the small island of **Easdale** with more old slate-workers' cottages and an interesting **Folk Museum** (☎ 300370), with displays about the slate industry, and life on the islands in the 18th and 19th centuries. It's open April to October, daily from 10.30 am to 5.30 pm (£1.75/1.25). Climb to the top of Easdale island (a 38m peak!) for a great view of the surrounding area (see Getting Around later in this section).

Places to Stay & Eat

For B&B, try the *Haven* (☎ 300468) at Clachan Seil, a village near the bridge. It charges from £14 per person for a double without bath. The **Willowburn Hotel** (☎ 300276), Clachan Seil, does dinner, B&B for £50 to £55 per person; it also has a good restaurant. The *Harbour Coffee Shop & Oyster Bar*, Easdale, does home baking and seafood, April to October, daily until 5 pm.

Getting There & Away

Oban & District (☎ 01631-562856) runs buses at least twice daily, except Sunday, from Oban to Ellanbeich and North Cuan (for the ferry to Luing).

Getting Around

Argyll and Bute Council (☎ 01631-562125) operates the daily passenger-only ferry service from Ellanbeich to Easdale (£1 return, bicycles free). Most runs are on request. To call the boat to Ellanbeich pier, sound the hooter during daylight, or switch on the light at night.

ISLE OF LUING
• pop 180   ☎ 01852

Luing is about 6 miles long and 1½ miles wide and has a fairly rugged western coast.

THE HEBRIDES

It's separated from the south end of Seil by the narrow Cuan Sound. There are two pleasant villages: **Cullipool** at the north end (2 miles from the ferry), which has a well stocked shop and post office; and **Toberonochy** in the east.

The main attractions are scenic including, just over a mile west of Toberonochy, the curious **Cobblers of Lorn**, a group of large knobbly rocks on a raised beach. The **slate quarries** of Cullipool were abandoned in 1965. About 1½ miles out to sea and west of Cullipool, you'll see the remains of the extensively quarried, bizarre slate islet, **Belnahua**. There are two Iron Age forts, the best being **Dun Leccamore**, about a mile north of Toberonochy.

In Toberonochy are the ruins of the late medieval **Kilchatton Church** and an unusual graveyard with slate gravestones. You can visit both villages, the fort, the ruined chapel and the Cobblers on a pleasant 8 mile circular walk, mainly on tracks.

Bardrishaig Farm (☎ *314364*), Cullipool, is open for lunch, afternoon tea and dinner. It also does B&B, with bath, for £17 per person; dinners are £7.

The vehicle ferry from Cuan (on Seil) to Luing (Argyll and Bute Council, ☎ 01631-562125) runs daily, roughly twice an hour (five minutes; £1 return, £5.20 for a car, free for bicycles).

There's a Monday to Saturday postbus service (☎ 01463-256200) around Luing which connects to Ellanbeich on Seil. In Cullipool, you can call ☎ 314256 for details of bike hire.

ISLE OF LISMORE
• pop 140   ☎ 01631

Lismore is a quiet and very fertile island in the Firth of Lorn, a few miles north of Oban. It's about 9½ miles long and just over a mile wide, with a road running almost its full length. There are a few scattered communities and two ferry terminals, one half way up the east coast, at Achnacroish, the other at Point, the island's northernmost tip. Lismore Stores is the main shop and post office, at Clachan, in the north.

Things to See & Do

The **Castle Coeffin**, 13th century ruins with a lovely coastal location, and **Tirefour Broch**, where double walls reach 3m in height, are both only half a mile from Clachan.

In Achnacroish, there's the **Lismore Historical Society museum** (☎ 760257), open at Easter and from May to September, Monday to Saturday from 10 am to 5 pm, and by appointment. The £1 admission includes tea and biscuits.

Lismore is a place to relax and enjoy the scenery. However, if you're feeling energetic the best walk on the island runs from Kilcheran, in the south, up to the top of **Barr Mór** (127m, 417 feet), then south-west along the ridge to the southern end of the island, returning to Kilcheran by track. It's about 6 miles for the round trip. Make sure to allow three to four hours to fully appreciate the fantastic views of the surrounding mountains.

Places to Stay & Eat

The *Old Schoolhouse* (☎ *760262*), just north of Clachan, does B&B for around £15 per person, including a light supper. Dinner is available for an extra £10. Nonresidents can also get meals (reserve in advance) during the day or evening; snacks and teas are available in the tearoom all day. *Mrs Carter* (☎ *760241*), Achnacroish, also does B&B for around £28 a double.

Getting There & Around

CalMac (☎ 566688) runs ferries from Oban to Achnacroish, with two to four sailings, Monday to Saturday (50 minutes; £2.15, £19.45 for a car). Argyll and Bute Council (☎ 562125) sails from Port Appin to Point, five to nine times daily. This 10 minute ferry takes passengers and bicycles only (85p, bikes for free).

The postbus (☎ 01463-256200) does several runs (Monday to Saturday), but only calls at Point at 12.40 pm. Lismore is great for cycling; contact Mr McKenzie on ☎ 760326 for details of bike hire (bikes are available at the Point ferry terminal).

ISLE OF MULL
• pop 2678

It's easy to see why Mull is so popular with tourists. As well as having superb mountain scenery, two castles and a narrow-gauge railway, and being on the route to the holy isle of Iona, it's also a charmingly endearing place.

Where else would you find a police station that used gerbils to shred important documents (really), or a stately home where notices actually encourage you to sit on the chairs? And there can be few places left in Britain where the locals don't lock their doors at night.

Despite the numbers of visitors who flock to the island, it seems to be large enough to absorb them all; and many stick to the well-worn route from Craignure to Iona, returning to Oban in the evening. If you're looking for budget accommodation, there's not much of it on Mull, so you'd be advised to take a tent.

Orientation & Information

About two-thirds of Mull's population is centred on Tobermory, in the north. Craignure is situated on the eastern coast and this is where most people arrive; it's a very small place.

There are TICs at Craignure (☎ 01680-812377), opposite the quay, and at Tobermory (☎ 01688-302182), at the CalMac terminal. The Craignure TIC is open all year, daily until 7 pm in summer, while the Tobermory TIC is only open from April to October, daily until 6 pm in summer.

Tobermory has a bank with an ATM. Elsewhere, you'll have to wait for a travelling bank. There are post offices and grocery stores in most villages – the Co-op supermarket, Main St, Tobermory, is the best for provisions.

There's a laundry in Tobermory but it's expensive; use the one at the youth hostel instead. The hospital (☎ 01680-300392) is centrally located at Salen. For a doctor in Tobermory or Bunessan, call ☎ 01688-302013 or ☎ 01681-700261 respectively.

Things to See & Do

There's little at **Craignure** apart from the ferry quay and the TIC. The Mull & West Highland Railway (☎ 01680-812494) is a toy train that transports passengers some 1½ miles south to Torosay Castle (10 minutes; £2.30/1.40 single). **Torosay Castle** (☎ 01680-812421) is a Victorian house in the Scottish Baronial style. 'Take your time but not our spoons', advises the sign, and you're left to wander at will. Set in a beautiful garden, the house is open from Easter to mid-October, daily from 10.30 am to 5.30 pm (£4.50/3.50 and £2 for children). Admission to the garden is available all year, daily from 10.30 am to sunset (£3.50).

A 40 minute walk beyond Torosay is **Duart Castle** (☎ 01680-812309), a formidable fortress dominating the Sound of Mull. The seat of the Maclean clan, this is one of the oldest inhabited castles in Scotland. The keep was built in 1360 and the castle was lost to the Campbells in 1745. In 1911, Sir Fitzroy Maclean bought and restored the castle. It has damp dungeons, vast halls and bathrooms equipped with ancient fittings. If Lady Mac is in residence, she'll take your £3.50 at the door (£3/1.75 student/child) and, in the excellent tearoom, you can try to get her Aussie employees to reveal what goes into her Chocolate Specials. The castle is open daily from May to mid-October from 10.30 am to 6 pm.

There are some interesting places to visit in the south, but you'll need to hitchhike, walk, or bring your own transport. At **Lochbuie**, there's the impressive **stone circle** and **Moy Castle**. Ask locally for the key to the castle. Farther west along the coast, at Malcolm's Point, you'll find the superb **Carsaig Arches** (see Walks later in this section).

Fionnphort (pronounced finni-fort) has lovely contrasts of pink granite rocks, sandy beaches and lovely blue/green seas. In the village, the **St Columba Exhibition and Welcome Centre** (☎ 01681-700660) has displays about the life of Columba, the Celts, and the history of Iona. It's open from

MULL, COLL & TIREE

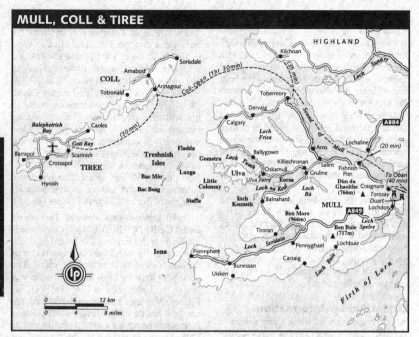

April to October, daily from 10 am to 6 pm; from 11 am on Sunday (£2/1.50).

In central Mull, one of the most scenic parts is around **Gribun**, where a huge rock fell on a house with a newly-wed couple inside. At Gruline, there's the pleasant **Loch Ba** and the **MacQuarrie Mausoleum**, complete with a sign erected by the NTS equivalent in New South Wales. MacQuarrie was a Governor-General of Australia, born at Gruline. Just north of Ulva Ferry, there's more wonderful scenery, and a great waterfall, **Eas Fors**, where a curious tree grows back on itself.

In the north of the island there's the beautiful little fishing port of **Tobermory**, Mull's capital. The brightly painted houses, reflected in the water, make this one of the most picturesque villages in Scotland. You can find out about local history in the **Mull Museum**, Main St. It's open April to October, weekdays from 10.30 am to 4.30

pm and Saturday until 1.30 pm (£1/50p). The **Tobermory Distillery** (☎ 01688-302645) does tours from Easter to October, Monday to Friday from 10 am to 4 pm. The entry cost (£2.50/1) includes a dram. You can't pass the chocolate factory without going in, but be warned – it's expensive. Somewhere out in the bay is the wreck of a ship that was part of the Armada, sunk here in 1588. No one is sure if the ship was the *Florida*, the *San Juan* or the *Santa Maria*, but rumours of a cargo of gold have kept treasure hunters looking ever since.

Eight miles west of Tobermory, at Dervaig, is the **Mull Little Theatre** (☎ 01688-400245). With only 43 seats, it's Scotland's smallest, and it has a good reputation. There are regular shows on summer evenings at 8.30 pm (around £10/6). One mile south of Dervaig, you'll find the **Old Byre Heritage Centre** (☎ 01688-400229), which is highly recommended. Displays comprise six cases of stuffed birds, a 40cm model of a midge, and excellent plasticine models of life on Mull and Iona, from the Stone Age to the present. The centre serves great inexpensive snacks and it's open from April to October, daily from 10.20 am to 6.30 pm. The **whale centre**, 1½ miles northwest of Dervaig, run by Sea Life Surveys (☎ 01688-400223), has cetacean displays and skeletons. It's open from April to October daily, except Saturday, from 10 am to 4 pm (closed from 1 to 2 pm).

Mull's best silver-sand beach is at **Calgary**, about 4 miles west of Dervaig. It's a wonderful place, flanked by cliffs, with views out to Coll and Tiree.

Walks

Ben More The highest peak on the island, Ben More (966m, 3168 feet), has spectacular views across to the surrounding islands when the weather is clear. If it's overcast or misty, wait until the next day because Mull's weather is notoriously changeable. A trail leads up the mountain from Loch na Keal, by the bridge on the A486 over the Abhainn na h-Uamha – the river 8 miles south of Salen. There's good wild camping by the roadside here (ask permission first). Return the same way, or continue down the narrow ridge to the eastern top, A'Chioch, then descend to the road via Gleann na Beinn Fhada. The glen can be rather wet and there's not much of a path. Allow five to six hours for the round trip.

Carsaig Arches One of the best walks on Mull goes along the south coast to the Carsaig Arches at Malcolm's Point. There's a good path below the cliffs all the way from Carsaig, but it becomes a bit exposed near the arches – the route climbs, then traverses a steep slope above a vertical drop into the sea. You'll see spectacular rock formations on the way, including one that looks like a giant slice of Christmas cake. The **Nun's Pass** is a gap in the cliffs through which some nuns from Iona fled after the Reformation. The arches are two sea-cut rock formations. One nicknamed 'the keyhole' is

a free-standing rock stack; another, 'the tunnel', is a huge cave with two entrances. The western entrance is hung with curtains of columnar basalt. This is an impressive place. Allow three to four hours walking time plus at least an hour at the arches.

Other Walks In the east, there's good walking on **Beinn Talaidh** (762m, 2499 feet) and **Dùn da Ghaoithe** (766m, 2512 feet). Beinn Talaidh is easiest to reach by its south ridge; look out for the aircraft wreckage near the top. Allow about four hours for the return trip. Dùn da Ghaoithe can be ascended from various places including Scallastle, about a mile north of Craignure. Allow around five hours.

Organised Tours

See Oban in The Highlands chapter for details of day tours by ferry and bus.

There are several companies running **wildlife tours**. You may see eagles, deer, otters, seals, dolphins and sharks. Andrew Jennings (☎ 01688-400223), Dervaig, is recommended and does five to seven-hour tours on weekdays (£15 to £20 per person). Isle of Mull Wildlife Expeditions (☎ 01688-302044), do a 7½ hour tour every day in summer (£23.50/17.50), which includes a picnic lunch. They leave from Tobermory at 10 am and from Craignure an hour later.

For sea safaris from Tobermory on the MV *Kelowna*, ring ☎ 01688-302111. A minimum of six persons is required. There are daily departures, from April to October; a six hour tour costs around £40 per head, but longer tours as far as Rum are possible. One mile north of Dervaig, at Torrbreac, Sea Life Surveys (☎ 01688-400223) operates Scotland's only whale research centre and runs **whale-watching trips**. A four hour family whale watch costs from £32/27.

There are also trips to the Treshnish Isles and Staffa (see Around Mull later in this chapter).

Special Events

The annual **Mull Music Festival** (☎ 01688-302383) takes place on the last weekend of

April and includes Celtic music and Irish folk music. The **Mull Highland Games and Dance** (☎ 01688-302001) is a one day event in late July. The **Tour of Mull Rally** (☎ 01688-302133), part of the Scottish Championship, is in early October. About 130 cars are involved and public roads are closed for parts of the weekend.

Places to Stay & Eat

Tobermory Here you'll find the best choice of places to stay. The newly renovated **Tobermory Youth Hostel** (☎ 01688-302481, Main St) is open from March to October. Beds are £6.10/4.95.

On Old Dervaig Rd, the *Cedars* (☎ 01688-302096) offers B&B from £16/30 for single/double. *Tom-A-Mhuillin* (☎ 01688-302164, Salen Rd) charges £14.50 to £18 per person. *Failte Guest House* (☎ 01688-302495, Main St) is very central and has rooms from £22 to £30 per person, all with bath. *Cuidhe Leathain* (☎ 01688-302352, Breadalbane St) has a great location above the harbour. B&B is £15 per person.

The *Harbour Guesthouse* (☎ 01688-302209, 59 Main St) has singles without bath for £18.50 and doubles with bath for £42. One of the top hotels on Mull, the *Western Isles Hotel* (☎ 01688-302012) charges from £38 to £87.50 per person. Bar meals, with vegetarian dishes, cost from £5. Its *Pisces seafood restaurant* has a good reputation and a nice atmosphere. À la carte main courses are from £10.50 to £12.75 and a four-course set meal is £25.50.

The *MacDonald Arms Hotel* (☎ 01688-302011, Main St) is popular with locals and it's the best place for a budget meal. Lunchtime snacks and meals are all under £4, and evening specials are £4.

For around the same price you can get a takeaway from *Posh Nosh*, upstairs at the CalMac ferry terminal. It does the usual fried food, as well as kebabs and scallops.

The *Mishnish Hotel* (☎ 01688-302009, Main St) is the place to drink and the food's good. Main dishes at this pub range from £4.50 to £12.50. There's often live music and sometimes a disco.

Dervaig & Calgary *Mucmara Lodge* (☎ 01688-400223), Torrbreac, Dervaig, has singles/doubles from £18/36, with dinner for £10 extra. It's run by Sea Life Surveys (see organised tours earlier in this section). Also in the Dervaig area, beside the theatre, is the upmarket *Druimard Country Hotel & Restaurant* (☎ 01688-400345), which charges from £57.50 per person. A four-course set meal is £22.50, but there's a pre-theatre meal for £19.50.

The *Old Byre Heritage Centre* (☎ 01688-400229) does great soup and snacks from £1.70. For a bar meal, you can try the *Bellachroy Hotel & Pub* (☎ 01688-400314), where main courses range from £3.50 to £10. It also does B&B year-round for £18 to £25 per person; some rooms with bath. From May to mid-October, there's live music every Thursday night – from folk and country to rock and roll.

In Calgary, the only place to stay is the *Calgary Farmhouse Hotel* (☎ 01688-400256). Singles/doubles cost £41/66. A three-course meal in the restaurant costs from £15 to £25.

Salen *Arle Farm Lodge* (☎ 01680-300343) is 4 miles north of Salen and offers hostel beds with duvets from £10 per night. It's a very well appointed place.

Salen Hotel (☎ 01680-300324) has singles/doubles from £20/48, some with bath. Bar snacks start around £1 and all main courses are under £6.

Craignure & Lochdon *Shieling Holidays* (☎ 01680-812496), Craignure, has camping charges from £5/8 for one/two persons. From May to October, hostel beds are available from £6.50 to £7.50. Two-person shieling accommodation costs around £18, but you must stay two nights. To get here, turn left from the ferry, then first left (around the bay); it's a 10 minute walk.

About 5 miles towards Tobermory and less than a mile from the Fishnish ferry terminal, *Balmeanach Park* (☎ 01680-300342) has a camp site, and dorm accommodation for £5. Although it doesn't have a kitchen you can use your own stove or eat at the camp site café.

Fois-an-Iolaire (☎ 01680-812423) is just over 350m from the Craignure ferry; B&B costs from £21/34. *Aon a'Dha* (☎ 01680-812318, Kirk Terrace), Craignure, is cheaper with prices from £15 per head.

By the ferry, the *Ceilidh Place* (☎ 01680-812471) does takeaway fish and chips for £3.35. Most main courses in the bar cost under £6.50.

Clachan House (☎ 01680-812439), Lochdon, has rooms for under £15 and dinner for an extra £7. The *Old Mill Cottage* (☎ 01680-812442), Lochdon, is a nice place to stay, with B&B for £30/50. It also serves three-course dinners (reservations required) for around £25 including wine.

Bunessan & Fionnphort In Bunessan, the *Argyll Tearooms* does inexpensive snacks. Bar meals are available in the *Argyll Arms* (☎ 01681-700240), mostly under £6. It also has *en suite* singles/doubles from £25 per head.

The upmarket *Ardfenaig House* (☎ 01681-700210) does dinner, B&B for £89 per person. Its four-course meals are highly regarded and the cost is £27.50 for nonresidents.

In Fionnphort, *Seaview* (☎ 01681-700235) does B&B from £16/26 for single/double. Next door, the *Keel Row* (☎ 01681-700458) does home-made bar meals and snacks for under £10. Specials, mainly local fish dishes, cost up to £15. There's also a basic snack bar down at the ferry. Camping is available at *Fidden* (☎ 01681-700427), 1¼ miles south of Fionnphort, from April to September for £2 per tent.

Getting There & Away

There are four to seven CalMac (☎ 01631-566688) ferries daily from Oban to Craignure (40 minutes; £3.25/22.70 for a passenger/small car). Smaller boats from Oban's North Pier can ferry passengers to Duart Castle; this is the cheapest way to reach Mull.

There's another ferry link between Fishnish and the mainland at Lochaline (15 minutes; £1.95/8.90 passenger/car), and boats run at least hourly every day. CalMac ferries also run from Tobermory to Kilchoan (35 minutes; £3.10/16.25 passenger/small car); from Monday to Saturday there are seven per day, and in July and August there are five sailings on Sunday. Call ☎ 01688-302017 for details. From November to March, there's only the weekday passenger service from Tobermory to Kilchoan run by Steading Holidays (☎ 01972-510262). It charges £4 single, £6 return. The Oban-Coll-Tiree ferry doesn't currently call in at Tobermory, but that may change.

Getting Around

There's a basic bus service run by Essbee Coaches (☎ 01631-566999) connecting the ferry points and main villages. The Craignure to Tobermory service (one hour; £2.65) goes up to five times a day all week (only once on Sunday, from Easter to October). The Craignure to Fionnphort service (1¼ hours; £3.10) is equally frequent. There's also a postbus (☎ 01463-256200) from Salen to Burg (Kilninian) via Ulva Ferry. RN Carmichael (☎ 01688-302220) runs the Tobermory to Dervaig and Calgary service.

For a taxi in Tobermory, call ☎ 01688-302204.

Cycling is a good way to get around, and you can rent bikes from a number of places. In Salen, try On Yer Bike (☎ 01680-300501). It also has an outlet in the craft shop near the ferry terminal in Craignure and charges £9/5 for a full/half day. In Tobermory, contact Mrs MacLean at Tom-A-Mhuillin (☎ 01688-302164), Salen Rd (similar rates).

AROUND MULL
Isle of Iona

- **pop 130**   ☎ **01681**

A five minute ferry ride (£3 return) from Fionnphort on the south-western tip of Mull brings you to Iona. St Columba landed here from Ireland in 563, before setting out to

Caledonian MacBrayne

Most travellers to Scotland's Hebridean islands will sail on one of Caledonian MacBrayne's distinctive vessels. The company, CalMac for short, traces its roots to David MacBrayne (1818-1907). MacBrayne was a Glasgow man from a family with shipping interests, so it's no surprise that he joined Hutcheson's shipping office at a young age. He inherited a west-coast steamship fleet which was developed steadily in following years. In 1878, MacBrayne became sole proprietor of a company with a virtual monopoly on passenger traffic (boosted by the expanding tourist trade) and shipping of agricultural goods to the islands.

After his death, MacBrayne's empire expanded into road haulage and bus transport. Nowadays, the successful merged company Caledonian MacBrayne prides itself with sailing to 23 Scottish islands. The company operates an efficient modern fleet with regularly serviced ships kept in tip-top operating order.

convert Scotland. A monastery was established and it was here that the Book of Kells, the prize attraction of Dublin's Trinity College, is believed to have been transcribed. It was taken to Kells in Ireland when Viking raids drove the monks from Iona.

The monks returned and the monastery prospered until its destruction in the Reformation. The ruins were given to the Church of Scotland in 1899, and by 1910 **Iona Abbey** was reconstructed by a group of enthusiasts called the Iona Community. It's still a flourishing spiritual community holding regular courses and retreats. The abbey (☎ 700404) is open to visitors at all times (free).

Iona is indeed a very special place, with some of the best beaches and coves in the Hebrides, but the stampeding hordes that pile off the tour buses daily make it difficult to appreciate. The best advice is to spend the night at one of the hotels or B&Bs here. After the crowds have gone, you can walk to the top of the hill, go to an evening service or look around the ancient graveyard where 48 of Scotland's early kings, including Macbeth, are buried. The grave of former British Labour leader John Smith is also here.

Iona has a Spar shop and post office, near the pier. You can visit the **Iona Heritage Centre** (☎ 700576), open from Easter to October daily except Sunday, from 10.30 am to 4.30 pm (£1.20/80p). The centre covers the history of Iona, crofting and lighthouses; home baking's available in the coffee shop.

For B&B try the *Bishop's House* (☎ 700306), near the abbey, or *Cruachan* (☎ 01681-700523), which serves herb teas and is half a mile from the ferry. Both charge from around £16 per person. The *Argyll Hotel* (☎ 700334) is the island's best and charges from £36/88 for a comfortable single/double. It does bar lunches for under £6 and four-course dinners for £19.50.

Meals are also available at the *Martyr's Bay Restaurant* (☎ 700382), near the pier. Lunch is under £4 and a three-course evening meal will cost from around £10.

Bicycle hire is available from Finlay Ross (☎ 700357).

Isle of Staffa

This uninhabited island is a truly magnificent sight, and you'll understand how it inspired Mendelssohn. Immense hexagonal basalt pillars form the walls, roof and floor of the cathedral-like **Fingal's Cave**. You can land on the island and walk into the cave via the causeway.

Boat Cave can be seen from the causeway, but you can't reach it on foot. Staffa also has a sizeable puffin colony, north of the landing place. In summer, Gordon Grant Marine (☎ 01681-700388) run once or twice-daily boat trips to Staffa from Fionnphort and Iona (2¼ hours; £10/5). Tours on the MV *Iolaire* (☎ 01681-700358), from Iona, are similar. You can also go from Ulva

Ferry on Mull with Turus Mara (☎ 01688-400242) for £10/7.

Treshnish Isles

This chain of deserted islands lies north-west of Staffa; two of them have ruined castles. The two main islands are the curiously shaped **Dutchman's Cap**, and **Lunga**. You can land on Lunga, walk to the top of the hill, and visit the shag, puffin and guillemot colonies on the west coast at **Harp Rock**. Camping is possible, but you need to bring all your drinking water.

Gordon Grant (☎ 01681-700388) sails to Staffa and Treshnish from Iona at 9.50 am on Tuesday, Wednesday, Thursday and Saturday (mid-May to July). For a six hour trip, the cost is £20/10. Turus Mara (☎ 01688-400242) sails to Lunga from Ulva Ferry on Mull; contact it for fares and schedule.

Isle of Ulva

- **pop 30**   ☎ 01688

Ulva is about 5 miles long and lies just off the west coast of Mull. It's linked by bridge to the even more remote island of Gometra. The ferry operators (☎ 500226) run an on-demand service for passengers and bicycles from Ulva Ferry (on Mull) to Ulva, from April to October, on weekdays from 8 am to 5 pm (two minutes; £2.50, 50p for bikes). There are also Sunday departures from June to August. At other times, phone to make arrangements. Ask them about camping on the island.

The island has reasonable tracks, great scenery, a 9th century Viking fort, **Dùn Bàn**, and an old chapel with a graveyard, **Cille Mhic Eoghainn**.

On the south coast at Caisteal Beag there are 10m-high **basalt columns**, suitable for difficult rock climbing.

The Boathouse Visitor Centre (☎ 500264) has displays about the history of the island; it's open Easter to October on weekdays from 9 am to 5 pm, and Sunday from June to August (£2.50/1.50). Its tearoom serves oysters with Guinness along with the more usual soup, toasties and filled rolls.

ISLE OF COLL

- **pop 172**   ☎ 01879

This lovely island, about 12 miles long and 3 miles wide, has a good sunshine record but can be very windy. On the western coast, the wind has formed sand dunes up to 30m high. Crossapol beach is one of the best spots on Coll. At the **Totronald RSPB reserve** (☎ 230301), in the far south-west of the island, there's a free information centre (open year-round); listen for the corncrakes on the machair. Two nearby castles, both known as **Breacachadh Castle**, were built by the Macleans. There was a clan battle here in 1593.

Coll Stores and the Corner Shop sell groceries; both are in the island's village, **Arinagour**, where the ferry docks. There's also a post office, and Coll Ceramics – pottery with art exhibitions.

Near the castles, and 4½ miles from Arinagour, *Garden House* (☎ 230374), Castle Gardens, offers B&B from £17 per person, plus £12 for the evening meal. It also runs the *camp site* (☎ 230374), with a nightly charge from £5 per tent. Phone to arrange pick-up from the pier.

The *Isle of Coll Hotel* (☎ 230334), Arinagour, has singles/doubles from £25/50 to £40/60 and a really good restaurant serving lobster (£15) and scallops, the local specialities. Bar meals cost from £4 to £12.50, and a set dinner is £25. For light meals and snacks, try the *Corner Café*.

CalMac ferries (☎ 230347) run daily, except Thursday and Sunday, to/from Tiree (one hour; £2.60, £15.35 for a car) and Oban (from 2½ hours; £10.50, £59 for a car). Sailings to Tobermory hopefully will resume in the future.

Mountain bikes can be hired in Arinagour from Tammie Hedderwick (☎ 230382), Coll Ceramics, for £7.50 per day.

ISLE OF TIREE

- **pop 768**   ☎ 01879

A low-lying island with some beautiful sandy beaches, Tiree has one of the best sunshine records in Britain, particularly during the early months of summer. It can also get breezy, which makes it an excellent location for windsurfing – there are annual competitions in October. Contact the windsurfing school (☎ 220399) for details about its courses and events.

There's a bank (without ATM), post office and Co-op store in Scarinish. Crossapol also has a shop. For the island's doctor, call ☎ 220323.

For the best view, walk up to Ben Hynish (141m, 462 feet), about 6 miles from Scarinish. It's got a radar installation on the top.

If you want to camp, make sure you get the landowner's permission first. *Mrs Cameron's (☎ 220503, The Shieling)*, Crossapol, 3 miles from Scarinish, does B&B for £16 per person. *Scarinish Hotel (☎ 220308)* is on the harbour and has rooms with bath for £25/46. Bar meals range from £4.50 to £20.

From Tiree airport (☎ 220309) you can fly to Glasgow with British Airways Express daily, except Sunday (from £97 return). CalMac ferries are as for Coll (see Isle of Coll earlier in this chapter). For car hire, contact MacLennan Motors (☎ 220555); for a taxi, call ☎ 220344. Bikes are available from Mr MacLean (☎ 220428). The postbus (☎ 220301) does daily runs (except Sunday), including an airport service.

Small Isles

The Small Isles consist of Muck, Eigg, Rum and Canna. Lying between the Ardnamurchan peninsula and the Isle of Skye, they are reached by ferry from Arisaig or Mallaig. Muck is flat and has great beaches. The tempestuous Isle of Eigg, with a notorious clan history and unfortunate recent disputes, at last seems to be settling down. Rum is a nature reserve, entirely owned by SNH, and the jewel of the Inner Hebrides – peaks soar to over 750m (2460 feet) and the glens are noted for their wildlife. Canna is owned by the NTS; it's an intriguing place, with interesting archaeology and a magnetic hill.

GETTING THERE & AWAY

The main ferry operator is CalMac (☎ 01687-462403). It sails various routes around the islands daily, except Sunday. To land on Rum (Monday, Wednesday and Saturday), you have to transfer to a lighter boat. Single fares to Muck/Eigg/Rum/Canna are £4.30/6.65/6.50/7.45.

Arisaig Marine (☎ 01687-450224) sails from Arisaig from May to September, with six runs per week to Eigg (£13 return), up to four per week to Rum (£17 return), and three per week to Muck (£13 return). The trip includes whale watching, with up to 15 minutes for close viewing.

Sailing times range from one to four hours.

ISLE OF MUCK

• **pop 24**   ☎ **01687**

Muck is tiny, measuring only 2 miles by a mile, but it's got a lot to offer. Walk to the top of **Beinn Airein** (137m, 449 feet) for the best views. There are corncrakes, a puffin colony, good beaches, and porpoises in the bays. The tearoom/craftshop, situated in a blackhouse-style building, does great snacks and sells fresh bread. You can ask here for permission to camp.

B&B and evening meal is available at *Port Mhor Guesthouse (☎ 462365)* for £33 per person, without bath. The three-course dinners here are recommended and they're available to nonresidents for £14 (reserve at least two hours in advance).

ISLE OF EIGG

• **pop 69**   ☎ **01687**

This small but distinctive island is dominated by the **Sgurr of Eigg**, a 393m-high (1289 feet) basalt peak with three vertical sides. It can be climbed easily by its western ridge. Eigg has two villages, Cleadale in the north and **Galmisdale** in the south. Ferries call at Galmisdale, where there's a post office, shop, and café for snacks, all by the pier.

There are several caves around the coast including **Uamh Fraing**, only half a mile from Galmisdale pier, where nearly 400

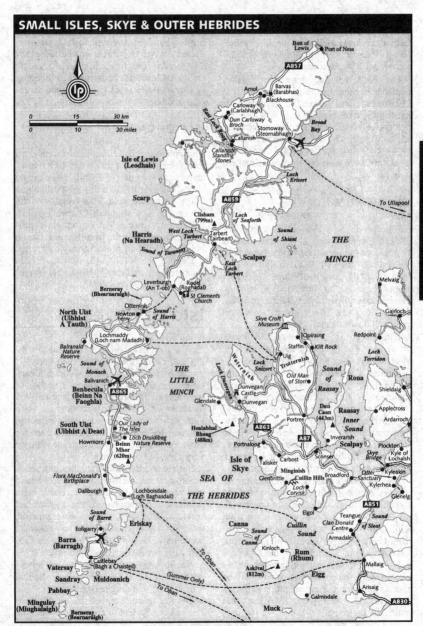

SMALL ISLES, SKYE & OUTER HEBRIDES

MacDonalds were killed by MacLeods from Skye in 1577. Located nearby, there's **Cathedral Cave**, used after the 1745 rebellion for banned Catholic services, and still occasionally in use today.

For B&B, try **Lageorna** (☎ 482405), with singles from £14 to £17, doubles from £12 to £15, and dinner for around £15. Room-only rates are £10 to £12. It also has two six-bed self-catering cottages for £180 to £380 per week. **Kildonan House** (☎ 482446) is similar for B&B – its evening meals are excellent, but you must make a reservation.

ISLE OF RUM
- **pop 26**   ☎ 01687

All the people who live on Rum work for SNH; the entire island is a nature reserve. You have to get permission to go there from the reserve office (☎ 462026). For various reasons, SNH puts restrictions on travel around the island, but they're not prohibitive. The island is noted for its wildlife, including deer, wild goats, Manx shearwaters, and golden and white-tailed sea eagles.

Kinloch is the main centre and ferries arrive here. The Spar shop has a good range of groceries; there's also a post office.

Kinloch Castle (☎ 462037) is the most extraordinary of the several buildings constructed by the Bullough family, who owned Rum from 1888 to 1957. It's decaying slowly but it's well worth a visit to see the furnishings, and it's even possible to stay here. There's also the **Bullough Mausoleum**, a 'folly' in Glen Harris, which wouldn't look out of place in Athens.

There's some great coastal and mountain scenery on the island, especially at **Guirdil** and **Dibidil**. It takes a couple of hours each way to walk the paths to either place from Kinloch. You can follow the main ridge from Hallival to the island's highest point, **Askival** (812m, 2663 feet) – the route involves rock scrambling and takes about six hours from Kinloch. Strong parties may be able to traverse the entire ridge as far as Sgurr nan Gillean (764m, 2506 feet) and return via the coast.

Camping is only allowed at Kinloch (☎ 462026). It's £1 per person, and a bit basic. There's **hostel and bothy** accommodation (☎ 462026) in various buildings for 26 people (£6 to £7.50). In the **castle** (☎ 462037), hostel beds cost £10 (bedding is extra), B&B is £15, and a good three-course dinner in the bistro is around £12.

ISLE OF CANNA
- **pop 20**   ☎ 01687

This pleasant little roadless island can easily be explored in a day. The ferry arrives at the hamlet of **A'Chill**. There are no shops, but you'll find a tiny post office in a hut, a **Celtic cross**, and the remains of the 7th century **St Columba's Chapel**. Just east of the ferry pier is **An Coroghon**, a jailhouse dating from the Middle Ages. Canna is linked to the adjacent Sanday by bridge.

Contact the NTS warden on ☎ 462466 for permission to camp. Indoor accommodation may also be available.

Isle of Skye

- **pop 8847**

Skye is a rugged, convoluted island stretching about 50 miles from end to end. It's ringed by beautiful coastline and dominated by the Cuillin, immensely popular for the sport of Munro bagging. Tourism is a mainstay of the island economy, so until you get off the main roads, don't expect to escape the hordes. Come prepared for changeable weather; when it's nice it's very very nice, but often it isn't!

Portree and Broadford are the main population centres. Getting around the island midweek is fairly straightforward, with postbuses supplementing the normal bus services. But here, as in the Highlands, transport dwindles to nothing at weekends, particularly in winter and even more dramatically (so it seems) when it rains.

Gaelic is spoken by half of Skye's residents and there's a Gaelic college, Sabhal Mòr Ostaig, at Teangue (An Teanga).

Despite the closing of the old Kyle of Lochalsh to Kyleakin ferry route when the

Skye Bridge opened in 1995, there are still two ways to travel over the sea to Skye – Mallaig to Armadale and Glenelg to Kylerhea (the latter in summer only). See Armadale and Kylerhea later in this section.

WALKS

Skye is one of the best places in Scotland for walking. There are many detailed guidebooks available. For the Cuillin Ridge, the best is *Black Cuillin Ridge – a scrambler's guide*, by SP Bull (Scottish Mountaineering Trust). You must obtain Ordnance Survey maps Nos 23 and 32 to appreciate the following routes. Don't attempt the longer walks without proper experience and avoid these routes in winter or in bad weather.

Easy low-level routes include Torrin to Luib (two hours); Sligachan to Kilmarie, via Camasunary (four hours); and Portnalong to Talisker, via Fiskavaig (four hours return).

Harder walks, but still on good paths, are: Kilmarie to Coruisk via the 'Bad Step', an exposed section of scrambling (at least four hours return); Glenbrittle camp site to Coire Lagan, a greatly improved path (at least three hours return); and The Quiraing, from the high point on the Staffin to Uig road – you'll need at least three hours to appreciate the pinnacles around The Table.

Longer walks include: from Orbost (3 miles south of Dunvegan) to MacLeod's Maidens, Glen Ollisdal, returning via Healabhal Bheag (488m, 1601 feet) – seven hours; Glenbrittle camp site to Coire Lagan and Sgurr Alasdair by the Great Stone Chute, with some airy scrambling near the summit – five to six hours; and Glenbrittle camp site to Coir' a'Ghrunnda and Sgurr Dubh Mór – six to seven hours of hard walking, with wet terrain and some difficult rock scrambling near the top.

ORGANISED TOURS

One of the best ways to see Skye is with Ted Badger Tours (☎ 01599-534169). His six-hour minibus tours around the island are very entertaining and cost £15 per person. You can book at the Kyleakin SYHA hostel.

PORTREE (PORT RIGH)
• pop 2561   ☎ 01478

Port Righ is Gaelic for King's Harbour, named after James V called here in 1540 to pacify local clan chieftains. Portree is Skye's biggest settlement with most of the facilities like banks with ATMs, petrol stations, and a post office with foreign exchange facilities.

There are also two supermarkets, including a large Co-op off Dunvegan Rd.

The harbour's very pretty and there are great views of the surrounding hills.

The TIC (☎ 612137), just off the central Somerled Square, is open all year, including Sunday from late May to mid-October. The hospital can be reached on ☎ 613200.

The annual Isle of Skye Highland Games, a one day event, are held in Portree in early August.

Things to See & Do

On the southern edge of Portree, the **Aros Experience** (☎ 613649) offers a lively introduction to Skye life. It's open daily from 9 am to 6 pm (11 pm in summer) and has a good restaurant. Admission is £3.50/2.50. Brigadoon Boat Trips (☎ 613718) runs **wildlife tours** three times daily out to the Sound of Raasay. Porpoises, seals and eagles are commonly seen, and you can explore sea caves in the boat. Charges are £9/4.50 for two hours. Fishing trips can also be arranged.

Places to Stay

Camping The *Torvaig Camping Site* (☎ 612209) is on the edge of town on the Staffin road. It charges £3 per person for camping.

Hostels *Portree Harbour Backpackers* (☎ 613332) is a basic backpacker's hostel on waterfront Douglas Row with beds for £7.50. Alternatively, there's *Portree Independent Hostel* (☎ 613737), in the old post office near Somerled Square (£8.50 per night), and *Portree Backpackers Hostel* (☎ 613641, *Dunvegan Rd*) which charges from £7.50 per night.

B&Bs & Hotels Portree is packed with B&Bs: try friendly *Benlee* (☎ 612664, *Bosville Terrace*) overlooking the harbour, with beds for £16; or *Coolin View (Bosville Terrace)* from £18 to £30 per bed. *Braeside* (☎ 612613, *Stormyhill Rd*) is another friendly place with beds from £14 to £18 per person. *Easdale* (☎ 613244, *Bridge Rd*) is similar. *Glendale* (☎ 613149, *2 Carn Dearg Place*) and *Oronsay* (☎ 612192, *1 Marsco Place*) are farther from the harbour. Both have some *en suite* rooms, and prices range from £18 to £23 per person.

Portree hotels include the *Tongadale* (☎ 612115, *Wentworth St*) with rooms from £20 to £30 per person. On Somerled Square, the friendly *Isles Hotel* (☎ 612129) costs from £24 to £35 per person, while the *Portree Hotel* (☎ 612511) is slightly pricier. The *Rosedale Hotel* (☎ 613131), right on the waterfront but only open May to October, costs from £35 to £45 per person.

Places to Eat

The *Granary Bakery (Somerled Square)* sells fresh bread and pastries. Its coffee shop serves snacks. The *Caledonian Hotel* (☎ 612641) is popular with locals and does bar meals for £2.50 to £7. It also has live music Tuesday to Sunday. The adjacent café is open from breakfast time; its snacks cost under £2. The *Bayfield Chip Shop* does good takeaway fish and chips for £2.75. The *Harbour View Seafood Restaurant* (☎ 612069, *Bosville Terrace*) is reasonable. There's pub food from £5.50 at the *Portree* or *Tongadale* hotels. You can even sample curry at the *Gandhi Indian Restaurant* (☎ 612681, *Bayfield Rd*). The excellent *Ben Tianavaig Bistro* (☎ 612152, *5 Bosville Terrace*) has an extensive vegetarian menu. Seafood kebabs cost £7.95.

The best places to eat in Portree are the *Bosville Hotel* (☎ 612846, *Bosville Terrace*) and *Portree House* (☎ 613713, *Home Farm Rd*). They both do bar meals for around £7 to £12. A three-course meal in the *Chandlery Seafood Restaurant* at the Bosville Hotel will cost around £23.

The *An Tuireann Art Centre Café* (☎ 613306) is out of town on the Struan road (B885). It caters for vegetarians and vegans and opens until 8 pm (5 pm Sunday and in winter). It also hosts contemporary art exhibitions.

The *Pier Hotel* is a popular waterfront drinking spot while the *Isles Hotel* features a Jacobean-theme bar with a flagstone floor and real fires.

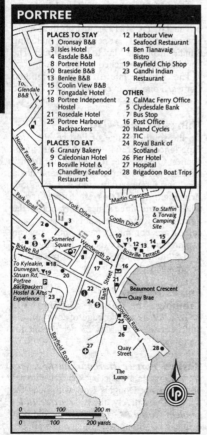

PORTREE

PLACES TO STAY
1 Oronsay B&B
3 Isles Hotel
4 Easdale B&B
8 Portree Hotel
10 Braeside B&B
13 Benlee B&B
15 Coolin View B&B
17 Tongadale Hotel
18 Portree Independent Hostel
21 Rosedale Hotel
25 Portree Harbour Backpackers

PLACES TO EAT
6 Granary Bakery
9 Caledonian Hotel
11 Bosville Hotel & Chandlery Seafood Restaurant
12 Harbour View Seafood Restaurant
14 Ben Tianavaig Bistro
19 Bayfield Chip Shop
23 Gandhi Indian Restaurant

OTHER
2 CalMac Ferry Office
5 Clydesdale Bank
7 Bus Stop
16 Post Office
20 Island Cycles
22 TIC
24 Royal Bank of Scotland
26 Pier Hotel
27 Hospital
28 Brigadoon Boat Trips

To Glendale B&B

To Staffin & Torvaig Camping Site

Martin Crescent
Coolin Drive
Park Road
York Drive
Somerled Square
Bridge Rd
Wentworth St
Bosville Terrace
To Kyleakin, Dunvegan, Struan Rd, Portree Backpackers Hostel & Aros Experience
Bank Street
Beaumont Crescent
Quay Brae
Douglas Row
Quay Street
Bayfield Road
The Lump

0   100   200 m
0   100   200 yards

Getting There & Away

Somerled Square is the Portree bus stop. Scottish Citylink (☎ 0990-505050) operates a Glasgow-Fort William-Kyle-Kyleakin-Portree-Uig route, three times daily in summer, taking three hours from Fort William to Portree (£12). It also runs the Inverness to Portree service three times daily Monday to Saturday, but only twice on Sunday (three hours; £10.50).

Getting Around

Bikes can be hired at Island Cycles (☎ 613121) for £7.50/12 for a half/full day.

KYLEAKIN (CAOL ACAIN)
• ☎ 01599

Even more than for Kyle of Lochalsh on the mainland, Kyleakin has had the carpet pulled from under it by the opening of the Skye Bridge. It's a pleasant wee place, but it's turning into backpacker city – there are four hostels and even a backpacker's pub.

The SYHA *Youth Hostel* (☎ 534585) charges £8.60/7.10 a night (£1 more in July and August) and is just doors away from friendly *Skye Backpackers* (☎ 534510) where beds cost £7 to £8.90. On the other side of the SYHA, there's the new *Corran Hostel* (☎ 534030), with dorm beds for £9. It has a laundry and kitchen; breakfast is available for £2. Near the old ferry quay, there's *Dun Caan Independent Hostel* (☎ 534087) which costs £8.50 per night. It hires bikes for £5/30 per day/week.

The *Pier Coffee House* on the waterfront does snacks and meals for 90p to £5.25. In the backpacker's pub, *Saucy Mary's*, you'll get main courses for £4 to £5.25. The best place to eat is the bright and airy *Crofter's Kitchen* (☎ 534134), where a three-course meal will cost from £10.

Castle Moil Seal Cruises (☎ 544235) charges £5.50/2.50 for its 1¼-hour cruises to see a seal colony on Eilean Mahl.

KYLERHEA (CAOL REITHE)

Kylerhea is about 4 miles south-east of Kyleakin and there's a car ferry from there to Glenelg on the mainland. Before crossing

to Glenelg, you can follow a 1½ hour nature trail offering the chance to see otters from a shoreline hide (☎ 01320-366581); entry is free. Even if the otters elude you, you should still see basking seals and assorted birds.

The ferry (☎ 01599-511302), for six cars, operates from April to mid-May, Monday to Saturday from 9 am to 6 pm; mid-May to August daily from 9 am to 8 pm (Sunday 10 am to 6 pm); and September and October daily from 9 am to 6 pm (Sunday first ferry at 10 am). Car and four passengers £5.50; foot passenger 60p; bicycle 40p.

ARMADALE (ARMADAL)
• ☎ 01471

It's still possible to arrive on Skye by boat from Mallaig. If you do that you'll wind up in Armadale, where there's a foodstore, post office, and hostel.

CalMac (☎ 01678-462403) runs the ferries (30 minutes; passengers £2.50, cars from £14.45), but cars are only taken during March to October.

If you visit the **Clan Donald Centre** (☎ 844305), in a restored part of ruined Armadale Castle, a guided tour will tell you all you ever wanted to know about the MacDonald clan. Family research facilities are available. It's open Easter to November, daily from 9.30 am to 5.30 pm (£3.50/2.50). There's a pleasant restaurant serving homemade soup and snacks for under £2.

It's just 350m from the Armadale ferry terminal to the SYHA *Youth Hostel* (☎ 844260), which is open from Easter to September and costs £6.10/4.95. At Kilmore (A'Chille Mhór), 3 miles from the ferry, there's the *Sleat Independent Hostel* (☎ 844440) which charges £7. Another mile along the road at Teangue is the *Hairy Coo Backpacker Hotel* (☎ 833231), a big, basic place with dorm beds for £8.50.

Try the *Galley* (☎ 844252) at Armadale pier for lunchtime snacks, and evening seafood and vegetarian dinners. *Hotel Eilean Armain* (☎ 833332), 8 miles from the ferry towards Broadford, does B&B for

£67.50/90 a single/double. The bar and restaurant meals are good.

Highland Country Buses (☎ 01478-612622) and Waterloo Bus Service (☎ 822630) do several runs on weekdays to Broadford, Kyleakin or Portree. You can hire a bike from the Ferry Filling Station (☎ 844249) for £6/30 per day/week.

BROADFORD (AN T-ATH LEATHANN)
• ☎ 01471

The TIC (☎ 822361) is by the large Esso petrol station. There's a new Co-op supermarket nearby. Also in the village there's a bank (with ATM) as well as a hospital (☎ 822491). The Esso station does free Gaelic car stickers with the legend 'cuir tigear na do thanc' – not difficult to translate! In the Serpentarium (☎ 822209) you can see and touch all sorts of snakes, some of them illegally imported, impounded by Customs and given refuge here. It's open Easter to October, Monday to Saturday from 10 am to 5 pm, and Sunday in July and August (£2.25/1.25).

The *Youth Hostel (☎ 822442)* is open all year, except January, and charges £7.75/6.50. The eight bed *Fossil Bothy* hostel *(☎ 822644, or ☎ 822297 evenings and weekends)*, at nearby Lower Breakish (Breacais), charges £7 a head. Friendly *Millbrae (☎ 822533)* does B&B for £13 to £18 per head, with shared bathroom. *Fairwinds (☎ 822270)* is a pleasant B&B by the Elgol road with rooms for £20 per person. The *Claymore (☎ 822333)* does good bar meals, with soup for £1.55 and main courses for £5 to £6.75. In Breakish, the *Seagull Restaurant (☎ 822001)* does excellent three-course meals for around £11.50 to £15.

Daily Citylink buses run to Portree, Inverness and Fort William. You can hire a mountain bike from Fairwinds Cycle Hire (☎ 822270) for £7 per day or rent a car from Skye Car Rental (☎ 822225).

ELGOL (EALAGHOL)

On a clear day, Elgol may well be the most scenic place on Skye, and the superb view from the pier towards **Loch Coruisk**, in the heart of the Cuillin, presents a magnificent scene.

A great way to appreciate the Cuillin and Loch Coruisk is on an organised boat trip. The *Bella Jane* (☎ 0800-7313089) costs from £12.50 return, and the *Nicola* (☎ 01471-866236) has similar fares. You sail into **Loch na Cuilce**, an impressive place with acres of rock-slab, and clamber ashore (on a calm day). You might see seals, otters and porpoises here. A short walk from the boat takes you to Loch Coruisk, connected to the sea by the River Scavaig.

Coruisk Guesthouse (☎ 01471-866330) in Elgol does B&B for £17.50 per person. The tearoom and seafood restaurant is highly recommended; during the day, snacks and meals are £2.75 to £6, and most evening main courses are £6 to £10. *Ach a'Chleat (☎ 01471-866235)* does B&B for £15 per head.

Postbuses run from Broadford to Elgol in the morning (Monday to Saturday) and afternoon (Monday to Friday), but you have to stay overnight in Elgol to do a boat trip.

THE CUILLINS & MINGINISH PENINSULA
• ☎ 01478

The rocky Cuillin Hills, west of Broadford, provide spectacular walking and climbing country. The complete traverse of the Black Cuillin ridge usually requires two days and involves real rock climbing; make sure you're properly equipped. The 986m (3234 feet) summit of the **Inaccessible Pinnacle** is a spectacular but not too difficult rock climb and abseil. **Sgurr Alasdair** at 993m (3257 feet) is the highest point and only involves a little scrambling. (See Walks earlier in this section for details.)

The camping ground at **Sligachan** (Sligeachan, ☎ 650333) is a popular jumping-off point for Cuillin climbers (£4 per head). The comfortable *Sligachan Hotel (☎ 650204)* has rooms from £20 to £40 per person. The bar serves real ales, and main courses cost around £6. The restaurant does three-course seafood dinners for £18.95.

In **Carbost** (Carbost), there's a store, a post office, and the Talisker Distillery (☎ 640314), open weekdays, and Saturday from July to September (£3). There are two hostels in **Portnalong** (Port nan Long), about 3 miles from Carbost: *Croft Bunkhouse (☎ 640254)* charges £6.50 to £8 (less for campers) and does bike hire for £7.50 per day. The *Skyewalker Independent Hostel (☎ 640250)* is at the Old School in Fiskavaig Rd and costs £7. Cheap but good bar meals are available close to the hostels at the *Taigh Ailean Hotel (☎ 640271)*, with snacks from £1 and all main courses under £6. There's also the *Old Inn (☎ 640205)*, Carbost, which is a favourite with walkers and climbers from Glenbrittle (Gleann Bhreatail), where a chickwich (really!) costs £1.80 and basket meals and specials are all under £7.

Talisker (Talasgair) is a magnificent place, with a sandy beach, sea stack and waterfall. There are two guest houses: *Talisker House (☎ 640245)*, in a magnificent whitewashed building with four-poster beds, charges from £42 per person B&B, and dinner is £22; *Bay View (☎ 640244)*, at the end of the public road, has rooms from £18. It serves seafood all day, and a three-course meal costs from £13.

The road to **Glenbrittle** (Gleann Bhreatail) gives great views of the central Cuillin. In the glen, most people head for the SYHA *Youth Hostel (☎ 640278)*. The hostel has a friendly manager and beds cost £6.10/4.95. There's also a camp site (☎ 521206) and shop down by the sea, but the midges can be diabolical. It's only £3.50 per person, including shower. Cars cost £1.75 extra.

Nicholson Bus Service (☎ 01470-532240) does weekday runs from Portree to Portnalong via Sligachan. Hitching to Glenbrittle can be slow, especially late in the day, so be prepared to walk.

NORTH-WEST SKYE

On the west side of the Waternish Peninsula, magnificent **Dunvegan Castle**, at Dunvegan (Dùn Bheagain), dates back to the 13th century although it was restored in romantic style in the mid-19th century. Inside you can see the dining room (with beautiful silver on display), lounge, a decidedly alarming dungeon and, right next door, an excellent drawing room with the famous Fairy Flag. The castle (☎ 01470-521206) is open daily from 10 am to 5.30 pm (from 11 am to 4 pm in winter); £5/4.50. It also runs daily loch and seal cruises for £8/6 and £3.80/2.50 respectively.

There are several other museums in the area, including the **Glendale Toy Museum** (☎ 01470-511240), admission £2, and the **Colbost Croft Museum** (☎ 01470-521296), about half way from Dunvegan to Glendale (Gleann Dàil), in a 19th century blackhouse (£1/80p).

See Walks earlier in this section for details of the excellent walks in the area. It's also worth taking a drive beyond Glendale, out to Waterstein, for great views of **Neist lighthouse**, **Waterstein Head**, and the Outer Hebrides.

The castle has the pleasant *MacLeod's Table Bistro (☎ 01470-521310)* for snacks and meals.

Of several possible places to stay, *Roskhill Guest House (☎ 01470-521317)* has beds from £24.50; and the *Tables Hotel (☎ 01470-521404)*, a mile from the castle, has beds from £25 and dinner from £14.

Monday to Friday, you can get to Dunvegan by Skyeways Travel (☎ 01599-534328) bus from Portree, leaving at 10 am and returning from the castle at 12.52 pm (you get two hours at the castle).

TROTTERNISH PENINSULA

North of Portree, Skye's coastal scenery is at its finest in the Trotternish Peninsula. Look out in particular for the rocky spike of the **Old Man of Storr**, the spectacular **Kilt Rock** and the ruins of **Duntulm Castle**. Near Staffin (Stamhain), the spectacular **Quiraing** also offers dramatic hill walking.

At the north end of the peninsula at Kilmuir (Cille Mhoire), the **Skye Museum of Island Life** (☎ 01470-552206) recreates crofting life in a series of cottages overlooking marvellous scenery. It's open April

THE HEBRIDES

to October, Monday to Saturday, from 9.30 am to 5.30 pm; £1.50/1.

The biggest settlement is **Staffin**, where you can stop for lunch or a drink at the *Oystercatcher (☎ 01470-562384)* except on Sunday. Three miles south of Staffin, at Culnaknock (Cùl nan Cnoc), the *Glenview Inn (☎ 01470-562248)* does B&B from £25 to £35 per person; the three-course dinners are recommended and cost around £13.

Three miles north of Staffin, in tiny **Flodigarry** (Flodaigearraidh), you can stay at the historic *Flodigarry Country House Hotel (☎ 01470-552203)*, with singles from £49 to £55 and doubles from £98 to £170. Meals here are also expensive. The home of Highland heroine **Flora MacDonald** is now part of the hotel, and her grave at Kilmuir indicates that she was a real victim of tourism – the 1955 memorial states, of the original memorial, that 'every fragment has been removed by tourists'.

The *Dun Flodigarry Hostel (☎ 01470-552212)* is much cheaper at £7.50 a head. For B&B, try *Achtalean (☎ 01470-562723)* in Stenscholl (Steinnseal) where rooms cost from £14 to £17 per person.

Skyeways Travel (☎ 01599-534328) run a weekday bus service from Portree to Flodigarry.

UIG (UIGE)

From Uig pier, CalMac has services every day to Lochmaddy on North Uist (1¾ hours; passengers £7.85, cars from £37) and from Monday to Saturday to Tarbert on Harris (same times and prices). Uig has good Scottish Citylink (☎ 0990-505050) bus connections with Portree, Inverness, Fort William and Glasgow. There's a TIC (☎ 01470-542404) in the terminal building; it's open Easter to October, including Sunday in July and August.

Flora MacDonald

The Isle of Skye was home to Flora MacDonald, who became famous for helping Bonnie Prince Charlie escape his defeat at the Battle of Culloden.

Flora was born in 1722 at Milton in South Uist and a memorial cairn marks the site of one of her early childhood homes. After her mother's abduction by Hugh MacDonald of Skye, Flora was reared by her brother and educated in the home of the Clanranald chiefs.

In 1746, she helped Bonnie Prince Charlie escape from Benbecula to Skye disguised as her Irish servant. With a price on the Prince's head, their little boat was fired on, but they managed to land safely and Flora escorted the Prince to Portree where he gave her a gold locket containing his portrait before setting sail for Raasay.

Waylaid on the way home, the boatmen admitted everything. Flora was arrested and imprisoned in the Tower of London. She never saw or heard from the Prince again.

In 1747, she returned home, marrying Allan MacDonald of Skye and going on to have nine children. Dr Johnson stayed with her in 1773 during his journey round the Western Isles, but later poverty forced her family to emigrate to North Carolina. There her husband was captured by rebels. Flora returned to Kingsburgh on Skye where she died in 1790 and was buried in Kilmuir churchyard, wrapped in the sheet in which both Bonnie Prince Charlie and Dr Johnson had slept.

Uig has a *Youth Hostel* (☎ *01470-542211)*, which is open from late March to October and costs £6.10/4.95. There's a cluster of bungalow B&Bs with beds for around £15.

The *Old Ferry Inn* (☎ *542242)* is pricier at £25 a head, the *Uig Hotel* (☎ *542205)* pricier still at £35 to £55, but both have fine positions overlooking the bay.

There's a shop and post office in the village. Both hotels do bar meals and there are three other places down by the pier. Fish and chips at the *Norseman Café* costs £2.95; meals at the *Pub at the Pier* and the *Uig Bay Bistro*, including their vegetarian dishes, are around £4 to £7.

ISLE OF RAASAY
- **pop 163**   ☎ **01478**

This long, narrow and very quiet island is reached by CalMac ferry from Sconser, between Portree and Broadford. In summer, the ferry operates up to 10 times daily, Monday to Saturday only (£2/8.45, passenger/car). There's no petrol on Raasay, but there is a traditional store and post office at **Inverarish**. Things to see include **Dùn Borodale** broch, by the village, and the extraordinary ruin of **Brochel Castle**, at the north end.

There are several good walks, including one to the flat-topped hill, Dun Caan (443m, 1453 feet), and also around the remote north end, but you have to cover 10 miles of road first – there's no bus here. Forest Enterprise publishes a free leaflet with suggested walks and forest trails.

To camp at the *Raasay Outdoor Centre* (☎ *660266)* costs from £4. There are bikes available for hire and its restaurant is quite good, with main meals for around £6. Outdoor activity courses here cost up to £35 per day. *Raasay Youth Hostel* (☎ *01478-660240)* is open from late March to October and costs £4.65/3.85. *Mrs Mackay* (☎ *660207, 6 Osgaig Park)* charges £14.50 per person for B&B. The *Isle of Raasay Hotel* (☎ *660222)* has a dinner, B&B rate of £40 to £50 per person. The bar meals are reasonable.

Outer Hebrides

Synonymous with remoteness, the Outer Hebrides (Western Isles) are a string of islands running in a 130 mile arc from north to south, shielding the north-western coast of Scotland. Bleak, isolated, treeless and exposed to gales that sweep in from the Atlantic, the Outer Hebrides are irresistibly romantic. They form one of Europe's most isolated frontiers and have a fascinating history, signposted by Neolithic standing stones, Viking place names, empty crofts and folk memories of the Clearances.

Immediate reality can be disappointing, however. The towns are straggly, unattractive and dominated by stern, austere churches. Although the ruins of traditional blackhouses can still be seen, they've been supplanted by unattractive (though no doubt more comfortable) concrete block bungalows. Rugged and apparently inhospitable though the islands are, they support a surprisingly large and widely distributed population and in summer the CalMac ferries disgorge a daily cargo of tourists.

The landscapes can be mournful, but they're also spectacular, with wide horizons of sky and water, dazzling white beaches, azure bays, wide peat moors, and countless lochs, mountains and stony hills. These are islands that reward an extended stay, especially if you travel on foot or by bike; a rushed tour will be less satisfying, and when driving you have to pay too much attention to the road (often single tracked and sheep-ridden) to appreciate the views.

The local culture is not very accessible to outsiders, but it is distinctive. Of the 18,000 crofts registered in Scotland, 6000 are on the Outer Hebrides. Of the 66,000 Scottish Gaelic speakers, around 25,000 live on the islands. Religion still plays a central role in island life, especially in the Protestant north, where the Sunday Sabbath is strictly observed – even the swings in Stornoway's playground are padlocked.

These are deeply conservative parts where a Scot from Glasgow is as much an incomer as someone from London. But the

EU is working to reduce the islands' isolation and many roads are being upgraded courtesy of loans from the European Regional Development Fund.

Life moves very slowly here, with supplies dependent on boats and planes. Often newspapers and bread are unavailable before 10 am. Bad weather can cause supplies to dry up altogether. Accommodation is in fairly short supply; book ahead in summer.

HISTORY
The first evidence of settlement dates back to around 4000 BC, when Stone Age farmers settled the islands.

They constructed massive stone tombs and the mounds can still be seen (as at Bharpa Langass, North Uist). Bronze Age Beaker People (named after their distinctive pottery) arrived around 1800 BC, and about this time groups of standing stones were set up, most notably at Callanish on Lewis.

Around 1000 BC, the climate deteriorated and the peat that now blankets much of the islands (in places to depths of 6m) began to accumulate.

Acidity increases when soil becomes permanently waterlogged, creating a sterile environment where bacterial activity slows, and where the dead grass, sedge, heather and moss build up in layers instead of rotting.

This spongy, nutrient-poor environment was no good for farming, and the population was forced onto the coastal fringe. When cut and dried, however, the peat provided the islanders with fuel. Every spring, families still cut it into bricks, which are wind dried in neat piles before being stacked outside homes.

The Iron Age, Gaelic-speaking Celts arrived around 500 BC and several defensive brochs remain from this period, the most impressive at Carloway on Lewis.

The Wee Frees & Other Island Creeds

Religion plays a complex and important role in island life, and priests and ministers enjoy powerful positions in the community. The split between the Protestants to the north of Benbecula and the Catholics to the south creates, or perhaps reflects, a different communal atmosphere.

Hebridean Protestants have developed a distinctive fundamentalist approach, with Sunday being devoted to religious services, prayer and Bible reading. On Lewis and Harris, virtually everything closes down. In general, social life is restricted to private homes and, as public drinking is frowned upon, pubs are mostly uninspiring.

The Protestants are further divided into three main sects with convoluted, emotionally charged histories. The Church of Scotland, the main Scottish church, is state-recognised or 'established'. The Free Presbyterian Church of Scotland and the Free Church of Scotland (or Wee Frees) are far more conservative and intolerant, permitting no ornaments, organ music or choirs. Their ministers deliver uncompromising sermons (usually in Gaelic) from central pulpits, and *precentors* lead the congregation in unaccompanied, but fervent psalm singing. Visitors are welcome to attend services, but due respect is essential.

The most recent split occurred in 1988 when Lord Mackay, Lord Chancellor and a prominent Free Presbyterian, committed the awful crime of attending a friend's Catholic requiem mass. The church elders threatened him with expulsion, and he and his supporters responded by establishing the breakaway Associated Presbyterian Church!

The Catholic Church south of Benbecula survived the Reformation. The priests were expelled early in the 17th century but, despite several missionary attempts, Protestantism failed to take hold. The Sunday Sabbath on South Uist and Barra is more easy-going, and the attitude towards the 'demon drink' more relaxed.

Vikings settled in the islands by 850, and many island clans, including the Morrisons, Nicolsons, MacAulays and MacLeods, are thought to have Norse backgrounds. The traditional island houses, the blackhouses that remained in common use into the 1930s, were essentially Viking longhouses. The Middle Ages saw a new influx of Gaelic-speaking Celts from Scotland and Ireland, and a weakening of the links to Norway, resulting in a Gaelic-speaking Celtic/Norse population.

LANGUAGE

Scottish Gaelic is similar to Irish Gaelic. About 75% of the islanders speak it (as opposed to just 1.5% of the total Scottish population), and recent efforts have ensured its survival. Many Gaelic television and radio programs are now produced.

All islanders speak English, and there's no reluctance to use it when speaking to outsiders. However, some road signs are only in Gaelic, which can cause confusion. When talking to outsiders, islanders use the anglicised version of a name, but this can bear little similarity to the Gaelic on the signs. The CalMac ferry company and the airlines also use anglicised names. One of the first purchases a visitor should make is a bilingual road map showing both names; Estate Publication's red covered *Official Tourist Map – Western Isles* (£3.75) is ideal.

This book uses English names where they are in common usage while the Gaelic name are given in brackets at the first main reference. See Scottish Gaelic in the Language chapter at the back of this book.

ORIENTATION & INFORMATION

Lewis and Harris are actually one island with a border of high hills between them. The northern half of Lewis is low and flat with miles of peat moors; southern Lewis and Harris are rugged, with some impressive stony mountains and glorious beaches. North Uist, Benbecula and South Uist are joined by bridges and causeways. Mostly these islands are low, flat, and green, half drowned by sinuous lochs and open to the sea and sky. Benbecula has a large army and air force base.

There are several TICs – one in every ferry port, open late for ferry arrivals up to midnight from April to mid-October.

The main Western Isles Tourist Board (☎ 01851-703088), 26 Cromwell St, Stornoway, PA87 2DD, produces a brochure which shows all accommodation possibilities, from hotels to B&Bs and self-catering cottages. *The Outer Hebrides Handbook & Guide* (Kittiwake, £7.95), written by local experts, gives lots of data on the islands' history, culture, flora and fauna.

ACCOMMODATION & FOOD

Camping grounds with facilities are scarce, but free camping is usually allowed, provided you get permission from the nearest house and remove all your rubbish. Some landowners may ask a small fee.

There are a few basic hostels in old crofts scattered around the islands, but most are difficult to get to without transport or a readiness to hike.

Most are run by the SYHA or the Gatliff Hebridean Hostels Trust, 71 Cromwell St, Stornoway, Lewis, PA87 2DG, in association with the SYHA. The Gatliff Trust hostels have bunk beds, blankets, cooking equipment, cold running water and open fires. Bring a sleeping bag and eating utensils. Local crofters look after them, but no advance bookings are accepted and they prefer people not to arrive or depart on a Sunday.

In recent years, several new independent hostels have opened. These tend to be very clean, modern and, consequently, more expensive than the Gatliff Trust or SYHA hostels.

The B&Bs provide opportunities to meet the islanders, who are famous both for their hospitality and the size of their breakfasts. Few offer private bathrooms, but they're usually comfortable and clean and offer hearty dinners as well. Most B&B hosts, especially on Lewis and Harris, appreciate guests booking ahead if they are going to stay on Sunday night.

THE HEBRIDES

A few B&Bs are handy for the ferry ports, but most are scattered around the countryside. The ports themselves are generally uninspiring but always have at least one pub where meals are available. If you do stay in the countryside – which is recommended – check whether there's a convenient pub, make arrangements to eat at your B&B, or take your own provisions to a hostel.

Self-catering cottages must be booked in advance.

Options for eating out centre on the pubs, which are few and far between and not particularly cheap. The picture for vegetarians is improving; most hotels with pubs manage at least one suitable dish.

GETTING THERE & AWAY
Air
British Airways Express (☎ 0345-222111) flies to the islands, and there are airports at Stornoway, on Lewis, and on Benbecula and Barra. The main airport, just 4 miles east of Stornoway, is served by regular British Airways Express flights from Glasgow and Inverness (Monday to Saturday); single/return fares start at £80/99 and £49/58 respectively. The company also has flights to Benbecula and Barra from Glasgow from Monday to Saturday, with additional Sunday flights in peak summer months – see their sections later for fare details. At Barra the planes land on the beach, so the timetable depends on the tides. Buses meet the Barra flights. British Airways Express also links Barra and Benbecula with Stornoway.

Bus
Regular bus services operating to Ullapool, Uig and Oban connect with the ferries and the principal operator is Scottish Citylink (☎ 0990-505050).

Train
Spectacular train services run as far as Oban, Mallaig and Kyle of Lochalsh from Glasgow and Edinburgh. In order to get to Ullapool, take the train to Inverness, then a bus to Ullapool. Phone ☎ 0345-484950 for rail details.

Boat
CalMac runs comfortable car and passenger ferries from Ullapool to Stornoway on Lewis (2½ hours; two or three times daily from Monday to Saturday); from Uig (Skye) to Tarbert on Harris and Lochmaddy on North Uist (around 1¾ hours; once or twice daily, six or seven days a week); and from Mallaig and Oban to Lochboisdale on South Uist and Castlebay on Barra (3¼ to seven hours; almost daily).

The timetables are complicated and, especially during summer, car space can fill up fast. Advance booking is essential, although foot and bicycle passengers should have no problems.

There are eight different Island Hopscotch fares for set routes in the Outer Hebrides, offering worthwhile savings (they're valid for one month). Island Rover Passes give unlimited travel on all CalMac routes for 8 or 15 days; convenient certainly, but make sure you will use enough services to recoup the cost.

For reservations and service details, contact CalMac (☎ 0990-650000 car reservations, ☎ 01475-650100 inquiries), The Ferry Terminal, Gourock, PA19 1QP.

A one-way ticket from Stornoway to Ullapool is £12 per person, plus £54 for a car. From Otternish to Leverburgh it's £4.30/20.20; from Lochboisdale to Castlebay £4.90/27.50; and from Lochboisdale or Castlebay to Oban £17.30/61. For a passenger this totals £38.50, for a car £162.70 – as against £35 and £147 for the equivalent hopscotch ticket. Allow at least a week to tackle this full north-south route. Bikes are carried free with a hopscotch ticket (otherwise, £7 on this routing).

GETTING AROUND
Bus
Bus transport is extremely limited, although a bare bones service allows crofters to get to the shops in the morning and return in the afternoon.

The TICs have up to date timetables and you can contact Stornoway bus station (☎ 01851-704327) for information about Lewis and Harris services. Visitors without their own transport should anticipate a fair amount of hitching and walking.

Car

Most roads are single track but the main hazard is posed by sheep wandering about or sleeping on the road. Petrol stations are far apart, expensive and usually closed on Sunday.

Cars can be hired from around £20 per day from Arnol Motors (☎ 01851-710548), Arnol, Lewis; Mackinnon Self Drive (☎ 01851-702984), 18 Inaclete Rd, Stornoway; Wildon Cameron (☎ 01859-502221), Tarbert, Harris; Maclennan's Self Drive (☎ 01870-602191), Balivanich, Benbecula; Ask Car Hire (☎ 01870-602818), Liniclate, Benbecula; and Laing Motors (☎ 01878-700267), Lochboisdale, South Uist.

Hitching

Hitching is feasible, although traffic is light and virtually stops on Sunday, especially on Harris and Lewis.

The islanders are generally hospitable, and it's definitely safer than around big cities. See also Hitching in the Getting Around chapter.

Bicycle

Cycling from north to south is quite popular but allow at least a week for the trip. The main problems are difficult weather, strong winds (you hear stories of people cycling downhill and freewheeling uphill) and sheep that seem to believe they have the right of way.

Bikes can be hired from Alex Dan's Cycle Centre (☎ 01851-704025), 67 Kenneth St, Stornoway, Lewis; DM Mackenzie (☎ 01859-502271), Pier Rd, Tarbert, Harris; Rothan Cycles (☎ 01870-620283), 9 Howmore, South Uist; and Barra Cycle Hire (☎ 01871-810284), 29 St Brendan's Rd, Castlebay, Barra. Booking is advisable.

LEWIS (LEODHAIS)

The northern half of Lewis (combined population with Harris: 21,737) is low and flat, and dominated by the vast Black Moor, a peat moor dotted with numerous small lochs. The coastal fringes have some arable land and are surprisingly densely populated, if not particularly attractive.

The old blackhouses (named after the soot left on the walls by the burning peat fire in the centre) may have gone, but most holdings are crofts that follow a traditional pattern dating back to medieval times. Most are narrow strips, designed to give everyone an equal share of good and bad land. Usually they run back from the foreshore (with its valuable seaweed), across the machair (the grassy sand dunes that were the best arable land), and back to the peaty grazing land.

Nowadays few crofts are economically viable, so most islanders supplement what they make from the land with other jobs. Many go away to work on oil rigs or ships, and others work in the fishing industry (including fish farming), service industries, or the traditional tweed weaving industry.

South of Stornoway and Barvas, the island is mountainous and beautiful, reminiscent of parts of the mainland's north-west coast. Three of the Outer Hebrides' most important sights – the Arnol Blackhouse, Dun Carloway Broch and Callanish Standing Stones – are also here.

Stornoway (Steornabhagh)
* **pop 6186**   ☎ **01851**

The island's only sizeable town may lie on a beautiful natural harbour, but it's not one of the most pleasant places in Scotland. There's a bit of a drug problem, perhaps because there's so little else to do. For tourists there are reasonable facilities and several things to see.

Stornoway is the Outer Hebrides' administrative and commercial centre, and the base for the Western Isles Council (Comhairle nan Eilan), a hospital and the islands' Gaelic TV and radio stations. There's an airport and a ferry link with Ullapool.

THE HEBRIDES

Orientation & Information The ferry docks in the town centre, which is compact and easy to get around on foot. The bus station is on the foreshore next to the ferry terminal. For ferry information, phone CalMac (☎ 702361).

Some of the residential areas (and B&Bs) are a fair hike without a car, and many people commute in from communities around the island to work and shop, so there's more traffic than you might expect.

The main Western Isles Tourist Board (☎ 703088) is a short walk from the ferry pier. In theory you could use this office to book B&Bs around the islands, but it's best to take the free accommodation list and make the calls yourself.

There are banks with ATMs as well as two supermarkets, all near the TIC. The Western Isles Hospital (☎ 704704) is three-quarters of a mile north of the town centre.

Things to See In Francis St, the **Museum nan Eilean** (☎ 703773) has a changing program of exhibitions. It's open daily, except Sunday, from 10 am to 5.30 pm, with shorter winter hours (free). The **Lewis Loom Centre** (☎ 703117), in the Old Grainstore, Bayhead St, does good 40 minute tours from April to September (closed Sunday), with demonstrations of Harris Tweed making (£2.50). There's also the **An Lanntair** gallery (☎ 703307) in the old Town Hall, with temporary art exhibitions (free) and a café.

Places to Stay The *Laxdale Holiday Park* (☎ 703234, 6 Laxdale Lane) is 1½ miles north of town off the A857. Charges start at £6.50 per person.

Stornoway Backpackers Hostel (☎ 703628, 47 Keith St) is a five minute walk from the ferry and bus station – walk east along pedestrianised Point St, which becomes Francis St, pass the post office, then turn left into Keith St. Dorm beds are £8 per night, including breakfast, and there's a self-catering kitchen.

Hollsetr (☎ 702796, 29 Urquhart Gardens) is a long walk from the centre, but

it's an immaculate and welcoming B&B, with a single, twin and family room from £16 per person. There are a few pleasant places on Matheson Rd, within walking distance of the ferry: *Ravenswood* (☎ 702673, 12 Matheson Rd) has a double and twin with bath from £18 a head; and *Fernlea* (☎ 702125, 9 Matheson Rd) charges similarly. *Mrs MacDonald's* (☎ 703254, 27 Springfield Rd) is just beyond the Nicholson Institute. B&B there costs from £16. Nearby, there's *Kildun* (☎ 703247, 14 Goathill Rd), with a single, a double and a twin room, from £16 to £18 per person.

Park Guest House (☎ 702485), with beds from £21 to £29, and *Tower Guest House* (☎ 703150), with beds from £18 to £36, are two comfortable guesthouses in Victorian homes in James St. To find them, follow the waterfront to the east then veer left at the signpost for the A866.

Continue east from the pedestrian mall to the old-fashioned *County Hotel* (☎ 703250, Francis St), a reasonable establishment, with singles for £40 and doubles at £60. The modern *Cabarfeidh Hotel* (☎ 702604, Manor Park) charges £69/92 for single/ double rooms. It does three-course set meals for £19.75.

Places to Eat During the day *Merchants Coffee House*, opposite the TIC, does snacky meals in pleasant surroundings – baked potatoes start at £1.85.

After 6 pm you'll only get food at the hotels and a few carry-out places. On Sunday, most carry-outs are closed. You can get a curry at the *Stornoway Balti and Kebab House* (☎ 706116, 24 South Beach St) from £6. It does takeaways and is open on Sunday. There's also the *Island Star* Chinese carry-out at the south end of Kenneth St, and a fish and chip shop on Church St.

The *County Hotel* does bar meals for £5 to £9. The *Royal Hotel* (☎ 702109, Cromwell St) has prices starting at £4.50, and a more expensive restaurant with a seafood slant (main courses around £16); it's a nice place, and it has half a boat attached to the

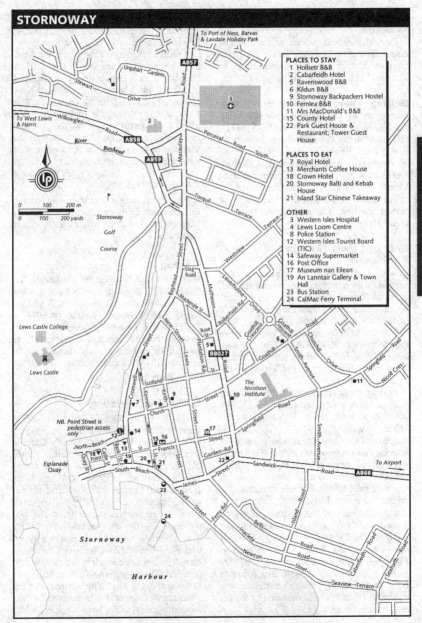

STORNOWAY

To Port of Ness, Barvas & Laxdale Holiday Park

A857

Urquhart Gardens

Stewart

Drive

Willowglen

To West Lewis & Harris

Road

River

Bayhead

A858

A859

Macaulay

Perceval Road

South

Street

Torquil

Terrace

Stornoway
Golf
Course

Westview

Terrace

Leverhulme

Drive

Stag
Road

Bayhead

Street

Matheson

Mackenzie St

Robertson Rd

Road

Coathill

Crescent

Coathill
Crescent

Road

Churchill Drive

Springfield Road

Lews Castle College

New Street

Rose
St

Coathill

St

6

Smith Avenue

Nicoll Cres

Lews Castle

Cromwell

Street

Kenneth

Lewis

Plantation Rd

5

B8027

St

4

The
Nicolson
Institute

Road

11

Scotland

Keith

9

Street

Street

Church

8

7

Springfield

Smith Avenue

NB. Point Street is
pedestrian access
only

12

14

15 16

17

Street

Garden Rd

22

Sandwick

Road

To Airport

A866

North Beach

St

19

Francis

Bank

St

Point St

Cromwell St
Quay

20

21

Esplanade
Quay

South Beach

James

Street

23

Shell Street

Ferry Rd

24

Bells

Island Road

Inaclete

Road

Caberfeidh Road

Seaforth Road

Stornoway

Newton

Road

Street

Seaview Terrace

Harbour

PLACES TO STAY
1 Hollsetr B&B
2 Cabarfeidh Hotel
5 Ravenswood B&B
6 Kildun B&B
9 Stornoway Backpackers Hostel
10 Fernlea B&B
11 Mrs MacDonald's B&B
15 County Hotel
22 Park Guest House & Restaurant; Tower Guest House

PLACES TO EAT
7 Royal Hotel
13 Merchants Coffee House
18 Crown Hotel
20 Stornoway Balti and Kebab House
21 Island Star Chinese Takeaway

OTHER
3 Western Isles Hospital
4 Lewis Loom Centre
8 Police Station
12 Western Isles Tourist Board (TIC)
14 Safeway Supermarket
16 Post Office
17 Museum nan Eilean
19 An Lanntair Gallery & Town Hall
23 Bus Station
24 CalMac Ferry Terminal

0   100   200 m
0   100   200 yards

ceiling. The *Crown Hotel (☎ 703181, Castle St)* also does bar meals.

One of the best places to eat is *Park Guest House (☎ 702485, James St)*. Main courses start at £13.25; it specialises in local seafood, shellfish and game.

Getting There & Away Buses from Stornoway to Tarbert and Leverburgh are run by Harris Coaches (☎ 01859-502441). Galson Motors (☎ 840269) run the service to Port of Ness and the circular route Stornoway to Arnol, Carloway, Callanish and Stornoway. Two or three buses run from Monday to Saturday on each route.

For details on CalMac ferries, see the earlier Getting There & Away section, Outer Hebrides.

Butt of Lewis (Rubha Robhanais)

Lewis' northern tip is windswept and rugged, with a lighthouse, pounding surf, seals, and large colonies of nesting fulmars. To get there, drive across the bleak expanse of Black Moor to **Barvas** (Barabhas), then follow the densely populated west coast to the north-east. **St Moluag's Church** is an austere, barn-like structure believed to date from the 12th century but still used by the Episcopal Church.

Port of Ness (Port Nis) is an attractive harbour with a popular sandy beach. It's possible to walk along the east coast for 16km between the roads at Tolsta (Tolstaidh) and Cuisiadar, near Ness (four to six hours). The route passes ruins of a chapel and lots of summer shielings – crofting families used to live on these moors in summer, until WWII. There's a natural arch on the shore near Filiscleitir.

Several places by the roadside sell Harris Tweed, and there are grocery shops in most villages. The *Cross Inn (☎ 01851-810378)* serves bar meals. Much better is *Galson Farm Guesthouse & Bunkhouse (☎ 01851-850492)*, South Galson, with single/double B&B from £35/58, pleasant hostel accommodation (with kitchen, shower etc) for £8, and dinners for £16.

Arnol Blackhouse Museum

The most interesting and beautiful part of Lewis is south of Barvas and Stornoway. Just west of Barvas off the A858, the **Arnol Blackhouse Museum** (☎ 01851-710395, HS) is the only authentically maintained, traditional blackhouse – a combined byre, barn and home – left on the islands. Built in 1885, it was inhabited until 1964 and now offers a wonderful insight into the old crofting way of life. It's open April to September, Monday to Saturday from 9.30 am to 6.30 pm, and October to March, Monday to Thursday (and Saturday), from 9.30 am to 4.30 pm (£1.80/1.30).

At nearby **Bragar** a pair of whalebones form an arch by the road, with the rusting harpoon that killed the whale dangling from the centre.

Dalbeg

West of Arnol, just before Carloway, lies this beautiful bay with a sandy beach backed with machair and flanked by cliffs and sea stacks. The *Copper Kettle (☎ 01851-710592)* is a pleasant place a few metres from the beach. You can get snacks (85p to £3.25), or evening meals (main courses around £18) with a reservation. It's closed on Sunday.

Carloway (Carlabagh)

Carloway looks across a beautiful loch to the southern mountains and has a post office and small store. At nearby **Garenin** (Na Gearrannan), some fascinating ruined blackhouses are quietly mouldering alongside new concrete cottages. Also here is the *Gearranan Crofters' Hostel*, itself a restored blackhouse (£4.65/3.85). It's open all year. To get to the hostel from the war memorial by the church, cross the bridge and turn left. Don't take the road that passes under the bridge. Pass the shop, but don't turn left; continue straight on at the next junction. The hostel is half a mile farther on at the end of the road. The warden, Mrs Pat Macgregor, lives at 3 Uraghag, one of the modern houses (with a large black and white cartwheel at its side), by the last road junction en route to the hostel.

Dun Carloway Broch (Dun Charlabhaigh) is a well preserved, 2000-year-old dry-stone defensive tower, in a beautiful position with panoramic views. The new **Dun Carloway Interpretative Centre** will be open by the time you read this.

Callanish (Calanais)

• ☎ 01851

The construction of the **Callanish Standing Stones** began around 4000 years ago, so they predate the Pyramids by 1000 years. Fifty-four large stones are arranged in the shape of a Celtic cross, with a circle where the arms cross, on a promontory overlooking Loch Roag. This is one of the most complete stone circles in Britain. Its great age, mystery, impressive scale and undeniable beauty have the dizzying effect of dislocating you from the present day.

The **Calanais Visitor Centre** (☎ 621422) is a *tour de force* of discreet design and provides a rare place to eat in the area. Snacks cost from 95p (baked potatoes are £2.39). It's open (free) daily from April to September from 10 am to 7 pm (4 pm the rest of the year). There's an exhibition about the stones (£1.50/1) and a souvenir shop. Ask for permission to camp in the field.

Just north of Callanish, there's the **Stones, Sky and Sacred Landscape Exhibition** (☎ 621277). Its interesting displays include astronomical items which relate to the Callanish stones. The exhibition is open Monday to Saturday, whenever someone is around.

There are a couple of pleasant B&Bs nearby; try *Mrs Morrison* (☎ 621392) in the house right by the stones (from £18), or the attractive *Eschol Guest House* (☎ 621357), half a mile back towards Carloway (from £25), which does good dinners for £17. *Tigh Mealros* (☎ 621333) does light lunches in summer from £2 and evening main courses from £7.50, including wild local scallops. The *Callanish Blackhouse Tearoom* is a bit dark inside.

Great Bernera

This rocky island is connected to Lewis by another 'bridge over the Atlantic'. At the hamlet of **Breaclete**, there's a **folk history museum** (☎ 01851-612331) with a tearoom serving home-baked goodies and snacks. It's open April to September from 11 am to 6 pm, except Sunday (£1). You can walk a half mile from Breaclete to a restored mill; there's also an on-going restoration of an **Iron Age house** at Bosta, where an entire village has been excavated. The beach at Bosta is excellent.

Mealista (Mealasta)

The road to Mealista (the B8011 south-west of Callanish, signposted to Uig) takes you through the most remote parts of Lewis. Follow the road round towards Breanais for some truly spectacular white-sand beaches, although the surf can make swimming treacherous. The famous 12th century walrus-ivory Lewis chess pieces were discovered in the sand dunes here in 1831; of the 78 pieces, 67 ended up in the British Museum in London. You can buy replicas from various outlets around the island.

The *Smuggler's Restaurant* (☎ 01851-672351) is at Aird, just 3 miles north of the biggest beach, Uig Sands, at Timsgarry (Timsgearraidh). It serves snacks, lunches and à la carte evening meals – bookings are essential for dinner. There's a B&B with an excellent location at *Baile na Cille* (☎ 01851-672242), Timsgarry, from £24 to £39 per head, but reports about the meals are not great.

HARRIS (NA HEARADH)

Harris has the islands' most dramatic scenery, combining mountains, magnificent beaches, expanses of machair and weird rocky hills and coastline.

North Harris is actually the mountainous southern tip of Lewis, beyond the peat moors south of Stornoway – Clisham is the highest point. South Harris, across the land bridge at Tarbert, is also mountainous but has a fascinating variety of landscapes and great beaches.

THE HEBRIDES

Harris is famous for Harris Tweed, high quality woollen cloth still handwoven in islanders' homes.

The industry employs 750 independent weavers and 400 millworkers. Tarbert TIC can tell you about weavers, and workshops you can visit.

Tarbert (An Tairbeart)
- **pop 500** ☎ **01859**

Tarbert is a village port midway between North and South Harris with ferry connections to Uig on Skye.

Not in itself particularly inspiring, it has a spectacular location, overshadowed by mountains on the narrow land bridge between two lochs. Tarbert has basic facilities: a petrol station, Bank of Scotland and two general stores. The Harris Tweed Shop stocks a wide range of books about the islands.

The TIC (☎ 502011) is signposted up the hill and to the right from the ferry. It's open April to October and occasionally at other times. For ferry information, phone CalMac on ☎ 502444. While you wait, the pleasant *Firstfruits* tearoom, open from April to September, does hot dishes, sandwiches and cakes. It's opposite the TIC. *Big D's*, open for lunch and dinner, does takeaways for under £3; like everything else, it's closed on Sunday. *Rockview Bunkhouse (☎ 502211, Main St)* has dorm beds for £8.50. It's extra for showers.

A good B&B is the cosy *Tigh na Mara (☎ 502270)*, a five minute walk from the ferry, with views of the east loch and beds from £15 to £16 per person. Dinner here is £10. *Hill Crest (☎ 502119)* overlooks the west loch and has rooms with bath for £16; dinner is about an extra £10.

Closer to the ferry terminal, *Waterstein House (☎ 502358)*, a bland building with three rooms, charges £14 per person.

Harris Hotel (☎ 502154), between the east and west lochs, has a range of rooms, some with bath, from £28 per head. It also has a good range of malt whiskies and serves good value pub meals (including vegetarian) from £5.

Harris Tweed

Previously an inexpensive type of cloth, warm, durable and relatively water resistant, Harris tweed is now a luxury item hand-woven by industrious Hebridean islanders in their own homes.

Weaving of Harris tweed originated on Amhuinnsuidhe Castle estate and it has now spread widely, with around 600 producers throughout Lewis and Harris. Since clothes made from Harris tweed have become expensive fashion statements, production in recent years has had to be cut back to avoid surpluses.

North Harris

North Harris is the most mountainous part of the Outer Hebrides. Only a few roads run through the region, but there are many opportunities for climbing and walking. **Clisham** (799m, 2621 feet) can be reached from the high point of the Stornoway to Tarbert road. The round trip takes about four hours and the views make it well worth the effort.

One road goes via **Amhuinnsuidhe Castle** to **Hushinish**, where there's a lovely silver-sand beach. Just north-west of Hushinish, the island of **Scarp**, now uninhabited, was the scene of bizarre attempts to send mail by rocket, in 1934. The first rocket exploded, but the second actually reached its destination.

The small village of **Rhenigidale** (Reinigeadal) has only recently become accessible by road. The *Reinigeadal Crofters' Hostel* can also be reached on foot (three hours and 6 miles from Tarbert). It's an excellent walk, but take all necessary supplies. From Tarbert, take the road to Kyles Scalpay for 2 miles. Just beyond Laxdale Lochs at a bend in the road, a signposted track, marked on OS maps, veers off to the left across the hills. The hostel is a white building standing above the road on the east side of the glen; the warden lives in the house closest to the shore. Beds cost £4.65/3.85.

The island of **Scalpay** (population 382), east of Tarbert, can now be reached by road. There's a couple of shops and B&Bs and interesting 'lazy-beds' on some of the crofts. Scalpay was the scene of great heroism during a storm in 1962 when local men set out in a small boat to rescue crew members of a ship that had run aground.

South Harris
• ☎ 01859

Beautiful South Harris is ringed by a tortuous 45 mile road. The beaches on the west coast, backed by rolling machair and mountains with views across to North Harris and to offshore islands, are stunning.

If your ancestors come from the Outer Hebrides, you may wish to get in touch with the genealogical centre, *Co Leis Thu?* (☎ 520258), at Northton.

The town of **Leverburgh** (An t-Ob) is named after Lord Leverhulme (the founder of the conglomerate Unilever), who bought Lewis and Harris in 1918 and 1919. He had grand plans for the islands, and for Obbe, as Leverburgh was then known, which was to be a major fishing port. It's now a sprawling, ordinary place but with a shop and several pleasant B&Bs. *Caberfeidh House* (☎ 520276) charges £15 per head (dinner is £10) and *Garryknowe* (☎ 520246) has doubles with/without bath for £18/16 per person. *Shieldaig House* (☎ 520378) does B&B for £18; dinner (including a vegetarian option) is £9. It supplies fishing rods and bicycles free of charge for residents. The *Anchorage Restaurant* (☎ 520225) is by the ferry terminal.

Three miles east, at attractive **Rodel** (Roghadal), stands **St Clement's Church**, mainly built between the 1520s and 1550s, only to be abandoned in 1560 after the Reformation. Inside there's the fascinating tomb of Alexander MacLeod, the man responsible for initial construction. Crude carvings show scenes of hunting, a castle, a galleon and various saints including St Clement clutching a skull. The church is open at all times and admission is free.

The east, or Bays, coast is traversed by the Golden Road, derisively nicknamed by national newspapers that didn't think so much money should be spent on building it. This is a weird, rocky moonscape, still dotted with numerous crofts. It's difficult to imagine how anyone could have survived in such an inhospitable environment. From late March to early October the SYHA operates the *Stockinish Youth Hostel* (☎ 530373) in the small village of Caolas Stocainis. It's 7 miles from Tarbert, costs £4.65/3.85, and you should bring all your supplies. This hostel may soon shut permanently so call the SYHA national office (☎ 01786-891400) before you visit.

Nearer Tarbert, at Drinishader, you'll find the hospitable *Drinishader Bunkhouse* (☎ 511255), with dorm beds for £6.50. There's also a camp site situated at nearby Plocrapool.

Getting Around
A passenger ferry goes from Leverburgh to Otternish on North Uist. In summer, it runs Monday to Saturday, three or four times daily; in winter, only once daily (one hour; £4.30, £20 for a car). Tarbert TIC has information, or you can phone CalMac on ☎ 01475-650100.

Getting Around
Buses from Tarbert to Scalpay, Stornoway and Leverburgh are run by Harris Coaches (☎ 01859-502441). Buses to Leverburgh and Rodel via Stockinish are operated by J Morrison (☎ 01859-530294).

BERNERAY (BEARNARAIGH)
• pop 141   ☎ 01876

The superb beaches of western Berneray are unparalleled. The new causeway to North Uist (to open in October 1998) shouldn't alter the peace and beauty of this place.

There are two shops for groceries on Berneray, and a *Gatliff hostel* (£4.65/3.85) at Baile, just under 2 miles from the causeway. It's open all year. *Mrs MacInnes*

(☎ 540253, 1 Borve) does B&B from £17 per person, and evening meals for £11. In summer, lunch and dinner are also available in the community hall for £3.25 to £5.

There are postbus services (☎ 500330), and Grenitote Travel (☎ 560244) buses, from Berneray to Lochmaddy.

NORTH UIST (UIBHIST A TUATH)
• pop 1404   ☎ 01876

North Uist is half drowned by lochs, and has some magnificent beaches on the north side. There are great views north to the mountains of Harris, especially from the top of hills like **Crogarry Mór** (180m, 590 feet), which is 5 miles from Lochmaddy, towards Sollas. The landscape is a bit less wild than on Harris but it has a sleepy, subtle appeal. For birdwatchers this is an earthly paradise, with huge populations of migrant waders – oystercatchers, lapwings, curlews and redshanks at every turn.

Lochmaddy (Loch nam Madadh)

There isn't much to keep you in tiny Lochmaddy, but it has the ferry terminal for sailings to Uig on Skye, and there are a couple of stores, a Bank of Scotland, a petrol station, a post office and a pub. To get the Long Island Hospital, call ☎ 500325. There's also the interesting **Taigh Chearsabhagh** museum and arts centre (☎ 500293) which is open March to December, Monday to Saturday from 10 am to 5 pm, with late Friday opening in summer (8 pm). The café next door does soup and sandwiches.

The TIC (☎ 500321) is open April to mid-October, Monday to Saturday from 9 am to 5 pm, and for late ferry arrivals. For ferry information, phone CalMac on ☎ 500337.

Lochmaddy's SYHA *Youth Hostel (☎ 500368)* is half a mile from the docks (signposted) and is open from mid-May to September for £6.10/4.95. An independent hostel at *Uist Outdoor Centre (☎ 500480)* has beds in four-bed rooms for £6.

The *Old Court House (☎ 500358)* is a comfortable B&B with two singles, a twin and a double, costing from £18 per person; the similarly priced *Old Bank House (☎ 500275)* is also good. Extremely comfortable and well presented is *Stag Lodge (☎ 500364)*, in a pleasing whitewashed building; beds start at £18 and are well worth it. There's also a small restaurant here serving snacks and meals for under £6.

For Peat's Sake

Visitors to the Outer Hebrides will not fail to notice peat stacks next to many houses. These interestingly constructed stacks are designed to allow wind to blow straight through, thus assisting the drying process before it can be used as fuel.

Peat is extremely wet in its raw state and it can take a few months to dry out. Initially it's cut from roadside sphagnum moss bogs, and cuttings are at least a metre deep. Rectangular blocks of peat are cut using a long-handled tool called a peat-iron (*tairsgeir* in Gaelic); this is extremely hard work and causes blisters, even on hands used to manual labour. Different types of tairsgeir are used in the islands. In Lewis, they cut relatively short brick-shaped blocks, while in Uist the blocks are somewhat longer. The peat blocks are transported to the cutter's house, then carefully built into a stack called a *cruach-mhonach*. The blocks are balanced on top of each other in a grid pattern so that there's a maximum of air space. Once the peat is dry it can be stored in a shed.

Peat fires in Hebridean homes are becoming increasingly rare due to the increasing popularity of oil-fuelled central heating. Peat burns much slower than wood or coal and it produces a pleasant smell and quite a lot of heat.

Lochmaddy Hotel (☎ *500331*) is a traditional hotel with a range of rooms (all with bath) from around £30 per person. Its restaurant serves excellent fish and seafood (main courses from £10.50 to £17.50), or you can get bar meals (most under £5.50) until 8.30 pm. It's also a good place to stay if you're into fishing (and North Uist is famous for fishing); you can buy permits here.

Car ferries for Leverburgh, on South Harris, leave from **Otternish**, near the Berneray causeway (see South Harris earlier in this section).

Balranald Nature Reserve
Eighteen miles west of Lochmaddy off the A865 there's an RSPB nature reserve (☎ 510730) where you can watch migrant waders and listen for rare corncrakes. A very basic visitors centre provides refuge from April to September if it's raining.

Bharpa Langass & Pobull Fhinn
The chambered Neolithic burial tomb of Bharpa Langass stands on a hillside 6 miles south-west of Lochmaddy, just off the A867. The 24m diameter and 4.2m high cairn is believed to date back 5000 years. Take care as the path can be boggy.

Pobull Fhinn (Finn's People) is a stone circle of similar age accessible from a path beside Langass Lodge Hotel. There are lovely views over the loch where seals can sometimes be seen. A marked circular route from the hotel takes less than an hour and takes in both sites.

Langass Lodge Hotel (☎ 580285) has single/double rooms for £36/60. It's noted for its food; a three-course bar meal here will cost around £9.

Clachan na Luib
This village has a shop and a few houses; Mermaid Fish Supplies does excellent smoked salmon. About a mile to the west, by the sandy tidal channel between North Uist and **Baleshare (Am Baile Sear) Island**, there's rather luxurious hostel accommodation at *Taigh mo Sheanair* (☎ 580246), with bunks for £8. Camping costs £4 per

person and bike hire can be organised with Iain Morrison (☎ 580211) for £7.50 per day.

The nearest places to eat are at Langass or the intriguing *Westford Inn* (☎ *580643*), north on the west-coast road, where bar meals are mostly under £6 and B&B is £20 per head.

Getting There & Away
Buses from Lochmaddy to Langass, Clachan na Luib, Benbecula and Lochboisdale are run by Royal Mail (☎ 500330), Hebridean Coaches (☎ 01870-620345) and Macdonald Coaches (☎ 01870-620288). There are usually two daily runs (not on Sunday).

BENBECULA (BEINN NA FAOGHLA)
- **pop 1803** ☎ 01870

Blink and you'll miss Benbecula, a low-lying island that's almost as much water as land, connected by bridge and causeway to both the Uists.

Although the number of British soldiers based here is declining, they still have a missile firing range. The troops and their families are quartered around functional **Balivanich** (Baile a'Mhanaich) where the big Naafi/Spar shop opens usual hours and on Sunday (until 1 pm). There's also a post office and a bank with an ATM.

The **Sgoil Lionacleit Leisure Centre** (☎ 602211), about 4 miles south of Balivanich, has a pool, games hall, and sauna. It's open to the public when not being used by the school.

The *Bunkhouse* (☎ *602522*) is near the airport – don't worry, flights are infrequent! Dorm beds cost £5 to £8.

Good food is available in the *Stepping Stone Restaurant* (☎ *603377*), which has lunchtime main courses under £4 and dinners under £9.

The *Café Bar* at the airport, and the *Low Flyer* pub, are more basic.

There's one daily flight (except Sunday) to Glasgow from £80 single, £99 return. For bus details see the North Uist Getting There & Away section earlier.

SOUTH UIST (UIBHIST A DEAS)
* pop 2106

South Uist is the second largest island in the Outer Hebrides. Once again, it lacks the drama of Harris, but although it's unassuming there's an expansiveness that has its own magic. The west coast is low, with machair backing an almost continuous sandy beach. The east coast is quite hilly, with spectacular **Beinn Mhor** reaching 620m (2034 feet), and is cut by four large sea lochs. The island rewards those who go beyond the main north-south road. One of the best areas to explore is remote Usinish on the east coast, where you'll find **Nicolson's Leap**.

As you drive from Benbecula, watch for the granite statue of **Our Lady of the Isles** standing on the slopes of the Rueval hill.

Lochboisdale (Loch Baghasdail)
* ☎ 01878

Lochboisdale has ferry links to Oban and Mallaig on the mainland and Castlebay on Barra.

The TIC (☎ 700286) is open April to mid-October, Monday to Saturday from 9 am to 5 pm, and for late ferry arrivals. For ferry information phone CalMac on ☎ 700288. There's a branch of Royal Bank of Scotland (no ATM) and petrol supplies. The nearest shop is at Daliburgh, 3 miles west. The medical centre and hospital (☎ 700311) is also there.

Of the B&Bs, friendly *Lochside Cottage* (☎ 700472) has beds from £13, while *Riverside* (☎ 700250) starts at £14. *Bay View* (☎ 700329) is nearer the pier and charges from £14 to £20 per person. *Lochboisdale Hotel* (☎ 700332), above the ferry terminal, has a variety of rooms, all with bath, for £36 to £42 a head. The pub has good food; bar meals and snacks range from £2 to £5.50.

For bus details, see the North Uist Getting There & Away section.

Howmore (Tobha Mor)

An attractive west coast village, Howmore has the *Tobha Mor Crofters' Hostel* (£4.65/3.85). To get to it, take the turn-off

from the A865 to Tobha Mor – the hostel is the white building with a porch by the church at the road's end. Watch out for the scrounging cat. The warden lives at Ben More House, at the junction with the main road. From the shed (☎ 01870-620283) at the junction you can hire a bike for £7.50/28 per day/week. There's a shop just down the road.

Two miles north there's the **Loch Druidibeg Nature Reserve**. SNH has an information office by the roadside, and you can take a 5 mile hike (two hours). A more demanding walk follows the north-east ridge of Beinn Mhor – beware of the precipitous cliffs on the north side, and carry OS map No 22. Allow six hours for the round trip from the hostel.

The North

The best place to eat in the Uists is the *Orasay Inn* (☎ *01870-610298*), Lochcarnan, with excellent bar meals, including seafood. B&B costs from £22 to £32 per person and all rooms are *en suite*.

The South

The southern tip of the island looks across to the islands of Eriskay and Barra. The scenery is particularly lovely around the *Polochar Inn* (☎ *01878-700215*) in Polochar (Pol a'Charra). B&B here costs £35/55 for singles /doubles and bar meals are around £6.

Hebridean Coaches (☎ 01870-620345) do at least three daily runs (except Sunday) from Ludag Pier to Lochboisdale.

From Ludag, there's a 15 minute car ferry to Eriskay (☎ 01878-720261) several times a day, except Sunday (£1, £3.60 for a car). The passenger ferry (☎ 01878-720238) to Eoligarry on Barra's northern tip also runs Monday to Saturday, twice per day (one hour; £4.50).

ERISKAY (EIRIOSGAIGH)
* pop 179   ☎ 01878

This romantic and beautiful island is where Bonnie Prince Charlie first set foot in Scotland, in 1745. More recently, the SS *Politician* sank just off the coast in 1941, and the islanders retrieved some of its cargo of around 250,000 bottles of whisky. After a binge of dramatic proportions, the police turned up and a number of the islanders landed in jail. The story was immortalised in good humour by Sir Compton Mackenzie in his book Whisky Galore, later turned into a film.

The island has a grocery store, post office, and pub, *Am Politician* (☎ 720246) which serves popular seafood meals. There's a well equipped *holiday chalet* (☎ 720274) available for £25 per night (minimum three nights), or £160 per week.

BARRA (BARRAIGH)
• pop 1244   ☎ 01871

Barra is a small island, just 14 miles around and ideal for exploring on foot. With beautiful beaches, machair, hills, Neolithic remains and a strong sense of community, it encapsulates the Outer Hebridean experience. Barra is connected by causeway to Vatersay, where there's a 4 mile heritage trail (three hours). For a great view, walk up to the top of Ben Tangaval (333m, 1092 feet) on Barra, and just north of the Vatersay causeway. Allow about two hours from the road.

The TIC (☎ 810336) in **Castlebay** (Bagh a'Chaisteil), the largest village, is open from April to mid-October. Castlebay has ferry connections with Lochboisdale (South Uist), Mallaig and Oban. For information, phone CalMac on ☎ 810306. There's a post office, a bank (no ATM), and Co-op and Spar foodstores.

Things to See
On an islet in the bay at Castlebay, there's **Kisimul Castle** (☎ 810336), first built by the MacNeil clan in the 12th century. It was sold in the 19th and restored in the 20th century by American architect Robert MacNeil, who became clan chief. A standard flies above the castle when his son and heir is in residence. You can visit the castle by boat on Monday, Wednesday and Saturday afternoons for £3/50p. Call the ferry operator on ☎ 810449.

The **Barra Heritage Centre** (☎ 810413), Castlebay, has Gaelic-theme displays about the island, and a tearoom. It's open April to September daily, except Saturday, from 11 am to 5 pm (£1). It also has a restored cottage at Craigston, 3 miles from Castlebay.

Places to Stay & Eat
By now there should be a new 23 bed *Gatliff Trust* hostel open in the old schoolhouse at Brevig, about 2 miles east of Castlebay. Check first with the TIC.

With only about 20 B&Bs scattered around the island and some ferries arriving late in the evening, it's best to book ahead. In Castlebay, try *Suidheachan* (☎ 890243), the former home of *Whisky Galore* author Sir Compton Mackenzie, with rooms from £16, all with bath; or *Faire Mhaoldonaich* (☎ 810441), where rooms with bath cost from £16. *Craigard Hotel* (☎ 810200) has a range of rooms, some with bath, from £29 to £32 per person.

The *Craigard Hotel* does bar meals from £4.50; three courses will be around £12. The *Kismul Galley* (☎ 810645), Castlebay, is open all week. It does soup and a roll for £1.95 and meals for under £7. At the north end of the island, the *airport tearoom* does snacks.

Getting There & Away
British Airways Express flies to Barra from Glasgow from Monday to Saturday, with additional Sunday flights in peak summer months (from £88/121, single/return).

See the Outer Hebrides Getting There & Away section for CalMac ferry details. The passenger ferry (☎ 01878-720238) to Ludag on South Uist runs Monday to Saturday, twice per day (£4.50).

Getting Around
There's a good postbus service (☎ 810312) around the island, connecting with flights at the airport.

MINGULAY (MIUGHALAIGH)
Mingulay is characterised by sea stacks and cliffs (over 200m high) on its western side,

and more gradual slopes in the east. It's about 2 miles by a mile and is uninhabited. The ruined village near the boat landing is a reminder of human occupation until 1912. The island cliffs have vast colonies of many types of sea bird.

A trip to Mingulay is highly recommended. A fine time to visit is during the puffin season from June to early August. Mr Campbell (☎ 01871-810303) in Castlebay, Barra, will sail to Mingulay for around £20 per person, depending on weather and numbers. You can also ask at the TIC in Castlebay.

ST KILDA
St Kilda, owned by NTS and leased to SNH, is a UNESCO World Heritage Site and consists of four main islands and several smaller ones. You can easily exhaust all superlatives to describe this collection of volcanic rock stacks and islands about 40 miles west of North Uist. The largest island, **Hirta**, measures about 2 miles east-west by a mile north-south. It has huge cliffs along most of its coastline.

History
Hirta was inhabited by Gaelic-speaking people until the well documented evacuation in 1930. Tourism and church influences in the 19th century assisted in the destruction of the community on St Kilda, but the islanders' habit of using fulmar oil on the umbilical cord of new-born babies killed about 80% of them. People survived here by keeping sheep, fishing, growing a few basic crops including barley, and climbing the cliffs without boots to catch sea birds and collect their eggs. Over the centuries, this resulted in a genetic peculiarity – St Kildan men have unusually long big-toes.

Organised Tours
The NTS charges volunteers for doing archaeological and conservation work in and around the village ruins. Archaeology/restoration trips run from mid-May to mid-August; you have to work 36/24 hours per week, and the cost is £400/450 (including transport from Oban in a converted lifeboat, and full board in dorm accommodation). Volunteers must be fit. There are 11 in each party, and the selection process takes place in January – get your application form from the NTS in November (for the following summer).

In your time off, you can wander up to the top of **Conachair** (430m, 1410 feet) to admire the view of **Boreray** (384m, 1260 feet) and the great rock towers of **Stac Lee** (172m, 564 feet) and **Stac an Armin** (196m, 643 feet). A visit will be arranged to the island of **Dun**. For an application form, ring ☎ 01631-570000.

Boat tours to St Kilda are expensive and landing is not usually possible. Rosa Hebridean Cruises (☎ 01851-702901) do three-day trips from April to October and charge £90 per person per day all inclusive. Robert Stevenson (☎ 01859-502192) departs from Harris and charges £80 per day. There's also Roddy Campbell (☎ 01859-511255), departing from Harris; and Western Edge (☎ 01224-210564), departing from Berneray on Saturday in summer.

Getting There & Away
Apart from the aforementioned organised trips, the only access to St Kilda is by private boat. Landing on all of the islands, except Hirta, is virtually impossible due to the ocean swell; even Hirta can be difficult in a southerly to north-easterly wind.

Orkney & Shetland Islands

These two groups of islands lie north of the Scottish mainland. They're popular with walkers, birdwatchers, anglers and divers and reward visitors who make the effort to get there with some spectacular scenery.

Orkney Islands

Just 6 miles off the north coast of the Scottish mainland, this magical group of islands is known for its dramatic coastal scenery, ranging from 300m-high cliffs to white, sandy beaches, for its abundant marine birdlife, and for a plethora of prehistoric sites, including an entire 4500-year-old village at Skara Brae.

Sixteen of the 70 islands are inhabited. Kirkwall is the main town and Stromness is a major port – both are on the largest island, which is known as Mainland. The land is virtually treeless, but lush, level and cultivated rather than rugged. The climate, warmed by the Gulf Stream, is surprisingly moderate, with April and May being the driest months.

Over 1000 prehistoric sites have been identified on Orkney, the greatest concentration of any place in Europe. Since there has always been a lack of wood, everything is made from stone. This explains the survival of ancient domestic architecture that includes a 5500-year-old house, Europe's oldest, on Papa Westray. The most impressive ancient monuments – the village of Skara Brae, the tomb of Maeshowe and the Ring of Brodgar – are all on Mainland.

Orkney's Pictish rulers were replaced by Norse earls in the 9th century. The Norse ruled until the mid-13th century and built the magnificent St Magnus Cathedral in Kirkwall. Even today, there are hints of those distant Scandinavian connections in the lilting accent with which Orcadians speak English.

Orkney is popular with birdwatchers and the RSPB runs several reserves. From May

HIGHLIGHTS

- Survey the prehistoric sites of Skara Brae, Maeshowe and the Ring of Brodgar

- Wander among stunning coastal scenery on Orkney's Hoy and Yesneby islands and at Eshaness and Hermaness in the Shetlands

- Experience sea angling off Whalsay or trout fishing in its lochs

- Enjoy excellent diving sites at Scapa Flow and in the Shetlands off Garth's Ness, Muckle Roe and Hillswick

- Sit among the puffins in North Unst, the northernmost point in Scotland

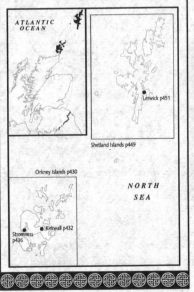

ATLANTIC OCEAN

Lerwick p451

Shetland Islands p449

Orkney Islands p430

NORTH SEA

Stromness p436

Kirkwall p432

to mid-July, vast numbers of seabirds come to nest on the cliffs. The clear waters around the islands attract divers, and Scapa Flow, south of Mainland, offers the most interesting wreck dive site in Europe.

ORKNEY ISLANDS

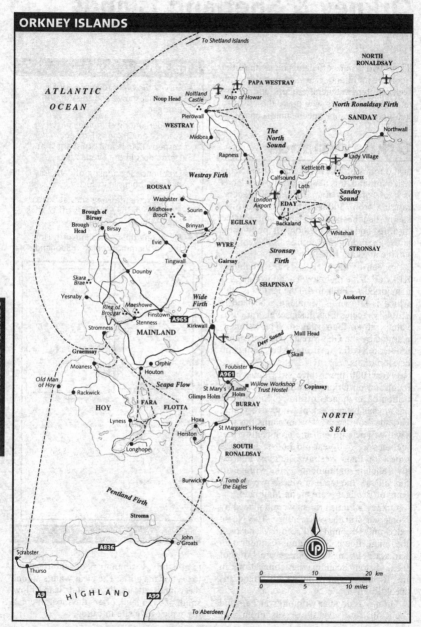

ATLANTIC
OCEAN

To Shetland Islands

NORTH
RONALDSAY

PAPA WESTRAY

Noltland
Castle
Noup Head
Knap of Howar

Pierowall

WESTRAY

Midbea

Rapness

The
North
Sound

North Ronaldsay Firth

SANDAY

Northwall

Calfsound

Loth

Lady Village

Kettletoft

Quoyness

Westray Firth

ROUSAY

Wasbister

Midhowe
Broch

Sourin

Brinyan

EGILSAY

London
Airport

EDAY

Backaland

Sanday
Sound

Whitehall

STRONSAY

Brough of
Birsay

Brough
Head

Birsay

Evie

WYRE

Gairsay

Stronsay
Firth

Tingwall

Skara
Brae

Dounby

Yesnaby

Ring of
Brodgar

Maeshowe

Finstown

Stenness

MAINLAND

A965

Kirkwall

SHAPINSAY

Auskerry

Wide
Firth

Deer Sound

Mull Head

Skaill

Stromness

Graemsay

Moaness

Old Man
of Hoy

Rackwick

Orphir

Houton

Scapa Flow

FARA

FLOTTA

HOY

Lyness

Hoxa

Herston

Longhope

Foubister

A961

St Mary's

Glimps Holm

Lamb
Holm

Willow Workshop
Trust Hostel

Copinsay

BURRAY

St Margaret's Hope

SOUTH
RONALDSAY

NORTH
SEA

Burwick

Tomb of
the Eagles

Pentland Firth

Stroma

John
o'Groats

Scrabster

Thurso

A836

A9

HIGHLAND

A99

To Aberdeen

0   10   20 km
0   5   10 miles

If you're anywhere in the area around mid-June, don't miss the St Magnus Arts Festival. Sir Peter Maxwell Davies, one of the greatest living British composers, usually contributes to the festival – he lives on Hoy. The poet and writer George Mackay Brown lived in Orkney. *Greenvoe*, or any of his other books set in Orkney, perfectly captures the special atmosphere of these islands.

INFORMATION

The Orkney Tourist Board (☎ 01856-872856), 6 Broad St, Kirkwall, KW15 1 NX, publishes a useful booklet detailing accommodation options in the islands. It also has a very useful guide called *The Islands of Orkney* which covers all the islands (except Mainland) in depth.

There are only two TICs, Kirkwall and Stromness, but they're both open all year.

GETTING THERE & AWAY
Air

There are flights to Kirkwall airport on British Airways/Loganair (☎ 0345-222111) daily except Sunday from Aberdeen, Edinburgh, Glasgow, Inverness and Shetland, with connections to London Heathrow, Birmingham, Manchester and Belfast. The cheapest return tickets (which must usually be bought 14 days in advance and require at least a Saturday night stay in Orkney) cost £214 from London, £126 from Glasgow and £113 from Inverness.

Bus & Boat

There's a car ferry from Scrabster, near Thurso, to Stromness, operated by P&O (☎ 01856-850655). The crossing can be exhilaratingly rough. If you're feeling like eating, the cafeteria serves good food (main courses for about £5). There's at least one departure a day all year, with single fares costing around £14 (10% student and senior reduction). For Scrabster, Scottish Citylink (☎ 0990-505050) has daily coaches leaving Inverness at around 1.30 pm, and you can connect with this service on early morning departures from Glasgow or Edinburgh, or from London on the overnight coach departing around 11 pm.

P&O also sails from Aberdeen (see the Central & North-East Scotland chapter).

John o'Groats Ferries (☎ 01955-611353) has a ferry (passengers and bicycles only) from John o'Groats to Burwick on South Ronaldsay, from May to September (two per day). A one-way ticket is £15, but it also offers an excellent deal to Kirkwall (£25 return). Bicycles cost an extra £3 each way. In Thurso, a free bus meets the train from Inverness at around 2.45 pm and a bus for Kirkwall (20 miles away) meets the ferry in Burwick. It also operates the Orkney Bus, a bus/ferry/bus through service between Inverness and Kirkwall via John o'Groats. Advance booking is essential. It runs from June to September, daily, departing Inverness at 7.30 am – a day return costs £40 (£20 for children), and the return journey takes 13½ hours.

From Lerwick (Shetland), P&O sails to Stromness on Wednesday (June to August) and Friday (all year). In the other direction, sailings are on Tuesday (June to August) and Sunday (all year). It's an eight to 10-hour trip and costs £37 each way (10% student and senior reduction).

KIRKWALL
* pop 6100   ☎ 01856

Orkney's capital is a bustling market town set back from a wide bay. Founded in the early 11th century by Earl Rognvald Brusson, the original part is one of the best examples of an ancient Norse town.

St Magnus Cathedral, one of Scotland's finest medieval cathedrals, is certainly worth a visit and there are a number of other things to see in the town; the whisky distillery tour is interesting.

Orientation & Information

Kirkwall is a fairly compact town and it's easy enough to get around on foot. The cathedral and most of the shops are set back from the harbour on Broad St, which changes its name several times along its

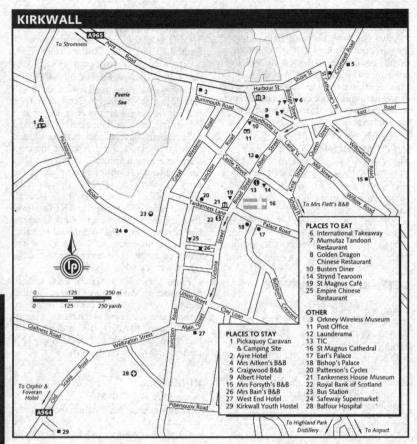

KIRKWALL

To Stromness

A965

Ayre Road

Peerie Sea

To Orphir & Foveran Hotel

A964

Pickaquoy Road

Great Western Road

Junction Road

Glaitness Road

Wellington Street

Union Street

Victoria Street

Main Street

Junction Road

Scapa Road

Old Scapa Road

Pipersquoy Road

Burnmouth Road

Castle Street

Albert Street

Mounthoolie La

Broad Street

Tankerness Lane

Clay Loan

Burnmouth Road

Laing St

King Street

Shore St

Bridge Street

Harbour St

St Catherine's Rd

Cromwell Road

East Road

Queen Street

Mill Street

Willowburn Road

Willow Road

Palace Road

Buttquoy Crescent

To Mrs Flett's B&B

To Highland Park Distillery

To Airport

0   125   250 m
0   125   250 yards

PLACES TO EAT
6   International Takeaway
7   Mumutaz Tandoori Restaurant
8   Golden Dragon Chinese Restaurant
10 Busters Diner
14 Strynd Tearoom
19 St Magnus Café
25 Empire Chinese Restaurant

OTHER
3   Orkney Wireless Museum
11 Post Office
12 Launderama
13 TIC
16 St Magnus Cathedral
17 Earl's Palace
18 Bishop's Palace
20 Patterson's Cycles
21 Tankerness House Museum
22 Royal Bank of Scotland
23 Bus Station
24 Safeway Supermarket
28 Balfour Hospital

PLACES TO STAY
1   Pickaquoy Caravan & Camping Site
2   Ayre Hotel
4   Mrs Aitken's B&B
5   Craigwood B&B
9   Albert Hotel
15 Mrs Forsyth's B&B
26 Mrs Bain's B&B
27 West End Hotel
29 Kirkwall Youth Hostel

length. Ferries leave from the harbour for the northern Orkney islands.

Kirkwall's only TIC (☎ 872856, www .orkneyislands.com) at 6 Broad St by the cathedral, opens daily April to September from 8.30 am to 8 pm and for the rest of the year Monday to Saturday from 9.30 am to 5 pm. It's a helpful place with a good range of publications on Orkney, and you can also change money.

Banks with ATMs are on Broad St and Albert St. The Launderama (☎ 872982), 47 Albert St, does a wash for £2 and dry for around 50p. It's closed on Sunday.

The Balfour Hospital (☎ 885400) is on New Scapa Rd.

St Magnus Cathedral

Founded in 1137 and constructed from local red sandstone and yellow Eday stone, St Magnus Cathedral (☎ 874894) was built by masons who had worked on Durham Cathedral. The interior is particularly impressive and, although much smaller than the great cathedral at Durham, the same powerful atmosphere of a very ancient faith pervades the place.

Earl Rognvald Kolsson commissioned the cathedral in the name of his martyred uncle, Magnus Erlendsson, who was killed by Earl Hakon Paulsson on Egilsay in 1115. Work began in 1137, but the building is actually the result of 300 years of construction and alteration, and includes Romanesque, transitional and Gothic styles.

The bones of Magnus are interred in one of the pillars in the cathedral. Other memorials include a statue of John Rae, the Arctic explorer, and the bell from HMS *Royal Oak*, torpedoed and sunk in Scapa Flow during WWII with the loss of 833 crew.

The cathedral opens April to September, Monday to Saturday from 9 am to 6 pm and Sunday from 2 to 6 pm. In winter it's open Monday to Saturday, from 9 am to 1 pm and 2 to 5 pm. There's a Sunday service at 11.15 am.

Earl's Palace & Bishop's Palace

Near the cathedral, and on opposite sides of the street, these two ruined buildings are in the care of HS (☎ 875461). They're open April to October, Monday to Saturday from 9.30 am to 6.30 pm, and from 2 pm on Sunday. Entry is £1.50/1.10 (child 75p) or £9/7 (child £2.50) for a ticket that also includes Maeshowe, Skara Brae, Skaill House, the Broch of Gurness and the Brough of Birsay.

The Bishop's Palace was built in the mid-12th century in order to provide comfortable lodgings for Bishop William the Old. There's a good view of the cathedral from the tower, and a plaque showing the different phases of the construction of the cathedral.

At one time the Earl's Palace was known as the finest example of French Renaissance architecture in Scotland. It was begun in 1600 by Earl Patrick Stewart, but he ran out of money and the palace wasn't completed.

Tankerness House Museum

This excellent restored merchant's house (☎ 873191) contains an interesting museum of Orkney life over the last 5000 years. Guided tours are available. The house and garden are open daily from May to September from 10.30 am to 5 pm (closed from 12.30 to 1.30 pm for lunch) and on afternoons only in winter; £2/free.

Orkney Wireless Museum

This museum (☎ 874272), Junction Rd, is a fascinating jumble of communications equipment dating from around 1930 onwards, especially relating to the Scapa Flow naval base. It's open daily April to September from 10 am to 4.30 pm (opening on Sunday at 2.30 pm); entry is £2/1.

Highland Park Distillery

Not only is Highland Park a very fine single-malt, but the tour of the world's most northern whisky distillery is also one of the best. You'll see the whole whisky-making process – this is one of the few distilleries that still does its own barley malting, known as floor malting.

There are tours of the distillery (☎ 874619) from April to October, Monday to Friday, every half-hour from 10 am to 4 pm, and at weekends in July and August (Saturday from 10 am to 4 pm; Sunday from noon to 4 pm). In winter there are weekday tours at 2 pm and by appointment. Your free dram's not free, though – tickets cost £3.

Organised Tours

Go Orkney (☎ 871871) has a good selection of bus tours, including a Monday afternoon visit to Skara Brae and the monuments around Stenness for £6.50/5 (child £3.50). A slightly longer version of this tour runs on Thursday and Saturday mornings. Wildabout Orkney (☎ 851011, or book at the TIC) is a small tour company with tours of various sights and birdwatching areas for around £9/17 (half/full-day). Also, Craigie's Taxis (☎ 878787) offers taxi tours for around £15 per hour for up to four people.

Special Events

The **St Magnus Festival** (☎ 872669) takes place in June and it's a celebration of music and the arts. An interesting event called **The Ba'** takes place on New Year's day; two teams chase each other and a ball around Broad St until one team reaches its goal.

Places to Stay

Camping The *Pickaquoy Caravan & Camping Site* (☎ 873535) is on the outskirts of town. It's OK but would be nicer if it were beside the sea. Charges are £3.50 for a tent.

Hostel The *Kirkwall Youth Hostel* (☎ 872243, Old Scapa Rd) is large and well equipped. It's a 20 minute walk from the harbour and costs £7.75/6.50 per night.

B&Bs & Hotels There's a good range of cheap B&Bs, though most are very small and few have rooms with attached baths.

Mrs Aitken's (☎ 874193, Whiteclett, St Catherine's Place) is central, with three doubles from £14.50 per person. There are several places on nearby Cromwell Rd. Try *Craigwood* (☎ 872006), which charges from £14 to £26.

Mrs Forsyth's (☎ 874020, 21 Willowburn Rd) is a small, friendly place, and costs £13 to £18 per person. Dinner is available for an extra £8. *Mrs Flett's* (☎ 872747, Briar Lea, 10 Dundas Crescent) is a comfortable B&B with two singles and two doubles for £15 to £17 per person.

Mrs Bain's (☎ 872862, 6 Frasers Close) is down a quiet lane near the bus station. There are three rooms, one with attached bath, costing £13 to £15 per person.

The *West End Hotel* (☎ 872368, Main St) dates from 1824 and has singles/doubles from £34/54 to £38/60, all with attached baths. It does good bar meals. The *Albert Hotel* (☎ 876000, Mounthoolie Lane) is central and has a couple of lively bars. Rooms are £35 to £45 single, £55 to £75 double.

Two miles from Kirkwall, on the Orphir road, there's the *Foveran Hotel* (☎ 872389), St Ola. All rooms are *en suite* and cost £45/70 single/double. It has a fine restaurant serving fresh seafood and local meats; try its Orkney bouillabaisse.

The harbourfront *Ayre Hotel* (☎ 873001) is the top place to stay. It's a very comfortable town-house hotel, built 200 years ago. B&B costs £54/80; the most pleasant rooms are those with a sea view.

Places to Eat

The *Safeway* supermarket, Pickaquoy Rd, is the best place for provisions.

St Magnus Café (☎ 873354), in the Kirkwall and St Ola Community Centre across the road from the cathedral, has good, cheap food – quiches, bacon rolls etc. Baked potatoes with fillings start at £1.85. It's open Monday to Saturday from 9.30 am to 4 pm and 7 to 10 pm, and also on Sunday afternoons in July and August. The *Strynd Tearoom*, Strynd, is also a great place for a snack.

There are several places to eat around Bridge St, near the harbour. *Mumutaz Tandoori Restaurant* (☎ 876596, 7 Bridge St) has a wide range of main dishes from £6 to £12, and does takeaways. Opposite, *International Takeaway* dishes up fairly good fish and chips for £2.70.

For Chinese food there are a couple of restaurants that also do takeaways: the *Golden Dragon* (☎ 872933, 25A Bridge St) and the *Empire Chinese Restaurant* (☎ 872300, 51 Junction Rd). The Empire is inexpensive and has lunch main courses for under £5.

Busters Diner (☎ 876717, 1 Mounthoolie Lane) is an American, Italian and Mexican place serving pizzas (from £3.30) and burgers (from £3.90). It's open daily until at least 10 pm, and also does takeaways.

For a great bar meal, go to the *West End Hotel* (☎ 872368, Main St) where main courses start at £4.50. Try the superb Orkney madeira marinated herring (£2.45) and roast North Ronaldsay lamb with skirlie (£6.20).

The restaurant at the *Ayre Hotel* is recommended but expensive. At the *Albert Hotel* main dishes are around £13, and it does three-course set meals for £18. Bar meals are cheaper, ranging from £4.25 to £11.90. For a really special occasion, go to the *Creel Restaurant* in St Margaret's Hope (see the section on South Ronaldsay later in this chapter).

Entertainment

The bar at the *Albert Hotel* is probably the liveliest place for a drink. On Thursday, Friday and Saturday there's Matchmakers disco; on Tuesday there's line dancing. The *West End Hotel* also has a pleasant bar.

Getting There & Away

The airport (☎ 872494) is 2½ miles from the town centre. For information on flying into Orkney, see the start of this section. For flights and ferries to the northern islands, see the following island sections.

From the bus station, JD Peace (☎ 872866) runs buses to Stromness (35 minutes, £2). There are eight buses a day on weekdays, six on Saturday. For Orphir and Houton (25 minutes, £1.20), there are also at least three buses a day from Monday to Saturday; they connect with ferries to Hoy. Causeway Coaches (☎ 831444) runs buses to St Margaret's Hope (£2), South Ronaldsay. The service between Kirkwall and Burwick is run by Shalder Coaches (☎ 850809), mainly for ferry passengers with through tickets, but pick-up or drop-off can be arranged. Rosie Coaches (☎ 751232) operates the service to Tingwall and Evie. Note that no buses run on Sunday in Orkney.

Getting Around

Car There are several rental places. Charges start from around £28 per day, or £150 per week (for a Renault Clio). Try Scarth Hire (☎ 872125), Great Western Rd, or John G Shearer & Sons (☎ 872950).

Taxi Call Craigies on ☎ 878787.

Bicycle Patterson's (☎ 873097), Tankerness Lane, rents mountain bikes for £7/42 for a day/week.

SOUTH MAINLAND

There are a few things to see at **Orphir**, a scattered community with no shop, about 9 miles west of Kirkwall. The Orkneyinga Saga Centre (no ☎) at Orphir opens all year, daily, from 9 am to 5 pm; entry is free. There are displays of the saga (a story about the Vikings in Orkney dating from 1136) and a wide-screen video show. For further details on the saga, get a copy of the leaflet *The Orkneyinga Saga – a guide to the saga sites*, compiled by the Department of Planning, Orkney Islands Council.

Just behind the centre is **The Earl's Bu**, the 12th century foundations of a manor house belonging to the Norse Earls of Orkney. There's also a remaining section of **St Nicholas' Church**, a unique circular building that was originally 9m in diameter. Built before 1136 and modelled on the rotunda of the Church of the Holy Sepulchre in Jerusalem, it was popular with pilgrims after the capture of the Holy Land by the first Crusade. The church was in use until 1705, then it was partly demolished in 1756. Both sites are always open and admission is free. For bus details, see the Kirkwall Getting There & Away section. From the main road, a 10 minute walk will get you to the centre.

King Haakon of Norway beached his ship at **Houton** in 1263, after his defeat at the Battle of Largs, and he died in Orkney soon afterwards. There's not much there except a ferry terminal and a hotel. *Houton Hotel* (☎ 01856-811320), Houton Bay, Orphir, does B&B for £27.50/45 single/double. It's a modern sort of place and it's also very spacious and pleasant inside. Bar snacks start from £1.50 (soup and a roll) and bar meals are from £5.25 (typically £10 for three courses).

For details on ferries from Houton to Hoy and Flotta, see Hoy later in this chapter.

WEST & NORTH MAINLAND
Stromness
* pop 2400   ☎ 01856

P&O ferries from Scrabster dock at this attractive little grey-stone town. As a place to stay, many visitors prefer Stromness to Kirkwall – it's smaller, it has more of the feeling of a working fishing village, and it's convenient for the island of Hoy. The streets and closes of Stromness have lots of interesting buildings – you can spend a while strolling around here. There are some excellent places to stay, including two hostels. The winding main street has a most civilised selection of shops that includes no less than three bookshops and even a place that does tarot readings.

Although Stromness was officially founded in 1620, it had been used as a port by the Vikings in the 12th century, as well as by earlier visitors. Its importance as a trading port grew in the 18th century and in

the 19th century it was a busy centre for the herring industry. Until the beginning of the 20th century, ships from the Hudson's Bay Company would stop to take on fresh water from Login's Well.

The TIC (☎ 850716) is at the ferry terminal and opens daily all year, staying open later when ferries dock. Its exhibition **This place called Orkney** will give you an introduction to the islands. Ask for the *Stromness Heritage Guide* leaflet.

There's a Royal Bank of Scotland ATM in Victoria St just behind the TIC, and a laundry at 20 Ferry Rd.

Things to See & Do The **Stromness Museum** (☎ 850925, 52 Alfred St) opens daily all year from 10 am to 5 pm (including Sunday from May to September). There are maritime, natural history and temporary exhibitions covering (among other things) fishing, whaling, and the German fleet. Admission costs £1.50/35p.

The Diving Cellar (☎ 850055), 4 Victoria St, does a diving package from £225 per week, including seven nights accommodation, transport and six days diving.

If the weather's bad, consider a visit to the **swimming pool** (☎ 850552), by the road to Kirkwall.

Special Events The annual Orkney Folk Festival (☎ 851331, www.orkneyislands.com/folk) is a lively event held on a May weekend in Stromness.

Places to Stay *Ness Point Caravan & Camping Site* (☎ 873535) overlooks the bay at the south end of town, although it can be a little breezy. It costs £3.50 for a tent.

Stromness Youth Hostel (☎ 850589, Hellihole Rd) is a 10 minute walk from the ferry terminal. Beds here cost £6.10/4.95. *Brown's Hostel* (☎ 850661, 45 Victoria St) is a very popular independent place. Open year-round, it has 14 beds (£7.50 each) and there's no curfew.

For B&B, try *Mrs Hourston's* (☎ 850642, 15 John St), from £15 per person. Out in the direction of the camping ground, there's *Mrs*

STROMNESS

1 Mrs Hourston's B&B
2 Ferry Inn
3 TIC
4 Royal Bank of Scotland
5 Stromness Hotel
6 Bus Stop
7 The Café
8 Post Office
9 Brown's Hostel
10 Royal Hotel
11 Hamnavoe Restaurant
12 Braes Hotel
13 Youth Hostel
14 Museum

To Kirkwall
John Street
Ferry Road
Bank Lane
North Pier (P&O Ferries)
Back Road
Khyber Pass
Boys Lane
New Pier (Boats to Hoy)
Church Rd
Christie's Brae
Manse La
Springfield Cres
Franklin Rd
Victoria Street
Franklin Rd
Hellihole Road
Spring Street
Alfred Street
Whitehouse Lane

0   50   100 m
0   50   100 yards

To Ness Point Caravan & Camping Site & B&Bs

Worthington's (☎ *850215, 2 South End*) with singles/doubles from £19/34. *Stenigar* (☎ *850438*), a little farther south, on Ness Rd, is a pleasant old house with views of Hoy. B&B here starts at £25 single, £30 double.

With good harbour views, the *Braes Hotel* (☎ *850495*) has rooms for £17/34. It also has rooms with bath attached. Near the harbour, the *Ferry Inn* (☎ *850280*) has rooms, most with attached baths, from £18/34.

Places to Eat Self-caterers can stock up at *Mill Stores (North End Rd)*, beyond the north end of John St. The *Café* (☎ *850368, 22 Victoria St*) does toasties from £1.40, pizzas, burgers and baked potatoes – to eat in or take away. Seafood dishes start at £4.80. There's also a *fish and chip shop* near the Royal Hotel.

There's a good bar at the *Ferry Inn* and a restaurant serving seafood with main dishes from around £6. The bar at the *Stromness Hotel* does meals from £5. The three-course Sunday lunch is only £5.95 (£4.95 for seniors). For a pint try Orkney Dark Island, Dragonhead Stout or Red Mc-Gregor, the local brews (£1.80). The most popular place to drink is the *Royal Hotel*, mainly because it stays open late.

The top place to eat is the *Hamnavoe Restaurant* (☎ *850606, 35 Graham Place*). Main dishes at this excellent seafood restaurant are around £9.50, with cheaper vegetarian options around £8. It's closed on Monday.

Getting There & Away For information on ferries to Scrabster, Lerwick and Aberdeen, see the start of the Orkney section. For boats to Hoy, see Hoy later in this chapter.

JD Peace (☎ 872866) runs buses to Kirkwall (35 minutes, £2), from Monday to Saturday. Shalder Coaches (☎ 850809) has a bus to Birsay (90p) on Monday only.

Stenness

This village is little more than a petrol station (with a shop which sells outrageous hats) and the *Standing Stones Hotel*

(☎ *01856-850449*), with rooms for £39/72 and bar meals from around £5. A mile east, however, are some of the most interesting prehistoric monuments on Orkney. Since the road between Stromness and Kirkwall passes through, you can travel by bus every day except Sunday. Hitching is also easy.

Maeshowe Constructed about 5000 years ago, this is the finest chambered tomb in western Europe. A long stone passage leads into a chamber in the centre of an earth-covered mound which is over 6.7m high and 35m across. The passage is aligned with sunset in mid-winter.

No remains were found when the tomb was excavated in the 19th century. It's not known how many people were originally buried here or whether they were buried with any of their worldly goods. In the 12th century, however, Vikings returning from the Crusades broke into the tomb, searching for treasure. They found none, but left a wonderfully earthy collection of graffiti, carved in runes on the walls of the tomb. Some of it's pretty basic – 'Thorni bedded Helgi Carved', but 'Many a woman has walked stooping in here' is a little more subtle – you have to stoop to get through the passage. There's also some Viking artwork including a crusader cross, a lion, a walrus and a knotted serpent.

Maeshowe (☎ 01856-761606) opens from April to September, from 9.30 am to 6.30 pm (on Sunday, from 2 pm), and for shorter hours in winter; £2.30/1.75 (£1 for children). There's also a combined ticket for £9/7 (child £2.50) that includes Skara Brae, Skaill House, the Broch of Gurness, the Brough of Birsay and the Bishop's and Earl's Palaces. Get your ticket in Tormiston Mill, on the other side of the road from Maeshowe, where there's a café serving snacks and light meals, a gift shop, small exhibition and a 15 minute video about Orkney's prehistoric sites.

Standing Stones of Stenness Near Maeshowe stand only four of the original 12 mighty boulders that once formed a ring.

ORKNEY & SHETLAND ISLANDS

They were erected around 2500 BC; one is over 5m high. There's no entrance charge.

Barnhouse Neolithic Village This reconstruction of a Neolithic village is very close to the Stenness stones. It's thought that the inhabitants were the builders of Maeshowe. Admission is free.

Ring of Brodgar About a mile along the road from Stenness towards Skara Brae is a wide circle of standing stones, some over 5m tall. Thirty-six of the original 60 stones are still standing among the heather. It's an impressive sight and a powerful place (especially so in a mid-winter blizzard!). These old stones, raised skyward 4500 years ago, still attract the forces of nature – on 5 June 1980, one was struck by lightning.

There's no entrance charge and the monument is always open.

Skara Brae & Skaill House

Eight miles north of Stromness, idyllically situated by a sandy bay, is northern Europe's best preserved prehistoric village. Even the stone furniture – beds, boxes and dressers – has survived the 5000 years since a community first occupied it. It was hidden under the sand until 1850, when a severe storm blew the sand and grass away, exposing the houses underneath.

Skara Brae (☎ 01856-841815) is in the care of HS; entry times are all year, Monday to Saturday, from 9.30 am to 6.30 pm (on Sunday, from 2 to 6.30 pm in summer, and 2 to 4.30 pm in winter), and admission prices are £4/3 (child £1.20), which include the new visitors centre and nearby Skaill House. It's worth buying the guidebook, which gives a guided tour involving eight viewpoints.

Skaill House (☎ 01856-841501) is an early 17th century mansion with displays including Captain Cook's dinner service. It's open April to September, Monday to Saturday, from 9.30 am to 6.30 pm, and Sunday from 11 am.

To get to Skara Brae and Skaill House you need your own transport, except on Monday when there's a bus to Birsay. You can also go

on a guided tour. Alternatively, it's possible to walk along the coast from Stromness via Yesnaby and the Broch of Borwick. There are several blow holes in the area.

Yesnaby Sea Stacks

Six miles north of Stromness are some spectacular but easy coastal walks. Less than half a mile south of the car park is the Yesnaby Castle sea stack, similar to the Old Man of Hoy. The ugly brick-built ruin at the car park was a WWII lookout post. Watch out during the nesting season in early summer, as seabirds will dive-bomb you to scare you away from their nests.

Birsay

The small village of Birsay is 6 miles north of Skara Brae; it has the grandly named *Palace Stores* shop with post office. The ruins of the **Earl's Palace** (always open; free) are in the centre of Birsay. There are several interesting and informative information boards on site. The palace was built in the 16th century by despotic Robert Stewart, Earl of Orkney, on an even grander scale than the palace in Kirkwall.

Brough of Birsay When the tide is low (for two hours around low tide), you can walk out to the Brough of Birsay, three-quarters of a mile from the Earl's Palace. On the island, you'll find extensive ruins of a Norse settlement and the 12th century St Peter's Church. There's a replica of a Pictish symbol stone which was found here, with eagle and human figures. St Magnus was buried here after his murder on Egilsay in 1117, and the island was a place of pilgrimage until a few centuries ago.

Places to Stay & Eat *Birsay Hostel (☎ 01856-873535, ext 2404, office hours only)* was formerly the village school; now it provides accommodation for groups of a minimum of 12 people. There are 30 beds and the charge is £6.10 per night each. It's open all year. There's B&B accommodation at *Primrose Cottage (☎ 01856-721384)*, overlooking Marwick Bay (2 miles south of

Birsay) for £14/28 or £36 for a double with bathroom attached. Evening meals are an extra £8. Meals are also available at the *Barony Hotel* (☎ *01856-721327*), by Boardhouse Loch, about half a mile south of Birsay.

Evie

Broch of Gurness About 1½ miles down a track from the tiny village of Evie, and past a sandy beach, you'll find the broch on an exposed headland. Although not nearly as impressive as Mousa Broch in Shetland, this is the best preserved example of a fortified stone tower in Orkney. Look out for the interesting stone dish – it was probably used as a grinder. Built around 100 BC, the broch is surrounded by a ditch and the remains of a large village. Opening times are April to September, Monday to Saturday, from 9.30 am to 6.30 pm (open on Sunday from 2 pm). The entrance fee is £2.30/1.75.

Places to Stay & Eat The *Eviedale Centre* (☎ *01856-751270*), in the village, has a small bothy with four beds (£5 each), and a camping ground (two people with tent for £5). A range of outdoor activities is offered at this centre, including canoeing and windsurfing. *Woodwick Stores* has a restaurant and serves high teas. *Woodwick House* (☎ *01856-751330*) does B&B for £34/46 without bath, £38/56 with bath. It also has a fine restaurant where a three-course meal costs £20.

EAST MAINLAND, BURRAY & SOUTH RONALDSAY

After a German U-boat sneaked into Scapa Flow and sank the battleship HMS *Royal Oak* in 1939, Churchill ordered better protection for the naval base. Using concrete blocks and old ships, the channels between some of the islands around Scapa Flow were blocked. The **Churchill Barriers**, as they're known, now link the islands of Lamb Holm, Glimps Holm, Burray and South Ronaldsay to Mainland. There are good sandy beaches by Barrier Nos 3 and 4.

East Mainland is mainly agricultural. There are large colonies of nesting seabirds at Mull Head, and the shores of Deer Sound attract wildfowl. The *Willow Workshop Trust* (☎ *01856-781324*), Ritchmond, Holm, has a little hostel with kitchen facilities and charges £5.50 per night for a bed. Bring a sleeping bag.

On the island of Lamb Holm, the **Italian Chapel** (☎ 01856-781268) is all that remains of a POW camp that housed the Italian prisoners who worked on the Churchill Barriers. They built the chapel in their spare time, using two Nissen huts, scrap metal and their considerable artistic and decorative skills. One of the artists returned in 1960 to restore the paintwork. It's quite extraordinary inside and definitely worth seeing. The chapel opens all year during daylight hours; entry is free.

On Burray, the road passes the **Orkney Fossil and Vintage Centre** (☎ 01856-731255), a quirky collection of local furniture and clothes, and 360 million-year-old fish fossils. Entry is £2/1 and the teashop is excellent. There's a general store and post office in Burray village; and the *Sands Motel* (☎ *01856-731298)* does bar meals.

The main village on South Ronaldsay is St Margaret's Hope, named after Margaret, the Maid of Norway, who was to have married Edward II of England but died here in 1290. There are two grocery stores, a post office and several pubs (most serve bar meals).

There's a summer-only ferry from John o'Groats which docks in Burwick, on the south coast of South Ronaldsay. See the start of the Orkney section for details.

Tomb of the Eagles

A visit to this tomb (☎ 01856-831339), Liddle Farm, Isbister, is highly recommended. The 5000-year-old stalled burial chamber was discovered by local farmers, the Simisons, who now run this privately owned visitors' attraction. It's as interesting for their entertaining and informative guided tour as for the tomb itself. After handling some of the human skulls and sea-eagles' claws found in the tomb, you walk across the fields, put on knee pads and crawl down the entrance passage. It's possible that sky burials occurred here; there's evidence that the dead people had been stripped of their flesh before being put in the tomb, possibly by being placed on top of wooden platforms just outside the tomb entrance, providing the eagles with a feast. You'll also see a **burnt mound**, an impressive Bronze Age kitchen. The tomb opens to visitors April to October, daily, from 10 am to 8 pm; the rest of the year from 10 am to noon. It's well worth the £2.50/2 ticket.

Places to Stay & Eat
Mrs Watt's (☎ 01856-731217), Ankersted, is an excellent B&B on Burray, with rooms with attached bath for £16/30. Diving trips to the wrecks in Scapa Flow (for experienced divers only) can be organised.

St Margaret's Hope on South Ronaldsay is a good place to stay. *Bellevue Guest House* (☎ 01856-831294) charges £15/30 for a room without bath, and £18/36 for a room with bathroom attached. *Barswick Farm* (☎ 01856-831259) does B&B from £15 single/twin.

The *Creel Restaurant* (☎ 01856-831311, Front Rd) is arguably the best place to eat in Orkney, and also has B&B accommodation for £40/60. Main dishes are £15.50; there's a three-course dinner for £26. Orcadian fish stew is excellent. It's open daily from April to September.

Wheems Bothy (☎ 01856-831537), Eastside, is a very pleasant hostel offering basic bed and organic breakfast for £5.50; it's open from April to October. You can camp if the hostel is full.

Getting There & Away
Between Kirkwall and St Margaret's Hope, Causeway Coaches (☎ 01856-831444) runs four buses a day on weekdays, two on Saturday (£2).

Shalder Coaches (☎ 01856-850809) runs the Kirkwall-Burwick service that connects with the ferries.

HOY
- ☎ 01856
The highest hill in Orkney is Ward Hill (479m, 1571 feet) on Hoy, the second-largest island in the group. Hoy means 'High Island'.

Things to See & Do
There's spectacular cliff scenery in the northern part of the island, including some of the highest vertical cliffs in Britain – St John's Head rises 346m (1135 feet) on the west coast. Hoy is probably best known for the **Old Man of Hoy**, a 137m-high (449 feet) rock stack that can be seen from the Scrabster-Stromness ferry, first climbed in 1966 by a party led by the eminent mountaineer Chris Bonnington. The northern part of Hoy has been maintained as a nature reserve by the RSPB since 1983.

There's basic hostel accommodation in Rackwick, a two hour walk by road from the Moaness pier through the beautiful **Rackwick Glen**. You'll pass the 5000-year-old **Dwarfie Stone**, the only example of a rock-cut tomb in Scotland, and, according to Sir Walter Scott, the favourite residence of Trolld, a dwarf from Norse legend. On your return, you can take a path via the **Glens of Kinnaird** and you'll see **Berriedale Wood**, Scotland's most northerly native forest.

The most popular walk goes to the edge of the cliffs opposite the Old Man of Hoy. The path climbs steeply westwards from Rackwick, then curves northwards, descending gradually to the cliff edge; allow about seven hours for the return trip from Moaness Pier, or three hours from Rackwick.

Lyness, on the eastern side of Hoy, was an important naval base during both world wars, when the British Grand Fleet was based in Scapa Flow. With the dilapidated remains of buildings and an uninspiring outlook towards the Elf Oil Terminal on Flotta Island, this isn't a pretty place, but the **Scapa Flow Visitors Centre** (☎ 791300) is well worth a visit. It's a fascinating naval museum and photographic display, located in an old pumphouse which fed fuel to the ships. It's open year-round on weekdays, from 9 am to 4 pm, and also mid-May to September weekends from 10 am to 4 pm; £2/1.

On both sides of Longhope Bay you'll see defensive towers dating from the Napoleonic Wars; they were built to protect convoys heading for the Baltic. The **Hackness Tower** on the south side of the bay, 3 miles from Longhope pier, opens to the public. For details of the current keyholder, call HS on ☎ 0131-668 8800.

Places to Stay & Eat

Hoy Outdoor Centre (☎ 873535, ext 2404, office hours only) is just over a mile from Moaness Pier and it's open from May to September. Beds cost £6 to £6.50 per person. Bring your own sleeping bag and supplies. Near the post office and the pier, the *Hoy Inn (☎ 791313)* is a bar with a restaurant serving good seafood; the garlic clams are excellent. The RSPB has a small information centre here.

In Rackwick Glen, the *Rackwick Youth Hostel (☎ 873535, ext 2404, office hours only)* has eight beds in two dorms; bring your own sleeping bag and food. The nightly charge is £6.10/4.95 and the warden comes by to collect it each evening.

There are several B&Bs on the island, with accommodation at around £16 per

Scapa Flow Wrecks

The wrecks that litter these clear waters make Scapa Flow the best diving location in Europe. Enclosed by Mainland, Hoy and South Ronaldsay, this is one of the world's largest natural harbours and has been used by vessels as diverse as King Hakon's Viking ships in the 13th century and the NATO fleet of today.

It was from Scapa Flow that the British Home Fleet sailed to meet the German High Seas Fleet at the Battle of Jutland on 31 May 1916. After the war, 74 German ships were interned in Scapa. Conditions for the German sailors were poor and there were several mutinies as the negotiations for the fate of the ships dragged on. When the terms of the armistice were agreed on 6 May 1919 with the announcement of a severely reduced German navy, Admiral von Reuter, who was in charge of the German fleet in Scapa Flow, decided to take matters into his own hands. On 21 June, a secret signal was passed from ship to ship and the British watched incredulously as every German ship began to sink.

Most of the ships were salvaged, but seven vessels remain to attract divers. There are three battleships – the *König*, the *Kronprinz Wilhelm* and the *Markgraf* – which are all over 25,000 tons. The first two were subjected to blasting for scrap metal, but the *Markgraf* is undamaged and considered one of the best dives in the area. Four light cruisers (4400 to 5600 tons) – the *Karlsruhe*, *Dresden*, *Brummer* and *Köln* – are particularly interesting as they lie on their sides and are very accessible to divers. The *Karlsruhe*, though severely damaged, is only 30 feet below the surface. Its twisted superstructure has now become a huge metal reef encrusted with diverse sea life.

As well as the German wrecks, numerous other ships litter the Scapa Flow sea bed. HMS *Royal Oak*, which was sunk by a German U-boat in October 1939, with the loss of 833 crew, is now an official war grave.

If you're interested in diving in Scapa Flow, contact the following: Dolphin Scuba Services (☎ 01856-731269), Garisle, Burray; the Diving Cellar (☎ 01856-850055), 4 Victoria St, Stromness; or Scapa Scuba (☎ 01856-851218), 13 Ness Rd, Stromness. Scapa Scuba runs half-day courses for beginners.

person, with dinner for around £8 extra. **Mrs Rendall** (*☎ 791262, The Glen*), Rackwick, does farmhouse B&B with one double room. At Lyness, **Mrs Budge's** (*☎ 791234*) has two rooms with attached bath. **Mrs Taylor** (*☎ 701358*) does B&B in the Old Custom House at Longhope and has two rooms without bath.

The newly opened **Hoy Hotel** (*☎ 791377, South Rd*), Lyness, has five pleasant rooms for £25 per person, including breakfast. It also serves lunches and evening meals.

The **Anchor Bar** (*☎ 791356*) at Lyness does bar lunches, and there's also a *café* for snacks at the Scapa Flow Visitors Centre. Groceries can be bought at the shop/post office in Lyness and the shop in Longhope.

Getting There & Away
Orkney Ferries (*☎ 850624*) runs a passenger ferry between Stromness and Moaness pier (30 minutes, £2.30), at 7.45 and 10 am and 4.30 pm on weekdays, and 9.30 am and 6 pm at weekends, with a reduced winter schedule (mid-September to mid-May). In the other direction, the service departs five minutes after its arrival on Hoy. All boats can call at Graemsay Island.

Orkney Ferries (*☎ 811397*) also sails to Hoy (Lyness and Longhope) and the island of Flotta from Houton on Mainland, up to seven times daily (Monday to Saturday), for £2.30 each way (£6.90 for a car). A more limited Sunday service runs from May to September.

Flotta and Houton are 20 minutes and 45 minutes from Lyness, respectively.

Getting Around
Transport on Hoy is very limited. North Hoy Transport (*☎ 791315*) runs a minibus service both ways between Rackwick and Moaness to meet the 10 am weekday boat from Stromness. Otherwise, call the same number for a taxi. If there are up to four of you, guided tours are an option; Louise Budge (*☎ 791234*) charges £40 for the group and this includes lunch at her farm.

Hitching is possible, but there's not much traffic.

FLOTTA
Unless you're interested in oil terminals, Flotta will not hold much for you. About 10% of Scotland's oil passes through here, which helps explain the prosperity of Orkney.

The island is flat and measures approximately 3 miles by 2 miles. There are lots of relics from the two world wars, and the only scenery of note is the **Cletts** in the southeastern corner, where there are sea-stacks and blow holes.

See Hoy for details of ferries.

NORTHERN ISLANDS
The group of windswept islands that lies north of Mainland provides a refuge for migrating birds and a nesting ground for seabirds; there are several RSPB reserves. Some of the islands are also rich in archaeological sites.

However, the beautiful scenery, with wonderful white sand beaches and limegreen to azure seas, is the main attraction.

The TICs in Kirkwall and Stromness have a useful brochure, *The Islands of Orkney*, with maps and details of these islands. Note that the pronunciation of the 'ay' ending of each island name is 'ee' (ie Shapinsay is pronounced shapinsee).

Orkney Ferries (*☎ 01856-872044*) operates an efficient ferry service. From Kirkwall you can day-trip to many of the islands (except North Ronaldsay; see that section) on most days of the week, but it's really worth staying for at least a few nights.

Shapinsay
Just 20 minutes by ferry from Kirkwall, Shapinsay is a highly cultivated, low-lying island. **Balfour Castle**, completed in 1848 in the Scottish Baronial style with several turrets, is the most impressive sight and there are tours on Wednesday and Sunday afternoon, May to September, leaving Kirkwall pier at 2.15 pm. These must be arranged in advance at the TIC in Kirkwall; prices are £13.95/6.95, including the ferry, admission to the castle and afternoon tea.

Shapinsay Heritage Centre (☎ 01856-711258), the Smithy, Balfour Village, has a wide range of displays about the island. It's open daily in summer and has a café for snacks.

About 4 miles from the pier, at the far north-eastern corner of the island, is the Iron Age **Burroughston Broch**, one of the best in Orkney. It has a central well. It's open at all times and admission is free.

There are two general stores and a post office on the island.

There's B&B for £16/32 at *Mrs Wallace's* (☎ *01856-711256)*, Girnigoe. With home-made bread and jam, the breakfasts at this farmhouse are excellent, and it also does four-course dinners for £9. It's also possible to stay at *Balfour Castle* (☎ *01856-711282)*, where dinner, B&B costs £88 per person. The castle has a private chapel seating about 20 which is becoming popular for weddings. A boat is available for residents for island trips, birdwatching and sea fishing.

There are about six sailings every day (including Sunday in summer) between Kirkwall and Shapinsay (20 minutes; £2.30, £6.90 for a car).

Rousay

This hilly island, with a population of around 200 people, is known as 'the Egypt of the North' for its numerous archaeological sites. It's mostly an SSSI but it also has the important RSPB **Trumland Reserve** and three lochs for trout fishing.

Marion's shop, and a post office that looks like a hen coop, are 2½ miles north of the pier, at Sourin. Bikes can be rented for £5.50 per day from ABC (☎ 01856-821398), near the pier, and the island's one road makes a pleasant circuit of about 13 miles.

Things to See West of the pier are four prehistoric burial cairns and a broch, open at all times and with free admission. Close to the road and near the hostel, the two-storeyed **Taversoe Tuick** contained the remains of at least five people and a large amount of pottery when it was excavated in

Victorian times. It's an amazing and most unusual structure. **Blackhammer** is a stalled Neolithic chambered cairn dating from 2500 BC, less than a mile west of Taversoe Tuick. Like many of these structures, it originally had a corbelled roof. The **Knowe of Yarso** stalled cairn is a wet half-mile walk from the road; it contained the remains of 29 adults, and had been in use from 2900 BC to 1900 BC.

Midhowe Cairn is the most extraordinary of them all. It's housed inside a modern barn-like building, about 5½ miles west of the pier, and a 550m walk down from the ring road. Containing the remains of 25 people and dating from the 3rd millennium BC, the 'Great Ship of Death', as it's called, is the longest chambered cairn in Orkney. As well as the human remains, there were bird and animal bones too – perhaps meant as food for the deceased?

Nearby, **Midhowe Broch** is the best example of a broch in Orkney. It was built in the 1st century AD and housed a powerful local family.

The TICs on Mainland have a useful leaflet, *Westness Walk*, describing the mile-long walk from Midhowe Cairn to Westness Farm via a Norse cemetery.

Organised Tours Rousay Traveller History Tours (☎ 01856-821234) run on Tuesday and Friday, June to August, meeting the ferry from Tingwall at 11.15 am (£13/11, £6 for children). In six hours, you'll be driven around the island in a minibus and you'll get to explore the main sites.

Places to Stay & Eat *Rousay Farm Hostel* (☎ *01856-821252, Trumland Farm)* is half a mile from the ferry. There's excellent dormitory accommodation for £6 (bring a sleeping bag), single rooms for £7 to £8.50 and tent sites for £2.50. Laundry facilities are available for £1/50p wash/dry. You can get basic groceries, and bar meals from £4.25 to £12, with vegetarian choices, at the *Pier Restaurant* (☎ *01856-821359)*. Its opening hours are complex so phone for details.

Taversoe Hotel (☎ *01856-821325)*, about 2 miles south-west of the pier, has B&B accommodation for £25 per head. The meals are inexpensive and highly recommended: a three-course dinner is about £10, and bar meals main courses start at around £3. Local produce, including seafood, are specialities. There are superb views from the restaurant and a good selection of malt whiskies in the bar. It's closed on Monday for nonresidents.

Getting There & Away A small car ferry connects Tingwall (Mainland) with Rousay (30 minutes; £2.30 for a passenger, £6.90 for a car) and the other nearby islands of Egilsay and Wyre about six times every day. Reversing a car onto the boat in icy conditions is an interesting experience. For bookings phone ☎ 01856-751360.

Egilsay & Wyre

These two small islands lie east of Rousay. On Egilsay, a cenotaph marks the spot where Earl Magnus was murdered in 1116. After his martyrdom, pilgrims flocked to the island and St Magnus Church, now roofless, was built. It's a rare example of a round-towered Viking church. Much of Egilsay is an RSPB reserve; listen for the corncrakes at the south end of the island.

Wyre is even smaller than Egilsay. It was the domain of the Viking baron Kolbein Hruga ('Cubbie Roo'); the ruins of his castle, built around 1145, and the nearby 12th century St Mary's Chapel, can be visited free. At Taing, on the south-west corner of Wyre, look out for seals.

These two islands are reached on the Rousay-Tingwall ferry (see the Rousay section above), but you have to ask if you wish to land.

Stronsay

In the 18th century, the major industry on this island was the collection and burning of seaweed to make kelp, which was exported for use in the production of glass, iodine and soap. In the 19th century, it was replaced by herring-curing, and Whitehall harbour became one of Scotland's major herring ports, until the collapse of the fisheries in the 1930s. Currently, Whitehall has shops, a post office and a hotel. The old **Stronsay Fish Mart** (☎ 01857-616360) now has a herring-fishing interpretation centre (open daily May to September from 11 am to 5 pm, admission free), a hostel and a café.

Just across the harbour from Whitehall is the small island of **Papa Stronsay**, where Earl Rognvald Brusason was murdered in 1046. There's lots of wildlife and seals can be seen on the shore. Ask in Whitehall for boat transport to the island.

A peaceful and attractive farming island, Stronsay now attracts seals, migratory birds and a few tourists. There are good coastal walks and some sandy beaches. In the east, the **Vat o'Kirbister** is the best example of a gloup (natural arch) in Orkney. There's a good trail from the road, and it's a 10 mile round trip from Whitehall.

At the southern end of the island, you should visit the **seal-watch hide** on the beach and under 300m from the camping barn (see Places to Stay & Eat later in this chapter). There's also a chance to see otters at nearby **Loch Lea-shun**.

Organised Tours Two eight-seat minibuses are used by friendly Mr Williamson (☎ 01857-616255) for tours of the island. He can take you on any day of the week, all year, depending on the times of the school bus runs. July and August are the best months; Tuesday and Thursday are not good for a tour, unless you're staying on Stronsay. Tours last at least three hours and visit sites of historical and natural interest; there's no minimum number of participants and the fare is good value at £4 to £5 per person.

Places to Stay & Eat The *Stronsay Hotel* (☎ *01857-616213)* in Whitehall has three rooms for £12 per person. In the bar you can get reasonable pub grub from around £4. The *Stronsay Fish Mart café* (☎ *01857-616360)* at Whitehall is fairly good. It's open all day for takeaways, snacks and meals. Basket meals cost around £4 to £6, and three-course dinners are around £12. There is also the *Stronsay Fish Mart Hostel* (☎ *01857-616360 or 01856-616346)*, open all year; a bed costs £7.50. If you catch the *Woodlea Takeaway* open, it can be very good.

At *Stronsay Bird Reserve* (☎ *01857-616363)*, on Mill Bay, a 40 minute walk from the ferry, there's B&B for £14 and you can also camp for £5 per tent.

Down at the south end of the island, there's *Torness Camping Barn* (☎ *01857-616314)*, on the environmentally-friendly Holland Farm, and only a few metres from the beach. It's a basic but rather pleasant place, sleeping about eight, with kitchen and toilet, but there isn't a shower yet and you'll need a sleeping bag. An overnight here costs only £3. Phone from the pier for pick-up.

Getting There & Away BA Express (☎ 01856-872494) has two flights a day, Monday to Friday, from Kirkwall (£29/58 for a single/return).

A ferry service links Kirkwall with Stronsay (1½ hours, two per day, £4.60, £10.35 for a car), and Stronsay with Eday (35 minutes, one per day, £2.30). There's a reduced service on Sunday (one per day; no run to Eday).

Eday

Eday supplied some of the stone for St Magnus Cathedral in Kirkwall, and peat for most other northern islands. It has a hilly centre and cultivated fields around the coast. Occupied for at least the last 5000 years, Eday has numerous chambered cairns, and also one of Orkney's most impressively located standing stones, the **Stone of Setter**, which is over 5m high. Close to the stone are the chambered cairns **Braeside**, **Huntersquoy** and **Vinquoy**. Huntersquoy is a two-storeyed cairn, like Taversoe Tuick on Rousay. From nearby **Mill Loch bird hide** you can observe red-throated divers.

The early 17th century **Carrick House** (☎ 01857-622260) is worth a visit. It's open

from June to September on Sunday afternoons and at other times by arrangement (there's a small admission charge). The pirate John Gow was captured here in 1725, during a failed raid on the house (there's still a blood stain on the floor). The pirates were later executed in London. Guided tours are available in French.

It's worth getting hold of the *Eday Heritage Walk* leaflet, which details an interesting four hour ramble from the Community Enterprises shop up to the Cliffs of Red Head (red sandstone) in the north of the island. There's also an easy one hour walk in the south of the island, to Warness Point.

Organised Tours The Eday Heritage Tour runs from Kirkwall at 9.20 am on Sunday from mid-June to mid-September. It lasts 10½ hours and the £28.50/25.50 ticket includes ferries, guided walks, lunch and admission to Carrick House. Book with Orkney Ferries (☎ 01856-872044), Kirkwall TIC, or pay on the boat.

Places to Stay & Eat The basic *Eday Youth Hostel* (☎ *01857-622283)*, run by Eday Community Enterprises, is centrally located, 4 miles from the ferry. You'll need to have a sleeping bag. There are 24 beds; £4.65/3.85 per night. Ask permission for camping.

There's dinner, B&B at *Mrs Popplewell's* (☎ *01857-622248, Blett)*, Carrick Bay, opposite the Calf of Eday. She has one single and one double for £23 per person. There's also a fully equipped self-catering croft-house nearby, for three people, at only £10 per person per night. Mrs Popplewell bakes fresh bread daily, and she serves snacks and meals at her craft shop. *Mrs Cockram's* (☎ *01857-622271)*, in a comfortable farmhouse at Skaill, near the church, charges around £29 per person for dinner, B&B.

Getting There & Away There are flights from Kirkwall (£29/58 per single/return) to London airport – that's London, Eday – on Wednesday only. The ferry service from Kirkwall sails via Stronsay (1¼ to two hours, £4.60, £10.35 for a car), but some-times it's direct. There's a link between Sanday and Eday on Monday, Friday and Sunday.

Getting Around Alan Stewart (☎ 01857-622206) runs the local minibus and taxi service. He charges around £3 for a trip along the length of Eday. Ask locally about bicycle hire.

Sanday

This island is aptly named, for the best beaches in Orkney are here – dazzling white sand of the sort you'd expect in the Caribbean.

The island is almost entirely flat, apart from the cliffs at Spurness; it's 12 miles long and growing due to sand build-up.

There are several archaeological sites, the most impressive being the **Quoyness chambered tomb**, similar to Maeshowe, and dating from the 3rd millennium BC. It has triple walls, a main chamber and six smaller cells. Open at all times, admission is free. At the north-eastern tip of Sanday, there's **Tofts Ness**, with around 500 prehis-toric burial mounds.

The island is known for its knitwear, which is sold in Lady village, at the Wool Hall. There are several shops and post offices on Sanday. Cars and taxis can be hired from Kettletoft Garage (☎ 01857-600321). For bicycle hire, try Bernie Flett (☎ 01857-600418).

Organised Tours Bernie Flett (☎ 01857-600418), Quivals Garage, does 9½-hour day tours of the island on Wednesday and Friday, late May to early September, leaving Kirkwall pier at 10.10 am. There's a minimum number (four people), and the charge is £28/20 per person.

Places to Stay & Eat With permission, you can camp on the island, but there's no hostel. There are several B&Bs charging around £15 per person, including *Mrs Flett* (☎ *01857-600418*), Quivals, where pick-up may be possible. The *Kettletoft Hotel*

(☎ *01857-600217*) costs £17 per person (rooms without bath); dinner is available for £6. There's comfortable accommodation at the *Belsair Hotel* (☎ *01857-600206*), Kettletoft, which has six rooms, three with attached baths. Charges are from £19.50 per person and dinner is £6 extra.

Getting There & Away Flights from Kirkwall (£29 single, £58 return) operate to Sanday and Westray twice daily from Monday to Friday, and once on Saturday. There's at least one ferry a day between Kirkwall and Sanday (1½ hours, £4.60, £10.35 for a car) year-round.

Westray

This is the largest of the northern islands, with a population of around 700. It's quite a varied island, with prehistoric sites, some sandy beaches, great cliff scenery and the impressive ruins of **Noltland Castle**, a 16th century fortified Z-plan tower house (access at all times; free).

It's also famous for the RSPB reserve at Noup Head Cliffs, which attracts vast numbers of breeding seabirds.

Pierowall is the main village and one of the best natural harbours in Orkney, once an important Viking base. It has grocery shops, a post office and a hotel. By the ruins of the 17th century **St Mary's Church**, you'll find some interesting gravestones. In the village, there's the **Westray Heritage Centre**, with local history and nature displays. It's open daily from early May to late September from 2 to 5 pm and admission is £2/1.50 (child 50p). Ferries from Kirkwall dock at Rapness, about 7 miles south of Pierowall.

Organised Tours Island Explorer (☎ 01857-677355) runs daily 5½ to nine-hour nature tours of the island from Easter to September, leaving Rapness pier after ferry arrivals. There's no minimum number, and the charge is around £20 per person, in-cluding lunch if you arrive around midday. Your guide, Alex Costie, is a retired fisher-man and he'll entertain you with colourful descriptions of island life.

Places to Stay & Eat With permission, you can camp almost anywhere. Several places offer B&B from around £15/30. Try *Mrs Groat's* (☎ *01857-677374*) at Sand o'Gill (where there are a couple of bikes for hire); she also has a camp site, and a six-berth van for between £50 and £80 per week. The *Pierowall Hotel* (☎ *01857-677208*) is a popular pub with accommodation at £16/30 without bath, £21/38 with bath. It does home-made bar meals for around £4 to £6, including its popular fish and chips (£3.60).

The most comfortable place to stay is the *Cleaton House Hotel* (☎ *01857-677508*), a refurbished Victorian manse about 2 miles south-east of Pierowall. B&B costs from £29 to £32 per person and all rooms are *en suite*. It serves good bar and restaurant meals.

Getting There & Away For information on flights, see under Sanday. A ferry service links Kirkwall with Rapness, with at least two trips a day (1½ hours, £4.60, £10.35 for a car) in each direction; the winter service (mid-September to mid-May) is once or twice daily. There's also a ferry from Pierowall to Papa Westray, two to six times daily (25 minutes), with the same fares. In winter (late October to May) the boat sails by arrangement (☎ 01857-677216). On Tuesday and Friday in summer, there's a through service from Pierowall to Kirkwall via Papa Westray for the same fare. It takes 1¾ hours.

Papa Westray

This tiny island (4 miles long and a mile wide) attracts superlatives – Europe's oldest domestic building is the **Knap of Howar** (built about 5500 years ago), the world's shortest scheduled flight is the two minute hop over from Westray, and a colony of about 6000 arctic terns, the largest in Europe, is at North Hill. The island was also the cradle of Christianity in Orkney – **St Boniface's Church** was founded in the 8th century, but most of the recently restored structure dates from the 12th century.

Jim Davidson (☎ 01857-644259) runs boat trips from May to September to the Holm of Papay, a small island about a half-mile east of Papa Westray, for £3 per person. The main reason for a visit is to see the huge **chambered cairn**, with 16 beehive cells and wall carvings. You enter through the roof and there's a torch so you can see your way as you crawl around in the gloomy interior.

Places to Stay & Eat The excellent *Papa Westray Hostel* (☎ *01857-644267*) opens all year and it's just over a mile north of the ferry. There are 16 beds and the nightly charge is £7.75/6.50. The community co-op, which runs the hostel, also has four comfortable rooms with attached bathrooms on a B&B basis for £26/46. There is also a small shop and restaurant here; lunches are served, and evening meals are available for £11.50 (reserve in advance).

The *Beltane House Hotel* (☎ *01857-644267*) is in a row of converted farm-workers' cottages. It has four rooms with attached bath for £26/46 single/double. Dinner is a further £14.50. Ask to be picked up from the airport or ferry terminal.

Getting There & Away Flying to Papa Westray or North Ronaldsay from Kirkwall is an amazing deal compared with other flights in Orkney – about twice the distance for half the price. To either island it's £14/28 for a single/return, and there are flights twice daily from Monday to Saturday.

There's a ferry from Pierowall on Westray to Papa Westray, two to six times daily from May to October (25 minutes, £4.60, £10.35 for a car). On Tuesday and Friday, there's a through service from Kirkwall (1¾ hours, with the same fares).

North Ronaldsay

Pity the poor sheep on this remote, windswept island – they're kept off the rich farmland by a 13 mile-long wall and forced to feed only on seaweed, which is said to give their meat a unique flavour.

North Ronaldsay, population 50, is only 3 miles long and almost completely flat. There's a shop and a pub which serves

ORKNEY & SHETLAND ISLANDS

meals. The island has Scotland's tallest land-built lighthouse (33m), and seal and cormorant colonies nearby. North Ronaldsay is also an important stopover point for migratory birds. The *Bird Observatory* (☎ *01857-633200)* at the pier offers solar-powered accommodation and ornithological activities from £24 to £27 per person including dinner. *Mrs Muir (☎ 01857-633244),* Garso Guest House, is about 3 miles from the pier; charges are £25 per head for dinner, B&B. There's also a self-catering cottage (minimum let one night), sleeping five, for £20 per night. Mr Muir does car hire for £25 per day, including petrol, but you're unlikely to use much! He also does a taxi and minibus service.

See Papa Westray for details of flights. There's also a weekly sailing from Kirkwall, not always on the same day of the week. Phone ☎ 01856-872044 for details.

Shetland Islands

Sixty miles north-east of Orkney, the Shetland Islands remained under Norse rule until 1469, when they were given to Scotland as part of a Danish princess' dowry. Even today these remote, windswept, virtually treeless islands are almost as much a part of Scandinavia as of Britain – the nearest mainland town is Bergen, Norway.

Much bleaker than Orkney, Shetland is famous for its varied birdlife, teeming seabird colonies and a 4000-year-old archaeological heritage that includes the ancient settlement of Jarlshof. Also, its rugged, indented coastline offers superb cliff-top walks and good fishing.

Almost everything of interest is on the coast rather than inland, so you're much more aware of the presence of the sea than on Orkney's Mainland. In fact, in Shetland it's impossible to get farther than 3 miles from the sea. There are some impressively located places to stay, and budget accommodation includes six camping böds (barns).

Covering an area of 547 sq miles, the Shetlands are made up of 100 islands, of which about 15 are inhabited. Mainland is by far the largest and Lerwick is the capital. Shetland is the base for the North Sea oilfields, and pipelines feed Europe's biggest oil refinery at Sullom Voe, in north Mainland. Oil has brought a certain amount of prosperity to these islands; there are well-equipped leisure centres in many villages. With the exceptions of Lerwick and Scalloway, most villages are collections of scattered settlements.

GETTING THERE & AWAY
Unlike Orkney, Shetland is relatively expensive to get to from mainland Britain.

Air
The oil industry ensures that air connections are good. The main airport is at Sumburgh, 25 miles south of Lerwick. There are at least four flights daily between Sumburgh and Aberdeen (50 minutes), on British Airways (☎ 0345-222111) and Business Air (☎ 0500-340146). The standard fare is around £130 return. You can also fly direct from Inverness, Glasgow, Edinburgh, Belfast and London.

British Airways operates low-flying ATPs daily between Orkney and Shetland (35 minutes, £85 return).

Boat
P&O (☎ 01224-572615) runs car ferries from Lerwick to Aberdeen and Stromness (Orkney); see those sections for details. For details of the ferry link between Lerwick and Bergen (Norway) see the Getting There & Away chapter.

GETTING AROUND
Bus
There are several bus operators. For detailed information on all services call ☎ 01595-694100.

Car
The wide roads seem more like motorways after Orkney's tiny, winding lanes. A cheaper option is to rent a car in Lerwick rather than at the airport. Try Star Rent A

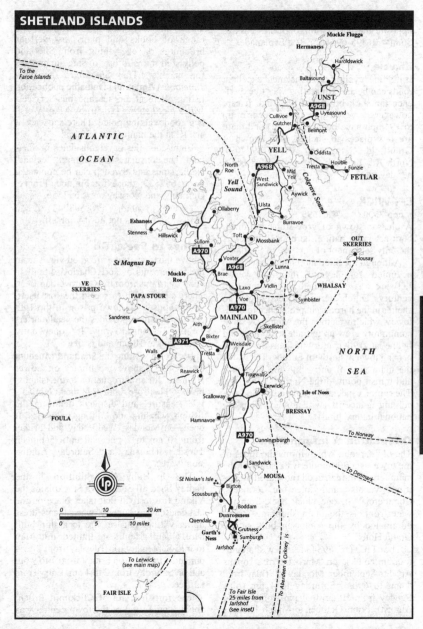

SHETLAND ISLANDS

Muckle Flugga
Hermaness
Haroldswick
Baltasound
UNST
A968
Uyeasound
Cullivoe
Gutcher
Belmont
Oddsta
Tresta
Houbie
Funzie
FETLAR
To the
Faroe Islands
ATLANTIC
OCEAN
North
Roe
Yell
Sound
YELL
A968
Mid
Yell
West
Sandwick
Aywick
Ulsta
Colgrave Sound
Ollaberry
Burravoe
OUT
SKERRIES
Eshaness
Stenness
Hillswick
Sullom
Toft
Mossbank
Housay
A970
Voxter
A968
St Magnus Bay
Muckle
Roe
Brae
Lunna
VE
SKERRIES
Laxo
Vidlin
WHALSAY
PAPA STOUR
Voe
Symbister
Sandness
A970
MAINLAND
Aith
Skellister
Walls
A971
Bixter
Weisdale
NORTH
Tresta
SEA
Reawick
Tingwall
Scalloway
Lerwick
Isle of Noss
BRESSAY
Hamnavoe
FOULA
A970
Cunningsburgh
To Norway
Sandwick
MOUSA
To Denmark
St Ninian's Isle
Bigton
Scousburgh
Boddam
Dunrossness
Quendale
Grutness
Garth's
Ness
Sumburgh
Jarlshof

0   10   20 km
0   5   10 miles

To Lerwick
(see main map)

FAIR ISLE

To Fair Isle
25 miles from
Jarlshof
(see inset)

To Aberdeen & Orkney Is

ORKNEY & SHETLAND ISLANDS

Car (☎ 01595-692075), 22 Commercial Rd, opposite the bus station, or John Leask & Son (☎ 01595-693162), The Esplanade.

Bicycle

If it's fine, cycling on the islands' excellent roads can be an exhilarating way to experience the stark beauty of Shetland. It can, however, be very windy (windspeeds of up to 194mph have been recorded!) and there are few places to shelter. Eric Brown at Grantfield Garage (☎ 01595-692709), North Rd, Lerwick, hires bikes for £6/35 per day/week.

LERWICK

• pop 7500   ☎ 01595

A pleasant town of grey-stone buildings built around a natural harbour, Lerwick is the only settlement of any size in Shetland.

Although the Shetland Islands have been occupied for several thousand years, Lerwick was established only in the 17th century. Dutch herring fleets began to shelter in the harbour, in preference to Scalloway, which was then the capital. A small community grew up to trade with them and by the late 19th century this was the largest herring town in northern Europe. Today, it's the main port of entry into the Shetlands and transit point to the North Sea oil rigs. The centre, especially Commercial St, is receiving a facelift (with money from the national lottery fund).

Orientation & Information

The old harbour, which forms the focus of the town, is a 20-minute walk south of the main ferry terminal, and is now used by visiting yachts and pleasure cruisers. Commercial St, one block back from the waterfront, is the main shopping street, dominated by the Victorian bulk of the Grand Hotel.

The TIC (☎ 693434, www.shetland-tourism.co.uk), on Market Cross, opens April to September, Monday to Friday from 8 am to 6 pm, Saturday to 4 pm (plus Sunday from 10 am to 1 pm from June to August). From October to March it opens

on weekdays from 9 am to 5 pm. There's a *bureau de change* here. The TIC has a good range of books and maps, as well as brochures on everything from Shetland pony stud farms to lists of safe anchorages for yachts. The *Shetland Transport Timetable* (70p) is an invaluable publication listing all local air, sea and bus services. *Walks on Shetland* (£6.50) by Mary Welsh is a good walking guide. There's a seasonal TIC at the main ferry terminal.

Eight countries have consulates in Shetland. The consulates for Denmark, Iceland, Netherlands and Sweden can be contacted on ☎ 692533; those for Finland, France, Germany and Norway on ☎ 692556.

Lerwick Laundry (☎ 698043) is on Market St, but it's not do-it-yourself.

Things to See & Do

Above the town, there are good views from the battlements of **Fort Charlotte**, built in 1653 by troops from the Cromwellian fleet. There's not much to see in the fort itself, which housed the town prison in the 19th century and now provides the headquarters for the Territorial Army. It's open daily from 9 am to 10 pm and is free.

It's worth visiting the **Shetland Museum** (☎ 695057), above the library on Lower Hillhead, for an introduction to the islands' history. There are replicas of the St Ninian's Isle treasure, and displays detailing the fishing, whaling and knitting industries. It opens on Monday, Wednesday and Friday from 10 am to 7 pm, and until 5 pm on Tuesday, Thursday and Saturday. Admission is free.

The **Up Helly Aa Exhibition**, in the Galley Shed off St Sunniva St, explains the Viking fire festival that takes place on the last Tuesday in January, when locals dress up as Vikings and set fire to a ship built here. Opening hours are limited: mid-May to mid-September, on Tuesday from 2 to 4 pm and 7 to 9 pm, on Friday from 7 to 9 pm and on Saturday from 2 to 4 pm. Entry costs £2/free.

The fortified site of **Clickimin Broch**, about a mile west of the town centre, was

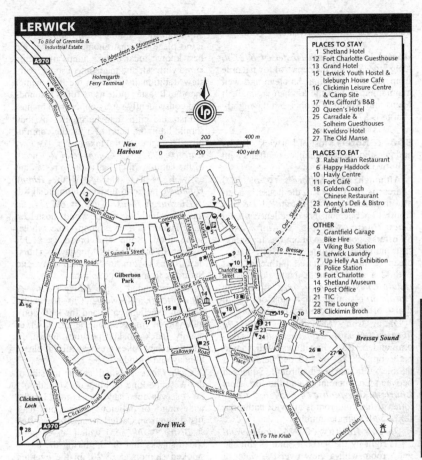

occupied from the 7th century BC to the 6th century AD. It's always open and is free. The entrance to the path leading to the site is opposite the BP service station.

The **Böd of Gremista**, about a mile north of the ferry terminal, was the birthplace of Arthur Anderson, one of the founders of P&O. It has been restored as an 18th century fishing booth; there's also a small exhibition about Anderson. It's open June to mid-September, on Wednesday to Sunday, from 10 am to 1 pm and from 2 to 5 pm, costing £1.50/1.

There's a cliff-side walk south to the headland known as **The Knab**, where you can watch the ferries coming in.

Special Events
It's well worth being here for the Folk Festival in April/May, or the Fiddle and Accordion Festival in October.

Places to Stay
Camping *Clickimin Caravan & Camp Site* (☎ 741000) is behind Clickimin Leisure Centre by the loch on the western edge of

town. It charges £5.60 for a small tent and includes use of the shower in the centre.

Hostel *Lerwick Youth Hostel (☎ 692114, King Harald St)* in the centre of town a mile from the ferry terminal, is clean and well maintained though the kitchen is small. It opens mid-April to October and the nightly charge is £7.75/6.50.

B&Bs & Hotels Most of Lerwick's B&Bs and guesthouses are small, cosy affairs with only two or three rooms.

Although *Mrs Gifford's (☎ 693554)* address is 12 Burgh Rd, the house is actually in a small lane off Burgh Rd. B&B is from £17 per person. The excellent *Solheim Guest House (☎ 695275, 34 King Harald St)* offers a good range of options for breakfast including yoghurt and fruit. Large, clean rooms with shared bathroom cost £18/32 a single/double. Next door, *Carradale Guest House (☎ 692251, 36 King Harald St)* is similar with rooms for £19/36; it also offers evening meals on request.

Dating from 1685, the charming *Old Manse (☎ 696301, 9 Commercial St)* is recommended. B&B in singles with shared bathroom is £18, or £20 per person in a double with attached bathroom. Squeezed between Commercial St and the fort, *Fort Charlotte Guesthouse (☎ 695956, 1 Charlotte St)* has four rooms all with bathroom for £25/40 a single/double.

Queen's Hotel (☎ 692826, Commercial St) is right by the harbour, and, if you can get a room with a view over the water, a pleasant place to stay. Singles/doubles are £59/90.

Also in the centre, the fully refurbished *Grand Hotel (☎ 692826, Commercial St)* offers *en suite* rooms for £62/85.

The top hotel, *Kveldsro House Hotel (☎ 692195)*, is just off Greenfield Place, overlooking the harbour, though the small, narrow streets can make it difficult to find. Pronounced kelro, it's a very comfortable, small hotel with 17 rooms for £88.50/105.50. If it isn't busy at the weekend you may be able to negotiate a special deal.

Places to Eat

Although there's good fresh fish, Shetland is no place for gastronomes. Restit is the best known local dish – lumps of mutton cured with salt and made into a soupy, salty stew traditionally eaten in the long winter months. It tastes quite as awful as it sounds and consequently rarely appears on menus.

Fish and chips can be good – as they should be in the heart of a fishing community. There are several takeaways. Try *Fort Café (☎ 693125, 2 Commercial Rd)* north of the centre, which has a cheap restaurant as well as a takeaway, or the *Happy Haddock*, farther round on Commercial Rd.

Islesburgh House Café (☎ 692114), in the same building as the youth hostel on King Harald St, serves good-value, wholesome food. Soup and bread is £1.15, lasagne £3.60. It opens Monday to Thursday from 11 am to 9 pm, Friday and Saturday from 11 am to 5 pm.

Recommended is the *Havly Centre (9 Charlotte St)*, a Norwegian Christian centre with an excellent café, and the staff don't quiz you on your religious beliefs. It serves mainly snacks (baked potatoes are £2.50) and its gooey cakes are heavenly; it closes Sunday and Monday.

Caffe Latte, is a small café at the side of the Westside Pine building on Mounthooly St. It serves open sandwiches for £3 and a wide range of delicious coffees and teas. Just down from Caffe Latte is *Monty's Deli & Bistro (☎ 696555)* which serves good cheap snacks and meals during the day – smoked salmon is £3.20; in the evening mains range from £7.20 to £13.50. It's closed on Sunday.

Raba Indian Restaurant, near the bus station, is the best curry house in Shetland. The large *Golden Coach (☎ 693848)*, Hillhead, is the only Chinese restaurant; lunchtime mains are around £5.

There's a good restaurant at the *Queen's Hotel*, with four-course dinners for £15.75, but secluded *Kveldsro House Hotel* is the place to go for a really special occasion. It serves a four-course dinner plus coffee/tea for £23.50, and also does cheaper bar meals.

Entertainment

The best place to drink is at the *Lounge*, Mounthooly St near the TIC. There's live music some evenings and Saturday lunchtimes. *Captain Flint's* nearby also has live music. The town's only nightclub is *Posers*, at the Grand Hotel. The Shetland Fiddlers play at a number of locations, and it's worth attending their sessions – inquire at the TIC.

Shopping

Best buys are the woollen jerseys, cardigans and sweaters for which Shetland is world-famous. There are numerous shops selling woollens, but for bargains you must go to the factories. One is Judane (☎ 693724), on the industrial estate north past the power station. It sells plain sweaters for £11, patterned ones for £15. Most sought-after are real Fair Isle sweaters, which cost from £25.50. To qualify as such, they must not only have the distinctive OXOXO pattern, but must also have been made on Fair Isle.

Getting There & Away

See the introductory Getting There & Away section to Shetland and the Getting There & Away chapter. Ferries dock at Holmsgarth terminal, a 20 minute walk from the town centre. From the main airport at Sumburgh, Leask's (☎ 693162) runs regular buses to meet flights (£1.90 one way).

Getting Around

If you need a taxi call Kings Taxi ☎ 696500.

AROUND LERWICK
Bressay & Noss

Two islands lie across Bressay Sound east of Lerwick. The 21-sq-mile island of Bressay (pronounced bressah) shelters Lerwick from the North Sea making the town's harbour one of the finest in Britain. There are some interesting walks especially along the cliffs and up Ward Hill (226m, 742 feet) which offers good views of the island.

Colonies of birds can be seen at the Ord and Bard Head cliffs in the south. For serious **birdwatching** though, it's worth visiting Noss (NNR) east of Bressay, to see the huge numbers of seabirds nesting on the island's 183m (600 feet) cliffs. Noss can only be visited mid-May to August when Scottish Natural Heritage operates a small visitors centre at Gungstie.

May to August, Bressaboats (☎ 693434) runs three-hour cruises from Lerwick around Bressay and Noss for £15/7.50; check with the TIC.

There's B&B accommodation on Bressay at the *Maryfield Hotel* (☎ 820207), near the ferry terminal, but you can't stay on Noss.

Getting There & Away From the dock below Fort Charlotte in Lerwick, there are hourly ferries (☎ 01426-980317) daily to Bressay (five minutes, £1.10). It's then 2½ miles across the island (some people bring rented bikes from Lerwick) to take the inflatable dinghy to Noss. The dinghy shuttles across the water Friday to Sunday and Tuesday and Wednesday from 10 am to 5 pm (£2.50/1 return). Check with the TIC before leaving Lerwick as the Noss dinghy doesn't operate in bad weather.

CENTRAL & WEST MAINLAND
Scalloway

The former capital of Shetland, Scalloway (pronounced scallowah), on the west coast 6 miles from Lerwick, is now a busy fishing village. During WWII, the Norwegian resistance movement operated from here, carrying arms and transporting refugees in fishing boats. This link was known as the 'Shetland Bus'.

Things to See The ruins of **Scalloway Castle** (HS) rise above the warehouses of the port. It was built in 1600 by the cruel Patrick Stewart, Earl of Orkney and Lord of Shetland, and consists of a four-storey rectangular main block, with a wing of the same height at one corner. If the gate is closed, get the key from the Shetland Woollen Company shop just up the hill. The small, volunteer-run **Scalloway Museum**,

Birdwatching in the Shetlands

Lying on the north-south and east-west migration routes, this island group is internationally famous for its birdlife, and is one of Britain's top birdwatching locations. As well as being a stopover for migrating Arctic species, there are large seabird breeding colonies.

Out of the 24 seabird species that nest in the British Isles, 21 are found here; June is the height of the breeding season. The bird population vastly outnumbers the human population of 24,000 – there are said to be around 30,000 gannets, 140,000 guillemots, 250,000 puffins and 300,000 fulmars.

The Shetland Islands boast a puffin population of 250,000.

The Royal Society for the Protection of Birds (RSPB) maintains reserves on south Mainland at **Loch of Spiggie**, which attracts wildfowl in autumn and winter, **Lumbister** on Yell, a 4000-acre moorland reserve, and on the remote island of **Fetlar**, which supports the richest heathland bird community, known particularly for its snowy owls.

There are national nature reserves at **Hermaness**, where you can't fail to be entertained by the clownish antics of the almost tame puffins – known here as the tammy norrie – and on the **Isle of Noss**, which can be reached from Lerwick. **Fair Isle**, owned by the National Trust for Scotland (NTS), supports large seabird populations and there's accommodation at the bird observatory.

Lerwick TIC has lots of ornithological leaflets. Take care when out birdwatching, as the cliff-edge sites can be dangerous. Also watch out for skuas ('bonxies') that will dive-bomb you if you go near their nests. Since they aim for the highest part of your body, it's wise to walk with a stick, pointing it above your head if they approach. And don't get too close to nesting fulmars or you'll be the target for their smelly, oily spittle!

Main St, is interesting for its displays on the 'Shetland Bus'. It opens from May to September, Tuesday to Thursday from 2 to 4.30 pm, Saturday from 10 am to 12.30 pm, and from 2 to 4.30 pm. A donation is requested.

Places to Stay & Eat There are two B&Bs in Upper Scalloway, which both have *en suite* singles/doubles: *Broch Guest House* (☎ 01595-880767) costs £19/34, *Hildasay Guest House* (☎ 01595-880822) £20/36. Hildasay also arranges fishing trips. Down in the village close to the waterfront on Main St, the refurbished *Scalloway* *Hotel* (☎ 01595-880444) has 24 rooms all with bathrooms from £40/60 including breakfast. It has bar meals and a restaurant as does the nearby *Kiln Bar*.

The *Da Haaf Restaurant* (☎ 01595-880328) is situated in the North Atlantic Fisheries College and specialises in local seafood which is quite often prepared by the students. It's open on weekdays from 9 am to 8 pm.

Getting There & Away Buses run up to six times daily from Lerwick (20 minutes, 95p); there are no buses on Sunday.

Tingwall Valley

North of Scalloway, the B9074 follows the western shores of the two lochs, Asta and Tingwall, through the fertile Tingwall Valley. In June and July the wildflowers are particularly beautiful. Both lochs are good for trout **fishing** and home to several species of birds including swans. The promontory at the northern end of the Loch of Tingwall is called the **Law Ting Holm**. In the days of Norse rule, this was where Shetland's annual parliament or *althing* was held.

Beyond the loch and Tingwall Kirk, **Tingwall Agricultural Museum** (☎ 01595-840344), in an 18th century granary, houses an intriguing collection of crofting, fishing and domestic implements. It opens from June to August, Monday to Saturday, from 10 am to 1 pm, and 2 to 5 pm; £1.50/1.

Weisdale

North-west of Tingwall, on the A971 there are great views of Shetland from **Wormadale Hill**, while below past the Loch of Strom, the head of **Weisdale Voe** is a good spot for viewing wading birds. Nearby, the restored **Weisdale Mill** (☎ 01595-830400) is now a gallery and café.

In the 19th century the mill was part of the estate of Kergord (then called Flemington), about half a mile north. No crofters' cottages are found here because in the 1850s tenants were 'cleared' by the laird to make way for sheep. Stones from the cottages were used to build the estate house which, in the 1940s, was the headquarters of the Shetland Bus operation. Today around Kergord, tree plantations attract woodland birds such as the rook and chaffinch.

On the western shore of Weisdale Voe, south of the mill, are the ruins of the house where John Clunies Ross (1786-1853) was born. In 1827 he settled in the Cocos Islands in the Indian Ocean where he proclaimed himself 'king'.

The West Side

The area west of Weisdale, notable for its varied scenery of bleak moors, sheer cliffs, rolling green hills and numerous cobalt-blue lochs and inlets, is great for walking, cycling and fishing.

There are also a number of interesting archaeological sites including **Stanydale**, a Neolithic settlement, and the **Scord of Brewster**, a prehistoric farm at Brig of Waas, both signposted off the road between Bixter and Walls.

Out in the Atlantic Ocean, about 15 miles south-wespt of Walls is the remote, windswept, 5-sq-mile island of **Foula** (Bird Island). It competes with Fair Isle for the title of Britain's most isolated inhabited island. It supports a community of around 40 people and 1500 sheep plus 500,000 seabirds, including the rare Leach's petrel and Britain's largest colony of great skuas. All this amid dramatic cliff scenery, particularly the awesome, sheer Kame (372m, 1220 feet). There's no shop on the island, but accommodation is available at *Mrs Taylor's* (☎ *01595-753226*), Leraback, who offers dinner, B&B for £22 per person. Foula is reached by twice-weekly ferries (four hours; £4 return, £39.36 for a car and driver) from Walls (☎ 01595-753232) and flights (£40 return) from Tingwall (☎ 01595-840246).

North-west from Walls, the road crosses desolate moorland then descends through green fields before arriving at the small crofting community of **Sandness**. Visible about a mile offshore is the island of **Papa Stour**, home to huge colonies of auks, terns and skuas. It's mostly made up of volcanic rock which has eroded to form sea caves, underground passages, arches and columns. Access to the island is by ferry from West Burrafirth (east of Sandness), which runs four times weekly (£4 return; £39.36 for a car and driver); book with W Clark (☎ 01595-810460).

SOUTH MAINLAND

From Lerwick, the main road south winds 25 miles down the eastern side of this long, narrow, hilly tail of land that ends at Sumburgh Head. South of Sandwick, a minor road loops around to the west coast at

ORKNEY & SHETLAND ISLANDS

Bigton before returning to the main road at Boddam.

Catpund

About 10 miles south of Lerwick, Catpund is an interesting archaeological site. From neolithic to medieval times this former large quarry was mined for soapstone, which was used to make various utensils and implements. It was excavated in the 1980s and evidence of the workings can be seen along the stream.

Sandwick & Around

Opposite the small, scattered village of Sandwick is the **Isle of Mousa** (SSSI), on which stands the impressive double-walled fortified tower, **Mousa Broch** (13m). The well preserved broch was built between 100 BC and 100 AD from local sandstone and features in two Viking sagas. The island is also home to many seabirds and waders, particularly the storm petrel. Common and grey seals can be seen on the beach and among the rocks at West Voe.

From April to September there are regular boat trips (15 minutes, £5/2.50 return) from Leebitton harbour in Sandwick, allowing 2½ hours on the island. Phone Tom Jamieson (☎ 01950-431367) in advance for reservations.

Mrs J Stove (☎ *01950-431410)*, Sandwick, has one room with B&B for £15 per person. *Barclay Arms Hotel* (☎ *01950-431226)*, has full *en suite* facilities and B&B for £26/50 a single/double; it also offers evening meals.

There are five buses a day, Monday to Saturday, between Lerwick and Sandwick (25 minutes, £1.30).

Bigton & Around

Buses from Lerwick stop twice daily in Bigton on the west coast, but it's another couple of miles to the **tombolo** (a narrow isthmus) that connects Mainland with St Ninian's Isle. The site is of geological importance and is an SSSI. It's the largest shell-and-sand tombolo in Britain; most other similar tombolos are made of gravel or shingle.

Across the tombolo is **St Ninian's Isle** where you'll find the ruins of a 12th century church, beneath which are traces of an earlier Pictish church. In 1958 during excavations, Pictish treasure, probably dating from 800 AD and consisting of 27 silver objects, including shallow bowls and dishes, was found beneath a broken sandstone slab. They're now kept in the Museum of Scotland in Edinburgh, but you can see replicas in the Shetland Museum, Lerwick.

Boddam

From this small village there's a side road that leads to the **Shetland Crofthouse Museum** (☎ 01595-695075). Built in the 1870s it has been restored, thatched and furnished with 19th century furniture and utensils. It's open daily May to September, from 10 am to 1 pm, and 2 to 3 pm; £1.50/1. The bus stops right outside.

Quendale

South of Boddam, a minor road runs southwest to Quendale where you'll find the small, restored, fully working, 19th century **Quendale Mill**, the last of Shetland's water mills. It's on a working farm and the £1.50/50p entry fee includes an interesting 10 minute video. It's open daily from May to September, from 10 am to 5 pm. The bus stops in Quendale from which it's about a mile (signposted) to the mill.

The village overlooks a long, sandy beach to the south in the Bay of Quendale. West of the bay there's dramatic cliff scenery and **diving** in the waters between Garth's Ness and Fitful Head and to the wreck of the oil tanker *Braer* off Garth's Ness. About 2 miles north of the village, the RSPB reserve of **Loch of Spiggie** is a refuge in autumn and winter for wildfowl, especially whooper swans. Other migrating birds that stop over are kittiwakes, arctic terns and greylag geese. Nesting birds include ducks, oystercatchers and curlews.

You're not allowed into the reserve, but there are good views from the road.

From Lerwick there are two buses daily, Monday to Saturday.

Sumburgh

At the southern tip of Mainland, this village is the location of the international airport and **Jarlshof** (☎ 01950-460112, HS), Shetland's most impressive archaeological attraction. This large settlement, with buildings from prehistory through Norse times to the 16th century, was hidden under the sand until exposed by a gale at the end of the 19th century. The original Stone Age settlement is topped by a medieval broch, wheelhouses, a Norse farmhouse and the remains of a 16th century mansion. The site gets its name from Sir Walter Scott; Jarlshof is what he called the mansion in his novel, *The Pirate*.

The short guidebook available from the visitors centre interprets the ruins from a number of vantage points. It's an interesting place, but the modern world impinges with the airport and hotel so close. It opens daily April to September, from 9.30 am to 6.30 pm; £2.30/1.

Near Jarlshof you can visit **Sumburgh Head**, an RSPB reserve. The lighthouse here isn't open to the public, but you can view the many birds that inhabit the cliffs below. At various times there are puffins, kittiwakes (20,000 pairs breed at the head), fulmars, guillemots (5000 pairs breed here), razorbills and cormorants (500 pairs). The other important birdwatching area is the **Pool of Virkie**, the bay just east of the airport.

At Old Scatness next to the airport, **Betty Mouat's Cottage**, a crofter's cottage, is now a camping böd. Betty became famous in 1886 when, on a routine sailing trip to Lerwick on board the fishing smack *Columbine*, the captain was swept overboard. His two crewmen went to rescue him, leaving Betty alone; they were unable to return to the smack which drifted for nine days before ending up in Norway, however Betty survived.

East of the airport, **Grutness** is the port for the ferry to Fair Isle.

Places to Stay *Betty Mouat's Cottage*, Old Scatness, is a camping böd sleeping up to eight people. It's open from April to October and costs £3 per night; book in advance at Lerwick TIC. *Sumburgh Hotel* (☎ *01950-460201*), next to Jarlshof, is a large, upmarket hotel with a bar and restaurant. Singles/doubles cost from £40/58.

Getting There & Away To get to Sumburgh from Lerwick take the airport bus (50 minutes, £1.90) and get off at the second-last stop.

FAIR ISLE

Twenty-four miles south-west of Sumburgh, about halfway to Orkney, and only three by 1½ miles in size, Fair Isle is one of Britain's most remote inhabited islands. It's probably best known for its patterned knitwear, still produced in the island's co-operative, Fair Isle Crafts.

However, it's also a paradise for birdwatchers, who form the bulk of the island's visitors. Fair Isle is in the flight paths of migrating birds and thousands breed here. They're monitored by the **Bird Observatory** which collects and analyses information year-round; visitors are more than welcome to participate.

The island also has 240 species of flowering plants, and grey and golden seals can be seen around the shores, especially in late summer.

Fair Isle was given to the NTS in 1954 by George Waterston, who had bought it earlier and set up the first bird observatory. In the same year it was declared a National Scenic Area.

The small **George Waterston Memorial Centre** (☎ 01595-760244), has photos and exhibits on the island's natural history, crofting, fishing, archaeology and knitwear. It's only open May to mid-September, Monday and Friday from 2 to 4 pm, and on Wednesday from 10.30 am to noon; donations are welcome.

Places to Stay

Accommodation must be booked in advance and includes meals. The *Fair Isle Lodge & Bird Observatory* (☎ *01595-760258)* has full-board accommodation, charging £25 in the dorm and £40/70 for singles/doubles. Locals also offer rooms with meals, at around £28/50. Try *Mrs Riddiford* (☎ *01595-760250)* in Schoolton or *Mrs Stout* (☎ *01595-760247)* in Barkland.

Getting There & Away

Air From Tingwall (☎ 01595-840246) there are two return flights a day (25 minutes, £70 return) on Monday, Wednesday, Friday and Saturday. A day return allows about six hours on the island, seven on Monday.

Boat From May to September, the *Good Shepherd IV* ferry sails from Grutness (near Sumburgh) to Fair Isle (2½ hours, £19.68) on Tuesday, Saturday and alternate Thursdays, and from Lerwick (4½ hours) on alternate Thursdays. Book with JW Stout (☎ 01595-760222). On the trip you may see dolphins and porpoises.

NORTH MAINLAND
Voe

Old Voe is a pretty collection of buildings beside a tranquil bay on the southern shore of Olna Firth. It's sheltered from the wind by the surrounding hills on which the newer part of the township has spread. Shetland would be an ideal place to harness wind energy and on one of the hills you can see a single modern windmill.

In old Voe, Selkie Charters (☎ 01806-588297) offers diving trips, training courses and equipment hire.

In previous incarnations, the red *Sail Loft* by the pier was a fishing shed and knitwear factory, but is now a camping böd, open from April to October, charging £3 per person. Food is available opposite at the *Pierhead Restaurant & Bar* (☎ *01806-588332)* run by an ex-pat New Zealander; a fisherman's basket is £6.

There are up to five buses daily from Lerwick to Voe, Monday to Saturday.

Whalsay & Out Skerries

South of Voe, the B9071 branches east to Laxo, the ferry terminal for the island of Whalsay. This is one of the most prosperous of Shetland's islands owing to its large fishing industry whose fleet is based at the modern harbour of **Symbister**.

The Hanseatic League, a commercial association of German towns that existed between the 14th and early 18th centuries, set up trading booths at the harbour. One of these, **Pier House** (☎ 01806-566362), has been restored and inside is an exhibition on the trade and about the island. It opens from April to September on weekdays from 9 am to 1 pm and 2 to 5 pm; 50p/free. Whalsay is popular for sea angling and for trout fishing in its lochs. There are also scenic walks in the south and east where colonies of seabirds breed and where you may catch sight of seals.

At Sodom not far from Symbister, *Grieve House*, Hugh MacDiarmid's former home, is now a camping böd (£3). There are regular ferries daily between Laxo and Symbister (30 minutes, £2.20 return). To book, call ☎ 01806-566259.

North-east of Whalsay, another thriving fishing community occupies the 2 sq miles of Out Skerries (or just Skerries). It's made up of the three main islands of Housay, Bruray (these two connected by a road bridge) and Grunay, plus a number of islets. Their rugged cliffs teem with birdlife. There are ferries between Out Skerries and Lerwick on Tuesday and Thursday (2½ hours), and the rest of the week to Vidlin (1½ hours) about 3 miles north-east of Laxo. The return passenger fare is £4.20, or £5.60 for cars. To book, call GW Henderson (☎ 01806-515226).

Brae & Around

There's little in Brae itself, but it does have a fair amount of accommodation and would make a good base. There's fine **walking** on the peninsula west of Brae, and to the south on the red-granite island of **Muckle Roe** which is connected to the peninsula by a bridge. Muckle Roe also offers good **diving** off its west and north coasts.

Places to Stay & Eat *Mrs Wood* (☎ *01806-522368*), Westayre, offers B&B on a working croft and has rooms from £16 per person. Evening meals are available. At *Valleyfield Guest House* (☎ *01806-522450*), all the rooms have adjoining bathrooms and cost £25 per person. It also does evening meals and there are a couple of sites for tents and caravans. *Busta House Hotel* (☎ *01806-522506*), about 1½ miles south-west of Brae, is a luxurious country-house hotel with singles/doubles from £53.50/80. The restaurant, considered to be the best in Shetland, offers four-course dinners for £25. Brae also has two coffee shops, *Valleyfield* and *Drumquin*.

Getting There & Away Buses from Lerwick to Eshaness and Sullom Voe stop in Brae (40 minutes, £1.50 one way).

Eshaness & Hillswick

About 11 miles north-west of Brae, the road ends at the red, basalt lava cliffs of Eshaness which form some of the most impressive coastal scenery in Shetland. This is superb **walking** country and there are panoramic views from the lighthouse (not open to the public) on the headland.

A mile east, a side road leads south to Tangwick Haa and the small **Tangwick Haa Museum**, where the difficulties and dangers of fishing and whaling, and the hardship of domestic life are shown through photographs and displays. It's open May to September on weekdays from 1 to 5 pm and on weekends from 11 am to 7 pm; entry is free.

At **Hamnavoe**, which you reach from another side road, about 3½ miles east of Eshaness, is *Johnny Notions Camping Böd* (£3, book at Lerwick TIC). This was the birthplace of Johnny 'Notions' Williamson, an 18th century blacksmith who inoculated several thousand people against smallpox using a serum and method he devised himself.

Offshore from **Hillswick**, 7 miles east of Eshaness, there's excellent **diving** around The Drongs, a series of exposed sea stacks. In Hillswick, B&B accommodation is available at *St Magnus Bay Hotel* (☎ *01806-503372*), which is built of timber brought from Norway. Rooms cost from £28/42. Down on the quay, the *Booth Restaurant & Café* (☎ *01806-503348*) is in one of Shetland's oldest buildings – a former Hanseatic trading post. It's open daily in summer, weekends only the rest of the year. It serves vegetarian food and has live music some nights. Proceeds go to the local wildlife sanctuary.

Buses from Lerwick run (evenings only) as far as Hillswick (1¼ hours, £1.90 one way), from which there's a feeder service to Eshaness. You should contact Shalder Coaches (☎ 01595-880127).

Sullom Voe

Sullom Voe is the name given to both the northern headland jutting into Yell Sound and the long sea inlet that provides a deep-water harbour for the huge Sullom Voe oil terminal. You can see the terminal to the left en route to **Toft**, the ferry terminal for Ulsta on Yell.

THE NORTH ISLES

The North Isles are made up of the three islands of Yell, Unst and Fetlar, all connected to each other by ferry.

Yell

Yell is a desolate island covered mostly by heather moors atop a deep layer of peat. There are, however, some good coastal and hill walks, especially around the **Herra Peninsula**, about halfway up the west coast.

Across Whale Firth from the peninsula is the RSPB **Lumbister Reserve** where red-throated divers (called 'rain geese' in Shetland), merlins, bonxies, arctic skuas and other bird species breed. The reserve is home to a large otter population too. They can be best viewed near the shores of Whale Firth, where you may also spot common and grey seals.

In the Daal of Lumbister, a short, narrow gorge between the Loch of Lumbister and the west coast, there are bright displays of wildflowers such as juniper, honeysuckle and thyme. The area immediately north of the reserve provides some excellent walking along the coast and over remote moorland.

South of the reserve on the hillside above the main road, stand the reputedly haunted ruins of **Windhouse**, dating from 1707. About a mile east of here is **Mid Yell**, the island's largest village and a natural harbour. The road north to Gutcher passes **Basta Voe** where many otters inhabit the shores. In the north, around the village of **Cullovoe**, there is more good walking along the attractive coastline.

From Ulsta, the road leads 5 miles east to Burravoe. Here, the **Old Haa Visitor Centre** (☎ 01957-722339) is in Yell's oldest building, built in 1672. There's an interesting exhibition on local flora, fauna and history and a small gallery. It's open mid-April to September, from Tuesday to Thursday and Saturday from 10 am to 4 pm and on Sunday 2 to 5 pm. Admission is free.

Places to Stay & Eat *Windhouse Lodge* (£3, book at Lerwick TIC) is a camping böd below the haunted ruins of Windhouse. There are a number of B&Bs around the island. The friendly *Gutcher Post Office* (☎ 01957-744201), Gutcher, run by Margaret Tulloch, is close to the ferry terminal. B&B costs £14 per person. In Burravoe *Mrs Leask's* (☎ 01957-722274) has good views and B&B also for £14 per person. Both offer evening meals as well.

While you're waiting for the ferry in Gutcher, you can snack at the *Seaview Café*, while in Burravoe the *Old Haa Visitor Centre* has a small café serving home-made food. In Mid Yell the *Hilltop Restaurant & Bar* (☎ 01957-702333) opens for lunch and dinner; main courses cost from around £3.50.

Getting There & Away Yell is connected with Mainland by ferry between Toft and Ulsta (20 minutes). Each ferry costs £1.10 per passenger or £2.80 for a car and driver. Although you don't need to book in advance, from May to September traffic is constant so it's wise to do so. Call ☎ 01957-722259.

Two buses daily (8 am and 4.05 pm), Monday to Saturday, leave Lerwick for Toft ferry pier (55 minutes, £1.90 one way). There are connecting buses at Ulsta for other parts of the island.

Unst

Unst has an area of 45 sq miles and with its population of around 1000, is Scotland's northernmost inhabited island. A geological fault line runs from Belmont in the south to Burrafirth in the north; to the east of the line the rocks are serpentine and gabbro, to the west mainly gneiss and schist. As a result, there is a wide variety of vegetation – over 400 different plant species. Some of the most unusual examples can be seen at the 74-acre **Keen of Hamar NNR** north-east of Baltasound.

In the north-west is the wonderfully wild and windy reserve of **Hermaness** (NNR). Here you can sit on the high cliffs, commune with the thousands of seabirds and Shetland's largest colony of puffins and gaze across the sea into the Arctic Circle. The more energetic might enjoy the superb cliff-top walk along the west coast.

Hermaness Visitor Centre (☎ 01957-711278), Shore Station, near the reserve's entrance, will provide information on the island's wildlife. It opens daily late April to mid-September from 8.30 am to 6 pm. Admission is free.

Robert Louis Stevenson wrote *Treasure Island* while living on Unst and the map in the novel is reputedly based on Unst. Stevenson's uncle built the lighthouse on **Muckle Flugga**, one of the group of rocks off Hermaness; another of the rocks is **Out Stack**, Scotland's most northerly point.

On the way to Hermaness, you might want to pause to mail a card at Scotland's northernmost post office in **Haroldswick**. There's also an RAF radar tracking station here and near to it is **Unst Boat Haven**, housing an interesting collection of photographs, boats and maritime artefacts. It's open daily May to September from 2 to 5 pm and admission is free.

Open the same hours and also free, **Unst Heritage Centre** is an active community centre as well as a museum on local history and family trees.

North of Haroldswick there are some fine sandy beaches at Burrafirth, Norwick and Skaw.

In the south about 3 miles east of Uyeasound are the remains of **Muness Castle** (HS), a late 16th century tower house. There's some gentle walking around the bay a little to the north, past the beach at Sand Wick, with the chance to see some otters and seals.

Places to Stay & Eat *Gardiesfauld Hostel* (☎ *01957-755298*), Uyeasound, has all modern facilities and charges £6.95/5.85 for dorm beds. It's open from May to October and hires out bicycles to residents.

In Haroldswick *Mrs Ritch* (☎ *01957-711323*), Gerratoun, offers B&B in a converted croft house for £14 per person. *Mrs Firmin* (☎ *01957-755234, Prestegaard*), Uyeasound, has two rooms in a large Victorian house for £17 per person; evening meals are available.

Baltasound has the greatest range of accommodation. At *Clingera Guest House* (☎ *01957-711579*), Mrs Mouat offers B&B in three *en suite* rooms for £18 per person. The notorious Burke and Hare stayed at *Buness House* (☎ *01957-711315*) and there are views of the otters down on the shore; B&B costs £25 per person.

The solid *Baltasound Hotel* (☎ *01957-711334*) has singles/doubles for £36/50 or £45/54 with bathroom. It's open to nonresidents for snacks and meals all day.

Nornova Tearoom near Muness Castle serves sandwiches and snacks.

Getting There & Away There are flights from Sumburgh and Tingwall to Unst, from Monday to Friday for £88 return.

Unst is connected with Yell by a small car ferry between Gutcher and Belmont (£1.10 one way, £2.80 for a car). To book, call ☎ 01957-722259.

Haroldswick is 55 miles from Lerwick, and if you don't have a car you must spend the night on Unst as buses only run twice a day. From Lerwick, if you catch the 8 am bus you can make connections with ferries and other buses to reach Haroldswick before noon. It's then only a couple of miles to either Hermaness or Keen of Hamar.

Fetlar

Fetlar is the smallest (5 by 2 miles) but most fertile of the North Isles. The name Fetlar is derived from old Norse meaning 'fat land' as there is good grazing and a rich variety of plant and bird life. Much of the island is designated a Site of Special Scientific Interest. Although the whole island is good for birdwatching, the 1700 acres of grassy moorland around Vord Hill (159m, 522 feet) in the north form the **North Fetlar RSPB Reserve**. Snowy owls sometimes visit here in winter and large numbers of auks, gulls and shags breed in the cliffs. Common and grey seals can also be seen on the shores. The reserve opens all year, but there is restricted access during the breeding season mid-May to early August; contact the warden (☎ 01957-733246) at Bealance.

Fetlar is home to one of Britain's rarest birds, the red-necked phalarope, which breeds in the loch near **Funzie** (pronounced finnie), in the island's east. You can view them from an RSPB hide in the nearby marshes. The whimbrel, a cousin of the curlew, also breeds here.

Scenic **walking** is possible on much of the island, especially around the bay near Tresta, at Urie and Gruting in the north and Funzie in the east.

There's no petrol or diesel on Fetlar, but there is a shop and post office in **Houbie**, the main village. Houbie also has the excellent **Fetlar Interpretive Centre** (☎ 01957-733206), with photos, audio recordings and videos on the island and its history. It opens from May to September,

Tuesday to Sunday from noon to 5 pm and entry is free.

Places to Stay & Eat *Garth's Campsite* (☎ *01957-733227*) overlooks the beach at Tresta and has flush toilets, showers and sites for £3.60. At the friendly *Gord* (☎ *01957-733227*) in Houbie the rooms all have their own bathroom; B&B costs £15 per person. The *Glebe* (☎ *01957-733242*), a

listed building overlooking Papil Water, provides B&B for £14/16 per person without/with bathroom. Both also offer dinner and the shop in Houbie serves teas.

Getting There & Away Regular ferries from Oddsta in the island's north-west connect with Gutcher on Yell and Belmont on Unst. The journey time is 25 minutes; £1.10 one way, £2.80 for car and driver.

Language

SCOTTISH GAELIC

Scottish Gaelic (*Gàidhlig* – pronounced. *gallic* in Scotland) is spoken by about 80,000 people in Scotland, mainly in the Highlands and Islands, and by many native speakers and learners overseas. It is a member of the Celtic branch of the Indo-European family of languages which has given us Gaelic, Irish, Manx, Welsh, Cornish and Breton.

Although Scottish Gaelic is the Celtic language most closely associated with Scotland it was quite a latecomer to those shores. Other Celtic languages in the form of Pictish and Brittonic had existed prior to the arrival and settlement by Gaelic speaking Celts (Gaels) from Ireland from the 4th to the 6th centuries AD. These Irish settlers, known to the Romans as Scotti, were eventually to give their name to the entire country. Initially they settled in the area on the west coast of Scotland in which their name is perpetuated, Earra Ghaidheal (Argyll). As their territorial influence extended so did their language and from the 9th to the 11th centuries Gaelic was spoken throughout the country. For many centuries the language was the same as the language of Ireland; there is little evidence of much divergence before the 13th century. Even up to the 18th century the bards adhered to the strict literary standards of Old Irish.

The Viking invasions from 800 AD brought linguistic influences which are evident in many of the coastal place names of the Highlands.

Gaelic culture flourished in the Highlands until the 18th century and the Jacobite rebellions. After the Battle of Culloden in 1746 many Gaelic speakers were forced from their ancestral lands; this 'ethnic cleansing' by landlords and governments culminated in the Highland Clearances of the 19th century. Although still studied at academic level, the spoken language declined, being regarded as a mere 'peasant' language of no modern significance.

It was only in the 1970s that Gaelic began to make a comeback with a new generation of young enthusiasts who were determined that it should not be allowed to die. People from all over Scotland, and indeed worldwide, are beginning to appreciate their Gaelic heritage.

After two centuries of decline, the language is now being encouraged through financial help from government agencies and the EU. Gaelic education is flourishing from playgroups to tertiary levels. This renaissance flows out into the field of music, literature, cultural events, and broadcasting.

The Gaelic language has a vital role to play in the life of modern Scotland.

Grammar

The usual word order in Gaelic is verb-subject-object; English, by comparison, has a subject-verb-object word order, eg The girl (subject) reads (verb) the book (object). There are two forms of the pronoun 'you' in Gaelic: the singular *thu*, and the plural form *sibh* which is also used as a formal (ie polite) singular. We use the informal *thu* in the following phraselist.

Some English Borrowings from Gaelic

bard	bard – *baard* (poet)
ben	beinn – *beh-een* (hill)
bog	bog – *bohk* (soft, wet)
brogue	bròg – *bro-ck* (shoe)
caber	cabar – *cap-er* (pole)
claymore	claidheamh mòr – *cly-af mor* (big sword)
dune	dùn – *doo-n* (a heap)
galore	gu leòr – *gu lyor* (plenty)
loch	loch – *loch*
Sassenach	Sasannach – *Sasunach* (Englishman)
sporran	sporan – *sporan* (purse)
strath	strath – *strah* (mountain valley)

Pronunciation

Stress usually falls on the first syllable of a word. The Gaelic alphabet has only 18 letters:

Vowels

There are five vowels: , e, i, o and u – a, o, u are known as broad vowels, e, i are known as slender vowels. A grave accent indicates that a vowel sound is lengthened, eg *bata* (a stick), *bàta* (a boat).

Consonants

There are 12 consonants: b, c, d, f, g, l, m, n, p, r, s, t, and the letter h (only used to change other sounds).

Consonants may be pronounced in different ways depending on the vowel beside them. The spelling rule in Gaelic is 'broad to broad and slender to slender'. This means that if, in a word, a consonant is preceded by a broad vowel it must be followed by a broad vowel, and if it is preceded by a slender vowel it must be followed by a slender vowel. Consequently, we speak about broad consonants and slender consonants, eg *balach* (a boy), *caileag* (a girl)

Broad consonants sound approximately as their English equivalents.
Slender consonants are often followed by a 'y' sound.

c	always a hard 'k' sound; never an 's' sound
d	when broad, thicker than English 'd'; when slender, as the 'j' in 'jet'
l, ll	when slender, as in 'value'
n, nn	when slender, as in 'new'
s	when slender, as 'sh'
t	when broad, thicker than English 't'; when slender, as the 'ch' in 'chin'

When consonants are followed by 'h', a change of sound occurs:

bh mh	as 'v'
ch	when broad, as in *loch* (not 'lock'!); when slender, as the German *ich*
dh gh	when broad, voiced at the back of the throat
	when slender, as 'y' – there's no English equivalent
fh	silent
ph	as 'f'
sh	as 'h' if before a broad vowel
th	as 'h'

There are a number of Gaelic sounds, especially vowel combinations and consonantal changes brought about by the addition of the letter h, which cannot be reproduced satisfactorily in English. The help of a native speaker is invaluable in learning these.

Greetings & Civilities

Good morning.
  madding va
  Madainn mhath.
Good afternoon/Good evening.
  fesskurr ma
  Feasgar math.
Good night.
  uh eech uh va
  Oidhche mhath.
How are you?
  kimmer uh ha oo?
  Ciamar a tha thu?
Very well, thank you.
  gley va, tappuh let
  Glè mhath, tapadh leat.
I'm well, thank you.
  ha mee goo ma, tappuh let
  Tha mi gu math, tapadh leat.
That's good.
  sma shin
  'S math sin.
Please.
  mahs eh doh hawl eh
  Mas e do thoil e.
Thank you.
  tappuh let
  Tapadh leat.
Many thanks.
  moe ran ta eeng
  Mòran taing.
You're welcome.
  sheh doh veh huh
  'Se do bheatha.

I beg you pardon.
baaluv
B'àill leibh.

Excuse me.
gav mo lishk yal
Gabh mo leisgeul.

I'm sorry.
ha mee dooleech
Tha mi duilich.

Small Talk

Do you speak (have) Gaelic?
uh vil ga lick ackut?
A bheil Gàidhlig agad?

Yes, a little.
ha, beg an
Tha, beagan.

Not much.
chan yil moe ran
Chan eil mòran.

What's your name?
jae an tannam uh ha orsht?
De an t ainm a tha ort?

Who are you?
coe oosuh?
Co thusa?

I'm ...
is meeshuh ...
Is mise ...

Good health! (Cheers!)
slahntchuh va!
Slàinte mhath!

Goodbye. (lit: Blessings go with you)
B yan achd let
Beannachd leat.

Goodbye. (The same with you)
mar shin let
Mar sin leat.

Useful Phrases

It's warm today.
ha eh blah un joo
Tha e blàth an diugh.

It's cold today.
ha eh foo ur un joo
Tha e fuar an diugh.

The day is beautiful.
ha un la bree a uh
Tha an latha brèagha.

It's wet.
ha e flooch
Tha e fliuch.

It's raining.
ha un tooshku a woon
Tha an t uisge ann.

It's misty.
ha k yaw a woon
Tha ceò ann.

Has the rain stopped?
un daw skoor un tooshku?
An do sguir an t uisge?

Travel & Accommodation

Can you tell me ...?
un yee ish oo ghoe ...?
An innis thu dhomh ...?

I want to go to ...
ha mee ug ee urry uh gholl goo ...
Tha mi ag iarraidh a dhol gu ...

How do I get to ...?
kimmer uh yaev mee goo ...?
Ciamar a gheibh mi gu ...?

by bus
ir uh vuss   air a' bhus
by train
ir un tren   air an trean
by car
a woon un car   ann an car

a hotel
tuh ee awstu   taigh òsda
a bedroom
roowm caddil   rùm cadail
a toilet
tuh ee beck   taigh beag

rhinn (also 'rhin')   headland

Food

food & drink
bee ugh agus joch
biadh agus deoch

I'm hungry.
ha an tac russ orrom
Tha an t acras orm.

I'm thirsty.
ha am pah ugh orrom
Tha am pathadh orm.

I want ...
ha mee ug ee uhree
Tha mi ag iarraidh ...
I'd like ...
boo tawl lehum
Bu toigh leam ...
I don't like ...
chah tawl lehum
Cha toigh leam ...
That was good.
va shood ma
Bha siud math.
Very good.
gley va
Glè mhath.

a biscuit
briskatch   brioscaid
apple juice
sooh ooh al   sùgh ubhal
bread
aran   aran
broth, soup
broht   brot
butter
eem   ìm
cheese
kashuh   càise
cream
baahrr   bàrr
dessert
meehlshuhn   mìlsean
fish
eeusk   iasg
meat
fehyawl   feòil
oatcakes
aran korkuh   aran coirce
orange juice
sooh awhrinsh   sùgh orains

peas
pessir   peasair
porridge
lee chuh   lite
potatoes
boontahtuh   buntàta
salmon
brahdan   bradan
vegetables
glasreech   glasraich

Drinks

a cup of coffee
coopa cawfee   cupa cofaidh
a cup of tea
coopa tee   cupa tì
black coffee
cawfee dooh   cofaidh dubh
black tea
tee dhooh   tì dhubh
with milk
leh bahnyuh   le bainne
with sugar
leh shooh car   le siùcar
a drink of milk
joch vahnyuh   deoch bhainne
a glass of water
glahnyuh ooshkuy   glainne uisge
a glass of wine
glahnyuh feeuhn   glainne fìon
beer
lyawn   leann
red wine
feeuhn jerrack   fìon dearg
white wine
feeuhn gyahl   fìon geal
whisky
ooshkuy beh huh   uisge beatha

Glossary

AA – Automobile Association
abhainn – river
ABTA – Association of British Travel Agents
aye – yes/always

BABA – book-a-bed-ahead scheme
bag – reach the top of (as in to 'bag a couple of peaks' or 'Munro-bagging')
bailey – the space enclosed by castle walls
bairn – baby
ben – mountain
böd – originally a simple trading booth used by fishing communities, today it refers to basic accommodation for walkers etc
bothy – hut or mountain shelter
brae – hill
broch – defensive tower
BT – British Telecom
BTA – British Tourist Authority
burgh – town
burn – stream

cairn – pile of stones to mark path or junction, also peak
carry-out – take-away food
ceilidh – pronounced kaylee, informal entertainment and dance
close – entrance
craig – exposed rock

dirk – dagger
doocot – dovecote
dram – whisky measure
dun – fort

firth – estuary

glen – valley

haar – fog off the North Sea
Hogmanay – New Year's Eve
howff – pub
HS – Historic Scotland

kail – cabbage

ken – know
kipper – smoked herring
kirk – church
kyle – narrow strait of water

law – round hill
laird – estate owner
land – tenement
links – golf course
linn – waterfall

MBA – Mountain Bothies Association
merse – saltmarsh
motte – early Norman fortification consisting of a raised, flattened mound with a keep on top; when attached to a bailey it is known as a motte-and-bailey
MCS – Mountaineering Council of Scotland
muckle – big
Munro – mountain of 3000 feet (914m) or higher
Munro-bagger – someone who reaches the top of a Munro

neeps – turnips
ness – headland (Shetland)
NNR – National Nature Reserve, managed by the SNH
NTS – National Trust for Scotland

OS – Ordnance Survey

pend – arched gateway
Pict – early Celtic inhabitants (from the Latin pictus, meaning painted) after their body paint decorations
provost – mayor

RAC – Royal Automobile Association
reiver – raider
rhinn or **rhin** – headland
RSA – Royal Scottish Academy
RSPB – Royal Society for the Protection of Birds
RNLI – Royal National Lifeboat Institute

Sassenach – either an English person or Lowland Scot, depending on who's saying it and in what context, and almost always used in a derogatory sense

sett – tartan pattern

SNH – Scottish Natural Heritage, a government organisation directly responsible for safeguarding and improving Scotland's natural heritage

SMC – Scottish Mountaineering Club

sporran – purse

SRWS – Scottish Rights of Way Society

SSSI – Sight of Special Scientific Interest

strath – valley

STB – Scottish Tourist Board

SYHA – Scottish Youth Hostel Association

toastie – a toasted sandwich

TIC – Tourist Information Centre

tolbooth – courthouse or jail

tor – Celtic word describing a hill shaped like a triangular wedge of cheese

trows – mythical little people (Shetland)

twitcher – birdwatcher

uisge-bha – the water of life, whisky

vennel – narrow street

voe – inlet (Shetland)

way – walking trail

wean – child

wynd – lane

Some Alternative Place Names

The following places with their alternative Gaelic names are in the Hebrides.

Place	Gaelic Name	Island
Armadale	Armadal	Skye
Baleshare Island	Am Baile Sear	–
Balivanich	Baile a'Mhanaich	Benbecula
Barra	Barraigh	–
Barvas	Barabhas	Lewis
Benbecula	Beinn Na Faoghla	–
Berneray	Bearnaraigh	–
Broadford	An T-Ath Leathann	Skye
Butt of Lewis	Rubha Robhanais	Lewis
Callanish	Calanais	Lewis
Carloway	Carlabagh	Lewis
Carloway Broch	Dun Charlabhaigh	Lewis
Castlebay	Bagh a'Chaisteil	Barra
Dunvegan	Dùn Bheagain	Skye
Elgol	Ealaghol	Skye
Eriskay	Eiriosgaigh	–
Flodigarry	Flodaigearraidh	Skye
Glenbrittle	Gleann Bhreatail	Skye
Glendale	Gleann Dàil	Skye
Harris	Na Hearadh	–
Howmore	Tobha Mor	South Uist
Kilmuir	Cille Mhoire	Skye
Kyleakin	Caol Acain	Skye
Kylerhea	Caol Reithe	Skye
Leverburgh	An t-Ob	Harris
Lewis	Leodhais	–
Lochboisdale	Loch Baghasdail	South Uist
Lochmaddy	Loch nam Madadh	North Uist
Mingulay	Miughalaigh	–
Mealista	Mealasta	Lewis

Place	Gaelic Name	Island
North Uist	Uibhist A Tuath	–
Port of Ness	Port Nis	Lewis
Portree	Port Righ	Skye
Rhenigidale	Reinigeadal	Harris
Rodel	Roghadal	Harris
South Uist	Uibhist A Deas	–
Staffin	Stamhain	Skye
Stenscholl	Steinnseal	Skye
Stornoway	Steornabhagh	Lewis
Talisker	Talasgair	Skye
Tarbert	An Tairbeart	Harris
Timsgarry	Timsgearraidh	Lewis

Acknowledgments

Continued from page 6

The list of thanks includes: Myrtle Potter in Dunning, and Angus Potter in Biggar; Alison & Dave Clark, Glasgow; Ina Hamilton, Glasgow, for help with Islay; Stuart & Pamela Cornwallis, Oldmeldrum, who were enthusiastic about the north-east; Iain & Liz Cornwallis, Denny; Keith Hoban and family, Nairn and Inverness; Sandy MacLennan and family, Glen Nevis; Jeremy Inglis, for great help with the Oban map on a very wet night; Mairi Campbell, Drinishader, Harris; John Russell, Galson Farm, Lewis; Bessie Muir, for wonderful Orkney hospitality; Gavin Rees of Glasgow, for driving while I was sleeping; Julie Cook, from Queensland, Australia, for sleeping while I was driving; Petra Roessner and Christine Kurz for a good time on North Uist; Bob McFarlane, Glasgow, for help with Bute and Great Cumbrae; and Theresa at Aberdeen bus station, for her amazing knowledge of completely new bus timetables.

Also of great help were Moira Dyer (Greater Glasgow & Clyde Valley Tourist Board), Eveleen Hastings (Greenock TIC), Pam Wells (Aberdeen & Grampian Tourist Board), Amy Fraser (Aberdeen Art Gallery), Caroline Beaton (Elgin TIC), the entire staff at Dornoch TIC, Abbie Kirsop (Craignure TIC), Chirsty MacKinnon (Portree TIC) and Tom Rendall (Kirkwall TIC). Several companies and organisations assisted me in various useful ways, including Scotrail, Scottish Citylink, National Express (Sarah Hawes), P&O Scottish Ferries (Scott Colegate, who organised a midwinter Orkney trip), Caledonian MacBrayne (Mike Blair), Sabhal Mor Ostaig (Christine Cain, who provided lots of detail on Gaelic), the National Trust for Scotland (Hillary Horrocks), the Forestry Commission (Howard Hart), Patrick Connor (Historic Scotland) and last (but not least), Scottish Natural Heritage (Stuart Graham, Heather Shirra and several others).

LONELY PLANET

FREE Lonely Planet Newsletters

We love hearing from you and think you'd like to hear from us.

Planet Talk

Our FREE quarterly printed newsletter is full of tips from travellers and anecdotes from Lonely Planet guidebook authors. Every issue is packed with up-to-date travel news and advice, and includes:

- a postcard from Lonely Planet co-founder Tony Wheeler
- a swag of mail from travellers
- a look at life on the road through the eyes of a Lonely Planet author
- topical health advice
- prizes for the best travel yarn
- news about forthcoming Lonely Planet events
- a complete list of Lonely Planet books and other titles

To join our mailing list, residents of the UK, Europe and Africa can email us at go@lonelyplanet.co.uk; residents of North and South America can email us at info@lonelyplanet.com; the rest of the world can email us at talk2us@lonelyplanet.com.au, or contact any Lonely Planet office.

Comet

Our FREE monthly email newsletter brings you all the latest travel news, features, interviews, competitions, destination ideas, travellers' tips & tales, Q&As, raging debates and related links. Find out what's new on the Lonely Planet Web site and which books are about to hit the shelves.

Subscribe from your desktop: www.lonelyplanet.com/comet

LONELY PLANET

Lonely Planet Online
www.lonelyplanet.com *or* AOL keyword: lp

Whether you've just begun planning your next trip, or you're chasing down specific info on currency regulations or visa requirements, check out Lonely Planet Online for up-to-the minute travel information.

As well as mini guides to more than 250 destinations, you'll find maps, photos, travel news, health and visa updates, travel advisories, and discussion of the ecological and political issues you need to be aware of as you travel. You'll also find timely upgrades to popular guidebooks which you can print out and stick in the back of your book.

There's also an online travellers' forum where you can share your experience of life on the road, meet travel companions and ask other travellers for their recommendations and advice.

And of course we have a complete and up-to-date list of all Lonely Planet travel products including travel guides, diving and snorkelling guides, phrasebooks, atlases, travel literature and videos, and a simple online ordering facility if you can't find the book you want elsewhere.

Lonely Planet Diving & Snorkelling Guides

Known for indispensible guidebooks to destinations all over the world, Lonely Planet's Pisces Books are the most popular series of diving and snorkelling titles available.

There are three series: **Diving & Snorkelling Guides**, **Shipwreck Diving** series, and **Dive Into History**. Full colour throughout, the **Diving & Snorkelling Guides** combine quality photographs with detailed descriptions of the best dive sites for each location, giving divers a glimpse of what they can expect both on land and in water. The **Dive Into History** series is perfect for the adventure diver or armchair traveller. The **Shipwreck Diving** series provides all the details for exploring the most interesting wrecks in the Atlantic and Pacific oceans. The list also includes underwater nature and technical guides.

LONELY PLANET

Mail Order

Lonely Planet products are distributed worldwide.They are also available by mail order from Lonely Planet, so if you have difficulty finding a title please write to us. North and South American residents should write to 150 Linden St, Oakland, CA 94607, USA; European and African residents should write to 10a Spring Place, London NW5 3BH, UK; and residents of other countries to PO Box 617, Hawthorn, Victoria 3122, Australia.

ISLANDS OF THE INDIAN OCEAN Madagascar & Comoros • Maldives • Mauritius, Réunion & Seychelles

MIDDLE EAST & CENTRAL ASIA Arab Gulf States • Central Asia • Central Asia phrasebook • Iran • Israel & the Palestinian Territories • Israel & the Palestinian Territories travel atlas • Istanbul • Jerusalem • Jordan & Syria • Jordan, Syria & Lebanon travel atlas • Lebanon • Middle East on a shoestring • Turkey • Turkish phrasebook • Turkey travel atlas • Yemen
Travel Literature: The Gates of Damascus • Kingdom of the Film Stars: Journey into Jordan

NORTH AMERICA Alaska • Backpacking in Alaska • Baja California • California & Nevada • Canada • Florida • Hawaii • Honolulu • Los Angeles • Miami • New England USA • New Orleans • New York City • New York, New Jersey & Pennsylvania • Pacific Northwest USA • Rocky Mountain States • San Francisco • Seattle • Southwest USA • USA phrasebook • Washington, DC & the Capital Region
Travel Literature: Drive Thru America

NORTH-EAST ASIA Beijing • Cantonese phrasebook • China • Hong Kong • Hong Kong, Macau & Guangzhou • Japan • Japanese phrasebook • Japanese audio pack • Korea • Korean phrasebook • Kyoto • Mandarin phrasebook • Mongolia • Mongolian phrasebook • North-East Asia on a shoestring • Seoul • South-West China • Taiwan • Tibet • Tibetan phrasebook • Tokyo
Travel Literature: Lost Japan

SOUTH AMERICA Argentina, Uruguay & Paraguay • Bolivia • Brazil • Brazilian phrasebook • Buenos Aires • Chile & Easter Island • Chile & Easter Island travel atlas • Colombia • Ecuador & the Galapagos Islands • Latin American Spanish phrasebook • Peru • Quechua phrasebook • Rio de Janeiro • South America on a shoestring • Trekking in the Patagonian Andes • Venezuela
Travel Literature: Full Circle: A South American Journey

SOUTH-EAST ASIA Bali & Lombok • Bangkok • Burmese phrasebook • Cambodia • Hill Tribes phrasebook • Ho Chi Minh City • Indonesia • Indonesian phrasebook • Indonesian audio pack • Jakarta • Java • Laos • Lao phrasebook • Laos travel atlas • Malay phrasebook • Malaysia, Singapore & Brunei • Myanmar (Burma) • Philippines • Pilipino (Tagalog) phrasebook • Singapore • South-East Asia on a shoestring • South-East Asia phrasebook • Thailand • Thailand's Islands & Beaches • Thailand travel atlas • Thai phrasebook • Thai audio pack • Vietnam • Vietnamese phrasebook • Vietnam travel atlas

ALSO AVAILABLE: Antarctica • Brief Encounters: Stories of Love, Sex & Travel • Chasing Rickshaws • Not the Only Planet: Travel Stories from Science Fiction • Travel with Children • Traveller's Tales

LONELY PLANET

Lonely Planet Travel Atlases

Lonely Planet has long been famous for the number and quality of its guidebook maps. Now we've gone one step further and produced a handy companion series: Lonely Planet travel atlases – maps of a country produced in book form.

Unlike other maps, which look good but lead travellers astray, our travel atlases have been researched on the road by Lonely Planet's experienced team of writers. All details are carefully checked to ensure the atlas corresponds with the equivalent Lonely Planet guidebook.

- full-colour throughout
- maps researched and checked by Lonely Planet authors
- place names correspond with Lonely Planet guidebooks
- no confusing spelling differences
- legend and travelling information in English, French, German, Japanese and Spanish
- size: 230 x 160 mm

Available now: Chile & Easter Island • Egypt • India & Bangladesh • Israel & the Palestinian Territories • Jordan, Syria & Lebanon • Kenya • Laos • Portugal • South Africa, Lesotho & Swaziland • Thailand • Turkey • Vietnam • Zimbabwe, Botswana & Namibia

Lonely Planet TV Series & Videos

Lonely Planet travel guides have been brought to life on television screens around the world. Like our guides, the programmes are based on the joy of independent travel, and look honestly at some of the most exciting, picturesque and frustrating places in the world. Each show is presented by one of three travellers from Australia, England or the USA and combines an innovative mixture of video, Super-8 film, atmospheric soundscapes and original music.

Videos of each episode – containing additional footage not shown on television – are available from good book and video shops, but the availability of individual videos varies with regional screening schedules.

Video destinations include: Alaska • American Rockies • Australia – The South-East • Baja California & the Copper Canyon • Brazil • Central Asia • Chile & Easter Island • Corsica, Sicily & Sardinia – The Mediterranean Islands • East Africa (Tanzania & Zanzibar) • Ecuador & the Galapagos Islands • Greenland & Iceland • Indonesia • Israel & the Sinai Desert • Jamaica • Japan • La Ruta Maya • Morocco • New York • North India • Pacific Islands (Fiji, Solomon Islands & Vanuatu) • South India • South West China • Turkey • Vietnam • West Africa • Zimbabwe, Botswana & Namibia

The Lonely Planet TV series is produced by: Pilot Productions
The Old Studio
18 Middle Row
London W10 5AT UK

LONELY PLANET

Phrasebooks

Lonely Planet phrasebooks are packed with essential words and phrases to help travellers communicate with the locals. With colour tabs for quick reference, an extensive vocabulary and use of script, these handy pocket-sized language guides cover day-to-day travel situations.

- handy pocket-sized books
- easy to understand Pronunciation chapter
- clear & comprehensive Grammar chapter
- romanisation alongside script to allow ease of pronunciation
- script throughout so users can point to phrases for every situation
- full of cultural information and tips for the traveller

'...vital for a real DIY spirit and attitude in language learning'
– *Backpacker*

'the phrasebooks have good cultural backgrounders and offer solid advice for challenging situations in remote locations'
– *San Francisco Examiner*

Arabic (Egyptian) • Arabic (Moroccan) • Australian *(Australian English, Aboriginal and Torres Strait languages)* • Baltic States *(Estonian, Latvian, Lithuanian)* • Bengali • Brazilian • Burmese • Cantonese • Central Asia • Central Europe *(Czech, French, German, Hungarian, Italian, Slovak)* • Eastern Europe *(Bulgarian, Czech, Hungarian, Polish, Romanian, Slovak)* • Ethiopian (Amharic) • Fijian • French • German • Greek • Hill Tribes • Hindi/Urdu • Indonesian • Italian • Japanese • Korean • Lao • Latin American Spanish • Malay • Mandarin • Mediterranean Europe *(Albanian, Croatian, Greek, Italian, Macedonian, Maltese, Serbian, Slovene)* • Mongolian • Nepali • Papua New Guinea • Pilipino (Tagalog) • Quechua • Russian • Scandinavian Europe *(Danish, Finnish, Icelandic, Norwegian, Swedish)* • South-East Asia *(Burmese, Indonesian, Khmer, Lao, Malay, Tagalog Pilipino, Thai, Vietnamese)* • Spanish (Castilian) *(also includes Catalan, Galician and Basque)* • Sri Lanka • Swahili • Thai • Tibetan • Turkish • Ukrainian • USA *(US English, Vernacular, Native American languages, Hawaiian)* • Vietnamese • Western Europe *(Basque, Catalan, Dutch, French, German, Greek, Irish)*

Lonely Planet Journeys

JOURNEYS is a unique collection of travel writing – published by the company that understands travel better than anyone else. It is a series for anyone who has ever experienced – or dreamed of – the magical moment when they encountered a strange culture or saw a place for the first time. They are tales to read while you're planning a trip, while you're on the road or while you're in an armchair, in front of a fire.

These outstanding titles explore our planet through the eyes of a diverse group of international writers. JOURNEYS books catch the spirit of a place, illuminate a culture, recount a crazy adventure, or introduce a fascinating way of life. They always entertain, and always enrich the experience of travel.

MALI BLUES
Traveling to an African Beat
Lieve Joris (translated by Sam Garrett)

Drought, rebel uprisings, ethnic conflict: these are the predominant images of West Africa. But as Lieve Joris travels in Senegal, Mauritania and Mali, she meets survivors, fascinating individuals charting new ways of living between tradition and modernity. With her remarkable gift for drawing out people's stories, Joris brilliantly captures the rhythms of a world that refuses to give in.

THE GATES OF DAMASCUS
Lieve Joris (translated by Sam Garrett)

This best-selling book is a beautifully drawn portrait of day-to-day life in modern Syria. Through her intimate contact with local people, Lieve Joris draws us into the fascinating world that lies behind the gates of Damascus. Hala's husband is a political prisoner, jailed for his opposition to the Assad regime; through the author's friendship with Hala we see how Syrian politics impacts on the lives of ordinary people.

THE OLIVE GROVE
Travels in Greece
Katherine Kizilos

Katherine Kizilos travels to fabled islands, troubled border zones and her family's village deep in the mountains. She vividly evokes breathtaking landscapes, generous people and passionate politics, capturing the complexities of a country she loves.

'**beautifully captures the real tensions of Greece**' – *Sunday Times*

KINGDOM OF THE FILM STARS
Journey into Jordan
Annie Caulfield

Kingdom of the Film Stars is a travel book and a love story. With honesty and humour, Annie Caulfield writes of travelling in Jordan and falling in love with a Bedouin with film-star looks.

She offers fascinating insights into the country – from the tent life of traditional women to the hustle of downtown Amman – and unpicks tight-woven Western myths about the Arab world.

Index

Text

D

Bold indicates maps.
Italics indicates boxed text.

Bold indicates maps.
Italics indicates boxed text.

Boxed Text

MAP LEGEND

BOUNDARIES

━━━━━━━━ International
━━━━━━━━ State
━ ━ ━ ━ ━ Disputed

HYDROGRAPHY

Coastline
River, Creek
Lake
Intermittent Lake
Salt Lake
Canal
⊚ ≫ Spring, Rapids
Waterfalls
Swamp

ROUTES & TRANSPORT

Freeway
Highway
Major Road
Minor Road
Unsealed Road
City Freeway
City Highway
City Road
City Street, Lane

Pedestrian Mall
⊃= = = =⊂ Tunnel
⊢⊢⊢⊢●⊢ Train Route & Station
⊸●⊸ Metro & Station
Tramway
⊩⊩⊩⊩ Cable Car or Chairlift
━ ━ ━ ━ Walking Track
• • • • • • Walking Tour
━ ━ ━ ━ Ferry Route

AREA FEATURES

Building
✿ Park, Gardens
✛ ✛ ✕ ✕ Cemetery

Market
Beach, Desert
Urban Area

MAP SYMBOLS

✈ Airport
━ Ancient or City Wall
∴ Archaeological Site
θ Bank
ℵ Beach
Ä Castle or Fort
Cave
🕀 Church
Cliff or Escarpment
Ο Embassy
✛ Hospital
☪ Mosque
▲ Mountain or Hill
🏛 Museum

○ CAPITAL National Capital
◉ CAPITAL State Capital
● CITY City
● Town Town
● Village Village
○ Point of Interest

■ Place to Stay
Å Camping Ground
⊞ Caravan Park
⌂ Hut or Chalet

▼ Place to Eat
🍺 Pub or Bar

← One Way Street
Ⓟ Parking
)(Pass
★ Police Station
✉ Post Office
❖ Shopping Centre
🏛 Stately Home
▭ Swimming Pool
☎ Telephone
🗿 Temple
θ Toilet
❶ Tourist Information
♨ Transport
🐘 Zoo

Note: not all symbols displayed above appear in this book

LONELY PLANET OFFICES

Australia
PO Box 617, Hawthorn, Victoria 3122
☎ (03) 9819 1877 fax (03) 9819 6459
email: talk2us@lonelyplanet.com.au

USA
150 Linden St, Oakland, CA 94607
☎ (510) 893 8555 TOLL FREE: 800 275 8555
fax (510) 893 8572
email: info@lonelyplanet.com

UK
10a Spring Place, London NW5 3BH
☎ (0171) 428 4800 fax (0171) 428 4828
email: go@lonelyplanet.co.uk

France
1 rue du Dahomey, 75011 Paris
☎ 01 55 25 33 00 fax 01 55 25 33 01
email: bip@lonelyplanet.fr
minitel: 3615 lonelyplanet *(1,29 F TTC/min)*

World Wide Web: www.lonelyplanet.com *or* AOL keyword: lp
Lonely Planet Images: lpi@lonelyplanet.com.au